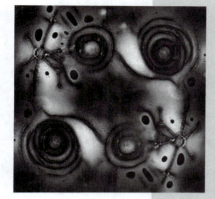

Teaching Science for Understanding

A Practical Guide for Middle and High School Teachers

James J. Gallagher
Michigan State University

PEARSON

Merrill
Prentice Hall

Upper Saddle River, New Jersey
Columbus, Ohio

Library of Congress Cataloging-in-Publication Data

Gallagher, James J.
  Teaching science for understanding / James Gallagher.—1st ed.
    p. cm.
  Includes bibliographical references and index.
  ISBN 0-13-114425-1 (paper back: alk. paper)
  1. Science—Study and teaching—United States. 2. Science teachers—United States.
I. Title.
Q183.3.A1G35 2007
507.1′2—dc22   2005028983

Vice President and Executive
  Publisher: Jeffery W. Johnston
Senior Editor: Linda Ashe Montgomery Bishop
Associate Editor: Meredith Saver
Senior Production Editor: Mary M. Irvin
Design Coordinator: Diane C. Lorenzo
Senior Editorial Assistant: Laura Weaver
Production Coordination and
  Text Design: GGS Book Services

Cover Designer: Jason Moore
Cover Images: Corbis
Production Manager: Pamela D. Bennett
Director of Marketing: David Gesell
Senior Marketing
  Manager: Darcy Betts Prybella
Marketing Coordinator: Brian Mounts

This book was set in Times Ten by GGS Book Services. It was printed and bound by Banta Book Group. The cover was printed by Coral Graphics.

Pearson Education Ltd.
Pearson Education Singapore Pte, Ltd.
Pearson Education Canada, Ltd.
Pearson Education—Japan

Pearson Education Australia Pty, Limited
Pearson Education North Asia Ltd.
Pearson Educación de Mexico, S.A. de C.V.
Pearson Education Malaysia Pte, Ltd.

10 9 8 7 6 5 4 3 2
ISBN: 0-13-114425-1

Preface

This book is for middle and secondary school science teachers—as well as those who are preparing to become teachers. It also is for those who teach them, because the new paradigm in teaching science for understanding requires new approaches in secondary school classrooms, laboratories, at the tertiary level and in professional development programs. This book is subtitled "a practical guide" because its approach develops the background knowledge and skills that teachers need to transform their teaching from more familiar models that often bypass development of understanding to newer models that foster understanding and application of science knowledge.

A fundamental premise of this book is that the work of secondary science teachers is far more complex than most people recognize. A common viewpoint held by members of our society, including many of those who make educational policy decisions, is that teaching is an easy career area that requires only a moderate amount of specialized expertise. Further, for many in our society, the key element for effective science teaching is the teacher's science knowledge. Little recognition is given to the importance of science teachers' pedagogical knowledge or skill, and few people recognize that teachers need specialized pedagogical content knowledge to be able to represent science ideas in ways that enable novice students to understand them. Moreover, the complexity of orchestrating all the elements of effective science teaching is rarely understood by most members of our society. The public generally has little appreciation for the demanding, skilled work that science teaching requires in putting together the appropriate science knowledge with knowledge about individual students and what they bring (or lack) as they enter class, knowledge of how to nurture development of students' interest and ideas, and skill in connecting students with science ideas and monitoring their progress toward sound educational goals. Not only is this a difficult viewpoint for the general public and policy makers to grasp, but it is equally difficult for many prospective teachers who see teaching as simply conveying information to students and then testing them to see that they have learned it.

A second fundamental premise of this book is that understanding cannot be transmitted from a teacher to students. Said another way, understanding is not a commodity that can be transferred. Instead each learner must create his or her own understanding. Teachers can support development of understanding in their students, but they cannot give understanding to them. Factual information can be transmitted, but understanding develops when a learner actively works to give meaning to experiences and ideas. Therefore, the work of teachers when they provide students with factual information is different from when they are supporting students in developing understanding and learning how to apply science knowledge. Most teachers are quite skilled at transmitting information to their students, but many need help in developing the knowledge and skills to support development of understanding. It is the latter set of skills that this book is about.

The book can be viewed as consisting of two parts. Chapters 1 through 7 provide a context or background for teachers to learn about the reasons for, and theoretical structures that underlie, the practices that middle and secondary school science teachers will use in teaching for understanding. This organization is based on a strong belief that theory is a very practical part of teachers' knowledge and that good practice is grounded in sound theoretical structures. Moreover, our theories in science teaching are both eclectic and developing. That is, they draw on many different fields of inquiry, including psychology, philosophy of science, and sociology, along with our own knowledge of students and classroom environments. In addition, our theories are undergoing development as teachers and teacher educators continue to learn more about our society's changing needs, how students learn, and new ways of teaching them. Therefore, the first seven chapters of the book deal with matters such as the changing social context in which science teaching occurs, and important features of what we know about how to support development of understanding of science in middle and secondary school students. Even though these chapters are theory based, they also have a practical side to them in showing how the ideas can be used in planning and enacting lessons with students.

Chapters 8 through 15 are designed to enable teachers to engage in a higher level of planning and enactment of instruction that leads to understanding. The eight chapters in Part 2 build on and extend the work in Part 1. Chapters 8 and 9 introduce you to a tool for evaluating science instructional materials that was designed by staff members at Project 2061. This tool has been modified for use in planning lesson sequences.

Chapters 10 through 14 show how the modified tool can be used to aid in the complex task of planning lesson sequences in five subject areas and grade level contexts—middle school physical science and earth science, and high school biology, chemistry, and physics. Further, the planning of all five lesson sequences is based on selected textbooks that are commercially available. An important idea underlying these five chapters is that textbooks can be valuable tools for supporting teachers in teaching more effectively. Textbooks should not dominate instruction, but they are valuable tools to help teachers and students meet intended objectives. When used properly, textbooks and other instructional materials can be powerful resources for teachers and students.

Chapter 15 serves another practical function in highlighting the need for long-term commitment to professional development. Not only is our work as middle and secondary school science teachers complex, it also is challenging and forever engaging! Therefore, the path to becoming an expert, effective science teacher is continual and exciting. It leads to both personal and professional growth over years as we strive to find and meet new challenges.

Some may criticize this book for what it lacks. First, it has not directly addressed one of the important purposes of the contemporary reform in science education: dealing with all students in our diverse society. However, the focus on teaching for understanding does address the needs of all students. Our experiences in urban and rural schools have shown us that students from varied cultural and economic backgrounds can achieve in science when teachers apply the principles that are incorporated in this book. Second, the book does not address some familiar topics for methods classes, such as lab safety and managing science laboratories, but there are many supplemental resources on these topics that can be used by methods instructors. However, the field lacks practical resources on the new paradigm for teaching science that this book provides.

Acknowledgments

Many people have influenced my thinking and understanding about how to teach science effectively. Most important among these have been the teachers with whom I have worked, especially a small group of twelve middle school science teachers in the public schools in Toledo, Ohio, and Lansing and Flint, Michigan, with whom I spent much of my work time and who dominated my thinking over a twelve-year period. To these people, I will be forever grateful.

During an even longer period, I also have learned from colleagues at Michigan State University and other universities. Charles (Andy) Anderson, Glenn Berkheimer, David Fortus, Perry Lanier, Joyce Parker, Gail Richmond, Kathleen Roth, Christina Schwarz, Edward Smith, Christopher Wheeler, and Sandra Wilcox were especially important in helping me form my ideas about teaching science for understanding. Graduate students (now professors at universities), including Rhibi Abu Snehneh, David Alao, Fernando Cajas, Armando Contreras, Don Duggan-Hass, Alejandro Gallard, David Kline, Benjalug Namfa, Letina Ngwenya, Josie Zesaguli, and many others, were sources of much of what I learned about learning and teaching. In addition, Barry Fraser, Leonie Rennie, and David Treagust from Curtin University in Australia, along with their colleague Ken Tobin, who worked with them and then came to work in our country, had a deep impact on my developing ideas. Work in Brazil, China, Panama, South Africa, Thailand, Taiwan, and Vietnam also added to my understanding about teaching science for understanding. Recently, my colleagues in the Center for Curriculum Materials in Science (Jo Ellen Roseman, George DeBoer, Betsy Davis, Joseph Krajcik, Danny Edelson, and Brian Reiser from Project 2061, University of Michigan, and Northwestern University, respectively) have added much to my perspective and understanding. I also have benefited from interactions with graduate students, post-doctoral fellows, and practicing teachers associated with this Center.

I would like to thank the reviewers of my manuscript for their comments and insights: Mary M. Capraro, Texas A&M University; Charles Cole, University of Illinois at Chicago; Ralph Feather, Bloomsburg University; Cheryl R. Grable, University of Arkansas at Little Rock; David Jelinek, California State University, Sacramento; Andrew C. Kemp, University of Louisville; Terrie Kielborn, State University of West Georgia; Michael Odell, University of Idaho; Scott Robinson, SUNY Brockport; Ted J. Singletary, Boise State University; Sherry Southerland, Florida State University; Heather Wilson-Ashworth, Utah Valley State College; and Robert E. Yager, University of Iowa.

Last, and most important, I thank Barb, who has provided for me in my work, my travels, and my happiness over a lifetime.

James J. Gallagher
East Lansing, Michigan

Your Class. Their Careers. Our Future. Will your students be prepared?

We invite you to explore our new, innovative and engaging website and all that it has to offer you, your course, and tomorrow's educators! Organized around the major courses pre-service teachers take, the Teacher Preparation site provides media, student/teacher artifacts, strategies, research articles, and other resources to equip your students with the quality tools needed to excel in their courses and prepare them for their first classroom.

This ultimate on-line education resource is available at no cost, when packaged with a Merrill text, and will provide you and your students access to:

Online Video Library. More than 150 video clips—each tied to a course topic and framed by learning goals and Praxis-type questions—capture real teachers and students working in real classrooms, as well as in-depth interviews with both students and educators.

Student and Teacher Artifacts. More than 200 student and teacher classroom artifacts—each tied to a course topic and framed by learning goals and application questions—provide a wealth of materials and experiences to help make your study to become a professional teacher more concrete and hands-on.

Research Articles. Over 500 articles form ASCD's renowned journal *Educational Leadership*. The site also includes Research Navigator, a searchable database of additional educational journals.

Teaching Strategies. Over 500 strategies and lesson plans for you to use when you become a practicing professional.

Licensure and Career Tools. Resources devoted to helping you pass your licensure exam; learn standards, law, and public policies; plan a teaching portfolio; and succeed in your first year of teaching.

How to ORDER *Teacher Prep* for you and your students:

For students to receive a *Teacher Prep* Access Code with this text, instructors **must** provide a special value pack ISBN number on their textbook order form. To receive this special ISBN, please email **Merrill.marketing@pearsoned.com** and provide the following information:

- Name and Affiliation
- Author/Title/Edition of Merrill text

Upon ordering *Teacher Prep* for their students, instructors will be given a lifetime *Teacher Prep* Access Code.

Contents

Chapter 1

Why Should We Teach Science for Understanding?

 While driving to my office on campus one autumn day in 1995, I noticed a bumper sticker that was far different from the usual ones I see that refer to our athletic teams or social causes. It was unusual, somewhat philosophical, in what it said:

"Subvert the Dominant Paradigm"

This caused me to ask myself, "What is the dominant paradigm[1] in science teaching? Should it be subverted and, if so, what should the new paradigm be?" At the time, I had been working as part of a large committee preparing the National Science Education Standards, and I had ready answers to these questions.

The dominant paradigm in science teaching in most classrooms in the United States from elementary school through college at that time, and even now, is as follows:

Teaching is perceived as transmitting information to students who are, more often than not, passive recipients. Learning tends to be perceived by both teachers and students as memorizing this information. And assessment is viewed as summative; that is, it comes in the form of a test at the end of an instructional unit or topic, and it is used to determine which students remembered the information so that a grade can be assigned to each student.

---

[1] Paradigm can be defined as "an example that serves as a pattern or model for something, especially one that forms the basis or a methodology or theory . . . in the philosophy of science a generally accepted model of how ideas relate to one another, forming a conceptual framework within which scientific research is carried out" (Microsoft Word dictionary). An example or a model (Morris, 1980).

Of course, there is much variation in how science is taught, and not all teachers follow this paradigm. However, it remains the dominant paradigm in science teaching and learning in spite of many efforts to enable a different approach.

A New Paradigm for Science Teaching and Learning

For over a century, reformers such as John Dewey and Alfred North Whitehead, along with many teachers, scientists, science teacher educators, and leaders in business and government, called for a different approach. Currently in the United States and in most nations of the world, reform leaders are promoting a new paradigm in which teaching is viewed as providing students with an array of experiences that enable understanding, and then guiding students toward understanding and use of science knowledge. In this paradigm, students must be active participants in doing science and constructing meaning from their experiences. Therefore, while learning always must involve some memorization, it is not the end point of the learning process. Students also must make personal sense of their experiences enroute to developing understanding and learning to apply their knowledge. Assessment does not just come at the end of instruction, but it is a continuous process that is used by both teachers and students to guide both teaching and learning. Moreover, in this new paradigm assessment is both teacher directed and student directed.

Teaching and learning science for understanding is not simple. It is a complex process that requires many new skills on the part of both students and teachers. It is far more complex than the "dominant paradigm" that most students and teachers have experienced throughout most of their school and college years. Of equal importance, this new paradigm also requires a transformation of "vision" about what it means to teach and to learn science. This transformation not only must be part of the education of science teachers, but also needs to be understood by students, school administrators, parents, and the general public.

Reflection & Discussion Questions

These questions occur throughout this book to stimulate you as a reader to reflect on the ideas presented, and to discuss them with your colleagues. Reflection and discussion represent an important part of your development of understanding about teaching science for understanding. Please take time to think about these questions and to discuss them with your associates. The first questions follow.

What is your paradigm for teaching science? How does it compare with the new and the old paradigms? How frequently have you experienced the new paradigm in any of the courses you have taken? Describe these experiences to your colleagues in this course.

Why Is a New Paradigm Essential?

A short history lesson will help you understand the rationale underlying the new paradigm for science teaching and learning. We will go back to 1957 to begin this lesson. At that time the world's two superpowers, the United States and the USSR, were locked in the Cold War, which involved superiority of ideologies and military might. In November of that year, Americans were caught by surprise when the USSR launched the first artificial satellite, which silently revolved around the earth every 90 minutes. It was perceived, and feared, that Sputnik (its Russian name) could be used to monitor our military actions and even be a tool for an attack on our nation. The response was overwhelming. The United States hurried to make an equivalent launch, but months of failure followed before we were able to successfully launch an artificial satellite similar to that launched by the Russians. Many people asked, "How could we be behind another nation in our technology? Were we not superior to the USSR?" As a result, scientists and educators entered into a huge effort to regain our technological superiority by seeking to improve science and mathematics curricula and strengthen our teaching force in science and mathematics. That effort resulted in new curricula and many intensive programs to increase science and mathematics teachers' understanding of the subject matter they were to teach. Such efforts continued for about fifteen years with strong federal support. However, like many valuable programs, these efforts fell from favor with our leaders in Washington as administrations changed, and their financial support was eliminated. The result was a period of apathy and confusion as the leadership in science education that had been provided by the National Science Foundation withered. The energy of that post-Sputnik era was lost, school programs in science languished, and students' achievement declined.

During the years that followed, leaders in education, business, and government became increasingly concerned about declining scores on university entrance examinations such as ACT and SAT. Experts were confident that the tests were not getting harder over time. They also were confident that the students taking them were less well prepared because schools, from kindergarten through high school, were not as effective as they had been in years past. Moreover, international studies showed that students in the United States were lagging far behind students from other industrialized nations in achievement, especially in science and mathematics. In 1983, the Secretary of Education, the member of the President's Cabinet who directs the United States Department of Education, issued a report titled *A Nation at Risk: The Imperative for Educational Reform*, which detailed the decline in the quality and effectiveness of our schools. It made the point that our schools were not producing a sufficient number of qualified graduates to enable the development of the high-tech workforce needed to maintain our economic and military leadership. The authors of this work identified a "diluted" curriculum in science and mathematics, low-level standards for learning, and poorly prepared teachers among the major reasons for the problem. The report claimed that students in the United States were not required to study science and mathematics in secondary schools at levels that were comparable to programs in other advanced nations. Moreover, a shortage of qualified teachers for both subjects was also identified as a serious problem in effecting a high level curriculum. The report also claimed that certification requirements for teachers were lax in many states and that teachers frequently were assigned to teach courses outside of their fields of expertise. Thus, the decline in the quality and effectiveness of our schools had placed our nation in jeopardy both economically and militarily, hence the title, *A Nation at Risk* (National Commission on Excellence in Education, 1983).

This report was hotly debated. Many teachers and school administrators were incensed with the level of criticism that followed the release of this report and many other reports that both preceded and followed its publication (Bracey, 2003). However, *A Nation at Risk* resulted in many important actions that changed the environment of schooling across the nation. Most states began or strengthened statewide testing programs to raise standards for both teaching and learning. Most states also developed new curricular and instructional standards to guide teachers, students, and test makers. Universities engaged in strengthening their teacher education programs. Many school districts across the nation responded with new curricula, textbooks, laboratory materials, organizational plans, and staff development efforts. In addition, there has been progress in student achievement since the report was issued even though the United States is still far from the top in international measures of achievement and is not producing enough science and mathematics teachers, scientists, and engineers to meet the our nation's needs (Forgione, 1998). In these areas, we continue to "import" highly qualified people from other nations to fill positions in our schools, universities, industries, and government because we are not educating enough U.S. citizens to fill these high-level jobs. Moreover, it appears that the condition will continue

for years to come (National Association of State Telecommunications Directors, 1998).

Formulating a New Paradigm for Science Education

At the national level, two major programs were developed near the close of the twentieth century that had important effects on science education in our nation. Beginning in 1985, Project 2061[2] was developed by leaders at the American Association for Advancement of Science. This began with the creation of a series of panels of specialists in science who were given the charge of thinking freely about how science teaching and learning should change so that students would be adequately prepared for the future. This freewheeling brainstorming activity extended over two years and resulted in the publication of an important book titled *Science for All Americans* (Rutherford and Ahlgren, 1989). This set out a highly integrated plan for science teaching and learning that included a far broader view of science than was found in most school programs. It included important science ideas that were a familiar part of school science, but it also added many other features such as an emphasis on the nature of science, and how science integrates with mathematics, technology, and design. It also emphasized the development of scientific ideas over time that included history of science, inquiry, and the habits of mind of scientists as important dimensions of science learning.

In addition to the broader view of science content, the book emphasized three other features. The first was implicit in the title of the book—*Science for ALL Americans*. It made the point that we must teach science effectively to a much larger segment of our nation's students than in the past. This presented a huge challenge to teachers, teacher educators, curriculum designers, and others who are part of the educational system, one that needs far more attention than it has received up to now. Another feature of the book was inherent in the language that it used, which described the high-level science knowledge expected of high school graduates in surprisingly simple terminology. In doing this, the authors set a standard for understanding science with a minimum of specialized language and terminology. In this way it brought an emphasis that has been captured by the slogans, "Less is better" or "Less is more." This couples with the feature *Science for All Americans*, central to this book, teaching science for understanding instead of only

---

[2] Project 2061 was named for the next return of Halley's comet, which passes by earth on a seventy-six-year cycle. The name was chosen to indicate the need for a long-term, future-oriented commitment to reform in science education.

memorizing information. Thus the goal was created for achieving understanding of science through reducing the amount of complex terminology, while guiding students to understand scientific ideas and their relationships to one another and to the real world.

Reflection & Discussion Questions

Think about and write down the four features of science education included in *Science for All Americans* that are listed in the last two paragraphs. Next think about and describe in writing how these are different from the science education you experienced. Also how do they compare with your "vision" of what you should teach? Does this constitute a new paradigm for science teaching and learning?

Does your list, or vision of science teaching, contain the four major elements of the new paradigm—the contemporary agenda for reform in science education?

- A broader vision of science
- Science for all
- Teaching and learning for understanding
- Reduction in the amount of science content

I encourage you to consider why each of these is an important component of the new paradigm and to think deeply about what each of these components of the new paradigm means as you continue your work in this book.

Science for All Americans created a new level of excitement for those who came to know it. It served as the basis for new standards in some states. It influenced research and development both at universities and within Project 2061 where a more detailed look was taken at the goals of science teaching at different levels from Kindergarten through grade 12. This work was detailed in a publication titled *Benchmarks for Science Literacy* (Project 2061, 1993). Subsequently, a series of concept maps were developed to show the connections among ideas and to aid in planning sequences of development of key ideas in science. This series of concept maps has been published as an *Atlas for Science Literacy* (Project 2061, 2001). Several other publications have been developed by this group, including a set of criteria to evaluate the quality of instructional materials, which is described in detail in Chapter 8.

Emergence of New Standards for Science in Schools

As a result of work done by the National Council of Teachers of Mathematics to develop national standards for teaching and learning, the National Research Council took leadership in developing *National Science Education Standards*. Beginning in 1993, three large working groups were formed to prepare standards for teaching, assessment, and science content. Several drafts of the *National Science Education Standards* were prepared and disseminated widely to gain national consensus among teachers, educational policy makers, legislators, teacher educators, and school administrators. A final draft of the *National Science Education Standards* (National Research Council, 1996) was published in 1996 containing chapters on standards for teaching, teacher professional development, assessment, and science content to be included in the school curriculum. Standards were also presented for programs and systems to guide district leaders and policy makers at local, state, and federal levels in planning for and providing the needed resources for effective science teaching. The six sets of standards incorporated in the *National Science Education Standards* (NSES) complemented the work done by the Project 2061 staff by providing guidance as people across the nation began to form and enact the new paradigm in science teaching, learning, and assessment.

The content standards reinforced the broad picture of science that was found in *Science for All Americans* by including eight content dimensions:

Unifying Concepts and Processes

Science as Inquiry

Physical Science

Life Science

Earth and Space Science

Science and Technology

Science in Personal and Social Perspectives

History and Nature of Science (National Research Council, 1996, p 189)

The combined work of Project 2061 and the *National Science Education Standards* had a substantial effect on the science education community among university faculties in science education and governmental agencies such as State Departments of Education. Professional organizations also responded to the *Standards*. For example, the National Science Teachers Association continues to make a concerted effort to support the dissemination of the *National Science Education Standards* through its publications, conferences, workshops, and Web site *(http://www.nsta.org/standards)*. Schools responded also, often at a slower pace. The prestige of the two sponsoring groups (National Research Council and the American Association for the Advancement of Science) added to the sense of importance of the reform agenda that was put forth. Most people saw the two efforts by Project 2061 and the National Research Council as compatible, although there were some differences in the organization of science content and in goals. In many ways the two efforts were complementary with different elements of reform highlighted. Both reports set forth the same broad agenda—science for all, teaching and learning for understanding, a broader vision of science, and reduction in the amount of science content as captured in the slogan "Less is better."

Reflection & Discussion Questions

Why are six sets of standards, such as those included in *National Science Education Standards*, essential?

Why are eight dimensions of science content included in the *National Science Education Standards?*

The documents from Project 2061 and National Research Council comprise a substantial part of the new paradigm in science teaching and learning. In your work, do you use any of the documents that are identified above? Are these documents important to you or are they peripheral to your work? Explain why.

Impact of Project 2061 and the *National Science Education Standards*

In addition to generating an agenda of reform in the United States, these programs prompted many other nations to reform their educational systems. Although some nations had begun earlier, by 1990 nearly all industrialized nations and many developing nations had initiated plans to improve education in mathematics and science as governmental, educational, and business leaders came to recognize the need for a workforce that can be competitive in a world of advancing technology.

Japan provides one interesting case in this reform. Japanese political, industrial, and educational leaders have long recognized the connection between economic strength and high-quality education in science for a wide segment of their society. Understanding science was seen as more important than memorization to create an effective workforce in this highly industrialized, high-tech nation. To achieve a high level of understanding across the population, the Japanese Ministry of Education took a bold move in 1985. They reduced the number of science concepts included in the science curriculum by approximately one-third. This step was taken to enable Japanese science teachers to provide more depth of understanding rather than a superficial coverage of science knowledge. What was even more surprising, in 2000 they further reduced the content by one-third for the same reason, recognizing that the curriculum was still too heavily packed with content knowledge. This reduced the amount of science content taught in Japanese schools to about half of what it was

prior to 1985. This is one example of the principal of "less being perceived as better" applied on a broad scale to achieve higher quality, more effective, science learning.

Other nations approached the improvement of science education differently. Korea placed more emphasis on more applications of science through technology. The Czech Republic, one of the high scoring nations in international assessments of science learning, continued to implement a highly structured curriculum and approach to teaching. The Netherlands was quite opposite in their approach to reform, encouraging a more open style of teaching in their science classes where students work independently or in small groups (Roth et al., in press). Taiwan reduced class size from about fifty students per classroom, which was typical in schools in most Asian nations, down to about thirty students over the period from 1990 to 2003. Taiwan also implemented a new integrated curriculum for grades 1 to 9, and entered into significant research and professional development work to foster more effective science teaching (Yang, 2003).

Serious reform of science teaching, learning, curriculum, and assessment is occurring in most nations as they compete for economic strength and security. Other factors that receive consideration include environmental sustainability and personal and public health in an attempt to balance more immediate and long-range survival goals.

A New, Long-Term Approach to Change in Science Curriculum, Teaching, and Assessment

In the United States, we have seen many important changes as a result of the current reform agenda. One important change, when compared with years prior to 1990, is that we have "stayed the course." The concept of long-term change, initially promoted by Project 2061, provides a beneficial climate for improvement in science for our schools. In the decades preceding 1990, change was more governed by fads, and teachers referred skeptically to new programs as "TYNT" (this year's new thing). In the most recent decade, educational reform has been guided more consistently by *National Science Education Standards* and Project 2061. We recognize that significant change in teaching, learning, and assessment does not occur easily, nor does it occur quickly. New curriculum materials and instructional resources need to be developed and teachers need to learn how to use them. Since most teachers and those who educate them "grew up" with the old paradigm, they need time to create their own new vision of teaching and learning that is compatible with the new paradigm. As a consequence of this realization, leaders in schools, universities, and government have initiated means to provide long-term support for teachers as they work to improve their teaching and students' learning. Curriculum guides and testing in most states have been influenced by some combination of *National Science Education Standards* and Project 2061. Publishers of educational materials for science have also responded to them. "Standards-based reform" has become a watchword for leaders in science teaching. Much has changed since Project 2061 and *National Science Education Standards* came on the scene. However, science teaching in most classrooms still needs much improvement before we can achieve the goals of this reform, which include having a wide segment of our citizenry understand science and able to use it in meaningful ways in their daily lives, including the workplace.

Now, as *No Child Left Behind* plays a larger role in science teaching and learning, science teachers across our nation have an additional demand on them. How can we reconcile this testing program and the ideas presented here about teaching science for understanding? Understanding and success on external tests go hand in hand. The mental skills and knowledge development that are part of teaching and learning science for understanding and application are the same as needed for success on external exams. When students understand science concepts and can apply science reasoning skills, instead of simply memorizing factual information, they score better on external tests (William and Black, 2000). Therefore, teaching for understanding matches the goals of high-quality testing programs that can be part of *No Child Left Behind*. Further discussion of this important point occurs in Chapter 7.

Reflection & Discussion Questions

How would you explain the slow change to the new paradigm in science teaching, when it has had so much publicity? What new vision, skills, and dispositions does the change require? What else must change to enable the effective enactment of the new paradigm for science in our schools?

How Have New Ideas about Learning Science Changed Our Thinking?

Economics and national security were not the only driving forces behind the new paradigm. These were politically important, but new knowledge about how students learn also was important in formulating Project 2061 and the *National Science Education Standards*. For decades, scholars who study learning

and teaching had increasingly recognized that learning required more than transferring information from someone who knew it to someone who didn't. This was especially important when it came to the understanding and use of knowledge (Bransford, Brown, and Cocking, 2000). The understanding of, and the ability to apply, knowledge cannot simply be transmitted. Factual knowledge can be transmitted rather easily, but understanding and application are more complex. They require that learners make personal sense of the new information and fit it in with what they already know. Therefore, learning with understanding requires that students make sense of ideas and experiences, and connect them with other, related ideas and experiences that form their prior knowledge. To apply knowledge also requires that students see the connection between the knowledge and its application. This takes some practice to develop the propensity to make this kind of connection.

In science classrooms, this is more complex than in most other subject fields because of the inquiry dimension of science. Guiding students through investigations to obtain reliable data and experience with scientific phenomena is not a simple process. Then helping students develop understanding at three levels—relating to the inquiry process itself, to the identification of patterns and meaning in the data, and then to the formation of explanations based on the experience—is demanding for both students and teachers. However, the connection among *investigations* and related experiences, finding *patterns* in data, and forming *explanations* lies at the heart of science learning.

Reflection & Discussion Questions

In the paragraph above, I claim understanding cannot be transmitted. Explain why this is an accurate statement. Do you accept this as accurate? If not, why do you disagree with it?

Also, people who have seriously studied learning believe that knowledge is socially constructed, meaning that understanding of science knowledge depends on interaction with both the real world and people who help to formulate ways of describing and giving meaning to data and experiences. This adds a dimension to learning that often is ignored by many teachers of science at all levels of schooling. Learning is not just an individual matter. It also is a social enterprise where we learn to describe ideas and hear other people's thoughts about them. This interaction allows people to clarify their understandings by comparing and contrasting their thoughts with those of others. This is quite different from the process where students sit alone and memorize information. It is also different from a small group of students working together to "quiz" each other on knowledge of facts (Bransford, Brown, and Cocking, 2000).

This may be better understood if you think about your college courses in science. Your professors typically lectured as a means of transmitting information about the subject matter. Often they would also provide you with hints about how the pieces of information fit together. Sometimes they would describe how this information was obtained through observations and experiments. Occasionally they would relate how this information had been applied to understand a real-world problem.

Does this sound like teaching for understanding and application? At the surface it may. However, two factors are missing in this scenario. First, it does not include you, the learner, processing this information to make personal sense of it and to fit it into your prior knowledge. Your professors all had a solution to this problem: you were expected to go back to your dorm room and study! That is where you would do the sense-making and connecting. The fallacy in this solution is that the task of making sense and making connections is complex and many students were not able to do it on their own. Moreover, if wiser and more experienced college students are not able to do it alone, what about less experienced learners in middle and high school? Some students can do this without much guidance from their teachers and professors. These are the students who get the high grades in courses. They were the ones who were not satisfied with just memorizing facts for the tests. They wanted to understand the subject. For these people, studying was not just to get better at memorizing, but it was to make sense of and connect the pieces, to create meaning from the facts and ideas.

The second missing factor is the process that involves interacting with phenomena and with people in the social construction of knowledge. To study alone has certain benefits, but it lacks the interaction among people as they work to organize their ideas and reasoning in a logical form so that others can understand them. Interaction with both phenomena and other people provides a validity check on emerging understanding to see that it matches the actual phenomenon and that people share a common "language" and meaning that allow them to communicate effectively about them.

Classroom management will differ with teaching science for understanding. On the surface, it may appear as though classroom management could become more difficult as students interact with each other in groups or engage in investigations, instead of spending the majority of time working alone or in activities that are teacher centered. However, the classroom environment can be developed so that it is more engaging for students, and when that occurs, management problems diminish. In addition, when teachers engage in formative assessment as part of teaching science for understanding, listening to students' ideas and attending to their reasoning, the climate of the classroom becomes more collaborative, which also diminishes management problems. Students show more respect for their teachers and are more highly motivated because their teachers, in turn, are giving them and their ideas more respect (Gallagher, 2000).

Reflection & Discussion Questions

What do we mean when we say that knowledge is socially constructed? Why is interaction with both phenomena and other people such an important part of science learning?

What we have come to understand in recent years is that this kind of learning can be available to all students if we provide them with help in *learning how to learn* (Bransford, Brown, and Cocking, 2000). We also have recognized that understanding science is too important to be left to chance or to be available to only a few highly motivated students. We need scientifically literate workers, citizens, consumers, and voters if we are to maintain our status as a leading nation on the world scene, our high standard of living, and a quality environment in the face of increasing population and resource use. However, it will require adopting a new paradigm for teaching and learning science.

How Should Science Teaching Change?

I will make a bold claim at the outset of this section: **Science is rarely taught effectively**.

To support this claim, I will state that most people in the United States fail to understand the science that they have studied, having substituted memorization of facts for understanding. It is rare that students in school or college comprehend the science content they have studied, and it is even rarer that they can apply the science they know effectively in contexts that are different from those in which it has been learned. Few school age students can give coherent explanations of even the most fundamental concepts in science. Even fewer can use what has been learned in school to make observations of objects or events they encounter each day. It is even more rare that adults have a useful knowledge of science. Most have forgotten the facts they learned in school, and they have not added to that knowledge in the interim. The knowledge of science that has been learned in school does not affect how they are able to interact with the world of daily experience. Typically, it does not help them make decisions about their personal health, about the health of the environment, or about how to diagnose problems with the technology that are a part of their daily life. More critically, their science knowledge does not help them in the workplace, even though it may be influenced by science in important ways.

Further evidence includes comments I have heard repeatedly from many teachers of science from elementary school through college, often make statements such as "My students don't understand and cannot apply the science I have taught them" or "Even the good students who memorize a lot of factual knowledge can't use what they have learned because they don't understand it." In the work that I do with pre-service secondary science teachers, I see the same problem. These bright, high-achieving, dedicated university students know a lot of science since they have both a major in one field of science such as chemistry, physics, earth science, or biology, and a minor in another field. They are seniors in college. They have good grade-point averages. They have a strong factual base in science, but they have not integrated that knowledge in a way that makes sense to them or enables them to use it effectively. It is "textbook knowledge," but it lacks the synthesis required to achieve understanding and application.

Much of this shortcoming in science learning is a direct consequence of the way in which science has been, and still is, taught in schools across the nation. The following story may give these assertions more meaning.

Many years ago, faculty at Antioch College in Ohio wanted to express their public gratitude to Charles F. Kettering for his many gifts to their institution. He had given many large cash donations to the college, and he also had helped them establish a work-study program that provided students with practical experience that added significantly to their academic knowledge. Kettering was a very rich man, quite old, and somewhat cantankerous. Because he was an engineer and a "tinkerer," who made important inventions, they decided the token of their appreciation would be a paper weight for his desk composed of a small screw driver and a pair of pliers embedded in clear plastic. On the day of the ceremony to honor Kettering, an official of the college presented him with the gift after a short commemorative speech. Kettering was very pleased in accepting the gift, but when he saw what it was he jokingly said, "Isn't this just like a group of educators—to give me a set of tools that I cannot use?"

This is a useful metaphor for the problem we face in science education. How often do we give students tools that they cannot use? How often do we teach people the gas laws or teach cellular respiration or teach about change of state without helping them grasp how these laws and concepts apply to the real world, inside their bodies, or outside of the classroom?

Further, how often do we transmit information about these important, basic ideas as facts to be memorized, without helping students integrate the facts into a meaningful "story" that leads to understanding of at least a small part their world? And as the school year progresses, when do we help the students build these small "stories" into a coherent "big picture"? Of equal importance in science, when do we help students learn *how we know*? That is, when do we help students grasp how scientists have been able to unravel the mysteries of nature and create the science knowledge that they are learning?

In the remaining chapters of this book, I will help prospective and practicing teachers of science think about what it means to teach science for understanding, and to develop some of the skills and techniques that will enable their students to learn science in ways that lead to understanding and the capability to use science knowledge in their daily lives. In the process, I hope that the teachers and their students will be empowered to be life-long learners in science because they have learned how to continue learning both from study and from experience.

Reflection & Discussion Questions

From your experience, do you agree or disagree with my statement that "science is rarely taught effectively"? What is your evidence for your answer?

What Does Teaching for Science Understanding Look Like?

What should science classes look like when teaching and learning for understanding is taking place? Will you see a teacher at the front of the room, presenting information to students? Yes. Will you see students working alone from their textbooks? Yes. However, these should not be the only means by which students gain new information and ideas. You should also see students and teachers engaged in laboratory or hands-on activities. You should see students planning investigations to answer questions that they have generated in their class discussions, from reading, and from their experiences both in and outside of school. You should see students engaged in investigations using science equipment, reference books, and the Internet. You should see students questioning experts in specific science fields by writing e-mail messages or preparing to interview them. You should see students engaged in analyzing and interpreting data and other information as they give meaning to it and relate it to other knowledge. You should also see students and teachers outdoors studying the natural and constructed world beyond the classroom, in natural settings, and in the community. You should also see students engaged in discussions of science ideas and data in small groups or as a whole class.

You also should see students writing and preparing posters and other representations of ideas to help them convey their ideas about their investigations to others. You should see students in heated discussions about the meaning of data and appropriate ways of interpreting data and presenting findings. The kinds of work will be varied as students engage in active learning.

Active learning, which leads to understanding, isn't just physical. It also is reflective, mental work. Sometimes it is quiet, as students think through an idea. It involves writing and creating models and diagrams to portray relationships. It can involve creating concept maps that show how ideas are connected with each other. It can involve drawing diagrams that represent ideas and the connections among them. It provides time and opportunities for students to work individually or in small groups to make sense of ideas and experiences. It also provides time and opportunities for, and may even require, students to find connections among ideas and connections between ideas and the real world.

Teaching for Science for Understanding IS Rocket Science!

We often hear an easy task described by the phrase, "It isn't rocket science!" However, teaching science for understanding is a demanding, high-level professional activity that requires much knowledge and many advanced skills.

What does the teacher do in classes where teaching and learning for understanding is the central theme? Although teaching for understanding may look easy, because responsibility for learning is shifted to students, the job is very demanding. One of the most difficult parts is to know when to withhold help, when to give help, and what help to give. Teachers must recognize that they cannot "give" their students understanding. Understanding has to be constructed by each student. But many individuals cannot always develop understanding alone. Interactions—among students, between the teacher and individual students, or between the small groups of students and the teacher—are essential in gaining understanding. Therefore, part of the teacher's role is to decide when and how to foster productive interactions.

Teachers also create the environment in which students can participate in the experiences and information gathering that form the basis of learning. Teachers help students determine effective ways to organize experiences and information so that they can construct

meaning about them. Then they guide and support students as their ideas develop from naïve understanding to more complete understanding. This work as a guide is grounded in the teacher's ability to listen and watch carefully; to grasp and interpret what students say, write, draw, and do as they work; and to assess continuously the ideas students hold, the information they have assembled, and the understanding they have formulated. Based on this, teachers then either determine the next action that is needed to move students from their current level of understanding to a higher level or, if students have reached the intended level of understanding, help them celebrate that accomplishment. One of the most demanding high-level tasks in teaching is processing a huge amount of information about all students, in ways that enable informed responses that advance students' learning, to whole class, small groups, or individuals.

Reflection & Discussion Questions

Have you seen the kind of teaching that is sketched in these two subsections of the chapter? Describe what you saw. Would you like to teach in this way? What will you need to learn in order to do so?

Classroom Management

If you are questioning how to manage students in a system such as this you are thinking appropriately. Classroom management is a matter of concern, as it affects learning in very significant ways.

If this sounds complex, you are perceptive! This is what we are asking teachers to do when we ask them to teach for understanding. As you can see, this involves use of a combination of high-level skills that are not commonplace. It also involves a vision of teaching and learning that is not commonplace. But this is what this reform is about—changing the views about teaching and learning from content coverage and memorization of science facts to understanding and being able to use science knowledge in the workplace, in our decisions about what we eat, our health and recreation, our purchases, and how we make decisions that affect people, our natural and constructed environment, and the world around us.

The purpose of this book is to help prospective and practicing teachers develop the vision, skills, and propensities that will enable them to teach science for understanding. The vision and propensities may come comparatively easily. Some people have them already. This vision of science teaching just makes sense to them. It feels right. For others it is not as "natural." It requires some time, discussion, reading, watching, and reflection before they see how it can become part of their teaching.

At the same time as a new vision of teaching and learning is developing, you can learn new skills to guide students, to clarify learning goals and objectives, to plan lessons and assessments, to learn how to implement plans for activities and assessments, to learn how to collect and interpret data from observing students at work, and to learn how to interpret this information and make judgments about what to do next when you have taught a lesson and students "didn't get it."

All of this takes years. It is what makes teaching science such a challenging and exciting career. You will continue to get better at it each day and week as you continue to develop new skills that support students' learning. As you learn, you also must develop confidence that your students are benefiting from their interactions with you and other students more than if they were seated in rows listening to you present facts and drill them on those facts. You also need to have confidence that as you become more proficient in teaching for understanding, they are benefiting more than if you presented them with a collage of interesting hands-on activities, but failed to nurture the development of their ideas and reasoning about these experiences. You also need to have confidence that your activities challenge students to think and reason because you are teaching them to use conceptual models to deepen their reasoning. Your increasing confidence will be based in the data and feedback you receive from your students as you observe them learning and finding excitement and joy in science.

In the remainder of this book, you will have many occasions to learn what it means to understand and develop viewpoints and skills that will help you to teach science for understanding. This can be the beginning of a grand experience in your professional growth.

Reflection & Discussion Questions

Why do I say "this can be the beginning of a grand experience . . ."?

Why Do You Need a Book on Teaching Science for Understanding?

Why not just concentrate on teaching for understanding in general? There are already books that present work on teaching for understanding (Wiske, 1999; Wiggins and McTighe 1999). There even is one on teaching science for understanding (Mintzes, Wandersee, and Novak, 1997). These are excellent resources, and I used them and many other sources to guide creation of this work. However, they do not provide adequate help in teaching science for understanding for three main reasons: First, teaching any topic for understanding is specific to that topic. It requires

specific knowledge of the content of the topic, specific knowledge of teaching strategies that are grounded in the content (*called pedagogical content knowledge*), specific knowledge of students' ideas and reasoning as they enter a topic, specific knowledge of ways of assessing students' knowledge as it develops, and specific knowledge of how to teach that particular content (Shulman, 1986). Such detailed knowledge is not adequately supported in these books that serve multiple subject fields. Second, none of these books adequately addresses one of the central issues in teaching science for understanding—that is formative assessment. Formative assessment is the means by which teachers continuously monitor students' learning as they move from naïve understanding and misconceptions to a fuller understanding of any topic. Without adequate attention to formative assessment, it is not possible to teach for understanding, as students and teachers will continually "talk past each other." That is, unless teachers monitor development of understanding of concepts in science recurrently during lessons, they probably will not realize when students are interpreting information and experiences differently than anticipated. Moreover, the teachers may also be interpreting students' words differently than expected. In addition, formative assessment is necessarily highly content specific. Formative assessment, like pedagogical content knowledge, differs for each specific topic taught. Third, teaching science in high schools and middle schools has not received the attention it deserves. As Kati Haycock, director of the Education Trust, said, "Almost all our reform energy has focused on elementary schools. High schools are the most stagnant part of our education system, followed by middle schools" (*Washington Post*, 2004). For these three reasons, a specialized book on teaching middle and high school science for understanding is a needed resource.

The remainder of this book is designed to help teachers and others grasp what teaching for understanding is about and the skills needed to enact it in their classrooms. The table of contents of this book sketches the complex vision, knowledge, skills, and techniques that are needed by teachers in order to teach science effectively for understanding and use. These topics range from philosophical ones—such as "What does it mean to understand science?" and "Why is formative assessment essential?"—to practical matters of lesson planning, assessment, and classroom management. All these taken together become the professional knowledge of teachers of science at middle and high school levels.

For prospective teachers, this book will be the start of a long journey to become a skilled, professional science teacher. The journey will take years, which is part of the excitement and challenge of the profession we have chosen. For practicing teachers, who have classroom experience, this book will lead your journey into new, exciting directions that will bring you closer to your students and to the science you teach. For all science teachers and your students, the journey will engender a closer connection to the world in which you live.

Journal Questions

You already have experienced Questions for Reflection and Discussion that are embedded at several points in the text. This concept is grounded in research studies by a scientist at Bell Labs, Ernst Rothkopf (1970), who found that questions embedded in written text improved readers' learning and comprehension of the material. Because these questions already are an integral part of the text, end-of-chapter activities need to be more integrative. Reflection and Discussion Questions have called attention to the fine-grained detail of the chapter. For end-of-chapter activities, you should be thinking about how to integrate ideas into a more comprehensive fabric. Therefore, I recommend the following plan for end-of-chapter questions.

You should keep a journal that records the development of your ideas and concerns about teaching science for understanding and application as you work through the chapters of this book. Your journal could be computer-based so that you can share your developing ideas and their representations with your colleagues and the instructor of your course or professional development project. On the other hand, there could be some reasons for keeping your journal as a more private record. This is a matter between you and your instructor.

I recommend inclusion of several components in your journal, and each of these should be structured in a way that the progression of your thinking and professional growth can emerge, and be recorded, over the weeks or months of the course or program. The following questions may serve as a guide for your journal:

1. What were the purposes or objectives of this chapter?
2. What were the key ideas presented in this chapter? (Note: Items 1 and 2 could be combined as a two-column table to show the parallel between the purposes of each chapter and the ideas presented.)
3. What important additions have you made to your vision of teaching science for understanding and application by studying this chapter and discussing it with others? This should be an ongoing narrative that highlights development of your personal paradigm for teaching and learning science.
4. I also recommend that you create a concept map that portrays your understanding about teaching and learning science for understanding and application and add new concepts and connections as you study each chapter of this book. This concept map can provide a visual representation of your developing new vision or paradigm of science teaching and learning that you developed in the previous item.
5. What new skills and techniques do you find you need to develop in order to enact your vision of science teaching? What progress are you making in developing those skills and techniques?
6. Finally, what concerns do you have about being able to implement your new vision, your new paradigm of science teaching with your students, in your classroom, laboratory, and fieldwork? How will you respond to these concerns?

Chapter 2

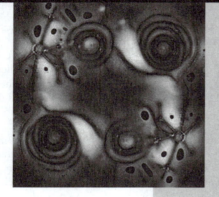

What Does It Mean to Understand Science?

The understanding, like the eye, whilst it makes us see and perceive all other things, takes no notice of itself; and it requires art and pains to set it at a distance and make it its own object. *(John Locke:* **An Essay Concerning Human Understanding, Introduction,** *c. 1690)*

Understanding is a concept that has puzzled people for centuries. The quote above from John Locke over three hundred years ago attests to this. What does it mean to understand something? What is understanding? How do you know if your students understand the subject matter you are teaching? How do you know if you understand it yourself? These are questions that have long been the subject of discussion and debate by philosophers, educators, and scientists.

Wiggins and McTighe (1998), in their book *Understanding by Design*, begin Chapter 3, titled "Understanding Understanding," with a telling statement:

> Up to now, we have presented understanding as if we understood it. The irony is that though we all claim, as teachers, to be after understanding we may not adequately understand our goal. (p. 38)

This point fits so well with Locke's statement. It also fits with my opening sentence to this chapter. Understanding is an elusive concept, yet what we mean by it is of great importance if we are to help our students achieve it.

If we, who claim to be in the business of helping our students understand, don't understand what understanding is, we could be in trouble! Part of the difficulty with understanding is displayed in the previous sentence. Talking about "understanding" presents a language problem. If you do a search on the World Wide Web about "understanding," nearly all of the findings will be about understanding a topic or an idea, such as understanding nutrition, understanding genetics, or understanding Web sites. There are few references to understanding as a stand-alone concept.

As teachers, you all need to know and be able to talk about something as central to your work as understanding. You need to be able to think and talk about the specific understanding you hope that your students will develop, such as understanding of genetics or inertia. However, you also need to be able to talk more deeply and abstractly about understanding. Therefore, the remainder of this chapter explores some ideas about understanding. Hopefully, as you read this chapter and discuss it with others, you will develop ideas and language that will be useful to you as a teacher striving to help your students understand the content and processes of science. I also hope to be able to help you deal with understanding in a deeper sense to allow you to design lessons that enable students to develop additional facets of understanding.

The following dictionary definitions of *understanding* provide some examples of what is meant by this term:

> To apprehend or comprehend fully
>
> To know or apprehend the meaning
>
> To interpret, to explain
>
> To interpret and explain the meaning of somebody or something
>
> To know or be able to explain to yourself the nature of somebody or something, or the meaning or cause of something
>
> To be able to use or apply knowledge in solving a problem

The first two definitions are rather vague. They don't help us to understand understanding in meaningful terms. The last four definitions all relate to actions—interpreting, explaining, or using knowledge for a purpose, such as solving a problem. The last three all imply that understanding is not abstract, but instead involves something or somebody to be understood. These definitions are more helpful to us as teachers. As we think about teaching science for understanding, we need to think in terms of understanding some aspects of science—its concepts, its processes, its applications, and its nature.

Ideas Underlying the New Paradigm

The following three subsections digress from the main line of "understanding understanding" to describe briefly three ideas that underlie the new paradigm in science teaching and therefore underlie our discussion of understanding science.

Science as Public Knowledge

In science, meaning is not merely "in the eye of the beholder." Scientific understanding is not only personal or individualistic. Understanding in science is public and shared among all people who comprehend a scientific idea or a science process. That is one of the strengths of science. When a scientifically literate person uses a science term or describes a scientific process, others who have an understanding of science gain the same meaning as the speaker. Interpretations and meaning often are created by an individual or a team and have become immersed in data, like Darwin in the decades after his voyage on the *Beagle*. When others become convinced that the data support a particular interpretation or meaning, that idea becomes part of the canon of science, which is shared, public knowledge. For Darwin building a sound argument about his findings from his world travels was an intellectual struggle of analysis and interpretation that took more than twenty years. For others to accept Darwin's ideas, a mechanism had to be found to enable explanation of how species could change and new species could evolve. That came with the rediscovery of Mendel's work on heredity and subsequent work in genetics, including understanding how mutations can occur.

Each of the great "discoveries" of science from Copernicus's heliocentric solar system in the sixteenth century to Watson and Crick's DNA structure in the twentieth century, to the latest discoveries, follows a similar pattern: interpreting data to give them meaning, and then convincing scientific peers of the validity of the interpretations and models used to explain them. In this process, scientific canon becomes public, shared knowledge that all members of the science community accept and find useful.

For students learning science, interpretation and creating shared meaning is an essential part of their learning. One of the difficulties with science learning is the creation of personal meanings by students that differ from scientific canon. This is one of the reasons for the new instructional approaches that have been found to be effective in science classrooms over the past few years. By continually connecting scientific ideas and the data on which they are based—through group work, individual and group writing, group discussions, and student-teacher interactions—students learn to communicate their ideas and make them public. Students also can learn that it often is possible to make different interpretations of the same data, and that seeking an interpretation that all can agree upon may not be easy, because individual students may be making different assumptions about the data or they may be working from different premises. As a result their logical reasoning may differ, even though each may feel that their own reasoning is sound. Through this process of helping students make their ideas and reasoning public, you can then identify when students are developing personal, idiosyncratic ideas that differ from the intended, scientific ideas, and then you can take corrective actions to guide students toward sound reasoning leading to an understanding that is aligned with scientific canon.

When this is handled effectively, students learn not only sound scientific ideas, but also about how science functions to validate science knowledge. However, as you undoubtedly have determined from the foregoing paragraph, the task is complex, especially as you think of twenty-five or more students in a class, each with their own interpretations of a set of observations from an activity. Moreover, this complexity is set in the varied personalities of individual students—some vocal, some introspective, some insecure, some curious, others not caring to engage in open discussion and protracted thought on the topic at hand. This is one of many elements that makes teaching for understanding both exciting and challenging. It also is what makes it necessary for you to learn new perspectives and skills that may be quite unfamiliar.

We will approach these new skills in later chapters, but for now, we will proceed to learn more about understanding.

Reflection & Discussion Questions

The creation of "stories" in science is a useful way for students to form sound meaning. Why is this so? What pitfalls must you be prepared to confront when students create science "stories"?

Understanding the Multiple Dimensions of Science

Science is complex. What is involved in understanding science? At least four dimensions of science must be understood if a person is to become scientifically literate:

1. Conceptual knowledge of science—the body of knowledge that comprises science. Said another way, this is *what we know*.
2. Science processes—the mental tools that scientists use to carry out inquiry and create the concepts that make up the body of knowledge. This concerns *how we know* the concepts that comprise the body of science knowledge.
3. Applications of science—the ways in which science concepts and processes are used in the world of experience. This concerns the *value or importance of science in daily life*.
4. Nature of science—the ways in which scientists work collectively in a professional milieu to generate, validate, and communicate scientific knowledge. This concerns the *internal workings of the scientific professions and their relationship to each other and to the larger society*.

The *National Science Education Standards* and *Science for All Americans* indicate a larger number of dimensions.

Figure 2.1 shows a comparison among the dimensions of science and the content recommendations of these two important documents.

My reason for bringing this before you at this point is to help you consider all four dimensions as we think about understanding science, as all four of these dimensions are a part of becoming scientifically literate. All too often, teachers of science at all levels tend to focus on one or two of these dimensions, yet all four are essential for understanding science in ways that are useful to people who will be citizens in a world strongly influenced by science. These dimensions are also essential in helping young people grasp a larger meaning of science as they explore potential careers that relate to science—careers that involve applying science, generating new science knowledge, or teaching science to others.

As we progress through this chapter, you will have some opportunities to think about understanding each of the four dimensions. In later chapters, you will explore these dimensions more deeply. For example, in Chapter 4 you will explore inquiry and the nature of science more fully. Later chapters will continue to touch on all four dimensions to demonstrate that understanding science involves all four of its dimensions.

Teaching and Learning with Understanding

Chapter 1 introduced the idea that understanding cannot be transmitted from you to your students. Instead, students must construct their own understanding from experience. To do this, they must make personal sense of the new information and fit it into what they already know. Therefore, learning with understanding requires that students make sense of ideas and experiences, and connect them with other, related ideas and experiences that form their prior knowledge. To apply knowledge also requires that students see the connection between

FIGURE 2.1 ■ Comparison of the Dimensions of Science and the Science Content Recommendations of *National Science Education Standards* and Project 2061

Dimensions of Science	National Science Education Standards	Science for All Americans, Project 2061
1. Conceptual knowledge of science	Physical science	The physical setting (encompassing both physical science and earth and space science)
	Earth and space science	
	Life science	The living environment The human organism Human society
2. Process of science	Inquiry	Inquiry (as a component of nature of science) Habits of mind
3. Applications of science	Science and technology	Nature of technology The designed world
	Science in personal and social perspectives	The human organism Human society The designed world The mathematical world
4. Nature of science	Unifying concepts and processes	Common themes Habits of mind
	History and nature of science	Nature of science Nature of mathematics Historical perspectives Habits of mind

the knowledge and its application. This is the essence of what is meant by "constructivism," which is a view of learning that is central to the new paradigm in science (Tobin, 1993).

The broad view of science, described above, that expands the content of science in the new paradigm also must be considered in the application of constructivist views of learning. How can inquiry and the nature of science be incorporated in constructivist views of learning science with understanding? This question probably cannot be answered directly at this point in your development, but should be kept in mind. The consideration of understanding is not limited to understanding conceptual knowledge, but also includes the other three dimensions of science described in the previous section. Further, it is essential that understanding inquiry and the nature of science is connected to a constructivist view of learning. This matter, too, will be considered in this and subsequent chapters.

As you read the remainder of this chapter, you will need to think how a constructivist view of learning will influence your role as a teacher who is teaching for understanding. How does constructivism, as part of teaching for understanding, change your instructional goals, what you view as knowledge, your actions as a teacher, your interactions with students, how and what you assess, and the milieu of the classroom? More will be said about this in Chapter 3, and the idea will underlie much of the remainder of this book.

Reflection & Discussion Questions

The two previous sections represent two significant changes in science teaching and learning that underlie the new paradigm. In each case, they require that teachers develop a new view of science, teaching, and learning. Write a few sentences in which you describe these views to a colleague or friend who is not familiar with them. Then you should share and discuss your writing with classmates or peers.

Understanding Is Demonstrated through Actions

In Martha Stone Wiske's (1998) book *Teaching for Understanding*, David Perkins provides the following definition of understanding: "the ability to think and act flexibly with what one knows" (p. 40). Similar to the last dictionary definition listed earlier, Perkins's definition adds a dimension of application to the meaning of understanding as being able to take actions based on what is known. In addition, Perkins calls for *performances of understanding*, instead of just reproducing information as a way of demonstrating understanding. Performances of understanding involve some action on the part of students. He explains that two ideas follow from this view:

> First to gauge a person's understanding at a given time, ask the person to do something that puts the understanding to work—explaining, solving a problem, building an argument, constructing a product. Second, what learners do in response not only shows their level of current understanding, but very likely advances it. (Wiske, p. 41)

This statement is important as it not only gives an operational definition of understanding, but also defines an instructional response. Tasks such as explaining, using ideas in science to solve problems, constructing arguments, or creating products are essential means of teaching for understanding. In requiring these tasks, teachers both aid advancement of students' understanding and gain insight into what students do and do not understand about the topic at hand. Therefore, such tasks are both instructive to students and useful tools for assessing students' understanding in ways that can guide both teachers in planning for teaching and students becoming self-directed learners.

In focusing on *performances of understanding*, Perkins incorporates application of knowledge into his definition of understanding. This emphasis on performance expands many people's definition of understanding away from that of verbal knowledge or knowledge of *propositions*, which too often is what science teaching and learning are about. It requires that students deal with their knowledge both verbally and in terms of action to demonstrate understanding. It is not just knowing ideas but also being able to use them in some appropriate way.

In reading and interpreting Perkins's work on understanding, we could think only about the conceptual content of science and its applications (Dimensions 1 and 3) and ignore the ways in which science knowledge is produced and validated (Dimensions 2 and 4). However, in thinking about performances of understanding we not only need to help students develop understanding of what we know and how to apply it, but also need to consider how the knowledge has been produced, validated, and communicated, and its value to our world.

Reflection & Discussion Questions

When you think of "understanding," what comes to your mind? What does it mean to understand? Is there a difference between knowing and understanding an idea like inertia or cellular respiration? How does Perkins's definition of understanding help you think about understanding?

How does the concept of *performances of understanding* help? How does the listing of the dimensions of science help you think about understanding?

Elements of Understanding

In their book *Probing Understanding*, White and Gunstone (1992) focus attention on Dimension 1, Conceptual Knowledge of Science, as they expand the elements of understanding to include understanding concepts, whole disciplines, single elements of knowledge, extensive communications, situations, and people. In understanding science, all of these are important, but some may be more critical than others. For the present, we will only consider the first four in this list and leave understanding situations and people outside our discussion, even though these two may be essential in students' personal development.

Understanding Concepts

Understanding concepts is a central part of understanding science. White and Gunstone (1992) include *propositions, images, episodes, intellectual skills, strings*, and *motor skills* as elements of understanding concepts (p.4). A brief description of each of these elements is summarized in Figure 2.2, along with an example.

This figure represents some important components of understanding. The first row highlights the importance of propositions in science and gives examples of three that are a part of the science curriculum. The last proposition ($E=mc^2$) represents an important idea from science that is often memorized but not understood. Therefore, you need to support students as they create meaning from this set of symbols. What does each part of the equation mean? The symbols stand for energy, mass, velocity of light. With c, the velocity of light, as a very large number being squared, it becomes evident that a small amount of matter can be converted into a huge amount of energy. The real-world connection is in nuclear reactors and bombs. If students are to

FIGURE 2.2 ■ Elements of Understanding Concepts According to White and Gunstone

Elements	Brief Description	Examples
Propositions	Facts, opinions, beliefs	There are many forms of energy; atoms are made of protons, neutrons, and electrons; $E=mc^2$
Images	Mental representations of sensory perceptions	The "feel of springiness" of the plunger in an air pump compressing air
Episodes	Memories of events that you experienced directly or vicariously	Recollection of an experiment you did in lab or a demonstration you observed
Intellectual skills	Capacities to carry out classes of mental tasks	Distinguishing among different forms of energy
Strings	Similar to propositions but in an unvarying form	Using "ROYGBIV" to recall the sequence of colors in the visible spectrum; reciting the Gettysburg Address from memory
Motor skills	Capacities to carry out physical tasks	Riding a bicycle; preparing a microscope slide and focusing a microscope

attain understanding, you need to help them "unpack" what the components of the equation represent and give meaning to the relationship that it conveys. This is only a beginning, as it is a big leap for students, intellectually, from understanding the fundamental meaning of the equation (Dimension 1—a small amount of matter can produce a huge amount of energy) to understanding its application (Dimension 3—nuclear reactors and bombs). Dimensions 2 and 4 also can become part of the discourse and inquiry about this topic as students investigate the basis of Einstein's formulation of this equation and how other scientists have empirically validated it.

Therefore, by starting with clarification of a proposition, you can help students give meaning to facts and relationships that are represented in the proposition. This then has the potential to enable understanding.

Another element of understanding included in Figure 2.2 is the role of images in developing understanding. A topic found in many programs at varied levels in the science curriculum is molecular theory, more specifically, the nature of gases as composed of moving molecules separated in space. The image that can emerge as a result of an experience with a syringe can help with understanding this structure of gases. By closing the orifice of a syringe, with the plunger midway in the barrel and pulling or pushing the plunger, students can experience the "springiness" of confined air in the syringe(Figure 2.3). This image can be important for students in comprehending the phenomenon of compressibility of gases. It can be helpful in understanding

the influence of intermolecular forces as a concept useful in explaining compressibility. Such an experience, and the related image, can have an important effect on students' understanding of the phenomenon of gas compression and expansion with changing pressure. Further, it can help students to understand the particle nature of gases and kinetic molecular theory. At another level of abstraction, this can show students how a theory or conceptual model can become a tool for explaining experiences.

Returning again to Figure 2.2, consider the intellectual skills that a student would apply in making sense of experiences and data from rolling metal balls and/or cylinders down an inclined surface and finding patterns and relationships among the variables. One skill would relate to designing experiments that would result in useful data. This could involve willingness to explore what happens when different balls or cylinders are rolled down an incline. This could lead to identification of variables that should be investigated. Another skill would relate to organizing data so that it would be more readily meaningful. A third skill relates to gaining meaning from these data and experiences that probably would involve asking questions such as "How does the mass of the object affect how long it takes the ball or cylinder to roll down the incline?" "What differences in time can be noted between balls and cylinders?" "How do times for hollow and solid cylinders differ?" "How does angle of the incline influence the time it takes for objects to roll the length of the incline?" A fourth intellectual skill relates to evaluating the connection

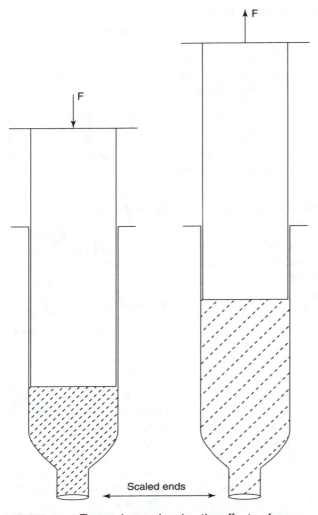

FIGURE 2.3 ■ Two syringes showing the effects of a compressing force ↓ and an expanding force ↑ on molecules of air inside.

between experimental techniques and the quality of data. For example, students should be concerned about the care taken in releasing the object at the top of the incline to be sure that the procedure does not vary from trial to trial. They also need to be thoughtful about how time is measured to ensure that a high level of precision is used in starting and stopping the timer. These concerns relate to the reproducibility of data, which is important in scientific work.

Reflection & Discussion Questions

How does understanding a science concept differ from memorizing a concept?

Think about inertia as an example. Many students can state a common textbook definition of inertia, "*An object at rest tends to remain at rest, or an object*

in motion tends to remain in motion in a straight line unless acted upon by an outside force." Does this mean they understand inertia? As a teacher, how could you tell when a student who can recite this statement understands inertia? What evidence could you collect that would indicate a student's understanding of this science concept?

Come up with another example of this on a topic you plan to teach, and think about how you would tell when a student understands versus just memorizing words.

Understanding Is Neither Dichotomous nor Linear. Many people, including students in school, equate understanding and memorizing. With memorizing a name, a concept, or a formula, learners either can recall it and state it correctly, or they cannot. Perkins refers to this kind of learning as *entity learning* where students believe that learning is something "they either get or they don't." White and Gunstone would refer to it as a dichotomous state. Guided by such a belief, students expect to understand the content they are studying by "getting it" and when this proves difficult, or when it takes more time than they wish to devote to the learning, they frequently give up and conclude that they lack the capability to learn this content.

Understanding fits what Perkins calls *incremental learning*, in which students' performances of understanding, like performances in sports or music, require attention, practice, and refinement to improve (Wiske, 1998). Understanding is not a dichotomous phenomenon. It is incremental, and it grows unevenly in time, with advances followed by plateaus. Sometimes learning with understanding is viewed using stair steps as a metaphor. That is, advances in understanding are like the risers and the plateaus like the treads on stairs. Like all metaphors, this one has limitations. For example, stairs usually are uniform in size while learning may occur in uneven advances, with irregular durations among them.

Reflection & Discussion Questions

How do the terms *entity learning* and *incremental learning* help you in thinking about the difference between memorizing and understanding? How does it affect your thinking about your teaching?

As White and Gunstone (1992) continue their analysis of understanding concepts, they make an important statement:

. . . understanding of a concept is not a dichotomous state but a continuum. . . . Everyone understands to some degree anything they know something about. It follows that understanding is never complete, for we can always add more knowledge, another episode, say, or refine an image or see new links between things we already know. (p. 6)

This statement deserves careful reflection as it has important pedagogical implications. First, as teachers you must recognize that development of understanding is a continuum. Second, you also must recognize that your students often have varying degrees of understanding when they come to you, based on their personal experiences and prior instruction. Third, the idea that understanding always is incomplete offers a viewpoint that is important for you, as teachers, to recognize about yourselves *and* to nurture in your students.

Understanding Whole Disciplines

White and Gunstone (1992) also explore what it means to understand whole disciplines, and they make a similar point. They raise the question, "Did Einstein understand physics?" To some, their answer may be surprising, as they say, "to a degree" (p. 7). They further explore whether Einstein understood physics better than Newton and answer affirmatively by saying that Einstein not only understood what Newton did, but also understood many ideas that were formulated in the centuries between their lives. However, their point that Einstein only understood physics "to a degree" highlights an argument that

> understanding of a concept or of a discipline is a continuous function of the person's knowledge, is not a dichotomy and is not linear in extent. To say someone understands is a subjective judgment, which varies with the judge and with the status of the person who is being judged. Knowledge varies in its relevance to understanding, but this relevance is also a subjective judgment. (White and Gunstone, 1992, p. 7).

How can you as teachers comprehend the significance of this statement? It has so much subjectivity, yet you must make decisions about your students' understanding, as well as what your goals in teaching should be, and how to proceed in helping your students attain them. Part of the answer lies in the guidance that is provided by the standards and benchmarks that national groups, states, and school districts have established. These give you a framework in which to make decisions about what should be taught in the disciplines you teach and what your instructional goals should be. Thus, you do not have to make all of the decisions. The professional community has given much thought to this and made judgments and decisions that you can follow. But in teaching your students within this guiding framework, you must also recognize that subjectivity exists in assessing each student's understanding. As professionals, you must be prepared to make intelligent, carefully reasoned, subjective decisions about

instructional moves that will enable students to progress toward better understanding of the subject matter you are attempting to teach.

Understanding Single Elements and Extensive Communications

Some of the ambiguity that White and Gunstone (1992) describe in understanding of whole disciplines is alleviated by considerations of the next elements in understanding that are described by these authors. Understanding single elements of knowledge and understanding extensive communications provide a focus that can help you expand your understanding of understanding. They make the point that understanding often begins with memorizing specific facts and rules. But it does not stop there. Understanding can, and should, be increased by helping students see connections and relationships among these specifics. This gives less emphasis to rote learning and helps students create meaning, instead of only memorizing. The authors then continue,

> When we talk of understanding of a proposition or a concept or a whole discipline, we are referring to a state of knowledge, the pattern of information that is linked to, or that constitutes, the target. It is a bit different. . . for an extensive communication such as. . . a block of text. When we talk about these. . . we refer to a process rather than a state, the analysis of the words and symbols to make a meaning. (White and Gunstone, 1992, p. 8)

Understanding an extensive communication, such as a textbook chapter or a complex diagram, requires grasping the meaning of each of the constituent parts, as well as grasping the meaning of the whole, which may not be directly expressed. Instead, forming understanding requires that students not only read the passage or examine the diagram with care, but also reflect on it to construct or create the meaning that approximates what the author or graphic artist has intended. In literature classes, the act of interpreting and giving meaning to literary works is part of what reading literature is about. It is less often experienced in science classes, but is an essential part of analysis of data from investigations, texts, diagrams, and lectures. Moreover, developing understanding of important "big ideas" in science also requires this dimension in learning, because it is an important part of learning with understanding.

Reflection & Discussion Questions

One of the headings in this section is "Understanding Is Neither Dichotomous nor Linear." What does this mean to you as a teacher of science? How has your thinking about understanding changed as a result of reading and reflecting on the information in this chapter up to this point? How have your conceptions of teaching and learning changed?

Model-based Reasoning

Science learning very often involves models, which have the characteristics of an *intensive* communication. That is, models often compress a large amount of information into a small space, representing several concepts and their connections to each other as a means of explaining a powerful science idea. Models of the structure of atoms and molecules are commonplace in science. Models that involve the motion of molecules are essential in understanding and explaining many phenomena, including evaporation, condensation, boiling, freezing, chemical reactions, and many others. Models of the cell, human body systems, food webs, the Krebs cycle, and energy flow are important in biology. Models of the structure of the earth, groundwater flow, galaxies, gravitational attraction, and weather fronts are central to earth and space sciences.

To reiterate an essential point, models typically encompass a large amount of scientific information and also show connections and relationships among the component parts. For example, the familiar model of the water cycle that is seen in textbooks shows the connections among several components of that cycle. Most diagrams represent evaporation from the ground and bodies of water, condensation in cloud formation, and precipitation. Because models show connections and relationships, they are important tools to help students understand and use science knowledge. In later chapters we will help you think more specifically about how scientific models can aid in advancing students' reasoning and understanding of the science content you are teaching.

Reflection & Discussion Questions

Pick one of your favorite models in science and reflect on how it helps you think about, and understand, some aspect of the natural world. For example, the water cycle is partly described in the previous paragraph. How does the model of the water cycle that you have seen in textbooks help you think about the "recycling of water" in nature?

Six Facets of Understanding

To further expand our knowledge of understanding, Wiggins and McTighe (1998) have identified six facets of understanding: explanation, interpretation, application,

perspective, empathy, and self-knowledge. For those of us in science, the first three are familiar, but the others may seem foreign. Explanation, interpretation, and application are different ways of using scientific ideas and processes to make sense of experiences and information. Each represents an important "performance of understanding." Self-knowledge also may seem reasonably comprehensible to us; we can see it as part of knowing what we know and what is still "fuzzy" or unclear in our minds. Perspective and empathy are more remote for most of us in science, but at one level of thinking they may be considered as representing deeper dimensions of understanding, whereas explanation, interpretation, and application are more foundational in their orientation.

Exploring each of these more fully in light of Wiggins and McTighe's description of them should be helpful.

Facet 1: Explanation

A central goal of science is explanation. It is what scientists are attempting to do. Most of the big ideas in science—theories—are attempts at explaining the natural world around us. These theories are based on large amounts of data from observations and experiments, and the patterns and relationships among them. In addition, they represent thoughtful reflections and debates about the connections between data and the explanation. Wiggins and McTighe (1998) describe explanation as

> the kind of understanding that emerges from a well-developed and supported theory, an explanation that makes sense of puzzling or opaque phenomenon, data, feelings, or ideas. (p. 46)

How does this relate to understanding? One level of understanding is the ability to use scientific theories, laws, concepts, and processes to explain events and phenomena in the world around us. An important part of science understanding is making the connection between ideas and the data on which they are based—a connection that frequently is missed in science classes. Consequently, students develop a dual misperception—misperception of the concept or theory they are learning *and* misperception of the character of science itself!

Anderson (2003) has pointed out the importance of the connection between data and explanation with an instructional sequence that includes *observations*, *seeking patterns* in the observations, and then creating *explanations* based on them. This three-part sequence highlights the connection between data and explanation, again reinforcing explanation as a central goal of science.

Facet 2: Interpretation

Interpretation is a part of sense making, which is essential to understanding. Scientists collect data. Interpretation is the means by which they make sense of it. It is a central act of science, parallel to explanation as a central goal. It is from interpretations of data that explanations and meaning evolve. Interpretation occurs in many ways. It can be in seeing patterns in a set of data that is presented in a table. It can be in recasting data as a graph. It can be in metaphors or analogies that help people make sense of observations and experiences. It can be in diagrams that show relationships or connections among components of the data. It also can be in models that are included in science textbooks, such as models of atoms, models that represent the structure of the earth, or models of predator-prey interactions.

Wiggins and McTighe (1998) indicate that "the object of interpretation is understanding, not explanation" (p. 48). These authors also state that a principal means of interpreting is by telling a story of what something is about. Creating valid stories that show relationships and connections between data and ideas, and among ideas, aids students in developing understanding. At times, the stories can be created by the teacher to help students see connections. However, understanding is not something passively acquired. Students must be involved in the process of interpreting and making connections if they are to develop understanding. Therefore, students should be involved in creating their own stories, instead of just adopting the teacher's stories. This is why Perkins places such importance on performances of understanding. Storytelling that fosters explanation or interpretation of science knowledge provides useful occasions for students to construct the coherent connections among experiences and data that constitute understanding of science ideas. Students' construction of science-based stories that make connections and show relationships also provides teachers with an important data source for formative assessment as students develop and clarify their understanding.

Students' stories must be reviewed by teachers, because students often construct meanings and connections that do not fit accepted science concepts and processes. Students can develop misconceptions that can be impediments to learning. For example, many students in middle and high school believe that as matter expands as a result of heating, the molecules increase in size. Conversely, contraction with cooling involves a decrease in size of molecules. This construction of experience is logical, given what students know about molecules. However, this construction does not fit accepted scientific knowledge. It ignores at least two concepts in kinetic molecular theory: first, that

molecules move faster when heating occurs; as a result, they occupy more space than when moving more slowly. Second, it ignores the fact that the size and structure of molecules are not affected by reasonable changes in temperature. Therefore, students' interpretations and story creation should be carefully monitored to ensure that students' misinterpretations and misconceptions are not left unchallenged.

Reflection & Discussion Questions

How has your reading and reflection on Facet 2—Interpretation—influenced your thinking about what understanding is and about your role as a teacher?

Facet 3: Application

The real test of understanding for many people is application. It is an important performance of understanding to evaluate understanding based on evidence that the knowledge a person has can be used in practical ways to shed light on, and solve, new problems. Another, perhaps less demanding, "test" of understanding is to use the knowledge in a different context than that in which it was taught. For example, students often learn about condensation from examples of water droplets forming on the side of a container of cold soft drink on a hot, humid day. However, there are many other examples in daily life where condensation can be observed, such as condensation on a range hood when water is being boiled for cooking spaghetti, condensation on the bathroom mirror after showering, condensation on the inside of car windows shortly after people enter the car. You most likely have your own favorite example of condensation.

Having students use the concept of condensation to explain what is occurring in such events is one level of application. Having students propose ways of removing the condensation is another level of application requiring greater understanding. For example, have you tried wiping down the "foggy" bathroom mirror after your morning shower only to find it steams up again? When this occurs, there are at least two ways to remedy the situation. One is to open the bathroom door. Another is to leave the bathroom door closed and use a hair dryer to clear the mirror.

So how does each of these two procedures work to clear the mirror? They are different. I will leave these to you to ponder and explain. But I will give you a hint: the hair dryer does not "blow the water away." Instead, the mirror clears for the same reason that rinsing glassware or dishes in hot water makes them easier to dry than if they are rinsed in cold water. That means that you must use your knowledge of evaporation along with your knowledge of condensation to explain this.

You will note that in the preceding paragraph, I have demonstrated several matters about sound teaching strategies that foster understanding. First, I did not give you the answer. Second, I presented a related, but challenging, task to explain. Third, I pointed you toward the use of prior knowledge (condensation) that is essential to the task. Fourth, I gave you some hints to provide a "scaffold" to help you get started on your effort at interpreting.

Another important part of the approach deals with the context of the problem. I highlighted several different contexts in which condensation can be observed, and then selected one for further exploration. This allows for more authentic experience for students in solving real problems. Addressing a concept in different contexts enables students to expand their understanding and develop the habit of mind that important ideas may be applied to many different situations.

Reflection & Discussion Questions

Think of another concept, different from evaporation and condensation, and describe some applications of it that can form the basis of learning experiences for students and lead to a performance of understanding. How has this reading about Facets 1 through 3 expanded your understanding of science? How has it expanded your understanding of understanding in science?

As stated at the end of the previous section, we will come back to these strategies for teaching for understanding in more detail in later chapters. Now we will proceed to examine three more facets of understanding that may be more difficult for science teachers to grasp than the first three facets.

Facet 4: Perspective

Wiggins and McTighe (1998) refer to perspective as "critical and insightful points of view" (p. 53). They go on to say that

> to understand in this sense is to see things from a dispassionate, and disinterested perspective. This type of understanding is not about any student's particular point of view but about the mature recognition that *any* answer to a complex question typically involves a point of view; hence, an answer is often one of many plausible accounts. (Wiggins and McTighe, 1998, p. 53)

In this sense, perspective furthers the analysis begun in interpretation. In interpreting data or experience, it is important to recognize that multiple interpretations are possible. Perspective delineates some of the tools that enable interpretation and identifying differences among points of view. As Wiggins and McTighe (1998) explain,

> In a critical-thinking sense of the term, students with perspective expose questionable and unexamined assumptions, conclusions and implications. When a student has or can gain perspective, she can gain a critical distance from the habitual or knee-jerk beliefs, feelings, theories, and appeals that characterize less careful and circumspect thinkers. (p. 53)

In the earlier quote above, the authors use the terms *dispassionate* and *disinterested* in connection with perspective. In the later quote, they talk about distancing from habitual or knee-jerk responses. Those who work with youth know how important this is, and that many young people, as well as some adults, have a habit of jumping to conclusions and not considering alternatives in both daily life or in science classes. Therefore, you have a responsibility to help your students consider alternatives and other viewpoints as they examine information, ideas, and the data that underlie them. As the authors state,

> Thus, perspective as an aspect of understanding is a mature achievement, an earned understanding of how ideas look from different vantage points. (Wiggins and McTighe, 1998, p. 54)

As teachers who are attempting to help students develop understanding, you need to make perspective part of your goals. Again, it further complicates the task of teaching. An additional point that these authors make relates to the importance of clear learning goals. This is a theme you will hear recurrently in later chapters. However, their advice is salient at this time:

> To develop fluency and flexibility in perspective taking—if understanding is to blossom—a student needs to have a clear performance goal and to keep that goal in constant view as different points of view emerge. (Wiggins and McTighe, 1998, p. 54)

This is important for you as teachers, as well as for your students. As you design and implement your lessons, you also need to have clear goals and keep them in "constant view." You need to help your students go beyond the surface of the ideas you are teaching if you hope to have them develop understanding and not just memorize facts without grasping their meaning. You must help them recognize what the scientists were trying to accomplish when they "discovered" the ideas that are being studied. You also can help students understand the different meanings that can be attributed to the data on which these ideas were based and how they resolved those differences to achieve the accepted scientific idea.

Perspective also relates to knowing the importance of an idea. The authors comment on this point by referencing the *Oxford English Dictionary* where the definition of *understand* includes "to know the import." They then state the following:

> By this criterion, our educational system is not very successful in causing understanding. Few students leave school with an understanding of the value of their schoolwork—and of the value of the discipline required to learn the disciplines. Few students can successfully ask and answer, What of it? (Wiggins and McTighe, p. 55)

However, all teachers know that students frequently ask the question, "Why are we learning this?" Unfortunately, we often view the question as impertinent and leave it unanswered or give it a superficial answer, such as "You will need it later." Instead teachers should design their lessons and units so that students can come away "knowing the import" of what they are learning.

As you explore models of teaching for understanding in the next chapter, you will learn about approaches that will emphasize helping students examine different points of view and "valuing the discipline required to learn the disciplines" as part of learning for understanding.

Reflection & Discussion Questions

What is meant by perspective?

Describe a place in the topics you have recently taught or intend to teach soon where perspective is important. What about that topic is important for your students to understand? Why do you think it is important? How will you help them come to regard it as important?

Facet 5: Empathy

Empathy is a difficult concept for many in science. Our usual definitions of empathy include consideration of other people's feelings. Further, empathy seems to fit the arts and humanities more readily than science. But that may be because we are using our commonplace definition of the term, such as "the ability to get inside another person's feelings." Wiggins and McTighe (1998) include an additional dimension within this definition by defining *empathy* as "the ability to get inside another person's feelings and worldview" (p. 55). With the addition of the term *worldview*, these authors show that empathy represents both cognition and affect (knowing and feeling), in that it focuses on understanding why people reason as they do.

In science you need to apply this broader definition of empathy at four levels. First, when you are helping students understand scientific ideas such as inertia or the germ theory, which represent important historical changes in worldview, students need help in seeing the intellectual struggle that the formulation and validation of these ideas represent. For Newton and his peers, who lived in an ox-cart world where objects only moved when forces were applied and stopped almost immediately when the force ceased, the concept of inertia commonly was seen as illogical. It seemed illogical because it was rarely demonstrated here on earth, but could be imagined in the astronomical world outside of earth. Pasteur's idea that spoilage of food could be prevented if invisible bacteria were kept away from it also appeared to violate the common sense of the time in which he lived. For Newton and Pasteur, these two ideas represented vast differences with the common mode of thought in their time. Thus, empathy is needed to understand why the science ideas we study in schools are important and what scientists went through to create them and persuade others of their validity and importance.

Second, many of the concepts in science represent a change in *worldview*, which is why they are so important. Also, science, itself, represents an important change in *worldview* in its connection of ideas and the data or experiences that constitute their foundation. To be effective teachers of science, you must understand and appreciate the changes that science has brought to people's ways of thinking about the world and to people's ways of reasoning, arguing, and persuading, in science, in contemporary medical practice, and in law, where evidence and sound reasoning based on conceptual models are at the cornerstone of practice. You also must understand how these differ from the ways of reasoning, arguing, and persuading that are found outside of the scientific and other evidence-based cultures. Moreover, you must include some of this content in your lessons so that your students grasp the important additions science has made, and will continue to make, to our way of thinking and our understanding of the world around us.

The third way in which empathy is important in science teaching and learning also relates to students' ideas and reasoning. Teachers need to grasp how and why their students are thinking as they do. As teachers, you must seek to understand what lies behind your students' ideas and reasoning. More importantly, you need to help students to develop the habit of mind to try to understand their peers' ideas and reasoning, so they can be clear about their own. Recognition of alternate interpretations of the same data by scientists, as well as by their classmates, is a first step. Coming to understand the reasoning processes that lead to different interpretations and conclusions can be an important factor in deepening understanding. As you learn more about teaching science for understanding, you will learn techniques that will enable you "to get inside your students' ideas and reasoning" and understand what prompts them to think as they do about the science ideas that are part of your curriculum. Attention to students' ideas and reasoning is an essential part of teaching science for understanding.

Fourth, empathy is important in understanding many of the current and future issues found in everyday life. For example, most environmental issues engender differing viewpoints from individuals and groups in our society. Use of fossil fuels and its relationship to global warming is one example. Many Americans purchase and drive "gas guzzler" automobiles instead of smaller, more fuel-efficient ones. Automobile manufacturers continue to advertise and promote this behavior. While others may disagree with these choices, it is important to understand the motivations that spur such actions. Similarly, the drivers and manufacturers of these automobiles should understand the concerns of people who oppose these actions.

Wiggins and McTighe (1998) continue their explanation of empathy with a section subtitled "A Form of Insight" in which they state that

> Empathy. . . involves the ability to get beyond odd, alien, seemingly weird opinions or people to find what is meaningful in them. Students have to *learn* how to open-mindedly embrace ideas, experiences, and texts that seem strange, off-putting, or just difficult to access if they are to understand them and their connection to what is more familiar. (p. 56)

Empathy is an important part of understanding, which teachers at all levels of schooling need to comprehend and to which they need to give far greater attention. Empathy is important as part of applying science knowledge in daily life, and it can take root in science classes as part of deepening understanding of science and its relevance to our world.

Reflection & Discussion Questions

What is meant by empathy? Why is it important in science teaching? Describe a place in the topics you have recently taught or intend to teach soon where empathy is important. What differences of viewpoint about that topic is important for your students to understand? Why do you think it is important?

Facet 6: Self-knowledge

According to Wiggins and McTighe (1998), self-knowledge is "the wisdom to know one's ignorance and how one's patterns of thought and action inform as well as prejudice understanding" (p. 57). For me, the

essence of this facet of understanding is examination of my own ideas and reasoning. To consider what I know and don't know about a topic is one component of self-reflection. To consider my own reasoning processes on this topic is another. To consider the actions I have taken to gather, organize, and interpret information about the topic at hand is still another.

The authors describe what self-knowledge requires of us:

> Self-knowledge is a key facet of understanding because it demands that we self-consciously question our understandings to advance them. It asks us to have the discipline to seek and find the inevitable blind spots or oversights in our thinking and to have the courage to face the uncertainty and inconsistencies lurking underneath effective habits, naïve confidence, strong beliefs, and worldviews that only seem complete and final. (Wiggins and McTighe, 1998, p. 59)

This statement opens a realm that many people do not consider—blind spots and oversights in thinking. It urges us to be thoughtful about what we *think* we know and understand, as it is easy for us to be self-deceptive in our perceptions of understanding. As you talk with adults and your students, it often is easy to see inconsistencies in their thinking. However, it is much harder to see those inconsistencies in your own thinking. In nurturing your students' self-knowledge as part of teaching science for understanding, you need to demonstrate the processes of questioning your own understanding and guide the students to do the same with their own ideas and reasoning.

An example may be of value here. Middle school students typically learn about mass and weight as part of the science curriculum. Mass of an object is often defined as the quantity of matter of that object. Weight is often defined as the gravitational attraction of the earth for the object. Students can memorize these definitions without reflecting on their meaning—without assessing their self-knowledge of them. What do the words *quantity of matter* and *gravitational attraction* actually mean? Does an object's mass influence its weight? Do objects that have more mass also weigh more? Does mass have anything to do with the number of molecules in the object? How does this connect with the concept of inertia? Do objects with more mass have more inertia? Questions such as these can help students examine their own knowledge. However, often students do not ask such questions. As teachers, you need to help students develop self-knowledge.

Reflection & Discussion Questions

Describe a situation where you have misunderstood a friend or one of your parents because you did not question your own understanding. Describe a situation where you have misunderstood a science idea because you did not question your own understanding. What caused you then to bring your understanding into question and enabled you to get on the right track? Identify ways in which you will help your students question their own understanding of a science idea or observation.

Each of the six facets of understanding laid out in this work adds to and deepens what is meant by understanding science knowledge. In retrospect, explanation, interpretation, and application are more familiar tools that you have used to construct your understanding of science. However, your understanding of science can be deepened by reflecting carefully on the elaborated meaning of them presented in this chapter and in the work by Wiggins and McTighe. Further, the additions to your *understanding of understanding* provided by reflection on perspective, empathy, and self-knowledge represent new ways for you, as teachers, to expand your own knowledge and that of your students.

Enriching Your Own Lives and Your Students' Lives

Two additional features that these six facets of understanding bring to you as science teachers are (1) the challenge to continually expand and deepen your own knowledge of science and (2) the challenge to guide your students in their formation of the habits of mind that will lead to their deep and effective understanding of science as life-long learners. This highlights the depth of your work as teachers of science. Teaching science is not only conveying science ideas and processes to students, as many in our nation believe. Teaching science also involves continual development of your own knowledge and understanding in an unending journey *and* an unending quest to help students along the same journey. This makes your work forever challenging.

Unfortunately, many teachers "flatten" their careers by not recognizing these exciting and stimulating personal and professional challenges that science teaching can entail. They "dumb-down" the professional work of teachers and their own professional growth. It is not their fault alone. Scientists, teacher educators, and administrators who should provide leadership for the profession often fail to enable teachers to see the superb challenges that are embedded in this career by not emphasizing the opportunities for personal and professional development that it offers to them both in enriching their own knowledge and understanding and that of their students.

Part of what this reform is about is enabling teachers and students to advance their personal growth in ways heretofore uncommon.

In this chapter, you learned the importance of what is meant by "understanding," especially as you think about the science you hope to teach. You learned that it is not easy to understand understanding because it is often hidden from your perception. Perkins identified a broad definition of understanding—"the ability to think and act flexibly with what one knows" (Wiske, 1998, p. 40). He also added "performances of understanding" as an assessment approach that includes both a means of improving understanding of science ideas and a means of assessing students' emerging understanding of them through their use of them in meaningful settings. Perkins also highlighted the difference between entity learning and incremental learning. From White and Gunstone, you learned about the complexity of *understanding* as an educational concept in their explanation of understanding concepts, single elements of knowledge, whole disciplines, and extensive communications. Further you learned from Wiggins and McTighe that the meaning of *understanding* is enriched by their explication of its six facets. Perhaps most important of all, you learned that understanding of a science idea is never complete, as there is always something new to enrich your understanding of any idea.

It is my hope that this chapter has been provocative of enriched thinking about what it means to understand, in your own personal and professional life and in the lives of those whom you teach.

Reflection & Discussion Questions

How has your understanding of understanding changed as a result of reading, discussing, and reflecting on this chapter?

Journal Questions

How has this chapter on understanding understanding advanced your new paradigm about teaching science for understanding and application? Make additions to the following sections of your journal.

1. What were the purposes or objectives of this chapter?
2. What were the key ideas presented in this chapter? (Note: These two could be combined as a two-column table to show the parallel between the purposes of each chapter and the ideas presented.)
3. What important additions have you made to your vision of teaching science for understanding and application by studying this chapter and discussing with others? This should be an ongoing narrative that highlights development of your personal paradigm for teaching and learning science.
4. I also recommend that you create a concept map that portrays your understanding about teaching and learning science for understanding and application and add

new concepts and connections as you study each chapter of this book. This concept map can provide a visual representation of your developing new vision or paradigm of science teaching and learning that you developed in the previous item.

5. What new skills and techniques do you find you need to develop in order to enact your vision of science teaching?

What progress are you making in developing those skills and techniques?

6. Finally, what concerns do you have about being able to implement your new vision, your new paradigm of science teaching with your students, in your classroom, laboratory, and fieldwork? How will you respond to these concerns?

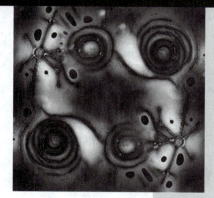

An Initial Planning Model for Teaching Science for Understanding: First Steps in Transforming Your Teaching and Students' Learning

This chapter begins with a presentation of part of a unit of instruction on photosynthesis. This practical approach will allow you to consider the connection between learning and teaching. Two story lines are woven together: one about photosynthesis and another about organizing instruction on this topic for middle school students. It makes the chapter a little different from chapters in many books like this. However, I feel that it is useful for you at this point in your learning about teaching science for understanding, as it integrates two major components of your work as a teacher—the content you teach and how you go about teaching it in a way that nurtures the development of your students' understanding of that content. I also introduce a planning model to aid you in thinking about your teaching. The chapter may become confusing at times as I move from one to the other, but it should help you think about the complexity of your work as a teacher, as you plan and teach specific science content to real students.

Teachers often plan in ways that shortcut careful thought about what they wish to have their students achieve or how they will measure achievement. Objectives of instruction and assessment of learning often are not central to planning. Instead, teachers tend to begin by suggesting activities that would make good lessons.

From a logical standpoint this approach has some serious weaknesses. To counter this tendency, Wiggins and McTighe (1998) have suggested what they call "backward design" in which planning for instruction begins with identification of the objectives of instruction, followed by consideration of the means of assessment of students' learning related to the objectives. The third element of the planning process involves identification of the learning activities. This concept of "backward design" may be backward in its relation to common practice, but it is logically sound as a way of approaching instruction.

The remainder of this chapter provides an initial journey through planning part of a lesson sequence on photosynthesis using this approach of planning objectives, assessments, and activities in a logical fashion. However, as you will learn from experience, the process is iterative. That is, each component of planning informs the others. As a result, while the planning process flows from objectives to assessments to activities, it is somewhat messy. Preparing assessments aids in the clarification of objectives and the identification of activities. Further, planning activities informs assessment and the clarification of objectives. In a final check of the lesson plans, all three must be logically connected.

A Useful Example of Planning Instruction

Understanding photosynthesis is an important goal of science instruction from middle school onward. I will focus on middle school instruction and learning for this example. Planning instruction often begins by identifying the content propositions that relate to the topic

National Science Education Standards *are quite general in describing goals for middle school that relate to photosynthesis. Statements are found in two locations—in the Content Standards for Life Science and in the section on Science in Personal and Social Perspectives. Some relevant statements from these sections are listed below (National Research Council, 1996):*

- *Plants and some organisms are producers—they make their own food. (pp. 157–158)*
- *For ecosystems, the major source of energy is sunlight [which is] transferred by producers into chemical energy through photosynthesis. (p. 158)*
- *Cells carry on many functions needed to sustain on life. They grow and divide, thereby producing more cells. This requires that they take in nutrients, which they use to provide energy for the work that cells do and to make the materials that a cell or an organism needs. (p. 156)*
- *Food provides energy and nutrients for growth and development. (p. 168)*

Even more general statements are found in the sections on Inquiry, Nature of Science, Science and Technology, and History of Science.

Expanding on these as guides, the following represent a sound beginning for a middle school unit on photosynthesis:

- *Plants make food (sugar) through a process known as photosynthesis.*

- *This process involves the use of two key raw materials, carbon dioxide and water, which plants combine, using light energy, to form sugar. Oxygen is a by-product of this production of sugar.*
- *Chlorophyll, the material that gives leaves and other plant parts their green color, is essential for this reaction to occur.*
- *Light is the essential energy source for this process.*
- *Plants transform sugar into hundreds of other products that they use for their growth and metabolism.*
- *The process of photosynthesis may be represented by the following chemical equation:*

$$6\ CO_2 + 6\ H_2O \rightarrow C_6H_{12}O_6 + 6\ O_2$$

These propositions represent the major content points for a middle school unit on photosynthesis. Before continuing with this example, we need to consider what the instructional goals should be for a middle school unit on photosynthesis. Instructional goals should include the key elements of content and appropriate emphasis on its applications. In addition, goals relating to inquiry and the nature of science need to be incorporated if we are to help students develop a valid picture of science. Here is one set of objectives that can guide instruction:

On completion of lessons on photosynthesis, students should be able to:

1. *Describe photosynthesis as the process in which plants use carbon dioxide and water to produce food (sugar) and oxygen.*
2. *Explain that, during photosynthesis, plants capture light energy, which allows them to reassemble molecules of carbon dioxide and water, release oxygen, make sugar molecules, and store the energy in sugar molecules.*
3. *Describe at least two experiments that provide evidence that plants carry out photosynthesis in the presence of sunlight.*
4. *Connect the role of each of the entities in photosynthesis (leaves of plants, light, chlorophyll, CO_2, H_2O, $C_6H_{12}O_6$, and O_2) into a clear, coherent story about the process and its importance.*
5. *Give some examples of the transformation of sugar by plants into new materials, new cells that enable plants to grow, and energy for plants' metabolism.*
6. *Describe a logical argument that led scientists to search for the connection between the production of sugar as the product of photosynthesis and its transformation into a wide variety of plant products.*
7. *Describe the importance of photosynthesis in our world.*

You will notice that all the objectives require *performances of understanding* of students (Wiske, 1998). They require students to do something to show what they have learned. Of these objectives for this lesson sequence, it is likely that only Objectives 1, 5 and 7 could be satisfied through memorization only. However, these two objectives are not limited to memorization but also could, and should, involve understanding and application of science knowledge. The other five objectives require forms of learning that involve reasoning, understanding, and application of knowledge. For example, to be able to provide the explanations or connections identified in Objectives 2 and 4 requires synthesis of many pieces of information within a structured framework. Objectives 3 and 6 deal with inquiry and the nature of science.

Teaching and Learning about Photosynthesis in Ways That Nurture Understanding

How can you help students learn about photosynthesis in a way that results in understanding this important biological process and the capability to use this knowledge, instead of only memorizing it?

To help students learn with understanding will require changes in what most teachers do with, and expect from, their students. It also will require changes in what most students do in class and expect from their time in school. Many students think that learning only involves memorizing. Moreover they sometimes complain that all we do is memorize and yet, paradoxically, some students may become very resistant when more is expected of them, especially when the added requirements include higher-order thinking and application of knowledge. Students want more than memorization, but often they are unwilling to accept the challenges that understanding and application of science knowledge require.

At the broadest level, learning with understanding requires that students become active in learning. At times you may want to have students in a passive role, but the portion of class time for passivity should be small. When you are giving directions, setting goals, or presenting new information, you may want students to act as passive "receivers." Even at these times, an interactive approach can be better. However, the majority of the time, students need to be actively engaged in exploring and investigating, in making sense of ideas, in giving personal meaning to ideas and experiences, and in grappling with connections among them. Active learning is more than having students busy with their hands. Their minds also need to be active to process new ideas, making sense of new information and experience, and making connections with what they already

know, instead of simply acting as "receivers" of information that is to be stored away.

To give credibility to the viewpoint expressed above, the words of a prominent researcher in the field are appropriate. Many educators and cognitive scientists believe that "meaning is constructed by the cognitive apparatus of learners" (Resnick, 1983). In other words, meaning is created in the mind of the student as a result of the students' sensory interaction with her or his world. Others add that students make sense of what teachers present to them by associating the new information with prior knowledge (von Glasersfeld, 1989; Appleton, 1997), *but students must construct the meaning.* The teacher cannot convey or transmit understanding or meaning (Saunders, 1992). Therefore, learning must change from a passive process to an active one, as students construct their own meaning from experience. The role of the teacher becomes one of guiding students as they construct meaning and make connections among ideas. The role of the teacher also becomes one of an assessor who monitors students' construction of meaning to ensure that it is sound and valid, and not erroneous.

Since learning involves the construction of meaning by learners, instead of the more common viewpoint that learning involves reception of information, the process is often described as a "constructivist view" of learning (Brooks and Brooks, 2001). Yager (1991) adds that, with constructivism, students' peers are very important in the learning process. Learning is an interpretive process, involving construction of meaning by individuals. However, there also is strong evidence that social collaboration helps individuals develop and clarify the language to convey meaning about science ideas. Knowledge is created through social interaction as individuals test the usefulness of their conceptual understandings in interactions with others and in contexts in which the knowledge is applied (Tobin, Briscoe, and Holman, 1993). The focus is on interaction of group members in developing and refining the language that gives meaning to experiences with scientific phenomena. Emphases in constructivist thought include considerations of constructs and processes seen to be internal to the learner (Freyberg and Osborne, 1985) as well as the influence of the social context and social interactions (Tobin, 1990). Therefore, the term *social constructivism* is often used to describe the contemporary view of learning.

Reflection & Discussion Questions

The previous four paragraphs are heavily laden with ideas about the role of students and teachers in an environment that nurtures understanding. What is your level of agreement with the viewpoints expressed? How can you help students develop an understanding of the science content that they are learning? How can you as a teacher create an active learning environment where students can develop an understanding of science concepts?

How are these ideas similar to, or different from, ideas held by your classmates or other teachers in your school?

Engagement of students in the work of learning—making sense, making connections, forming meaning from experience—is essential. So how do you, as a teacher, enhance students' engagement in active learning when they view their role as receivers of information that they are expected to memorize? After years in this role, you now ask them for something more demanding! Obviously, the answer is not simple and the essential change won't occur spontaneously or immediately. It will require time and support from teachers, like you, who formulate a clear sense of how to create, and function in, a different educational environment. Therefore, two changes are needed: first in you as a teacher to learn how to teach science for understanding, and second, in your students who also will need to develop a new view about learning and new skills to accompany the changed view.

Generating a Conversation with Students to Learn about Their Ideas

Engagement could begin by asking students to tell you what they know about photosynthesis. Perhaps this could begin with students in groups of three or four, telling each other what they know as a form of review to recall and reconstruct their prior knowledge. Working in small groups involves less risk for them. Students can be intimidated if they are required to make a public statement in front of the whole class on a topic that has become remote. By talking in a small group, the students get to review what they have seen and learned before, both inside and out of school. As they share their ideas with a few peers, they may be challenged to try to sort out their ideas and put them in a more coherent form. If they are then asked to prepare a group report to the whole class, the clarification of their ideas may take on more importance.

This procedure comprises an excellent preassessment of your students' knowledge. What you may learn from this is that students know some facts about photosynthesis, and that some essential ideas and relationships may be missing. Moreover, you may learn that students are not able to put the factual information that they have into a coherent story about photosynthesis. They have facts, but they have not made sense of how the facts fit together into a logical description or explanation about photosynthesis. For example, they

may know that carbon dioxide and water are turned into sugar by plants, but they haven't connected the idea that light energy is "captured by leaves and locked up in sugar." They probably don't know that the bonds between atoms of sugar molecules contain more energy than the bonds in between the atoms in molecules of carbon dioxide or water. They also probably don't know that the added energy in the sugar molecules came from the plant's capture of light. Yet all of these ideas are implied in objectives 2 and 4 listed above. More importantly, these ideas are essential if students are to be able to tell a coherent story about photosynthesis.

Reflection & Discussion Questions

Engaging students and assessing their knowledge at the outset of instruction are important parts of teaching. How does having students review their existing knowledge in groups enable both engagement and preassessment?

Examining Sample Objectives of the Photosynthesis Lesson

Objective 5—Transformation of Sugar by Plants

Objective 5 raises another point that is very often omitted from the "photosynthesis story," which makes for a big void in understanding. This point is about the growth of plants. All plants grow; some grow very fast. If you are a careful observer, you can see growth in some plants from one day to the next. So how do photosynthesis and the production of sugar connect with plant growth?

Look again at Objective 5: *Give some examples of the transformation of sugar by plants into new materials, new cells that enable plants to grow, and energy for plants' metabolism.*

What happens to sugar after it is produced by plants through the process of photosynthesis? It certainly does not all remain as sugar. Some does, in some plants like sugar cane and most fruits and the sap of maple trees. But even then it is changed from glucose into different sugars such as fructose and sucrose. Often it is changed into starch, which makes up many grains and starchy vegetables that we eat. Often sugar is converted into cellulose and lignin, which give plants the materials that enable them to become "woody" and stand upright. Plants also use sugar to form protoplasm from which the internal parts of cells are made. This enables plants to grow. It is also changed into other complex chemicals that result in the wonderful aroma and beautiful pigments of flowers and thousands of other chemicals, such as the waxes that protect apples from drying out or the chemicals that protect them from attack by insects. It is also transformed into amino acids and fats that make up plant proteins and oils such as corn oil, canola oil, and olive oil.

It also is the conversion of sugar into this varied array of chemicals that enables plants to produce cells and results in their growth. Plants convert sugar into complex chemicals and ultimately into new living cells, which enable plants to grow. This is a pretty major "miracle"! And it is an important idea that is omitted in many presentations about photosynthesis. Without this idea, the story is incomplete, making it difficult for students to relate photosynthesis to plants as growing entities that yield a multitude of different products, not just sugar! (Of course, a similar "miracle" occurs in your body—the food you eat is converted into living cells. It also is used to give you the energy to carry out all of the functions that keep you alive and give you your wonderful intellect, your creative spirit, and your engaging personality!)

The foregoing paragraphs about Objective 5 point out an important aspect regarding teaching science for understanding: the content of instruction must comprise a coherent story. Most instructional materials do not include the connection between photosynthesis and growth. Without this, the story omits a part about which students often wonder. When this is missing, students will be frustrated in attempting to make sense of a partial story. Therefore, in teaching science for understanding you must be sure that you formulate a coherent storyline as you plan your instructional units and lessons. It helps if you identify the "big ideas" that constitute your unit and be sure that the goals of your unit match them. It helps if you write out the "storyline" of your unit—the story you want students to be able to understand and tell when they have completed the unit. Another way of checking on the completeness of the content storyline is to write down what you want students to know about, and be able to do with, the subject matter at the end of the unit—another action that should be part of writing objectives.

Reflection & Discussion Questions

Summarize why Objective 5 is an essential part of a unit on photosynthesis.

Objectives 3 and 6—Inquiry and the Nature of Science

Inquiry and the nature of science are addressed with Objectives 3 and 6. Objective 3 calls for inclusion of some experimental evidence that give direct support to the claims that are being made about the production of sugar in plants. These experiments should be part of the

FIGURE 3.1 ■ Geranium with some leaves covered with opaque material.

instructional sequence that students experience. Two examples follow but others could be substituted or added to provide additional experiential data on which students can build their understanding.

Testing the effects of light on the production of starch: At the middle school level, one familiar demonstration involves covering a few leaves of a geranium plant with an opaque material so that light does not reach them (Figure 3.1). After a couple of days of strong exposure to light, these leaves are removed, boiled briefly in alcohol to remove the chlorophyll, and then tested for the presence of starch by adding a few drops of tincture of iodine to the surface of the leaves. Also other leaves that have been exposed to light are removed and tested in the same way. The hypothesis is that the leaves that have been exposed to light will turn dark when the iodine solution is applied, showing the presence of starch, whereas the leaves that had been covered with the opaque material will not show starch presence. (A key inference in this activity is that sugar changes to starch quickly in plant leaves. Part of the reason for using the starch test is that it is simple, while testing for the presence of sugar is more difficult. Also, the leaves of geranium plants readily show the presence of starch when exposed to light.)

Another simple demonstration that can be carried out involves inverting a large glass funnel over several

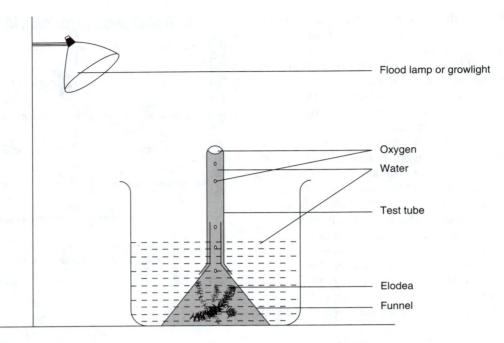

Flood lamp or growlight

Oxygen

Water

Test tube

Elodea

Funnel

FIGURE 3.2 ■ Elodea in a gas collection system.

sprigs of elodea, an aquatic plant that can be found in stores that sell fish and other supplies for aquaria. This system is submerged and a water-filled test tube is inverted over the stem of the funnel (Figure 3.2). Exposure to a strong light for a few hours will result in accumulation of a gas in an inverted test tube, displacing some of the water. Testing that gas with a glowing splint will show the presence of oxygen. This is a standard qualitative test that indicates the presence of oxygen if the glowing splint bursts into flame on insertion into the test tube.

The argument underlying Objective 6, which led scientists to search for the connection between the production of sugar by plants and its transformation into a wide variety of products had its beginnings in observations that are as old as humans. Throughout the ages people have depended on plants for many products including olive oil, waxes, fragrances from flowers, and many varieties of foods including the carbohydrates, proteins, and fats that are found in nuts, fruits, leaves, stems, roots, and even flowers. The question about how plants produced such varieties of materials and in such quantities became more pressing when scientists figured out that the raw material for all of these materials was sugar, the product of photosynthesis. The plants did not have another source of such material. Therefore, every one of these products is based in some way on a transformation of sugar (Ross, et al., pp. 91–96, 1996).

A Model to Guide Design and Planning

Establishing Objectives and Assessment

In the process described in the foregoing paragraphs, you have begun to attend to two of five important aspects of planning for your instruction: establishing your *instructional objectives* and *preassessment*, that is, how you will gain information about the ideas students bring with them on the topic. The remaining elements of planning include *summative assessment*, which occurs at the end of instruction; *formative assessment*, which is integrated throughout instruction; and the *activities* that constitute the learning opportunities for the students.

As you consider the objectives of instruction, you also should think about how you will determine whether students have actually met these objectives by the end of instruction. That is, how will you assess students at the end of the unit? Considering the summative assessment early in planning instruction is helpful as it offers more detailed meaning for the more abstract statements of objectives. Wiggins and McTighe (1998) describe this process as "backward design"—backward because many people plan lessons by thinking of assessment last in the process, after planning activities.

Earlier, the discussion included preassessment of students' ideas and reasoning about photosynthesis, which also served as an engaging activity. Two more aspects of instructional planning follow: (1) identifying learning activities that have potential to modify students' ideas and reasoning, and (2) determining formative assessments that monitor students' progress as they develop their new understanding of the topic.

As you can see, this instructional approach places a large emphasis on assessment. Preassessment, formative assessment, and summative assessment are each part of instructional planning. Learning activities that provide students with opportunities to learn with understanding and the accompanying assessment, especially formative assessment that is embedded within the activities, provide teachers and students with feedback on their progress toward the instructional objectives. Said another way, preassessment allows students and teachers to form a "picture" of where the students are in relation to the objectives at the start of instruction. Formative assessment allows both students and teachers to gauge progress toward the objectives during instruction. It also allows for corrective action when students fail to grasp ideas or form misconceptions, as they are being developed in the lesson sequence. Summative assessment allows teachers and students to take a holistic look at how students have created meaning on the topic. These three forms of assessment can all be included in one term—continuous assessment—which represents an important idea in teaching and learning for understanding.

Designing Learning Activities

Figure 3.3 provides a visual model of an approach to design and planning learning activities for sequences of lessons that support development of understanding.

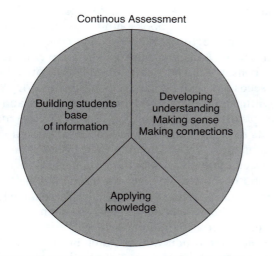

FIGURE 3.3 ■ A Model for Design and Planning of Lesson Sequences in Science

It shows the three instructional components in a backdrop of continuous assessment that includes preassessment, formative assessment, and summative assessment.

This model is based on my assertion that learning activities need to be of three types: (1) building an accurate base of experience and information about the topic to be learned, (2) developing understanding, including making sense of experiences and information and making connections among these components as well as between these components and what students already know, and (3) learning how to apply their new understanding to the real world in new contexts. To reiterate an essential point: all of this exists in a backdrop of continuous assessment that includes preassessment, formative assessment that blurs the lines between teaching and assessing, and summative assessment that occurs at the end of instruction.

This model needs some additional explanation. The three types of learning activities do not comprise a sequence, nor are they always distinct from each other in time. The sequence is not necessarily beginning with type 1, followed by type 2, and concluding with type 3. It is entirely possible to begin an instructional sequence with type 3, application. For example, engagement often can be enhanced by beginning instruction with an application of the concepts being studied. Also the boundaries among the types should be considered as fluid, so that students and teachers should be thinking about all three, even though they may be focusing on one of them. Moreover, three types may vary in proportion. The diagram shows them all of equal proportion, but it is not my intent that the three elements have equal time. In many college-level science courses, most of the time is spent on type 1 (building the information base) and virtually no time on type 3 (application). However, I recommend that a much larger portion of time needs to be spent on developing understanding and applying knowledge than is commonplace in science classes.

Figure 3.4 highlights an essential point: the three levels require different kinds of teaching strategies and learning activities. Building students' base of information requires familiar information transfer methods as well as methods that provide students with first-hand experiences with phenomena. Developing understanding requires activities that enable students to construct meaning from experience. These activities engage students in active learning as they write about, talk about, create diagrams and models of, and prepare presentations about scientific ideas and experiences. A key part of these activities is sense making and making connections between what they already know and new information and experiences. Applying knowledge involves further expanding understanding by connecting

FIGURE 3.4 ■ Teaching and Assessment Activities to Support Teaching and Learning Science for Understanding

Building Students' Base of Information	Developing Understanding	Applying Knowledge
Learning facts, concepts, and skills	Making sense and interrelating concepts	Applying concepts to real problems
Familiar Teacher-centered Methods	**New Methods of Active Learning**	**Even Newer Methods Beyond the Classroom**
Giving lectures and demonstrations	Writing to learn	Finding practical applications
Assigning reading	Participatingin group discussions	
Answering questions and problems that advance students' information base	Preparing and giving presentations	Finding applications to advance understanding
Watching videos	Formulating explanations	Finding applications that aid subsequent learning
Assigning hands-on activities and cookbook laboratory activities	Performing investigative or inquiry laboratory activities	Using science knowledge to solve real problems
Testing Recall of Facts and Concepts	**Assessing Performances of Understanding**	**Assessing Capability to Apply Science Knowledge**

beyond the classroom to the outside world. Activities include finding practical applications of the science ideas being studied and finding applications that advance understanding and aid subsequent learning. The bottom two rows in Figure 3.4 also show that different kinds of laboratory activities and different approaches to assessment are needed for each level of learning.

What this figure highlights is that many teachers will need to form both a new vision of learning and teaching and learn new teaching and assessment skills to enable enactment of that vision.

Reflection & Discussion Questions

Much of the experience you have had as a student involved only one of the three parts of the planning model described above and in Figures 3.1 and 3.2. Building a base of information has been a major part of science teaching, whereas nurturing understanding and application often have "taken a back seat." Why must these two parts move up in importance in science teaching and learning? How convinced are you that these need much more attention in your teaching than you experienced as a student? What are your key worries about this new focus in science teaching?

Using the Planning Model to Interpret Activities in Teaching Photosynthesis

Returning to the unit on photosynthesis, what kinds of learning and assessment activities are appropriate for each of the three levels described above?

Type 1, building students' base of information, would involve some information transfer via demonstrations, labs, hands-on activities, searching in resources (including books and the Internet), reading, videos, and lectures. Students also could germinate some bean seeds and observe their development as they consume the nutrients stored in the cotyledons of the seeds and then become self-sufficient through photosynthesis, as leaves and stems turn green and they start producing their own food. Leaves of more mature plants in bright sunlight could be tested for the presence of sugar. Transformation of sugar into starch can be tested for in plants such as geraniums where the test for photosynthesis involves the simple iodine test for starch after removing the chlorophyll by soaking leaves in hot alcohol. Covering parts of geranium leaves with opaque material, to inhibit photosynthesis, allows comparison in the production of starch in the covered and uncovered parts. In addition to providing direct experience via a laboratory activity or demonstration with these phenomena, you also can provide students with readings, videos, and lectures that will add to their information base.

Type 2 and type 3 activities are not entirely separate from type 1 activities. As you work with students in building their information base, you also can begin to help students build understanding. Making sense of the input from each activity and making connections among the activities is an important part of developing understanding. Asking questions such as "Why is it necessary to soak leaves in hot alcohol in order to test for starch?" or "What do you predict the difference will be between the covered parts and uncovered parts of leaves, when we test for starch?" advances the classroom discourse and students' thinking in ways that enable understanding. The first question may prompt students to recognize that the iodine test will be hard to observe on dark green leaves, but if the green chlorophyll is leached out by soaking the leaves in hot alcohol, then the presence of starch will be easier to determine on pale leaves. The second question should prompt a prediction that there will be evidence of starch in leaves that have been exposed to light, whereas there would be an absence of starch in leaves that were not exposed to the light.

As is shown in Figures 3.4, types 2 and 3 activities require students to make sense of the information and experiences gained in type 1 activities. They also require that students make connections among the experiences and with what they already know. This involves organizing and analyzing information to look for patterns and relationships; it involves giving meaning to experience.

What does this mean in terms of actions that the students and you will engage in? Let's work through the observations from the laboratory activity or demonstrations with the geranium leaves to provide an example. Students have observed that leaves and parts of leaves exposed to bright light, soaked in hot alcohol, and then tested with iodine appear very dark in color, nearly black. Leaves or parts of leaves not exposed to light simply show the color of iodine, deep orange, when tested.

Before we continue, we need to consider the objectives for doing the lab or demonstration. Let's assume that for the sake of safety, you do part of the lab as demonstrations such as boiling leaves in alcohol. There would be some additional objectives regarding safety and procedures if the all of the activities were carried out by students. By considering demonstration as the vehicle for this learning, it sharpens the focus on content knowledge, which helps to simplify an already complex matter.

Now it is important to consider objectives for these two activities. I suggest the following objectives.

At the end of the two demonstrations and follow-up activity, students should be able to:

- *Describe evidence that shows that light is essential for photosynthesis.*
- *Describe the process for comparing the presence of starch in leaves (and leaf parts) exposed and not exposed to light.*
- *Explain the origin or source starch in the leaves of the plants.*
- *Connect the demonstration to their developing understanding of photosynthesis.*

What follows is a set of questions that could be used to guide small-group or whole-class discussions about these observations. (Small-group discussions, typically in groups of four, are preferred, but students must be prepared for small-group work. This will be a topic of a later chapter.)

- *Why did we test for starch in these experiments when we have said all along that sugar is the product of photosynthesis?* (Note that this question should be discussed during your lab preparation. Following the demonstration, you now are checking to determine whether the students have included this central idea into their thinking.)
- *Describe the iodine test for starch. What color change occurs when starch is present? What happens when starch is not present?*
- *When we soaked the leaves in hot alcohol, the leaves became pale and the alcohol became green. Describe what occurred to cause these changes? Why was this step a necessary part of the process?*
- *Think about the leaves that had been partially (or fully) covered to keep light from reaching them. We soaked them in hot alcohol and then we placed iodine on them. What did we observe? Explain the cause of those observations.*
- *What did these two activities with the geranium leaves show you about photosynthesis? What did we observe? What did we infer from these observations? What did we assume about the production of starch? What did we conclude?*

While students are discussing these questions, and writing answers to them in small groups, you should spend time observing and listening to each group to make sure they are on task, to note the answers that individuals are giving, and to ask probing questions to cause students to think more deeply about the questions and their answers.

Reflection & Discussion Questions

What is meant by "probing" questions? Give a couple of examples of questions you could ask students that would probe their understanding of the demonstrations and give you more information than those listed above.

Why is it essential that you observe and listen to each group? In answering this question, think about both classroom management and students' learning.

As you can see from these questions, you are prompting students to reflect on the activities that they have just completed and helping them draw meaning from them. The next steps are to (1) have each group of students report on their discussions and the answers to questions and (2) then give them a short individual quiz about the topic. The reporting procedure could be to ask each group to give their answer to one of the questions and have other groups respond to that answer. To prompt responses from members of all groups, you could include questions such as "What do people from other groups think of that answer?" or "Do other group members have any additions or corrections to make to that response?"

The short quiz could ask questions like the following:

1. *Sugar is a product of photosynthesis, but in the activities we tested for starch. Why is this considered a valid strategy? Where did the starch come from? Why is it important to consider the origin of the starch?*

2. *Why was it necessary to soak the leaves of the geranium plant in hot alcohol before testing them with iodine?*

3. *Describe the results of placing iodine on a leaf that has been partly covered, exposed to light, and then soaked in alcohol.*

4. *In the activity, we covered parts of leaves, exposed them to light, soaked the leaves in hot alcohol, and applied iodine to them. We inferred that no starch was found in the covered parts, but starch was found in the uncovered parts. What did we observe that allowed us to make the inference? What did we conclude from these observations and inferences?*

The quiz serves at least two purposes. First, it is an individual check on an understanding of the activities and the related concepts. Therefore, it is a part of formative assessment. This is important because much of the activity is group or whole-class centered and it allows you, as the teacher, to learn whether individuals are progressing toward the intended goals. Second, the quiz is also a learning activity for the students. Because it is a writing task, students need to represent their ideas somewhat differently than they have previously in the lesson where most of the activity was group based, hands-on, and oral. Individual writing adds an additional dimension to the learning. Also, the particular questions are intended to prompt a deeper level of reflection that is grounded in the prior experiences of engaging in the activities and in discussing them in small groups and in whole-class discussion.

Reflecting on the Photosynthesis Activities

Up to this point, this chapter has focused on what probably would be two or three class periods within an instructional unit on photosynthesis. The discussion centered on two related demonstrations and the activities that surround them. At the beginning of the chapter, I presented a set of subject matter propositions about photosynthesis, followed by a statement of broad objectives for the instructional unit. Next, I described a planning model with three levels of activities dealing with (1) building students' information base, (2) developing understanding of the information and experiences that were part of level 1, and (3) applying knowledge in new contexts. I then used the planning model to help you think through some aspects of the teaching-learning process. This included the demonstrations, which were type 1 activities, small-group and whole-class type 2 activities, and the assessments that are an essential element of teaching and learning for understanding. I did not include some parts of lesson and unit planning that are also essential, such as considering where these activities fit into the instructional sequence or how to engage students in the activities.

I have not presented a complete lesson sequence. I started out considering the objectives for the lesson sequence and described part of the content. I then "zeroed in" on two aspects of the lesson sequence—a demonstration that provided the experiential, information-building part, and the follow-up activities that provide an example of the sense-making or understanding-building part of a lesson within the sequence. Clearly, there is much more to this lesson sequence than is represented here. More details will be provided in Chapter 6.

Even with this abbreviated lesson plan, you saw a degree of complexity in planning for teaching science for understanding that may have surprised you. This presentation clearly shows that teaching for understanding involves more than the teacher transmitting information to students. Time and activities must be devoted to helping students create meaning and understanding from their experiences. Here is where you must act as a facilitator by providing the right activities and asking the right questions at the right time. Also, you must be attentive to note students' progress toward understanding and any potential difficulties or misconceptions students may form or carry with them as they process information. This is where assessment is essential.

I hope you are forming agreement with the claim that understanding cannot be transmitted and that understanding can be nurtured through interaction with phenomena, written material in books or on line, and people, including you and other students. I hope that you recognize that understanding is developed through action and that you are comprehending what active learning entails. Moreover, I hope you agree with White and Gunstone (1992) that understanding is not a dichotomous state.

Reflection & Discussion Questions

To what degree do you concur with the following statements:

- Understanding cannot be transmitted, but can be nurtured through interaction with phenomena and people, including you and other students.

- Understanding is developed through action.

- Understanding is not a dichotomous state.

To what degree are you developing an understanding of what active learning entails?

Research-based Knowledge on Teaching for Understanding

The National Research Council assembled a group of prominent psychologists and educators to synthesize what is presently known about learning and how this knowledge can be used to improve teaching and learning in schools. Although their report is long and well documented, they recommended three essential elements of teaching for understanding:

- Attention to the ideas that students bring with them to the classroom, which constitute their personal understandings of how the world works. If their initial understandings are not addressed, they may fail to grasp the new concepts and ideas that are being taught, or they may learn them for the purposes of a test and revert to their preconceptions outside of the school environment.

- Building competence by supporting students' development of (1) a deep foundation of content knowledge, (2) understanding of facts and ideas in the context of a conceptual framework, and (3) an organization of that knowledge in ways that facilitate its retrieval and application.

- Helping students "learn how to learn," so they can become independent learners who take control of their own learning by defining learning goals and by monitoring their own progress in achieving them. (Bransford, Brown, and Cocking, 2000, pp.14–18)

To this list I must add an idea with which these authors also concur, that learning not only is an individual activity, but also is affected by the social and physical context in which it occurs. Most scholars who study the learning process agree that knowledge is socially constructed, and that too has implications for

teachers as they strive to help students understand the subject matter they teach (Lave and Wenger, 1991).

In what ways have the activities in the first part of this chapter reflected these essential elements? Look at the first essential element, *attention to students' ideas*. The section headed "Generating a Conversation with Students to Learn about Their Ideas" suggests ways for gaining information about what students already know about photosynthesis, including their naïve conceptions, and preconceptions, about it. This conversation about photosynthesis provides a window into students' thinking about the topic.

Also, as you have seen from the planning model, assessment is the backdrop in which all three levels of learning and teaching occur. Preassessment, of which this initial conversation is an example, is only one part of the assessment that this model requires. It also requires continuous, formative assessment as you and your students progress through the unit and summative assessment at the end of a topic or unit.

This expands the first essential element beyond "attention to the ideas that students bring with them to the classroom" (Bransford, Brown, and Cocking, 2000, pp. 14–15). It gives attention to students' ideas throughout the instructional process. Moreover, in the photosynthesis example, assessment occurred at many points—with the initial conversation, which may have taken half of a class period, again as the teacher was observing students working in small groups on the reflection questions following the demonstrations, and again using the quiz as an assessment of progress of individuals toward the objectives of the activities surrounding the demonstrations.

Reflection & Discussion Questions

You may not have observed formative assessment in science classes. Sometimes it is not there to observe. Sometimes it is not explicit and therefore somewhat invisible. What place do you think continuous, formative assessment should have in your science classes? What skills will you need to develop in order to be able to use formative assessment in significant ways with your students?

The second essential element has three component parts: "(1) a deep foundation of content knowledge, (2) understanding of facts and ideas in the context of a conceptual framework, and (3) an organization of that knowledge in ways that facilitate its retrieval and application" (Bransford, Brown, and Cocking, 2000, p. 16). Through the activities and demonstrations, I attempted to show how to go about building understanding of the content knowledge, including both important ideas that contribute to an understanding of photosynthesis itself *and* the processes by which scientists (and students) move from experience with a phenomenon to understanding of those experiences and the phenomenon. In doing so, I included activities that provided opportunities for students to examine information from the demonstrations and give it meaning. Part of the work in the photosynthesis example was at the early stages of building a conceptual framework that will aid in organizing information, ideas, and experiences for meaning and later retrieval.

One specific way that I attended to part 3, organizing knowledge for retrieval, was in the formulation of the content for the unit. As you will recall, I added two dimensions in the unit goals that typically are omitted in the content of instruction about photosynthesis. I added the connection between photosynthesis and plant growth. I also added attention to the multiple products that plants make by transforming sugar into cellulose, starch, lignin, oils, waxes, and substances that give flowers their color and aroma (see Objective 5). These two dimensions are important in organizing content knowledge for retrieval because they close a logical, conceptual gap that frequently has been left open in most instruction about photosynthesis.

Turning attention to the planning model, the three activity types—building an information base, developing understanding, and applying knowledge—map very closely onto the second essential element identified by the National Research Council study. The model attends to the first two parts of the second essential element directly. The third part, organizing for retrieval, is not explicitly covered by the planning model, and that needs more attention as we develop our ideas in later chapters.

The third essential element—helping students "learn how to learn"—also was addressed in the activities and in the planning model (Bransford, Brown, and Cocking, 2000). In addition to learning with understanding, "learning how to learn" is what the model is about. Activity types 2 and 3 on understanding and application form a foundation for learning how to learn, which is accentuated in the emphasis on assessment. Moreover, activities such as working in groups, preparing and giving oral presentations, and writing to learn were designed to help students develop skills and techniques that enable independence in learning. However, learning how to learn is less visible than other aspects of learning, partly because most people are less experienced with it. In addition, you may not have language that helps you describe it and give it meaning. That too will emerge as you work through subsequent chapters.

Finally, the point that I added to the three essential elements, about social construction of knowledge, is evident in the lessons that surround the two demonstrations about photosynthesis. Students worked in groups on two situations that provided a setting for

them to work together to clarify and construct meaning from the experiences with phenomena. The preassessment activity and the discussion following the demonstrations were both designed for small-group discussion followed by whole-class discussion. The interaction among students within small groups and again interactions with the whole class provide the physical context, and the questions that were listed provide the intellectual context for interaction that leads to socially constructed knowledge.

The planning model is not explicit about the importance of social construction of knowledge. This represents a limitation of the model. However, Figure 3.4 does emphasize group work, writing to learn, public presentations, and inquiry, all of which have a social component. In addition, the organization of this chapter, like previous ones, with "Reflection and Discussion Questions" interspersed throughout, emphasizes the need for social construction of your newly developing understanding about teaching and learning. I feel that interaction with colleagues is an essential part of your professional development, and I strongly encourage you to include this as part of your professional work. One important intention of this book is to help you experience the construction of your own understanding about both science content knowledge and approaches to teaching, learning, and assessment.

Reflection & Discussion Questions

Why is it important for you to develop concepts, language, experiences, and habits of mind that will enable you to engage in discourse about planning, teaching, learning, and reflecting on your work with your colleagues as a valuable part of your professional activity? How can this influence your professional development and your work as a teacher?

As you conclude this chapter, you should remember that if science instruction is to be effective in guiding students to understanding and developing the capability to use their science knowledge, you need to plan instructional activities in sequences that

1. Provide opportunities for students to engage with appropriate phenomena that pertain to the topic under study and with valid information, ideas, and reasoning about the topic.

2. Nurture students' developing ideas and reasoning as they process the information by engaging with it, making sense of it, and making connections with other related ideas.

3. Assess each student's ideas and reasoning as these develop, and also provide corrective action when it

appears that one or more students are developing incomplete or inaccurate personal knowledge about the content being taught.

This may be a very different view of teaching and learning than you may be used to. However, it is a view of learning that fits with our present-day knowledge from psychology and science education about how we can attain the goals set forth in the *National Science Education Standards*, Project 2061, and many state standards. Like all scientific, academic, and practical knowledge, it may change as new information and interpretive frameworks emerge. However, these documents represent the most sound framework for learning science with understanding that is available at present.

Reflection & Discussion Questions

You may hear a question like this from colleagues, parents, and even students: "Why not just present students the correct ideas and demonstrate the appropriate reasoning as a guide and have them learn how to use the ideas and reasoning processes correctly?" How will you answer this question when you hear it?

[Although I won't do this often, I will share my reaction to this question. You should expand on it. The suggestion is a good start, but it is inadequate. We have long history in which many thoughtful teachers have done just this and it is not very effective, because understanding cannot be transmitted. Understanding must be constructed individually, with teachers monitoring this construction and rectifying it when it deviates into unsound directions.]

A Final Note

After reading this chapter, you should now understand why the subtitle begins with "First Steps. . . .." The focus of the chapter is on teaching and its relationship to learning. The transformation you are about to make in your professional work is a substantial one. It involves transforming your views about science knowledge, about learning, about students, and about your roles as a teacher. The process involved in making a successful and lasting transformation is long and complex. Therefore, in this chapter, we began with some manageable steps. We will elaborate and expand these steps as we continue on this journey. We are consistent with the ancient Chinese proverb: "A journey of a thousand miles begins with one step."

Journal Questions

Add to your journal by revisiting the following questions that will help you monitor your progress as you make a paradigm shift in your teaching and your understanding of your students' learning for understanding and application in science.

1. What were the purposes or objectives of this chapter?
2. What were the key ideas presented in this chapter? (Note: Items 1 and 2 could be combined as a two-column table to show the parallel between the purposes of each chapter and the ideas presented.)
3. What important additions have you made to your vision of teaching science for understanding and application by studying this chapter and discussing with others? This should be an ongoing narrative that highlights development of your personal paradigm for teaching and learning science.
4. I also recommend that you create a concept map that portrays your understanding about teaching and learning science for understanding and application and add new concepts and connections as you study each chapter of this book. This concept map can provide a visual representation of your developing new vision or paradigm of science teaching and learning that you developed in the previous item.
5. What new skills and techniques do you find you need to develop in order to enact your vision of science teaching? What progress are you making in developing those skills and techniques?
6. Finally, what concerns do you have about being able to implement your new vision, your new paradigm of science teaching with your students, in your classroom, laboratory, and fieldwork? How will you respond to these concerns?

Chapter 4

Models of Teaching Science for Understanding through Inquiry

This chapter describes three models for teaching for understanding through inquiry and then shows how these models can be applied to teaching. This will give you a deeper look at teaching this topic than was presented in Chapter 3, and will help you grasp the complexity of the task of teaching science for understanding.

You will notice two shifts that have occurred as you begin this chapter. First, increased emphasis will be given to teaching, in addition to planning. Second, *inquiry* will be given greater prominence in planning and teaching. Both of these are important additions. Before continuing with the teaching models, I have provided you with the following short introduction to inquiry.

Inquiry as an Essential Part of Science Teaching

Inquiry was mentioned in Chapter 1, but not explained. It is one of the seven dimensions of science content in the *National Science Education Standards*. Inquiry was placed first on the list, indicating the importance given to it by the developers of that document.

What makes inquiry so important, when you may have had little experience with it, even though you have been studying science for a long time? Leaders in science education have been emphasizing inquiry for about a century and its importance has varied over that time. In the 1960s, it took on an important place in national projects to improve science curricula at all levels from kindergarten through college. It became a prominent, even a central, element in science programs and textbooks in elementary, middle, and high schools. Although inquiry was picked up by some science teachers, it did not reach wide-scale usage across the nation (Weiss, 1979). However, in spite of its minimal inclusion in classrooms during the closing years of the twentieth century, it had a "rebirth" in *National Science Education Standards*, as more people recognized its importance.

What is inquiry? Inquiry is a term that describes the processes scientists use to carry on investigations and research in generating knowledge and understanding about the natural world. Science has two major dimensions: (1) the concepts, principles, laws, and theories that comprise the *body of knowledge* that fills journals, textbooks, and all of the other repositories that hold scientific information, and (2) *inquiry*, which is "how we think about what we know, why we know, and how we have come to know" (National Research Council, 2000, p. 6). Educators and scientists who have given deep thought to science teaching and learning agree that both of these dimensions are essential to understanding science. Both groups recognize the importance of understanding *what we know* and *how we know* if people are to have a valid understanding of science. Knowing both dimensions helps in making the connection between the concepts, theories, and laws of science (which are abstract entities) and the data and experiences on which they are based. In addition to enabling deeper understanding of science knowledge and how scientists work and think, inquiry, when incorporated into science teaching, capitalizes on and enriches the natural, human curiosity that we all have about the world around us. Inquiry, therefore, not only is important for learning, but also has a positive effect on motivation.

Inquiry is a critical omission in the backgrounds of many pre-service and practicing secondary science teachers. In spite of their deep knowledge of the important theories and concepts in science, most science teachers learned them as abstractions, without fully grounding them in the data, experiences, and procedures on which they are based. As a result, these teachers lack the connections between what is known and how it came to be known. Consequently, when these teachers plan and enact lessons with their students, they are not able to help students make the connections between abstract ideas and the data, experience, and processes on which they are built. This leaves students with an incomplete picture of the nature of science and how it works to create knowledge. It also leaves them with a hollow grasp of the concepts and theories of science.

What does inquiry look like when scientists engage in it? What does it look like in school classrooms? For an elaborate description of inquiry in both of these settings, I recommend you read *Inquiry and the National Science Education Standards: A Guide for Teaching and Learning* (National Research Council, 2000). It is an excellent resource for you as you expand your knowledge about teaching science for understanding.

To give a short answer to the questions in the preceding paragraph, inquiry involves investigating. That includes being curious about something, asking questions, and using these questions to guide the search for information in books and other sources or by investigating through observing and doing experiments. Investigating, whether done by scientists or school students, also involves making sense of the information acquired and using it to answer the questions that curiosity prompted. Therefore, because inquiry involves sense making, it typically results in an advancement of understanding.

Inquiry uses a variety of skills and techniques as tools for investigating and making sense of the natural world, such as

- Asking questions that can be answered through "first-hand" observations and experiments, or through analysis of information and data collected by others.
- Making observations, which involves using your senses.
- Using words and diagrams to also describe observations and to note patterns that occur in them.
- Using numbers to describe and quantify observable events.
- Making inferences, seeking to identify patterns, and formulating predictions and hypotheses, which permit the investigator to go beyond the available information in ways that lead to new investigations and to deeper understanding of available information.
- Designing experiments to test predictions and hypotheses.
- Carrying out experiments, which involves changing one variable at a time and noting what happens.
- Recording observations by writing in notebooks or on computer disks.
- Analyzing and interpreting data to give meaning to the information that is recorded.
- Drawing conclusions from all of the above.

Figure 4.1 is a list of fundamental abilities necessary to do scientific inquiry taken from the *National Science Education Standards*. This list shows the Inquiry Content Standards for all three levels of schooling: K–4, 5–8, and 9–12. As you read the table, you should recognize that the standards are cumulative. That is, grades 5–8 build on and presume that students have developed those abilities from the prior level (K–4). Likewise, high school students are expected to have developed and are capable of using the abilities that are listed for both grades K–4 and 5–8.

FIGURE 4.1 ■ Content Standard for Science as Inquiry: Fundamental Abilities Necessary to Do Scientific Inquiry

Grades K–4

- Ask a question about objects, organisms, and events in the environment.
- Plan and conduct a simple investigation.
- Employ simple equipment and tools to gather data and extend the senses.
- Use data to construct a reasonable explanation.
- Communicate investigations and explanations.

Grades 5–8

- Identify questions that can be answered through scientific investigations.
- Design and conduct a scientific investigation.
- Use appropriate tools and techniques to gather, analyze, and interpret data.
- Develop descriptions, explanations, predictions and models using evidence.
- Think critically and logically to make the relationships between evidence and explanations.
- Recognize and analyze alternative explanations and predictions.
- Use mathematics in all aspects of scientific inquiry.

Grades 9–12

- Identify questions and concepts that guide scientific investigations.
- Design and conduct scientific investigations.
- Use technology and mathematics to improve investigations and communications.
- Formulate and analyze alternative explanations and models.
- Recognize and analyze alternative explanations and models.
- Communicate and defend a scientific argument.

(National Research Council, 2000, p. 19)

Reflection & Discussion Questions

After reading the previous paragraphs and studying Figure 4.1, what is your definition of inquiry? How does inquiry fit into your planning and teaching?

How Does Learning Occur through Inquiry?

As you review Figure 4.1, you can see that inquiry involves both physical and mental activity. It involves the physical acts of gathering information, from books, from talking to people, or from the actual empirical work of observing and experimenting often using tools to take measurements of distance, time, speed, temperature, light intensity, and so forth. It also involves the mental work of asking questions to guide information gathering or investigating. Of equal importance, it involves the mental work of making sense of new information in relation to what already is known. It is out of this combination of these physical and mental actions that learning occurs. It is how scientists, working in their laboratories and field studies, learn about and give meaning to observations and events in the natural world. It is also how students in schools can learn about, and give meaning to, observations and events in their world.

Inquiry requires students to mesh these abilities with scientific knowledge as they use scientific reasoning and critical thinking to develop their understanding of science. An important difference between early efforts with processes of science and this listing is the encouragement of students "to participate in the evaluation of scientific knowledge. At each of the steps involved in inquiry, students and teachers ought to ask 'what counts?' What data do we keep? What data do we disregard? What patterns exist in the data? Are these patterns appropriate for the inquiry? What explanations account for the patterns? Is one explanation better than another?" (National Research Council, 2000, p 18).

FIGURE 4.2 ■ Scientific Understanding as Connected Experiences, Patterns, and Explanations

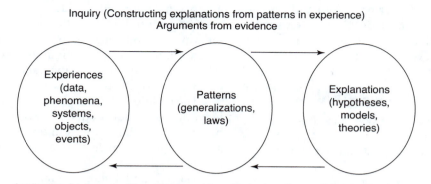

(Anderson et al., 2004)

Reflection & Discussion Questions

As you examine Figure 4.1 and then think about this section, what images of your work as a teacher come to mind? Have you or your students "participated in the evaluation of scientific knowledge"? Note how it is part of the *Standards* for grades 5 and above. It also is implied in the *Standards* for lower elementary school in the statement "Use data to construct a reasonable explanation." What would inquiry look like in a science classroom at the level you teach?

Figure 4.2 helps to clarify connections that occur between inquiry and learning in science. The diagram shows that learning through inquiry involves making connections among experiences, patterns, and explanations. Anderson and his colleagues (2004) claim that students must look for patterns within their experiences and then try to make sense of these patterns through explanations. They also imply an important connection between the work of scientists and the work of inquiring students as they engage in investigations. Scientists work to collect reliable data about phenomena, systems, objects, or events they are investigating. They then seek to create evidence-based arguments or generalizations that fit their data by saying that these specific cases, which have been observed, represent other, similar cases not yet investigated. These patterns then become the basis for explanations of the observations, which can take the forms of hypotheses that lead to further investigations, or models and theories that provide ways of understanding the observations or data that are available. Such reasoning is highlighted by the arrows pointing from left to right at the top of the diagram, which represent the construction of explanations from observable patterns in experience (Anderson et al., 2004).

Figure 4.2 also has a set of arrows pointing from right to left. These arrows show a relationship among experiences, patterns, and explanations that involves applying hypotheses, theories, and models in advancing understanding the world around us. Using abstract constructs as tools to help people make sense of specific patterns, data, or experiences that are part of daily life is also a part of the value of science learning. This two-way connection among experiences, patterns, and explanations is a very powerful model in thinking about science learning.

Reflection & Discussion Questions

How does Figure 4.2 help you think about planning and designing instruction? Think about the top arrows. How do they help you think about the foundation of theories in data, experience, and patterns? How does the diagram help you understand how inquiry can be a part of science teaching and learning? Further, how do the arrows at the bottom of the diagram help you think about applying theories and connecting them with the real world?

In summary, learning through inquiry is an important feature of learning in science. According to *National Science Education Standards*, it is a central part of learning science, where it is placed at the top of the list of content features, ahead of conceptual knowledge and applications. Inquiry receives this level of importance for several reasons: (1) inquiry represents how science works to formulate new knowledge, (2) it bases science learning on actual experience with phenomena, and (3) it has the effect of positive motivation.

With this brief introduction to inquiry, you are now better prepared to think about models of teaching science where inquiry holds a central place. However, there is much more to be learned about teaching science through inquiry, and your professional development over the next few years should give attention to expanding your knowledge about inquiry and your skills in using inquiry in your teaching.

Reflection & Discussion Questions

How would you describe the place of inquiry in science teaching and learning to parents and the children you teach? How is inquiry different from "hands-on learning"?

The Learning Cycle: Five Es/Seven Es

This model of learning and teaching has been around for about half a century, and as people come to understand learning more fully it has been further elaborated and adapted. In 1962, Atkin and Karplus developed it as a Learning Cycle with three parts: exploration, invention, and discovery. Exploration was a time for learners to do just that—explore a scientific phenomenon (such as the objects rolling down an incline to study acceleration, or observations of phototropisms in plants) in a controlled way so that all students in a class started with a common, shared experience about the topic of a sequence of lessons. Invention was the next step in which the teacher and students together reflected on the exploration activity and then "invented" a concept to help give meaning to their exploratory experiences. The invention phase was guided by the teacher, who introduced a valid science concept, because it seemed unrealistic to expect that students would generate an appropriate scientific concept to understand and give sound meaning to the exploratory experiences. Finally, the students were provided with experiences that allowed them to "discover" how the newly invented concept could help understand, and be applied to, new experiences that are similar to, but go beyond, the initial exploratory activity. This model has been widely accepted by the science education community, and many people worked to refine it in the years since its original formulation.

In the late 1980s, Rodger Bybee (1997), working on the development of an elementary science program for the Biological Sciences Curriculum Study, modified the Learning Cycle by changing the terminology in some significant ways and then added two more dimensions. The result was the 5E model. More recently Arthur Eisenkraft (2003) added two more Es to the model. Both are delineated in Figure 4.3, where you can see that exploration, invention, and discovery have been replaced in the newer models by explore, explain, and elaborate. Elaborate appears to have broader meaning

than discovery in the earlier version. Both imply application but elaborate includes student-centered clarification and understanding of the ideas that also is part of the teacher-centered explain. In addition, engage became the way of introducing the topic. This formerly was part of exploration, but by highlighting "engagement" Bybee emphasized the importance and difficulty of engaging all students in a lesson.

The addition of evaluate fills an important, obvious need in the earlier model. An evaluation component brings this model more in line with current thinking about the importance of evaluation as a part of the instructional cycle.

The 7E model adds two more elements: elicit and extend. Elicit appears to be a direct response to the advice from the National Research Council report (Donovan, Brandsford, and Pellegrino, 1999) that it is essential to attend to students' preconceptions, as these can have a significant effect on students' learning and understanding if teachers ignore them. Therefore, in teaching for understanding teachers need to find out about their students' ideas and reasoning on each instructional topic, so that they can use this information in planning and implementing lessons.

Eisenkraft explains the second addition as follows: "The addition of *extend* to the *elaborate* phase is intended to explicitly remind teachers of the importance for students to practice transfer of learning. Teachers need to make sure that knowledge is applied in a new context and is not limited to simple elaboration" (Eisenkraft, 2003, p. 59).

The successive additions to the Learning Cycle model over the years is in response to deepening understanding of what it takes to help students learn with understanding. The addition of steps in these models of learning also implies that it requires more time for understanding to develop than is commonly perceived. Another important feature of these models is that they recognize the role of the teacher in guiding students to understanding. That role varies as students progress from one part to another in the sequence. Beginning with engagement and exploration, the teacher works to bring students into the lesson and lead them to accepting responsibility for taking an active part in learning. This is followed by the teacher guiding students in creating meaning from their exploratory experiences, and it is further enriched by the teacher introducing a concept that enables students to form a sound, scientific meaning. Next, the teacher provides experiences that direct students toward applications of their newly acquired science concept in ways not previously experienced. Throughout this sequence of varied roles, the teacher is continuously observing students and listening to them to determine how well students are engaging in, and learning from, their experiences as part of a process of continuous assessment.

FIGURE 4.3 ■ The Learning Cycle and the 5E and 7E Models of Learning and Teaching

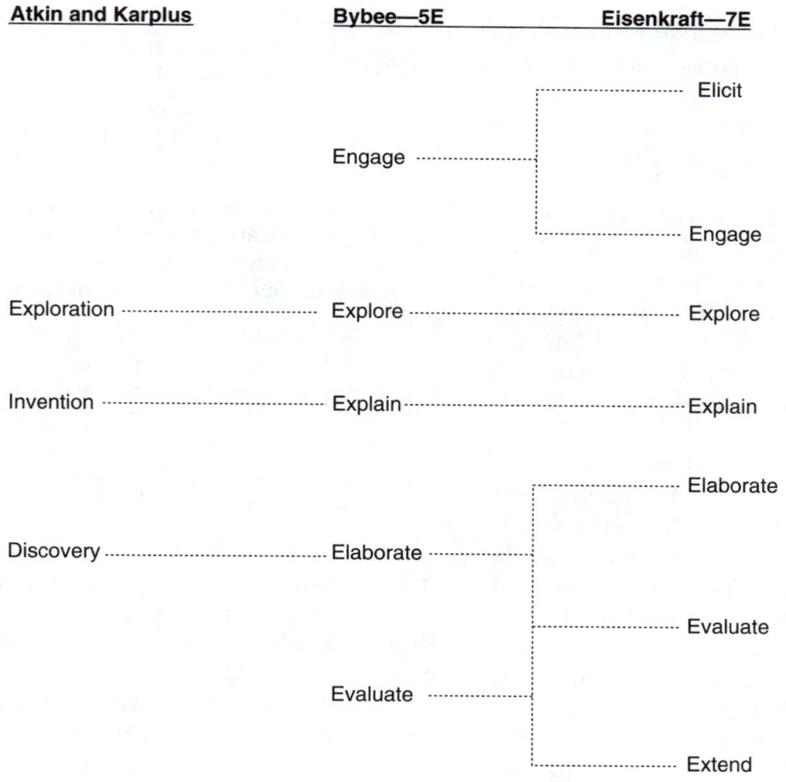

Atkin and Karplus	Bybee—5E	Eisenkraft—7E
		Elicit
	Engage	
		Engage
Exploration	Explore	Explore
Invention	Explain	Explain
		Elaborate
Discovery	Elaborate	
		Evaluate
	Evaluate	
		Extend

(Adapted from Eisenkraft, 2003)

Thus the teacher's role changes subtly, importantly and frequently during this lesson sequence.

Reflection & Discussion Questions

Summarize the changing role of a teacher as a lesson sequence progresses from introduction to conclusion using the 5e or 7e instructional model for a friend who is not a teacher. What skills are needed to implement these different roles? How does this instructional model help students learn science with understanding? What are its strengths? What about this model is difficult for you to grasp conceptually? What would be difficult for you to enact in your teaching?

The Apprenticeship Model: Modeling, Coaching, Fading

As its name implies, this model is based on the work of an apprentice learning new skills (Collins, Brown, and Newman, 1989). It involves three phases of learning: In the first phase the role of the students is that of an observer, where the teacher (or a master artisan) demonstrates a technique. This is called *modeling* the technique.

Consider a task such as teaching middle school students how to use a microscope. The teacher would demonstrate how to find a microscopic object on a slide by using a low power objective lens and by moving the course adjustment knob to raise the objective lens from its lowest point. This technique is essential to avoid breaking slides and damaging lenses, which can occur if the objective lens is lowered with the course adjustment knob while looking through the eyepiece. So the correct procedure is to lower the microscope tube only while watching from the side to see that the objective lens does not contact the slide on the microscope stage. To focus, the user then looks through the eyepiece and only uses the course adjustment knob to raise the lens system in the attempt to bring the object on the slide into focus. Finally, with the fine adjustment knob it is safe to move the lens system up or down to bring the object into sharper focus.

After the teacher or another skilled person demonstrates or models this technique, then the second phase, *coaching*, begins. Here the students are given an opportunity to apply the technique with close supervision and coaching from the teacher. Observation allows the teacher to see that students are applying the technique correctly and to provide feedback and corrective actions as they proceed.

The third stage is referred to as *fading* in which the teacher allows students to continue to practice the correct technique on their own to consolidate the learning. This is akin to what psychologists refer to as "overlearning." It follows the old adage that "Practice makes perfect."

You can easily see how the apprenticeship model fits learning particular techniques and skills. Modeling, coaching, and fading quite clearly apply to skill learning. It certainly fits learning laboratory techniques and even how to conduct scientific investigations and inquiry. However, it can also apply to learning concepts and scientific ideas. For example, consider how students learn to *use* a concept.

Students often learn concepts like evaporation and condensation from experience and definitions. Experiences such as swabbing water or alcohol on the backs of students' hands and noting its disappearance and the cooling effect are frequent means of introducing evaporation. Observing drops of water on the lid of a closed aquarium or the outside of a cold can of soft drink is often a means of introducing condensation. These experiences with observable phenomena provide direct experience with a concept and allow the concept to be identified and named. However, they do not help students to use the concept as a tool for making sense of the world around them.

Here is where modeling, coaching, and fading from the apprenticeship model relate to understanding and using concepts. Let's think about your morning routines as an example. You enter your bathroom and the mirror is clear and dry. You take a shower and the mirror becomes foggy. You wipe off the mirror with a towel and it fogs up again. You direct your hair dryer on a part of the mirror and a small area becomes clear, and stays clear, but the rest of the mirror remains foggy. It appears that the air from the hair dryer blew the water away! You drive to work and on some mornings your car windows become clouded over. You reach your hand up to wipe off the moisture and it clouds up again. You turn on the air conditioner or the defroster and it clears. How can you use the concepts of evaporation and condensation to understand these events? A sketchy explanation is given below. You may wish to elaborate it.

You step out of the shower and feel cold. Why is this? The water on your body is evaporating and cools your body.

Why did the dry mirror become "foggy" as you showered? Warm water from the shower spray evaporated into the air in your bathroom. It also warmed the air a

few degrees, but it did not warm the mirror as much. As a result, there is considerable moisture in the air. The warmer, moist air that is now in the bathroom contacted the cooler mirror and the moisture in it condensed on the mirror forming droplets, which "fogged" it. This is an application of the principle that condensation occurs when warm moist air comes in contact with cooler surfaces. Water vapor in the air condenses onto the cooler surface.

Why did wiping the mirror with a towel have little effect on clearing the mirror? The mirror is still cooler than the moisture-laden air so the moisture continues to condense out of the air onto the mirror.

Why did the hair dryer cause the fog to leave part of the mirror? It warmed part of the mirror so that condensation no longer occurred in that location. (It did not "blow the moisture off" as I stated above!) This is an application of the principle that evaporation occurs more rapidly when the liquid is warmer. Warming the surface of the mirror also warms the water on it.

The events with the car windows are similar to the mirror. However the use of the heater/defroster or the air conditioner to defog the windshield are different from each other. I will leave that to you to ponder and explain!

In the paragraphs above, I modeled some responses that show how to employ the apprenticeship model in teaching students how to use concepts and theories as tools to understand experiences beyond the classroom. This was introduced in Figure 4.2, at the bottom of the diagram, with the arrows pointing to the left. Here Anderson et al. (2004) indicate how a concept or theory (a general, abstract statement) can be applied to gain understanding of particular events, data, or observations.

Unfortunately, since I cannot interact directly with you as you read this book, I am not able to *coach* or *fade* in this activity. However, a teacher would provide students with added examples, such as the car windows in the previous paragraph, or ask a probing question such as "Why is it easier to dry dishes or glasses that are rinsed in hot water than if they are rinsed in cold water?" The teacher would then listen to students as they explained how the concept helped them to understand the example. The teacher could also evaluate written work on this topic. Such activities could be individual, small group, or whole class, or more likely a combination of these. Also these activities could involve either coaching or fading, depending on the teacher's perception of the students' capability to use these concepts.

Recently, Anderson (2003) made additions to this model. He suggested that *engaging* and *sustaining* (see Figure 4.5) also were essential elements of any model of teaching and learning, and therefore, the steps in his expanded apprenticeship model are engaging, modeling, coaching, fading, and sustaining. Also at all stages in this model, continuous assessment is implied even though it is not explicitly highlighted.

The apprenticeship model is an effective tool for teaching both *technical skills and techniques* and *how to use concepts*. This model allows students to see the action demonstrated by a proficient person (including actions such as applying a concept to a new observation), then have the benefit of supervised practice with corrective feedback, and then further practice on their own as the supervision is withdrawn.

Reflection & Discussion Questions

What skills are needed to implement this model in your planning and enactment of teaching? How does this instructional model help students learn science with understanding? What are its strengths? What about this model is difficult for you to grasp conceptually? What would be difficult for you to enact in your teaching?

Conceptual Change Model

Before thinking about conceptual change, it is necessary to address two related ideas that allow you to understand why conceptual change is an important topic for science teachers to consider and employ in their teaching. Both of these are based in research on students' learning.

Students' Ideas and Reasoning

The first of these consists of a huge body of research-based information about students' concepts that are misaligned with accepted science concepts. Research during the past 30 years that deals with students' naïve conceptions and misconceptions in science has expanded our knowledge about learning. Research on students' ideas in science became popular among science educators and others during the 1970s, and for many years researchers from all parts of the world investigated this domain, publishing a huge number of studies relating to most topics included in school science. Results of these studies showed that ideas held by students and adults on concepts in all fields of science, such as inertia, expansion of materials, evaporation, circulation of blood, "weightlessness," movements of glaciers, and chemical reactions, differ from ideas accepted by scientists. For example, many students and adults do not see motion as a natural state as indicated in the law of inertia. As a result, they fail to understand why objects in space continue to move, even though no force is there to propel them. The apparent "weightlessness" of astronauts in the space station is, for many students and adults, not seen as an example of inertia. Instead it is viewed as a result of lack of gravity, even though the gravitational force on objects at the distance above the earth at which the space station travels is about 90 percent of the gravity at the surface of the earth. Another example is the circulation of blood in mammals, including humans: many students and adults do not understand that the circulatory system is closed. That is, they do not envision blood confined to capillaries as it moves from arteries and arterioles to veinuoles and veins. Instead they envision blood leaving the capillaries and oozing around cells, then magically gathering into them as it returns to the heart.

The literature on students' concepts in science is extensive. Moreover it is part of the professional knowledge that science teachers should comprehend. Many valuable resources are available that will serve as ready references about this research, including the following:

Driver, Squires, Rushworth, and Wood-Robinson, *Making Sense of Secondary School Science*

Driver, Guesne, and Tiberghien, *Children's Ideas in Science*

Osborne and Freyberg, *Learning in Science*

A few of the many Web sites are as follows:

Minds of Our Own—*www.learner.org/resources/series26.html*

Private Universe Project—*http://www.learner.org/resources/series29.html*

Science Misconceptions Research and Some Implications for the Teaching of Science to Elementary School Students—*http://www. ericdigests.org/pre-925/science.htm*

Children's Misconceptions about Science—*http://www.amasci.com/miscon/opphys.html*

Earth Science Misconceptions—*http://k12s.phast.umass.edu/~nasa/misconceptions.html*

I strongly recommend that you add such resources to your professional library and learn about students' ideas related to the topics you teach. Further, you will need to give careful thought to students' misconceptions and naïve conceptions as you plan for, teach, and assess your students. This is where preassessment and formative assessment will play an important role in your success as a teacher, as well as in your students' success in developing and using science knowledge.

Reflection & Discussion Questions

From your own experiences as a student of science, and as an observer of others, what misconceptions and naïve conceptions are you familiar with? How have these ideas influenced learning accepted scientific ideas for yourself or for people you observed? In your own teaching, can you identify students' ideas that have affected their learning?

Piaget's Equilibration Model

The second related idea that constitutes a foundation for understanding conceptual change deals with a model of learning and human information processing that was developed more than a half century ago by a famous psychologist, Jean Piaget (1950). He devoted a great portion of his work to understanding how people process information as part of learning. His efforts resulted in the *equilibration* model. He indicated that learning involves reconciling newly encountered ideas and reasoning, such as those in a new experience or lesson, with the learner's existing ideas and reasoning. In other words, Piaget believed that people typically try to make sense of new information and experience in terms of what they already know, using the intellectual tools that work for them. Further he pointed out that equilibration involves two related, complementary processes, which he called *assimilation* and *accommodation*. Accommodation is what we normally think of as learning: new information is taken in by the learner and existing ideas are adjusted to fit with (or are accommodated to) the new knowledge. That is, a person's existing ideas are modified to account for or match the new information. Often, however, that is not what happens. Instead, *new information is adjusted (assimilated) to match the existing knowledge*. This is what Piaget called assimilation, which is the complementary process with accommodation.

To explain a bit further, new information often can be considered as creating disequilibrium or a discrepant event in a person's mind. There are two ways that people deal with a discrepancy, according to Piaget. Either they can modify their ideas to coincide with the new information, or they can adjust the incoming information to fit their existing ideas. For example, at one time I worked with a teacher whose last name was Newlon who told me that many people wanted to call him Newton. One experience he related happened during an interview for a teaching position. He was sitting with a school official who looked at his application and quietly crossed the *l* to make it a *t*, correcting what he interpreted as a spelling error! The school official was assimilating Mr. Newlon's name and making it fit his idea of how it should be spelled.

An example that is more relevant to science teaching can be found in a group of middle school students studying the movement of a pendulum. Many students believe that pushing a pendulum makes it swing (oscillate) at a faster rate; that is making more swings per minute. This often is based on their experience in pushing another person on a playground swing. Pushing makes the swing move faster and farther. However it has little effect on the number of oscillations per minute. When people interpret this experience, many often fail to distinguish between the faster movement of the child on the swing and the rate of oscillation in "swings" per minute. This should come as no surprise since few people pay attention to the rate of oscillation as they push a child on a swing. (Although I have observed kids on swings many times, I have never seen anyone timing the rate of oscillation while pushing a child on a swing.) Instead they usually are concerned with how high the swing moves, and the safety of the child in the swing.

In science classes, students are often engaged in studying pendulums. When they are directed to explore the factors that affect the period (or the number of oscillations per minute) of a pendulum, most will find quite quickly that the length of the pendulum is one factor. Longer pendulums require more time per swing and shorter ones require less time. Then they will look for other factors; "push" is one factor that commonly is tested by the students. They will compare the rate of swing of a pendulum that is "pulled" from the resting point (at the bottom of its swing) and released with one that is given a push (like pushing a child on a swing). The data from trials by six groups in a class are presented in Figure 4.4.

In spite of observing that the averages were nearly the same and that two groups found that the push method resulted in a lower number of swings, three groups found it resulted in higher number of swings, and one group found it resulted in the same number of swings as the pull method, most students retain their view that the pendulums that are given a push will

FIGURE 4.4 ■ Using Two Different Methods for Starting a Pendulum

Number of Swings per Minute		
Group	Pull and Release Method	Push Method
1	38	37
2	40	39
3	41	42
4	39	40
5	39	40
6	41	41
Average	39.7	39.8

swing faster. Their belief about pendulums is a stronger influence than the data from their experiment.

The same can be said about the weight of the pendulum bob. It is as though some students have constructed a "model" where lighter things move faster, whereas others believe that heavier things move faster. When comparisons are made between pendulums with different weights attached to a string, observational data have only a limited effect on the students' beliefs. Again, beliefs have a strong influence on thinking.

Students have developed ideas that work for them based on a combination of their own experiences, what they have heard from others or seen on TV or other places, and their own reflections and construction of this information. Like ideas from science, this personal set of ideas is interconnected. The parts of a student's constructed knowledge often are connected with each other, sometimes in very idiosyncratic ways, and to change one part can disrupt other parts. Such personal ideas about the natural world are logical to the student, and they differ from student to student. It is a *private universe*[1] that is constructed and it can be unique to each student. It is quite complex. If you think about Piaget's equilibration model, you can see how each student's private universe can be very different from others. Each student has had different experiences in a different sequence, with different family, school, and neighborhood influences. Add to this the different experiences from TV, books, travel, toys, and so forth. Each experience is assimilated differently into the child's mental framework. Each experience may have a different influence on the restructuring (accommodation) of that framework.

You should also be aware that researchers have found that there are common misconceptions that seem to pervade the thinking of many school students and adults. I have listed some examples in the previous pages. As you may recall, it is fairly commonplace for students to have what have been referred to as Aristotelian concepts of motion. These are the commonly held views of motion that prevailed in the scholarly community and among ordinary citizens in the centuries before Newton. These still prevail among many non-scientists since they are based in every day experiences. For example, most people hold that "motion requires a force," and they often do not fully comprehend the idea underlying Newton's First Law that deals with inertia. Also, most students have difficulty understanding that an object resting on a table has two forces on it, gravity pulling it downward and an equal, upward force that is exerted by the table on the object. Likewise, many students also view groundwater as being held in rivers and lakes underground (*http://www.dcnr.state.pa.us/topogeo/groundwater/bad_hydro.aspx*). Naïve conceptions about circulation of blood in the body have also been mentioned. The fact that there are common misconceptions and naïve conceptions somewhat eases the diagnostic work of teachers. However, it adds to the importance of teachers knowing about how to detect them as part of the professional knowledge of teachers.

Reflection & Discussion Questions

As you reflect on Piaget's equilibration model, think about how an understanding of assimilation and accommodation should influence your work as a teacher. As teachers, we often are confident that students incorporate new information accurately, but evidence suggests that they modify it or deal with it selectively so that it fits with existing ideas. What challenges does this present to us as teachers? How can we respond effectively to these challenges?

Piaget's concept of assimilation helps us to think about how misconceptions influence how students deal with new information and ideas. Thinking about assimilation as modification of new information to match existing ideas, new experiences and information often are modified by students to match their personal erroneous or naïve ideas. Thus, each student may actually perceive something different from what his/her teacher intended students to see or hear as a result of an experience.

An example might help. Anderson and Smith (1986) have worked on elementary and middle school students' concepts of "seeing" or vision. The scientific idea that they hoped that students would comprehend can be summarized as follows: We see because light from a source strikes an object, such as a flower, and is reflected to the viewer's eyes where it passes through the lens to the retina, which sends a message to the brain. The brain then recognizes the message as a flower. Therefore, the scientific idea is that "seeing" is a matter of light entering the eye.

For many students, their understanding of "seeing" differs from the scientific idea. Frequently, students' ideas are similar to Saturday morning cartoon representations. You may remember Road Runner and Wiley Coyote's antics in which Wiley is pursuing Road Runner, and a dotted line goes from Wiley's eye to the bird. This is a representation of a common misconception that seeing involves something going from the eye of the viewer to the object that is being seen. Moreover, for many students, the reason that light is important in seeing is that the light "lights up the object

---

[1] *Private universe* is a term taken from a video series prepared by the Harvard Smithsonian Astrophysics Laboratory about students' personal constructions of the natural world and the science ideas that help to understand it.

so it can be seen." That is, for many students, a reason it is not possible to see objects in the dark is that they are not illuminated.

Smith described what happens in many classrooms where vision is being studied: "Teachers are talking about the light, while students are talking about seeing. Part of the difficulty is that the teachers and students don't realize that they are actually saying something different" (Smith, personal communication, 1986). When the students hear the teacher talking about "light," they perceive that the teacher means that the light "lights up" the object so it can be seen. For students, the light is needed because a person cannot see in the dark! When students speak about "seeing," some teachers, who are not aware of students' misconceptions related to vision, will perceive that the student is actually referring to light entering the eye.

This example is just one of hundreds like it that teachers encounter when they attempt to teach science for understanding. An even more striking example of the difficulty of changing students' ideas and reasoning is presented in the Private Universe videos. At least two of the videos in this series begin by asking a sample of students (and faculty) at Harvard Commencement some basic questions such as "Why is it warmer in summer than in winter?" None of the students and faculty in the video give a satisfactory answer to the question, in spite of the fact that they are recognized as very intelligent and have completed highly esteemed programs of study. Instead of giving answers that match accepted scientific principles, the answers differ little from those of elementary school students, even though they have many additional years of schooling.

So how can we understand why this is occurring? To say that misconceptions are resistant to change only describes the condition. It does not explain the cause of the problem. To understand the cause, you must look at the schooling and testing that has occurred throughout most of these students' lives. The schooling has been strongly influenced by an information transmission model. Too little time has been invested in providing students with meaningful experiences with scientific phenomena and then guiding students in constructing logically sound, valid science ideas based on these experiences. Too little time has been devoted to seeking patterns in data and developing reasoning that help students formulate ideas based in data and experience. Too much time has been devoted to transmitting information and too little time has been devoted to guiding students' understanding of it. Testing frequently only measures recall of factual information and does not attend to students' understanding of ideas, the connections students are making among ideas, or their reasoning as it relates to understanding and application of ideas. Such assessment procedures rarely are able to identify that students have misconceptions.

Piaget's equilibration theory also helps us understand why misconceptions are so resistant to change. Assimilation of new experience frequently involves changing the meaning of an experience to match the existing conceptual framework. Therefore, classroom experiences that are intended to help students develop new, scientifically sound understandings may be assimilated in ways that conform to existing misconceptions. Therefore, new experience often may tend to reinforce the misconception instead of generating a change in it. This is why it is so essential for teachers to continuously monitor students' learning as instruction progresses, instead of waiting until the end of a unit or lesson sequence to assess understanding.

In addition, because students have been constructing meaning all through their lives independently as they play, listen to adults, watch television, and engage in all of the experiences of living, frequently without having any interaction or feedback about their ideas, you should not be surprised that they possess many erroneous ideas about science concepts and the world around them. The term *private universe* takes on much more meaning when thought of in this way. Unless students come from an uncommon environment, where ideas about science are talked of frequently, their ideas about the world around them will be individually constructed from the experiences that make up their daily lives and will become their private view of how the world works.

Reflection & Discussion Questions

Imagine that you have been asked to explain to a group of science teachers why students have difficulty in overcoming their science misconceptions. How would you describe misconceptions? What examples of misconceptions would you use? How would you use Piaget's concepts of assimilation and accommodation to give substance to your explanation? How would the phrase *private universe* help you with this explanation? What would you ask the teachers to do, other than listen attentively, as their role in learning about these ideas?

Conceptual Change Approach and Teaching for Understanding

Now that you have some added background, you can return to the main line of this development about conceptual change.

The conceptual change model of teaching recognizes that students come to science classes with many misconceptions and naïve conceptions that are firmly held and not easily changed. The authors of this model (Posner, Strike, Hewson and Hertzog, 1982) also recognized that misconceptions frequently impede learning of valid science ideas. They offer the conceptual change model to provide a strategy that guides teachers and students in addressing misconceptions and replacing them with appropriate science concepts that are reflected in the goals of instruction. The basis of their strategy is to confront misconceptions directly and to help students replace the misconceptions with valid, scientifically accepted concepts. Further, this model is based on the way in which scientists formulate ideas and make paradigm shifts in their thinking. To these authors, conceptual change in students is viewed as similar to a paradigm shift among scientists.

In its early formulation, the authors described four required conditions for conceptual change to occur:

1. The learners must become dissatisfied with their current conceptions.
2. The new conception to replace the current ones must be intelligible by, and make sense to, the learners.
3. The new conception must be plausible, leading them to useful explanations.
4. The new conception should fruitful of new investigations and explanations. (Posner, Strike, Hewson and Hertzog, 1982 p. 214)

An important part of the teachers' responsibility in teaching for conceptual change is to help students create the dissatisfaction with their own ideas about the topic being studied. Teachers also have the responsibility to guide students to grapple with the new conception so that it becomes intelligible, plausible, and fruitful, as indicated in the list above. As you might imagine, this has been difficult for teachers, as well as for students. As a result, the authors made a revision in the approach by recognizing the importance of addressing motives for dissatisfaction with current conceptions and the need for change to new conceptions.

The revised version of the conceptual change model gives more attention to students' motives and goals along with the nature of misconceptions and the bases of their development. The authors increased attention to what they labeled as "learners' conceptual ecologies." By this they mean the interconnected set of concepts, the experiences that engendered them, and the motivations that surround them. Such conceptual ecologies appear to be complex with specific science concepts being intricately connected to other concepts, beliefs, values, attitudes, and motivations. Conceptual ecologies include more than just the content of science. They also may be influenced by affective factors, such as cultural and religious beliefs, and by what students are convinced that they have "seen" or experienced. Thus experiences outside of school, events from television, folklore, and other matters, real and perceived, influence conceptual ecologies. As such, Condition 1 in the list above (engendering dissatisfaction) may be difficult due to factors in the conceptual ecology that have little to do directly with the misconception that is the center of classroom activity (Strike and Posner, 1992).

In adopting this broader view of the embedded nature of each misconception with a larger, connected system, conceptual change became an effort at changing conceptual ecologies in a more holistic fashion than simply working with the cognitive side of one concept at a time. This viewpoint requires that teachers who plan and teach students directly, as well as people who design instruction, become analytical about students' ideas and reasoning and the affective factors associated with each student's system of beliefs and values.

The four conditions presented above from the authors' earlier description of conceptual change do not match the practical reality of conceptual change. The later version of the conceptual change model is much "messier," because it attempts to deal with the interconnectedness of students' ideas, beliefs, and reasoning. However, in its complexity, it more closely aligns with the practical reality of teaching science in schools. And although it does not provide a simple formula to guide teachers' actions, it does provide a viewpoint that is important for teachers to keep in mind as they work toward teaching for understanding.

Reflection & Discussion Questions

What skills are needed to implement this model in your planning and enactment of teaching? How does this instructional model help students learn science with understanding? What are its strengths? What about this model is difficult for you to grasp conceptually? What would be difficult for you to enact in your teaching?

Applying the Models to Planning, Teaching, and Assessing Students

This chapter highlighted the place of inquiry as an important element in teaching science for understanding. A parallel was drawn between scientists as they work to advance the frontiers of knowledge and students in school in developing an understanding of the way science works and the concepts and theories of science. Scientists and students are both engaged in learning, and for both, investigation and reflection are essential elements of the process of learning. For both groups, inquiry lies at the heart of learning. Therefore, inquiry must have a central place in school science if students are to understand science—including both its concepts and theories and the ways in which scientists work together to produce and validate this body of knowledge.

The three models described in this chapter—the 5 (or 7) Es model, the apprenticeship model, and the conceptual change model—are aligned with inquiry teaching. Moreover, they are complementary to each other. Each one adds to our understanding about how to help students learn science with understanding. Further, they complement the planning model that was employed in Chapter 3. There, three elements of teaching and learning were identified: (1) building a base of information on science topics, (2) developing understanding of that information by making sense of it and finding connections between new information and ideas that students already hold, and (3) learning to apply the new understandings in new contexts. All three of these elements of teaching and learning lie at the foundation of the models described in this chapter.

Figure 4.5 presents key elements of all four models in a concise table that allows visual comparison. A quick inspection shows connections among like elements as well as gaps. For example, the planning model does not address engagement, whereas the other models all place emphasis on it. The conceptual change model has the most elaborated vision of engagement including goals, motives, and science concepts. However, in its focus on preassessment, formative assessment, and summative assessment, the planning model gives more attention to assessment than the others. The conceptual change model also implies a similar emphasis on continuous assessment, whereas the 5Es model appears to stress summative assessment, and the apprenticeship model does not include assessment explicitly. All four models attend to building a base of information, developing understanding, and applying new learning or constructs, although they vary in the level of detail that is provided. In reflecting on the apprenticeship and 5Es models, it seems that they do not convey the extensive time and the demanding nature of the work that is required to develop understanding of important concepts in science. Moreover, the models are not explicit in how to go

about teaching for application of knowledge. This is not surprising as application of science knowledge has a history of being undervalued in the academic science community (Cajas, 1998).

Reflection & Discussion Questions

How do the models summarized in Figure 4.5 help you think about your teaching, assessment, and students' learning? Which models do you find most readily applicable? Why are these easier for you to grasp? What added information do you need in order to make other models more accessible?

What is the message from this chapter for teachers who are planning science lessons, units, and courses? It seems that, just as a single approach to teaching is insufficient, one model may be inadequate for the task of planning and enacting instruction in science if understanding is to be attained. Moreover, a key message from Chapter 3 is reinforced:

- Teachers must attend to the ideas that students bring with them to the classroom, which constitute their personal understandings of how the world works. If students' initial understandings are not addressed, they may fail to grasp the new concepts and ideas that are being taught, or they may learn them for the purposes of a test and revert to their preconceptions outside of the school environment.

- Teachers must build students' competence by supporting development of (1) a deep foundation of content knowledge, (2) understanding of facts and ideas in the context of a conceptual framework, and (3) an organization of that knowledge in ways that facilitate its retrieval and application.

- Teachers must help students "learn how to learn," so they can become independent learners who take

FIGURE 4.5 ■ Comparing Models of Teaching and Learning

Planning Model	5Es Model	Apprenticeship Model	Conceptual Change Model
	Engage	Engage	Attending to motives and goals Creating dissatisfaction with existing conception
Build the base of knowledge	Explore	Model	Learning the new conception
Develop understanding	Explain	Coach Fade	Developing intelligibility and plausibility of the new conception
Apply in new contexts	Elaborate	Sustain	Using the new conception in new investigations and explanations
Prior elements occur in a framework of preassessment, formative and summative assessment	Evaluate		Exploring and monitoring conceptual ecologies of individual students

control of their own learning by defining learning goals and by monitoring their own progress in achieving them. (Bransford, Brown, and Cocking, 2000)

In addition we will expand the list to include the following:

- Teachers must develop knowledge and techniques that will allow them to deal with students' conceptual ecologies, including affective dimensions such as motivation, values, and beliefs.

- Teachers must learn how to engage in preassessment and in continuous, formative assessment so that they can monitor students' developing understanding and keep on a valid pathway that is consistent with scientific knowledge.

- Once teachers recognize that students have inaccurately constructed meaning about science ideas, they must also apply skills in how to nurture students to construct more accurate meanings that are in line with ideas that are accepted by the scientific community. Learning these skills will be an important part of their professional development that has both pedagogical and content dimensions.

In Chapter 6, we will explore a unit for middle school science that is based on a more comprehensive model of instruction that blends the approaches developed in this chapter. In the meantime, our next effort will be on teaching approaches that can be used to foster understanding.

Journal Questions

Add to your journal by revisiting the following questions that will help you monitor your progress as you make a paradigm shift in your teaching and your understanding of your students' learning for understanding and application in science.

1. What were the purposes or objectives of this chapter?
2. What were the key ideas presented in this chapter? (Note: These two could be combined as a two-column table to show the parallel between the purposes of each chapter and the ideas presented.)
3. What important additions have you made to your vision of teaching science for understanding and application by studying this chapter and discussing with others? This should be an ongoing narrative that highlights development of your personal paradigm for teaching and learning science.
4. I also recommend that you create a concept map that portrays your understanding about teaching and learning science for understanding and application and add new concepts and connections as you study each chapter of this book. This concept map can provide a visual representation of your developing new vision or paradigm of science teaching and learning that you developed in the previous item.
5. What new skills and techniques do you find you need to develop in order to enact your vision of science teaching? What progress are you making in developing those skills and techniques?
6. Finally, what concerns do you have about being able to implement your new vision, your new paradigm of science teaching with your students, in your classroom, laboratory, and fieldwork? How will you respond to these concerns?

Chapter **5**

Teaching Strategies That Foster Understanding

This chapter provides you with information on several strategies that will enhance your capability to teach science for understanding. It expands the ideas developed in Chapters 3 and 4, including Figure 3.2. In that chart, different teaching strategies were listed for each of the three elements of teaching—building a base of information about science phenomena and concepts, developing understanding of the phenomena and concepts, and applying these understandings in future learning and in daily life. By this time in your professional development, you should be confident that active learning is an essential part of learning for understanding and use of science knowledge. Therefore, we begin this chapter with a discussion of learning communities as an appropriate environment for active learning.

Creating an Environment for Active Learning

To begin our consideration of learning communities, I will introduce an integrated model that builds on the work of the previous chapter on models of teaching. This model was developed by Roth (1997) and is the basis for the unit plan that forms the content of Chapter 6. Therefore Roth's model serves multiple purposes, including the integration of the three models developed in Chapter 4, a platform for our discussion of learning communities in this chapter, and as the instructional model for understanding the unit presented in Chapter 6.

The title of Figure 5.1 is interesting and quite comprehensive in its triple focus on learner-centered instruction, conceptual change, and learning community. As you examine the center section of Roth's model, you will notice the similarities to the 5Es model with the steps elicit, explore, and explain. Then Roth shifts to bring in the apprenticeship model, with modeling, coaching, and fading. Last, she incorporates reflecting on and

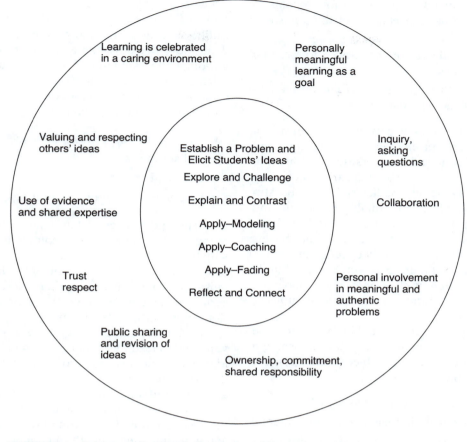

FIGURE 5.1 ■ A Learner-Centered, Conceptual Change Instructional Model and Learning Community

connecting ideas as a key part of her model. In Chapter 6, this part of the model will be discussed more fully. However, for now it is the outer circle of the model that should be the focus of attention.

The terms in the outer circle are especially important as a point of departure into learning communities. They highlight many important features of learning communities:

- Personally meaningful learning as a goal
- Personal involvement in meaningful and authentic problems
- Ownership, involvement, and personal commitment
- Inquiry and asking questions
- Use of evidence and shared expertise
- Valuing and respecting others' ideas
- Public sharing and revising of ideas
- Collaboration
- Trust and respect
- Learning is shared in a caring environment

These characteristics coincide with, and elaborate, a common definition of a learning community. Although there is no single definition of a learning community, a useful definition is:

> Any one of a variety of curricular structures that link together several existing courses—or actually restructure the material entirely—so that students have opportunities for deeper understanding and integration of the material they are learning, and more interaction with one another and their teachers as fellow participants in the learning enterprise. (Shapiro and Levine, 1999)

Although this definition is more aligned with college-level teaching, it certainly applies to middle and high school teaching as well. Learning community approaches in classrooms tend to share the following basic characteristics:

- Students are organized into small groups to enhance collaboration.
- Students are helped to learn skills that support group interaction that relates to learning with understanding academic and social support.

- A time and setting are established for students to be socialized to the expectations of the classroom and the subject field.
- Teachers and students are encouraged to focus on learning outcomes.
- Integration of the curriculum is encouraged to enrich understanding. (Shapiro and Levine, 1999)

Learning communities as part of classroom strategies are often found in elementary classrooms and in programs in colleges and universities, but they are less often incorporated as an essential part of secondary school instruction. However, middle and high school students need and benefit from a quality classroom and school environment that gives attention to building a community of learners, with shared values and beliefs about learning and the value of knowledge of subject matter content. Thus Figure 5.1 sketches a valuable way of thinking about how classrooms and schools can be organized to foster learning science, and all subjects, with understanding.

Returning to points represented in the outer circle on Figure 5.1, three elements deal with establishing a deep involvement between the subject matter content of instruction and the students:

- Personally meaningful learning as a goal
- Personal involvement in meaningful and authentic problems
- Ownership, commitment, and shared responsibility

How can this level of involvement be achieved? Teachers enable students to gain this involvement by beginning topics with time for students to describe what they already know about the topic and then asking what more they would like to know about it. In addition, if the topic or content is connected to the real world of students' experience, the topic becomes more meaningful and authentic. Ownership and personal commitment are enhanced. However, this emphasis on personal involvement needs to be nurtured throughout the lessons that pertain to the topic.

This is where the three additional items from Figure 5.1 come into play:

- Inquiry and asking questions
- Use of evidence and shared expertise
- Public sharing and revising of ideas

By engaging students in inquiry—acquiring data and experiences that relate to the topic—students' initial interest is nurtured. Having them work to make sense of data and connect experiences and data to ideas helps them to learn skills, which increases their competence and is motivating in itself. When students, working in groups, are able to share their ideas with the whole class or with other groups, and argue points of disagreement, engagement and motivation increase. Public sharing of ideas also is motivating, since students view it as developing an important competence, although they sometimes are reluctant to admit it. Further, reporting to the class can be threatening to some students, unless the following attributes are promoted as part of the "ground rules" for the class:

- Valuing and respecting others' ideas
- Collaboration
- Trust and respect
- Learning is celebrated in a caring environment

Trust and respect are key values of a learning community. Students need to feel confident that their ideas will be accepted and considered carefully without being "put down" by other students. The environment must be collaborative and caring, where ideas and concerns are dealt with in ways that support open discussion, appraisal, and development.

In developing an effective learning community, you need to lead by example in valuing and respecting ideas from students. You also must set up rules that students cannot make derogatory comments about another student's ideas or efforts. Rules of polite behavior also are an essential. Time needs to be devoted to setting these ground rules early in the year and to maintaining them throughout time. Periodic discussions with the class about the ways of making the learning community more effective are also an essential element in maintaining the appropriate spirit.

In Chapter 6, you will have several opportunities to see how a learning community can be enacted in a classroom.

Reflection & Discussion Questions

1. In what ways does your vision of teaching give attention to developing and maintaining a learning community?

2. What dimensions do you feel need to develop further in your vision and the skills needed to support an effective learning community in your classroom and with your students?

3. What concerns do you have about using learning communities in your teaching?

You will need at least three essential skills to enable students to form and maintain an effective learning community in science classrooms, laboratories, and field settings:

1. How to establish and sustain effective group work

2. How to employ writing as a learning tool in science

3. How to support effective classroom discourse that enriches and supports understanding and application of science

These three topics will comprise the remainder of this chapter.

Establishing and Sustaining Effective Group Work

With the emphasis on collaboration, sharing, and valuing the ideas of others found in effective learning communities, science teachers who wish to teach for understanding need to give attention to supporting effective group work in their classrooms and other instructional environments such as laboratories and field settings. In addition, the meta-cognitive skills that students acquire for effective group work have the potential for transfer to life roles in the workplace, in social and community settings, and in families.

Perhaps one of the most important concepts about group work for you to recognize is that secondary school students will need to learn how to work effectively in groups. Therefore, you will need to spend time teaching your students how to work collaboratively with their peers to learn and understand the subject matter.

Linking group work and subject matter content is an essential change that most students will encounter in your classes. Most students will have had some experiences with group work in prior grades, as it is quite common in elementary schools. However, much of the students' prior experience has related to learning how to work cooperatively with their peers, and the use of group work as a tool for supporting the development of understanding may be novel. Therefore, having students work together to comprehend variations in ideas about instructional topics may be a new experience for them (Lazarowitcz, 1994).

In addition, the social dynamics of middle and high schools is different from that in elementary schools. Student groupings tend to change from period to period through the school day. The time duration spent with a teacher during the day is less. In addition, secondary schools may have more social, economic, and ethnic diversity within the student body than elementary schools. Students in secondary schools may also have more firm convictions on important topics than their younger counterparts. Perhaps the most crucial element lies in the fact that some students have not learned how to collaborate with others, especially where different interpretations of information and experiences can occur. Therefore, you have an important job in helping forge a learning community and effective group participation from the diverse collec-tions of students that enter your classroom each hour of the day.

Reflection & Discussion Questions

1. What are your own attitudes about, and experiences with, group work? Do you value it, or do you not see its promise?

2. What factors in your background and experience have led you to this viewpoint?

Fostering Development of Skills for Effective Group Work in Science Classes

How should you begin? My advice is to start small, a position that is supported by research as well as experience (Sharan and Sharan, 1992). Also, you should initiate group work as early in the year as possible so that it becomes a normal part of life in your classroom. You can begin by giving students a specific task to work out with one or two students that are seated nearby. Also make the time frame for group work activities both specific and short, especially as you begin. For example, you could present students with a graph from a textbook or newspaper that addresses the present topic of instruction and ask the students to tell you what the graph shows. You could give the students two or three minutes to review the graph and prepare a statement about the graph. Then select several of the groups to report their interpretations. After two or more different interpretations are identified, you could speed the reporting process by asking for a show of hands from all groups about who had similar interpretations to each of the alternatives identified. You also should ask if there are any other interpretations by other groups.

If the graph you select is like many found in newspapers, you could ask a second question for groups to answer following the students' reports. Many graphs, especially those in advertisements, portray scales on the Y-axis that give misimpressions about the data presented, such as exaggerated differences because the scale does not begin at zero. Figure 5.2 contains an example. To an untrained eye, looking at the right-hand graph, Brand Y appears to be far better than Brand X. Therefore your second question could be, "Do the two graphs convey the same information about Brand X and Brand Y?" Again give students a couple of minutes to frame their response. Then elicit responses from a small number of students. Then continue with questions such as "How do the impressions created by the two graphs differ?" "Does one graph portray one product more positively than the other?" "In what way does it do so?" Questions such as these should generate thinking and discussion among students working in groups.

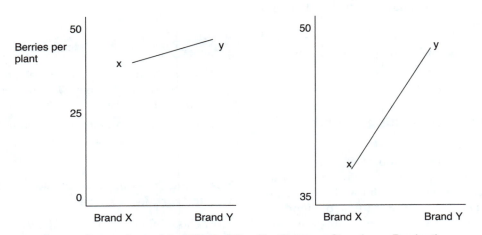

FIGURE 5.2 ■ Comparison of the Effect of Two Fertilizers on Strawberry Production

Activities such as these can be used to help students begin to work collaboratively on tasks that are related to the subject content. In this way students begin to develop collaborative skills to help in thinking about subject matter in a group setting.

As part of this initial process, you will also need to set out some rules. Students must answer the question posed. Time is limited so that students must focus on the question and not on "sidebar" conversations. Interaction is limited to the members of the group and not across groups. A report is expected from students at the end of the allotted time. All members of the group must contribute to answering the question.

To foster productive group work, researchers have created useful strategies, including one called the Four Stage Rocket (Cohen, 1994). This strategy requires the formation of groups of four to six students. Students are presented with an interesting topic or question that is part of a lesson sequence to be addressed in a group setting. For example, in a study of Great Lakes water, students were asked "What factors contribute to the changing levels of water in the Great Lakes from one year to another?" They then practice presenting their ideas about the topic using a sequence of four strategies.

Stage 1, Being Concise: A timekeeper makes sure that each person in the group speaks for only fifteen seconds. This teaches skills in being succinct in their discourse and gives practice in making a point in a way that speeds discussion.

Stage 2, Being Attentive: Select a new timekeeper. Each person can only speak for fifteen seconds again. However, before the next person can speak there must be three seconds of silence to enhance the likelihood that students will attend to and process the prior speaker's point.

Stage 3, Being Reflective: Select a new timekeeper. Continuing with the ideas in 1 and 2 (fifteen seconds to speak and three seconds wait time), each new speaker must refer to or repeat a part of the previous speaker's ideas then elaborate on it.

Stage 4, Enabling Participation of All Group Members: Select a new timekeeper. Maintaining all the rules from Stages 1 through 3, now require that no one may speak a second time until everyone has had a chance to speak the first time.

One feature of this approach relates to students' roles for group work. At each stage, a new timekeeper was selected. This exemplifies two important aspects of group work: the importance of identifying roles for students in group activities and in rotating these roles so that everyone in the group serves all roles. Timekeeper, recorder, reporter, equipment manager, and group leader (to keep the group on task) are among the possible roles for group work. Deciding on the roles is an important part of your planning for group activity. Further, these roles must be rotated among the group members so that all students can learn the skills associated with each role. This also is an important part of a learning community, since high status could be associated with some roles such as leader and low status to other roles such as recorder, which would mitigate against the goals of cooperation and personal development that effective group work in learning communities can foster.

Your role is to ensure that the rules are followed, and then to lead a discussion about students' success or difficulties in employing the strategies with their peers. To aid this approach in fostering effective group interaction on both interpersonal and cognitive fronts, you should also give appropriate attention to the content of the discussions. You should also ask students to frame and present a short report on the factors that contribute to changing water levels in the Great Lakes. In addition, you have the responsibility to observe what is occurring in each group as part of your role in continuous assessment. You must move around the room, carefully listening and watching what is occurring in each group. You also should be prepared to take corrective action when groups are off task or heading down an unproductive pathway in their interactions.

Careful attention to the students' self-management in group activities, and your role in planning appropriate group tasks and questions, as well as your role in assessing actions of group members will be necessary to help students develop the skills needed for quality interactions in dealing with substantive issues related to subject matter content.

Lonning's work expands this effort further. He suggests training sessions where students are asked to focus on five areas of positive collaborative learning behaviors. *Positive independence* is the idea that the group is learning together and that the success of any individual in the group depends on group success. *Face-to-face interaction* discusses the skills students will need to interact physically and verbally within their group. It also explains the importance of interaction in the group. *Individual accountability* reminds students of the point of positive independence that in order for success to occur everyone in the group must understand the material. As a result it is the responsibility of all students to give help to students who do not understand, and to monitor the understanding of all group members. *Interpersonal and small-group skills* focus on ways of functioning effectively in a group such as creating positive group dynamics and learning how to ask for help when it is needed. In the group process, the value of *feedback for group members* is emphasized in order for improvement to occur (Lonning, 1993).

The importance of helping students develop the skills and willingness to ask for help when needed, and to provide help for others, cannot be overemphasized. It is an important part of learning community and successful group work. It also is essential in teaching and learning for understanding. Webb and Palincsar (1996) found that students who asked direct and specific questions about what was not understood clearly made larger improvements in understanding than others. Those who practiced this questioning technique most often showed the biggest improvement between pretest and posttest scores. Help givers were instructed to give elaborated responses and detailed explanations as opposed to just giving an answer. Use of this technique also gave help givers an opportunity to identify

their own misconceptions and understandings (Webb and Palincsar, 1996).

Reflection & Discussion Questions

1. How can you apply these ideas in your classroom to create an environment in which students are willing and able to work cooperatively and productively in groups?

2. How can you help students develop the skills needed to enable effective interactions that foster high-level learning?

3. How can the ideas from Cohen, Lonning, and Webb and Palincsar help you?

Supporting Responsibility of Group Members

Students also should learn that they have responsibility for the learning of all group members, in addition to their own learning. This may not be easy for some students and their parents as they see schooling as a competitive enterprise. Therefore, helping others is seen to be a disadvantage to the help giver, which may be the case when learning is viewed as memorization. However, by viewing learning as developing understanding and use of science knowledge, the situation changes. Experience shows that help givers learn at least as much as others simply because giving others assistance in understanding an idea or procedure requires that the givers organize their knowledge to express it in an comprehensible form to others. This is similar to the improved understanding that a new teacher undergoes as part of the change in role from student to teacher.

Helping students and their parents understand the role of group work as part of teaching for, and learning with, understanding should be a part of the support you give your secondary school students. This will highlight differences between memorization and understanding for both students and their parents and will ease some concerns that students have about working in groups. Further, the work cited in the previous section has relevance here, as students must learn how to talk with fellow students both to ask for help when they fail to understand an idea or procedure and to give help in a supportive way when they perceive that others are facing difficulty with understanding. This not only requires a high degree of motivation and some sophistication regarding the subject matter content, but also requires that students take a mature approach to interaction with peers. Quite disturbingly, neither of these attributes are modeled very frequently in the popular media, including TV and movies. Too often, the antithesis of these attributes makes for popular scripts for such entertainment. To counter this commonplace societal effect, one creative middle school teacher reacted to her students' lackadaisical responses to her questions with phrases like "I don't know" with a question: "How could you respond to me in a way that showed more thought and interest?" The students then turned this challenge into a game in providing more thoughtful, intelligent-sounding replies to questions, such as "I have not thought about that question before, and I don't have an answer for you now" (Gonzales-Lantz, 1998). Although this was only a start at generating higher-quality responses, it was a way of countering an artifact of popular culture.

Reflection & Discussion Questions

1. What attitudes do your students have about group work?

2. What skills for effective group work do your students bring with them?

3. What skills need further development?

4. What actions have you tried to motivate students to take more responsibility for their own learning and those of their peers?

5. What actions do you intend to try because of what you learned in this chapter?

Organizing Students in Groups

How teachers organize students into groups is an important factor in the success of group work. Group membership should not be a matter of chance or even student choice. Assignment of students to groups requires substantial thought, and knowledge of student qualities, on the part of teachers. Several research studies support this viewpoint and provide information on how to implement it in your classroom.

Research by McManus and Gettinger (1996) shows the importance of diversity of group membership, because it allows lower-achieving students to receive needed help from more able students. Diverse groups can also help students of non-Western backgrounds voice their opinions; whereas, in teacher-led discussions, students from Western cultural backgrounds tend to dominate conversations. These researchers also advise that the teacher choose groups to insure this diversity.

In a study of group work in high school science classes, Mitchell, Reilly, and Bramwell (2004) explored teacher versus student choice in configuring groups for collaborative learning. Student and teacher opinions were taken into account as to whether teachers or students should choose group members. Students felt that they knew their classmates better than their teachers

and as a result could choose better group mates. They claimed that they knew with whom they would work well, and who would work hard in the group. Students also pointed out that grades are not always a good measure of the potential effectiveness of a group member. However, when students were invited to choose their own groups, they often chose their friends. Choosing a group member had little to do with the elements they previously stated to be important. Group members were often chosen by means of social status (often influenced by physical appearance and athletic capability). Higher-level students worked together, and lower-level students were left in a group to "fend for themselves." Further, lower-level students felt that they were often relegated to a group with students who were in the "same boat" and that they could not be helped by groups comprised in this manner.

The researchers then comprised groups that maximized diversity in learning styles, ability, gender, and ethnicity. The students worked in these groups and were asked again at the end of the study which method students preferred for choosing group members: teacher's choice or students' choice. Many of the students agreed that better groups were comprised when the teacher chose groups. Female students perceived that teacher placement of students in groups took pressure off of them to choose their friends. An important conclusion of the study is that teachers must be aware of the social pressures students face when choosing their own groups. The researchers also reiterated a point made earlier—that training for students to work effectively in groups is essential.

When working with a new class, using such strategies as "think, pair, share" provide opportunities for the students to learn about your expectations about group activities and interactions. Such strategies also provide time for you to develop knowledge about the skills students already possess for working productively in groups. Equally important, it creates opportunities for you to learn where students need help in developing skills to improve productive group interaction that focuses on developing understanding. Finally, it provides an opportunity for you to appraise your students' understandings of the science content that is the basis of lessons (Baumeister, 1992). These are important data elements that can be useful in assigning students to groups.

These studies and practical experience show that group work in science classes is improved if you take leadership in assigning group membership to enhance diversity of group membership. In addition, changing group assignments occasionally throughout the semester or year may be advisable for two reasons: to enable more productive groupings and to reduce the formation of dependencies among students in working groups.

1. What has been your experience with group work as both teacher and student?

2. In what ways does your experience support the findings from research that groups are more effective if membership is determined by the teacher based on adequate knowledge of students' capabilities?

3. How can you assemble the information that is needed for effective group assignments?

4. What pitfalls must be avoided in assigning students to groups?

In closing this section on the use of groups as an effective strategy in teaching science for understanding, keep in mind that its value is enhanced when you

- Possess and employ high-level skills for supporting group work.

- Are thoughtful about assignment of group membership.

- Plan tasks carefully, including appropriate allocation of time for them.

- Monitor group activity frequently, asking probing questions to guide students in their work and providing feedback and appropriate support.

- Follow group activities with opportunities for students to report publicly on the results of their collective work.

Employing Writing as a Learning Tool in Science

Writing is an important tool in helping students gain understanding of ideas and processes in science. Because writing is by nature an active process, it is a useful vehicle for active learning. *Writing to learn*, or WTL, gained popularity among educators in the 1960s and 1970s. In the intervening years, WTL has been defined in many different ways by its advocates. In its original form, its purpose was to increase learning by having students write for purposes of personal expression, with little attention to discipline-specific goals or constraints (Ochsner and Fowler, 2004). As the movement gained support, the nature of WTL in different subject areas was the topic of much debate. The original emphasis on expressive writing led many science teachers to perceive writing as unrelated to attainment of science learning goals. However, some people saw potential for writing as a useful tool in science learning along two lines: one emphasizing writing as a tool to aid the understanding and application of knowledge, and the other helping students understand and become skilled in writing as a tool for conveying the results of research and scholarship, much the way scientists use writing.

Although people may disagree on the exact nature of WTL in science, many agree that it can help to alleviate the frequent passive character of science classrooms that so often leaves students feeling disenchanted, unmotivated, or disengaged with science learning (Gallagher, 2000; Rivard and Straw, 2000).

How Does Writing Help Students Learn Science?

An essential value of WTL is that it helps students learn, in an active, participatory manner, about the central place of communication and debate about ideas and data in science:

> The application of writing to learn strategies encourages the concept of science literacy advocated in the national standards of having students communicate to broader audiences than just the teacher or class, for such purposes as arguing, persuading, and explaining science concepts for themselves and others. (Hand, Wallace, and Yang, 2004, p. 132)

Given the fact that traditional science classrooms typically have given little attention to expository writing as a tool for learning, the addition of writing as a tool to nurture active learning represents a substantial change. However, Anderson (1999) warns that even when writing is present, learners tend to "treat inscriptions as parts of school tasks rather than as tools for expanding their experience and reducing it to order" (p. 973). This points up the need for helping students value writing as a tool to help them with understanding and not just "busy work" that needs to be completed for the teacher. This concern is also present in other subjects, where argumentative techniques are similar to those in science (Rowell, 1997). With the increasing use of WTL in many academic subjects, the shift in attitudes about writing as a tool for learning with understanding may be easier for students than it has been in the past.

An important reason for including WTL strategies in science curricula is to help students develop an understanding of science content. Writing is a tool that can help students as they try to make sense of new information and ideas and connect them with those they already possess. Regarding the complex process of interpreting and integrating experiences, information, and ideas that are essential in understanding science, "[p]eer discussion may be sufficient for the retention of facts and simple concepts, but may have to be augmented by writing for the retention of more complex integrated knowledge" (Rivard and Straw, 2000, p. 578). For students to benefit from writing to learn, teachers need to guide their attention toward the relationships among experiences and data, patterns and relationships, and explanations. Therefore, the questions that teachers pose to guide writing will be critical if they are to stimulate deep thought and the construction of understanding of science ideas. Further, teachers may also be learning about these relationships at the same time as their students. Over my many years as a teacher, the process of continually coming to understand the experiential and empirical basis for science ideas has been one of the exciting (and challenging) parts of teaching science for understanding. The addition of writing to learn as part of my teaching repertoire had the unpredicted benefit of boosting my own understanding of the very science content that I had previously thought I understood quite well.

Reflection & Discussion Questions

Suppose you were asked by your department to prepare a short justification for writing as part of science classes for parents and the school board members. What points would you raise about writing as a tool for helping students learn science?

To help you learn more about how to prepare writing activities that foster understanding of science topics, I suggest that you give special attention on the writing prompts that are included in Chapter 6 for upper elementary school students. Also, as you proceed to Chapters 10 through 14, you will see new approaches to planning lesson sequences in middle and high school science that provide examples of writing prompts that foster understanding of specific subject matter ideas. In each of these cases, you will see that the writing activities are subject specific and highly dependent on the objectives of the lessons. Therefore, designing writing prompts that support understanding is not a generic skill, but is closely aligned with the subject matter content, reasoning skills, and the objectives of instruction. An obvious, general point that can be made about writing prompts is that they need to guide students in integrating two or more "things" such as data and ideas about patterns or connections. Therefore, they will require that students write sentences and paragraphs, not just abbreviated, telegraphic responses. For students, this may be a difficult change that will take time and support.

Helping Students Get Started in Writing in Science Classes

Getting students to write expository paragraphs about data, experiences, patterns, relationships, and explanations may not be easy. A few years ago, a colleague and I worked with two seventh-grade teachers in an urban middle school. The teachers were advocates of writing to learn in science. At the beginning of the year, they set out to help their students, many of whom had a history of low achievement, use writing as a tool for improving the quality and amount of their school learning. Each day, the teachers gave the students at least two writing tasks. Although the students' initial responses to writing prompts about hands-on experiences and short readings and videos were limited to a few words, the teachers remained undaunted. They encouraged students to be more expansive in their writing and gave them help in doing so. As a result, the few words students wrote in response to prompts in September turned into sentences by October, paragraphs by November, and pages by January. More important, students developed a positive stance toward writing about their experiences with lab work, reading, videos, and classroom discussions. Also, writing was not always an individual task. Frequently, pairs or triads of students worked together to write a report about experiences, connections among ideas, or explanations of observations. This was incorporated often enough to be supportive, but not exclusively, to avoid creation of dependencies between students that could limit learning.

Many teachers also have used *quick writes* at the beginning of class as a review of ideas that were part of the prior lesson or to help students make connections among experiences and ideas. Typically, the writing prompts are presented on the chalkboard or overhead projector for students to see as they entered the room. Students then are given five to seven minutes to respond to the prompt, while the teacher records attendance and takes care of other routines. The writing prompt usually is collected and reviewed by the teacher as a form of embedded assessment and returned the next day. Frequently, teachers use the writing prompt as a springboard for the day's activity, sometimes asking students to describe their responses to the prompt to the whole class, other times responding to students' questions arising from the experience of writing they had just completed.

An example may be helpful to further see the value of quick writes or pre-writes as they are often called. In a lesson sequence on change of state, where students completed a set of activities on evaporation the previous day, students are presented the following question on the chalkboard when they enter the room:

> Using the ideas we discussed yesterday, describe why you usually feel cold when you are drying off after a shower or swimming.

This is an activity to connect the previous lesson and the current one. It calls for application of the concepts from yesterday's lesson. The writing task not only forms a bridge in time between two or more lessons, but it also bridges between school and the students' experiential world. In addition, the teacher then has access to information about each student's ideas on evaporation as a change of state from liquid to gas and its connection with heat or energy transfer—the idea that change of state from liquid to gas requires heat.

Many teachers also use writing as a key part of group work. Teachers often alternate between short oral reports and written reports as a consequence of a group activity. Group tasks in science classes frequently require that students show relationships among observations, data, and ideas, or show connections among ideas. In either case, group activity may involve assignment of a specific task, a time allotment for completing it, and instructions about what students are to produce as a result. When students are asked for an oral report, often the teacher recommends preparation of an overhead transparency or poster to serve as an organizer for the oral presentation and a focus for the classroom audience. This comprises one kind of writing task. In contrast, written reports require a stand-alone document, containing enough information and organized in a manner that the teacher, other students, or an outsider could read and understand the description, relationship, or explanation being made as a result of the task.

Some writing tasks include more than writing. Other tools for representing ideas can be included in writing such as diagrams, graphs, and tables of data. In cases like these, the written discourse usually focuses on clarifying the meaning of these graphical representations of data or relationships. Writing tasks like these are of value to students because they encourage students to use multiple representations of science ideas or relationships, including the data on which they are based. For example, an explanation of acceleration is made more meaningful if it includes a table of data showing time and distance measurements about spheres rolling down an inclined plane, or a table that shows the speed of a car versus time, as it starts from rest until it reaches a constant speed.

Reflection & Discussion Questions

1. How do you (or will you) help your students initiate writing as part of science learning?

2. What difficulties have you had, or do you anticipate, with students in initiating writing that compare with those encountered by the two teachers with their grade 7 students in the description above?

3. Do you have the persistence that these two teachers had?

4. What would cause you to be persistent?

5. How do you feel about using multiple means of generating students' expression of ideas such as those included above?

Concept Maps

Concept maps are another form of expressing ideas on paper. The value of concept maps in advancing science understanding is well documented. Moreover, they have become widely used by science teachers because they show connections and relationships among science ideas in a clear pictorial form. In addition, they have been used with students of all ages, backgrounds, and skill levels.

Concept maps take on different forms, but for students from grades 4 or 5 through high school, I recommend a form of concept maps in which boxes or ovals contain nouns (concepts) and the connecting arrows show direction and are labeled with verbs to describe the connection between the two concepts. The simple example in Figure 5.3 shows the placement of the verbs on directional arrows that show relationships among components of plants.

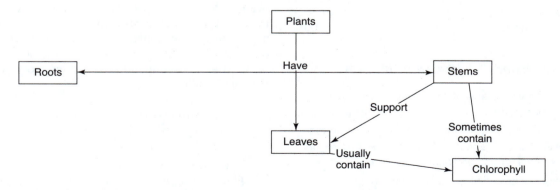

FIGURE 5.3 ■ A Partial Concept Map of Parts of Plants

As with other tasks designed to elicit students' ideas and reasoning and aid in nurturing understanding, the benefit comes from the mental engagement that they demand. Creation of a concept map during an instructional activity sequence can become a meaningful small-group activity to help students clarify the connections and relationships that are inherent in the topic of study. One way of beginning this activity is to develop a list of terms that portray the key ideas in the topic either as a whole class or a small-group activity. In certain circumstances, you could use a prepared list. For the partial map begun in Figure 5.3, the list could include the five terms in Figure 5.3 plus *flowers*, *seeds*, *food*, *petals*, *stamens*, *pistils*, *pollen*, and more words depending on the level of detail that is consistent with your instructional objectives. Then students, in groups of two to four, are given the task of creating the concept map and allotted an appropriate amount of time for it, which may be about fifteen minutes. You should allocate enough time so that students can be reflective about where the arrows go and what should be written on them. They also need to be able to debate relationships among the terms with members of their group. Writing the terms on small *Post-it notes* allows greater flexibility in placement, which stimulates deeper thinking about relationships among the terms. Completing the concept map on a sheet of poster paper aids in presenting it to classmates and in discussing different representations of relationships from the various groups in your classroom.

This section has presented examples of successful techniques to incorporate writing into your science classroom. The teachers who used these approaches have noted benefits to students. In addition, research data show the benefits to a wide range of students. Heath (1983) found that WTL-related strategies were successful not only in improving a group of low-income students' conceptual knowledge, but also in increasing engagement with science, and helping to create a community of learners around science issues in their community (Rowell, 1997). Other researchers have found WTL to increase student engagement with science as well (Hand, Wallace, and Yang, 2004). WTL also can promote language development through contextualization and authentic communication for all students, including second language learners (Stoddart et al., 2002; Yore, 2000).

Reflection & Discussion Questions

1. How can you use writing as a tool to aid learning with your students?

2. In what ways do the approaches described in the previous paragraphs add to your repertoire of techniques for use of writing?

3. What concerns do you have about writing in science classes?

Inquiry and Writing

Researchers agree that writing can aid inquiry learning. It can be a tool to "extend and support the overall inquiry process regarding the nature of science and science concepts, rather than as a product of grading purposes" (Rowell, 1997, p. 38). WTL strategies may also be used to address inquiry and nature of science in scientifically valid ways (Keys et al., 1999). Individual and group writing tasks can also be included that help students reflect on inquiry processes used in their own investigations. Keys and her colleagues have formulated and used a *Science Writing Heuristic* to guide students in writing about investigations in ways that support learning with understanding. This heuristic encourages reflection on the question, methods, data, interpretations, meaning, and connections regarding an investigation (Keys et al., 1999). The questions are straightforward and helpful in guiding the interpretive process:

A. Beginning ideas and questions—*What are my questions about this experiment?*

B. Tests and Procedures—*What will I do to help answer my questions?*

C. Observations—*What did I see when I completed my tests and procedures?*

D. Claims—*What can I claim?*

E. Evidence—*What evidence do I have for my claims? How do I know? Why am I making these claims?*

F. Reading and Discussion—*How do my ideas compare with ideas held by others?*

This heuristic guides students through a series of steps that gives meaning to investigations. Moreover, it can help students be reflective about how scientists construct knowledge of the natural world from research data. Helping students continually recognize that scientific discoveries and ideas are based in observations and sense making can foster this understanding about science. It can also help students understand the role of written discourse that is used by scientists.

Since not all inquiry is empirically based, the Science Writing Heuristic could be expanded to include investigations that are based in review of available information from other sources such as research reports from other scientists, interviews with experts, and the Web. In these cases, I recommend modifications to items C and E in the list above:

C. Observations—*What did I see when I completed review of data obtained from other people's research and analysis?*

E. Evidence—*What evidence do I have for my claims? How confident am I that the evidence presented is valid?* (Note: This is a serious concern with some

Web-based information and interpretations, because it may not have been reviewed by peers.) *How do I know? Why am I making these claims?*

1. How do you use writing as part of inquiry in science teaching?

2. Are there ways that you feel that you could improve the quality and effectiveness of student investigations through the use of writing?

Writing and Assessment

In concluding this section on WTL, we must turn attention to assessment. Writing has many benefits for students, but an important benefit that often escapes attention is its utility in helping students claim ownership of the assessment process in their own education (Treagust et al., 2001). Providing students with occasions and skills that can foster self-assessment advances students' self-knowledge and autonomy in learning.

Assessment of writing is a novel matter for many science teachers. Obviously, it requires skills that some will need to develop. Scoring rubrics are useful in guiding teachers in assessing writing, and when they are shared with students they can support students' self-evaluation. In preparing scoring rubrics for writing that is directed toward building understanding, *facets of understanding,* which were described in Chapter 2, come into play (Wiggins and McTighe, 1999). Depending on the objectives of a lesson, assessment of writing should incorporate one or more of these facets (explanation, interpretation, application, perspective, empathy, and self-knowledge). The reason for highlighting the facets is to ensure that scoring rubrics foster writing that addresses understanding. Sometimes, scoring rubrics focus so specifically on the components of an idea that integration needed for understanding is missed. In a nutshell, rubrics are important and helpful in scoring writing, but care should be taken ensure that the desire for specificity does not trivialize the writing process.

More will be said about assessment of writing in Chapter 7. However, there are questions that are appropriate at this point:

1. What are the criteria on which you grade or evaluate students' written work?

2. How do these criteria support students' learning with understanding?

3. Is this an area that needs more attention in your professional growth agenda? Explain why you answered this as you did.

Supporting Effective Classroom Discourse That Enriches and Supports Understanding and Application of Science

The previous sections of this chapter have emphasized students' interactions in learning communities, group work, and writing to learn. Oral discourse is essential in at least two of these. Moreover, research shows that students learn more when writing and group interaction are combined in a supportive learning environment (Rivard and Straw, 2000). Therefore, oral discourse can be an adjunct to effective writing.

Researchers and educational theorists have given attention to the role of language and discourse in science classrooms beginning in the 1960s. Since 1990, attention to this area has grown significantly, with increasing emphasis on the place of argumentation in science (Osborne, Erduran and Simon, 2004). He states:

> The general point. . . is that argumentation, the coordination of evidence and theory to support or refute an explanatory conclusion, model or prediction (Suppe, 1998) is a critically important epistemic task and discourse process in science. Situating argumentation as a central element in the learning of sciences has two functions: one is as a heuristic to engage learners in the coordination of conceptual and epistemic goals and the other is to make student scientific thinking and reasoning visible to enable formative assessment by teachers or instructors. (Osborne, Erduran and Simon, 2004, p. 995).

These authors further explain the importance of this direction for science teachers:

> In addition, from a societal perspective, contemporary science impinges directly upon many aspects of people's lives. Individuals and societies have to make personal and ethical decisions about a range of socioscientific issues based on information available through the press and other media. Contemporary developments in science and technology (e.g., genetic engineering, reproductive technologies, food safety) often pose dilemmas. . . , particularly where they are based on equivocal findings or contested claims whose resolution depends not simply on a knowledge of science but also on the application of moral and ethical values. Evaluating media reports. . . is not straightforward as it requires the ability to assess whether the evidence is valid and reliable, to distinguish correlations from causes, and to assess the degree of risk. Within the context of a society where scientific issues dominate the cultural landscape. . . there is, therefore, and urgent need to improve the quality of young people's understanding of the nature of argument in general and argument in a scientific context in particular (Osborne, Erduran and Simon, 2004, pp. 995–6)

How can teachers foster productive classroom interaction and verbal discourse in whole-class and small-group settings? Experience shows us that students need help in learning how to talk with one another about science ideas in ways that support learning with understanding and effective intellectual growth. Left alone, students' talk rarely will be about science and when they do, their discourse may only occasionally enhance their understanding of science. Moreover, Kuhn (1991) has shown that both adults and school-age students have limited capacity to formulate and express a reasoned argument. Her research demonstrated that people frequently lack the ability to coordinate and construct a relationship between data and ideas, essential to a valid argument. More recently, researchers have provided additional data to support this claim (Hogan and Maglienti, 2001). Further, Koslowski (1996) pointed out that the reason for this inability lies in the lack of understanding of science ideas and theories and the data in which they are grounded. Therefore, lack of knowledge of relevant theories and concepts often constrains people's ability to reason effectively (Koslowski, 1996). This supports a belief that rational use of science knowledge in personal and group decision making requires a knowledge of scientific theories, a familiarity with their supporting evidence, and skill in constructing and/or evaluating their inter-relationship (Osborne, 2002).

 Reflection & Discussion Questions

The introduction to this section sets out some important ideas about why we teach science. Reflect on the ideas about the reasons for, and goals of, science teaching and learning that are embedded within these justifications for attention to oral discourse in science classes. What is added to, or reinforced in, your understanding of the goals and purposes of science teaching by the paragraphs that open this section?

Strategies for Improving the Quality and Effectiveness of Classroom Discourse

Teaching for the kind of understanding and application of science knowledge described in the paragraphs above places additional responsibilities on teachers to support students in learning how to use science knowledge in personal and social decision making. As you will recall, this is one of the eight components of the content standards in the *National Science Education Standards* (National Research Council, 1996). Osborne, Erudan and Simon (2004) clarify a dimension of this component by identifying argumentation as "the

coordination of evidence and theory to support or refute an explanatory conclusion, model or prediction. The authors also emphasize the importance of understanding the theories and their bases in being prepared to use science knowledge wisely. He and others further stress the important place of oral discourse in students' learning for understanding and use.

Therefore teachers need to provide an environment and tasks that engage students in productive talk about the science where data, patterns, explanations, and applications are integrated and become meaningful. Such an environment must be "low risk" for students, so that ideas can be explored and discussed without fear of ridicule from peers or lowered grades from the teacher. As in the previous work in writing and group activity, my advice is to start slowly with a specific goal or purpose in mind and a task that is clear for both you and the students. Moreover, while some degree of flexibility in timing is beneficial with classroom discussions, you must have a solid idea about the purpose you intend and one or more pathways toward that purpose that would be practical. Therefore, planning is an essential element for generating and maintaining the kind of discourse that will enrich students' understanding and ability to use science knowledge. You must be clear about the purpose and objectives of classroom discussion to prevent the conversation from drifting in irrelevant directions that cause more confusion than clarity. Additionally, you will need to use the chalkboard, overhead projector, or poster paper to help students focus on what can be a rapidly shifting ideational environment in whole-class discussion. Small-group discussions will need your careful monitoring, and persons assigned the role of group leader will need your support to prevent unproductive, off-task discourse.

Setting the topic for a whole-class discussion in ways that engage all students is an essential task. It will take time and planning. As part of planning for effective classroom discussions, you should answer the following questions:

- What is the question to be discussed?
- What is the purpose and objective for this discussion?
- Is whole-class or small-group organization the appropriate environment for this discussion?
- How will I introduce the question to the students so that it engages them?
- How will I ensure that all the students participate in the discussion?
- What component questions will I ask to ensure that the discussion stays on track and continues to serve the objective of the discussion?

- How will I help students maintain focus as several ideas or viewpoints emerge? How should these differing ideas or viewpoints be recorded so that students can follow the discussion?

- How will I help students gain meaning from the discussion?

- What signals should I look for to assess the direction and effectiveness of the discussion?

- How long should this discussion run? How will I bring closure to the discussion?

- What should be the next action after the discussion? How will the discussion help to advance my larger goals for this lesson sequence?

In addition to your own learning about leading effective discussions, students will need to learn how to carry on effective discourse in both whole-class and small-group discussions. Strategies for effective group work, which were part of an earlier section of this chapter, will aid students here. In whole-class discussions, students will need to develop strategies for maintaining attention to, and keeping pace with, what may be a rapidly shifting set of points made by different speakers, including both the teacher and students. Therefore, students will need assistance in developing skills in engaging and maintaining focus during discussion.

Further, all students need to be encouraged to participate in discussion. In starting a discussion, you may need to do a "round robin" so that everyone speaks early in a whole-class discussion. This "breaks the ice" and gives all students "a voice" at the outset of the session. Keeping track of ideas as they emerge in a discussion is a learned skill that can be aided by students taking brief notes, which can aid in maintaining attention and participation. You should encourage note taking so that it becomes part of the way in which students respond to whole-class discussions. Also, students need to learn how to be concise in making points and in not dominating the discussion. On the other hand, students need to be persistent when they have a point that they feel is essential and sound. Students' judgments about the appropriate response to the conflicting needs for conciseness and persistence will require guidance from you as the teacher.

In discussions in science, students will need to comprehend and apply Facets 4 and 5 on perspective and empathy (Wiggins and McTighe, 1998) as they try to understand the viewpoints of other students in the class. This applies not just to controversial issues, but also to students' personal conceptions about science phenomena. In addition, many discussions should focus on linking data and theory in making arguments based in students' developing understanding of science ideas and processes.

A valuable resource for helping teachers see effective classroom discourse in action is a video from the Annenburg Foundation that shows a teacher, Robert Tai, and a grade 7 class struggling with the question "Is it gravity or friction that causes a ball in a U-shaped track to stop its oscillations?" This video shows how classroom discussion can be an effective tool in helping students think deeply about alternative explanations regarding this engaging phenomenon. It presents several days of "intellectual wrestling" by the students as they try to understand the phenomenon, their own ideas, and scientists' ideas about it. I have found it a very powerful tool for helping teachers to think about classroom discourse in whole-class settings.

In the previous paragraphs, I have addressed discourse in whole-class settings, and only occasionally mentioned discourse in small groups. The potential for learning is at least as great in small-group settings, because the opportunity for all voices to be heard is greater. Moreover, each voice has more "air time" in small groups than in whole-class settings. On the other hand, the teacher has less opportunity to be a part of this discussion.

Reflection & Discussion Questions

1. How do you plan for discussion in your science classroom now and in the future?

2. What added skills and techniques do you feel you need to enable your students to engage in more productive classroom discourse?

3. What skills do your students need to improve in order to have more effective discussions?

4. How will you use classroom discourse as a tool for assessing students learning?

This chapter has offered many ideas to consider as you continue to improve in teaching science for understanding. Many challenges were presented that represent promising directions for your professional growth over the months and years ahead. I encourage you to experiment with these ideas and strategies. Moreover, I recommend that you work with a colleague so that the two of you can offer each other guidance and support as you explore new ways of teaching and guiding students toward understanding of science. Finally, don't be discouraged if initial trials are less successful than you hope for. Both you and your students need to be persistent in learning new ways of interacting with each other and in understanding the subject matter and processes of science. It can be an exciting, albeit long, journey.

Journal Questions

Add to your journal by revisiting the following questions that will help you monitor your progress as you make a paradigm shift in your teaching and your understanding of your students' learning for understanding and application in science.

1. What were the purposes or objectives of this chapter?
2. What were the key ideas presented in this chapter? (Note: These two could be combined as a two-column table to show the parallel between the purposes of each chapter and the big ideas presented.)
3. What important additions have you made to your vision of teaching science for understanding and application by studying this chapter and discussing with others? This should be an ongoing narrative that highlights development of your personal paradigm for teaching and learning science.
4. I also recommend that you create a concept map that portrays your understanding about teaching and learning science for understanding and application and add new concepts and connections as you study each chapter of this book. This concept map can provide a visual representation of your developing new vision or paradigm of science teaching and learning that you developed in the previous item.
5. What new skills and techniques do you find you need to develop in order to enact your vision of science teaching? What progress are you making in developing those skills and techniques?
6. Finally, what concerns do you have about being able to implement your new vision, your new paradigm of science teaching with your students, in your classroom, laboratory, and fieldwork? How will you respond to these concerns?

Chapter 6

Examining *Food for Plants*

As this chapter begins, I will make the claim that understanding how plants get the food they need to live, grow, and reproduce is not easy. Why do I say this? Experienced teachers know, and research on students' ideas and reasoning shows, that plants are a source of many naïve and incorrect understandings for students over a wide range of age and experience.

What comes to mind when you hear the term *food for plants*? A common response to this question is "the liquid or powder from a local garden store used to fertilize their houseplants or garden." A person who gives this response implies that food for plants consists of the materials that are absorbed through the roots along with water. While this response is common among both children and adults, it is inconsistent with accepted science knowledge about food for plants. Moreover, it is grounded in an inappropriate analogy that plants take in food through their roots in a way that is similar to animals eating.

The scientific view is that plants make their own food through photosynthesis, using water and minerals absorbed through the roots and carbon dioxide taken in through the leaves to capture and lock energy from the sun in the form of sugar. Therefore, it is sugar (glucose) that is food for plants!

The purpose of Dr. Roth's unit, *Food for Plants*, is to help students in grades 5 through 7 put aside the commonplace misconception that is deeply ingrained in our societal language and beliefs and to understand the scientific conception. As stated earlier, this is not easy for students, and it puts substantial demands on their teachers. Significantly, this unit has been carefully designed and tested to provide a sound strategy for teachers to aid students in attaining the intended understandings about this important process.

Food for Plants

This unit can be found at the following Web site: *http://ed-web3.educ.msu.edu/rothk/*. The Web version of *Food for Plants* has a different title, *A Plant Exploration Unit: How Plants* Really *Get their Food*. Although there are small differences between the print version and the Web-based version, I urge you to study the unit in detail, especially if you are using this book as part of a science methods course or extended professional development program. Working through the unit can be a valuable experience as you can see its full detail and richness. Moreover, it is organized to give you and your students a high level of support in teaching and learning science for understanding. When you go to the Web site, click on Explorations for Teachers and you will find that the material for the unit is organized to give you a rich background on several relevant topics, including:

1. Daily Lesson Organization
2. Teaching Model, which includes a representation of the learner-centered, conceptual change instructional model and unit sequence overview (which you have already seen in Figure 5.1)
3. Unit Objectives
4. Unit Concepts
5. Student Ideas
6. List of Activities, which includes both student pages and teacher pages for over twenty activities that comprise the unit
7. Pre- and Posttests
8. Sample MEAP Questions (the state science examination for Michigan)
9. Video (clips that expand on those embedded in several of the items in this list)

There also is a button on the home page that is titled "Explorations for Students" containing experiments, activities, and more video clips. At the time of publication, there were a small number of buttons that were not active.

Some parts of the unit are reproduced in the pages that follow to accompany my description of the activities that make up the *Food for Plants*. I encourage you to read the materials in items 1 through 5 above with care as these provide many important ideas about teaching science for understanding that relate to this unit. Item 6 contains detailed materials about each lesson in a very useful format. Each Teacher's Page provides detailed guidance about the purposes of the activity, directions about how to proceed with it to guide students toward the objective or purpose of the activity, the larger goals of the unit, and materials needed to carry out the activity. The Teacher's Pages often contain a possible narrative for the teacher to use

in framing, conducting, and leading students in reflection about the activity. In addition some activities contain information on topics such as

- Common Student Responses and Suggested Teacher Interpretations and Actions
- Being Sensitive to Student Diversity
- Additional Teacher Background Resources

By clicking the Student's Page button near the top of each Teacher's Page, the materials for students are made available. The Student's Pages are written to give students needed information and activities that will guide them in attaining the learning objectives of that specific lesson.

In the pages that follow in this chapter, I will highlight several important features of this instructional unit, which could be a useful supplement to your examination of it. I will begin by the goals and approaches used. However, I am not able to provide the level of detail and organization that is contained in the materials that were developed by Dr. Roth and her colleagues. To see that level of richness, you must go to the Web site and study the unit itself. It is a treasure chest of information and ideas about teaching science for understanding that you should explore, even if you do not plan to teach about plants or photosynthesis or to teach at middle school. There are no other resources that provide so much richness about teaching for understanding and application of science!

The Objectives of the Unit

Food for Plants draws its objectives from *Benchmarks for Science Literacy* (Project 2061, 1993) and *National Science Education Standards* (National Research Council, 1996). The unit objectives and the related objectives from *Benchmarks* and *National Science Education Standards* are presented in Figure 6.1. As you can see from careful examination of these unit objectives, they deal with content understandings (Objectives 1, 2, 3, 4, 5, and 7), and science processes (Objectives 6, 8, 9, and 10). You also will note that Objectives 6, 9, and 10 can be thought of as serving a double duty as both science process objectives and meta-cognitive objectives.

Reflection & Discussion Questions

1. Describe the similarities and differences among the three kinds of objectives listed above.
2. Why are all three kinds of objectives important to students in middle grades in understanding science?
3. Why would they be important to students of any age?

FIGURE 6.1 ■ Objectives and Main Ideas: Matching to *Standards* and *Benchmarks*

Food for Plants Unit Objectives

1. Describe the <u>functions of seed parts</u>.
2. Identify examples and non examples of food as energy-containing material.
3. Describe the process of <u>food production, food storage</u>, and <u>food use</u> in plants.
4. Describe <u>evidence</u> that plants make and store food.
5. Identify <u>energy and matter changes</u> during the food making process in plants.
6. Use <u>models</u> to represent processes in the plant that you cannot see.
7. Know that <u>hypotheses</u> are valuable even if they turn out not to be true, if they lead to fruitful investigations (Benchmarks, 6–8)
8. Develop <u>descriptions, explanations, predictions, and models using evidence</u>. (NSES, 5–8)
9. Think critically and logically to make the relationships between <u>evidence and explanations</u>. (NSES, 5–8)
10. Trace all food energy back to plants and photosynthesis, categorizing plants as producers and animals as consumers.

Food for Plants Unit Main Ideas

National Science Education Standards

A. Plants are producers—they make their own food. (5–8, p. 158).
B. Food provides energy and nutrients for growth and development. (5–8, p. 168)
C. All animals, including humans, are consumers, which obtain food by eating other organisms. (5–8, p. 158)
D. Plants use solar energy to combine carbon dioxide and water into complex, energy rich compounds. This process of photosynthesis provides a vital connection between the sun and energy needs of living systems. (9–12, p. 184)
E. The energy for life primarily derives from the sun. Plants capture energy by absorbing light and using it to form energy-rich food. (9–l2, p. 186)
F. Evidence consists of observations and data on which to base scientific explanations. (p. 117)
G. Models are tentative schemes or structures that correspond to real objects, events, or classes of events, and that have explanatory power. Models help scientists and engineers understand how things work. Models take many forms. (p. 117)
H. Scientific explanations incorporate existing scientific knowledge and new evidence from observations, experiments, or models into internally consistent, logical statements (p. 117).
I. Different terms, such as hypothesis and theory, are used to describe different types of scientific explanation (p. 117)
J. It is normal for scientists to differ with one another about the interpretation of the evidence or theory being considered. Ideally, scientists acknowledge such conflict and work towards finding evidence that will resolve their disagreement. (5–8, p. 171).

Benchmarks for Science Literacy

a. Food provides the fuel and building material for all organisms. Plants use energy from the light to make sugars from carbon dioxide and water. This food can be used immediately or stored for later use. Organisms that eat plants break down the plant structures to produce the materials and energy they need to survive. (6–8, p. 120)
b. Some source of energy is needed for all organisms to stay alive and grow. (3–5, p. 119)
c. Almost all food energy comes originally from sunlight. (6–8, p. 120)
d. Energy appears in different forms. (6–8, p. 85)
e. Models are often used to think about processes that happen too slowly, too quickly, or on too small a scale to observe them directly. (6–8, p. 269)
f. Scientists' explanations about what happens in the world come partly from what they observe, partly from what they think. Sometimes scientists have different explanations for the same set of observations. That usually leads to their making more observations to resolve the differences. (3–5, p. 11)
g. Scientists do not pay much attention to claims about how something they know about works unless the claims are backed up with evidence that can be confirmed and with a logical argument. (3–5, p. 11)
h. Graphs, diagrams, sketches, maps, and stories can be used to represent objects, events, and processes in the real world, although such representations can never be exact in every detail.

K. Roth, *A Plant Exploration Unit: How Plants Really Get Their Food*

As you review Figure 6.1, you should see connections between the objectives for this unit and the *Benchmarks* and *National Science Education Standards*. As a teacher, you will need to make connections between the objectives of lessons and units that you plan and the standards and benchmarks that have been adopted by your school district and your state. Even though you may have a high degree of autonomy as a teacher in choosing your teaching approaches, you are not a "free agent." You are responsible to guide your students toward achievement of objectives set by your district and state. Therefore, making connections between your lessons and instructional units and those of the district and state is an important aspect of instructional planning and design. One way of doing this is to create a table with the following headings, so that you are clear about those connections:

Objectives of My Unit	District Objectives	State Objectives

Understanding the Teaching Model Employed in the Unit

Another important feature of the *Food for Plants* unit is its instructional model, which is described as a leaner-centered, conceptual change instructional model. This is represented in two ways in the unit. First as a diagram (see Figure 5.1) that shows its "learner-centered" quality, including a learning community feature and the steps of the instructional model. *Learning community* was a key part of Chapter 5. In its most basic form, learning community occurs in classrooms where the teacher and students work together in a cooperative atmosphere that has the features identified in the outer circle shown in Figure 5.1. These qualities of instruction may be among the reasons you entered teaching. However, they are accompanied by a set of interactional skills that need to be developed by both students and teachers.

The steps of the instructional model used in *Food for Plants* are found within the inner circle in Figure 5.1. These steps are elaborated in Figure 6.2. As you can see, it is a combination of the models described in Chapters 4 and 5.

Reflection & Discussion Questions

1. Take a careful look at Figure 6.2 and determine how it combines the 5E model, the apprenticeship model, and the conceptual change model that were the subject of Chapter 4. Then identify the model (or models) of teaching that form the basis of each of the seven steps listed in Figure 6.2.

2. Describe in your own words why each step of the learner-centered, conceptual change instructional model is needed to enable students to understand and use the science knowledge contained in the *Food for Plants* unit.

3. Would the learner-centered, conceptual change instructional model be of value in teaching other topics? Give reasons for your answer.

As you may have seen from your examination of the learner-centered instructional model (Figure 6.2), Steps 1 through 3 are much like the conceptual change model, but it also is blended with the 5E model and the apprenticeship model. In Step 1, *elicit students' ideas* corresponds to the first condition in the conceptual change model, and *establish a problem* sounds like engagement, Step 1 of the 5E model and the apprenticeship model. Step 2, *explore phenomena and challenge students' ideas*, is strongly associated with the conceptual change model, but *exploring* is the second E in the 5E model. This also shows how the authors of the unit blended models to come up with this learner-centered instructional model. Step 3, *introduce new ideas and contrast them with students' ideas*, also blends to these two models, but the shift here is toward the 5E model with explaining and contrasting the new idea with students' ideas. The conceptual change model comes through in the "fine print" in step 3, where it states "New ideas and concepts are not explained to students until their explorations have convinced them of a need for a new explanation." The remainder of the elaboration of Step 3 in Figure 6.2 is strongly associated with the conceptual change model as it highlights the need to make the new idea comprehensible and plausible.

Steps 4 through 6 become more focused on the apprenticeship model and blend it with the fourth E in the 5E model. The term used in the latter model is *expand*, which has at its base, application of the new idea. Connecting with the conceptual change model, Steps 4 through 6 all include *reconciliation* of the new idea with students' ideas. The sequence of development in Steps 4 through 6—*modeling, coaching,* and *fading*—comprises the core of the apprenticeship model.

Step 7, *reflect on changes in students' ideas and connect with new ideas*, is implicit in all three models, but not explicitly part of any of the models. Step 7 and

FIGURE 6.2 ■ A Learner-centered, Conceptual Change Instructional Model

1. *Establish a problem and elicit students' ideas.* Introduce the central question in a way that will engage students' interest and elicit their many different ideas about the question. Students should see that other students have different ways of explaining the same phenomenon.

2. *Explore phenomena and challenge students' ideas.* Engage students in experience with phenomena (direct, hands-on experience whenever possible) that allows them a chance to think through their ideas, to gather new evidence relevant to the central question, and to consider whether their initial ideas still really make sense in light of the evidence. Activities are designed to challenge students' preconceptions—to get them finding their initial ideas incomplete or unsatisfying in some way.

3. *Introduce new ideas and contrast them with students' ideas.* New ideas and concepts are not explained to be students until their explorations have convinced them of a need for a new explanation. New concepts need to introduced in ways that are likely to make sense from the students' perspectives. Use a variety of representations to explain new ideas (models, role playing, charts, diagrams, etc.). Compare end contrast students' ideas with scientific explanations. Encourage students to critique the new explanation: Does it make sense in light of the evidence we have gathered?

4. *Apply new ideas and reconcile them with students' ideas—Teacher Modeling.* Students need opportunities to *practice using new concepts* to explain real world situations. The teacher at first plays an important role as director in this process, at first providing lots of modeling of scientific ways of thinking. For example, after students have attempted an explanation of a problem situation, the teacher might point out aspects of their attempts that are scientifically strong and say, "these are the ways scientists would use this concept to think about this situation."

5. *Apply new ideas and reconcile them with students' ideas—Teacher Coaching.* Students need numerous opportunities to practice using new concepts to explain real world situations. Teacher modeling in one context is not enough. A variety of activities and questions that engage students in using scientific concepts and in refining their understanding of these concepts will help students see the wide usefulness of the concepts. During these activities, the teacher should actively coach students, providing them with feedback about ways in which their thinking is strong and ways in which they need to be more scientific in their thinking.

6. *Apply new ideas and reconcile them with students' ideas—Teacher Fading* Understanding is not occurring until students are able to use new ideas to explain novel situations independently. So it is essential that the teacher coaching fade out as students become more comfortable with working with the ideas.

7. *Reflect on changes in students' ideas and Connect with new ideas.* Students need to reflect often on the ways in which their ideas are changing and why. Frequently, the teacher asks: "How did today's activities give you any new ideas about our question? Did you change any of your ideas today? What evidence convinced you to do so? What is confusing to you today? What do we still need to know to help us answer our question?" As students reflect their understanding by becoming comfortable using new concepts without teacher coaching, it is especially important to take time to have students look back at the progress of their thinking and learning. Their awareness of their own conceptual change plays an important role in their valuing of the scientific process.

K. Roth, *A Plant Exploration Unit: How Plants Really Get Their Food*

the three prior steps (4 through 6) highlight the need for multiple experiences if students are to understand and be able to use new ideas from science in their daily lives. This idea is so central to planning lessons and enacting teaching for understanding that it needs to become part of your plan of operation as you think about and carry out your work with students. This learner-centered, conceptual change instructional model represents a significant step forward in thinking about how to help students understand and apply science knowledge. Without these multiple experiences, students will not be able to attain the under-standing and capability to apply knowledge that is essential.

Reflection & Discussion Questions

1. Why do you think that multiple experiences or activities surrounding an objective are needed to help students learn with understanding?

2. How does the learner-centered, conceptual change model help you understand what is required to enable students to understand and use ideas in science?

The Teacher's Role

Even though this model is labeled as "learner-centered," the roles of the teacher are very important. The teacher is not a purveyor of information. Instead, the teacher's role places much more emphasis on providing guidance to students and assessing their progress toward the goal. Clearly the teacher has an important role in helping students draw meaning from all of the activities and reconcile new ideas with their existing ideas.

There is one place, however, where the approach becomes teacher centered: Step 3, *introduce new ideas and contrast them with students' ideas*. Here the teacher must provide a new scientific explanation for the students because it is quite unlikely that they will formulate the intended, valid, scientific model on their own. Further, the teacher will not just present the new scientific idea. The teacher's role is to guide students in comparing and contrasting their ideas with it. As a teacher, you should be sure to note that introduction of the new scientific model is not done without careful preparation of students so that "their explorations have convinced them of a need for a new explanation." Your skills as a teacher will be critical in attaining the needed levels of cognitive engagement and preparation for students to undergo the conceptual change that is an essential part of learning and then to consolidate the change so that the new understanding becomes useful.

There is delicate balance among teacher roles in (1) setting up the environment for engagement in thoughtful exploration of the phenomena related to the instructional topic, (2) challenging students' initial ideas, (3) assessing when students have reached a point where they are ready for the new explanation as a result of their exploration and challenges to their existing ideas, (4) presenting the new explanation in a manner that is clear and meaningful to the students, and (5) helping students contrast the new explanation with the ideas that they currently hold. This is a very demanding set of roles for you as the teacher.

In later steps in the instructional model sections of the *Food for Plants* unit, the focus shifts to application of the conceptual model regarding photosynthesis to new situations. The purpose here is to help students *transfer* their new learning that plants have the special ability to make their own food from simple materials—carbon dioxide and water—and turn it into complex materials that store energy. Students must be able to comprehend this idea not just in the context in which it is developed in the lesson, but also in contexts that abound in the world in which they live, both within and outside of school. The learning model also shifts to the apprenticeship model where the teacher *models* (demonstrates) a use of the new concept in a new context, then *coaches* (supports) students as they try to use the new concept, and then *fades* (gives responsibility for the application to the students) so they can gain confidence and experience in using the concept. Several lessons are found in these two sections, providing multiple experiences with application of the photosynthesis concept in new situations.

The last step of the instructional model, *reflection*, carries this even further. Here, as in other places in the unit, students are encouraged to evaluate their own thinking and understanding of the ideas. They are urged to compare their new understandings about plants with those they had at the start of the unit. An additional comparison is generated by the posttest, which is exactly like the pretest. By making such comparisons, students can see how their ideas have changed as a result of the experiences in the unit, and their actions related to it.

Perhaps you are asking yourself at this point, "Why is Gallagher spending so many words on this? Does he think we are 'dense' and don't get it?" My reason is that it may be easy in concept, but it is difficult in practice. For most people, it represents a substantial paradigm shift from the one we most likely experienced during most of our time as students and may have carried with us into our teaching to the new paradigm in science teaching and learning that *Food for Plants* exemplifies. Moreover, the learning model and the process are complex. It is unusual for science teachers to provide this sequence of guidance, support, practice, and reflection for their students. And this is one reason why so few students succeed in understanding and being able to use—in practical, meaningful ways—the science knowledge learned in school.

Reflection & Discussion Questions

1. How would you categorize my presentation in relation to Figure 6.2 in this chapter up to this point?

2. Since I cannot interact with you personally, as I would in a classroom, I must attempt to engage you with the problem and do as much as I am able to help you work through the seven steps in Figure 6.2. To what degree am I being successful in "practicing what I am preaching"?

3. In what ways does the learner-centered, conceptual change instructional model make sense to you? In what ways does it appear to be inappropriate for your use?

Where Is Assessment in This Model?

In spite of the important addition that this model provides in our thinking about teaching and instructional planning, its use of formative, embedded assessment may not be obvious. However, assessment is found in each of the seven steps. To find it requires being able to understand the model at a deeper level.

The model does an excellent job with preassessment in Step 1, as it highlights the need to *elicit students' ideas*. Step 2 emphasizes giving responsibility to students "to consider whether their initial ideas still really make sense in the light of the evidence. Activities are designed to challenge students' preconceptions—to get them to find their initial ideas incomplete or unsatisfying in some way." Making students responsible for evaluating their own ideas in relation to new evidence is an important meta-cognitive learning skill, and it represents an important scientific value—to be skeptical. Throughout their efforts in Step 2, listening to students as they describe their struggle with existing and new ideas provides information about the meanings they are giving to experiences and thought.

Step 3 can be highly teacher centered in presenting the new idea to students. However, it also can be interactive, and students' responses to the new idea that the teacher is introducing become a source of assessment information for the teacher. This approach depends on the teacher's attending to students' ideas and reasoning as they ask questions, respond to the teacher's questions, and begin using the new idea to attempt explanations or applications. Attention to students' talk and actions is essential, not just here in Step 3, but in all aspects of teaching, including every step in this approach to teaching.

In Step 4 of the Learner Centered Conceptual Change Instructional Model for *Food for Plants*, assessment and giving feedback are given added importance. For example, after students have attempted an explanation of a problem situation, the teacher might point out aspects of their attempts that are scientifically strong and say "This is how scientists would use this concept to think about this situation."

In Step 5, *coaching* depends on the teacher making assessments continuously, figuring out how to support the students' correct thoughts and actions, figuring out what to do when thoughts and actions are incorrect, and then responding in a way that fosters improvement. Therefore, assessment lies at the heart of coaching.

Step 6 grows out of Step 5. Knowing when to *fade* is also based on assessment of when students are able to take independent action in applying the new explanation or idea to new situations in a valid way. *Fading* requires careful and continuous assessment as the teacher observes how students are using the new concept independently.

In Step 7, *reflection* is a tool for transferring responsibility for assessment from the teacher to students and making students more responsible for their own learning. Step 7 also is designed to engage students in self-assessment. Reflection is a meta-cognitive

act, in which students think about the changes in their thinking that result from the experiences they have had during instruction, based on the steps of the learner-centered, conceptual change instructional model.

One limitation of *Food for Plants* may be that it does not support the teacher adequately in taking action when formative assessment shows that students are not attaining the objectives. Said another way, how does the unit help the teacher when the students are *not* getting it? This is a matter we will explore as we examine the unit in detail.

Reflection & Discussion Questions

Even though the Learner-centered, Conceptual Change Instructional Model is not explicit about the role of formative assessment in its description, assessment is very important within it. How would you demonstrate the important place of formative assessment to a colleague who is interested in this instructional model?

Getting into Activities in *Food for Plants*

Now that you know about the instructional model underlying *Food for Plants*, and its objectives, you can explore structure and organization of the unit. The unit consists of twenty-two activities developed in a sequence based on the instructional model. The extensive table in Figure 6.3 presents a map through the unit, which also identifies the storyline for the unit.

As you can see from reviewing Figure 6.3, the activities form a carefully designed developmental sequence. *Food for Plants* is divided into five parts that coincide with the instructional model as follows:

1. ESTABLISH THE PROBLEM and ELICIT STUDENTS' IDEAS.
2. EXPLORE activities and CHALLENGE students' ideas.
3. EXPLAIN scientific concepts and CONTRAST them with students' ideas.
4. APPLY activities to practice using and coming to new concepts in relation to students' perceptions.
5. REFLECT AND CONNECT activities to monitor learning, to raise questions and new explorations, to assess conceptual change.

A Closer Look at *Food for Plants*

In the next several pages, we will "walk through" the *Food for Plants*, highlighting particular features that make this an exemplary instructional unit. I strongly urge you to go to the Web site for this unit and follow

FIGURE 6.3 ■ *Food for Plants* Map and Storyline

Engage and Elicit Activities

Activity (Task)	Description	Objectives
1. Wondering about Plants	Eliciting Students' Ideas	
2. Pretest	Eliciting Students' Ideas	1–5, 8–10
3. The Seed and the Log	Establishing a Problem and Eliciting Students' Ideas	7
4. What Is Food for Plants?	Establishing a Problem and Eliciting Students' Ideas	2
5. Plants and People: Is Their Food the Same?	Establishing a Problem and Eliciting Students' Ideas	2

Explore and Challenge Activities

6. Are Seeds Food for Plants?	Explore and Challenge	1, 7, 8, 9
7. Creating Models of Bean Plants	Explore and Challenge: Is the seed food for plants?	
8. Grass Plant Experiments	Explore and Challenge: Are water, sun, and soil food for plants?	
9. Dr. Van Helmont, "Is soil food for plants?"	Explore and Challenge	
10. Counting Calories: Measuring Food Energy	Explore and Challenge: Are minerals and plant fertilizers food for plants?	

EXPLAIN Scientific Concepts

Activity (Task)	Description	Objectives
11. Read about photosynthesis	Read and talk about what scientists have discovered about how plants get their food.	3
12. Bean books with photographs	Looking at stages of bean growth and explaining how the plant is getting its food at each stage of growth.	1, 3

APPLY Activities to practice using and coming to new concepts in relationship to students' preconceptions

Activity (Task)	Description	Objectives
13. Visit from a plant with a problem	Visiting plant challenges us to use idea of photosynthesis to tell her how to get her food now that she has run out of the food stored in the cotyledon.	1, 2, 3, 5
14. Sand plant models	Investigating cells and chlorophyll and where food is made in the plant; how food travels in a plant to all cells.	3, 5
15. Testing plant parts for starch	Investigating plant parts to see if they have starch; tracing where that starch came from— how it was produced in the leaves and stored in various parts of the plant.	1, 2, 3, 4, 10
16. Visit from a plant with a problem	Visiting plant challenges us to use idea of photosynthesis to tell her what those strawberries are that have started to grow on her and where they came from.	1, 2, 3, 5,10
17. Creating Models	Students create skits and/or word pictures to put their ideas together to explain how plants get their food.	3, 6, 7

(Continued)

Activity (Task)	Description	Objectives
18. Snickers Science	Students analyze ingredients in a Snickers bar and consider the question: If all the plants in the world died, could we still live? Where does the food in Snickers bars come from?	3, 10
19. Application Problems Student-Designed Experiments		Various Various

---

Reflect and Connect Activities to monitor own learning, to raise questions and new explorations, to assess conceptual change

---

Activity (Task)	Description	Objectives
Ongoing Reflect and Connect Activities	Each lesson throughout the unit should include Reflect and Connect opportunities. The FAR lesson plan format (Frame, Activity, Reflect) emphasizes this continual assessment of student thinking by both the teacher and the students.	
20. Revisiting Your Initial Ideas	Look back at ideas at beginning of unit and consider how those ideas have changed and why.	1, 2, 3, 4, 5
21. Writing stories about the time I really felt like a scientist in this unit	Students write a story about a time I felt like a scientist during this unit.	Will vary
22. Teaching with Transparencies	Students take turns teaching the class at the overhead projector using Transparency Masters 1A through 7A.	All

K. Roth, *A Plant Exploration Unit: How Plants Really Get Their Food*

the more detailed development of these ideas as you read the remainder of this chapter. As you do, it will be valuable for you to read the *Purposes* the authors have stated for each lesson and to reflect on how those purposes are achieved. In addition, each activity is accompanied by about a half page *Possible Teacher Narrative* that usually includes three sections that help you understand the actions that teachers can make to foster student learning:

> FRAME—suggestions on how to engage students at the initiation of the lesson
>
> ACTIVITY—suggestions about how to organize the students for the lesson
>
> REFLECT—suggested activities that engage students in reflection about their learning, usually near the end of the lesson

PART 1 ■ Activities That Engage Students in the Problem and Elicit Students' Ideas

The first activity in Part 1, *Brainstorming Questions and Observations about Plants*, is used to engage students so that they will be ready for a pretest in Activity 2.

The pretest can be found on the Web site for *Food for Plants* (*http://ed-web3.educ.msu.edu/rothk/*) below the list of activities in the Assessment Items section. You should take time to review the pretest to see the kinds of questions asked there.

Reflection & Discussion Questions

1. What might students' responses to these questions tell you, if you were to administer the pretest to a group of students?

Activity 3 raises the question about how a tiny pine seed can grow into a large pine tree with many branches and leaves. It also raises an additional question, "How does the seed get its food to grow?" which is related to the central question for the unit. From there, the sequence begins a process of defining food in Activity 4. In Activity 5 students are directed to write down their ideas in answering the question "What is food for plants?" Three questions are given to prompt their writing:

1. Write down YOUR ideas about how plants get food (put down the ideas you have TODAY; we know that your ideas may change).

2. Write YOUR ideas about what kind of food plants use to live and grow (put down the ideas you have TODAY; we know that your ideas may change).

3. Draw arrows to show how you think food moves in a plant. Why does it move this way? (*How Plants Really Get Their Food*, Web site, Activity 5, Student's Pages)

The lesson plan shifts at this point from the lesson content to an activity titled "Getting ready to talk!" In this activity students are introduced to ways in which scientists talk with each other about scientific ideas. This is an important excursion from the main ideas so that students learn RULES OR GUIDELINES FOR SCIENCE TALKS (Web site, Activity 5, Student's Pages). Activity 5 concludes with a response sheet titled "Reflect and Connect: Having a Scientific Discussion," which helps students think this about the meta-cognitive component. It consists of seven completion questions and a checklist of how YOU were a thoughtful scientist in today's discussion. The items in the checklist begin with phrases such as "I shared...," "I listened...," "I described...," and "I gave reasons for..." The closing item on the checklist states "I did a lot of hard thinking and wondering about how plants get their food" (Web site, Activity 5, Student's Pages). This excursion provides students with an opportunity to learn a set of skills about reflective conversation that are new to many students. Activities such as these are important in helping students learn appropriate, *meta-level strategies* that will enable attainment of the specific learning goals. Another relevant meta-level strategy that is closely related to this one is how to work effectively with class members in small-group settings.

By the end of Activity 5, several developments should have occurred. First, the teacher has learned much about ideas that students hold regarding plants, especially about how and where they think plants get their food. Second, the students have been encouraged to question some general ideas about plant growth and development from seeds. Third, they have been prompted to think about what constitutes food for plants and where it comes from. Fourth, they should begin to recognize that some students have ideas about food for plants that differ from theirs. Fifth, they should

be started on a pathway that will enable them to question and reason about the natural world in ways that are similar to those used by scientists. Most important, they should be prepared to explore different ideas about food for plants with a somewhat open mind.

Reflection & Discussion Questions

1. Five of the twenty activities in this unit (all of Part 1) have focused on giving the teacher insight into the students' ideas and reasoning and preparing the students to learn the subject matter of the unit. Why is this so important?

2. Would it differ in other topics such as in a middle grade physical science or earth science unit?

3. Would it differ with students in a high school class in biology or chemistry?

4. Would it differ if you were teaching high school students who had a history of low achievement? Give reasons for your answers to these questions.

PART 2 ■ Activities to Explore Phenomena and Challenge Students' Naïve Ideas

Next students engage in an investigation that asks the question, "Are seeds food for plants?" (Web site, Activity 6). In this activity, students compare the growth of four configurations of bean seeds—the whole seed, one cotyledon with an embryo, one cotyledon alone, and the embryo alone. Preparing for the investigation includes careful observation of different kinds of seeds. Designing the investigation is also part of the preparation. The observations from this investigation are intended to be informative regarding the effects on growth. Students place each of the four entities listed above on moist paper towel and seal the combination inside a container and then observe what occurs over several days. An important part of Activity 6 in the Student's Pages is making predictions. Students are asked, "Which seed parts will grow? Why do you think so?" Having the students make predictions and give their reasons before any data are produced through their experiment is an excellent thought process and a useful diagnostic tool. It will yield precise information about students' ideas and reasoning. Naïve conceptions will surface as students write their predictions and reasons for them.

Observing, drawing diagrams to record observations, discussing what is observed, reflecting on observations and discussions, and writing about observations and their meaning comprise the component activities relating to this investigation. Thus this activity will take several days of class time as the various parts of the seed either germinate or fail to do so. Also, because several small groups of students have set up the experiment there will be simultaneous, multiple replications of it. Students should compare results from all groups, not just their own. It will be important to see how all of the multiple replications turned out and to try to understand any variations in the results.

In subsequent days, students make and record observations. When more than a week has elapsed, the activity shifts to examination of the results over the duration of the experiment (Web site, Activity 6, Student's Pages). The students then "reflect on and connect" their experimental data with their predictions and background information. As part of this, they evaluate three explanations of the events that they have been observing about the source of food that enables the development of the embryo. Two of the explanations are incomplete and one is appropriate for middle grades students. Activity 6 continues with students discussing their ideas and reading about how scientists would think about this experiment. Activity 6 concludes with students, working individually, preparing a written response to questions about how their ideas have changed as a result of the experiment and its accompanying tasks.

As you studied this section, I hope that you have developed a clearer idea of the depth and complexity of the task of teaching students about this experiment about seeds as food for plants. The activity shows how a skillful teacher has designed a hands-on activity, developed a plan for introducing it to a group of middle grades students, guided them as they conducted the experiment and recorded and interpreted data from it. The result is a rich learning environment in which the teacher guides students toward understanding of the important scientific concept. The example provides an opportunity to see how a skilled teacher thinks about the sequence of activities, including when the students must give meaning to their experiences and when the teacher adds frameworks to advance their own efforts at creating meaning.

Reflection & Discussion Questions

1. What is the conceptual framework that students should be developing as a result of Activity 6?

2. Locate the places in Activity 6 where the teacher becomes the source of a conceptual framework, where the students must use their own frameworks, and where the students must find information from the experiment.

3. What conditions support the students in bringing together these ideas and experiences in a way that is meaningful to them?

This section on Exploring and Challenging Students' Ideas about food for plants continues with four more rather extensive activities (Activities 7–10). The *exploring* activities provide students with new experiences that are relevant to developing a scientific perspective on food for plants, and for the concept of photosynthesis that will be introduced in Activity 11. However, introduction of that concept will be preceded by these four activities designed to prepare students to understand this new concept.

Activity 7 consists of skits that students will prepare as a representation of what occurred with the parts of the bean seed. The task is presented on the Student's Pages as follows:

Your group's task is to create a model that explains what you are thinking about how a bean gets its food to begin to grow. Use ideas from your experiment!

This model will show how something works that you cannot really see. We will use the model to imagine what is happening inside bean seeds.

Models take on many forms. We will put our model in the form of a skit that your group will create and perform.

Work in your group to create a skit model that shows that you understand how the embryo gets its food and that you can support your ideas with evidence.

Here are the rules for this model creation:

1. You must use all the following words: Food, energy, embryo, seed, cotyledon, evidence.
2. You must have each person in the group speak at least once.
3. You can only use the props your teacher provides.
4. Your skit must be scientifically accurate based on our experiment.
5. End with one idea about how the food gets into the cotyledon and one question that you are wondering about.

Presenting the Skit Models

Watch each skit carefully and think about how good a model it is. How well does it represent what you think is happening inside bean seeds? Models can never represent things 100% accurately. So think about ways in which each model is and is not scientifically accurate. You will write feedback for each group on the chart. And you will have a chance to share your feedback after each group's presentation.
(From Web site, Activity 7, Student's Pages)

The feedback form can be found on the Web site (Activity 7, Student's Pages). Five questions are listed on which students must give feedback:

1. Used words accurately? Which ones were not used accurately?
2. Did everyone speak?
3. What was the group's hypothesis about how the food gets into the cotyledon?
4. What was the group's question?
5. Name one way the model was NOT exactly like real plants.

In Activity 8, students set up a grass plant experiment to determine if water, light, or soil provide food for plants. The plan, as in previous activities, is to design experiments to answer a question, to carry out the experiments, and then to interpret the results. Reflection, connections to prior knowledge, and writing about the meaning that can be gained from the experiments are key parts of the activity. This is a pivotal activity in the developmental sequence as it provides evidence that will challenge many of the naïve conceptions that students hold as is explained in the purpose of the lesson:

Purpose: This is a very simple experiment that can be used to explore and challenge students' conceptions that water, soil, and sunlight are possible sources of food for plants. Grass plants are grown in soil in the light and dark. The plants in the dark begin to grow (using food from the cotyledon), but then die without sunlight. The plants in the dark die even though they have water and soil. So the activity challenges the hypotheses about water and soil being food for plants. It emphasizes the necessity of light. For many students this activity gets them wondering whether plant food is a combination of things. Ideally, students will finish this experiment saying something like: "Well, I'm not sure about water anymore. It seems important but it is not enough. Plants need sunlight, too. I'm not sure." When students get to this point of wondering about their hypotheses, they are ready for the concept of photosynthesis to make sense to them! (Web site, Activity 8, Teacher's Pages)

In Activity 8, as in every activity, you should read the entire Teacher's Page and Student's Page so that you are able to see the detail of planning and preparation that is included. It also will help you further understand the richness of the work of teaching for understanding.

Activity 9 takes an historical approach by having students study the classic "Dr. Van Helmont: Is Soil Food for Plants?" Again the purpose statement shows the significant position of this activity:

Purpose: On the students' pages, students' ideas about soil as food for plants are challenged as they think about the experiment done by the Belgian Jan Van Helmont in 1642. In this experiment he showed that plants do not use food from the soil to support their growth. (Web site, Activity 9, Teacher's Page)

As you may recall, in 1642, Jan Van Helmont began a five-year observational experiment by planting a young tree, weighing 5 lbs in 200 lbs of soil. Five years later, after watering the tree carefully, the tree weighed 169 lbs and the soil weighed 199 lbs 14 oz. Students work through this historical presentation about the experiment in a manner similar to previous activities, except, quite obviously, they do not perform the experiment. However, they discuss the experiment and its findings, and reflect on their meaning.

Activity 9 is an excellent example of the use of historical materials as a basis for student inquiry. They can "look over the shoulders" of a scientist and understand the intellectual struggle that took place in developing an understanding of the natural world. Coming to understand how an idea was formulated by reading about their experiments and interpreting their data is an important vehicle for understanding how ideas emerged over time from experiments, and at the same time, it allows students an opportunity to gain some understanding about how science functions.

In Activity 10, students explore fertilizers and minerals that are sold as "plant food" to determine if they are the source of energy for plants. Using the analogy of vitamins pills for people, the argument is made that plants need minerals to be healthy, but minerals do not provide the energy plants need to survive and grow. Students study labels from "plant food" products, fertilizers, and minerals for plants, along with labels from vitamins for people. They also examine labels from foods and drinks that students often consume to see how they are sources of energy for humans. In this activity, students explore the following hypothesis and seek evidence to *support and challenge* it. The task takes on a scientific posture in the manner in which it is presented:

Hypothesis: Plant food or minerals and fertilizers are food for plants.

Evidence: Can we find any evidence to support this hypothesis?

Can we find any evidence to challenge this hypothesis?

Not surprisingly, the familiar format of activities follows the path of predicting, observing, recording data, and then reflecting on its meaning. Activity 10 closes with an activity titled "Reflect and Connect" in which students reflect on both the Van Helmont experiment and the meaning that is gained from all of the experiments done so far in the unit. Students are asked three questions and also to give reasons for their answers:

1. Are you convinced that water is not food for plants? Why or why not?

2. Are you convinced that soil is not food for plants? Why or why not?

3. Are you convinced that minerals in the soil are not food for plants? Why or why not? (Web site, Activity 10, Student's Pages)

The authors explain the importance of this reflection activity:

> **Purpose:** The purpose of these questions is to challenge students to think across all of the experiments they have done and to consider whether they are convinced by the arguments that say that water, soil, and minerals are not food for plants. It is not enough for students to memorize the argument given in the text on p. 41. These arguments must make sense to the students. If they do not make sense, it is important for the teacher to elicit this from the students at this point.
>
> Whether or not students are convinced about water, soil, and minerals, you should proceed at this point to introduce the idea of photosynthesis. Hopefully, students will be at least uncertain about the role of water, soil, and minerals and ready to hear a new way of making sense of the data they have been exploring. (Web site, Activity 10, Teacher's Pages)

As a result of this sequence of explorations and reflections, students should be prepared for the next phase of the unit, Explaining Scientific Concepts.

Reflection & Discussion Questions

1. In the statement of purpose for this most recent activity, the claim was made that, "It is not enough for students to memorize the argument given in the text on page 41. These arguments must make sense to the students." Why is this statement important? Use your knowledge about conceptual change and other viewpoints about learning to explain the significance of this statement. How does this statement capture the essence of the

structure of this unit both up to this point and for the future parts of the unit?

2. In Part 2 of this unit, students are guided in drawing meaning from five different activities that all are focused on challenging their naïve, entry-level ideas as preparation for a new idea that replaces them. How does the teacher support students in keeping track of, and drawing meaning from, all of these activities? How does the teacher help them use the new information to change their ideas?

PART 3 ■ Activities That Present New Ideas Using a Variety of Representations That Can Help Make Clear the Contrast with Students' Initial Ideas

Two activities comprise this part of *Food for Plants*. However, the nature of these activities is different from the prior ones. In terms of the 5 Es model developed in the previous chapter, this is the explanation phase. It is where the teacher introduces a new concept to the students to help them synthesize and give deeper meaning to the experiences they have shared during the exploration phase of that model. It is a more teacher-centered, teacher-directed part of the unit. But at the same time, students are not passive recipients of the teacher's ideas. Instead, the activities are highly interactive between teacher and students, and among students.

The title of Activity 11 is "How Plants Use Sunlight To Make Their Own Food." The purpose of the unit is stated as follows:

> This activity introduces the idea of photosynthesis for the first time. Students are encouraged to see the idea of photosynthesis in contrast with many of the hypotheses they suggested. (Web site, Activity 11, Teacher's Pages)

The activity begins with students reading an introduction to photosynthesis. Two reading activities are provided, one that appears to be a whole-class reading (Web site, Activity 11, Student's Pages), and a second one that is organized as a small-group activity with specific rules to guide the students in reading thoughtfully and in giving meaning to the paragraphs.

The first reading sets the stage for answering the question, "Is sunlight food for plants?" It reviews the experiment in which seeds were germinated in both light and dark conditions. Then it states:

> To find out if light is food for plants, you need to know more about plants than we can observe in this experiment. A good explanation of why plants in the light live and why plants in the dark die must tell us more than what happened. It must tell us more than "plants need

light." We want to know why the plants need light. What do they do with the light? Is it their food?

Scientists have developed good explanations for these observations. They have done many complicated experiments, and they have done lots of thinking and imagining about what goes on inside of plants. What happens to light when it goes into the leaves of plants? Scientists have found that the sun is not eaten or digested by plants. It is not food for plants.

BUT sunlight does have something to do with food for plants. Scientists have found that plants are able to do something amazing with energy that comes from the sun. No humans or animals are able to do what plants can do. Neither worms, fish, birds, monkeys, nor people can do what plants can do with the sun's light energy.

Plants can use light from the sun to make their own food inside their leaves. They do not have to go out and catch or buy their food like people do. Read the next section to find out how plants make food inside their leaves. (Web site, Activity 11, Student's Pages)

Only part of the reading and other resources for Activity 11 have been reproduced here. You should read the entire plan on the Web site.

Reflection & Discussion Questions

1. How is this reading selection similar to what you would find in many science textbooks for students of this age?
2. How does it differ?

The next reading in Activity 11 is done in small groups of approximately four students, who are advised of the following rules that are designed to foster active comprehension:

a. Go around your circle and take turns reading the paragraphs.
b. After reading a paragraph, the reader should ask the group:
   - Did this paragraph give you any ideas about how plants get their food? Give examples.
   - Did this paragraph say something different than you thought before? Give examples.
   - Did this paragraph challenge any of the hypotheses on our class data chart? Which ones?
   - Do you have any questions about this paragraph? Is it clear? Could it be clearer?

The second reading is presented in Figure 6.4. Careful examination of the reading shows the "invention" of the idea we know as photosynthesis. This is not an idea that students can construct without substantial external help, as important parts lie beyond an attainable experiential base for them. Therefore, the teacher and this reading are the key sources of invention of this concept of photosynthesis.

Reflection & Discussion Questions

As you study the reading in Figure 6.4, reflect on how the complex concept of photosynthesis is developed, building on the prior work that students have done up to this point in the unit.

1. What experiences serve as a foundation for the reading?
2. How is the idea of photosynthesis developed so that students can understand it?

The reading in Figure 6.4 alone will not enable most students to understand the miracle of photosynthesis. Therefore, the designers of this unit added the activity shown in Figure 6.5. It is somewhat theatrical but it seems to be appropriate to give added meaning to the material that students have read. It also can be found on the Teacher's Pages for Activity 11.

As you read about this activity in Figure 6.5, note how the theatrics serve as a basis for important discussion about models at a meta-cognitive level, while also adding a useful representation of photosynthesis.

The activity presented in Figure 6.5 is supplemented by a writing activity in which students reflect on and write about their ideas about photosynthesis (Web site, Activity 11, Teacher's Pages). The sequence on this page is designed to help students expand their understanding of photosynthesis by

a. Reflecting on their early ideas about how plants get their food, which they have written about at the beginning of the unit, and then using the idea of photosynthesis to explain how plants get their food.

b. Reflecting on the meaning of the grass experiment and using the ideas of plants making their own food to explain why plants in the light survived while the plants in the dark died.

c. Reading about photosynthesis from another source, describing a new idea gleaned from this reading, and then comparing the two explanations to assess which makes more sense to them.

d. Revisiting the Van Helmont experiment to use the idea of photosynthesis to explain how the tree gained its weight.

Reflection & Discussion Questions

1. What purpose does each of these four elements of the worksheet serve in helping students to understand photosynthesis? Note that in Figure 6.5, it is suggested that perhaps a whole day might be devoted to analysis and discussion of this activity by including one or more additional readings. What would be the advantages and disadvantages of this choice?

FIGURE 6.4 ■ Reading to Introduce the Concept of Photosynthesis

Activity Eleven: How Plants Use Sunlight To Make Their Own Food

Plants are the only living things that can make their own energy-containing food out of water and air. *Water and air??!* How can plants turn water and air into food that they eat, food that we eat?

The secret is the <u>sunlight</u>. Green plants have a special substance in their leaves that makes them green. This substance is special because it can trap the sun's light energy. It is called chlorophyll. After the sunlight is trapped by the chlorophyll, the plant can do something quite amazing—it can use that energy to transform air and water into energy-containing sugars.

To make their own energy-containing food, plants need three things: <u>water</u>, <u>sunlight</u>, and <u>carbon dioxide</u> from the air. As you read, label the picture to show where each of these three things enters the plant. Then think about what happens to each of these three things when the plant turns them into food.

The <u>sunlight</u> is soaked into the leaves. A green substance in the leaf cells (called chlorophyll) is able to trap the sun's energy in the leaf. Plants take in <u>water</u> from the soil. The water travels from the roots up tubes inside the plant. The water then goes up the stem. Finally, the water reaches the cells in the leaf. <u>Carbon dioxide</u> goes into the leaves through tiny holes in the leaf (they are so tiny that you needs a microscope to be able to see them). When sunlight, water, and carbon dioxide are in the leaf cells, the plant can begin making food in the leaves.

The leaf cells use energy from the sun to mix water and air together to make a totally new material out of them—food! This food is not water. It is not air. It is made out of water and air, but it is a new material. It contains energy that living things can use to live and grow. The food it makes is in the form of sugar.

The way that plants make food is called <u>photosynthesis</u>. "Photo" means light and "synthesis" means putting together. Photosynthesis is using light energy to put together air and water to make food energy.

ONLY plants are able to use sunlight to make their own food inside their bodies. Imagine if people could make food that way! All we would have to do when we were hungry is to get plenty of air and water and to stand in the sun. No more trips to the grocery store or to McDonald's!

The ONLY way plants can get food is <u>to make it for themselves</u>. They do <u>not</u> get food from the soil, of from water, or from the grocery store. They get all the food they need by making it themselves.

K. Roth, *A Plant Exploration Unit: How Plants Really Get Their Food*

2. It also suggests two optional activities, which present photosynthesis at the cellular and molecular levels. How might these help students? Under what circumstances might these tasks be inappropriate?

(Note: Teachers have many decisions to make as they progress through a unit. Professional knowledge, as well as data from assessment, can help with these decisions.)

Activity 12 is also a part of the explaining section of the unit. This activity "challenges students to use their knowledge about photosynthesis to describe how a bean plant is getting its food at each stage of development" (Web site, Activity 12, Teacher's Pages).

The teacher's role in this activity is to coach if necessary but to try to "fade" and let students coach each other, as they examine photos of bean plants developing from seeds. You will recall that during Activity 6,

FIGURE 6.5 ■ Activity to Represent Photosynthesis Visually

Activity

As another way of representing photosynthesis, do a teacher demonstration model of the photosynthesis process:

"I'm going to show you a model of how I think photosynthesis happens. I want you to listen carefully and give me feedback based on my model. Based on what you have read about photosynthesis, is my model accurate? In what ways? In what ways is it inaccurate?"

For extra effect, you might want to wear an apron and a chef's hat!

Have a student helper pour water in the bowl.
Have another student helper pour carbon dioxide in the bowl.
Have another student helper shine a flashlight on the contents of the bowl.
Use wire whisk or mixer to mix up the water and carbon dioxide.

Then surreptitiously (magically!?) throw out a sugar cube from the bowl.
"Look what was made from water and carbon dioxide and light!!! What is it?"

Ask students to name what each part of this model represents.

> Bowl: Leaf and cells in the leaf
> Wire whisk: What starts the chemical reactions between the water and carbon dioxide

What are the strengths of this model?

> Shows that water and carbon dioxide get turned into something completely new—sugar!
> Helps you imagine what is going on inside of each cell.

What are the limitations/inaccuracies of this model?

> There is no human chef cooking the sugar in photosynthesis—it is done by each green, leaf cell.
> The water and carbon dioxide are not poured into the leaf by humans.
> It is more than just simple mixing that occurs in the leaf—the mixing involves a chemical change from one substance to another.

Work through the questions on p. 46 with the students. You might want to take extra time with #3 and make a whole day's session focus on this activity. You could have different groups read different explanations of photosynthesis and then have them compare findings. Alternatively, you could read an explanation to them and ask them to listen for new or different ways of explaining photosynthesis.

> How Do Plants Get Food by Meish Goldish (Raintree Stock-Vaughn Publishers, Austin TX, 1992) is a picture book that you could read to the class.

A MORE DETAILED EXPLANATION—CELLS (OPTIONAL)

If you want students to think more about cells and cell activity in photosynthesis, use Transparency Masters 13.1 through 13.8. This series helps students zoom in closer to a leaf and its cells. You could pair this discussion with work with microscopes and looking at leaf cell cross sections.

A MORE DETAILED EXPLANATION—MOLECULES (OPTIONAL)

If you get into more about the molecules and chemistry of the photosynthesis reaction, you could use the factory analogy as represented on the last handout in the blackline masters section of this guide.

K. Roth, *A Plant Exploration Unit: How Plants Really Get Their Food* students observed different parts of bean seeds, some of which germinated. The discussion about observations in this activity focused on where the food for growth came from. It was decided that the cotyledon was the source of food.

Now, the photographs in this lesson provide additional views as the bean plant consumes the food in the cotyledon and develops roots, stems, and leaves, finally making its own food in its leaves. Students should also note that the cotyledons and stems become green like the leaves and support photosynthesis.

Reflection & Discussion Questions

1. In Activity 11, the students were introduced to the microscopic (cellular) and submicroscopic (molecular) structure of the plant. In Activity 12, they returned to the macroscopic level (whole plant). Why are all three levels important for your students?

2. How should you guide students to make connections among these three levels of structure?

PART 4 ■ Activities to Practice Using, and Coming to, New Concepts in Relationship to Students' Preconceptions

In the Web-based version of *Food for Plants*, this section is more elaborately titled, "Apply and practice using new ideas in a variety of real-world contexts with the teacher modeling appropriate thinking processes, then coaching students, then fading support" (Web site, Teacher and Student Links, Apply Activities). How descriptive of what this section is about!

Seven different activities are included in this application section. These are designed to enable students to use their new concept about photosynthesis to give it greater meaning and utility. As a teacher, you must recognize that at this point in the unit, many students still hold on to their initial concepts that plants get food from soil. It is deeply ingrained in their experiential and cultural background. It is highly connected within their conceptual ecology of knowledge, beliefs, and values. It is a model that has worked for them since they first thought about plants. It is grounded in the fact that people and all other animals they know about ingest food from their surroundings. So to them it is logical that plants need food too and that they take it in through their roots. The old model just doesn't go away—it is still there, in their minds, as a useful tool. Therefore, in your role as teacher, you need to guide students through these activities so that photosynthesis

becomes a useful and dominant tool for your students to understand how plants get food and energy for growth and life processes.

As you can see from Figure 6.3, the activities form an engaging developmental sequence. *Activity 13* has students visit a strawberry plant that has run out of food when the food stored in the cotyledons has been exhausted. Students must tell the plant what to do in order to get food. The students' task is to write a letter to Ms. Strawberry telling her what she must now do to obtain food.

The purpose of this activity as stated by the author is as follows:

> This activity provides a context for students to practice using the idea of photosynthesis to explain how a plant gets its food at different stages of growth. They use their knowledge to explain to a strawberry plant how to make her own food after her cotyledon is used up. (Web site, Activity 13, Teacher's Pages)

In Activity 13, the suggested teacher role is "Assessment—try to fade and not do any coaching" (Web site, Activity 13, Teacher's Pages). This activity is an embedded assessment activity to allow the teacher to learn how students are able to apply the new concept to a new setting, now that they have recently observed the development of bean plants from embryo to adult.

Activity 14 engages students in examining plants more closely to learn that plants are made of cells—all parts of the plant, not just the leaves—and that every cell needs to be able to receive food made in the leaves in order to stay alive and do its particular job for the plant. The medium for this lesson is to construct a sand painting to represent a plant, with sand grains representing individual cells. Again the limitations of models to represent ideas are part of this lesson, as it had been in the earlier lessons.

The purpose of this activity is described as:

> This activity focuses students' attention on the fact that the plant is made up of cells and that each cell needs to get food that is made in the leaf. Students typically think about plants making food for US to eat, and forget that plants need food, too! (Web site, Activity 13, Teacher's Pages)

The teacher's role in this lesson is described as coaching students' understanding of cells to help them come to realize that "it is not just that there are cells in plants. Rather the entire plant is built of cells" (Web site, Activity 13, Teacher's Pages). This probably will be a new concept for students. Therefore, they will need help in understanding the idea that plants like all living things are comprised of cells. Moreover, the idea that the whole organism is constituted of cells may not be easily grasped by them. As a result, students will need support with this idea as they work through the sand plant model they create in this activity. Teachers will need to ask students questions to get them to think about what the sand grains represent and to see that the whole painting is made of sand grains just as the plant is made of individual cells and that the whole plant is made of them.

Reflection & Discussion Questions

Activities 13 and 14 expand students' ideas on different levels moving from the big idea about photosynthesis as a source of food to the microscopic structure of plants. In this way they revisit ideas that have been introduced previously. How do these activities help your students grasp and use both ways of looking at plants? Why are both important?

Activity 15 is an extensive lesson that raises the question "What happens to food after it is made in the leaf?" In this activity, students learn (a) that sugar produced in leaves during photosynthesis is transported to all other parts of the plant to provide energy and raw material for growth for each and every cell, and (b) that sugar is often changed to starch and stored by plants. This is followed with activities that test various parts of vegetable plants to see where starch is located. Students perform a simple test with iodine that shows the presence of starch by its purple or black color when iodine contacts it.

The main ideas developed in this activity are

1. Food travels from the cells in the leaf all over so that food reaches each cell in the plant to provide it with the food energy it needs to live and function.
2. The plant has structures such as veins to help food travel through the plant.
3. Extra food that the cells do not immediately use is stored in different parts of the plant—seeds, fruits, vegetables. (Web site, Activity 15, Teacher's Pages)

Following the experimental activity, students then make sense of their findings by discussing and answering series of questions, including

1. Which parts of the plants that you tested had starch in them?
2. Can the cells in seeds make their own food? Why or why not?
3. Where does the food stored in a peanut seed come from?
4. Draw arrows to show how starch reached the cotyledons in the seeds. Where did the food come from?
5. Draw arrows to show how the starch got to the potato and to the banana. Where did the starch come from?
6. Draw arrows to show how the starch got to the stem of the celery plant.
7. If you look carefully at the cut edge of a celery stem, you will notice little circles. These are actually long tubes that go the length of the celery stem. You may have found that starch was stored in some of these tubes. The tubes carry food from one part of the plant to another. Do you think that the food in the celery stem moves up the stem or down the stem? (Web site, Activity 15, Student's Pages)

In this activity, teachers would model (demonstrate) how to test for starch and how to interpret how it came to be in the places it is found in plants. Then coaching would be useful as students begin to use this new technique to test for starch and to make sense of the findings from their test. Linking the long tubes in celery (question 7) to the big ideas of this lesson may require some further coaching.

Activity 16 revisits the strawberry plant, personified as Ms. Strawberry J. Plant. She is happy and healthy, but is concerned about something that is happening to her—she has red things growing all over her, and she wants to know what they are, where they come from, and if she should be worried about them! She even thinks they are "tumors or something bad." Students are to write her a letter to solve her puzzle.

This could be another embedded assessment to see how students are linking ideas. Therefore, you may want to fade here, at least for time. If students need support in making the connections among ideas to answer Ms. Strawberry J. Plant's problem, then coaching may be required.

Activity 17 provides a different look at application. It has students creating skits and drawing concept maps to show how plants get their food. Again, students not only create these models, but also critique them to determine their usefulness and their limitations. Some modeling and coaching may be needed with concept maps, but the skits may need only a little coaching to ensure that students do not become so "creative" with the skit that they miss the underlying science involved in showing how plants get their food.

Activities 18 and 19 provide a series of added activities, beginning with determining plants that are capable of producing each of the ingredients that are included in a Snickers bar. Having students recognize that the chocolate, nuts, and sugar in the Snickers bar were all produced by plants will be important in showing that plants produce many different products— carbohydrates, proteins, fats, waxes, oils, and thousands of other materials. This should help to reinforce the idea that all of these products come from a transformation of one basic product—sugar—which plants produce through photosynthesis. It should set them wondering how plants are able to make all of these transformations to produce so many different products.

In Activity 19, students compare food for humans and food for plants as an additional application of the photosynthesis concept. Also, Activity 19 begins an exploration of how plants and animals living in northern climates survive winter. Where do they get their food to allow them to survive the winter when most plants are not producing food? These activities most likely begin by drawing out students' ideas and then coaching them as they try to create a meaningful synthesis of ideas from their own experience and this unit on photosynthesis. Helping students sort out ideas and clarify naïve conceptions will be an important part of the teacher's role at this stage of the unit.

Reflection & Discussion Questions

1. Have you thought about the wide diversity of materials that plants produce and their transformation from sugar within the plant? Have you realized that plants transform sugar into such a wide array of products including materials from which new cells are made? Students need opportunities to understand this, too!

   Take a few minutes to summarize the applications of photosynthesis that students experienced with the seven lessons in this part of the unit.

2. How have these helped students to understand how plants make food?

3. Why are so many activities needed in this part of the unit?

The next section in the unit is titled "Students reflect on how activities help them change their ideas; students connect new ideas and activities with previous ones." This section consists of seven activities. If you think back to our initial planning model, developed in Chapter 3, this section of *Food for Plants* fits the developing understanding component of that model as it has students making connections between ideas and making sense of experiences. However, that model was only a precursor of the more elaborated models of teaching and learning that are involved in this unit, but it does help to comprehend "the big picture" of why this unit is so detailed.

Activity 20 actually revisits the pretest given at the beginning of the unit. Students are now asked to answer four questions and compare the current and pretest responses:

1. How would you now describe how plants get their food?

2. How would you use arrows to show how food travels in plants? A diagram of a plant is provided and students are also asked to "explain your arrows." (Web site, Activity 20, Student's Pages)

3. Describe how your ideas about food for plants have changed:

   Before I thought that plants got their food

   _____
   _____.

   But I changed my mind about

   _____.

   I changed my mind because

   _____
   _____.

4. I thought the best evidence we got about how plants got their food was

   _____
   _____
   _____
   _____.

Reflection & Discussion Questions

1. Why are Activities 13 through 20 so important in the developmental sequence of this unit?

2. What do these activities add that is so often omitted in unit plans in textbook programs?

3. How do these features of *Food for Plants* enable you to support students' understanding and application of science?

The unit comes to an end with a posttest that is found in the Web site. It is a rich experience for students following the instructional model laid out at the beginning. The activities in Part 4 follow an approach of modeling, coaching, and fading—the apprenticeship model—so that students are given more responsibility for taking charge of their learning and understanding.

Reflection & Discussion Questions

Take time to reflect on the learning model for this unit (Figure 5.1 and 6.2) and how it was implemented in the unit to foster understanding and application.

Additional Valuable Resources

Figure 6.6 provides a listing that compares students' naïve conceptions and the conceptions that are the desired outcomes of *Food for Plants*. The goal conceptions listed in this figure are aligned with the ideas and ways of thinking of scientists, whereas the naïve conceptions represent ideas and reasoning that are often observed among middle grades students. Studying

FIGURE 6.6 ■ Students' Ideas about Food for Plants

Comparing Student Conceptions and Ways of Thinking with Scientists' Conceptions
and Ways of Thinking. . . About Plants and their Food

Issue	Goal Conceptions	Naïve Conceptions
Plants' source of food	Plants make their own food internally using carbon dioxide, water, and sun in a process called photosynthesis. This is plants' only source of food.	Plants take in their food from the outside environment. Plants have multiple sources of food.
Nature of food	Food made by green plants; is matter that organisms can use as a source of energy. It is an energy-containing material.	Food is the stuff that organisms eat, chew, take into their bodies.
Function of food in plants	Food supplies the energy that each cell of a plant needs for internal life processes (functional explanation).	Food is needed to keep plants alive, to grow (nonfunctional explanation).
Matter transformation (chemical change)	Water and carbon dioxide taken into plants is changed into new matter as a result of a chemical reaction. In this chemical change, nonenergy-containing matter (carbon dioxide and water) is rearranged and recombined to make energy-containing food (glucose).	Water and carbon dioxide taken into plants are not changed. They are used unchanged to support two separate life processes—drinking/eating the water and breathing the carbon dioxide.
Movement of matter	Water and carbon dioxide travel to cells in the leaf where they are involved in one process—photosynthesis.	Water and carbon dioxide travel throughout the plant where they are used for two separate processes—eating/drinking the water and breathing the carbon dioxide.
Energy transformation	During photosynthesis, light energy from the sun is changed into chemical energy stored in the food that plants make.	Plants need sun to live, grow to be green. (No notion of energy being absorbed, needed, or changed) OR Plants get their energy directly from the sun—this is their food. (No notion of light energy being transformed into food energy)
Importance of food-making process for plants	Most important product is food. This food is the plant cells' only source of energy.	The food-making process in plants is something they do for the benefit of people/animals. Plants are important because they give us oxygen and food.
Importance of food-making process for people/animals	Animals depend on plants for food as well as oxygen. Only green plants can change light energy from sun into chemical energy stored in food. Thus, only green plants can make energy-containing food that all living things need.	Plants are important because they make oxygen for people and animals to breathe. (Focus on oxygen production, not food production) Plants are also an important source of food for animals, but they are not the only source.

K. Roth, *A Plant Exploration Unit: How Plants* Really *Get Their Food*

Figure 6.6 will result in valuable additions to your knowledge as a professional in the field of science teaching. This knowledge will "put you on the alert" as a listener and observer of your students. You will be increasingly able to interpret your students' oral and written expressions in ways that will be helpful to you as a teacher. For example, examination of the first two rows in the figure shows fundamental differences between the understanding you hope students will take away from this unit and what they most likely bring to it. With this knowledge, you will be able to interpret students' words more effectively to determine whether they hold the naïve conception or are seriously entertaining the goal conception. If you ask your students "Where do plants obtain their food?" and your students say "From the soil," you then should ask "Tell me more about what you mean?" If students say "Plants take in water and minerals and that is their food," then you know that students are holding on to the naïve conception. You also can be quite sure that students have not constructed the goal conception that plants make their own food.

Another valuable resource about students' ideas and reasoning is found on the Web site under Teacher and Student Links. Click on the button Student Ideas and you will find another treasure of information from research that adds to your knowledge about students' thinking about photosynthesis. Like so many other sections of the Web site, video clips are included that give you an opportunity to observe Dr. Roth working with students (Web site, Teacher and Student Links, Student Ideas).

Reflection & Discussion Questions

1. As you study Figure 6.6 and Student Ideas on the Web site, how has your understanding about plants and their food been affected?

2. How have your ideas about students' learning been affected?

3. What are the major clues to students' ideas and reasoning processes that you would watch and listen for as a result of studying these resources?

Where Is Inquiry in This Model?

Some reviewers of this chapter have commented that they did not see inquiry present in it. This was surprising to me, because I view the unit as highly based in inquiry. At every stage in the unit, the work of the students is guided by such questions as "What is food for plants?" and "How do plants get their food?" At every stage in the unit, students are engaged in investigations that vary from empirical data collection to interpreting data from prepared sources to examining data from their world of experience. At every stage in the unit, students are working to give meaning to data and to making connections among experiences, data, and ideas.

Returning to Figure 4.1 on what *National Science Education Standards* says about inquiry for grades 5 through 8, the following points are listed:

- Identify questions that can be answered through scientific investigations.
- Design and conduct a scientific investigation.
- Use appropriate tools and techniques to gather, analyze, and interpret data.
- Develop descriptions, explanations, predictions, and models using evidence.
- Think critically and logically to make the relationships between evidence and explanations.
- Recognize and analyze alternative explanations and predictions.
- Use mathematics in all aspects of scientific inquiry.

Each of these points, except the last one, is exemplified frequently in the unit. Perhaps the critics did not see the investigations as being sufficiently "scientific"? However, investigations in the unit do relate to students' experiential world and to their level of development. Perhaps the critics felt that too many activities focused on analysis of data and events that dealt with literacy skills, but all of these activities were strategically placed in the unit to foster students' development of a new paradigm about "what is food for plants" and "where plants get their food." Perhaps critics saw this unit as being too teacher directed. If you view the teacher as an active part of the learning community, instead of "sitting above it," then the role of the teacher is heavily invested in guiding and interacting with students. Whole-class activities will occur, and the teacher may be quite directive in his/her interactions. However, this is not all that the teacher does. More frequently, the teacher is attending to students' ideas and reasoning in order to understand them and determine what actions would be most valuable in helping students make the paradigm shift about what constitutes food for plants and how plants obtain the food needed for growth and other activities. In short, the teacher must fill a role that sometimes has the traditional responsibilities of providing information to students, and a newer role supporting them as they struggle with ideas and create meaning on their own. Through all of this, the teacher must continually assess students' progress toward the instructional objectives and determine what steps are needed to foster that progress most effectively. It is this part of the teacher's role that is the subject of the next chapter. These actions exemplify formative assessment, which is detailed in Chapter 7.

Reflection & Discussion Questions

1. Do you feel that this unit is based in an appropriate model of inquiry for middle school students? Explain why or why not.

2. How would you ensure that your students and people who observe your work in this unit (or one like it that you teach) would see it as a valid inquiry-based experience?

As you conclude work on this chapter, consider how your ideas have changed as a result of this experience.

Reflection & Discussion Questions

1. As a teacher for middle grades or high school, how has this unit influenced your thinking about teaching and learning science?

2. What changes do you need to make in your teaching to support students' understanding of the subjects you teach?

3. What changes do you need to support in your students as they try to learn with understanding?

Journal Questions

Add to your journal by revisiting the following questions that will help you monitor your progress as you make a paradigm shift in your teaching and your understanding of your students' learning for understanding and application in science:

1. What were the purposes or objectives of this chapter?

2. What were the key ideas presented in this chapter? (Note: These two could be combined as a two-column table to show the parallel between the purposes of each chapter and the ideas presented.)

3. What important additions have you made to your vision of teaching science for understanding and application by studying this chapter and discussing with others? This should be an ongoing narrative that highlights development of your personal paradigm for teaching and learning science.

4. I also recommend that you create a concept map that portrays your understanding about teaching and learning science for understanding and application and add new concepts and connections as you study each chapter of this book. This concept map can provide a visual representation of your developing new vision or paradigm of science teaching and learning that you developed in the previous item.

5. What new skills and techniques do you find you need to develop in order to enact your vision of science teaching? What progress are you making in developing those skills and techniques?

6. Finally, what concerns do you have about being able to implement your new vision, your new paradigm of science teaching with your students, in your classroom, laboratory, and fieldwork? How will you respond to these concerns?

Chapter 7

Why Is Formative Assessment Essential?[1]

The purpose of this chapter is to (1) explain the essential role of formative assessment in teaching science for understanding and (2) present strategies that help teachers learn to use formative assessment as a vehicle for improving their teaching effectiveness and students' learning.

Formative assessment fits between preassessment and summative assessment. As you should recall from Figure 3.1, the initial planning model sits in a backdrop of continuous assessment, which consists of preassessment, formative assessment, and summative assessment. Formative assessment is deeply integrated into, or embedded within, instruction, which is why it often is called embedded assessment or continuous assessment. In fact, many learning activities in which students are engaged also offer teachers opportunities to gain information about students' progress toward the instructional goals and impediments to learning that block students from developing the level of understanding that teachers seek.

A key reason that assessment forms the backdrop for the initial planning model lies in the importance of assessment in both planning and teaching. Assessment allows teachers to add a higher degree of specificity to planning than is commonly the case in considering objectives alone. Lists of instructional objectives for a unit or even a sequence of lessons can become confusing if they are too long and detailed. However, by its nature, assessment is more specific. Therefore, thinking about assessment allows teachers to increase the level of detail in planning, while doing something that is practical and important. This is an important reason that Wiggins and McTighe (1998) stress "backward design" in planning lesson sequences, units, and courses. The potential for teachers to think carefully

[1] Research reported in this chapter was supported by National Science Foundation Grant Number MDR9252881, Eisenhower Higher Education Fund, and Michigan State University.

about the substance of lessons, lesson sequences, and units is enhanced when they think carefully about instructional goals and objectives along with assessments that will be used to monitor achievement of them. Moreover, thinking about goals, objectives, and assessments prior to assembling learning activities helps teachers to more strategically direct them toward specific purposes.

Thinking about formative assessment further enhances the opportunity to increase specificity and detail about what you intend your students to know and be able to do as a result of a lesson sequence. Moreover, it enables you to integrate teaching, learning, and assessment in ways that are not attainable otherwise. Adding formative assessment to your repertoire of teaching will add a dimension to your teaching that will enrich both your students' learning and your effectiveness as a teacher and provide you with deeper insights into your students' thought processes and factors that can inhibit learning and understanding.

Reflection & Discussion Questions

The purpose of the previous paragraphs is to help you make connections between this chapter on formative assessment and prior chapters on planning and teaching science for understanding. Take a few minutes to reflect on the ideas you have encountered up to now that form a foundation for thinking about assessment in general and formative assessment in particular.

What Is Formative Assessment?

Formative assessment, or embedded assessment, is merged with teaching and is designed to help give feedback to teachers and students about progress toward the objectives of instruction. Unlike traditional assessment, which often is a test or quiz administered to determine what students have learned (or not learned) *after* teaching is completed, formative assessment involves the use of teaching and learning activities that reveal developments in students' thinking *while* they are learning (Bybee, 1997). Therefore, with formative assessment, the line between teaching and assessment is blurred. Further, my definition of formative assessment also includes *teachers' use of newly gained knowledge of students' understanding to guide subsequent instructional decisions and actions.* With this definition, formative assessment becomes a cyclical, ongoing process whereby teachers (1) gather information about students' understanding as they teach, (2) analyze the information formally or informally, and (3) use the analysis to plan or adjust their teaching. Adjustments can be made immediately as a lesson progresses, during

next hour, in tomorrow's class, or as late as next year when the topic is taught again. Also, because the next day's teaching includes formative assessment, the cycle repeats itself.

Said another way, formative assessment involves assessing students as they participate in learning activities, interpreting the results of the assessment, and using that information to modify teaching. Modifications in teaching most frequently involve determining what to do next when some portion of the students in the class fail to comprehend what you are teaching. What can you do when one or more students fail to grasp what is being taught? What actions can you take when students are not attaining the objectives you have set for them? Formative assessment, as defined here, could help you fine-tune your teaching in cases where feedback from formative assessment shows that students are not understanding the subject matter as you had intended. This is what formative assessment is about!

As the *National Science Education Standards* point out, effective science teachers must be "skilled observers of students" in order to "guide and facilitate learning" (National Research Council, 1996, p. 33). Teachers can neither guide students nor plan activities that fit their emerging ideas on the topic of lessons unless they are able to gain access to detailed information about their students' ideas and reasoning before and during instruction. This is especially important because as students engage in learning, their ideas change. As a result, teachers must be able to access information about their students' ideas and reasoning before, during, and after instruction. All of this requires a set of skills for (1) gaining information about students' thinking throughout the learning process, (2) interpreting this information so that it becomes useful in guiding both day-to-day and longer term instructional planning, and (3) using the information to make adjustments in teaching. However, these skills are frequently absent from the repertoire of many teachers, and they tend to be "off the radar screen" of most preservice and novice teachers. Another complication is that, even though generic, formative assessment skills and techniques can be identified, implementation of formative assessment is highly topic specific. That is, although formative assessment in a high school biology class studying two topics, such as the structure of cells and genetics, may use similar formative assessment strategies, the different subject contexts make the task quite different. Therefore, formative assessment must be explicitly and systematically included in teacher education and staff development efforts. Moreover, high-quality instructional materials will provide guidance for teachers in carrying out formative assessment, but until such materials are commonplace, the responsibility for designing and using formative assessment tasks will fall to teachers.

1. How does this view of formative assessment fit into your view of teaching?
2. How does it expand your understanding of what teaching for understanding involves?

A Conceptual Model for Formative Assessment

A conceptual model that Joyce Parker and I developed as part of the project noted in footnote 1 has three main elements that describe teachers' actions:

- *Gathering information about students' understanding* as students work on tasks that expose their ideas and reasoning while they learn. Information can be derived from oral, written, or graphic products; from watching students at work; from listening to them during informal conversation; or in response to probing questions.

- *Engaging in deep analysis* of this body of information to determine what students appear to understand, and what they seem to be struggling with, yields clues as to their reasoning and the ideas they hold, which may be influencing their learning about the topic.

- *Deciding next instructional moves* based on analysis of the information, taking into account the learners, the learning goals, and possible courses of action for making progress toward those goals. (Gallagher and Parker, 1996a; Gallagher, 2000a)

Figure 7.1 shows the role of formative assessment in effective science teaching, as a continually recurring set of related activities.

How can formative assessment facilitate and support the change from traditional teaching to teaching science for understanding? The starting point includes teachers who embrace the reform movement goals of focusing on teaching powerful science concepts and processes, and teaching for understanding. If teachers accept these goals, they will need to incorporate formative assessment into their teaching because it is not possible to teach for understanding without it. Teachers can start by including a teaching activity that focuses on the specific learning goal and reveals students' thinking (not just a final answer). For example, during a study of change of state, middle school students could be asked to write a description of what occurs when molecules of water leave the liquid state and enter the gaseous state. They then could be asked to work in groups to develop a physical enactment of how this occurs. Or during a study of electricity, physics students

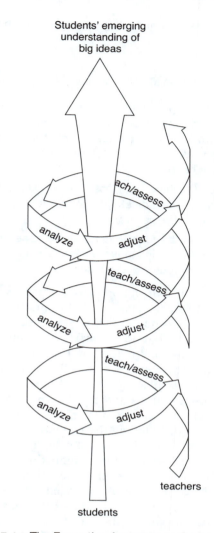

Students' emerging understanding of big ideas

teach/assess

analyze   adjust

teach/assess

analyze   adjust

teach/assess

analyze   adjust

teachers

students

FIGURE 7.1 ■ The Formative Assessment Cycle

could be asked to describe what occurs in a coil of wire when a magnet is brought close to it. These tasks not only can be considered as learning activities, but also can be thought of as giving teachers information about students' ideas and reasoning. Conversely, if they are thought of as assessment activities, they provide students with opportunities to construct meaning from experiences they have had earlier in the study of electricity or change of state. In addition to allowing teachers to assess students' progress, activities such as these make instruction more student centered, because students need to explain phenomena using a concept or theory that has been introduced to aid understanding. The focus of activities such as these is on making sense of experiences and ideas and applying constructs, rather than just giving correct answers. Usually this kind of assessment reveals the complexity of learning and creates an awareness of the need for teachers to guide students in clarifying their view of relationships among ideas. It also can produce evidence about what students know and how they are thinking about the topic.

Reflection & Discussion Questions

1. Reflect on Figure 7.1 for a moment and think how that model is useful in thinking about how you would design a sequence of activities for your students. What does it provide that previous models have not provided?

2. How do the three parts (assessing while teaching, analyzing, and adjusting) expand your thinking about formative assessment?

3. How does the idea that formative assessment needs to be continuous influence your understanding of your role as a teacher?

Collection of information from activities such as those in the two examples is only the first step. Next, teachers must interpret students' responses to determine what is understood and what is missing in students' factual base and reasoning. Then teachers must figure out the next course of action. For example, if students suggest that placing a magnet next to a coil of wire will cause electrons in the coil to move or if they say that the electrons go from the magnet into the coil, they are not understanding the phenomenon of electromagnetic induction. In the first case, "placing" indicates a static condition, whereas induction of electric current in the coil requires that the coil and magnet must move in relation to each other. In the latter case, a serious misconception is indicated. Electrons do not move from the magnet to the coil. Instead the moving magnetic field surrounding the magnet is interrupted by wires in the coil, which causes electrons in the wires to move. Like many phenomena, this phenomenon can be understood and interpreted at many levels, some of which are descriptive while others are highly abstract and mathematical.

The final step is to think about what actions can occur to help students correct any misconceptions that became evident through the activity and also to foster deeper understanding. One strategy that is both effective and reasonably simple to create lies in the use of students' answers or responses to such tasks. For example, a physics teacher could assemble a few examples of students' responses to the question about electromagnetic induction and create a learning task that addresses some of the difficulties that were uncovered, as shown in Figure 7.2. These could be used as an excellent learning activity to follow a formative assessment.

Information gathered from formative assessment about student learning is important, regardless of the form of instruction that you are using. For example, when you are presenting information to your whole class, information about what students already know and understand on the topic can help you "connect" with your students. It will help you avoid "going over their heads" or boring them with information they already possess. In what may be a common difficulty in presenting information and ideas to students who have some information on the topic you are teaching, their knowledge often is neither integrated with other relevant ideas nor complete. That is, students often have "bits and pieces" of information on a topic, and it is not connected to a larger framework of an earth science unit or course. For example, in the familiar topic of air movements across mountains, students may know that the windward side of mountain ranges receives more precipitation and that the leeward side can be quite dry. They also know that as you ascend mountains the air temperature decreases. These are essentials, but they have not created a coherent "story" about them in their own mind. Moreover, they may be missing the idea that as air is pushed over mountains by prevailing winds, it expands and cools, and when air descends the leeward side it is compressed and warms at a rate that is higher than its cooling rate. Students may be clueless about why this accounts for deserts on the leeward side of mountains. Also, most students will not be able to make connections with kinetic molecular theory to explain why the temperature of air decreases as it expands or increases as it is compressed. Continuous assessment is needed to determine what students do

FIGURE 7.2 ■ Using Student Work to Reteach Missed Understandings

After yesterday's class I reviewed your answers to the question on electromagnetic induction, and I saw some confusion in them. I'd like you to work on undoing the confusion. Study these responses and think about how these could be modified to make them scientifically correct. Think about the items on the list individually for about five minutes and rewrite it correctly. Then work in groups to check each other's answers, and then we will have a class discussion of the group work.

Here are three statements from yesterday's work for you to work on:

1. Electrons moved from the magnet into the coil of wire producing an electric current in the coil.

2. Placing a magnet next to a coil of wire induces a current in the wire.

3. As a magnet and coil are moved relative to each other, a direct current is induced in the wire.

not know and understand about a topic so that you can organize information in ways that are meaningful to students.

In addition, as you are presenting information, you must check on the meaning that students are creating from your presentation and other learning experiences. Therefore, you should engage in formative assessment as you proceed, or certainly as you conclude a presentation.

Preassessment could be in different forms. You could ask students to write a paragraph describing what they remember from their previous classes about the affects of air movements over mountain ranges on the climate of places on the windward and leeward sides. You could also have them draw a concept map about what they already understand about adiabatic cooling and warming, either individually or in small groups of two or three. Multiple-choice, matching, or fill-in-the-blank questions are also possibilities, but while they have the advantage of being easier to evaluate, they don't require students to construct a representation of what they know and understand. This is a severe limitation for the purposes of assessment for you as a teacher who is trying to teach for understanding.

Formative assessment enables you to identify specific problems that occur in students' understandings that can be addressed through instructional actions when you and students work together. This is empowering for both you and students. Rather than wondering why students do poorly on a unit test or are disengaged during class, you have information on how to help students improve their understanding at a time when it can be acted on, and before confusion and inappropriate conceptions deepen and solidify. In addition, some students who do not usually achieve well in traditional classrooms appear to understand more when instruction includes, and is based on, formative assessment. Most important, the results from formative assessment reward and guide you toward more effective teaching and more satisfied students (Gallagher and Wilcox, 1995).

Reflection & Discussion Questions

1. List at least six benefits that can accrue to you and to your students as a result of using formative assessment in your classes.

2. Describe how you would share information about the benefits of formative assessment with your students, their parents, and your colleagues.

Our Research and Development Project

A team of colleagues and I developed the conceptual model described above during the course of a four-year project supported by National Science Foundation and Michigan State University. We worked to better understand formative assessment and to develop a conceptual model and resource materials to aid teachers in employing formative assessment in science classes at the middle school level. You already have seen the conceptual model in Figure 7.1. In this section the resource materials are described.

During the project we worked with a team of teachers whose experience ranged from three to twenty-five years. These particular teachers were selected because their schools were already involved in collaborative projects with us. We also worked with over fifty leaders in staff development from schools and other agencies in Michigan to learn more about large-scale implementation of the work across the state of Michigan.

The resource materials consist of seven booklets. One of the booklets is a compendium of general teaching/assessment strategies that teachers in our project use to teach, and at the same time assess, their students' ideas and reasoning in science. These strategies are each described briefly and one or two practical examples are provided to show how these general strategies can be adapted to a variety of subjects. The teachers in our project who were skilled in the use of formative assessment planned their teaching by creating an orchestrated series of these teaching/assessment activities adapted to each big idea in a unit.

The six remaining booklets each correspond to an instructional topic that is commonly included in the middle school science curriculum. The topics were also included in the content for middle school in *National Science Education Standards*, Project 2061 *Benchmarks for Science Literacy*, and guidelines for science from several state education departments. This adds to the likelihood that these topics will be part of future curricula in science. The booklets' topics are

- Structure of Matter
- Force and Motion
- Astronomy
- Forces that Shape the Earth (Geology)
- Ecology
- Human Body Systems

Each booklet is organized around "key ideas." For each key idea, we describe the difficulties that students typically have with the idea, several teaching/assessment strategies, and assessment criteria that help the teacher analyze students' responses. For at least one activity included with each key idea, we have included samples of students' work, analysis of the work, and suggestions for how to use the analysis to guide the next steps in teaching. Below is a more complete description of each component of the booklets, including its connection to the new ideas about science education and how it can help teachers.

Key Ideas. For each topic, five or six key ideas are identified that comprise the major concepts appropriate for students at the middle school level. The key ideas form the basis of content organization for both teachers and students. The key ideas are meant to be indices to the booklets that can be used by teachers regardless of the curricula that they are using. Thus a teacher who is looking for examples of how to use formative assessment when teaching about the effects of temperature on matter would turn first to Key Idea 3 in *Structure of Matter*, which states:

> As a material is heated, its particles move faster. When it is cooled, the particles move slower. (p. 23)

Another reason for organizing around key ideas arose from our observations in classrooms, where we noted that many teachers and students "became lost" in the details of science content and were not able to delineate the main ideas that they were teaching or learning. This was also noted by other researchers (Wiggins and McTighe, 1998; Wiske, 1998). As a result, facts, concepts, principles, and theories were seen as being of equal importance. Little or no hierarchical structure was given to knowledge, which limited teachers' ability to help students organize information, focus on overarching ideas, and identify supporting facts. Moreover, experiences and data on which concepts and theories are based were not viewed in perspective.

A focus on central ideas mirrors *Benchmark's* delineation of a "common core" of ideas that form a foundation for scientific literacy and *National Science Education Standards'* call for a focus on powerful ideas that are useful, have many applications, and enrich students' lives (Project 2061, 1993; National Research Council, 1996). In addition, we consulted with scientists to make sure that the key ideas were formulated in such a way that they accurately conveyed their centrality in the discipline. In this respect, they somewhat resemble the generative topics described in the Teaching for Understanding Project (Wiske, 1998).

Reflection & Discussion Questions

1. Why is attention to key ideas of a topic so important?
2. Is this a new concept for you?
3. How would inclusion of key ideas in your lesson plans help you be clearer about the purposes and goals of instruction?
4. How would they help your students' learning?

Students' Difficulties. For each key idea, we provide a description of selected data from the extensive body of research on students' misconceptions and naïve concepts in science (see, for example, Driver, Guesne, and Tiberghien, 1985; Driver et al., 1994) and from teachers' practical knowledge about the difficulties that students encounter when learning the concept or principle. For each key idea, we have included both narrative text on students' difficulties and a table that summarizes and juxtaposes *intended understandings* and *naïve conceptions*. Presenting the information in two forms was done to make this essential component of formative assessment as "user friendly" as possible.

Information about students' ways of thinking about particular topics forms an important part of science teachers' professional knowledge (Magnusson et al., 1997). It can (1) heighten teachers' awareness of their students' ideas and reasoning so that teachers can structure their teaching around them and (2) guide their interpretation of students' words, work, and actions in the classroom. As you recall from Chapters 3 and 4, one foundation of the new theories of learning is that students have existing frameworks of understanding that often are strongly held, and new, lasting understanding occurs only when students can incorporate their personal theories and new information. Knowing about ways that students may go astray in the process of developing and refining their ideas allows teachers to formulate appropriate reinforcements into their teaching at those points.

Thus when preparing to teach about the effects of temperature on matter, teachers with an awareness that many students do not associate the effects of heating with changes in molecular behavior can plan several activities that provide students with experience with heating and cooling. Subsequently, the students are guided in developing explanations of their observations in terms of molecular motion. If teachers are also aware that students may think that the reason "substances expand when heated, is because the molecules in them get bigger," they will be prepared for students whose actions, discourse, or representations imply this conception (Gallagher and Parker, 1996, p. 24). Teachers can then plan follow-up activities that help students revisit important ideas such as expansion and change of state from a perspective of molecular motion.

Reflection & Discussion Questions

1. Why is attention to student difficulties in understanding about science topics so important?
2. Is this a new concept for you?
3. How would inclusion of difficulties students encounter in learning into your lesson plans help

you be clearer about the purposes and goals of instruction?

4. How would they help your students' learning?

Teaching/Assessment Activities. For each key idea, four to six or more teaching/assessment activities are included. These activities are designed to simultaneously nurture and assess students' understanding of the key idea. These teaching/assessment activities "blur the lines" between teaching and assessment. They are designed to show teachers that most activities can be used for the dual purpose of teaching and assessing, and to aid teachers in making assessment a more integral part of teaching.

The activities provide a range of opportunities for students to demonstrate their ideas and reasoning. Activities include opportunities for students to (1) write about their understanding and applications of scientific ideas through activities called *mind stretchers* in our booklets (sometimes labeled quick writes by others); (2) represent them in graphic form using pictures, diagrams, and models including concept maps; (3) use analogies; (4) engage in group discussion and group writing; (5) analyze each others' work in a whole-class or group format called *peer analysis*; and many other strategies that use both individual and group techniques to elicit information about students' understanding of, and ability to apply, science concepts and reasoning skills.

The variety of activities is intended to achieve several goals. First, activities are designed to "be engaging to students with different interests and experiences," an important feature of ongoing assessment as described by the *National Science Education Standards* (National Research Council, 1996, p. 85). Second, the variety is meant to model the multiple opportunities to make sense of new ideas that modern learning theories show are needed by students as they construct understanding. In addition, strategies like group work and peer analysis help develop communities of learners and orchestrate discourse among learners. These are components of effective teaching included in the new learning theories and described by the *National Science Education Standards* (National Research Council, 1996, pp. 27–53).

The teaching/assessment activities for Key Idea 3 in *Structure of Matter* are shown as examples in Figure 7.3. These booklets are not structured curriculum guides. Instead, they are resources for teachers to use as supplements with any of several programs and curricula for middle school science.

Reflection & Discussion Questions

1. What does it mean that many teaching activities can also be assessment activities?

2. What does it mean that any assessment activity can also be a teaching activity?

3. Explain why blurring the lines between teaching and assessment is important in teaching science for understanding?

4. What characteristics of teaching/assessment activities distinguish them from more familiar teaching or assessment activities?

Assessment Criteria. For each teaching/assessment activity, assessment criteria are presented to guide teachers in interpreting the students' responses. These criteria refocus teachers' attention on students' understanding and application of the science content, helping teachers grasp what students' had already learned, and had yet to learn, to achieve a suitable level of understanding and application of the key idea. Many teachers initially have difficulty moving beyond judgments about whether their students' responses are adequate or inadequate. The assessment criteria are meant to guide teachers to consider, more thoroughly, other aspects of

FIGURE 7.3 ■ The Teaching/Assessment Activities for Key Idea 3, *Structure of Matter*

Key Idea 3 states, "As a material is heated, its particles move faster and faster. When it is cooled, the particles move slower."

	Activity Title	Type of Teaching/Assessment Strategy
A	Food coloring in hot water	Experiment
B	Ball through a ring	Laboratory demonstration and picture drawing
C	Thermometers	Inquiry project
D	Melting chocolate	Student predictions
E	Cooling balloons	Role playing
F	Balloon sellers	Design project and presentations

their students' work. As an example, the assessment criteria for the thermometer inquiry project for Key Idea 3 in *Structure of Matter* are shown in Figure 7.4. In this activity students describe, draw pictures of, experiment with, and watch in action a variety of thermometers. They use their findings to explain how liquid-in-glass thermometers indicate temperature.

Reflection & Discussion Questions

1. How do these assessment criteria help you think about the learning goals for this lesson?
2. How would assessment criteria help you be more effective in planning and enacting your lessons?
3. How would they help your students learn more effectively?

Student Work. For at least one teaching/assessment activity in each key idea, examples of students' work are included, often in the students' original handwriting. This allows teacher and staff developers to have actual examples of students' work for discussion, analysis, and interpretation. In addition, we include examples of the "Analysis of Student Work" that had been done by the teachers who cooperated with us on the project development. We also include examples of "Teacher's Actions" or recommendations for actions that teachers would take as next steps in working the students whose work had been displayed, which provides a model of actions that we are encouraging among middle school science teachers to improve teaching and learning.

Reflection & Discussion Questions

1. Why are analysis of students' work and determining next actions important parts of your work as a teacher?
2. Do you feel you have all of the knowledge and skills needed for these professional tasks?
3. What knowledge and skills do you already have for this work?
4. What knowledge and skills do you feel you need to add to your repertoire to be fully effective in using formative assessment as part of your teaching?

An Example from a Middle School Classroom

The classroom example of the use of embedded assessment that I have chosen returns to Key Idea 3 in *Structure of Matter*:

> As a material is heated, its particles move faster. When it is cooled, the particles move more slowly. (p. 23)

Explaining the common observation that most objects expand when heated and contract when cooled often is difficult for middle school students, especially when the expectation is that students use kinetic molecular theory in their explanation. The difficulty usually lies in their misunderstanding of what happens to molecules on heating and cooling. According to kinetic molecular theory, molecules move faster and occupy more space or volume when heated. Conversely, when objects decrease in temperature, the molecules that comprise them move more slowly and occupy less volume.

FIGURE 7.4 ■ The Assessment Criteria for the Thermometer Inquiry Project for Key Idea 3 in *Structure of Matter*

Assessment Criteria	Focus of Criteria
Do students' explanations include a description of the liquid in the thermometer expanding as the surrounding temperature increases? Do they state that this is due to the increase speed of the particles in the liquid?	Students' ability to recognize and then explain the critical features
Do students keep complete, accurate, and organized records? . . . Does the log describe what they actually did, or what they thought they should do?	Students' record keeping—a goal in itself and a factor that affects their ability to generalize
Have students asked themselves useful questions as they try to figure things out, or do they operate without a plan on the spur of the moment?	Students' sense making process—a goal in itself and a factor that affects their ability to generalize

A common misconception that students hold about expansion and contraction is that molecules change in size with heating and cooling. Many middle school students, as well as those in higher grades and even college students, will say that the reason objects expand on heating is that the molecules themselves expand. Many also will say that contraction is the result of molecules contracting.

In the example below, students in a sixth-grade class observed a demonstration of expansion of air in which a balloon was slipped over the mouth of a bottle. The bottle was placed in the hot water bath, causing the air in the bottle to expand, partially inflating the balloon. After some discussion in class about what was observed and how it could be explained using a molecular model, students were asked to write their explanation. Below are answers from four students in the class.

Student 1. Balloons blew up because when the water was heated, the heat rose up but couldn't escape. So it went into the balloon and blew up.

Student 2. The air compressed and blew it up.

Student 3. The hot water made the molecules of air expand.

Student 4. The atoms separated. The only place they could go was into the balloon. (Gallagher and Parker, 1996, p. 29)

Analysis and interpretation of the results of this task showed that explanations were brief and incomplete. Also, several students explained their observations in a manner similar to Student 1, centering on a commonplace, but incomplete, concept that fits their experience: "hot air rises." Other students presented views like Student 2 whose logic and conceptual content is flawed in his terse statement that "air compressed." This student used a "science term" as part of his/her explanation, trying to give an explanation that sounded scientific. However, this student chose an inappropriate concept on which to base the answer. This occurs frequently when students have inadequate understanding and guess at what would be a correct answer. Like others in the class, Student 3 gave an answer that was based on the misconception that molecules expand when heated. Student 4 centered his/her explanation on the desired concept (atoms separated), but the statement is incomplete and lacked sound logical connections. Two of the four examples given above provide a logically sound idea that the only place that would allow for expansion was the balloon, implying (though not stating) that it could stretch, whereas the bottle had a fixed volume.

Reflection & Discussion Questions

What would be your next instructional actions if your students expressed ideas like these?

The teacher, who taught both science and language arts, provided the following plan for the next steps with this class:

Because the most common problem with students' responses was their incompleteness, she realized that she needed to model the type of reasoning that she wanted her students to use in formulating and presenting explanations. Therefore, as a class, they developed an explanation for what was observed in the "balloon and bottle" demonstration. The teacher recommended that the explanation should start with "The hot water heated the bottle and the air inside it" and end with "This caused the balloon to inflate." The subject of each sentence in between should be "the molecules." She also pointed out that a statement would be needed to describe the effect of heat on the molecules of air. She then directed students to work individually to write explanations. This was followed by students working in groups of three, comparing their answers and constructing a group answer on an overhead transparency. Finally, the groups presented their answers for review and suggestions for improvement from others in the class. (Gallagher and Parker, 1996, p. 30)

This action on the part of the teacher represented a very thoughtful approach. It was not a simple attempt to "fix the misconception." The teacher looked into the conceptual ecology to try to understand what underlay students' tendency to give incomplete explanations. She then used a template to help students formulate more complete explanations. Her work was effective, as it helped students focus on the fact that the hot water caused the air to expand and the effect of heating on molecules. Following this activity, explanations were longer, more detailed, and showed connections among science concepts, as in the following:

The hot water heated the bottle and the air inside it. As the air warmed up, the air molecules moved faster. Faster moving molecules need more room to move around in. The only place the air molecules could find more room was in the balloon. This caused the balloon to inflate.

This example shows several features of our work with formative assessment. First, it shows the utility of the resources that were developed to aid teachers in thinking deeply about teaching and learning in the framework of assessment as an integral part of instruction. Second, it shows the value of key ideas as tools to help teachers focus their instructional activities on understanding concepts and principles of science rather than on unconnected facts (National Research Council, 1996; Schmidt et al., 1999). In this case, the key idea guided the teacher to focus on expansion and contraction as related to motion of molecules as opposed to the often seen emphasis on vocabulary. Third, the section on student difficulties alerted the teacher to identify the students' naïve concepts noted in explanations that they wrote. Even though only a few of her students demonstrated one of the major naïve concepts that persists among students, "Molecules expand when heated," it alerted the teacher to the fact the incomplete answers could be the result of students' poor grasp of what an explanation should contain. Fourth, it led the teacher to come up with a plan of action based on the information found in students' explanations, which focused on the form and logic of an explanation. Difficulties with conceptual understandings that were evident in some explanations were set aside temporarily, to be addressed after students' ideas were more clearly formulated. The content of explanations was dealt with in small groups as they worked on writing explanations.

Finally, it implies the continuing, cyclic nature of the formative assessment. The teacher developed a plan of action based on her interpretation of the information that was generated from the teaching/assessment activity. The plan of action was strongly influenced by the teacher's background as a teacher of both science and language arts. Moreover, the strategy of writing explanations with a constrained format automatically lead to another round of collection of information about the effect it had on students' expression of ideas and reasoning. The teacher next must examine the effect of her plan on all students. Did her recommendations about the form of explanation result in explanations that were more logically and scientifically sound than those presented previously by students? Another question to explore pertains to those students whose ideas were influenced by the commonplace viewpoint the "heat rises." Was the teacher's prompt "Heat made the molecules in the flask. . . " sufficient to refocus students' attention from their simple view that many observations can be adequately explained by "heat rises" to the more complex idea that molecular motion and heating are connected? Have the students, in fact, internalized this connection in any practical way that allows them to apply it to this situation? For the teacher to continue to guide students to a more complete understanding of this key idea, she will need to continue appraisal of the responses to new tasks that inform her of the ideas and reasoning.

Reflection & Discussion Questions

1. In what ways did the example help you to think about strategies for enacting the formative assessment cycle in your classroom?

2. How did it help you understand formative assessment more completely?

3. What questions do you still have about formative assessment as a tool to improve your teaching

and the social and intellectual climate of your classroom?

How Experienced Teachers Use Formative Assessment

Our research and development team was surprised to find that formative assessment was not a more natural part of most teachers' teaching. Our assumption at the start of our work was that nearly all teachers were effective in monitoring students' behavior and taking actions to correct counterproductive behaviors, and that most would also engage in similar actions regarding learning. Therefore, we saw formative assessment as the cognitive counterpart of classroom management, but our experience showed that many teachers did not demonstrate these actions in their classrooms on a consistent basis. Although many teachers exhibited some aspects of formative assessment in their classes, their use of it tended to be intermittent, instead of commonplace and systematic. Moreover, many teachers tended to look upon students' naïve conceptions as interesting, often humorous curiosities. They tended to minimize the importance of addressing misconceptions and naïve concepts in learning and teaching science. Few were able to use this information to understand their students' ideas and reasoning, and even fewer used it to guide instructional decisions and actions to rectify naïve concepts and unsound reasoning.

Over time, the teachers with whom we worked incorporated formative assessment into their teaching more systematically. For some, it required a substantial paradigm shift—replacing a model of teaching that can be summed up in the phrase "teach, test, and proceed to the next topic" with an approach consistent with the formative assessment cycle shown in Figure 7.1. They also used assessment more broadly to include formative assessment to guide their instructional decisions, which added to their more limited use of assessment largely for the purpose of assigning grades to students' work. When applying the formative assessment cycle, teachers developed skills that enabled them to monitor students' ideas and reasoning to determine their progress toward the desired understanding and application of scientific knowledge, to interpret this information, and then to use it to modify their teaching to make it more effective in helping students advance toward their intended goal for the lesson or instructional unit.

The frequency and the means of monitoring varied. Some teachers were continuous observers, listening carefully as students asked and answered questions. These teachers also read students' written work and made mental notes of what they wrote, the diagrams they drew, and how they expressed their ideas.

They also watched and listened carefully as students worked in class and spoke during whole-class interactions. This careful and continuous observation gave teachers clues about their students' ideas and reasoning. These data became the "raw material" for making instructional decisions about next actions with their students.

Some teachers gave a brief writing assignment at the beginning of each class period that served to re-engage students with the previous lesson and to check their understanding of it. Such tasks have various names: quick writes, pre-writes, mind stretchers, and primers are some examples. Others gave summary tasks near the end of the class period. Still others used homework in this way. Whatever their name or form, these classroom and homework tasks were carefully designed to elicit students' ideas and reasoning about the understandings that were inherent in the instructional topic.

Seeing the changes in vision and action on the part of both experienced and prospective teachers was rewarding. We have witnessed the paradigm shift in teachers with whom we worked on our research and development project whose experience ranged from three to more than twenty-five years of teaching. We have also witnessed changes in our prospective science teachers, with whom we worked for two years in a methods course that begins during their senior year of college and continues through the following intern year. In addition to becoming an important part of these pre-service teachers' teaching, an emphasis on formative assessment helped them broaden their focus—from being concerned mainly about their own actions as teachers to considering the effects those actions have on their students. This is an important step in the new teachers' professional development.

Reflection & Discussion Questions

In what ways did the section above on experienced teachers' use of formative assessment add to your knowledge of how to use formative assessment with your students?

Support Needed by Teachers

To make the changes needed to incorporate formative assessment into their teaching, both prospective and practicing teachers need considerable support. First, they need to be helped in making the paradigm shift from using assessment predominately as a tool for giving grades to the use of assessment as a guide to teaching and learning. This is a fundamental change in beliefs and actions related to teaching. To give this change in viewpoint substance, other changes are needed that also require considerable support. In particular, teachers need support in

- *Learning new assessment strategies* to obtain information about students' ideas and reasoning regarding the science concepts, principles, and processes that make up the content of their lessons and units *as students learn*. Thus, teachers need to develop a repertoire of teaching/assessment strategies that are different from those commonly observed in science classrooms. These strategies require students to be more active in expressing their ideas and reasoning processes about the content of lessons. Some examples of strategies include pre-writes, quick writes, or primers, which already have been mentioned. These can be structured in ways that elicit explanations, interpretations, and applications of concepts that students are in the process of studying. Another strategy that is useful is to have students create concept maps that show the connections they are making among ideas. Drawing diagrams to represent ideas is also a useful source of information that is less dependent on language skills. A most essential assessment strategy is to develop skills that allow you to be more observant of students' ideas and reasoning. Listening and hearing students is a key source of information. Watching them as they work and attending to the ideas they use in their interactions with you and their peers can be a major source of information. Reading and interpreting their written responses to classroom tasks also is an excellent source of information that requires a high level of professional skill.

- *Deepening understanding of the concepts, principles, and processes* that are part of the curriculum. Work on formative assessment typically "pushes" teachers' knowledge of the subject matter to new levels of understanding. As one of our colleagues put it, "Learning about students' ideas also exposes our own naïve concepts." As staff members of the project, we also can attest to how this experience helped us deepen our understanding of the fundamentals of the subject matter that are included in the school science curriculum and standards. It became increasingly evident to us that teachers would be more able to teach for understanding and application if greater emphasis were placed on teaching for understanding and application in college courses in science. This is one of the serious problems that higher education needs to face (Tyson, 1994; Floden and Gallagher, 1994; Duggan-Haas, 2000).

- *Developing increased knowledge of the research literature on naïve conceptions, misconceptions, and students' thinking*. The benefits here are threefold: (1) It makes teachers more aware of the potential areas of difficulty that their students may encounter as they are trying to learn particular new content; (2) it provides clues for teachers about what to look for as they listen to students, watch them at work, and examine products of their work; and (3) it suggests new activities and techniques to add to their repertoire of assessment strategies. Thus more attention should be given to expanding teachers' professional knowledge of the research literature on students' concepts in science as part of teacher preparation and staff development activities.

■ *Learning to interpret students' work and discourse.* Collecting information about students is only a first step in the process of formative assessment. Making sense of what students say, what they write, the pictures they draw, the models they build, the successes they have, and the mistakes they make is at the foundation of formative assessment. This requires the propensity to ask "What does this action or statement by a student tell me about his/her ideas and reasoning?" It also requires some insight into how to make sound judgments in answer to this question. This is where both the art and science of teaching coalesce. However, it is a dimension of teachers' professional knowledge that is seriously underdeveloped in many teacher education programs (Salish, 1997).

■ *Deciding what to do next.* For many teachers, this is the most difficult part of formative assessment because they have only limited ideas about alternative actions to remedy inadequate performance or understanding by students after an initial attempt at teaching. The next instructional activity can often begin with students analyzing the work of their peers (with names removed) or the work of students from other classes at the same level. Analysis of responses to a task, some of which are acceptable, some at least partly acceptable, and some that are quite unacceptable, can be a useful beginning at reteaching an idea that was not fully grasped on the first round. One important reason for this is that the center of students' difficulty in learning often is in not integrating ideas into a sound explanation—in not making a coherent story out of the facts. Therefore, an important instructional step is to have students (1) review other students' attempts at creating a coherent explanation, (2) identify the strengths and weaknesses of them, and (3) improve on them and then reflect on and discuss their suggested improvements. This approach is effective in helping students develop deeper understanding of subject matter *and* become more adept at expressing their understanding of it (Keys, 1999). This approach also is relatively easy for the teacher because the raw material for these tasks is right there in the students' work, ready for the teachers and students to examine and rework. It only takes a little time for the teachers to select varied examples from their students' work, make them anonymous, and then engage students and guide them as they work through the task reviewing and improving on the sample explanations.

Another strategy for helping students revise or clarify problematic ideas that is both a formative assessment and an instructional activity is to pose a question that requires an integrated, explanatory answer, and then to ask the class "How many of you think you can answer this question?" When I first observed this strategy in action, the class had been studying respiration and circulation, and the teacher wanted to determine how well students were integrating their ideas on these related topics. The challenge he gave to students was

How many of you think you can explain how a molecule of air gets from the air outside your body to a cell in your big toe?

The teacher then had those students who responded affirmatively serve as leaders of small groups to discuss appropriate answers to the question for five minutes. During this time, students reviewed and organized ideas that they had studied earlier to come up with explanations of the movement of oxygen to remote body cells. He then re-asked how many think they can answer the question, and a few students indicated they were still uncertain. He then directed the class to reorganize into groups around these students and spend about four minutes helping them understand the ideas more clearly. Finally he had two students teach the whole class, while the remainder of the students evaluated the presentation and gave feedback to the presenters. In this way, the class was engaged in serious analysis of the question and potential answers to it for an extended duration, perhaps as much as half of a class period. With careful selection of questions that require synthesis of ideas and demonstration of integrated understanding, this strategy can be effective in helping students develop a high level of understanding. These are only two of many possible strategies for reteaching and deepening understanding of a concept.

Reflection & Discussion Questions

1. What learning advantages do the strategies described above hold for students?

2. How can these approaches help students increase their understanding of the subject matter being taught?

Teachers need to seek out resources and help in adding formative assessment to their repertoire of skills. Also, more attention needs to be given in methods courses and professional development activities to helping teachers develop a repertoire of effective, alternative instructional strategies that can be used for teaching and reteaching scientific ideas to advance students' understanding and application of scientific concepts and processes.

Finally, all of the teachers with whom we worked were emphatic in their reports to us that they could not undergo these demanding changes without the support of a group of like-minded peers who met regularly.

In summary, formative assessment is an essential tool for attainment of the central goals of contemporary reforms including deepening students' understanding of, and ability to apply, scientific knowledge. It also shows promise for advancing attainment of the goal of science for all. However, teachers need substantial staff development and support if they are to use this approach systematically and effectively in the classroom.

Reflection & Discussion Questions

This would be a good time to write a synopsis of your views on formative assessment. You should summarize the key ideas you hold about formative assessment, its advantages, and questions or concerns you have about it. Be sure to include assessments that involve both paper-and-pencil work and those that facilitate students in using other modes of expression of ideas. Your synopsis should then be discussed with peers.

Positive Effects of Formative Assessment

Effects on the Classroom and School Environment

Observations of classrooms where teachers are using formative assessment and interviews with those teachers point to several important outcomes of formative assessment. For teachers, one of the most significant is an improved classroom environment. Students in middle school science classrooms where teachers are using formative assessment as a continuous, integral part of their instruction became more engaged in science and were less disruptive. When teachers began to listen carefully to students, and provide supportive responses to their ideas, positive changes occurred in their behavior that resulted in a more wholesome classroom environment (Gallagher, 2000). This finding supports the literature on learning communities.(Gabelnick, 1994)

Teachers who use formative assessment as an integral part of their teaching report that they work harder and yet find their work increasingly rewarding. Moreover, teachers who work in the same department or school who use formative assessment find that they have a new basis for interaction with their peers, grounded in the multiple components of this approach. This is more positive than the usual sharing of complaints about students' behavior, which do little to improve the teachers' situation. Benefits of this work affect interactions with peers, parents, and administrators in positive ways. This finding is related to the literature on effective teaching (William and Black, 1996).

Effects on Students' Learning and Motivation

The literature on student motivation clearly shows that one of the most potent motivators is success (Ames and Archer, 1988). Because the goal of formative assessment is to maximize student success in understanding and applying science, it is not surprising that we find that students are more enthusiastic about learning in classes where teachers use formative assessment systematically in their teaching. When the emphasis is on students' understanding, they feel more Supported by the teacher. This is in contrast to traditional teaching where an undeclared message often may be " We will go on to the next topic regardless of what you learned about the current one."

The positive effects of formative assessment are most evident among students who experience this kind of teaching. Conversely, some students who have performed well by memorizing or who are used to traditional teaching may feel that their usual method for success has been undermined or the rules have been unfairly changed on them. Teachers report that these students resist change or may even be openly hostile. Teachers have reported to us in debriefing seminars and during interviews that they need to be very explicit about expectations, and be patient and persistent in helping students develop the new skills that help them understand and apply science. Moreover, when these obstacles are dealt with, nearly all students can come away from the activity with a sense of accomplishment and improved self-confidence that has a positive effect on motivation.

Scoring and Grading

Assessment has a long history of connection with the assignment of grades to students. With formative assessment, the major emphasis is on understanding students' progress toward educational goals, but this also can be coupled with assignment of grades. Teachers can use the output of teaching and assessment tasks in two ways: (1) as sources of information about students' ideas and reasoning and (2) to assign grades. Any written work can be used for both purposes. However, it may (and perhaps should) take more than one review of this work to tease out meanings related to students' understanding of the content and to assign grades to the product. In addition, you can use observations of students working in groups and individual responses of students as a source of grades.

There are some dangers in grading formative assessment tasks—a key one being that grading may inhibit students from being open about their ideas if they feel that their candid expression of developing ideas could depress their grade. Therefore, you may wish to only occasionally incorporate formative assessment data in grading, and instead derive grades largely from summative assessment data.

Relation of Formative Assessments and External Examinations

Most states require that students take an external examination in science at various grade levels to monitor progress toward the goals of that state. Often these tests are administered near the end of elementary, middle, and high school. For example, some states require these tests in grades 4 or 5, 8, and 11. In some states passage of the test is part of the requirement for graduation from high school. Typically these tests are developed to assess the instructional goals for science in each state. As a result, there is some difference in the character and level of the examinations.

In 2007, a new examination plan for science will be in effect as a result of federal legislation known as *No Child Left Behind*. The focus of this new requirement is on ensuring that *all students* have opportunities for quality instruction in all subjects and that all achieve at an appropriate level. The concerns that need attention in mathematics and science cited by the President of the United States in support of this legislation include:

- Eighty-two percent of our nation's twelfth graders performed below the proficient level on the 2000 National Assessment of Educational Progress (NAEP) science test.

- The longer students stay in the current system the worse they do. According to the 1995 Third International Mathematics and Science Study, U.S. fourth graders ranked second. By twelfth grade, they fell to 16th, behind nearly every industrialized rival and ahead of only Cyprus and South Africa.

- As the U.S. Commission on National Security in the Twenty-First Century reports, "More Americans will have to understand and work competently with science and math on a daily basis . . . the inadequacies of our

systems of research and education pose a greater threat to U.S. national security over the next quarter century than any potential conventional war that we might imagine." (*http://www.ed.gov/print/nclb/methods/science/science.html*)

Further, it is stated that "over the last decade, researchers have scientifically proven the best ways to teach reading. We must do the same in science. America's teachers must use only research-based teaching methods and the schools must reject unproven fads." (*http://www.ed.gov/print/nclb/methods/ science/science.html*)

Although this legislation has been in effect for reading and mathematics, science is also included as follows:

- States must develop plans with annual measurable objectives that will ensure that all math and science teachers are "highly qualified" by the end of the 2005–2006 school year. (Highly qualified means all teachers must be certified or licensed, hold a bachelor's degree, and have demonstrated competencies in his or her teaching area, as determined by the state.)

- Beginning in 2007 states must measure students' progress in science at least once in each of three grade spans (3–5, 6–9, 10–12) each year (*http://www.ed.gov/print/nclb/methods/science/science.html*).

- States, school districts, and schools must be accountable for ensuring that all students, including disadvantaged students, meet high academic standards. States must develop a system of sanctions and rewards to hold districts and schools accountable for improving academic achievement (*http://www.whitehouse.gov/news/reports/no-child-left-behind.html#1*).

As a result of this legislation, elementary, middle, and high school students are to be assessed in science on a regular basis using external examinations that are based in state-level objectives for science. Moreover, schools that do not show adequate progress toward improving achievement for all students will be sanctioned.

External examinations are a form of summative assessment with significant consequences to school districts, teachers, and students. How do they relate to formative assessment? Are formative assessments marginalized by emphasis on these high-stakes summative assessments?

Formative assessments support learning that can make a difference in students' performance on summative assessments, including state-level examinations.

FIGURE 7.5 ■ Percentage of Students Attaining Proficiency on the State Middle School Science Examination

(Years 1–3 provide baseline data; year 4 follows staff development in School A on teaching for understanding, including formative assessment.)

	Baseline Data			After Staff Development
	Year 1	Year 2	Year 3	Year 4
School A	14.0	13.1	15.6	23.0
District Mean	11.4	12.5	11.3	14.1
State Mean	21.5	17.5	22.0	24.0

In my own work in a school in an urban district where my colleagues and I provided extensive staff development that dealt with teaching for understanding using formative assessment, students showed improved achievement when contrasted with other schools in the same district where this professional development was not occurring. Figure 7.5 shows results of baseline data over a three-year period for schools in this district. Our work was in School A. The district mean shows the results for four middle schools including School A. The results in Year 4, following intensive work with the science teachers in that building, show remarkable gains, which brought the percentage of students attaining proficiency on the state's middle school science examination within one percentage point of the state mean and nearly 9 percentage points above the district mean.

Similar results were found in another urban district in a different state with a different external examination. In that study, we also observed and recorded student and teacher behaviors and found that student achievement on the statewide middle school science test was greater in classrooms where teachers used embedded assessment more frequently. Moreover, we also noted that students in these classes attempted to solve problems on external examinations and local summative examinations more frequently than students in classes where teachers followed more traditional, teacher-centered approaches (Gallagher, 2000). William and his associates (2004) also found a similar result in a study in six schools in two districts.

It therefore is reasonable to conclude that the use of strategies involving active learning with formative assessment help students become more willing to try difficult, unfamiliar problems, which leads to higher achievement results. When this information is coupled with other data that show higher achievement and less disruptive, more attentive students, a compelling case

emerges for the use of formative assessment as part of active learning in a positive learning community.

Reflection & Discussion Questions

1. How do formative and summative assessments fit together in your vision of teaching and learning?

2. What elements of summative assessment, including both end-of-unit or end-of-marking-period tests and external examinations, do you consider important?

3. How do formative assessments support higher achievement on summative assessments?

Journal Questions

Add to your journal by revisiting the following questions that will help you monitor your progress as you make a paradigm shift in your teaching and your understanding of your students' learning for understanding and application in science.

1. What were the purposes or objectives of this chapter?
2. What were the key ideas presented in this chapter? (Note: These two could be combined as a two-column table to show the parallel between the purposes of each chapter and the big ideas presented.)
3. What important additions have you made to your vision of teaching science for understanding and application by studying this chapter and discussing with others? This should be an ongoing narrative that highlights development of your personal paradigm for teaching and learning science.
4. I also recommend that you create a concept map that portrays your understanding about teaching and learning science for understanding and application and add new concepts and connections as you study each chapter

of this book. This concept map can provide a visual representation of your developing new vision or paradigm of science teaching and learning that you developed in the previous item.

5. What new skills and techniques do you find you need to develop in order to enact your vision of science teaching? What progress are you making in developing those skills and techniques?

6. Finally, what concerns do you have about being able to implement your new vision, your new paradigm of science teaching with your students, in your classroom, laboratory, and fieldwork? How will you respond to these concerns?

Chapter 8

Criteria to Guide Planning and Teaching Science for Understanding: An Advanced Model for Planning

In this chapter, you will begin the formulation of a more sophisticated model for planning and teaching science. This is the culmination of a process that you began in Chapter 3 with the initial planning model and expanded in Chapters 4, 5, and 7. In Chapters 9 through 14, you then apply this model in varied contexts as you continue to develop understanding and skills with the contemporary paradigm for science teaching and improve your effectiveness as a science teacher.

Planning lessons that can guide you in the complex process of teaching science for understanding is an important part of your work as a teacher. In the early stages of your career, you probably will spend as much time (sometimes more) planning each lesson as you will spend in teaching it. Experienced science teachers who transform their teaching from teaching for memorization and recall to teaching for understanding and application will also spend a sizable amount of time in planning new kinds of lessons and assessments to aid their transformation. As one whose work involves designing instructional materials, I spend far more time planning and designing activities and lessons than is required to teach them. As a teacher, you need to develop new knowledge and skills that allow you to select and adapt instructional materials and resources and turn them into lessons that match your students' educational needs—lessons that enable your students to understand and use science knowledge.

That is the goal of this chapter—to help you in planning effective lessons that will help your students understand and use the science knowledge that is part of the curriculum plan for the courses or grades you teach. This chapter describes a powerful tool to help you with this important part of your work as a teacher. The task of planning effective lessons and lesson sequences may seem rather complicated as you progress through the chapter, and that perception is correct. It is a complex task.

Planning effective lessons requires much more than simply identifying the content you want your students to learn. In the next several pages, more than twenty criteria to guide the design of effective lesson sequences will be described. But don't be too overwhelmed with this long list. These criteria are grouped into seven categories that help to organize the planning task and make it somewhat more manageable.

In Chapter 9, I will provide some ways of approaching the complexity of the work that make it more feasible. Later chapters will show how to use this resource in planning lessons on various topics and levels of teaching.

Project 2061 Criteria for Evaluating Instructional Materials

In 2000, the staff of Project 2061 developed a tool to examine and evaluate instructional materials called the *Mathematics and Science Instructional Categories and Criteria* (Project 2061, 2000). This tool was designed to guide careful analysis of instructional materials to see how well they supported effective teaching for understanding and use of science and mathematics. In addition to the categories and criteria indicated in the title, the tool also has extensive lists of *indicators* of effective support for teachers within the materials. These indicators provided reliable ways of analyzing materials that enabled different reviewers to obtain reproducible results, which were important to people doing these reviews. In the pages below, I have included modified indicators for the first two categories. However, I elected not to continue to include indicators, as they made the chapter somewhat cumbersome to read. For those who wish to study the unmodified indicators for Categories III through VII, can be found by accessing the Web site (*http://www.project2061.org/tools/textbook/mgsci/criteria.htm*).

In addition to its importance as a tool for analyzing instructional materials, the Project 2061 *Categories and Criteria* provides a framework to guide your work in planning and for examining instructional plans. This resource also enables deep reflection on your teaching. As a result, it can be used for us to think about what effective science instruction looks like. To make this more relevant to planning and teaching lessons, instead of analysis of instructional materials, I have modified some of the wording. Most notably, I have substituted "lesson sequence" for "instructional materials" in applying the Project 2061 *Categories and Criteria*. In addition, I have modified selected *Indicators* prepared by the Project 2061 staff so that they fit instruction more directly. This represents a modification in their original design framework of evaluating instructional materials. As you study and apply indicators in the

Web site, you will need to make a mental transformation of them since your purpose is not to evaluate science materials, but to use the criteria and indicators to guide instructional planning.

The term *lesson sequence* is meant to signify a related set of lessons that may involve a week or more of work for you and your students. You also can apply these criteria to planning for an instructional unit. However, unit plans often do not contain the high level of detail that is typically found in lesson plans. These criteria are useful in preparing and examining more detailed plans, but they don't work well with a single lesson because it is impractical to meet all of the criteria in a single lesson. Therefore, I recommend that you think of a "lesson sequence" or a "cluster of lessons" when using these criteria in planning or reviewing plans. A week or longer seems like an appropriate time frame for application of these criteria.

How Can These Criteria Help You Teach More Effectively?

Planning sequences of lessons that build toward instructional goals is an essential step in effective teaching. These criteria can guide you to think about the multiple dimensions required to teach science for understanding.

The model of teaching and learning that underlies the Project 2061 *Mathematics and Science Instructional Categories and Criteria* is very rich and highly elaborated in terms of the multiple dimensions that are part of effective teaching. It consists of seven categories and over twenty criteria that relate to effective science instruction. Each criterion typically has three to six indicators, making the list of indicators very long. In this chapter, I will present the structure of this tool and describe its strengths and limitations. I also will show how it can help identify and understand the attributes of effective teaching for understanding in science classrooms. In addition, inquiry in teaching is underrepresented in the Project 2061 *Categories and Criteria*. Therefore, I have added four additional criteria to deal with inquiry in science teaching and a related topic—nature of science.

When using these criteria in planning and reflecting on lessons, you will need to recognize that the categories, criteria, and indicators do not comprise a shopping list or a to-do list. They are not a "must-do" list. They represent a vision of what excellent, highly effective lessons should be like. They represent a demonstration of the complexity of what we do as science teachers when we do our very best instructional planning and enactment of lessons.

However, high quality plans need to be implemented in real classrooms and so there is more to effective teaching than having good plans. But you must remember, good teaching is too complex to occur without having good plans. Therefore, the modified *Categories and Criteria* that follow can provide guidance to teachers in planning more effective lessons.

To understand this complex tool, I encourage you to examine the seven categories and then study the criteria and indicators that provide an elaboration and clarification of each. The categories are presented first as an overview of this complex set:

> *Category I:* Formulating Goals and a Sense of Purpose
>
> *Category II:* Taking Account of Student Ideas and Reasoning
>
> *Category III:* Engaging Students with Relevant Phenomena
>
> *Category IV:* Developing and Using Scientific Ideas
>
> *Category V:* Promoting Student Thinking about Phenomena, Experiences, and Knowledge
>
> *Category VI:* Assessing Student Progress
>
> *Category VII:* Enhancing the Science Learning Environment

Reflection & Discussion Questions

1. The seven categories listed above represent the attributes of effective lesson plans. Write a sentence to describe what each of these seven categories means to you when you think about planning lesson sequences. Then share your sentences with a couple of your colleagues to get their ideas.

2. Consider Categories III through VI together as making up a basic set of ideas about what occurs in classrooms as you teach a lesson or a short series of lessons.

   How does the list of categories expand your thinking about teaching for understanding?

Mathematics and Science Instructional Categories and Criteria

Category I: Formulating Goals and a Sense of Purpose

As you review this list of categories and criteria, you may realize that one important matter that we have discussed is missing. The developers of the categories and criteria placed it in a different ranking as a prerequisite to their review and so it did not appear in this list. The missing element is the list of learning goals for the lesson sequence. Therefore, a Criterion I.0 needs to be included in the list that addresses the learning goals for the lesson sequence you are planning.

Criterion I.0. Stating Learning Goals for the Lesson Sequence. Do the learning goals define what students are expected to learn and the performances expected of them as a result of the lesson sequence? Do the learning goals include the context in which performance is anticipated?

Indicators for Meeting Criterion I.0

Do learning goals include clear statements about

1. the content understanding that is to be developed?
2. relevant inquiry processes to be developed?
3. not only what is known, but also how it came to be known?
4. applications of the content knowledge that can be used as performance assessments to document students' learning?
5. connections to related concepts and processes from earlier lessons?
6. meta-cognitive expectations that students should attain as a result of the lesson sequence?

As you can see from these indicators, writing learning goals for a lesson sequence will require time and careful thought about what is to be taught, the level of understanding that is intended to result from instruction, its applications, and the related meta-cognitive skills to be nurtured.

Reflection & Discussion Questions

1. How does this description of learning goals and the related indicators correspond with your thinking about developing goals as part of instructional planning?

2. Why have I chosen to place this high level of emphasis on goals?

Category I deals with purposes and goals of lesson sequences. Criteria I.A and I.B, which are stated below, are quite similar except in terms of their scope. Criterion I.A concerns a larger unit level or even a course level, whereas Criterion I.B deals with the purposes and goals of specific lessons or even at a finer grain size of activities that comprise lessons. I report them as they were originally stated even in spite of my earlier statement about the desirability of applying these criteria to a lesson sequence because they cause you to think about "sense of purpose" at different levels, such as the lesson and the unit or lesson sequence.

Criterion I.A. Conveying Unit[1] Purpose. Does the unit plan convey an overall sense of purpose and direction that is motivating to students and aimed at the learning goals[2]?

Criterion I.B. Conveying Lesson or Activity Purpose. Does the plan for the lesson convey to the students a purpose for each lesson or activity (aimed at the learning goals) and relate it to other lessons or activities?

Why is it important to consider both immediate purposes and goals of a lesson or activity as well as the longer-term purposes of a lesson sequence or even a whole unit? The answer to this question lies in how students view their educational experience. Students tend to focus on the immediate and often fail to make connections among activities, from lesson to lesson, or from unit to unit. Effective teachers tend to keep all levels of purposes and goals of their teaching in front of their students by describing how current lessons contribute to the larger picture of the unit, course, and year. Criteria I.A and I.B work together to highlight this important element of effective teaching.

In Figure 8.1, you will find a list of indicators that further elaborate what is meant by Criteria I.A and I.B in terms of items that can be observed in unit plans and lesson plans. Moreover, these should also be evident as part of actual teaching, because they help students answer a recurring question: "Why are we learning this?" Clear descriptions of goals and purposes of instruction are not just "window dressing" to make unit plans or lesson plans look good. Instead, they are essential elements of teaching, because they keep students informed about the teacher's intentions and how the sequence of activities and events of instruction fit together for coherent development of understanding. Even more important, clear statements about purposes are guides for you as a teacher to help you become clear about what you intend to accomplish with the series of activities and lessons.

Criterion I.C implies three important instructional elements that further develop the need for clarity of instructional purposes. Included are (1) sequencing of activities, (2) consideration of students' perspectives, and (3) systematically building toward attainment of learning goals that pertain to understanding. The three indicators provide a valid way of thinking about these three aspects (see Figure 8.2). The indicators included in Criterion I.C deserve special mention. Logical sequencing of ideas that recognize the student's level of knowledge and skills and that build toward the intended educational goal is at the heart of instructional planning and teaching.

---

[1] *Unit* is used here to denote an extended sequence of lessons that might be labeled differently in various materials, e.g., unit, chapter, module. As stated earlier in this chapter, I prefer to think about lesson sequences.

[2] A *learning goal* (sometimes just *goal*) is a recommendation for what all students should end up knowing or being able to do—that is, understanding and being able to apply in varied contexts. For example, "Everything on or anywhere near the earth is pulled toward the earth's center by gravitational force."—grades 6–8 goal (*Benchmarks for Science Literacy*, AAAS, 1993).

FIGURE 8.1 ■ Indicators for Criteria I.A and I.B

Indicators for Meeting Criterion I.A—Conveying Unit Purpose

1. The lesson sequence or unit explicitly presents to the students a unit purpose—in the form of a statement, problem, question, or representation—that is aimed at the learning goals.
2. The purpose is likely to be comprehensible to students.
3. The purpose is likely to be interesting and/or motivating to students.
4. The lesson sequence gives students an opportunity to think about and discuss the purpose.
5. Most activities or lessons are consistent with the purpose.
6. The lesson sequence returns to the purpose at the end of the unit or lesson sequence.

Indicators for Meeting Criterion I.B—Conveying Lesson or Activity Purpose

1. The lesson explicitly presents to students the purposes of the lesson or activity—in the form of statements, problems, questions, or representations—that are aimed at the learning goals.
2. The purpose of each lesson or activity is likely to be comprehensible to students.
3. The lesson conveys to students how each lesson or activity relates to the unit purpose.
4. Each lesson or activity encourages each student to think about its purpose.
5. The lesson periodically engages students in thinking about what they have learned or done so far and what they need to learn or do next.

FIGURE 8.2 ■ Indicators for Criterion I.C

Instructional Elements	Indicators for Meeting Criterion I.C
Activities are in a logical order	1. The activities are systematically sequenced.
Consideration of students' perspectives	2. The sequence of activities reflects consideration of students' initial ideas and skills and builds strategically toward a more accurate understanding of the learning goals.
Systematically building toward understanding	3. The sequence of activities is based on a rationale that can be stated succinctly, making clear the function of each activity in relation to the purposes of the lesson and sequence of activities.

Criterion I.C. Justifying the Lesson Sequence. Does the material involve students in a logical or strategic sequence of lessons or activities (versus being just a collection of lessons or activities)?

Although concern about students' ideas is dealt with more thoroughly in the next category in the Project 2061 *Categories and Criteria*, you need to consider students' ideas when identifying purposes and goals of instruction and when planning sequences of activities. Therefore, I encourage you to keep learners, their ideas, and their reasoning in mind at all stages of planning and implementing instruction.

Reflection & Discussion Questions

1. How would you describe the importance of the three criteria in Category I in your own words?

2. How would you describe the importance of conveying sense of purpose as part of effective teaching to a friend who was not a teacher?

3. How would you explain the importance of Criterion I.C to this person?

4. How might you convey the ideas behind Criterion I.C to your students?

Category II: Taking Account of Students' Ideas and Reasoning

Category II addresses four criteria that focus on students' ideas and reasoning. I added reasoning to this category because teaching for understanding requires that both the ideas students hold and the ways they use them in thinking and reasoning must be given attention by teachers. Understanding requires both sound ideas and sound reasoning.

The four criteria for Category II are as follows:

Criterion II.A. Attending to Prerequisite Knowledge and Skills. Do your plans for the lesson sequence specify and address the prerequisite knowledge and/or skills that are necessary for understanding the subject matter of the learning goals?

Criterion II.B. Highlighting Commonly Held Student Ideas. Do the instructional plans highlight commonly held student ideas (both troublesome and helpful) that are relevant to the learning goals and described in the learning research literature?

Criterion II.C. Identifying Students' Ideas and Reasoning. Do your plans for the lesson sequence include questions and/or tasks to help you identify what your students think about familiar situations and phenomena related to the learning goals before these goals are introduced?

Criterion II.D. Addressing Students' Ideas and Reasoning. Do your plans for the lesson sequence assist you in explicitly addressing students' ideas and their reasoning relevant to the learning goals?

The indicators for *Criterion II.A—Attending to Prerequisite Knowledge and Skills*—are quite helpful in clarifying how the lesson sequence should address the necessary foundational knowledge for success in learning the content and reasoning that are the intended outcomes of them. Indictors for Criterion II.A state that in planning lesson sequences, teachers should be clear about specific prerequisite ideas or skills that are necessary for understanding each of the learning goals. Learning goals and prerequisites should be matched, and the connection between them should be made clear. Students should be alerted to prerequisites that are assumed to have been learned so that students know the entry-level expectancies, and they should be made aware of where or when these prerequisites were learned. Further if the prerequisites are to be developed or reviewed as part of the current lesson sequence, teachers should make that known to their students as it is important that both teachers and students are aware of the prerequisites, why they are essential to attainment of the learning goals, and where or when the prerequisites were supposed to have been learned. At very least, teachers should check to see whether students are in command of the prerequisite knowledge and skills, and take appropriate actions if they are not. Often a review of prerequisites is important both as a diagnostic tool and as a way of refreshing knowledge and skills that have become remote in students' repertoire.

Criterion II.B—Highlighting Commonly Held Student Ideas—is also an important part of planning and preparing to implement lessons. Teachers should have knowledge of common misconceptions and naïve understandings and reasoning skills that students may hold. This is part of the particular pedagogical content knowledge that teachers need for each topic they teach. This knowledge will help in designing and implementing lessons, as it will enable teachers to appraise students' statements, questions, and actions more adequately. Knowledge of students' misconceptions and naïve conceptions will help teachers make sense of students' responses and comprehend at least some of the causes of the difficulties students encounter when learning the particular subject matter. With this knowledge, teachers will be able to provide guidance and experiences that will benefit students in gaining the intended understandings more effectively and quickly. They also will have at their disposal information on which they can base changes in instructional plans when students are encountering difficulty reconciling their own personal ideas and reasoning with the ideas and reasoning that the teacher is working to achieve.

Therefore, as part of instructional planning, teachers should draw on relevant resources to enable them to list *specific* commonly held ideas that are relevant to the learning goals and described in the learning research literature (rather than just stating that students have difficulties with particular ideas or topics). They should also use resources that enable them to identify how ideas might appear and how they might be reflected in student responses (including examples of student work when appropriate or practical).

This is a part of science teachers' professional knowledge that needs to be given greater attention during pre-service and professional development courses. Moreover, teachers can gain access to topic-specific information on students' ideas and reasoning through readings such as Driver, Guesne, and Tiberghien, *Children's Ideas in Science* (1985) and Driver et al. *Making Sense of Secondary Science* (1994), as well as from many other sources, including some excellent Web sites such as *http://www.learner.org*, *http://www.geocities.com/lclane2/misconceptions.html*, and *http://www.huntel.net/rsweetland/science/misconceptions/*. (I also will add a note of caution about some Web sites, which treat misconceptions as "cute" or as "curiosities" instead of important educational concerns. These are not particularly helpful in understanding students' thinking and in planning instruction. Instead there are many useful resources that can aid instructional planning and add significantly to your pedagogical content knowledge.)

Criterion II.C—Identifying Students' Ideas and Reasoning—requires teachers to have the professional knowledge, or pedagogical content knowledge, described in Criterion II.B, but also skill in determining their own students' knowledge and beliefs related to the specific learning goals for lessons. Teachers need to determine what ideas their students may hold, including misconceptions, since these ideas can have important influences on what students learn and fail to learn. Determining students' concepts or misconceptions on a topic can be quite difficult as students often are quite circumspect about their ideas and cover up their misconceptions quite well. This is one important reason for the emphasis on Criterion II.B as part of teachers' professional knowledge, because it will help them become alert to clues about students' misunderstanding. However, this knowledge alone is not enough. Knowing how researchers have "uncovered" information about students' naïve conceptions can be an additional resource for discerning naïve conceptions among students.

The indicators for Criterion II.C recommend that teachers be prepared with specific questions and/or tasks to identify *their own* students' ideas related to the learning goals before lessons addressing the goals are introduced. This helps you do some "detective work" in your own class to understand your students' ideas and reasoning relevant to the topic of your lessons. Such questions and tasks should go beyond identifying students' knowledge of terms. The questions and tasks should include making predictions and/or giving explanations of concepts, procedures, or phenomena. Yet these questions and tasks must be comprehensible to students who are not familiar with the concepts, procedures, or vocabulary introduced in the unit. Moreover, these should be explicitly identified as serving the purpose of identifying students' ideas and reasoning at the outset of instruction to help identify the starting points and strategies for instruction.

The professional knowledge of teachers should also include knowing how to interpret students' responses to ascertain their thinking and level of understanding. To enable teachers to do this, teacher educators and curriculum designers will need to provide samples of student responses to specific questions, along with interpretations. Also, annotated samples of student work with interpretations by expert teachers will be helpful as resources. Finally, curriculum resources and instructional materials will need to provide additional guidance to teachers in identifying and interpreting statements, actions, and drawings that expose students' ideas and reasoning. This will be the subject of later chapters.

The reason for all of the foregoing actions within lessons is to meet the challenge set by *Criterion II.D—Addressing Students' Ideas and Reasoning*. The indicators for meeting this criterion represent a powerful statement about how lessons and instructional units should be planned and implemented to respond effectively to the knowledge of students' ideas and reasoning obtained as part of instruction procedures.

Indicators for Meeting Category II.D

1. The lesson sequence includes teaching strategies to address commonly held student ideas described in the learning research literature that are relevant to the learning goals.

2. The lesson sequence goes beyond simply contradicting commonly held student ideas and addresses them using specifically described strategies, such as

    a. Challenging students' ideas by comparing their predictions about a real world example/phenomenon to what actually happens or pointing out inconsistencies with other ideas.

    b. Prompting students to contrast specific commonly held student ideas with the mathematically or scientifically accepted ideas and to resolve differences between them using evidence that the lesson makes available—or presenting such contrasts and resolutions directly.

    c. Suggesting additional tests that students could carry out or data that they could collect to resolve differences.

    d. Presenting tasks that require students to extend their commonly held ideas into situations where their limitations become evident.

3. The lesson sequence contains explicit strategies to address the specific commonly held ideas.

4. The lesson sequence includes general strategies for addressing other unanticipated ideas (those not identified in the learning research literature). Strategies might include

    a. Suggesting that the teacher challenge students' ideas by comparing their predictions about a real world example/phenomenon to what actually happens or pointing out inconsistencies with other ideas, as identified by the teacher.

    b. Suggesting that the teacher prompt students to contrast specific student ideas with the mathematically or scientifically accepted ideas and try to resolve differences between them.

    c. Having students (or teacher) design tests or ways to collect evidence to resolve differences.

    d. Extending useful commonly held ideas that have limited scope, as identified by the teacher.

Although these recommendations are all valid, they imply an important additional strategy that is essential—being able to initiate, manage, and sustain group work and classroom discourse effectively so that students' ideas and reasoning can be nurtured through direct teacher intervention and productive student-to-student interaction. This was part of Chapter 5, which dealt with group work and classroom discourse. Because enabling effective group work and classroom discourse require skills that may be new to many science teachers, additional work with the ideas in that chapter may be needed.

Reflection & Discussion Questions

1. How do the four criteria in Category II, dealing with students' ideas and reasoning, expand your views about your work as a teacher?

2. Do you see this as adding dimensions that you had not considered previously? Explain your thinking.

3. What additional professional knowledge and skills will it demand of you? How and when will you develop such knowledge and skills?

Category III: Engaging Students with Relevant Phenomena Category III is where the actual planning of activities for teaching and learning begin. Up to now, the work has been in preparation for instruction—identifying goals and purposes, and accounting for students' ideas. The foundational actions in Categories I and II will strongly influence what you do as an effective teacher throughout the remainder of the planning cycle and during enactment of the lesson sequence with your students. In addition, the learning activities you create in Categories III, IV, and V comprise the science content of your teaching and the experiences that form much of the basis of students' learning.

Engaging students with phenomena and real world examples, the experiential substance of science, also requires planning and preparation. The two criteria for this category are stated below:

Criterion III.A. Providing a Variety of Relevant Phenomena and Real World Examples. Do your plans for the lesson sequence provide multiple and varied phenomena and real world examples to support the key ideas in your learning goals?

Criterion III.B. Providing Vivid Firsthand and Vicarious Experiences. Do your plans for the lesson sequence provide an appropriate balance of firsthand and vicarious experiences with phenomena that are explicitly linked to the learning goals?

As with previous criteria, the indicators provide important elaboration and clarification of the features and attributes of potentially effective lessons. You should go to the Web site (*http://www.project2061. org/tools/textbook/mgsci/crit-used.htm*) and review the indicators to develop a deeper understanding of each criterion. The phenomena should be relevant to the learning goals. For example, in studying rocks and minerals, students should have firsthand experiences with several samples of igneous, metamorphic, and sedimentary rocks and the common minerals that comprise them. In studying accelerated motion, middle or high school students should have ample opportunities to experience acceleration in many forms, including some readily controlled instances such as actual experiences with spheres rolling down inclines as well as practical vicarious examples such as accelerating and decelerating vehicles, drag racing, and airplanes landing and taking off. Moreover, both the learning goals and the phenomena that support the goals should be appropriate for the experiential and developmental levels of the students so that the experiences are engaging.

In addition direct, firsthand experiences should be provided where possible, but when not feasible, due to time required to observe the phenomenon, its distance from the students, its size, or the danger it entails, vicarious experiences are appropriate. Opportunities for students to observe "weightlessness," volcanic eruptions, or scanning electron microscope views of electron clouds of atoms are beyond reasonable experiences for most students. However, with the myriad opportunities that the Internet and video recordings present, such experiences can become commonplace in all classrooms. Moreover, these vicarious experiences can be excellent bases for classroom activities in analyzing observational data. A final consideration: experiences with phenomena should be efficient, so that the costs in time, effort, and money do not overshadow their benefits.

In this category, the authors omitted what I perceive to be an important criterion, having to do with inquiry. This was not an oversight on their part. It was because inquiry is not a presence in many of the textbooks they intended to review. However, *National Science Education Standards* (National Research Council, 1996) highlighted the importance of inquiry in science teaching by placing it at the top of the list of elements in the content standards. It is important so that students can grasp how scientists work to create new knowledge about the natural world. Inquiry also provides students with direct experience with phenomena, and it can be engaging for students. Therefore, I have expanded Category III with the addition of a criterion dealing with inquiry.

Added Criterion III.C. Providing Opportunities for Students to Engage in Inquiry. Do your plans for the lesson sequence provide appropriate opportunities for students to engage in inquiry as a way of simultaneously experiencing both phenomena and ways of investigating them that simulate how scientists create new knowledge?

Since this criterion does not have indicators available on the Web, as is the case for other criteria, some examples are provided below.

Indicators for Meeting Criterion III.C

1. When practical and appropriate, the material provides opportunities for students to engage in firsthand inquiry that is explicitly linked to the learning goals.

2. The material provides other experiences that give students a sense of how scientists have engaged in inquiry to create knowledge relevant to the topic of the lesson sequence.

3. The set of experiences is efficient, i.e., the potential benefits justify the costs in time and money.

Reflection & Discussion Questions

1. Why is it essential to engage students with phenomena and real world examples as part of science instruction?

2. Describe how you would justify this to a friend who is not a teacher but who believes that the lecture method is acceptable as the dominant approach to teaching.

3. Describe how you would explain inquiry to this person so that she or he understands its importance in science instruction.

Category IV: Developing and Using Scientific Ideas

If Category III represents a beginning for instruction and learning, Category IV represents where instruction and learning mature and take on strength. Category IV builds on the experience with phenomena highlighted in Category III and gives it meaning and connections. The criteria in this category are the core of science instruction as they provide evidence to support the ideas, reasoning, and understanding that we are seeking. This is where terms and ideas that constitute the conceptual and logical frameworks of science are learned and given meaning. It is also where connections are formed among ideas and where science knowledge is given meaning by students. In addition, it is where students gain practice in using science ideas and processes to solidify their experiences into meaningful understandings.

The authors of the *Categories and Criteria* provide a useful and succinct introduction to Category IV:

> Science literacy requires that students understand the link between scientific ideas and the phenomena that they can explain. Furthermore, they should see the ideas as useful and become skillful at applying them. This category consists of criteria for determining whether the curriculum material expresses and develops the key ideas in ways that are accessible and intelligible to students, and that demonstrate the usefulness of the key ideas and provide practice in varied contexts. (*http://www.project2061. org/tools/textbook/mgsci/crit-used.htm*)

The criteria in Category IV include:

Criterion IV.A. Building a Case. Do the plans develop an evidence-based argument for key ideas? Do your plans use scientific evidence to support students in learning and suggest ways to help students develop a sense of the validity of the science knowledge and skills encompassed by the learning goals for the lesson sequence?

Criterion IV.B. Introducing Terms and Procedures Meaningfully. Do your plans for the lesson sequence introduce terms and procedures in the context of experiences with phenomena and use them to effectively communicate about the learning goals, understandings, and skills that underlie them?

Criterion IV.C. Representing Ideas Effectively. Do your plans for the lesson sequence include accurate and comprehensible representations[3] of the conceptual understandings and skills that underlie the learning goals?

Criterion IV.D. Connecting and Synthesizing Ideas. Do your plans for the lesson sequence explicitly make appropriate connections among individual instances of ideas and skills to support achievement of specific learning goals?

Criterion IV.E. Demonstrating Skills and Use of Knowledge. Do your plans for the lesson sequence demonstrate skills and the use of knowledge related to the learning goals?

Criterion IV.F. Providing Practice. Do your plans for the lesson sequence provide questions and/or tasks in a variety of situations for students to practice knowledge or skills related to the learning goals?

(Reminder: The indicators for meeting these criteria are found at the Web site: *http://www.project2061. org/tools/textbook/mgsci/crit-used.htm.*)

Reflection & Discussion Questions

1. This category contains a lot of information! Why is this category on "Developing and Using Scientific Ideas" so important that it receives so much space in this list of criteria?

2. What important messages are presented in Category IV for you, as a teacher?

3. Describe how would you explain the importance of the criteria in Category IV to a teaching colleague.

Category V: Promoting Student Thinking about Phenomena, Experiences and Knowledge

Students of all ages, as well as many adults, have difficulty reasoning from experiences to ideas. In addition, many also are not facile in reasoning from words to ideas to actions. Moreover, students often are not adept at reasoning from general principles to specifics, and conversely, they are even less adept at reasoning from specifics to general principles. Using different words to convey a similar meaning, many people, including school students, are not skilled in deductive and inductive reasoning.

These kinds of reasoning are important in science and in daily life. Part of understanding science is to know how scientific ideas have been formed, by understanding the reasoning processes that underlay their formulation. An overarching, long-term goal of science teaching is to help students be able to use scientific reasoning and logical reasoning because they are important not only in science, but also in a practical sense. Moreover, science is an especially fertile ground for nurturing development of logical reasoning.

Reasoning from observations about phenomena to the noting of patterns in observations to explanations of

---

[3] By representations we mean drawings, diagrams, graphs, images, analogies, and metaphors or other verbal statements, models, and simulations, role-playing, etc.

observations is a hallmark of science both for scientists and for people learning it. Here is one example of scientific reasoning based on observations and data. Scientists who study glaciers, for example, note that nearly every glacier in the world is receding. The glaciers at Glacier Bay in Alaska have receded more than fifty miles in approximately two hundred years since they were first recorded by the famous explorer Captain Cook. This pattern, which has been observed in many places around the world, has led glaciologists to speculate that the earth is warming. Other scientists have taken other measures and found data that also suggest that the average temperature of the earth has been increasing for more than a century. To describe this phenomenon a scientist invented the term *global warming*. Many see this trend as being connected with people's increased use of fossil fuels since about 1750 and feel that at least part of the cause can be explained by increasing levels of what have been called "greenhouse gases" that slow the radiation of heat from earth into space.

In another example, in school laboratories all around the globe, many students study pendulums. One observation about pendulums is that shorter pendulums also have a shorter duration of swing. Also, unless pushed occasionally, all pendulums will gradually over time swing through a progressively smaller arc and eventually stop swinging. This pattern of reduction in the angle of the swing, and stopping, also calls for an explanation. Students often debate whether the cause of the reduced movement and stopping is gravity or friction. (Recall the mention of this and a video about it that was described in Chapter 5.) This provides another simple example of how students can be helped to learn about phenomena and the processes by which science moves from observations to noting of patterns, sometimes called recurrent regularity, to explanations and speculations about causes.

An essential part of science learning involves helping students develop the habit of mind to reason from data to seeking patterns to explanations, while forming and testing hypotheses along the way to test alternative explanations. It is essential because it helps students experience how scientists and science work. It also is essential because it helps students learn to reason logically and scientifically—to develop a scientific habit of mind!

The criteria below for this section need expansion to incorporate the cognitive or minds-on features of inquiry into the planning for this category—Promoting Student Thinking about Experiences and Knowledge. Therefore, I have added three criteria to the list: Criterion V.0, because it seems to precede the three criteria in this category, and Criteria V.D and V.E, which logically follow the three already included. Criterion V.0 deals with grounding understanding in data from investigations and experiences. Criteria V.D and V.E

aid students in recognizing that knowledge in science is dynamic and socially constructed. Thus all three of the additions are designed to advance students' understanding of inquiry and nature of science.

All of the criteria in this category, including the three new ones, are directed to the development of scientific reasoning and understanding the ways in which scientists and science operate. These six criteria follow, with the indicators included for the three new ones:

Added Criterion V.0. Encouraging Students to Base Their Understanding in Data from Investigations and Experiences. Do your plans for the lesson sequence routinely require that all students connect their ideas and explanations with data from observations and investigations? Do your plans for the lesson sequence build on students' investigations when feasible, and if not feasible, on data or resources used by scientists to formulate the ideas being studied?

Indicators for Meeting Criterion V.0

1. Lesson sequences are designed help students base their developing science knowledge in data and experiences either gained directly from investigations or resources that show how scientists made those connections in their work.

2. Lesson sequences help students comprehend how scientific knowledge is an attempt to make sense of, and provide a coherent explanation for, existing data.

3. Lesson sequences help students understand that hypotheses testing, empirical work, data interpretation, and explanation are essential parts of scientific reasoning.

4. Lesson sequences help students comprehend the connections that exist between data and conceptual frameworks, models, and theories.

Reflection & Discussion Questions

1. Think about experiences/observation, patterns, and explanations. Also think about inquiry. Are you finding these to be important ideas underlying your work as a science teacher? How do they fit into this category on Promoting Student Thinking about Experiences and Knowledge?

2. Select a topic that is familiar and describe the data you would use as the basis for it by sketching out the experiences/observations, patterns, and explanations that underlie it.

Criterion V.A. Encouraging Students to Explain Their Ideas. Does your plan for the lesson sequence routinely require that all students express, clarify, justify, interpret, and represent their ideas about the topic and phenomena underlying the learning goals? Does your plan include having students get feedback?

Criterion V.B. Guiding Interpretation and Reasoning.

Does your plan for the lesson sequence include questions and tasks that guide students' interpretation and reasoning about experiences with phenomena, representations, and/or readings related to the topic and phenomena underlying the learning goals?

Criterion V.C. Encouraging Students to Think about What They Have Learned.

Does your plan for the lesson sequence suggest ways to have students check and reflect on their own progress toward the learning goals, following instruction related to the topic and phenomena?

Reflection & Discussion Questions

1. Think about a lesson sequence that you planned recently. How did this lesson reflect the four criteria just listed (V.0–V.C)?

2. If you did not include one or more criteria, how would you improve the lesson based on these criteria?

Added Criterion V.D. Encouraging Students to Recognize that Science Knowledge Is Dynamic.

Does your plan for the sequence of lessons provide students with a perspective that science knowledge can change as a consequence of new data and/or new ways of viewing existing data?

Indicators for Meeting Criterion V.D

1. Lesson sequences provide examples of changes in scientific ideas due to new data, new instrumentation, and new ways of thinking about available data.

2. Lesson sequences show that scientific ideas that are no longer accepted as valid resulted from appropriate interpretation of data and perspectives that existed at an earlier time.

3. Lessons do not present ideas that are no longer accepted by scientists as foolish or the result of bad thinking. Instead they remind students that these ideas represented sound thinking in terms of the evidence and perspectives of that former time, but new data and perspectives provide more satisfying explanations of the natural world. Sometimes this is the result of new instrumentation or techniques, but many times it is the result of the formulation of new perspectives.

Reflection & Discussion Questions

Think about a science idea that you teach that has changed over time, such as the replacement of the geocentric model with the Copernican model of the solar system. Describe how formulation and acceptance of that model was the result of one or more of the following changes: new instrumentation, new data, and new perspectives about interpretation of the data.

Added Criterion V.E. Encouraging Students to Recognize that Science Knowledge Is Socially Constructed and Validated.

Do your plans for lesson sequences help students recognize that science knowledge is constructed by scientists from their interpretations of data from observations and experiments? Do lessons help students recognize that the scientific enterprise operates on an agreed-upon set of rules for validating scientific knowledge?

Indicators for Meeting Criterion V.E

1. Lesson sequences include specific questions and/or tasks about how scientists came to change their ideas as new evidence or paradigms became available.

2. Lesson sequences include some tasks that help students understand that, while individual or small teams of scientists make discoveries or formulate new paradigms, other members of the scientific community must be able to replicate and/or evaluate their work as a means of validating it.

3. Lesson sequences should also show that new scientific ideas and research discoveries must stand the test of scrutiny by scientific peers before they are accepted.

4. Lesson sequences should also provide information about important debates and disagreements that occur in science and how these come to resolution.

Reflection & Discussion Questions

1. Using a topic that is familiar to you, describe how an idea within that topic was constructed by scientists from their interpretations of data from observations and experiments.

2. What does it mean when we say that the scientific enterprise operates on an agreed-upon set of rules for validating scientific knowledge?

3. Why are replication and publication of scientists' observations and experiments an important part of scientists' work?

1. How does this category on Promoting Student Thinking differ from the previous one on Developing and Using Scientific Ideas?

2. What important components to your plans are added in Category V that are missing in Category IV?

3. How do the criteria listed in this category relate to inquiry?

   This is the key place where inquiry and nature of science are highlighted in these criteria. What components of inquiry are included in these criteria? What components are omitted?

Category VI: Assessing Student Progress

Assessment is a key part of the work of teachers. Its importance lies far beyond providing data for assigning grades to students. Assessment also is essential as the source of information that guides both students and teachers in learning and teaching as shown in the previous chapter. The multiple functions of assessment need to be included in teachers' plans for lessons and instructional units. Thoughtful use of assessment can be an important asset in both teaching and learning for understanding.

Criterion VI.A. Aligning Assessment to Goals. Assuming a match between the content of the lesson sequence and the learning goals, are questions and tasks included that assess student achievement of the learning goals?

Criterion VI.B. Probing Student Understanding. Do your plans for the lesson sequence include assessment questions and tasks that require students to show, use, apply, explain, or otherwise demonstrate their understanding of the knowledge and skills specified in the learning goals?

Criterion VI.C. Assessing Effectively. Are the questions and/or tasks likely to be effective in assessing the knowledge and/or skills specified in the learning goals, or do they only test recall of factual information without emphasis on understanding and application of knowledge?

Criterion VI.D. Informing Instruction. Does your plan monitor students' progress toward learning goals within the lesson sequence, not just at the end? Does your plan include ideas about using assessment results to choose among or modify activities to address the learning goals? Is assessment organized to give students useful feedback on their progress toward the goals of lessons?

1. What did the authors of these criteria have in mind when they included Criterion V.A?

2. What do Criteria VI.A, VI.B, and VI.C have in common?

3. What guidance do these three criteria give you when you take all three of them together?

4. Does Criterion VI.D sound familiar? Would it be more recognizable if it were labeled the formative assessment cycle?

5. How does this category help you comprehend formative assessment as activities that are part of a sequence of lessons?

Category VII: Enhancing the Science Learning Environment

Creating the appropriate environment in which learning for understanding takes place is also an important task for teachers. Three features of this environment include being supportive, encouraging, and welcoming. These are represented by the three criteria below. [Note that the first criterion refers to how your lesson plans support enrichment of your understanding of the content. This is a change, since all of the criteria excepting this one refer to supporting students' understanding.]

Criterion VII.A. Providing Teacher Content Support. Do your plans for the series of lessons support and enrich *your* understanding of the science, mathematics, and technology concepts needed for teaching the lesson?

Criterion VII.B. Encouraging Curiosity and Questioning. Do your plans for the lesson sequence help to create a classroom environment that welcomes student curiosity, rewards creativity, encourages a spirit of healthy questioning, and avoids dogmatism?

Criterion VII.C. Supporting All Students. Does the material or teacher help to create a classroom community that encourages high expectations for all students, enables all students to experience success, and provides all different kinds of students with a feeling of belonging in the classroom?

Reflection & Discussion Questions

1. Setting a high standard, while making the environment appealing to all students, may seem like a contradictory matter as you examine Criterion VII.C. How may the other two criteria in this category about the instructional environment reduce the contradiction?

2. What new perspectives on the learning environment have these three criteria engendered in your mind?

3. When planning lessons, do you typically think about the learning environment in your classroom?

Application of Criteria by Teachers

As was stated at the opening of this chapter, the Project 2061 *Mathematics and Science Instructional Categories and Criteria* show considerable potential for helping science teachers and others involved with the field to provide substance to the reform paradigm in science education. It offers a framework for thinking about effective science and mathematics instruction at a level of detail not otherwise available. Moreover, it shows so richly the depth of the work of an effective science teacher.

In the next chapter, we will explore how to apply these criteria to your work in selecting high-quality instructional materials, planning instruction, and enacting it in your classroom.

Acknowledgement: Criteria III.C, V.0, V.D, and V.E were prompted by a paper prepared by Kristin Gunckel (2003) (see References). I thank Kristin for her thoughtful work on this paper and for the inspiration it provided me to create these additional criteria.

Journal Questions

Add to your journal by revisiting the following questions that will help you monitor your progress as you make a paradigm shift in your teaching and your understanding of your students' learning for understanding and application in science.

1. What were the purposes or objectives of this chapter?
2. What were the key ideas presented in this chapter? (Note: These two could be combined as a two-column table to show the parallel between the purposes of each chapter and the big ideas presented.)
3. What important additions have you made to your vision of teaching science for understanding and application by studying this chapter and discussing with others? This should be an ongoing narrative that highlights development of your personal paradigm for teaching and learning science.
4. I also recommend that you create a concept map that portrays your understanding about teaching and learning science for understanding and application and add new concepts and connections as you study each chapter of this book. This concept map can provide a visual representation of your developing new vision or paradigm of science teaching and learning that you developed in the previous item.
5. What new skills and techniques do you find you need to develop in order to enact your vision of science teaching? What progress are you making in developing those skills and techniques?
6. Finally, what concerns do you have about being able to implement your new vision, your new paradigm of science teaching with your students, in your classroom, laboratory, and fieldwork? How will you respond to these concerns?

Chapter 9

A Plan for Planning: Using Criteria to Select Resources and Plan Instruction

The previous chapter presented an important, useful, but complicated tool for teachers that can be a guide for the multiple tasks that lead to effective teaching. How should you begin to work with this tool to select instructional materials, adapt them to your work, and plan and enact high-quality lessons?

Using Modified Criteria to Select Instructional Materials

Often teachers have little or no control over the selection of the textbook or other instructional resources used in their school. This is especially true when you first enter a school district, because textbooks usually are adopted for a period of five years or more. If you are a new teacher, the textbook for your course or program probably was selected prior to your arrival and new resources will not be adopted until a few years in the future. However, both new and experienced teachers frequently make choices about supplemental materials that augment the adopted textbooks or programs used by school districts.

The Criteria to Guide Planning and Teaching from Chapter 8 is a promising tool to guide you in adapting your current instructional resources to engender deeper learning. Further, many supplemental resources are available including other textbooks, books, articles from science-related magazines, newspapers, resources from libraries, and instructional materials that are available online. Teachers frequently use supplemental resources to complement textbooks that have been adopted and purchased by their district. Here is where the criteria from Chapter 8 also can be useful. Recall that Chapter 8 is based on Project 2061 *Mathematics and Science Instructional Categories and Criteria*, which were designed for evaluation of textbooks in science and mathematics. Given this history, you can use the criteria to evaluate and select supplemental resources for your program. For example, if you find that your text is deficient in materials that promote student thinking (Category V), you can seek supplemental materials that provide added support for you and your students in this dimension.

In reviewing materials for adoption or use as supplements, you should seek materials that have a high degree of conformity with the goals for science in your state or district so that your efforts are on target with the intentions of your school. Then seeking materials that contain as many dimensions of the criteria as possible will make your work easier. For example, materials that help you learn about students' ideas and reasoning by providing background information and assessment tasks that uncover students' concepts will ease your work and improve your effectiveness. The same can be said about materials that provide resources for you and your students related to Categories III, IV, and V, dealing with the multiple dimensions of providing students with meaningful experiences and help in translating experiences into ideas and understandings. Choosing high-quality materials that are faithful to the criteria described in Chapter 8 can ease your work and improve your effectiveness in advancing your students' understanding. Therefore, I strongly encourage you to give careful thought to Chapter 8 as you select textbooks and other resources for your courses.

Using Criteria to Plan Lesson Sequences: Building Synergy among Teachers, Students, and Instructional Resources

Attention will now be directed to how you can make the most out of the instructional resources, including textbooks, that are available to you. This chapter, and several that follow, will focus on the question "How can you teach for understanding with materials provided by your district, which may be directed more toward presenting content and may offer only limited support for developing understanding?"

In this chapter, as well as throughout the book, my premise is that many teachers can improve their effectiveness in using textbooks and other instructional resources. I often hear teachers say that they do not follow the textbook very closely, if at all. Some teachers create their own units and instructional resources, which is a demanding and time-consuming task. Moreover, a great deal of work, thought, and instructional experience underlies the production of most textbooks. As a result, textbooks provide teachers with valuable resources that include a logical presentation of information on each topic that usually is based on an instructional model. If teachers use these strengths of textbooks in

planning and enacting teaching in ways that combine the resources therein with their own intentions that are based in the particulars of the local context, a synergy can emerge among the teacher, students, and the text that can be more productive than the teacher working independently. Therefore, teachers must examine the textbooks that have been provided by the district with an open mind to appraise the strengths of them and determine how to capitalize on them to achieve their own instructional goals.

Reflection & Discussion Questions

1. How does the image of textbooks presented in the previous two paragraphs coincide with your views?

2. If you disagree, please keep an open mind on the idea as you read the remainder of this chapter.

In addition to helping teachers utilize the power of textbooks, the criteria can be used to guide adaptations to textbooks so that they better serve your intentions for your science courses. If you find that your textbook has little or no material that helps you attend to students' ideas and reasoning, for example, the criteria at least help you to recognize that this is an area needing attention. They also give you some hints as to ways that you may adapt your course or unit to be attentive to students' concepts. For example, Criterion II.C—Identifying Students' Ideas and Reasoning—is followed by the question, "Do your plans for the lesson sequence include questions and/or tasks to help you identify what your students think about familiar situations and phenomena related to the learning goals before these goals are introduced?"

This criterion recommends that you have some form of preassessment for your students that will provide you with information about their understandings on the topic you are teaching, to guide you in planning and initiating lessons on the topic. It also implies that you need to incorporate formative assessment in your plans so that you can monitor development of students' ideas and reasoning during lessons. The indicators for this criterion also suggest that you will need to have specific questions and tasks to help you identify your students' ideas about the topic. This requires that your planning for the lesson sequence entails either developing appropriate questions or tasks that will elicit students' ideas or searching the Web, or other sources, to find some ready-made questions that you can use to uncover your students' concepts.

The same can be said for each of the categories and criteria, as planning instruction also should include careful thought about goals and purposes; the three aspects of activities addressed in Categories III, IV, and V;

assessment; and the learning environment that you create in your classroom, lab, or field setting. By following the modified set of categories and criteria included in Chapter 8, your work in planning will be much richer and more detailed. This will result in higher-quality teaching and improved student learning.

Reflection & Discussion Questions

1. What is your reaction to the idea that you have an obligation to find ways of supplementing the resources that your school provides for you to use with your teaching so that you can do your job effectively?

2. Describe why this is a part of your professional responsibility?

3. How do you think this will affect the time you need for planning instruction?

4. Do you agree that this added work will result in improvements in your teaching and in student learning?

Planning Effective Lesson Sequences that Result in Students' Learning with Understanding

Before we get into the details of using the criteria in planning lesson sequences, we need to think about two fundamentals of planning that have been developed by Wiggins and McTighe (1998). Their first fundamental is called the *backward design process*, which recommends that planning begin with identification of desired results (in the language of the criteria, "listing of learning goals" and "statement of purposes") for the lesson sequence. This is followed by the determination of acceptable evidence, which means you need to consider how you will assess students' learning. And last in the planning activity, you will plan the learning experiences and instructional activities (Wiggins and McTighe, 1998).

Why do they call it backward design? Those of us who work with beginning and experienced teachers have observed that the most common approach to instructional planning is to select a topic and then to begin thinking about the activities that will comprise the sequence of lessons for it. The goals and purposes of instruction on the topic typically are only vaguely described, and if it is a group-planning project, members of the team can have quite different, and often unstated, purposes in mind. In Wiggins and McTighe's backward design process, determining purposes of instruction (including goals and objectives) becomes a starting point. Therefore, the following question becomes

the first priority in planning once you have decided on a substantive topic for your lesson sequence or unit, such as "refraction" or "light" or "the cell" or "body systems" or "plate tectonics" or "writing and balancing chemical equations":

> **What are you hoping students will know, understand, feel, and be able to do when they finish the lesson sequence?**

Notice that your goals and purposes for the lesson sequence include four components—knowing, understanding, attitudes, and actions or applications. Each of these is an essential part of understanding the topic, and each needs to be recognized as you identify the desired results of your instruction. This is where you make important decisions about what you intend to accomplish with your students. Also this is where the *second* fundamental from Wiggins and McTighe comes into play. They say that you need to be thoughtful about what is included as learning expectations for your students. They suggest that in planning instruction you need to establish priorities for the content of lesson sequences by thinking about the following distinctions:

1. What is worth being familiar with? The broad background information and ideas that are part of the topic.

2. What is important to know? The important facts, concepts, principles, attitudes, and skills including processes, strategies, and methods that form the basis of the topic.

3. What enduring understanding do you want students to develop and hold over the long duration? The big ideas and how to apply them that students will find useful in many situations beyond the walls of school.

In their book, Wiggins and McTighe presented them as shown in Figure 9.1.

These two important ideas adapted from Wiggins and McTighe are key parts of identifying the instructional objectives and purposes for lesson sequences. The three parts of Figure 9.1 relate somewhat to time. Enduring understanding can be thought of as including the "big ideas" that underlie a topic of instruction. For example, in a study of motion in physics, the big ideas that you want students to learn relate to understanding uniform motion, its distinction from accelerated motion, and its connection to Newton's Laws of Motion. These are ideas you want students to carry with them through life as a result of the study of motion. Being able to solve problems using Newton's Second Law is important, because it helps to deepen the enduring understanding, but it is of restricted utility beyond physics classes, except for those who specialize

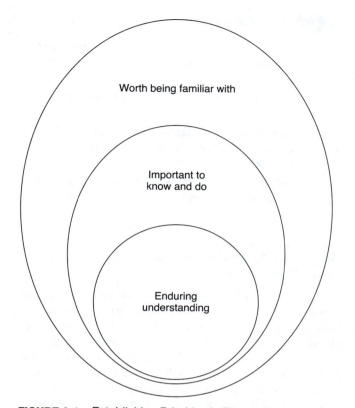

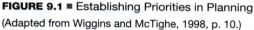

FIGURE 9.1 ■ Establishing Priorities in Planning
(Adapted from Wiggins and McTighe, 1998, p. 10.)

consider what facts, concepts, attitudes, and skills or applications fit into each of the three priorities.

The second part of the backward design process, determining acceptable evidence to show that students have achieved the desired results, leads you to consider an assessment of students' learning. How will you assess students' learning? What evidence will you collect to measure what students are learning as a result of the lesson sequence? To measure learning, you will need to think about the changes in students' knowledge, understanding, attitudes, actions, and applications. Measuring changes implies that you have some indicators of these components before and after instruction. Therefore, pretests and posttests are essential. In addition, information from a pretest can help you with planning, because you will have some information about students' background relevant to the topic and goals as they begin the topic.

What will constitute evidence of learning by your students on the topic of your lesson sequence? My use of the term *test* can be taken to mean familiar forms of assessment including test items such as multiple-choice questions, matching questions, labeling diagrams, completion questions, and questions that require students to construct a written response or to draw and label a diagram. But as you plan your assessments you can think about formative assessment (Chapter 7), including other assessment tools, such as informal checks of understanding in oral questioning, presentations by students, and demonstration of skills and techniques. These performance tasks are useful additions to your set of tools for assessing students.

Why is it important to bring up assessment at this point in the planning process? I believe there are two major reasons for doing so. First, consideration of what will constitute evidence of students' achievement of the purposes of a lesson sequence helps you to sharpen the clarity of your instructional intentions—your goals and objectives. Also, it adds specific meaning to the rather general statements of purpose. Second, it sets your purposes in a context. That is, what examples and details do you want to include in your plans?

Let's think for a moment about a high school biology teacher planning a lesson sequence that addresses the following benchmark related to cells:

> Within the cell are specialized parts for the transport of materials, energy capture and release, protein building, water disposal, information feedback, and even movement. In addition to these basic cellular functions common to all cells, most cells in multi-cellular organisms perform some specialized functions that others do not. (Project 2061, 1993, p. 113)

In your assessment, you would identify which of the several specialized parts of cells you would include

in a particular field of engineering and design. Many activities and demonstrations that help students understand inertia are worth being familiar with, and students should be able to describe their connection to inertia, but the concept of inertia is the enduring understanding. Taking another example from the study of circulation of blood in the human body, an enduring understanding is that the heart is a muscle that needs to be supplied with oxygen and nutrients, and this is accomplished by circulation of blood through the coronary arteries, veins, and capillaries. When this circulation is impeded, the heart cannot function properly. It is important to know that diet and exercise are factors that contribute to the good or poor health of the system of coronary circulation. Many facts about the health of this system are worthy of knowing, but they are only useful information in the context of the big idea or enduring understanding.

Discussion and Reflection Questions

Think about the significance of the identifying priorities for lesson sequences, units, and courses you teach. Pick a topic that is important to you as a teacher, and in your lessons and the level of knowledge and understanding you would expect of students. For example, do you want students to be able to name certain specialized parts, to identify them on an unlabeled diagram of a cell, or to describe the function of several of them in the overall working of a cell? Also, how detailed do you want your students to be able explain protein building in cells, or are you willing to have students simply say that the mitochondria are the "factories" within the cell in which proteins are synthesized? Finally, what evidence will you seek to measure students' learning in this lesson sequence? Will you use familiar objective test questions or will you ask students to construct a more interconnected "story" about what each of the parts of a cell do and how they work together, which might look like a "travelogue" through a cell? Such decisions will be aided by distinguishing among information that is *worth being familiar with*, ideas that are *important to know*, and understandings of the functions of cells and their parts that should be *enduring* (Figure 9.1). Thus, the need for clarity of purposes is highlighted when you think about assessment, showing how setting instructional goals and developing assessment plans reinforce each other.

The third step in the backward design process is planning learning experiences and instruction. The terminology here is important—why "learning experiences and instruction"? This terminology signifies two "players" in the classroom—students and the teacher. Learning experiences are what the students do. Instruction is what the teacher does to guide students through the learning experiences toward the instructional objectives, to monitor their progress along the way, and to nurture their development based on feedback about any difficulties they are encountering in that "journey." Therefore, as you plan activities for lesson sequences you must think about what students will be doing to learn, and what information, guidance, monitoring, and support you will provide. It is the coordination of these two sets of activities that are important.

As you use backward design, you also should be aware that this approach is strengthened by viewing it as iterative. That is, as you move from stating goals to defining the assessments you will use, you will inadvertently further clarify your goals. Similarly, as you plan activities, you may also gain insights into deeper meanings of your goals, and some new assessments may become evident. Therefore, I suggest that you keep an open mind about all aspects of the lesson sequence, since developing plans for lesson sequences, and then trying them out with your students can be an educative process for you, and your ideas about teaching, learning, your students, and the content of lesson sequences will expand and become clearer as you engage in the effort!

Reflection & Discussion Questions

1. Why is it important to coordinate development of the purposes and goals of instruction with the assessments?

2. Why would you call instructional planning an iterative process?

3. Why is it also important to coordinate development of all three parts of lesson sequences (purposes, assessments, and activities)?

4. What are the dangers of not having a plan that ensures that these three are logically consistent?

Importance of Having Clear Purposes and Objectives

What does research tell teachers about the value of being clear about their own instructional intentions and purposes, and what does it say about the importance of teachers making their intentions and purposes clear to students? The findings from research are quite straightforward. When teachers are clear about their goals and intentions for their teaching, they have lesson sequences that provide richer experiences for students and they have fewer irrelevant diversions from the main purposes of their instruction. Most important, when teachers convey their purposes and goals to students in a meaningful way, students' achievement also improves. These findings show that time spent by teachers in clarifying their purposes and conveying them to their students is valuable. It leads to positive payoff!

Kesidou and Roseman (2002) state the following in their article on the importance of clarifying objectives:

> The positive effects of providing students with a clear understanding of the purpose, goals, and content of an activity have been repeatedly confirmed by educational research (Boulanger, 1981; Wise & Okey, 1983). If students are to derive the intended learning benefits from engaging in an activity, their interest in or recognition of the value of the activity needs to be motivated (Blumenfeld, Soloway, Marx, Krajcik, Guzdial, & Palincsar, 1991; Malone & Lepper, 1987). Moreover, students need to understand the activity's goals and what these imply about how they should respond to the activity (Tasker & Freyberg, 1985). This category includes criteria to determine whether the curriculum material attempts to make its goals clear and meaningful to students, either by itself or by instructions to the teachers. (p. 530)

Ausubel (2000) also reinforces this idea in a report that compared students' achievements when they were told in advance what an activity was about, what a unit was about, and other kinds of primers with their achievements when they weren't given this information. Students who understood the purposes and goals of instruction achieved higher.

Using Criteria: Getting Started in Selecting Materials and Planning Instruction

The criteria have an obvious drawback for teachers who lack experience with teaching for understanding. The list can be overwhelming since it is hard to deal with more than twenty criteria, each of which represents complex ideas and relationships. Novice teachers may be even more overwhelmed since basic skills of classroom management and content representation consume such a large part of their available cognitive and emotional "space."

As you begin to think about using the criteria as a guide to planning, one way to simplify them is to think of grouping them in the following way:

- Category I (Formulating Goals and a Sense of Purpose for Students) deals with identifying desired results, or the goals and objectives of instruction. Category VII (Enhancing the Learning Environment for Students) also is useful in thinking about purposes, especially Criterion VII.B.—Encouraging Curiosity and Questioning.

- Category II (Taking Account of Students' Ideas and Reasoning) and Category VI (Assessing Students' Progress) focus on assessment—collecting information about students' ideas and reasoning

and determining acceptable evidence of attainment of the desired results. These four categories (I, II, VI, and VII) guide you in laying the essential foundations for a lesson sequence.

- The other three categories (III—Engaging Students with Relevant Phenomena IV—Developing and Using Scientific Ideas, and V—Promoting Student Thinking about Phenomena, Experiences, and Knowledge) provide guidance in planning learning experiences and instruction.

This represents an important way of conceptualizing the long list of criteria according to their utility in thinking about planning. You also probably noticed that the organization bears a strong association with Wiggins and McTighe's backward design. This is no accident as backward design is a powerful approach for planning instruction and designing lesson sequences.

Reflection & Discussion Questions

1. How is this way of conceptualizing the categories and criteria helpful to you as a teacher?

2. What are the limitations of this conceptualization of them?

This chapter concludes with a summary table (Figure 9.2) of the categories and criteria that will be useful as a ready reference for you. It lists each category and criterion in a condensed form that summarizes the development in Chapter 8. In Figure 9.2, the categories are listed in the three groups described in the previous section. This makes the system more

FIGURE 9.2 ■ Summary Listing of Project 2061 Categories and Criteria with Additions

Category	Criteria	Questions to Guide Planning	Degree Incorporated in My Lesson Sequence
I: Formulating Goals and a Sense of Purpose with Students	I.0. Listing of Learning Goals for the Lesson Sequence	Do the learning goals define what students are expected to learn and the performances expected of them as a result of the lesson sequence? Do the learning goals include the context in which performance is anticipated?	
	I.A. Conveying Unit Purpose	Does the unit plan convey an overall sense of purpose and direction that is motivating to students and aimed at the learning goals?	
	I.B. Conveying Lesson or Activity Purpose	Does the plan for the lesson convey to the students a purpose for each lesson or activity (aimed at the learning goals) and relate it to other lessons or activities?	

(Continued)

FIGURE 9.2 ■ *(Continued)*

Category	Criteria	Questions to Guide Planning	Degree Incorporated in My Lesson Sequence
	I.C. Sequencing Activities	Does the material involve students in a logical or strategic sequence of lessons or activities (versus being just a collection of lessons or activities)?	
VII: Enhancing the Learning Environment for Students	VII.A. Providing Teacher Content Support	Do your plans for the series of lessons support and enrich your understanding of the science, mathematics, and technology concepts needed for teaching the lesson?	
	VII.B. Encouraging Curiosity and Questioning	Does the lesson sequence help to create a classroom environment that welcomes student curiosity, rewards creativity, encourages a spirit of healthy questioning, and avoids dogmatism?	
	VII.C. Supporting All Students	Does the material or teacher help to create a classroom community that encourages high expectations for all students, enables all students to experience success, and provides all different kinds of students with a feeling of belonging in the classroom?	
II: Building on Students' Ideas and Reasoning	II.A. Attending to Prerequisite Knowledge and Skills	Does the lesson sequence specify and address the prerequisite knowledge and/or skills that are necessary for understanding the learning goals?	
	II.B. Highlighting Commonly Held Student Ideas	Do the instructional plans highlight commonly held student ideas (both troublesome and helpful) that are relevant to the learning goals and described in the learning research literature?	
	II.C. Identifying Students' Ideas and Reasoning	Does the lesson sequence plan include questions and/or tasks to help teachers identify what their students think about familiar situations and/or phenomena related to the learning goals before these goals are introduced?	
	II.D. Addressing Students' Ideas and Reasoning	Does the lesson sequence assist teachers in explicitly addressing students' ideas relevant to the learning goals?	
VI: Assessing Student Progress	VI.A. Aligning Assessment to Goals	Assuming a content match between the content of the lesson sequence and the learning goals, are questions and/or tasks included that assess student achievement of the learning goals?	
	VI.B. Probing Student Understanding	Does the lesson sequence include assessment questions and/or tasks that require students to show, use, apply, explain, or otherwise demonstrate their understanding of the knowledge and skills specified in the learning goals?	
	VI.C. Assessing Effectively	Are the questions and/or tasks likely to be effective in assessing the knowledge and/or skills specified in the learning goals?	
	VI.D. Informing Instruction	Does the plan monitor students' progress toward learning goals within the lesson sequence, not just at the end? Does the plan include ideas about using assessment results to choose among or	

FIGURE 9.2

Category	Criteria	Questions to Guide Planning	Degree Incorporated in My Lesson Sequence
		modify activities to address the learning goals? Is assessment organized to give students useful feedback on their progress toward the goals of lessons?	
III: Engaging Students with Phenomena and Real World Examples	III.A. Providing a Variety of Relevant Phenomena	Does the lesson sequence provide multiple and varied phenomena to support the key ideas in the learning goals?	
	III.B. Providing Firsthand and Vicarious Experiences	Does the lesson sequence provide an appropriate balance of firsthand and vicarious experiences with phenomena that are explicitly linked to the learning goals?	
	III.C. Providing Opportunities for Students to Engage in Inquiry	Does the lesson sequence provide appropriate opportunities for students to engage in inquiry as a way of simultaneously experiencing both phenomena and ways of investigating them that simulate how scientists create new knowledge?	
IV: Developing and Using Scientific Ideas	IV.A. Providing Evidence for Learning and the Learning Goals	Does the lesson sequence use scientific evidence to support learning, and suggest ways to help students develop a sense of the validity of the science knowledge and skills encompassed by the learning goals for the lesson sequence?	
	IV.B. Introducing Terms and Procedures Meaningfully	Does the lesson sequence introduce terms and procedures in the context of experiences with phenomena and use them to effectively communicate about the learning goals, understandings, and skills that underlie them?	
	IV.C. Representing Ideas Effectively	Does the lesson sequence include accurate and comprehensible representations[1] of the conceptual understandings and skills that underlie the learning goals?	
	IV.D. Connecting and Synthesizing Ideas	Does the lesson sequence explicitly make appropriate connections among individual instances of ideas and skills to support achievement of specific learning goals?	
	IV.E. Demonstrating Skills and Use of Knowledge	Does the lesson sequence demonstrate skills and the use of knowledge related to the learning goals?	
	IV.F. Providing Practice	Does the lesson sequence provide questions and/or tasks in a variety of situations for students to practice knowledge or skills related to the learning goals?	
V: Promoting Student Thinking about Experiences and Knowledge	V.0. Encouraging Students to Base Their Understanding in Data from Investigations and	Does the lesson sequence routinely require that all students connect their ideas and explanations with data from observations and investigations? Does the lesson sequence build on students' investigations?	

(Continued)

FIGURE 9.2 ■ *(Continued)*

Category	Experiences Criteria	Questions to Guide Planning	Degree Incorporated in My Lesson Sequence
	V.A. Encouraging Students to Explain Their Ideas	Does the lesson routinely require that all students express, clarify, justify, interpret, and represent their ideas about the topic and phenomena underlying the learning goals and for having students get feedback?	
	V.B. Guiding Interpretation and Reasoning	Does the lesson include questions and/or tasks that guide students' interpretation and reasoning about experiences with phenomena, representations, and/or readings related to the topic and phenomena underlying the learning goals?	
	V.C. Encouraging Students to Think about What They Have Learned	Does the lesson suggest ways to have students check and reflect on their own progress toward the learning goals, following instruction related to the topic and phenomena?	
	V.D. Encouraging Students to Recognize that Science Knowledge Is Dynamic	Do lessons provide students with a perspective that science knowledge can change as a consequence of new data and/or new ways of viewing existing data?	
	V.E. Encouraging Students to Recognize that Science Knowledge Is Socially Constructed	Do lessons help students recognize that science knowledge is constructed by scientists from their interpretations of data from observations and experiments? Do lessons help students recognize that the scientific enterprise operates on an agreed-upon set of rules for validating scientific knowledge?	

[1]By representations we mean drawings, diagrams, graphs, images, analogies, and metaphors or other verbal statements, models and simulations, role-playing, etc.

(Adapted from Project 2061, 2000.)

functional to me. In addition, I have added a fourth column that makes it a potential checklist for planning. The table has at least two potential uses:

1. It can serve as a guide to planning so that you are reminded of the factors you should consider as you plan lesson sequences.

2. It also can serve as a checklist as you near the end of planning to remind you of items you may have overlooked in the complex process of planning.

For the latter purpose, you may wish to use a response system like the following:

A—I feel that I have responded to this criterion adequately.

P—I feel that I have partially responded to this criterion. This could serve to remind you that you will come back to it a later time, such as when you

teach this topic again. (This implies that you will be reusing the lesson sequence and will keep these plans as a basis for teaching it the next time.)

N—I am not able to respond to this criterion at this time.

It would be appropriate to have some of each letter included in your checklist in your first round of development of lesson sequences, but as time goes on, you should be able to refine your plans so that more of the criteria receive the S rating.

Journal Questions

Add to your journal by revisiting the following questions that will help you monitor your progress as you make a paradigm shift in your teaching and your understanding of your students' learning for understanding and application in science.

1. What were the purposes or objectives of this chapter?
2. What were the key ideas presented in this chapter? (Note: These two could be combined as a two-column table to show the parallel between the purposes of each chapter and the big ideas presented.)
3. What important additions have you made to your vision of teaching science for understanding and application by studying this chapter and discussing with others? This should be an ongoing narrative that highlights development of your personal paradigm for teaching and learning science.
4. I also recommend that you create a concept map that portrays your understanding about teaching and learning science for understanding and application and add new concepts and connections as you study each chapter of this book. This concept map can provide a visual representation of your developing new vision or paradigm of science teaching and learning that you developed in the previous item.
5. What new skills and techniques do you find you need to develop in order to enact your vision of science teaching? What progress are you making in developing those skills and techniques?
6. Finally, what concerns do you have about being able to implement your new vision, your new paradigm of science teaching with your students, in your classroom, laboratory, and fieldwork? How will you respond to these concerns?

Chapter 10

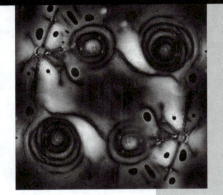

Planning a Middle School Lesson Sequence on Newton's Second Law

A Plan for Planning

The intention of this chapter is to apply the plan for planning developed in Chapter 9 to formulating a lesson sequence for eighth grade science based on a popular textbook. Individual teachers will modify such a plan to suit their own needs and their students' capabilities. However, what follows is a plan for planning that is based on the expanded categories and criteria from Chapter 8. In working through this plan for planning, you will examine the content of the lesson sequence, the purposes for teaching it, the means of helping students understand and use this content knowledge, the science processes that are related to the content, and how to assess students' learning. Also you will think about what you will do when you work with real students in your classroom.

This chapter is very detailed and it deals with a difficult topic that may lie outside of your field of expertise and interest. In spite of these possibilities, I urge you to go through this chapter with care, as it is designed to help you develop an approach to planning that is important in your professional development. The level of detail in this chapter, which exceeds that in later chapters, is precisely what makes it so important for you.

A note of caution as you begin: Teaching for understanding is complex and multifaceted. Therefore, this chapter on planning is long and intertwined. Give it the time and reflection that is needed to determine its strengths and to overcome its weaknesses.

The plan for planning begins, quite obviously, by selecting a topic and examining the instructional materials and resources that are available for your use in teaching the topic. The importance of careful study of the available instructional resources should not be underestimated. These are tools you can use in your teaching that are available to you and to your students. Determining the potential of these resources, as well as

their deficiencies, is an important part of your planning activity.

When you have selected the topic of instruction, the categories and criteria (summarized in Figure 9.2)

FIGURE 10.1 ■ Selected Pages from *Focus on Physical Science*
From *Prentice Hall Science Explorer—Focus on Physical Science California Version Teacher's Edition*
© 2001 by Pearson Education, Inc., publishing as Prentice Hall. Used by permission.

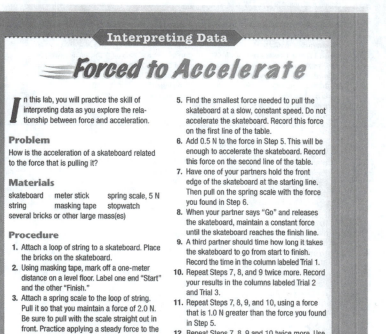

Skills Lab

Interpreting Data

Forced to Accelerate

Preparing for Inquiry

Key Concept An unbalanced force causes an object to accelerate.
Skills Objectives Students will be able to
- make observations of time and distance and calculate velocity and acceleration.
- graph data of acceleration vs. force;
- infer the relation between force and acceleration for constant mass.

Time 45 minutes
Advance Planning Ask volunteers to bring skateboards from home. Check calibration of the spring scales. Practice the experiment.
Alternative Materials You may be able to borrow carts or use old-fashioned roller skates in place of skateboards.

Guiding Inquiry

Invitation Put a skateboard on the floor and put a brick on it. Have a student accelerate it for about 1 meter using a spring scale. Ask students why the skateboard accelerated. Ask the students how they could investigate how acceleration depends on force.

Introducing the Procedure
- If needed, demonstrate how to zero and use a spring scale.
- Review the concepts of average speed and acceleration.
- Ask the students: **What are the manipulated and responding variables in this experiment?** *(Manipulated variable—force with which they pull the skateboard; responding variable—acceleration of the skateboard)*

Troubleshooting the Experiment
- If more mass is needed to keep the final velocity low, add bricks. Keep mass constant during the experiment.
- Be sure students zero the spring scale each time they use it. Point out that scale must be held horizontal and pulled straight.

42

Skills Lab

Interpreting Data

Forced to Accelerate

In this lab, you will practice the skill of interpreting data as you explore the relationship between force and acceleration.

Problem
How is the acceleration of a skateboard related to the force that is pulling it?

Materials
skateboard   meter stick   spring scale, 5 N
string   masking tape   stopwatch
several bricks or other large mass(es)

Procedure
1. Attach a loop of string to a skateboard. Place the bricks on the skateboard.
2. Using masking tape, mark off a one-meter distance on a level floor. Label one end "Start" and the other "Finish."
3. Attach a spring scale to the loop of string. Pull it so that you maintain a force of 2.0 N. Be sure to pull with the scale straight out in front. Practice applying a steady force to the skateboard as it moves.
4. Make a data table in your notebook like the one below.

5. Find the smallest force needed to pull the skateboard at a slow, constant speed. Do not accelerate the skateboard. Record this force on the first line of the table.
6. Add 0.5 N to the force in Step 5. This will be enough to accelerate the skateboard. Record this force on the second line of the table.
7. Have one of your partners hold the front edge of the skateboard at the starting line. Then pull on the spring scale with the force you found in Step 6.
8. When your partner says "Go" and releases the skateboard, maintain a constant force until the skateboard reaches the finish line.
9. A third partner should time how long it takes the skateboard to go from start to finish. Record the time in the column labeled Trial 1.
10. Repeat Steps 7, 8, and 9 twice more. Record your results in the columns labeled Trial 2 and Trial 3.
11. Repeat Steps 7, 8, 9, and 10, using a force that is 1.0 N greater than the force you found in Step 5.
12. Repeat Steps 7, 8, 9 and 10 twice more. Use forces that are 1.5 N and 2.0 N greater than the force you found in Step 5.

DATA TABLE

Force (N)	Trial 1 Time (s)	Trial 2 Time (s)	Trial 3 Time (s)	Avg Time (s)	Avg Speed (m/s)	Final Speed (m/s)	Acceleration (m/s²)

42

- If the spring scale is calibrated in grams, multiply by 0.01 to obtain newtons.
- Remind students that for Steps 6–12, they should try to pull with constant force, not at a constant speed. Students should practice this before starting to record data.
- Be sure students round off their results to an appropriate number of digits.
- Remind students to measure force when the skateboard is moving, not the initial force to get it started moving (which will be higher).

- Students may want to pull using forces of 0.5 N, 1.0 N, and so on. Be sure to add the force reading from Step 5. For example, if it takes 0.2 N to keep the skateboard moving at constant speed, then the students should pull with 0.7 N, 1.2 N, and so on.
- In Question 3, students calculate the final speed from the average speed. They can do this because the acceleration is constant. Average speed = (Final speed − initial speed)/2. Since the initial speed is zero, Final speed = Average speed × 2.

Note: Please note that the actual text pages are full color.

FIGURE 10.1 (contd.)

Analyze and Conclude

1. For each force you used, find the average of the three times that you measured. Record the average in your data table.
2. Find the average speed of the skateboard for each force. Use this formula:

   Average speed = 1 m ÷ Average time

   Record this value for each force.
3. To obtain the final speed of the skateboard, multiply each average speed by 2. Record the result in your data table.
4. To obtain the acceleration, divide each final speed you found by the average time. Record the acceleration in your data table.
5. Make a line graph. Show the acceleration on the y-axis and the force on the x-axis. The y-axis scale should go from zero to about 1 m/s². The x-axis should go from zero to 3.0 newtons.
6. If your data points seem to form a straight line, draw a line through them.
7. Your first data point is the force required for an acceleration of zero. How do you know the force for an acceleration of zero?
8. According to your graph, how is the acceleration of the skateboard related to the pulling force?
9. **Think About It** Which variable is the manipulated variable? Which is the responding variable?

Design an Experiment

Design an experiment to test how the acceleration of the loaded skateboard depends on its mass. Think about how you would vary the mass of the skateboard. What quantity would you need to measure that you did not measure in this experiment? Do you have the equipment to make that measurement? If not, what other equipment would you need?

Chapter 2   **43**

Sample Data Table

Force for zero acceleration: 0.2   N

Force (N)	0.7	1.2	1.7	2.2
Trial 1 Time (s)				
Trial 2 Time (s)				
Trial 3 Time (s)				
Avg. Time (s)	4.4	3.2	2.5	2.0
Avg. Speed (m/s)	0.23	0.31	0.40	0.50
Final Speed (m/s)	0.46	0.62	0.80	1.00
Acceleration (m/s²)	0.11	0.19	0.32	0.50

Safety

The skateboard can achieve a significant speed. It is safest to perform the experiment on the floor rather than on tables. Review the safety guidelines in Appendix A.

Program Resources

◆ **Unit 1 Resources** Chapter 2 Skills Lab, pp. 53–54

Expected Outcome

◆ The students should complete a data table similar to the sample provided.
◆ After calculating acceleration, the students should produce a graph showing that acceleration is proportional to force.
◆ Probable sources of error include improper use of the spring scale, calculating errors, and failing to pull with a constant force.

Analyze and Conclude

1. Answers may vary. If the mass is about 4 kg, and the force is 2.2 N, the time to accelerate for 1.0 m will be approximately 2 s.
2. Answers may vary. For the same combination, the average speed will be around 0.5 m/s.
3. Answers may vary. For the same combination, the final speed will be around 1 m/s.
4. Answers may vary. For the same combination, the acceleration will be around 0.5 m/s².
5. Answers may vary. Be sure to check for accuracy of graphing and comprehension of what the graph results mean.
6. Show students how to draw a "best-fit" line. Do not allow them to "connect the dots."
7. The force for an acceleration of zero was measured in Step 5 (at constant speed).
8. Acceleration is proportional to accelerating force.
9. The manipulated variable is the force; the responding variable is the acceleration.

Extending the Inquiry

Design an Experiment The new experiment should be essentially the same except that students should vary the mass (change the number of bricks) and keep the force constant.

43

Note: Please note that the actual text pages are full color.

can be used to guide your description of the goals and purposes of the lesson sequence or unit that you are planning. As you identify the purposes, you also may wish to think about the learning environment that enables you to achieve the purposes you intend.

Therefore, you will make use of Categories I and VII as you begin your planning.

The next stage in planning will be to continue on the path of *backward design* and think about Categories II and VI—students' ideas and reasoning

FIGURE 10.1 (contd.)

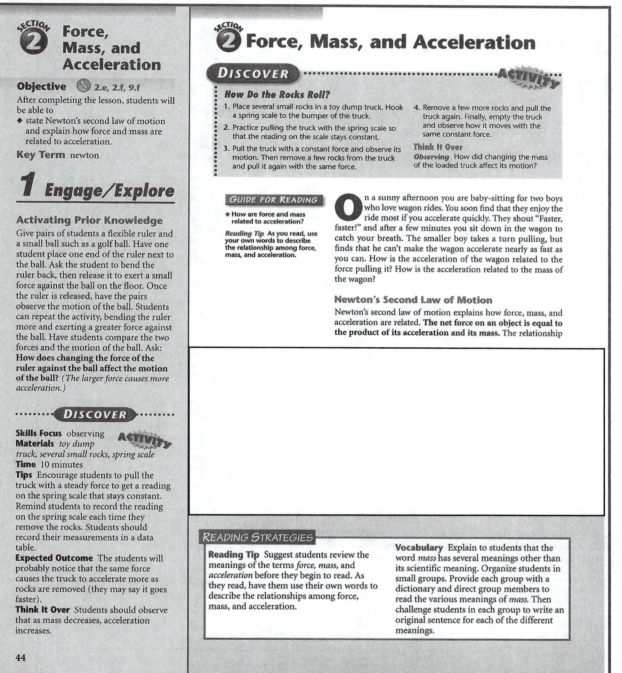

SECTION 2 Force, Mass, and Acceleration

Objective 2.e, 2.f, 9.f

After completing the lesson, students will be able to

◆ state Newton's second law of motion and explain how force and mass are related to acceleration.

Key Term newton

1 Engage/Explore

Activating Prior Knowledge

Give pairs of students a flexible ruler and a small ball such as a golf ball. Have one student place one end of the ruler next to the ball. Ask the student to bend the ruler back, then release it to exert a small force against the ball on the floor. Once the ruler is released, have the pairs observe the motion of the ball. Students can repeat the activity, bending the ruler more and exerting a greater force against the ball. Have students compare the two forces and the motion of the ball. Ask: **How does changing the force of the ruler against the ball affect the motion of the ball?** (*The larger force causes more acceleration.*)

DISCOVER

Skills Focus observing
Materials *toy dump truck, several small rocks, spring scale*
Time 10 minutes
Tips Encourage students to pull the truck with a steady force to get a reading on the spring scale that stays constant. Remind students to record the reading on the spring scale each time they remove the rocks. Students should record their measurements in a data table.
Expected Outcome The students will probably notice that the same force causes the truck to accelerate more as rocks are removed (they may say it goes faster).
Think It Over Students should observe that as mass decreases, acceleration increases.

44

SECTION 2 Force, Mass, and Acceleration

DISCOVER ············ ACTIVITY

How Do the Rocks Roll?

1. Place several small rocks in a toy dump truck. Hook a spring scale to the bumper of the truck.
2. Practice pulling the truck with the spring scale so that the reading on the scale stays constant.
3. Pull the truck with a constant force and observe its motion. Then remove a few rocks from the truck and pull it again with the same force.
4. Remove a few more rocks and pull the truck again. Finally, empty the truck and observe how it moves with the same constant force.

Think It Over
Observing How did changing the mass of the loaded truck affect its motion?

GUIDE FOR READING

◆ How are force and mass related to acceleration?

Reading Tip As you read, use your own words to describe the relationship among force, mass, and acceleration.

On a sunny afternoon you are baby-sitting for two boys who love wagon rides. You soon find that they enjoy the ride most if you accelerate quickly. They shout "Faster, faster!" and after a few minutes you sit down in the wagon to catch your breath. The smaller boy takes a turn pulling, but finds that he can't make the wagon accelerate nearly as fast as you can. How is the acceleration of the wagon related to the force pulling it? How is the acceleration related to the mass of the wagon?

Newton's Second Law of Motion

Newton's second law of motion explains how force, mass, and acceleration are related. **The net force on an object is equal to the product of its acceleration and its mass.** The relationship

READING STRATEGIES

Reading Tip Suggest students review the meanings of the terms *force, mass,* and *acceleration* before they begin to read. As they read, have them use their own words to describe the relationships among force, mass, and acceleration.

Vocabulary Explain to students that the word *mass* has several meanings other than its scientific meaning. Organize students in small groups. Provide each group with a dictionary and direct group members to read the various meanings of *mass.* Then challenge students in each group to write an original sentence for each of the different meanings.

Note: Please note that the actual text pages are full color.

and assessment. Finally, you will think about Categories III, IV, and V—engaging students with phenomena and real world examples, developing and using scientific ideas, and promoting students' thinking about experiences and knowledge.

In this example, we will focus on planning a lesson sequence on Newton's Second Law. The resource we will use for this lesson is found in Prentice Hall's *Science Explorer—Focus on Physical Science* (California Edition) (Needham, MA: Prentice Hall, 2001). This textbook series

FIGURE 10.1 (*contd.*)

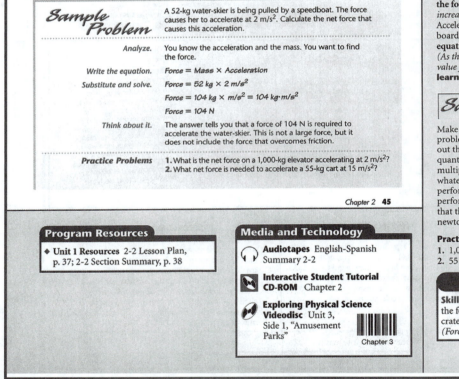

among the quantities force, mass, and acceleration can be written in one equation.

$$Force = Mass \times Acceleration$$

People often refer to this equation itself as Newton's second law of motion.

As with any equation, you must pay attention to the units of measurement. When acceleration is measured in meters per second per second (m/s^2) and mass is measured in kilograms, force is measured in kilograms × meters per second per second ($kg \cdot m/s^2$). This long unit is called the newton (N), in honor of Isaac Newton. One **newton** equals the force required to accelerate one kilogram of mass at 1 meter per second per second.

$$1\,N = 1\,kg \times 1\,m/s^2$$

A student might have a mass of 40 kilograms. Suppose she is walking, and accelerates at $1\ m/s^2$. You can easily find the force exerted on her by substituting mass and acceleration into the equation. You find that 40 kilograms × $1\ m/s^2$ is 40 newtons.

Sometimes you may want to write the relationship among acceleration, force, and mass in a different form.

$$Acceleration = \frac{Force}{Mass}$$

This form is found by rearranging the equation for Newton's second law.

Sample Problem

A 52-kg water-skier is being pulled by a speedboat. The force causes her to accelerate at $2\ m/s^2$. Calculate the net force that causes this acceleration.

Analyze. You know the acceleration and the mass. You want to find the force.

Write the equation. Force = Mass × Acceleration

Substitute and solve. Force = 52 kg × 2 m/s^2

Force = 104 kg × m/s^2 = 104 kg·m/s^2

Force = 104 N

Think about it. The answer tells you that a force of 104 N is required to accelerate the water-skier. This is not a large force, but it does not include the force that overcomes friction.

Practice Problems 1. What is the net force on a 1,000-kg elevator accelerating at 2 m/s^2?
2. What net force is needed to accelerate a 55-kg cart at 15 m/s^2?

Chapter 2 **45**

Program Resources

◆ **Unit 1 Resources** 2-2 Lesson Plan, p. 37; 2-2 Section Summary, p. 38

Media and Technology

🎧 **Audiotapes** English-Spanish Summary 2-2

💿 **Interactive Student Tutorial CD-ROM** Chapter 2

💿 **Exploring Physical Science Videodisc** Unit 3, Side 1, "Amusement Parks"

Chapter 3

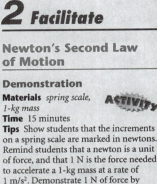

2 *Facilitate*

Newton's Second Law of Motion

Demonstration

Materials *spring scale, 1-kg mass*
Time 15 minutes
Tips Show students that the increments on a spring scale are marked in newtons. Remind students that a newton is a unit of force, and that 1 N is the force needed to accelerate a 1-kg mass at a rate of $1\ m/s^2$. Demonstrate 1 N of force by attaching the spring scale to the 1-kg mass and dragging the mass along a table. You can minimize friction by pulling the mass over beads, ice, or vegetable oil. Ask: **How can you tell the amount of force it took to pull the mass?** *(Read the measurement on the spring scale)* Demonstrate forces less than and greater than 1 N. Ask: **What happens to the acceleration when the force on the mass increases?** *(It increases.)* Write the equation Acceleration = Force ÷ Mass on the board. Ask: **How does Newton's equation represent what you observed?** *(As the value of the force gets larger, the value for acceleration also gets larger.)*
learning modality: visual

Sample Problem

Make sure that students practice good problem solving skills. Have them write out the formula, substitute the known quantities, cancel the units and do the multiplication. Remind students that whatever mathematical operations are performed on the values are also performed on the units. Remind them that the kg·m/s^2 has a special name, the newton (N).

Practice Problems
1. 1,000 kg × 2 m/s^2 = 2,000 N
2. 55 kg × 15 m/s^2 = 825 N

Ongoing Assessment

Skills Check Have students calculate the force needed to accelerate a 25-kg crate of bananas at a rate of 1.5 m/s^2. *(Force = 25 kg × 1.5 m/s^2 = 37.5 N)*

45

Note: Please note that the actual text pages are full color.

is widely used across the nation, and a special edition has been made to meet California's educational standards. The material for this topic is found on pages 42 through 46 of this eighth grade science text. These pages of the text and teacher's guide pages are reproduced here for your convenience (Figure 10.1). Take time to review these pages carefully, including both the student pages and the notes to teachers, which surround the student pages in this copy. As you examine the textbook material, reflect on the content that is included, how it is presented, the meanings that can be derived from the diagrams, and the instructional approach that is implied in these pages.

FIGURE 10.1 (*contd.*)

Changes in Force and Mass

Using the Visuals: Figure 6

Draw attention to this photograph to help students visualize how mass and acceleration are related. Ask:

◆ **How could you decrease the mass so that acceleration could increase?** (*Ask a child to step out of the wagon.*)

◆ **How could you increase acceleration without changing mass?** (*Increase force by pulling harder.*)

◆ **How could you apply what you learned about mass, force, and acceleration to make the wagon accelerate as much as possible?** (*Increase force and decrease mass at the same time.*)

learning modality: visual

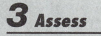

3 Assess

Section 2 Review Answers

1. Force, mass, and acceleration; Force = Mass × Acceleration.
2. The acceleration increases.
3. You need to know the mass of the shopping cart.
4. If you double the net force acting on an object, you have to double the mass of the object to keep the acceleration unchanged.

Check Your Progress

At this point, students should begin to sketch possible vehicle designs. Allow them to discuss their designs in small groups so that they can improve their vehicles. Have them brainstorm ways of increasing force or decreasing mass. For example: three wheels have less mass than four.

Performance Assessment

Oral Presentation Have students explain why the same force accelerates an empty wagon more than a wagon full of bricks. (*According to Newton's second law, if the mass is smaller, acceleration is larger for the same force.*)

46

Figure 6 The acceleration of an object depends on the force acting on it and the object's mass.

Changes in Force and Mass

How can you increase the acceleration of the wagon? Look again at the equation for acceleration: Acceleration = Force ÷ Mass. One way to increase acceleration is by changing the force. According to the equation, acceleration and force change in the same way. An increase in force causes an increase in acceleration. So to increase the acceleration of the wagon, you can increase the force you use to pull it. You can pull harder.

Another way to increase acceleration is to change the mass. According to the equation, acceleration and mass change in opposite ways. This means that an increase in mass causes a decrease in acceleration. It also means that a decrease in mass causes an increase in acceleration. So to increase the acceleration of the wagon, you can decrease its mass. Instead of you, the boys should ride in the wagon.

Section 2 Review

1. What three quantities are related in Newton's second law of motion? What is the relationship among them?
2. When the net force on an object increases, how does the object's acceleration change?
3. Suppose you know the acceleration of a shopping cart as it rolls down a supermarket aisle. You want to find the net force with which it was pushed. What other information do you need in order to find the force?
4. **Thinking Critically Problem Solving** Suppose you doubled the force acting on an object. In what way could you change its mass to keep its acceleration unchanged?

46

Check Your Progress

CHAPTER PROJECT

The vehicle for your project will need to accelerate from a resting position. From Newton's second law of motion, you know that Acceleration = Force ÷ Mass. This means you have two ways of increasing acceleration: increasing force or decreasing mass. How can you either increase the force acting on your vehicle or decrease its mass?

Background

Facts and Figures In the U.S. Customary system of measurement, the pound is a unit of force, not mass. In this system, the unit for mass is the *slug*. The weight of an object that has a mass of 1 slug is 32.17 pounds. This unit of mass measurement is used widely by engineers but is rarely used by anybody else. When people say they want to take off a few "pounds," they probably mean they want to lose mass.

Program Resources

◆ **Unit 1 Resources** 2-2 Review and Reinforce, p. 39; 2-2 Enrich, p. 40

Note: Please note that the actual text pages are full color.

Reflection & Discussion Questions

As you examined the materials, what did you learn about (1) the content that is included, (2) how the content is presented, (3) representations of content included to aid learning, (4) resources that are valuable for you as a teacher, (5) the instructional approach that is implicit?

Identifying and Clarifying Goals and Purposes for the Lesson Sequence

Now, let's begin with thinking about the goals and purposes that are appropriate for students of this age (grade 8) to accomplish with this particular sequence of lessons.

FIGURE 10.2 ■ Categories and Criteria I and VII

Category	Criteria	Questions to Guide Planning
I: Providing a Sense of Purpose for Students	I.0. Listing of Learning Goals for the Lesson Sequence	Do the learning goals define what students are expected to learn and the performances expected of them as a result of the lesson sequence? Do the learning goals include the context in which performance is anticipated?
	I.A. Conveying Unit Purpose	Does the unit plan convey an overall sense of purpose and direction that is motivating to students and aimed at the learning goals?
	I.B. Conveying Lesson or Activity Purpose	Does the plan for the lesson convey to the students a purpose for each lesson or activity (aimed at the learning goals) and relate it to other lessons or activities?
	I.C. Sequencing Activities	Does the material involve students in a logical or strategic sequence of lessons or activities (versus just being a collection of lessons or activities)?
VII: Enhancing the Learning Environment for Students	VII.A. Providing Teacher Content Support	Do your plans for the series of lessons support and enrich your understanding of the science, mathematics, and technology concepts needed for teaching the lesson?
	VII.B. Encouraging Curiosity and Questioning	Does the lesson sequence help to create a classroom environment that welcomes student curiosity, rewards creativity, encourages a spirit of healthy questioning, and avoids dogmatism?
	VII.C. Supporting All Students	Does the material or teacher help to create a classroom community that encourages high expectations for all students, enables all students to experience success, and provides all different kinds of students with a feeling of belonging in the classroom?

(Adapted from Project 2061, 2000.)

Figure 10.2 provides you with a reminder of the criteria in Categories I and VII that are useful in defining the purposes and goals of this lesson sequence.

At the outset, you should identify the appropriate standards and benchmarks for your school. Since I have chosen the California version of this text, I will begin by examining the *Benchmarks* from Project 2061, and the California Standards for Grade 8 Science (*http://www.cde.ca.gov/be/st/ss/scgrade8.asp*).

The Project 2061 benchmarks relevant to this topic come from three levels. Benchmarks from grades 3–5 show what may be expected as prerequisite knowledge that students may have as you begin the topic. One benchmark is stated for this topic from the grade 3–5 list:

Something that is moving may move steadily or change its direction. The greater the force is, the greater the change in motion will be. The more massive the object is, the less effect a given force will have. (Project 2061, 1993, p. 89)

A single benchmark is given for each of the two higher levels. For grades 6–8 the benchmark is as follows:

In the absence of retarding forces, such as friction, an object will keep its direction of motion and its speed. Whenever an object is seen to speed up, slow down, or change direction, it can be assumed that an unbalanced force is acting on it. (Project 2061, 1993, p. 90)

For grades 10–12, the benchmark listed is a statement of Newton's Second Law:

The change in motion of an object is proportional to the force applied and inversely proportional to the mass. (Project 2061, 1993, p. 91)

The California Standards for Grade 8 Science on the topic of Force (which is the relevant set that follows standards for Motion) are presented below. The full set of standards is included to provide context; the most relevant standards are highlighted.

Forces

2. Unbalanced forces cause changes in velocity. As a basis for understanding this concept:
   a. *Students know* a force has both direction and magnitude.

b. *Students know* when an object is subject to two or more forces at once, the result is the cumulative effect of all the forces.

c. *Students know* when the forces on an object are balanced, the motion of the object does not change.

d. *Students know* how to identify separately the two or more forces that are acting on a single static object, including gravity, elastic forces due to tension or compression in matter, and friction.

e. ***Students know* that when the forces on an object are unbalanced, the object will change its velocity (that is, it will speed up, slow down, or change direction).**

f. ***Students know* the greater the mass of an object, the more force is needed to achieve the same rate of change in motion.**

g. *Students know* the role of gravity in forming and maintaining the shapes of planets, stars, and the solar system. (Author's note: This part of the standard appears to go beyond the scope of the lessons being planned.)

9. Scientific progress is made by asking meaningful questions and conducting careful investigations. As a basis for understanding this concept and addressing the content in the other three strands, students should develop their own questions and perform investigations. Students will:

a. Plan and conduct a scientific investigation to test a hypothesis.

b. Evaluate the accuracy and reproducibility of data.

c. Distinguish between variable and controlled parameters in a test.

d. Recognize the slope of the linear graph as the constant in the relationship $y = kx$ and apply this principle in interpreting graphs constructed from data.

e. Construct appropriate graphs from data and develop quantitative statements about the relationships between variables.

f. **Apply simple mathematic relationships to determine a missing quantity in a mathematic expression, given the two remaining terms (including speed = distance/time, density = mass/volume, force = pressure × area, volume = area × height).**

g. Distinguish between linear and nonlinear relationships on a graph of data.

What will be the purposes and objectives of this lesson sequence? The authors of the textbook indicate that this topic addresses three benchmarks (2e, 2f, and 9f), which are highlighted above. Drawing on the two sets of benchmarks, students should know and be able to do the following when they complete this set of lessons:

1. Describe what is meant by change of motion, using terms such as *velocity*, *speed*, *acceleration*, *speeding up*, *deceleration*, *slowing down*, and *changing direction*.

2. When examining a system in which a change in motion is noted, describe the change in speed and/or direction *and* identify the unbalanced force(s) acting on the object that change the object's motion to demonstrate a sound understanding of the concept of acceleration.

3. When examining a system in which motion is occurring, describe, demonstrate, and give examples of the following:

a. Different changes in motion, including changes in speed and changes in direction;

b. The effect of an unbalanced force in increasing, decreasing speed, or changing direction;

c. The effect of different strength of forces on change in motion for a particular mass;

d. The effect of a particular strength of force in changing the motion of different masses.

(This can also be stated as follows: The change in motion of an object is proportional to the force applied and inversely proportional to the mass.)

4. Identify and use *newton* as a unit of force that is consistent with the metric system.

5. Evaluate the accuracy and reproducibility of data from empirical investigations.

Let's reflect on these objectives. First, what do we want students to know about Newton's Second Law? The textbook uses such terms as *force*, *mass*, and *acceleration*, and it also shows the mathematical relationship among these, that is

$$\text{Force} = \text{Mass} \times \text{Acceleration } and$$
$$\text{Acceleration} = \text{Force/Mass}$$

By introducing the term *inversely proportional* in Objective 3 above, we have included understanding the mathematical relationships in Newton's Second Law as part of the purposes of this lesson sequence. Also, since the textbook uses language that is commonplace, the terms in Objective 1 are appropriate. Moreover, the precise distinctions between terms such as *velocity* and *speed* that are part of a physics course are not made in these lessons and would only add unnecessary complications at this point. Moreover, velocity is not used in the textbook pages for this lesson sequence.

Another aspect of the purposes of this lesson sequence is to allow students to both develop an understanding of Newton's Second Law and to learn how and when to use it. Therefore, the objectives include the terms *demonstrate* and *give examples*.

One complicating factor in the presentation of the material in the textbook is the use of *newtons* as the force unit, which has not been introduced earlier in the text. This is not a familiar unit for students. Another

FIGURE 10.3 ■ Indicators for Category I.A

1. The lesson sequence or unit explicitly presents to the students a unit purpose—in the form of a statement, problem, question, or representation—that is aimed at the learning goals.
2. The purpose is likely to be comprehensible to students.
3. The purpose is likely to be interesting and/or motivating to students.
4. The lesson sequence gives students an opportunity to think about and discuss the purpose.
5. Most activities or lessons are consistent with the purpose.
6. The lesson sequence returns to the purpose at the end of the unit or lesson sequence.

(Adapted from Project 2061, 2000.)

complication is that the distinction between *mass* and *weight* does not appear to have been made as yet in this textbook, so students probably will not be familiar with this aspect of the topic. Benchmark 9f from the California Standards also adds a complication in that it requires that students can use a formula to calculate the missing term such as finding a numeric value for acceleration when the mass of an object and the force applied to it are known. Therefore, Objective 4 was added to account for these points.

How do the *indicators*, shown in Figure 10.3, help you in expressing purposes in a clear and comprehensible manner? All of the indicators are important.

Reflection & Discussion Questions

1. Why has so much time and space been devoted to objectives for this short lesson sequence?

2. Why is this an essential part of planning?

3. How has each of the resources presented above been useful in identifying the objectives?

4. Why is each of the resources necessary?

5. What important resource should be included as you plan the lesson for your students that was not present if you teach somewhere other than California?

Creating a Supportive, Motivating Environment for Students

You must admit that the set of five objectives above don't seem too exciting for grade 8 students. So how can you make it more appealing to your students? I suggest that there are two aspects of making this topic more appealing: one is to address something of interest and the other is to address an aspect of science that may be intriguing to students' developing view of the world. For the first, I suggest that the favorite sports of

your students may be an important vehicle for incorporating some "life" into your purposes. Let's assume that soccer is popular with your students, as it is with both male and female students at middle school level in many parts of the country. A soccer ball goes through many changes in motion during each minute of play. All of these involve acceleration resulting from unbalanced forces acting on the ball. Most people have observed hard kicks that have sent the ball through long distances at high rates of speed. Most people have seen the ball change direction and noted that the force causing the change has been associated with a person's feet, head, or body. Therefore, this is a good topic to use to enhance interest in the topic. If you add softball or basketball, you can further enrich interest if your students are engaged in these sports.

This leads us to the formation of a central or driving question for this topic. Here is one suggestion; perhaps you can identify one, such as extreme skateboarding, for your class that is more appealing:

How can we understand the motion of a soccer ball during play?

The intention here is to use the motion and changes in motion of a soccer ball to develop understanding of motion in general. When kicked, stopped, or headed, soccer balls change their motion. How does this relate to the forces applied to them? What if a soccer ball became water soaked? How does this change its mass, and what affect does this have on its change in motion? What if soccer were played with a heavier or lighter ball? What if it were played with a larger ball with more air resistance? Questions such as these can enliven interest in this topic.

Choosing a central question that allows you to transform your study of science into a topic that connects with students' lives is an important part of instructional design. It needs thoughtful attention from teachers who are aware of, and capitalize on, their students' interests and motivations. This thoughtful approach to making the subject matter more appealing to students is an example of Category VII, especially Criterion VII.B, Encouraging Curiosity and Questioning.

The second aspect of bringing "life" to the purposes is to give attention to how scientists think about, talk about, and understand motion. This will help students to understand the scientific habits of mind that have enabled scientists to give meaning to experiences and investigations with natural phenomena. It will help them understand what underlies the terms and rules that scientists use. Therefore, I recommend a second driving question as follows:

> How do scientists think about and describe motion of objects?

I also suggest that these two questions be displayed in a prominent place in your classroom and remain there for the duration of this lesson sequence, and perhaps longer, as they may also be useful during subsequent lesson sequences in this unit, including the study of friction and motion.

Reflection & Discussion Questions

1. How has the emphasis on Category VII helped you to think differently about this topic?

2. In what ways do the two guiding questions about soccer and how scientists think improve the lesson sequence?

3. What alternative would you recommend as guiding questions?

A Missing Element that You Must Provide

An essential component for understanding this topic is missing from both of these sets of statements about educational goals, and it is only implicit in the textbook. That component is a deep understanding of acceleration—that it is a change in either speed or direction of motion that occurs over some period of time. What makes it difficult to grasp is the fact that in many familiar instances the period of time is very short. Kicking a ball is a good example. How and when does acceleration of a soccer ball during a kick occur? It is only in the fraction of a second that the kicker's foot is in contact with the ball. In that short time, the ball's motion changes from no motion to motion at a high speed. If you think about throwing a ball, your arm swings through an arc, moving the ball from zero speed to a speed of many miles per hour in the fraction of a second it takes to complete the movement of your arm and release the ball. Acceleration of the ball occurs in that fraction of a second. The force on the ball that causes acceleration is from your hand. The speed of the ball after it leaves your hand is only as great as you, the thrower, impart to it.

Students can also observe negative acceleration, or deceleration, as soccer balls slow down when rolling across the grass. The retarding force is friction with the grass and air. Deceleration of a rolling soccer ball occurs over a longer duration and therefore is easier to study. Deceleration also can occur in an extremely short time duration when a moving ball is blocked. In such instances, the ball will go through a very rapid deceleration, from a high speed to a stop and then often rebound at a high speed. In less than a second, the ball will decelerate to zero speed and then accelerate to a high speed in a different direction. The forces involved in these changes are often quite large, as you know if you are the blocker! The forces on the rolling ball, which has a smaller deceleration, are also smaller. These differences can be understood in terms of Newton's Second Law: $a = f/m$.

In this lesson sequence, one important objective will be to help students understand acceleration deeply. Many different examples will be needed to help students attain this understanding. It also will require many different activities, including participating in hands-on experiences, reflecting on those experiences, talking about them, writing about them, and representing them and the meaning behind them in various ways. One difficulty is that most students will have a naïve concept about acceleration "as something related to speed." Enhancing and clarifying that concept will be a critical, foundational part of your work in this unit. Unless you ensure that this understanding emerges, many of your students will miss the importance and meaning of this lesson sequence.

Reflection & Discussion Questions

Return to Figure 10.2 and rate the development on objectives and purposes according to the plan outlined in Chapter 9. Rate each item as S, P, or N, based on your interpretation of the adequacy of the development up to this point. Be reflective in assigning your ratings. It may be useful to have a group or whole-class discussion based on this task.

Students' Ideas and Assessment

Looking next at Categories II and VI we will begin to examine how to build on students' ideas and to consider assessment as part of backward design. These are summarized in Figures 10.4 and 10.5 for your convenience.

What are the common misconceptions that students have on this topic of changing motion? Figure 10.6 contains one set I found on the Internet at the following site that deals with force and motion: *http:// nasalearn.org/teacher_support_alerts_misconceps_ physci.htm*. Although these misconceptions relate in

FIGURE 10.4 ■ Category II. Building on Student Ideas

II: Taking Account of Students' Ideas and Reasoning	II.A. Attending to Prerequisite Knowledge and Skills	Does the lesson sequence specify and address the prerequisite knowledge and/or skills that are necessary for understanding the learning goals?
	II.B. Highlighting Commonly Held Student Ideas	Do the instructional plans highlight commonly held student ideas (both troublesome and helpful) that are relevant to the learning goals and described in the learning research literature?
	II.C. Identifying Students' Ideas and Reasoning	Does the lesson sequence plan include questions and/or tasks to help teachers identify what their students think about familiar situations and/or phenomena related to the learning goals before these goals are introduced?
	II.D. Addressing Students' Ideas and Reasoning	Does the lesson sequence assist teachers in explicitly addressing students' ideas relevant to the learning goals?

(Adapted from Project 2061, 2000.)

FIGURE 10.5 ■ Category VI. Assessing Student Progress

VI: Assessing Student Progress	VI.A. Aligning Assessment to Goals	Assuming a content match between the content of the lesson sequence and the learning goals, are questions and/or tasks included that assess student achievement of the learning goals?
	VI.B. Probing Student Understanding	Does the lesson sequence include assessment questions and/or tasks that require students to show, use, apply, explain, or otherwise demonstrate their understanding of the knowledge and skills specified in the learning goals?
	VI.C. Assessing Effectively	Are the questions and/or tasks likely to be effective in assessing the knowledge and/or skills specified in the learning goals?
	VI.D. Informing Instruction	Does the plan monitor students' progress toward learning goals within the lesson sequence, not just at the end? Does the plan include ideas about using assessment results to choose among or modify activities to address the learning goals? Is assessment organized to give students useful feedback on their progress toward the goals of lessons?

(Adapted from Project 2061, 2000.)

some way to Newton's Second Law, the three that are highlighted are the most closely related.

Reflection & Discussion Questions

1. This list of common misconceptions deserves careful analysis and thought. It is a great source of information for teachers. As you examine this, do you find that you are in agreement with any of the points listed? If so, you also hold a misconception, and you need to reexamine your ideas so that you are able to be an advocate for valid scientific knowledge. (Note: Don't be ashamed that you have a few misconceptions. It is not your fault, unless you fail to do something to correct the situation.)

2. The box above shows the importance of, and difficulty for, students developing a deep understanding of acceleration. This will be a major challenge in achieving the intended objectives of the lesson sequence. How will you keep this component of the lesson in the foreground of your thinking as you teach this lesson?

FIGURE 10.6 ■ Some Common Misconceptions Relating to Motion

1. Constant motion requires a constant force—if you want to keep moving along a horizontal track, you have to keep pushing, otherwise you will run out of force and just stop. This represents a failure to distinguish the role of friction as a separate force.
2. *Reaction* forces are less real than *real* forces. For example, students are told that when they hit (or exert a force on an object), that object "exerts" a force back. It is difficult for many students to attribute an active word to a passive object. (They believe stationary objects like tables do not exert a force.)
3. All things fall down due to gravity but heavy things always fall fastest.
4. Objects fall because of two things acting separately—gravity and the weight of an object.
5. Students do not equate weight with the force of gravity.
6. **If a body is not moving there is no force acting on it.**
7. **The amount of motion (speed and distance traveled) is proportional to the amount of force.**
8. **If a body is in motion, there is a force acting upon it in the direction of motion.**
9. Force is something that is a property of an object and gets used up.

The following resource books by Rosalind Driver and her associates also are excellent sources of information about misconceptions. These books are important as resources not just for this topic, but for many topics in science:

Children's Ideas in Science
Making Sense of Secondary Science

The latter book has two excellent chapters that pertain to this lesson sequence: Chapter 21 is on "Forces" and Chapter 22 on "Horizontal Motion." Both chapters provide you with detailed information on the common misconceptions that students bring with them. Many of these misconceptions are quite enduring and therefore need attention as part of schooling. Chapter 22 contains a list of several misconceptions that pertain to this section, including the following:

1. If there is motion, there is a force acting.
2. There cannot be a force without motion, and if there is no motion then there is no force acting.
3. When an object is moving, there is a force in the direction of motion.
4. A moving object has a force within it, which keeps it going.
5. A moving object stops when its force is used up.
6. Motion is proportional to the force acting, and a constant speed results from a constant force. (Driver, et al., 1994, pp. 157–158)

In addition to the common misconceptions about the relationship between force and motion, Newton's Second Law is not easy to comprehend as it requires that students address some conceptual difficulties that are difficult to grasp. For example, Newton's Second Law is about acceleration, which is a concept that students do not readily understand beyond the notion that it has something to do with going faster. Acceleration means that during each second an accelerated object goes faster than it did in the previous second, which is an idea that does not come easily to students. Many students think about change of speed as being instantaneous, instead of a gradual matter. Their experience with sports reinforces this view. For example, when a moving soccer ball is kicked, so that its direction of motion and its speed changes abruptly, the change does not appear to be gradual. When someone pulls a child's wagon as shown on pages 44 and 46 of the *Focus on Physical Science* text (see Figure 10.1), gradual acceleration is not easy to infer. Also the unit of acceleration (meters/second/second) seems strange to students. Such understandings often are referred to as naïve conceptions.

Driver and her associates report on a point that I made in describing the motion of soccer balls. They noted that students "tend to see objects either at rest or moving. The period of change, when for example an object speeds up from rest to a steady speed or slows down and stops is less frequently focused on by children" (Driver et al., 1994, p. 155). Driver and her associates go on to indicate that students do not appear to use the term *acceleration* until it is introduced in science classes, and that everyday terms such as *going faster* are used in ambiguous ways to describe a high speed and to indicate increasing speed. Moreover, they point out that even college students exhibit much confusion about acceleration. Driver and her associates conclude this section with the advice for science teachers "that children need to develop the language tools to describe motion appropriately (including vocabulary, graphical representations and numerical formulations, for example $v=d/t$) prior to developing an understanding of dynamical principles" (Driver et al., 1994, p. 155). This is important advice for this lesson, which reiterates a point I have made recurrently in this text—students need to be able to write about, talk about (use vocabulary), draw diagrams of (graphical representations), and use other representations of experiences–observations (e.g., numerical formulations) as part of developing understanding.

To help students with the concept of acceleration, you may need to deal with acceleration of cars, such as how long it takes a car to go from 0 to 60 miles per hour. This is often part of the advertisement or specifications that are listed for sports cars and some students will know about it. For example, 0 to 60 miles per hour in 6 seconds is quite a rapid rate of acceleration. This means that the car probably increases its speed to 10 mph at the end of the first second, to 20 mph at the end of 2 seconds, and to 30 mph at the end of the third second, and so forth to 60 mph at the end of 6 seconds. The fact that at the end of each second the speed is 10 miles per hour faster than at the end of the previous second is an idea that can make sense to students, and it helps them to comprehend acceleration. They can see that the rate of increase (acceleration) is 10 miles per hour (a speed unit) in each second (a time unit) or 10 mi/hr/sec (specifies change in speed in a unit of time). With this idea made clear, the unit for acceleration—meters/second/second (also shows change of speed in a unit of time)—is made somewhat clearer.

Two additional concepts that are difficult for students have to do with the metric unit of force—the newton, and the distinction between mass and weight. The mass of an object is an unchanging quantity under normal circumstances, whereas the weight of an object depends on the force of gravity (see Figure 10.6, misconception 5). Because the force of gravity can change with location (you probably recall that the surface of the moon has about one-sixth of the gravity that occurs on the surface of the earth), the weight of an object on the moon would be about one-sixth of its weight on earth. Following this logic further, because weight is the result of the force of gravity and mass is a property of matter that is unchanging except in unusual circumstances, force units must be different from mass units. According to Newton's Second Law, force is equal to the product of mass and acceleration ($f = ma$). Therefore, the unit of force would be equal to kilogram meters per second per second. This is a cumbersome term that has been renamed by scientists as the *newton*. A force of 1 newton is approximately equal to the force of gravity on a mass of 100 grams or 0.1 kilogram that is at the surface of the earth. Therefore, if you slowly lift a 100-gram mass with your hand, you are lifting with a force of about 1 newton. Or if you hold a 1-kilogram mass with your hand, you are exerting an upward force of about 10 newtons to counterbalance the downward force of gravity on this 1-kg mass. (Notice the precise terminology used here. This is part of the difficulty that grade 8 students will have with this lesson sequence. Eighth graders typically are not in the habit of using language in this precise manner.)

The need for precise language makes this difficult for students. Notice how I said "slowly lift" to imply no acceleration. Also notice how I said "you are exerting an upward force of about 10 newtons to counterbalance the downward force of gravity on this 1-kg mass." This precision in language is not easy for middle school students. Neither is the complex, interconnected logic familiar to them. Therefore, as a teacher you have several complications to deal with in teaching this topic. However, these are important parts of the habit of mind of scientists, and they will be important as you work with students to help them understand motion from the perspective that scientists use in describing and explaining motion. This connects with the second driving question, How do scientists think about and describe motion of objects?

As you work with students, you need to help them understand that a goal of science is to see commonalities where they may exist. Scientists also strive to formulate scientific laws and explanations that apply to many different examples of the same phenomenon. Therefore, Newton's Second Law applies to changes of motion of a great many objects from soccer balls and cars to planets and stars. Comprehending the commonalities in motion of so many different objects is not easy for students to see. However, it is one of the habits of mind that is an important outcome of this unit, as reflected in the second driving question listed above.

In summary, what is important to keep in mind about students' ideas and reasoning as you prepare for and teach this topic? The following list may help:

1. Acceleration must be approached in a way that enables students to understand that it represents a change in speed, second by second. Moreover, to produce a uniform acceleration over several seconds by pulling on a scale attached to a skateboard with a constant force of a few newtons, as suggested on pages 42 and 43 of the *Focus on Physical Science* text (see Figure 10.1), will require some practice and patience. The technique is not easy to hone to the level that produces good experimental results and meaningful data. Moreover, the examples pictured in the *Focus on Physical Science* text on pages 44 and 46 that show one person pulling two others in a wagon may present counterexamples of acceleration. In neither case do these two pictures give a strong image of acceleration. On the contrary, when I look at them, they both imply motion at a constant speed. Examine these pictures and see what your impressions are.

2. The distinction between force and mass must also be approached, and it will require some examples that go beyond what is presented in the text. However, I do not encourage you to use examples of "weightlessness" that are shown in videos of spacecraft like the space shuttle. Unless this is developed more extensively than is implied in this

chapter, discussion of the "weightlessness" experienced by astronauts in the space shuttle can be a source of further misconceptions. Instead, I recommend that you use comparisons between earth and moon to help students develop a concept of the constancy of mass and the dependency of weight on the force of gravity on a mass.

3. The unit of force, the *newton*, can be approached in a factual manner for most middle school students. It may be enough just to explain to students that the unit of force is called a *newton* and that it is about equal to the gravitational pull on a 100-gram mass at the surface of the earth. Then let students hold a 100-gram and a 1-kilogram mass and inform them that the force of gravity downward on their hand is 1 and 10 newtons, respectively. Although this may not engender understanding of this point, it does help to keep students from getting lost with the details of the force unit and keep their attention on the unit goal, which is to teach about Newton's Laws of Motion.

4. Finally, the inclusion of discussions of scientists' views about developing explanations that address multiple examples of a phenomenon is related to a topic from earlier chapters in this book that show the connection among experiences and data, identification of patterns in these, and the goal of explanation that leads to understanding the natural world. This is a habit of mind that characterizes science and is part of the goals of science teaching.

Reflection & Discussion Questions:

1. Did you realize that planning for instruction was this complex? And you have only begun the planning task!

2. Create your own summary of the difficulties that you anticipate that students will have in understanding changes in motion using Newton's Second Law. Do you think that identifying common misconceptions and difficulties that students may encounter in learning a topic is an important part of planning lesson sequences?

3. How would you explain the importance of this to a friend who is not a teacher?

Reflection & Discussion Questions:

1. Return to Figure 10.4 and rate the development on students' ideas and reasoning that you have prepared, according to the plan outlined in Chapter 9. Rate each item as S, P, or N, based on your interpretation of the adequacy the consideration of

students' ideas and reasoning in the section above.

2. Are there ideas that need further development? If so, what are they?

Planning Assessment of Students' Learning

With this knowledge about potential difficulties that students may encounter in learning this subject matter, we need to consider assessment at three levels—preassessment, summative assessment at the end of this lesson sequence, and formative assessment to monitor students' progress along the pathway of learning. What questions will you ask for preassessment of students to guide your initial steps in teaching? How will you monitor students' progress during instruction, and what questions will you ask as you conclude the topic? Figure 10.5 provides a summary of Category VI, Assessing Student Progress, and its criteria.

Using a backward design approach, how should you assess students at the end of instruction on this topic? Obviously, you need to return to your purposes and objectives for the lesson sequence to answer this question. As you can see from the following questions, the summative assessment mirrors the objectives of this lesson sequence.

A Sample Summative Assessment

Here are some sample questions that could be used as a summative assessment.

1. A board, one meter in length, is set up in the hallway of the school to make a small incline as shown below. A soccer ball is released from the top of the incline and allowed to roll down the board and continue along the hallway floor. Describe your prediction of the motion of the ball using some of the following terms: *velocity, speed, acceleration, speeding up, deceleration, slowing down,* and *changing direction.*

2. Using the same board to make a similar incline in a room that is carpeted, describe the forces acting on a ball as it rolls down the incline and along the carpet

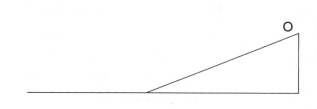

for 4 meters, gradually slowing down until it stops. Be sure to identify the forces acting on the ball in all three conditions:

a. Rolling down the incline,

b. Rolling along the floor, and

c. After it stopped.

3. At the start of a race, a runner accelerates from the starting line to a speed of 8 meters per second in 2 seconds and then runs the remaining race at that speed.

a. What is the acceleration of the runner during the first 2 seconds?

b. If the runner has a mass of 40 kg, what force must she exert to accelerate at the rate you found in part a?

c. What is the speed of the runner during the remainder of the race?

d. What is the acceleration of the runner during the remainder of the race?

4. A car accelerates from 0 to 30 m/sec (which is approximately 100 km per hour or 60 mph) in 6 seconds.

a. What is the rate of acceleration? Show your calculations and your answer in this space.

b. If the car has a mass of 900 kg, what force is required to accelerate it at that rate? Show your calculations and your answer in this space.

c. What units do you use for your answer? Why do you use these units?

5. A child's wagon is loaded with ten bricks, which give it a total mass of 15 kg. A force of 30 newtons is applied to the handle for 4 seconds.

a. What acceleration will this force give to the cart? Show your calculations and your answer in this space. (Note: Assume that this is a very high quality wagon with excellent tires and bearings in the wheels so that friction is small.)

b. Describe the motion of the cart during the 4 seconds.

c. Fill out the following table to show its speed at the end of each second.

Time (sec)	Speed (m/sec)
0	0
1	
2	
3	
4	

d. If the force were no longer applied at the end of the 4 seconds, what would happen to the speed of the wagon? I predict that it would

1. Continue to increase its speed

2. Keep on moving at the same speed

3. Slow down gradually

4. Stop immediately

Explain your choice.

e. If more bricks were added to the wagon and the same force were applied, would the acceleration increase, decrease, or remain the same?

6. Newton's Second Law is about how forces cause motion to change. If an object speeds up, slows down, stops motion, or changes direction, scientists claim that an unbalanced force has been applied to it. Why is this simple explanation thought of as such an important idea in science?

Reflection & Discussion Questions

Review the posttest above to see if it addresses the key objectives that were described for this lesson sequence. To do so, create a matrix that has the objectives on one axis and the question in the other. This will give you a "visual report" on the coverage of the objectives by the test items.

Now we need to turn our attention to a preassessment so we have information about what students understand and how they think about this topic as you initiate your lessons. Here are some items that can be used for preassessment, which could be given as part of the first day of the lesson sequence or a few days prior to the start of the unit so that you have time to use the data from it in planning lessons. In either case, you will need to explain to students why you are giving this preassessment.

A Sample Preassessment

P1. From your own experiences, describe what happens to a ball that is allowed to roll down an incline and then across a level *floor that is carpeted*, as in the following diagram.

P2. Explain what causes the ball to behave in the way you describe.

P3. As you ride in a car on a street with stoplights, describe the changes in motion that you and the car go through as the traffic lights change. Use terms such as *accelerate* (speed up) and *decelerate* (slow down). Also talk about the forces that the car and the seat belts exert on you as the car starts up from a red light and slows to a stop at another red light.

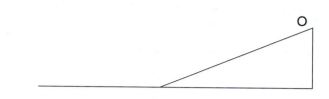

P4. Explain why an ordinary passenger car, a "hot" (powerful) sports car, and a large truck carrying a heavy load "get away" from red lights at different rates of speed. How does the weight of the three vehicles affect how quickly they are able to move away from the red light (accelerate)? How does the size or power of the engine affect how they are able to accelerate?

P5. Think for a moment about a sports event such as a football, baseball, or soccer game. How do terms like *acceleration, motion, change of speed, change in motion, change in direction*, and *force* help you describe what happens to the ball in these events? Choose one sporting event and use these terms to describe the motion of the ball during a play in that sport.

Analyzing Preassessment Data

An essential step in planning is to review the data from your preassessment to determine what it tells you about students' ideas and reasoning on the topic. What terms did your students use in explaining the motion of the ball in P1 and P2? Were these scientific terms or every day terms? What concepts did students use? Were they sound or naïve? What terms and what concepts and relationships did students use in responding to questions P3 and P4 about motions of vehicles? Was there consistency between their views about the rolling ball and the motion of the vehicles? What did P5 add to

your understanding of your students' ideas and reasoning about the connections among force, motion, and acceleration? As you look over these data, what inferences can you draw about your students' understanding about acceleration? How will this information influence your plans for this lesson sequence?

Formative assessment is developed as part of the instructional plan because it is integrated with instruction. Moreover, many instructional activities can also be assessment activities and many assessment activities can be instructional activities.

Reflection & Discussion Questions

Return to Figure 10.5 and rate the development on assessment according to the plan outlined in Chapter 9. Rate each item as S, P, or N, based on your interpretation of the adequacy of the development up to this point. It is obvious that VI.0, will receive a rating of N, as indicated in the previous paragraph.

Organizing Activities

As you think about organizing learning activities for your students, the Project 2061 criteria developed in the previous chapter include three categories that are relevant:

Category III, Engaging Students with Relevant Phenomena and Real World Examples

Category IV, Developing and Using Scientific Ideas

Category V, Promoting Student Thinking about Phenomena, Experiences, and Knowledge

All three of these are essential, and we will begin with Category III. This category is reproduced in Figure 10.7 to remind you of its details.

In addition to using the criteria included in these three categories, along with embedded assessment from

FIGURE 10.7 ■ Category VII. Engaging Students with Phenomena

III: Engaging Students with Phenomena	III.A. Providing a Variety of Relevant Phenomena	Does the lesson sequence provide multiple and varied phenomena to support the key ideas in the learning goals?
	III.B. Providing Firsthand and Vicarious Experiences	Does the lesson sequence provide an appropriate balance of firsthand and vicarious experiences with phenomena that are explicitly linked to the learning goals?
	III.C. Providing Opportunities for Students to Engage in Inquiry	Does the lesson sequence provide appropriate opportunities for students to engage in inquiry as a way of simultaneously experiencing both phenomena and ways of investigating them that simulate how scientists create new knowledge?

(Adapted from Project 2061, 2000.)

Category VI, you also will need to consider the instructional models you will use to guide your approach. It may be that you will need to use a combination of models, such as was described in Chapter 6 in *Food for Plants*. (Refer to Figure 6.2 to review this model.)

As you plan the activities for students in your lesson sequence, you need to give thought to its enactment in the classroom with your students. An instructional model like the one used in Chapter 6 can help as you think about what each activity does to

- Engage your students in learning
- Provide them with experiences with relevant phenomena on which to base science ideas and confront their existing naïve ideas and misconceptions
- Develop understanding of science ideas about the natural world by identifying patterns and relationships from their experiences
- Develop appropriate reasoning and reflection about the science content
- Understand how scientists create and validate new science knowledge
- Provide you and the students with information about their progress toward the educational objectives
- Contribute to long-range goals about understanding science, inquiry, its nature, and its place in students' lives
- Help them reflect on the ideas and their own understanding of and ability to use, these ideas

You also need to plan the sequence in which you schedule the activities, the time that each will require, and how that fits into the blocks or periods of your schedule. In addition, you need to consider the routines you wish to establish or maintain in your classroom. For example, many teachers use a "quick write" or "primer" at the beginning of class to help students recall ideas from the previous class meeting and other experiences, and to provide a springboard for the rest of the class. Others have a short writing or discussion activity at the end of the class to summarize the experiences of that day. In either case, these provide feedback to teachers about their students' progress toward goals. Activities like these also provide students with feedback about their learning and highlight important ideas for them.

PART 1 ■ Introducing Acceleration

This lesson sequence follows lessons on Newton's First Law of Motion, which precedes it in the *Focus on Physical Science* text. Therefore, students have some experience with two prerequisite concepts—force and

inertia. As a result, these concepts should be used in this lesson sequence. One idea that bridges Newton's First and Second Laws is that force is needed to affect the inertia of an object. That is, a force is needed to change the motion of an object, whether it is moving or not.

Another idea encompassed in Newton's First Law that is difficult for students to internalize is that motion is a natural state. That is, moving objects will keep moving in a straight line unless some force retards or increases their motion or changes their direction. A force is not needed to keep the object moving.

This idea is very simple! However, it lies outside of everyday experience. For us, here on earth, motion does not appear to be a natural state. Instead, rest seems more natural, because if we stop pushing, moving objects stop either immediately or after a short time. The idea that motion is natural was part of the genius of Newton who saw the commonality between motion on earth and motion of objects in the heavens. This is the idea of inertia. It is a way of thinking about motion that scientists have accepted for about three hundred years. It is different from our common experiences, but it is an effective way of thinking about motion. As we work to understand Newton's Second Law, we also need to make some adjustment in our way of thinking about how objects speed up and slow down.

Activity 1. As you make the transition from the prior topic to this lesson sequence, students should be reminded that we are trying to understand motion at many levels and through many examples. You could begin by setting the stage for the first activity presented in the *Focus on Physical Science* textbook on pages 42 and 43 by discussing the motion of a soccer ball in a game. (I suggest having a soccer ball in the room as a prop that can be used to simulate the moves described below; or you can substitute your own favorite sport, using the appropriate prop.) Here is a possible scenario for the introduction:

We are going to continue our study of motion by talking about changing motion–we will look at changes in the direction or speed of motion. To begin, let's think for a few minutes about a soccer game. We will focus on a single play, which I have diagrammed on the chalkboard. Imagine that two forwards (X_1 and X_2) on our team are

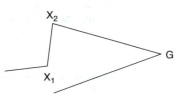

bringing the ball toward the opposing team's goal. X_1 kicks a lateral pass to X_2, who then kicks the ball toward the goal. The goalie (G) blocks the kick and knocks it back away from the goal net. How would you describe the motions of the ball? Let's use this diagram to help us understand what is occurring:

These are some questions you can pose to engage students:

- What causes the ball to change direction?
- Does it also change its speed?
- Why did it change direction and/or speed?
- What did X_1, X_2, and G do to make the ball change direction and/or speed?

Reflection & Discussion Questions

1. How do the activities represented in the previous paragraphs reflect Category III (Figure 10.7) on engagement? What is missing at this point? What would you add?

2. Do you think that engagement is a one-time concern or is it a part of every activity?

At this point in the lesson sequence you will begin helping students develop and use the experiences and ideas that were part of the engagement activity, Activity 1. The focus now shifts to Categories IV and V, which are displayed in Figure 10.8.

Activity 2 and Assessment. The questions raised in Activity 1, and those below, are designed to deepen the conversation and engage students in thinking about acceleration and the forces that cause it. This activity not only serves to foster learning about the topic, but also can be a source of information about students' understanding as they begin the study. Therefore, it provides additional data about students' ideas and reasoning. Your role is to listen carefully to students' responses. To help you and the students process the data, you may wish to record key ideas that come from this discussion on the chalkboard or your overhead projector. This gives you a record of these ideas that you can review after class to learn more about your students' thinking.

In enacting this section of the lesson as a whole-class discussion, be sure to engage all students in it so that you can learn about their ideas at the same time as you introduce the concept of acceleration and its connection to forces. You may continue the lesson with questions like those that follow:

- Let's suppose that X_2 stopped the ball and then kicked it toward the goal. How would you describe the motion of the ball as it went from being stopped to moving rapidly toward the goal?

- Was there a short period of time when X_2 caused the ball to slow down and stop? Was there also a short period of time when X_2 kicked the ball that it was speeding up? (What does this have to do with coaches stressing the importance of "follow through" when you throw, hit, or kick a ball?)

- Can you identify the force that was exerted on the ball when X_2 made it stop? What force made it accelerate toward the goalie? Then, as it traveled toward the goal, do you think it would have maintained its speed or did it slow down? What might have made it slow down?

- As the goalie connected with the ball and changed its direction, was there a time when it was first slowing down very quickly and then speeding up very quickly in the opposite direction?

During this time, you can introduce the terms *acceleration* and *deceleration* to help the students talk about how force from the players' feet and bodies causes the ball to speed up, slow down, and change direction. You should use terms that relate to *inertia* as part of the discussion here to further expand students' ability to use that concept. (Note: The previous discussion could be done as a whole-class group or by small groups of students followed by a shorter whole-class discussion. There are advantages and disadvantages to either approach. Which approach to follow is a decision you must make.)

Activity 3. After a time discussing acceleration (changes in motion) and its relation to forces on the ball, you can segue into the activity on pages 42 and 43 of the *Focus on Physical Science* text. The activity on these pages is nicely described, with adequate directions, except for lack of guidance on *techniques* needed to obtain meaningful results. However, you will need to provide students with guidance on these techniques, including how to pull with a uniform force of 2 newtons. You will need to give special attention to items 3 and 5 in the student text. The details on the teacher's pages also provide important hints for you about extensions of the lesson.

You also will need to guide students in how to determine acceleration. Students will find this quite difficult because they cannot measure acceleration directly. Instead they will measure time required for the skateboard to travel across a distance of 1 meter, starting from rest, when a constant force is applied to it. Then they will need to calculate acceleration using the procedure described in Steps 1 through 4 of "Analyze and Conclude" on page 43. The table at the bottom of student page 42 provides students with a way of keeping track of their data and also helps them keep organized as they do their calculations. An example is provided in the table at the bottom of teacher page 43.

FIGURE 10.8 ■ Categories IV and V

Category	Criteria	Questions to Guide Planning
IV: Developing and Using Scientific Ideas	IV.A. Providing Evidence for Learning and the Learning Goals	Does the lesson sequence use scientific evidence to support learning, and suggest ways to help students develop a sense of the validity of the scientific knowledge and skills encompassed by the learning goals for the lesson sequence?
	IV.B. Introducing Terms and Procedures Meaningfully	Does the lesson sequence introduce terms and procedures in the context of experiences with phenomena and use them to effectively communicate about the learning goals, understandings, and skills that underlie them?
	IV.C. Representing Ideas Effectively	Does the lesson sequence include accurate and comprehensible representations[1] of the conceptual understandings and skills that underlie the learning goals?
	IV.D. Connecting and Synthesizing Ideas	Does the lesson sequence explicitly make appropriate connections among individual instances of ideas and skills to support achievement of specific learning goals?
	IV.E. Demonstrating Skills and Use of Knowledge	Does the lesson sequence demonstrate skills and the use of knowledge related to the learning goals?
	IV.F. Providing Practice	Does the lesson sequence provide questions and/or tasks in a variety of situations for students to practice knowledge or skills related to the learning goals?
V: Promoting Student Thinking about Phenomena Experiences and Knowledge	V.0. Encouraging Students to Base Their Understanding in Data from Investigations and Experiences	Does the lesson sequence routinely require that all students connect their ideas and explanations with data from observations and investigations? Does the lesson sequence build on students' investigations?
	V.A. Encouraging Students to Explain Their Ideas	Does the lesson routinely require that all students express, clarify, justify, interpret, and represent their ideas about the topic and phenomena underlying the learning goals and for having students get feedback?
	V.B. Guiding Interpretation and Reasoning	Does the lesson include questions and/or tasks that guide students' interpretation and reasoning about experiences with phenomena, representations, and/or readings related to the topic and phenomena underlying the learning goals?
	V.C. Encouraging Students to Think about What They Have Learned	Does the lesson suggest ways to have students check and reflect on their own progress toward the learning goals, following instruction related to the topic and phenomena?
	V.D. Encouraging Recognition that Science Knowledge Is Dynamic	Do lessons provide students with a perspective that science knowledge can change as a consequence of new data and/or new ways of viewing existing data?
	V.E. Encouraging Recognition that Science Knowledge Is Socially Constructed	Do lessons help students recognize that science knowledge is constructed by scientists from their interpretations of data from observations and experiments? Do lessons help students recognize that the scientific enterprise operates on an agreed-upon set of rules for validating scientific knowledge?

[1]By representations we mean drawings, diagrams, graphs, images, analogies, and metaphors or other verbal statements, models and simulations, role-playing, etc.

(Adapted from Project 2061, 2000.)

Unfortunately, this table is not oriented in the same way as the students' table on page 42, which adds another possible confusion.

Informal Assessment. As you move around the room and watch students carry out the initial experiment with the skateboard, you should look for successes and problems, especially problems with techniques and concepts that will impede collection of useful data and developing the intended understanding. Are the students accelerating the skateboard with a constant force over the 1 meter track? Do they interpret the motion of the skateboard as acceleration? Do they see its motion as gradually increasing in speed as a result of the force being applied? Feel free to ask questions as you observe. General questions such as "What are you trying to show with this experiment?" and "Are your results what you expected?" are important. More specific questions also can be helpful to students. For example, "Why is it important to keep a steady force of 1 newton as you pull the skateboard?" or "Show me how you were able to pull with a force of 1 newton steadily?" or "What data have you recorded so far?"

Activity 4 and Assessment. Before the students continue with "Design an Experiment" on page 43, discussion of results will be useful when students conclude the first lab activity described on pages 42 and 43 to help them create personal meaning from the experiences that it provided. Many students have difficulty making the connection between activities and ideas that they represent. To help focus your discussion, you may wish to have groups of students record their data on the chalkboard so that it can be examined by all class members. To lead off a discussion with either small groups or the whole class, you should ask questions such as:

- What were the results of your activities with the skateboard? (This open question may engender a list of difficulties that students encountered with measuring techniques. These need attention, but you should have students move on after a time to consider the data that they acquired.)

- What did these results show you about acceleration and its relation to the force applied and the variations in mass of the skateboard that were tested?

- How did you measure acceleration of the skateboard? Were you able to measure it directly? What were the steps in determining acceleration? Do they make sense to you? How would you describe the process of measuring acceleration so that a classmate who missed today's class would understand it and be able to carry out the investigation?

Activity 5 and Assessment. Following this discussion, you should ask students to write a summary of their findings and the meaning that they drew from them, either as individual work or as a group activity. These written summaries are important learning opportunities for students *and* useful sources of information about students' progress toward the objectives of the lesson sequence.

Reflection & Discussion Questions

1. In the instructional sequence above, I have attempted to show how assessment, especially preassessment and formative assessment, can be integrated into instruction. This allows you to continuously monitor students' progress toward objectives and the difficulties they are having with the subject matter. How might this make your work as a teacher easier? What additional demands does this approach place on you?

2. I also have tried to show how a single hands-on activity really is five activities as you (1) set the stage for it, (2) informally pre-assess students' comprehension of the concepts underlying the activity, (3) do the hands-on activity, (4) help students create meaning from the experience, and (5) assess students on their understanding of the concept underlying the activity. Did you realize how complex your work is, especially when you are teaching for understanding? Explain why this complex approach is essential if students are to understand and be able to use the ideas and skills they learn in science.

3. As in previous cases, you may want to think about how you would explain this to a friend who is not a teacher. Or you could think about how you would explain it to an experienced colleague who tends to teach using the "old" paradigm.

Activity 6. The last paragraph on student page 43, under the heading "Design an Experiment" gives a useful hint at how to expand the highly directed observational activity into a valid inquiry activity. I strongly encourage you to include this activity as part of your plan so that students can have a controlled experiment in which the mass of the skateboard is changed by loading it with objects such as one, two, and three books to increase the mass, and then repeating the experiment as described on page 42. However, it will be important to only change one variable at a time. That is, measure the effect of 2 newtons of force pulling on a skateboard with one book, then two books, then three books. This could be followed with another experiment in which you use a force of 3 newtons with one, two, and three books on the skateboard. If your students are highly motivated and high achievers, you also could have them determine the mass of the skateboard and its different loads in kilograms, making this experiment more quantitative to enable use of the formulas shown on page 45. However, it is not necessary for most students as it adds an additional dimension to the topic that will be addressed in high school physics.

PART 2 ■ Formalizing Ideas about Acceleration

Moving on to the next part of this lesson sequence, you see that the purpose here is to formalize the experiences from the lab with the skateboard using Newton's Second Law as an organizing concept. Two hands-on activities are suggested, one in the teacher's pages and one in at the top of student page 44 of *Focus on PhysicaleScience* text. They are different as one focuses on the effect of force on acceleration of a constant mass, whereas the other measures the effect of mass on acceleration when force is held constant. On student page 44, "How do rocks roll?" is quite similar to the activity on page 43, "Designing an Experiment," although it is not cast as an inquiry. Instead it is highly directive. "Activating Prior Knowledge" on teacher page 44 is somewhat less directive. Both activities reinforce what was learned on the two previous pages.

Reflection & Discussion Questions

Teachers must make many instructional decisions each day. Whether to use one or both of these activities is one such decision. What information would you use to decide whether or not to use these activities? How would you decide?

In these activities, you could ask students to make predictions of the outcomes and then test their predictions to foster that level of scientific thinking. You also should make a point in these two activities about the importance of controlling variables, allowing only one variable to change at a time.

Both provide firsthand experience with the connection among force, mass, and acceleration. Because acceleration is not an easy topic for students to comprehend, especially because it is not directly measurable, students should benefit from more practice in determining it.

Activity 7. A possible course of action would be to divide your class in half, and have each half, working in small groups, do one of the activities and then report on their results. The group that conducted "Activating Prior Knowledge" would study the effect of changing force on the acceleration of an object while holding mass constant, and the other group ("How do rocks roll?") would study the effect of changing the mass of the object being accelerated with the force being held constant. Having the two halves of your class then report their findings could be a useful outcome. Part of this reporting could deal with identifying the differences between the two investigations.

As the groups of students engage in either of these studies, you will need to help the students keep their focus on acceleration. Students will tend to think about the results only in terms of speed. *Therefore, you will need to have each group identify how they will measure acceleration.* To help students design a means of measuring acceleration, you can have them refer to the skateboard activity. There, they had a means of measuring acceleration by measuring the time required for the skateboard to travel one meter, and then they calculated the acceleration.

The students doing "Activating Prior Knowledge" have a new challenge because the force causing acceleration of the golf ball only acts on the ball for a very short time. Therefore, the acceleration is not easy to measure. This could be treated simply as a descriptive or qualitative experience with acceleration; or it could be a high-level experience, where students must design the means of measuring acceleration that happens in a fraction of a second. A productive activity could be to have your students engage in some hands-on activities with the bent ruler and golf ball, and then engage in "thought experiments" about how to measure acceleration of the ball.

Informal Assessment. As your students engage in these activities, you should be an astute observer of their talk and actions. As you watch and listen, what are they saying about their procedures? Are they talking about acceleration and speed appropriately, as two different phenomena? Or are they confusing them or failing to distinguish between them? Also, in their data tables, do they have a sense of the connection between time that an object is being accelerated and the distance covered by the object? Do they see that these two numbers allow them to calculate average speed over the time of acceleration? Do they then understand how final speed is calculated, and how acceleration is derived from it? As you can tell from these questions, measuring acceleration is complex. The concept may be easy to comprehend at one level, but it is also is easy to become confused when you try to quantify it. One pitfall with "Activating Prior Knowledge" lies in measuring the time and distance in which the force is being applied to the golf ball with the bent ruler.

Activity 8 and Assessment. Following completion of the tasks above, some significant thought and activity will be needed to help students further their understanding of what they have just done and how it connects with (a) what they did in the skateboard experiments and (b) the driving questions of this lesson sequence:

These activities should help students get a clear picture of the difference between acceleration and

---

How can we understand the motion of a soccer ball during play?

How do scientists think about and describe motion of objects?

---

speed. They also need to be designed to help students comprehend how acceleration is measured. You might start with a question such as the following:

We now need to think about what we have been able to learn from these two activities and how they connect with the activities we did yesterday with the skateboard. How were the activities today like the activities we did yesterday, and how were they different?

A few minutes of this discussion with important differences and similarities listed on the board will give you an idea of what students are understanding and the connections they are making. It also should help students further grasp the concept of acceleration and how the force that is exerted and the mass of the object being accelerated are related.

Then you could shift to the following pair of questions since two different activities were just completed:

- In "How do rocks roll?," how was acceleration measured?
- What ideas did you come up with to measure acceleration in "Activating Prior Knowledge" in which the golf ball was accelerated with the bent ruler?

(Note: You may want to change the activity grouping here from whole class to small groups for a few minutes to give students a chance to construct an answer that is appropriate for the task they completed. Small-group settings increase the opportunity for students to participate actively. The answers to these questions are complex, and giving the students four or five minutes to construct an answer should result in higher participation, as more students will have ideas to contribute.)

Students in the former group, who placed rocks in the toy trucks to measure the affect of changing the mass on acceleration, should be able to repeat the procedures that they used in the skateboard activity. This is a rather direct transfer of learning from one task to another one that is very similar. This should be a good review and consolidation of ideas from the previous activity and application to a new, similar task. Questions such as the following will be helpful as you observe groups and when you return to whole-class discussion after a few minutes in the small groups:

- How did you determine the average speed of the truck across the distance? Did you use one meter as the distance? If not, what distance did you use?
- How did you obtain the final speed of the truck in each case?
- How did you find the acceleration of the truck in each case?

You may need to ask additional questions and record specific data on the chalkboard or overhead to help students grasp the logic of the procedure to measure acceleration. The skateboard activity and this one may be the first time that students have been asked to determine a quantity by indirect means. Therefore, it won't be easy for them. However, it is a good opportunity for them to participate in scientific reasoning from data to one indirect measure (average speed) to further indirect measures (final velocity and acceleration) and to understand what these indirect measures tell us about motion.

To discuss the golf ball activity, you will need to be sure that students are "tuned in" to the meaning that the activity with the trucks has for understanding (1) the relation between mass and acceleration and (2) Newton's Second Law. Specifically *do your students understand that when the amount of force causing acceleration is not changed, increasing the mass of the object being accelerated results in a smaller rate of acceleration? Conversely, do your students understand that as the mass is decreased, with force being constant, acceleration increases?* Said more simply, when force is not changed, increased mass decreases acceleration *or* decreased mass increases acceleration. This is an *inverse* relationship!

Now you will need to address the more difficult task of measuring the accelerating force and the acceleration of the golf ball. This could be done, but it is not easy, especially for students of this age. However, the experience could be handled in a descriptive manner so that students are able to construct some meaning from it.

The essential feature of this activity lies in the fact that things happen rapidly over a short distance, similar to the soccer example. You could begin by asking two students to describe and demonstrate the activity for their peers who did not participate in it. You or these students need to be sure to point out that the force causing the acceleration only affected the ball during the fraction of a second that it was in contact with the ball. Questions such as the following will be good prompts for a meaningful discussion:

- When was the ball being accelerated?
- What was the force that caused the ball to accelerate?

(Note: If you wanted to go high tech, you could make a video of a few examples of the ruler accelerating the golf ball and then play it on a video editing program so that you could see the ball accelerating each 1/30 of a second.)

Students may have difficulty comprehending the idea that acceleration is occurring only when the ruler is contacting the ball, and that time is very short. You may wish to use a diagram like the following to help students see this:

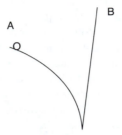

Ask the following questions:

- The curved line represents the bent ruler and the straight line is the ruler after it is released. What does the distance from A to B represent?
- When is the ball being accelerated?
- How could you measure the time that it takes for the ruler to move from A to B?
- How could you measure the force on the ball while it is being accelerated? If you were to pull the ruler back (to the left) half as far as shown in the diagram above, what force would the ruler exert on the ball when released? Would it be more, less, or the same as in the condition shown in the diagram?
- Which position would result in a greater acceleration for the golf ball?

Can you obtain agreement on the answers to these questions? Do students differ in their ideas on this? If so, what are their reasons for the different answers? (Note: This may be an excellent access to students' misconceptions that are emerging as they progress through the lesson sequence.)

Depending on time that is available and students' interest, you may wish to present this challenge to students:

How could you measure the speed of the ball or its acceleration?

As with the previous activity, before you leave it and go on to the introduction of Newton's Second Law, you will need to be sure that students are "tuned in" to the meaning that this activity has for understanding (1) acceleration, (2) the relation between force and acceleration, and (3) Newton's Second Law. Specifically, *do your students understand that when the mass being*

accelerated is not changed, increasing force of the object being accelerated results in a greater rate of acceleration? Conversely, do students understand that as the force is decreased, with mass being constant, acceleration decreases? Do they also understand that force and acceleration are directly proportional when mass is held constant? For example, do they understand that smaller masses are easier to accelerate than larger ones? Do they comprehend the meaning of the following statements?

- When mass is held constant, force and acceleration are directly related.
- Mass and acceleration are inversely related if force is constant.

Can they describe these ideas effectively using their own terminology?

You may also need to reinforce the concept of acceleration with activities like those shown below.

Activity 9 and Assessment. Present students with a problem like the following:

A car starts moving forward from a stopped position and reaches a speed of 50 km/hr in 5 seconds. (50 km/hr is approximately 30 miles per hour or 15 meters/second.) What is the rate of acceleration?

Students should be able to calculate this and obtain the answers quite easily with appropriate units. Ask them to complete the following table showing the speed of the car each second from 0 to 5 seconds.

Time (sec)	Speed (m/sec)	Speed (km/hr)	Speed (miles/hr)
0	0		
1			
2			
3			
4			
5			

Have students state the acceleration of the car from this table.

Reflection & Discussion Questions

1. Why was this labeled as both activity and assessment?
2. How would you use it as a learning activity? How would you use it as an inquiry activity?
3. What does it teach about the nature of science?
4. How does it become an assessment activity? What does it help you to assess?

Note: You could give very glib answers to these questions, but it would be much more meaningful if you were to ponder them seriously and discuss them with professional colleagues and others in your life.

Activity 10. Connecting with the Driving Questions of This Lesson Sequence

How do the activities thus far in this lesson sequence connect with the driving questions?

- How can we understand the motion of a soccer ball during play?
- How do scientists think about and describe motion of objects?

It is possible for you to ignore them, but it may diminish the effectiveness of the lessons to do so, because some students may not be excited by accelerating skateboards and toy trucks. Movements of soccer balls may be more exciting to eighth graders. However, the bent ruler and golf ball are closely related to the first driving question, because this activity represents the rapid changes in motion of soccer balls more closely than do accelerating skateboards and toy trucks.

This makes a good connection with the motion of the soccer ball in a game. It may be helpful here to ask the following question:

How is the bent ruler and golf ball system similar to the soccer ball when it is kicked or headed?

The soccer ball changes direction and speed many times in a minute, but the acceleration of the ball only occurs when a foot or another body part is exerting a force on the ball. Each of those contacts between the ball and a player's foot or other part of their body, which is the accelerating force, lasts only a small fraction of a second and the acceleration occurs very quickly over a short distance. With the bent ruler and golf ball you have a similar condition. The force that causes the acceleration only lasts a fraction of a second and it occurs over a short distance. Much more can be said about this in a later section of the textbook on this topic, especially during the section on Newton's Third Law.

What should students have learned about how scientists think about and describe motion from their experiences thus far in the lesson sequence? You may want to ask the following question and have students in groups spend five to ten minutes discussing it, followed by a few minutes of reporting students' ideas. Then you can hold a whole-class discussion on the topic. The question to open discussion in small groups might be:

From your experiences with skateboards, toy trucks, and golf balls over the past few days, how would you respond to the second driving question about how scientists think about and talk about motion?

What should you expect from students at this time? You may need to add some prompts to help students think about this topic. For example, you may need to help the students focus on the use of terms like *average speed, final speed, acceleration, force,* and *mass.* You also may need to ask about how scientists obtain and use data through careful measurements, so that they can find agreement and reproduce results. Another point could be that various groups compare and discuss results as part of the process of giving meaning to data and experiences. You might also raise the issue of taking three trials and averaging them as a way of increasing reproducibility of results and agreement among different working groups.

Reflection & Discussion Questions

1. Why is a sequence of activities like the one suggested above (i.e., "have students in groups spend five to ten minutes discussing it, followed by a few minutes of reporting students' ideas. Then you can hold a whole-class discussion on the topic.") beneficial and worthy of the time it requires?

2. Why is talking about how scientists think and talk about motion an important topic for consideration?

Reflection & Discussion Questions

Refer to Figure 10.8 and make a check to see which of the criteria have been addressed in the plans thus far. For those that have been addressed, make a judgment of the adequacy of the opportunities for students to learn that are provided by the activities. A few notes on this point at this time would be useful in further plans.

PART 3 ■ Exploring Newton's Second Law

Looking at the *Focus on Physical Science* text on pages 44 through 46, you can see that the emphasis shifts from collecting and interpreting data to an examination of Newton's Second Law. Activities up to this point have been designed to prepare students to consider Newton's Second Law. Without this background, including an understanding of acceleration, the law is not very meaningful. A combination of readings, thought experiments with visuals, and quantitative problem solving is included in the textbook to assist students in understanding Newton's Second Law.

You will also note near the beginning of the first paragraph on page 44 that the textbook authors included a question and a tip to guide reading. The question keeps the key point of the lesson sequence in front of students: "How are force and mass related to acceleration?" The reading tip also reinforces this idea, "As you read, describe in your own words the relationship between force, mass and acceleration." More important, it suggests that students create their own way of stating the relationship, which adds an important action in learning.

The text materials can be helpful to you and your students, but there are some pitfalls to avoid. First, students may interpret the illustrations as showing constant motion, or no motion, instead of acceleration. Also, students very probably learned before they reached grade 8 that it is hard to pull a wagon with two people in it and generate a constant acceleration. Because students often confuse speed and acceleration, you will need to be watchful that some students don't misinterpret the diagrams on pages 44 and 46. However, teacher page 46 has a section with the title "Using the Visuals: Figure 6" that provides you with some useful questions to guide your effective use of the illustrations. Also, the first paragraph of the reading focuses students on acceleration and its relation to force and mass. Second, it is predictable that students will need help in comprehending the formulas on page 45 and in connecting them to the hands-on experiences they have had in the lesson sequence so far. Third, the demonstration activity suggested on teacher page 45 under the heading "2. Facilitate Newton's Second Law of Motion" is tricky to execute and get good results. You will need to practice the demonstration a few times before class so that you are able to make it work well.

There is a sample problem and two practice problems on page 45 for your use. These can be helpful in formulating your plan for helping students use the book to guide their learning. Page 46 provides a two-paragraph synopsis of the previous page on Newton's Second Law and a review activity. Questions 1, 2, and 4 in this review are useful, but question 3 reintroduces fuzziness about speed and acceleration. It asks:

> Suppose you know the acceleration of a shopping cart as it rolls down a supermarket aisle. You want to find the net force with which it was pushed. What other information do you need in order to find the force?

This could become a useful puzzle for the students. You could ask them such questions as the following to try to make sense of the question:

- What mistake did the writer of this question make? (Unless the supermarket aisle is sloping substantially, the cart will not roll down the aisle and accelerate. It needs a force to accelerate and the term *rolling* implies that it is not being pushed—that it is moving on its own.)

- Or did we make a mistake in thinking that acceleration must always mean "speeding up"? Could the author have meant a "negative acceleration" or deceleration in this question?

- How could the question be rephrased to make it scientifically correct? (One possibility is to say, "A supermarket shopping cart is rolling along an aisle and slowing down (decelerating) at a rate that you know. You want to find out the force of friction that is slowing it down. What other information would you need to know in order to find the force?") This parallels the first question and the answer is "mass of the cart."

- Another question that could be asked is "How many ways could you think of to find out the force of friction that is slowing the cart?" This becomes a creative problem-solving question for students.

Activity 11 and Assessment. As you begin to develop the quantitative use of Newton's Second Law, on pages 44 and 45, most students will need conceptual help with drawing meaning from the text reading and the equations. Also, this is where the students will develop the main understandings about the connection among force, mass, and acceleration, which is what Newton's Second Law is about. Students can easily memorize a concise statement of this law, without understanding its meaning or without being able to use it. A multistep approach will be necessary here to permit students to (a) process the information on these pages, (b) come away with an understanding of Newton's Second Law, and (c) be able to use it in thinking about motion in their daily lives. Students will need guidance to interpret and understand the content of these two pages. A possible strategy follows:

Step 1: Give students about ten minutes to read and study the six short paragraphs on text pages 44 and 45.

Step 2: Talk with them about what they read, referring back to the text material so that they draw meaning from their experience over the last few days and their reading of the printed material on these two pages, including the equations that are presented. Students probably will need support and help from you to do this, as the representations in the text are likely to be new to them. Even if your grade 8 students have studied algebra, the connection between the equations and the experiences the students have had in the last few lessons on force and acceleration probably will be weak.

For your students, representing physical events with equations probably is a new way of thinking about the world.

The first equation ($F = ma$) and the representation of the newton ($1N = 1$ kg $\times$ 1 m/s^2) are the subject of the demonstration on the same teacher page.

Step 3: I suggest that you link these by doing the demonstration as part of your presentation and the discussion. This will enable students to revisit the idea of acceleration and its relation to force and mass.

Step 4: As part of the demonstration, you can reiterate the idea of representing acceleration units as m/s^2. These units can be problematic unless you reiterate a point that you made earlier that acceleration is the rate of increasing speed, measured in m/s, for each second of acceleration. Therefore, acceleration is how much the speed in meters per second changes each second, or meters per second per second. The shorthand for this is m/s^2. Not an easy set of ideas for students! It takes time and thought for students to comprehend the meaning!

Step 5: The second equation ($a = f/m$) is the central representation of Newton's Second Law for this lesson sequence. As force on an object increases, so does its acceleration, if the mass does not change. If you add mass to the object being accelerated, its acceleration will decrease if force does not change. For example, a heavily loaded truck will not accelerate as rapidly as the same truck with a smaller load. Giving examples of fractions here makes a connection for students with their experiences in mathematics. As the denominator of a fraction increases, the quantity that the fraction represents decreases. For example, 1/4 is smaller than 1/2, and 1/100 is smaller yet. The same holds for $a = f/m$.

Step 6: Now it is time to give students a few minutes to reflect the meaning they now have regarding Newton's Second Law as represented by $a = f/m$. You can ask your students:

- What do you understand from the term *acceleration*?
- What does the right hand side of the equation mean?
- What does this equation tell you about the motion of objects such as skateboards, cars, and soccer balls?

(Bringing up specific examples here would be useful to connect their experiences with the representation of the law.)

Step 7: A formal application of the law to a familiar scene regarding acceleration would be helpful here. Have students consider 1000 kg car and a 4000 kg truck in city traffic. Ask questions like the following about the two as they move along from one traffic light the next one:

- What would you predict about their acceleration if the two vehicles were to exert the same force when the light changed to green? (Note: Be sure to have students make a qualitative description based on this question, before moving on to the quantitative description on the next question.)
- If the engine of each vehicle delivered a force of 2000 newtons, what would the acceleration of each vehicle be?
- If these two vehicles were to start ahead when the light changes to green, and accelerate at the same rate, what would you know about the force that is accelerating each?
- Suppose the two vehicles are traveling side by side at the same speed as they approach the next traffic light and the light changes. Both come to a stop at the same time. What could you predict about the force exerted by the brakes on each vehicle?

Reflection & Discussion Questions

1. Why are the seven steps in Activity 11 important? What is the purpose of this set of activities at this time?

2. What potential or opportunities to learn does Activity 11 provide for your students' knowledge and understanding?

3. Why are both qualitative and quantitative applications of Newton's Second Law useful?

Activity 12. Question 4 in the Review on page 46 would be beneficial for groups to talk about for three or four minutes. It asks, "Suppose you doubled the force acting on an object. In what way could you change its mass to keep its acceleration unchanged?" Students need to be able to justify their answer. Therefore, students should be alerted to the fact that you will expect them to explain why they believe their answer to this question is correct. After a few minutes of small-group discussion, you could have students take one of three actions:

1. Reconvene and present their answer and their justification orally to the group.

2. Write their answers and justifications as a group task.

3. Write answers and justifications individually.

Each of these options presents an opportunity for the students to reflect on and construct deeper meaning about acceleration and Newton's Second Law. Each also provides you with an excellent opportunity to monitor students' ideas and reasoning on this topic.

Activity 13 and Assessment. As you bring this lesson sequence to a close, you need to return to the original purposes set out at the beginning. Activity 13 deals with the first of the two driving questions, and Activity 14 deals with the second.

On revisiting the topic of soccer again, you could pose a question about a long-kick contest where players all line up with a ball in front of each player. Then each kicks the ball with as much force as possible to give it the maximum acceleration. The questions for students, working in groups of three or four, about this contest are as follows:

- Why might a player with long legs have an advantage over players with shorter legs?
- What would a short-legged player need to do to beat a long-legged player in this contest?
- What do you predict would be the result if three players of equal leg strength and leg length were to compete and one had a ball placed in front of him/her that had gotten very wet, another had a normal soccer ball, and one had a lighter ball that had only half the mass of a normal soccer ball? Whose ball would travel the farthest? Whose would travel the least distance? Why do you think that your prediction is correct? How could you design an experiment that would test your prediction?

This would be a good activity to be introduced to the whole class and then allow for small-group discussion for a few minutes, followed by more whole-class discussion. This enables students to think about, and discuss, the problem in a low-risk setting, then to formulate an answer, and finally to report it to the whole class where comparisons can be made. You may want to record the results of each group's thinking as they report, and then use these data as a basis for the discussion, as it is likely that all three ball masses will be thought by one or more groups as showing the longest flight. Of course, it is students' reasoning and logical argument that constitute the important outcome of this activity for both students and you as an assessor.

Activity 14 and Assessment. One more consideration is the second driving question about *how scientists think about and talk about motion.* Ask students how they would answer the question now that they have come nearly to the end of this lesson sequence. This could be a useful whole-class discussion that might begin with students making some notes, individually, about how they

would answer it before discussion started. That would cause all students to give it some thought instead of relying on the more vocal students to answer for them.

Appropriate responses are described earlier in this chapter. Please refer back to that description.

Reflection & Discussion Questions

Return to Figures 10.7 and 10.8 and rate the development on assessment according to the plan outlined in Chapter 9. Rate each item as S, P, or N, based on your interpretation of the adequacy of the development up to this point.

This task will require more than just a few minutes. You should reflect on the work that has been presented here and assess whether it matches the framework developed in Chapters 8 and 9. Also, take time to think about and describe why this assessment task is of value.

Developing a Schedule of Activities

It has been a long journey to plan this series of activities. Now you need to think about putting them in a daily sequence and what might be appropriate homework (indicated by HW in the Figure 10.9) activities and what would best be done in class. If we assume that your class periods are about fifty minutes duration, Figure 10.9 provides that organization. If class periods are of a different duration, you will need to do some modification to enable it to fit into your time blocks.

Reflection & Discussion Questions

1. Why is scheduling activities so that they fit in the available time an important part of the planning process? Would you find it easier if you were to think about scheduling at the same time you think about planning activities than to leave the scheduling to the end?

2. What else needs to be done to prepare for enactment of the lessons, now that planning has progressed this far?

3. What might cause you to modify your plans as you are in the process of enacting them?

I hope that this experience has been meaningful to you. It highlights the complexity of planning a lesson sequence. It also highlights the high-level professional knowledge that teachers must have to be effective in teaching complex ideas, which constitute science knowledge. It also highlights the difficulties and demands on teachers that arise in teaching using inquiry.

FIGURE 10.9 ■ Scheduling Activities

Day	Activity	Time	Purpose
1	Pretest	15	Obtain data on students' entry-level knowledge of the topic
	1	10	Introduce students to the lesson sequence
	2	20	Engage students with ideas about acceleration and motion
	3	20	Introduce the skateboard activity and give students practice with using a constant force to produce acceleration
2	3	20	Conduct the skateboard lab activity
	4	20	Discuss data and meaning from skateboard activity
	5	10	Individual writing about the meaning of the skateboard experience
	HW		Describe at least three examples of acceleration that you see outside of school including the mass that was accelerated and the nature of the force causing the acceleration
3	HW	10	Check students' findings from homework by recording different categories of objects being accelerated; e.g., change of direction or speed of vehicles, people, balls in sports, etc.
	6	50	Design and conduct an experiment about the relation of force, mass, and acceleration; include pre-lab discussion, the lab activity, and post-lab discussion
4	7	20	Lab activities to further explore accelerated motion
	8	30	Use data from days 2–4 to develop a clear definition of acceleration and the relationships with mass and force
	HW		Students are given the following task: Write a letter that explains acceleration to a friend in another class. Use diagrams to aid your explanation. Be sure to include the ideas of acceleration as change of speed and/or direction, and as result of a force on a mass
5	HW	10	Collect letters and evaluate them to determine students' understanding of acceleration as change of speed and/or direction, and as result of a force on a mass. Take a few minutes to hear students' reactions to the assignment. For example, ask, "How did the assignment help improve your understanding of acceleration?"
	9	15	Apply quantitative ideas on acceleration
	10	15	Consideration of the driving questions: Apply what has been learned up to this point in the lesson sequence
	11	10	Introduce Newton's Second Law with Steps 1 and 2 of Activity 10.
6	11	40	Revisit Steps 1 and 2 and then continue on with Steps 3–7 to nurture understanding and application of Newton's Second Law
	HW	10	Assign the practice problems at the bottom of page 45 as homework; guide the students through the sample problem.
7	HW	5	Collect and evaluate homework, giving feedback on the papers
	12	20	Application of Newton's Second Law
	13	25	Application of the Second Law to a sporting event
8	14	30	Reflection on how scientists think about and talk about motion
	Test	20	Assessment of students' learning from the lesson sequence

Journal Questions

For Chapters 10–14, the journal questions have been modified so that they relate more closely to the practical matters of planning lesson sequences. The original set of journal questions used in Chapters 1–9 will be revisited one more time as part of Chapter 15, to allow you to synthesize your learning about teaching science for understanding resulting from this book. The new set of journal questions follows.

In your journal, reflect on how the process of planning this lesson sequence has *deepened your understanding* and *strengthened your skills* related to:

1. The subject concepts that are incorporated in the textbook chapter.
2. Inquiry and the process of science.
3. The nature of science including the historical development of scientific concepts as well as the connections that exist between concepts and processes.
4. Applications of science to your students' experimental world.
5. Students' ideas, reasoning, and conceptual difficulties including potential misconceptions.
6. Instructional models and approaches to teaching.
7. The complexity of the planning process.

Chapter **11**

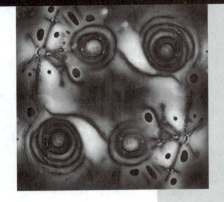

Planning a High School Lesson Sequence on Cells

Cells hold an important place in biology; therefore, understanding cells is an essential part of a high school biology program. Given the organization of instruction in American schools, much of the responsibility for development of these understandings falls on high school biology teachers, even though some of this knowledge is developed in earlier grades. To help teachers place cells in an appropriate context in a high school biology course, I have begun this chapter with three readings from Project 2061. First is a selection from Chapter 5 of *Science for All Americans* (Rutherford and Ahlgren, 1989), in which they provide their view on what students should know about cells when they graduate from high school.

The second selection is from *Benchmarks for Science Literacy* (Project 2061, 1993). This selection describes how ideas about cells develop across the grades, with special attention to developments that are recommended in previous grades, especially in grades 6 through 8. A short selection is also added from *Atlas for Science Literacy* (Project 2061, 2001).

One of the challenges that face high school students in biology classes is the heavy load of new terms that comprise most courses. One of the interesting features of these two selections is the way in which science content is expressed with a reduction of emphasis on terminology, while increasing the emphasis on understanding biological concepts. As you read the following selections, note how they have accomplished this remarkable feat, and also consider how you can apply it to your teaching not only in the context of this lesson sequence on cells, but also in all parts of your teaching.

Science for All Americans: The Living Environment

CELLS

All self-replicating life forms are composed of cells—from single-celled bacteria to elephants, with their trillions of cells. Although a few giant cells, such as hens' eggs, can be seen with the naked eye, most cells are microscopic. It is at the cell level that many of the basic functions of organisms are carried out: protein synthesis, extraction of energy from nutrients, replication, and so forth.

All living cells have similar types of complex molecules that are involved in these basic activities of life. These molecules interact in a soup, about 2/3 water, surrounded by a membrane that controls what can enter and leave. In more complex cells, some of the common types of molecules are organized into structures that perform the same basic functions more efficiently. In particular, a nucleus encloses the DNA and a protein skeleton helps to organize operations. In addition to the basic cellular functions common to all cells, most cells in multicelled organisms perform some special functions that others do not. For example, gland cells secrete hormones, muscle cells contract, and nerve cells conduct electrical signals.

Cell molecules are composed of atoms of a small number of elements—mainly carbon, hydrogen, nitrogen, oxygen, phosphorous, and sulfur. Carbon atoms, because of their small size and four available bonding electrons, can join to other carbon atoms in chains and rings to form large and complex molecules. Most of the molecular interactions in cells occur in water solution and require a fairly narrow range of temperature and acidity. At low temperatures the reactions go too slowly, whereas high temperatures or extremes of acidity can irreversibly damage the structure of protein molecules. Even small changes in acidity can alter the molecules and how they interact. Both single cells and multicellular organisms have molecules that help to keep the cells' acidity within the necessary range.

The work of the cell is carried out by the many different types of molecules it assembles, mostly proteins. Protein molecules are long, usually folded chains made from 20 different kinds of amino acid molecules. The function of each protein depends on its specific sequence of amino acids and the shape the chain takes as a consequence of attractions between the chain's parts. Some of the assembled molecules assist in replicating genetic information, repairing cell structures, helping other molecules to get in or out of the cell, and generally in catalyzing and regulating molecular interactions. In specialized cells, other protein molecules may carry oxygen, effect contraction, respond to outside stimuli, or provide material for hair, nails, and other body structures. In still other cells, assembled molecules may be exported to serve as hormones, antibodies, or digestive enzymes.

The genetic information encoded in DNA molecules provides instructions for assembling protein molecules. This code is virtually the same for all life forms. Thus, for example, if a gene from a human cell is placed in a bacterium, the chemical machinery of the bacterium will follow the gene's instructions and produce the same protein that would be produced in human cells. A change in even a single atom in the DNA molecule, which may be induced by chemicals or radiation, can therefore change the protein that is produced. Such a mutation of a DNA segment may not make much difference, may fatally disrupt the operation of the cell, or may change the successful operation of the cell in a significant way (for example, it may foster uncontrolled replication, as in cancer).

All the cells of an organism are descendants of the single fertilized egg cell and have the same DNA information. As successive generations of cells form by division, small differences in their immediate environments cause them to develop slightly differently, by activating or inactivating different parts of the DNA information. Later generations of cells differ still further and eventually mature into cells as different as gland, muscle, and nerve cells.

Complex interactions among the myriad kinds of molecules in the cell may give rise to distinct cycles of activities, such as growth and division. Control of cell processes comes also from without: Cell behavior may be influenced by molecules from other parts of the organism or from other organisms (for example, hormones and neurotransmitters) that attach to or pass through the cell membrane and affect the rates of reaction among cell constituents. (Rutherford and Ahlgren, 1989, pp. 62–64)

Reflection & Discussion Questions

1. This section from *Science for All Americans* is included to help you "get the big picture" of the place of cells in a high school biology course. What does this convey about the nature of the objectives for your students?

2. What does this section convey to you about the nature of vocabulary that should be taught to students?

3. Describe how you could employ these ideas with the students you teach.

Benchmarks for Science Literacy

C. CELLS

Students can proceed far in their study of organisms before they need to learn that all activities within those organisms are performed by cells and that organisms are mostly cells. The familiar description and depiction of cells in blood sometimes lead students to the notion that organisms contain cells rather than that organisms are mostly made up of cells. Imagining the large number of cells is also a problem for young students. Large organisms are composed of about a trillion cells, but this number means little to middle-school students. A million millions might have a better chance of making an impression.

Students may have even more difficulty with the idea that cells are the basic units in which life processes occur. Neither familiarity with functions of regular-sized organisms nor observation of single-celled organisms will reveal much about the chemical activity going on inside single cells. For most students, the story should be kept simple. The way to approach the idea of functioning microscopic units is to start with the needs of macroscopic organisms.

Information transfer and energy transformation are functions of nearly all cells. The molecular aspects of these processes should wait until students have observed the transformation of energy in a variety of physical systems and have examined more generally the requirements for the transfer of information. Information transfer may mean communication among cells within an organism or passing genetic codes from a cell to its descendants.

Kindergarten through Grade 2

Emphasis should be placed on examining a variety of familiar animals and plants and considering things and processes they all need to stay alive, such as food and getting rid of wastes. Students should use hand lenses to make things appear 3 to 10 times bigger and more detailed and should be encouraged to wonder what they might see with more powerful lenses.

By the end of the 2nd grade, students should know that:

- **Magnifiers help people see things they could not see without them.**
- **Most living things need water, food, and air.**

Grades 3 through 5

Students' experiences should expand to include the observation of microscopic organisms, so the scale of magnification should increase to 30- or 100-power (dissection scope or low power on microscopes). Watching microorganisms is always informative, but some events are so rare that prepared materials are a necessity. Students can observe films of living cells growing and dividing, taking in substances, and changing direction when they run into things. Some students may reason that because these tiny cells are alive, they probably have the same needs as other, larger organisms. That can stimulate discussions about how single-celled organisms satisfy their need for food, water, and air.

By the end of the 5th grade, students should know that:

- **Some living things consist of a single cell. Like familiar organisms, they need food, water, and air; a way to dispose of waste; and an environment they can live in.**
- **Microscopes make it possible to see that living things are made mostly of cells. Some organisms are made of a collection of similar cells that benefit from**

cooperating. **Some organisms' cells vary greatly in appearance and perform very different roles in the organism**.

Grades 6 through 8

Once they have some "magnification sense," students can use photomicrographs to extend their observations of cells, gradually concentrating on cells that make up internal body structures. The main interest of youngsters at this level is the human body, so they can begin with as many different kinds of body cells as possible—nerve, bone, muscle, skin—and then move on to examining cells in other animals and plants. This activity can show students that cells are the fundamental building blocks of their own bodies and of other living things as well. Also, once students see that tissue in other animals looks pretty much the same as tissue in humans, two important claims of science will be reinforced: the ubiquity of cells and the unity of nature.

By the end of the 8th grade, students should know that

- **All living things are composed of cells, from just one to many millions, whose details usually are visible only through a microscope. Different body tissues and organs are made up of different kinds of cells. The cells in similar tissues and organs in other animals are similar to those in human beings but differ somewhat from cells found in plants.**
- **Cells repeatedly divide to make more cells for growth and repair. Various organs and tissues function to serve the needs of cells for food, air, and waste removal.**
- **Within cells, many of the basic functions of organisms—such as extracting energy from food and getting rid of waste—are carried out. The way in which cells function is similar in all living organisms.**
- **About two thirds of the weight of cells is accounted for by water, which gives cells many of their properties.**

Grades 9 through 12

The individual cell can be considered as a system itself and as part of larger systems, sometimes as part of a multicellular organism, always as part of an ecosystem. The cell membrane serves as a boundary between the cell and its environment, containing for its own use the proteins it makes, equipment to make them, and stockpiles of fuel. Students should be asked to consider the variety of functions cells serve in the organism and how needed materials and information get to and from the cells. It may help students to understand the interdependency of cells if they think of an organism as a community of cells, each of which has some common tasks and some special jobs.

The idea that protein molecules assembled by cells conduct the work that goes on inside and outside the cells in an organism can be learned without going into the biochemical details. It is sufficient for students to know that the molecules involved are different configurations of a relatively few kinds of amino acids, and that the different shapes of the molecules influence what they do.

Students should acquire a general picture of the functions of the cell and know that the cell has specialized parts that perform these functions. This can be accomplished without many technical terms. Emphasizing vocabulary can impede understanding and take the fun out of science. Discussion of what needs to be done in the cell is much more important than identifying or naming the parts that do it. For example, students should know that cells have certain parts that oxidize sugar to release energy and parts to stitch protein chains together according to instructions; but they don't need to remember that one type of part is a mitochondrion and the other a ribosome, or which is which.

By the end of the 12th grade, students should know that

▪ **Every cell is covered by a membrane that controls what can enter and leave the cell. In all but quite primitive cells, a complex network of proteins provides organization and shape and, for animal cells, movement.**

▪ *Within every cell are specialized parts for the transport of materials, energy transfer, protein building, waste disposal, information feedback, and even movement. In addition, most cells in multicellular organisms perform some special functions that others do not.*

▪ **The work of the cell is carried out by the many different types of molecules it assembles, mostly proteins. Protein molecules are long, usually folded chains made from 20 different kinds of amino-acid molecules. The function of each protein molecule depends on its specific sequence of amino acids and the shape the chain takes is a consequence of attractions between the chain's parts.**

▪ **The genetic information encoded in DNA molecules provides instructions for assembling protein molecules. The code used is virtually the same for all life forms. Before a cell divides, the instructions are duplicated so that each of the two new cells gets all the necessary information for carrying on.**

▪ **Complex interactions among the different kinds of molecules in the cell cause distinct cycles of activities, such as growth and division. Cell behavior can also be affected by molecules from other parts of the organism or even other organisms.**

▪ **Gene mutation in a cell can result in uncontrolled cell division, called cancer. Exposure of cells to certain chemicals and radiation increases mutations and thus increases the chance of cancer.**

▪ **Most cells function best within a narrow range of temperature and acidity. At very low temperatures, reaction rates are too slow. High temperatures and/or extremes of acidity can irreversibly change the structure of most protein molecules. Even small changes in acidity can alter the molecules and how they interact. Both single cells and multicellular organisms have molecules that help to keep the cell's acidity within a narrow range.**

▪ **A living cell is composed of a small number of chemical elements mainly carbon, hydrogen, nitrogen, oxygen, phosphorous, and sulfur. Carbon atoms can easily bond to several other carbon atoms in chains and rings to form large and complex molecules. (Project 2061, 1993, p. 110–114).**

Atlas for Science Literacy

CELL FUNCTIONS

As the basic units of life, cells have needs and functions that are very similar to those of whole organisms. Students' understanding of the functions of cells develops along three major strands of benchmarks: the basic needs of organisms, the basic functions that are performed in organisms, and the structure of organisms and cells.

These strands of benchmarks first come together in middle school, where the benchmarks include the idea that the basic functions of organisms are carried out in cells. Later, when students know something about the structure of matter, they can understand the synthesis of protein molecules and the interactions of molecules within and between cells. This map has some important relationships to topics that will be mapped in the next edition of *Atlas*, including basic human functions and the commonalties evident within the diversity of life.

Notes: In 9–12, ideas about the functions common to all cells are further extended to the benchmark that different parts of the cell carry out specialized functions and eventually that the proteins made in the cell carry out its work. (Project 2061, 2001, p. 72)

Reflection & Discussion Questions

1. Part of the utility of *Benchmarks for Science Literacy* and *Atlas for Science Literacy* lies in their developmental sense. What do these resources tell you about what students might have learned about cells in prior grades?

2. How will you be able to determine what students learned about cells in earlier grades? Is this information important? (Hint: Think about what you know about the effects of students' misconceptions on further learning.)

Description of Prentice Hall *Biology*

Prentice Hall Biology (Miller and Levine, 2004) is the textbook selected for this chapter on planning a lesson sequence on cells for high school biology. This section is part of Unit 3 and it follows Unit 1, The Nature of Life, and Unit 2, Ecology. By the time students in introductory biology who use this book begin the study of cells, they have been presented with an overview of biology that includes three main features: An overview of the science of biology, a chapter of the chemistry of life, and an ecological perspective that shows the interconnectedness of life and some of the relationships that occur among living things and between living things and the physical environment. In Unit 2 on ecology, they also have learned concepts of energy flow and matter cycling and their application to ecosystems, communities, populations, and people's impact on the biosphere.

Unit 3 contains four chapters:

Chapter 7: Cell Structure and Function
>   7-1 Life Is Cellular
>   7-2 Eukaryotic Cell Structure
>   7-3 Cell Boundaries
>   7-4 The Diversity of Cellular Life
Chapter 8: Photosynthesis
Chapter 9: Cellular Respiration
Chapter 10: Cell Growth and Division

This lesson sequence will be based on Section 7-2, Eukaryotic Cell Structure, which deals with a small but important part of the larger story about cells described above in the selections from *Science for All Americans* and *Benchmarks for Science Literacy*. That story is developed over Chapters 7 through 10 in this textbook. Therefore, the plan for this lesson sequence will be a small part of a larger plan that a teacher would develop dealing with Unit 3. This is a challenging lesson sequence because it contains a high demand on vocabulary and because so much of the content lies beyond the experiential background of high school students. As one indicator of this, much of the understanding of the internal structure of cells came into being only with the development of electron microscopy during the latter half of the twentieth century.

As specific preparation for learning about eukaryotic cell structure in Section 7-2, the previous section provides readings and suggested activities designed to develop an understanding of the cell concept in biology, a brief history of the development of scientists' understanding of cells (beginning with Robert Hooke's identification and naming of cells in the seventeenth century), the development of the cell theory nearly two hundred years later in the early to mid-nineteenth century (1838–1855), and more recent developments with electron microscopy. It has the potential for inquiry that could serve as a foundation for Section 7-2, using photos from various electron microscopes. Section 7-1 concludes by making the distinction between prokaryotic cells and eukaryotic cells.

Section 7-2 is contained on textbook pages 174 to 181, which are reproduced below. You should read these pages carefully so that you are clear on the concepts that are part of this lesson sequence. Also note that cell boundaries are addressed in the next section of this text. Therefore, that part of cell structure is not included in this lesson sequence, but can be dealt with immediately afterward.

As in previous chapters, be sure to examine the strengths of the materials presented in this section of the textbook. Also think about where you will need to supplement it and whether you may need to omit parts of the content.

Planning the Lesson Sequence

As in Chapters 9 and 10 of this book, I will use the guidelines provided in the modified Project 2061 Categories and Criteria as the organizing framework, beginning with goals, purposes, and learning environment. In its design, this chapter applies the apprenticeship teaching approach, as it moves from modeling, which was provided in Chapters 5, 9 and 10, to coaching, which will be provided in the following pages with the assistance of the course instructor.

Categories I and VII: Goals, Purposes, and Learning Environment

As you think about the goals for this topic, you will need to make many decisions about the importance of terms, concepts, and big ideas related to the structure of cells. The decision-making model from Wiggins and McTighe (1998), which I described in Chapter 9, will be important to keep in mind. As you will recall, those authors indicated that teachers should distinguish among three levels of knowing that arise from the following questions:

1. What is worth being familiar with? The broad background information and ideas that are part of the topic.

2. What is important to know? The important facts, concepts, principles, attitudes, and skills, including processes, strategies, and methods that form the basis of the topic.

3. What are the enduring understandings you want students to develop and hold over the long duration? The big ideas and how to apply them that students will find useful in many situations beyond the walls of school.

Because the structure of cells is complex and descriptions of cells are heavily laden with highly specialized terms, you will need to decide about the enduring understandings you hope to foster with your students; the important facts, concepts, principles,

FIGURE 11.1 ■ Selected Pages from Prentice Hall Biology

Section 7–2

1 FOCUS

Objectives

7.2.1 *Describe* the function of the cell nucleus.

7.2.2 *Describe* the functions of the major cell organelles.

7.2.3 *Identify* the main roles of the cytoskeleton.

Guide for Reading

Vocabulary Preview

Pronounce each Vocabulary word and have students repeat the pronunciation as a class. Pay special attention to words that are difficult for English language learners.

Reading Strategy

To help students begin their understanding of the differences between plant cells and animal cells, have them preview Figure 7–6 and answer the caption question.

2 INSTRUCT

Comparing the Cell to a Factory

Build Science Skills

Using Models Divide the class into small groups, and have groups make a labeled, two-dimensional drawing of a typical cell. First, have groups meet before reading the section to discuss what the inside of a cell might contain. Then, ask groups to meet again after learning about the structures of a cell to make the labeled drawing. **L2**

7–2 Eukaryotic Cell Structure

Guide for Reading

Key Concept
• What are the functions of the major cell structures?

Vocabulary
organelle
cytoplasm
nuclear envelope
chromatin
chromosome
nucleolus
ribosome
endoplasmic reticulum
Golgi apparatus
lysosome
vacuole
mitochondrion
chloroplast
cytoskeleton
centriole

Reading Strategy: Building Vocabulary
Before you read, preview the vocabulary by skimming the section and making a list of the boldface terms. Leave space to make notes as you read.

At first glance, a factory is a puzzling place. A bewildering variety of machines buzz and clatter, people move quickly in different directions, and the sheer diversity of so much activity can be confusing. However, if you take your time and watch carefully, before long you will begin to identify patterns. What might at first have seemed like chaos begins to make sense.

Comparing the Cell to a Factory

In some respects, the eukaryotic cell is like a factory. The first time you look at a microscope image of a cell, such as the one in **Figure 7–5**, the cell seems impossibly complex. Look closely at a eukaryotic cell, however, and patterns begin to emerge. To see those patterns more clearly, we'll look at some structures that are common to eukaryotic cells, shown in **Figure 7–6**. Because many of these structures act as if they are specialized organs, these structures are known as **organelles**, literally "little organs."

Cell biologists divide the eukaryotic cell into two major parts: the nucleus and the cytoplasm. The **cytoplasm** is the portion of the cell outside the nucleus. As you will see, the nucleus and cytoplasm work together in the business of life.

▶ **Figure 7–5** This electron micrograph of a plant cell shows many of the different types of structures that are found in eukaryotic cells. The cell has been artificially colored so that you can distinguish one structure from another.

In the student version of the text , a picture of a magnified plant cell appears here.

(magnification: 1500×)

SECTION RESOURCES

Print:
• *Teaching Resources,* Section Review 7–2
• *Guided Reading and Study Workbook,* Section 7–2
• *Lesson Plans,* Section 7–2

Technology:
• *iText,* Section 7–2
• *Transparencies Plus,* Section 7–2

Note: Please note that the actual text pages are full color.

Source: From *Prentice Hall Biology* by Kenneth R. Miller and Joseph Levine © 2004 by Pearson Education, Inc., publishing as Pearson Prentice Hall. Used by permission.

FIGURE 11.1 *(Contd.)*

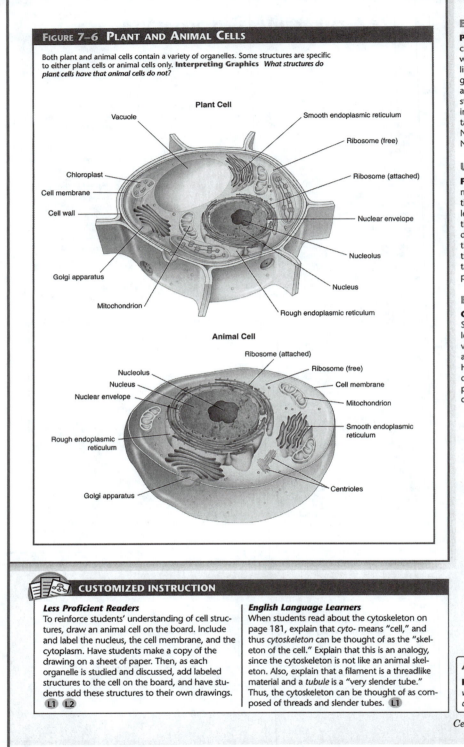

FIGURE 7–6 PLANT AND ANIMAL CELLS

Both plant and animal cells contain a variety of organelles. Some structures are specific to either plant cells or animal cells only. **Interpreting Graphics** *What structures do plant cells have that animal cells do not?*

Plant Cell

- Vacuole
- Chloroplast
- Cell membrane
- Cell wall
- Golgi apparatus
- Mitochondrion
- Smooth endoplasmic reticulum
- Ribosome (free)
- Ribosome (attached)
- Nuclear envelope
- Nucleolus
- Nucleus
- Rough endoplasmic reticulum

Animal Cell

- Nucleolus
- Nucleus
- Nuclear envelope
- Rough endoplasmic reticulum
- Golgi apparatus
- Ribosome (attached)
- Ribosome (free)
- Cell membrane
- Mitochondrion
- Smooth endoplasmic reticulum
- Centrioles

Build Science Skills

Predicting Ask students what specific functions a one-celled organism would need to carry out in order to live. Then, divide the class into small groups, and ask each group to make a table of predictions about what structures would likely be found inside a one-celled organism. The table should have two columns: Necessary Function and Structure Needed to Carry Out Function. **L2**

Use Visuals

Figure 7–6 Encourage students to make copies of these labeled illustrations in their notebooks. As they learn about the various structures that make up a cell, they can add definitions and descriptions of functions for each of the labels. Point out that when they have completed this task, they will have made the best possible tool for review. **L1 L2**

Build Science Skills

Comparing and Contrasting
Set up microscope stations at several locations around the room, and provide prepared slides of an animal cell and a plant cell at each location. Have students make labeled drawings of each and write a paragraph comparing and contrasting the two types of cells. **L2 L3**

![icon] **CUSTOMIZED INSTRUCTION**

Less Proficient Readers
To reinforce students' understanding of cell structures, draw an animal cell on the board. Include and label the nucleus, the cell membrane, and the cytoplasm. Have students make a copy of the drawing on a sheet of paper. Then, as each organelle is studied and discussed, add labeled structures to the cell on the board, and have students add these structures to their own drawings. **L1 L2**

English Language Learners
When students read about the cytoskeleton on page 181, explain that *cyto-* means "cell," and thus *cytoskeleton* can be thought of as the "skeleton of the cell." Explain that this is an analogy, since the cytoskeleton is not like an animal skeleton. Also, explain that a filament is a threadlike material and a *tubule* is a "very slender tube." Thus, the cytoskeleton can be thought of as composed of threads and slender tubes. **L1**

Answer to . . .

Figure 7–6 *Plant cells have a cell wall and chloroplasts. Many plant cells also have a large, central vacuole.*

Cell Structure and Function **175**

Note: Please note that the actual text pages are full color.

FIGURE 11.1 (Contd.)

7–2 (continued)

Nucleus

Use Visuals

Figure 7–7 Ask students: What is the nucleolus? *(It is a small, dense region of the nucleus where the assembly of ribosomes begins.)* Where is the DNA that a nucleus contains? *(The DNA is part of the chromatin, which is spread throughout the nucleus most of the time.)* Why is DNA important? *(It holds coded instructions for making proteins and other important molecules.)* Point out that the genetic information is the coded instructions for making molecules. (L1) (L2)

Build Science Skills

Inferring Remind students that prokaryotes do not contain a nucleus. Then, ask: If the nucleus controls most cell processes in eukaryotes, how can prokaryotes live without a nucleus? *(Some students might suggest that the lives of prokaryotes aren't as complex as those of eukaryotes. Others might correctly infer that the most important part of a nucleus is the DNA it contains, and prokaryotes have DNA without having a nucleus.)* (L2) (L3)

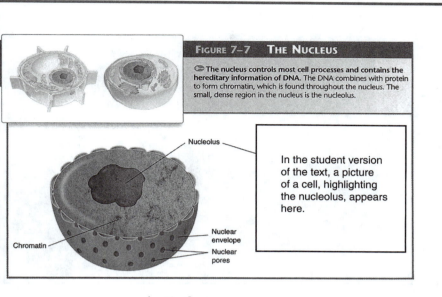

FIGURE 7–7   THE NUCLEUS

⊙ The nucleus controls most cell processes and contains the hereditary information of DNA. The DNA combines with protein to form chromatin, which is found throughout the nucleus. The small, dense region in the nucleus is the nucleolus.

Nucleolus

Chromatin

Nuclear envelope

Nuclear pores

In the student version of the text, a picture of a cell, highlighting the nucleolus, appears here.

Nucleus

In the same way that the main office controls a large factory, the nucleus is the control center of the cell. ⊙ **The nucleus contains nearly all the cell's DNA and with it the coded instructions for making proteins and other important molecules.** The structure of the nucleus is shown in **Figure 7–7.**

The nucleus is surrounded by a **nuclear envelope** composed of two membranes. The nuclear envelope is dotted with thousands of nuclear pores, which allow material to move into and out of the nucleus. Like messages, instructions, and blueprints moving in and out of a main office, a steady stream of proteins, RNA, and other molecules move through the nuclear pores to and from the rest of the cell.

The granular material you can see in the nucleus is called **chromatin.** Chromatin consists of DNA bound to protein. Most of the time, chromatin is spread throughout the nucleus. When a cell divides, however, chromatin condenses to form **chromosomes** (KROH-muh-sohms). These distinct, threadlike structures contain the genetic information that is passed from one generation of cells to the next. You will learn more about chromosomes in later chapters.

Most nuclei also contain a small, dense region known as the **nucleolus** (noo-KLEE-uh-lus). The nucleolus is where the assembly of ribosomes begins.

✓ CHECKPOINT   *What kind of information is contained in chromosomes?*

BIO INSIGHTS   HISTORY OF SCIENCE

The nucleus controls the cell
During the 1930s and 1940s, researchers performed a series of experiments that demonstrated the link between a cell's nucleus and the physical characteristics of the cell. Two species of *Acetabularia* algae were used in the experiments. This marine alga, though 5 cm long, consists of a single cell. Each cell includes a holdfast at the bottom, a stalk, and a cuplike cap at the top, and the cell's nucleus is in the holdfast. The two species that were used had different-shaped caps. Researchers cut the cap off one cell, removed the nucleus from its holdfast, and transplanted a nucleus from a cell of the second species into the holdfast of the first cell. The cell regenerated a new cap, and researchers cut off that one. Eventually, the cap that grew was the shape of the cap from the second species, from which the transplanted nucleus came, and not the shape of the first cap.

Note: Please note that the actual text pages are full color.

FIGURE 11.1 *(Contd.)*

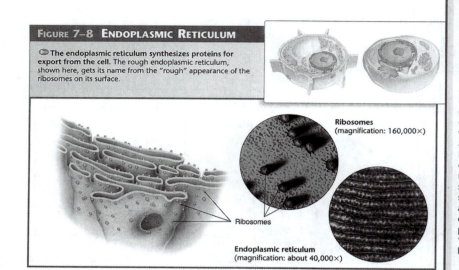

FIGURE 7–8 ENDOPLASMIC RETICULUM

The endoplasmic reticulum synthesizes proteins for export from the cell. The rough endoplasmic reticulum, shown here, gets its name from the "rough" appearance of the ribosomes on its surface.

Ribosomes
(magnification: 160,000×)

Ribosomes

Endoplasmic reticulum
(magnification: about 40,000×)

Ribosomes

One of the most important jobs carried out in the cellular "factory" is making proteins. **Proteins are assembled on ribosomes. Ribosomes** are small particles of RNA and protein found throughout the cytoplasm. They produce proteins by following coded instructions that come from the nucleus. Each ribosome, in its own way, is like a small machine in a factory, turning out proteins on orders that come from its "boss"—the cell nucleus. Cells that are active in protein synthesis are often packed with ribosomes.

Endoplasmic Reticulum

Eukaryotic cells also contain an internal membrane system known as the **endoplasmic reticulum** (en-doh-PLAZ-mik rih-TIK-yuh-lum), or ER. **The endoplasmic reticulum is the site where lipid components of the cell membrane are assembled, along with proteins and other materials that are exported from the cell.**

The portion of the ER involved in the synthesis of proteins is called rough endoplasmic reticulum, or rough ER. It is given this name because of the ribosomes found on its surface. Newly made proteins leave these ribosomes and are inserted into the rough ER, where they may be chemically modified.

Ribosomes

Build Science Skills

Using Analogies Read aloud the sentence in the text that compares a ribosome to a machine. Use this comparison to discuss how a eukaryotic cell is like a factory. Then, encourage students who need an extra challenge to work together in writing a short play based on the analogy of the cell as a factory. Explain that a good play needs some conflict or danger. The "factory" might be under economic threat or some environmental threat. Advise students to include the functions of as many parts of the factory—cell organelles—as possible. Once the play has been written, encourage the "playwrights" to recruit class members to act out the drama. **L3**

Endoplasmic Reticulum

Use Visuals

Figure 7–8 Ask students: **What are ribosomes composed of?** *(RNA and protein)* **Where are ribosomes produced?** *(In the nucleolus)* **What do ribosomes produce?** *(Proteins)* **What happens to these proteins after they're produced by ribosomes?** *(Membrane proteins are inserted directly into the ER membrane. Many of the proteins produced on the rough ER are released or secreted from the cell.)* **If this were an illustration of smooth ER, how would it be different?** *(The ER would not have ribosomes on its surface.)* **What is the function of smooth ER?** *(The smooth ER contains enzymes that help synthesize lipids, such as steroids. Smooth ER also helps to detoxify and process chemicals.)* **L1** **L2**

BIO INSIGHTS HISTORY OF SCIENCE

Learning from sea urchin nuclei
The German cytologist Theodor Boveri (1862–1915) performed an experiment before the invention of microdissection that demonstrated the importance of the nucleus. By vigorous shaking, Boveri removed the nuclei from the eggs of sea urchins of the genus *Sphaerechinus*. He then fertilized the eggs (which had no nuclei) with sperm from sea urchins of the genus *Echinus*. In a practical sense, fertilization resulted in the substitution of one nucleus for another. The larvae that developed had only the traits of *Echinus*, even though the sperm contributed little more than a tiny bit of nucleus to the developing organism.

Answer to . . .

✔CHECKPOINT *Chromosomes contain the genetic information that is passed from one generation to the next.*

Cell Structure and Function **177**

Note: Please note that the actual text pages are full color.

FIGURE 11.1 (*Contd.*)

7–2 (continued)

Golgi Apparatus

Build Science Skills

Comparing and Contrasting
Students often confuse the Golgi apparatus with the endoplasmic reticulum, because both are usually represented as folded membranes within the cytoplasm. Have students compare the illustrations in Figure 7–8 with those in Figure 7–9. Then, call on students at random to explain the differences in functions between ER and the Golgi apparatus. **L2**

Lysosomes

Build Science Skills

Observing Divide the class into small groups, and give each group access to a paramecium culture and a yeast suspension, as well as to a microscope slide, coverslip, toothpick, dropper pipette, and microscope. (Prepare the yeast suspension by adding a pinch of Congo red indicator to a thick mixture of yeast and water. Then, bring it to a gentle boil for 5 minutes. Cool before using. Transfer some paramecium culture from the stock culture at least a day ahead of time, and then limit the food supply to the transferred culture.) Have each group prepare a slide of live paramecia using the dropper pipette. Students should focus the slide under the low-power objective of the microscope. They should then obtain a small sample of the yeast solution. The indicator in the solution is red above pH 5 and blue below pH 3. The next step is to use a toothpick to transfer a small drop of yeast suspension to the edge of the slide and observe the paramecia under the microscope for 5 minutes. (*Students should observe that the paramecia sweep the yeast through their oral grooves and form vacuoles to enclose it. The vacuoles become blue at first and eventually red, as lysosomes fuse with the vacuole and release acids that digest the yeast.*)
L2 **L3**

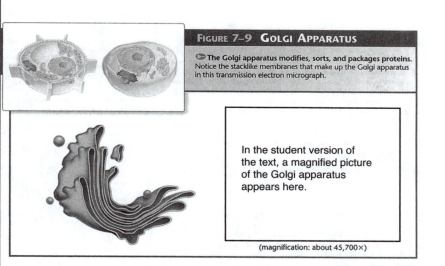

FIGURE 7–9 GOLGI APPARATUS

The Golgi apparatus modifies, sorts, and packages proteins. Notice the stacklike membranes that make up the Golgi apparatus in this transmission electron micrograph.

In the student version of the text, a magnified picture of the Golgi apparatus appears here.

(magnification: about 45,700×)

Proteins that are released, or exported, from the cell are synthesized on the rough ER, as are many membrane proteins. Rough ER is abundant in cells that produce large amounts of protein for export. Other cellular proteins are made on "free" ribosomes, which are not attached to membranes.

The other portion of the ER is known as smooth endoplasmic reticulum (smooth ER) because ribosomes are not found on its surface. In many cells, the smooth ER contains collections of enzymes that perform specialized tasks, including the synthesis of membrane lipids and the detoxification of drugs. Liver cells, which play a key role in detoxifying drugs, often contain large amounts of smooth ER.

Golgi Apparatus

Proteins produced in the rough ER move next into an organelle called the **Golgi apparatus**, discovered by the Italian scientist Camillo Golgi. As you can see in **Figure 7–9**, Golgi appears as a stack of closely apposed membranes. **The function of the Golgi apparatus is to modify, sort, and package proteins and other materials from the endoplasmic reticulum for storage in the cell or secretion outside the cell.** The Golgi apparatus is somewhat like a customization shop, where the finishing touches are put on proteins before they are ready to leave the "factory." From the Golgi apparatus, proteins are then "shipped" to their final destinations throughout the cell or outside of the cell.

BIO INSIGHTS   FACTS AND FIGURES

Important products of the Golgi apparatus
One of the most important cell components packaged and distributed by the Golgi apparatus is material for the membranes of the cell and its organelles. Lysosomes, which are essentially membranous bags filled with enzymes, are products of the Golgi apparatuses. These enzymes would destroy the cell if they were not surrounded by membrane. An example of how lysosomes function in cells can be seen in the way paramecia digest their food. Upon contact with a food organism or some other particle, the paramecium envelops the food in a vacuole. Lysosomes then fuse with the vacuole and release acids. The acids quickly digest the contents of the vacuole.

178   *Chapter 7*

Note: Please note that the actual text pages are full color.

FIGURE 11.1 *(Contd.)*

Lysosomes

Even the neatest, cleanest factory needs a cleanup crew, and that's what lysosomes (LY-suh-sohmz) are. **Lysosomes** are small organelles filled with enzymes. One function of lysosomes is the digestion, or breakdown, of lipids, carbohydrates, and proteins into small molecules that can be used by the rest of the cell.

Lysosomes are also involved in breaking down organelles that have outlived their usefulness. Lysosomes perform the vital function of removing "junk" that might otherwise accumulate and clutter up the cell. A number of serious human diseases, including Tay-Sachs disease, can be traced to lysosomes that fail to function properly.

✓CHECKPOINT   *What is the role of lysosomes?*

Vacuoles

Every factory needs a place to store things, and cells contain places for storage as well. Some kinds of cells contain saclike structures called **vacuoles** (VAK-yoo-ohlz) that store materials such as water, salts, proteins, and carbohydrates. In many plant cells there is a single, large central vacuole filled with liquid. The pressure of the central vacuole in these cells makes it possible for plants to support heavy structures such as leaves and flowers.

Vacuoles are also found in some single-celled organisms and in some animals. The paramecium in **Figure 7–10** contains a vacuole called a contractile vacuole. By contracting rhythmically, this specialized vacuole pumps excess water out of the cell. The control of water content within the cell is just one example of an important process known as homeostasis. Homeostasis is the maintenance of a controlled internal environment.

Mitochondria and Chloroplasts

All living things require a source of energy. Factories are hooked up to the local power company, but what about cells? Most cells get energy in one of two ways—from food molecules or from the sun.

Mitochondria   Nearly all eukaryotic cells, including plants, contain **mitochondria** (myt-oh-KAHN-dree-uh; singular: mitochondrion). **Mitochondria are organelles that convert the chemical energy stored in food into compounds that are more convenient for the cell to use.** Mitochondria are enclosed by two membranes—an outer membrane and an inner membrane. The inner membrane is folded up inside the organelle.

One of the most interesting aspects of mitochondria is the way in which they are inherited. In humans, all or nearly all of our mitochondria come from the cytoplasm of the ovum, or egg cell. This means that when your relatives are discussing which side of the family should take credit for your best characteristics, you can tell them that you got your mitchondria from Mom!

Figure 7–10 Vacuoles have a variety of functions. In the *Coleus* plant cell (top), the large blue structure is the central vacuole that stores salts, proteins, and carbohydrates. The paramecium (bottom) contains contractile vacuoles that fill with water and then pump the water out of the cell. **Applying Concepts** *How do vacuoles help support plant structures?*

Vacuole

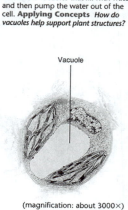

(magnification: about 3000×)

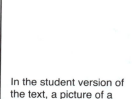

In the student version of the text, a picture of a paramecium appears here.

Cell Structure and Function   **179**

Note: Please note that the actual text pages are full color.

FIGURE 11.1 (*Contd.*)

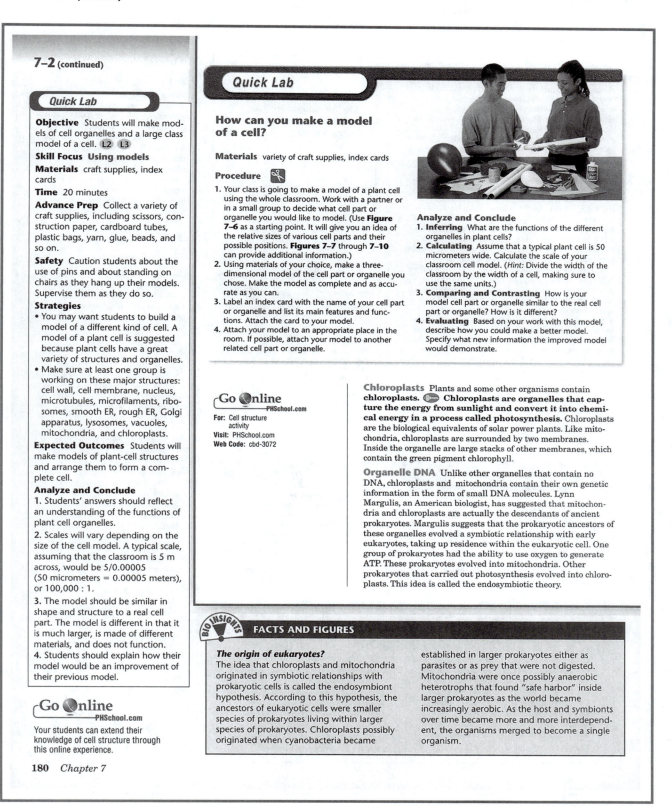

7–2 (continued)

Quick Lab

Objective Students will make models of cell organelles and a large class model of a cell. (L2) (L3)

Skill Focus Using models

Materials craft supplies, index cards

Time 20 minutes

Advance Prep Collect a variety of craft supplies, including scissors, construction paper, cardboard tubes, plastic bags, yarn, glue, beads, and so on.

Safety Caution students about the use of pins and about standing on chairs as they hang up their models. Supervise them as they do so.

Strategies

• You may want students to build a model of a different kind of cell. A model of a plant cell is suggested because plant cells have a great variety of structures and organelles.

• Make sure at least one group is working on these major structures: cell wall, cell membrane, nucleus, microtubules, microfilaments, ribosomes, smooth ER, rough ER, Golgi apparatus, lysosomes, vacuoles, mitochondria, and chloroplasts.

Expected Outcomes Students will make models of plant-cell structures and arrange them to form a complete cell.

Analyze and Conclude

1. Students' answers should reflect an understanding of the functions of plant cell organelles.

2. Scales will vary depending on the size of the cell model. A typical scale, assuming that the classroom is 5 m across, would be 5/0.00005 (50 micrometers = 0.00005 meters), or 100,000 : 1.

3. The model should be similar in shape and structure to a real cell part. The model is different in that it is much larger, is made of different materials, and does not function.

4. Students should explain how their model would be an improvement of their previous model.

Go Online
PHSchool.com

Your students can extend their knowledge of cell structure through this online experience.

180   *Chapter 7*

Quick Lab

How can you make a model of a cell?

Materials variety of craft supplies, index cards

Procedure ✂

1. Your class is going to make a model of a plant cell using the whole classroom. Work with a partner or in a small group to decide what cell part or organelle you would like to model. (Use **Figure 7–6** as a starting point. It will give you an idea of the relative sizes of various cell parts and their possible positions. **Figures 7–7** through **7–10** can provide additional information.)

2. Using materials of your choice, make a three-dimensional model of the cell part or organelle you chose. Make the model as complete and as accurate as you can.

3. Label an index card with the name of your cell part or organelle and list its main features and functions. Attach the card to your model.

4. Attach your model to an appropriate place in the room. If possible, attach your model to another related cell part or organelle.

Analyze and Conclude

1. **Inferring** What are the functions of the different organelles in plant cells?

2. **Calculating** Assume that a typical plant cell is 50 micrometers wide. Calculate the scale of your classroom cell model. (*Hint:* Divide the width of the classroom by the width of a cell, making sure to use the same units.)

3. **Comparing and Contrasting** How is your model cell part or organelle similar to the real cell part or organelle? How is it different?

4. **Evaluating** Based on your work with this model, describe how you could make a better model. Specify what new information the improved model would demonstrate.

Go Online
PHSchool.com

For: Cell structure activity
Visit: PHSchool.com
Web Code: cbd-3072

Chloroplasts Plants and some other organisms contain chloroplasts. ▸ **Chloroplasts are organelles that capture the energy from sunlight and convert it into chemical energy in a process called photosynthesis.** Chloroplasts are the biological equivalents of solar power plants. Like mitochondria, chloroplasts are surrounded by two membranes. Inside the organelle are large stacks of other membranes, which contain the green pigment chlorophyll.

Organelle DNA Unlike other organelles that contain no DNA, chloroplasts and mitochondria contain their own genetic information in the form of small DNA molecules. Lynn Margulis, an American biologist, has suggested that mitochondria and chloroplasts are actually the descendants of ancient prokaryotes. Margulis suggests that the prokaryotic ancestors of these organelles evolved a symbiotic relationship with early eukaryotes, taking up residence within the eukaryotic cell. One group of prokaryotes had the ability to use oxygen to generate ATP. These prokaryotes evolved into mitochondria. Other prokaryotes that carried out photosynthesis evolved into chloroplasts. This idea is called the endosymbiotic theory.

BIO INSIGHTS   FACTS AND FIGURES

The origin of eukaryotes?
The idea that chloroplasts and mitochondria originated in symbiotic relationships with prokaryotic cells is called the endosymbiont hypothesis. According to this hypothesis, the ancestors of eukaryotic cells were smaller species of prokaryotes living within larger species of prokaryotes. Chloroplasts possibly originated when cyanobacteria became established in larger prokaryotes either as parasites or as prey that were not digested. Mitochondria were once possibly anaerobic heterotrophs that found "safe harbor" inside larger prokaryotes as the world became increasingly aerobic. As the host and symbionts over time became more and more interdependent, the organisms merged to become a single organism.

Note: Please note that the actual text pages are full color.

Cytoskeleton

A supporting structure and a transportation system complete our picture of the cell as a factory. As you know, a factory building is supported by steel or cement beams and by columns that support its walls and roof. Eukaryotic cells have a structure—the **cytoskeleton**—that helps support the cell. **The cytoskeleton is a network of protein filaments that helps the cell to maintain its shape. The cytoskeleton is also involved in movement.** Microfilaments and microtubules are two of the principal protein filaments that make up the cytoskeleton.

Microfilaments are threadlike structures made of a protein called actin. They form extensive networks in some cells and produce a tough, flexible framework that supports the cell. Microfilaments also help cells move. Microfilament assembly and disassembly is responsible for the cytoplasmic movements that allow cells, such as amoebas, to crawl along surfaces.

Microtubules, as shown in **Figure 7–11**, are hollow structures made up of proteins known as tubulins. In many cells, they play critical roles in maintaining cell shape. Microtubules are also important in cell division, where they form a structure known as the mitotic spindle, which helps to separate chromosomes. In animal cells, tubulin is also used to form a pair of structures known as centrioles. **Centrioles** are located near the nucleus and help to organize cell division. Centrioles are not found in plant cells.

Microtubules also help to build projections from the cell surface, which are known as cilia (singular: cilium) and flagella (singular: flagellum), that enable cells to swim rapidly through liquids. Cilia and flagella can produce considerable force; and in some cells they move almost like the oars of a boat, pulling or pushing cells through the water. You will learn more about cilia and flagella in later chapters.

In the student version, a picture of microtubules appears here.

(magnification: 1000×)

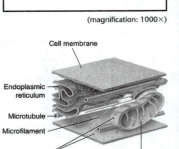

Cell membrane
Endoplasmic reticulum
Microtubule
Microfilament
Ribosomes
Mitochondrion

▲ **Figure 7–11** The cytoskeleton is a network of protein filaments that helps the cell to maintain its shape and is involved in many forms of cell movement. The micrograph shows the microtubules of kidney cells. Microtubules are part of the cytoskeleton that help maintain cell shape.

Cytoskeleton

Build Science Skills

Using Analogies Show students a photo of a house that's being built, with only the foundation laid and the basic frame constructed. Builders call this initial stage "framing" the house. Ask: **How is this house frame like a cell's cytoskeleton?** (*Just as a cytoskeleton is a network of protein filaments that helps a cell maintain its shape, the frame of a house is a network of boards and timbers that forms the shape of the house.*) **L1** **L2**

3 ASSESS

Evaluate Understanding

Have students make a Venn diagram to show organelles that are found only in prokaryotic cells, those that are found only in eukaryotic cells, and those that are found in both types of cells.

Reteach

Ask students to make a compare/contrast table that lists all the parts of a typical cell, including nucleus and organelles. Column heads might include *Name*, *Structure*, and *Function*.

Writing in Science

Students' letters may vary. The focus of all letters, though, should be to explain the endosymbiotic theory—the idea that mitochondria and chloroplasts are actually descendants of ancient prokaryotes. Because this explanation must be clear to people without a biology background, students should explain in simple but accurate terms what mitochondria, chloroplasts, and prokaryotes are, as well as how such symbiotic relationships could evolve.

iText

If your class subscribes to the iText, use it to review the key concepts in Section 7–2.

7–2 Section Assessment

1. **Key Concept** Describe the functions of the endoplasmic reticulum, Golgi apparatus, chloroplast, and mitochondrion.
2. Describe the role of the nucleus in the cell.
3. What are two functions of the cytoskeleton?
4. How is a cell like a factory?
5. **Critical Thinking** **Inferring** You examine an unknown cell under the microscope and discover that the cell contains chloroplasts. What type of organism could you infer that the cell came from?

Writing in Science

Persuasive Writing Image that you are Lynn Margulis. Write a persuasive letter to the editor of a magazine, explaining your idea. Your explanation should be clear to people who do not have a biology background. *Hint*: Review the concept of symbiosis in Section 4–2.

7–2 Section Assessment

1. Rough ER makes membranes and secretory proteins. Smooth ER makes lipids and helps in detoxification. The Golgi apparatus modifies, sorts, and packages proteins and other materials from the ER for storage or secretion. Chloroplasts capture the energy of sunlight and convert it into chemical energy. Mitochondria convert stored chemical energy into compounds that the cell can use.
2. It is the control center of the cell.
3. It helps the cell maintain its shape and also is involved in movement.
4. Answers may vary. A typical response will compare ribosomes to factory machines and the cytoskeleton to a supporting structure. Students should also compare other organelles to various parts of a factory.
5. Students should infer that the organism would either be a plant or some other organism that carries out photosynthesis.

Note: Please note that the actual text pages are full color.

processes, strategies, and methods that they should know; and the background information that they should be familiar with. Sorting out these different levels of knowing will be part of the decision making about the objectives for this lesson sequence.

One of the goals presented in *Benchmarks for Science Literacy* for grades 9 through 12 fits this Section 7-2 and this lesson sequence very well. It states that:

> Within every cell are specialized parts for the transport of materials, energy transfer, protein building, waste disposal, information feedback, and even movement. (Project 2061, 1993, p. 113)

The objectives for this section are stated in the textbook as follows:

> 7.2.1 Describe the function of the cell nucleus.
>
> 7.2.2 Describe the functions of the major cell organelles.
>
> 7.2.3 Identify the main roles of the cytoskeleton.

To these objectives, I recommend that the following objectives be added to this section to provide students with a base of experience for their work on cell structure:

- Using photomicrographs, students should be able to identify cell organelles.

Addition of this objective allows for reification of the organelles as visible entities whose function has been determined through the research of many scientists over several decades, using new technologies as they were developed. Therefore, I recommend the following objective:

- Students should appreciate the long history of the development of current concepts of the cell, based on technological developments and the work of many different scientists from different nations.

I also recommend that students should understand that individual cells must carry on functions that are similar to whole, multicellular organisms, and that organelles support these functions.

As a result of these additions, the expanded list of objectives for Section 7-2 on eukaryotic cell structure is as follows:

> On completion of this lesson sequence, students should be able to
>
> 1. Identify cell organelles shown in photomicrographs.
> 2. Describe the function of the cell nucleus.
> 3. Describe the functions of the major cell organelles.
> 4. Identify the main roles of the cytoskeleton.
> 5. Compare and contrast cell functions with functions of whole, multicellular organisms.

> 6. Describe the key elements of the long history of development of contemporary concepts of cell structure and function and link them to technological developments in microscopy.

The purpose of this lesson sequence is to help students develop an appreciation and understanding of the complexity of cells and to be able to show the similarities that exist between cellular functions and the functions of multicellular organism. The lesson sequence should also instill a sense of awe at two levels: (1) the complexity of both structure and function that occurs at the microscopic level within a cell and (2) the capability that scientists have shown in determining both the structure and the functioning of the organelles within cells.

As you plan and carry out this lesson sequence, I urge you to follow the admonition from *Benchmarks for Science Literacy*, which is repeated below:

> Emphasizing vocabulary can impede understanding and take the fun out of science. Discussion of what needs to be done in the cell is much more important than identifying or naming the parts that do it. For example, students should know that cells have certain parts that oxidize sugar to release energy and parts to stitch protein chains together according to instructions; but they don't need to remember that one type of part is a mitochondrion and the other a ribosome, or which is which. (Project 2061, 1993, p. 113)

Obviously, an alternative position suggests that knowledge of cells is one of the fundamentals of biological science; therefore, students need to both understand the structure and functions of cells and be at least reasonably fluent in the terminology used to describe the structure and function. Striking a balance between these two positions is a challenge that we all must address, and our response will vary depending on the age of students, their ability, and their aspirations. However, ability to use and appreciate this knowledge should be paramount.

Two driving questions for this section might be:

- How do individual cells and whole organisms compare in the ways they carry out the life functions?
- How have scientists been able to determine the structure and function of cells?

Reflection & Discussion Questions

1. Do these goals and purposes seem appropriate?
2. How are these similar to, or different from, the goals and purposes you have experienced in courses you have taken or those you have taught?
3. How do these goals address understanding of the content of this lesson sequence?

Reflection & Discussion Questions

1. Given this background, what objectives and purposes do you choose for this lesson sequence?

   (Note: At this point, you should write out your list of goals, objectives, and purposes for the lesson sequence using the material provided from Project 2061, from the textbook, and the foregoing commentary that I have written.)

Regarding the learning environment, this section needs special attention to keep it from falling into a common trap that occurs in science classes and in high school biology in particular. That "trap" is the tendency to focus on learning complex new vocabulary without developing an understanding of its meaning and the connections among the biological concepts and principals that are part of the topic. The large number of new terms shown in the vocabulary list on page 174 of the *Biology* textbook attests to the need to go beyond emphasizing only the vocabulary in this lesson sequence. This was my motive for including two additional objectives shown above. By basing the work in a study of photomicrographs and by comparing and contrasting cells and whole organisms, you can help students develop understandings that go beyond memorization of vocabularies.

Reflection & Discussion Questions

1. Several years ago, Mary Budd Rowe, a valued colleague, studied the vocabulary demands in high school biology textbooks and found that about 1800 new words were introduced in them. That is an average of 10 new words per day through the whole school year. This was twice as many words as were introduced in a one-year course in a foreign language. Also, the words in a foreign-language course typically represented familiar concepts, whereas those in biology represented complex, unfamiliar concepts. What do you think about Dr. Rowe's observation? Should we consider reducing the vocabulary demand in high school biology?

2. Review the section from *Science for All Americans* that is presented in the opening pages of this chapter, and consider how that piece was written without a high use of specialized vocabulary, but still represented the concepts meaningfully. Can we organize our teaching in ways that alleviate the high demand on vocabulary development and at the same time, teach essential biological principles with understanding?

Reflection & Discussion Questions

1. Return to Figure 9.2 and rate the development on objectives and purposes according to the plan outlined in Chapter 9. Rate each item as S, P, or N, based on your interpretation of the adequacy of the development up to this point. Be reflective in assigning your ratings. It may be useful to have a group or whole-class discussion based on this task.

Categories II and VI: Students' Ideas and Assessment

Research on students' learning about cells is summarized in Driver and colleagues (1994). There are several confusions that affect students' thinking related to cells. The most common of these is a confusion that persists about order of magnitude among cells, macromolecules such as proteins and DNA, and smaller molecules. Students appear to aggregate "small things," or as one researcher suggested, students have a generalized concept of small units that make up larger things, which have been called the "molecell" (Driver et al., 1994, p. 25).

Data also show that an overwhelming majority of students indicated that living things are not made up of molecules, but heat and energy are. This points to a belief that molecules are confined to physics and chemistry and are not part of biology. Perhaps the introductory work on chemistry of life in Unit 1 of the *Biology* textbook will help to alleviate this problem, but you need to be aware of the common confusion that exists so that you can address it as you encounter it among your students.

Other research demonstrates that 16-year-olds show similar confusion about orders of magnitude and levels of organization. Students thought that protein molecules were larger than the size of cells and that single-celled organisms contained organs like lungs and intestines. Experience with students also shows that they frequently view cells as two-dimensional, instead of three-dimensional. This arises from their interpretations of the pictures and diagrams they have seen and from experiences with microscopes if they have not been coached in the use of the fine adjustment as a tool for "seeing the third dimension" of microscopic objects (Driver et al., 1994, p. 25).

Given the various ways that students have constructed meaning from their prior experiences, you have a challenge ahead of you in teaching about the structure of the cell. This requires that you remain alert to students' potential misconceptions and naïve understandings, and at the same time find ways of probing their ideas and reasoning.

1. What ideas about cells and this hierarchy (atoms, molecules, cells, organs, and organisms) gave you difficulty as you were learning biology?
2. In your experience, what have you noticed about the misconceptions that students hold regarding levels of organization from molecules to cells to organisms?
3. What other concepts related to cells do students find difficult or confusing?

Preassessment As a preassessment, you may want to give students an individual writing or drawing task that addresses their ideas about levels of organization within a multicelled organism such as a person. For example, you may try asking students to draw a diagram of a cell and label its parts based on what they already know. This will tap into what ideas and misconceptions students already have about cells. You could also ask students to describe the functions of each part.

You also might ask students to place the following in order of size from smallest to largest:

A cell, a water molecule, a protein molecule, a cell nucleus, a molecule of DNA, an oxygen molecule, and a mite (a very small arthropod that can only be seen when magnified).

After students have worked with ordering this list for a few minutes, then students could engage in an initial learning activity by comparing their results with one or two neighboring students and by discussing any differences they have to try to reconcile them. Finally, this could be the basis for a whole-class discussion to help students come to understand the connectedness of these entities in a living organism. You may also wish to conclude with asking a question about the similarities and differences among a cell in a multicelled organism, a single-celled organism, and a mite. Then you could ask if all three contain protein molecules, DNA molecules, and water molecules. You may also wish to ask which ones contain a heart, intestines, and nerves. Discussions like these can be very productive in identifying misconceptions and in helping students gain an understanding of levels of organization.

1. What will preassessment questions, such as the ones described above, tell you about your students' ideas and reasoning about cells?
2. Identify other questions you should be asking.

Summative Assessment As an essential part of planning your lesson sequence, you should plan your summative assessment, based on the objectives for the lesson sequence. I suggest the following items may be useful as you create the summative assessment.

One possibility is to include a matching question that relates names and functions of part of eukaryotic cells as shown in item 1 below. (Note: You may shorten the list of items in this question depending on the level of your students. In its present form, it tends to violate the advice given in *Benchmarks for Science Literacy* about emphasis on details. However, some knowledge of details about the gross structure of cells and the function of organelles is appropriate. Therefore, you may want this question to have six to eight pairs of items for matching instead of the twelve that are listed.)

1. Match the names of the cell parts and the appropriate functions by placing the appropriate letter in the blank column ahead of the related function.

a. vacuoles	Granular material that condenses to form chromosomes
b. mitochondria	Aid in breakdown and removal of materials from cells
c. chromatin	Enables movement of material in and out of the nucleus
d. chromosome	Contains most of the cell's DNA
e. nucleolus	In plants, fill with water to provide support
f. nucleus	Contains genetic information used in cell reproduction
g. chloroplast	Modifies, sorts, and packages proteins for varied uses
h. lysosomes	Initiates the assembly of ribosomes
i. Golgi apparatus	Gives cells their shape and aids in movement
j. endoplasmic reticulum	Converts food into usable forms for the cell
k. cytoskeleton	Capture sunlight and convert it into chemical energy
l. nuclear envelope	Uses ribosomes to assemble proteins and RNA

Another type of summative assessment task that assesses a different level of understanding is an essay question that requires a constructed response. An example is provided below. For obvious reasons, the two should not be used on the same test.

2. List the names of eight cell parts and describe the function of each in one or two sentences. (Note: Again the number eight is arbitrary. You may wish

to use a larger or smaller number depending on the students in your class. Also, a variation on this would be to list an appropriate number of the structural members of cells, and then have students describe the function of your preestablished list.)

Yet another type of summative task could include presentation of photomicrographs of cells from a Web site such as the following:

http://ghs.gresham.k12.or.us/science/ps/sci/soph/cells/anat/cellquiz.htm

http://micro.magnet.fsu.edu/micro/gallery.html

There are many good Web sites on cell biology, but relatively few have good electron microscope photos that are useful for showing the organelles of cells in place in cells. Too often, the photos are replaced by drawings. The following is an example; while excellent, it does not enable students to see what scientists had to work with in developing their ideas about cell structure:

http://web.mit.edu/esgbio/www/cb/cbdir.html

Then have students identify and describe several cell organelles that appear in the photos. Again, the number of organelles to be identified can be modified. Also, you may wish to name particular organelles that you expect students to be knowledgeable about.

3. Using the photomicrographs provided (the teacher should select the appropriate ones), identify and describe at least four cell organelles.

The following items revisit two of the preassessment tasks, the first of which (item 4 below) contains only a minor modification:

4. Order these items from largest to smallest: (a) a cell from your skin, (b) a water molecule, (c) a protein molecule, (d) a cell nucleus, (e) a molecule of DNA, (f) a carbon-dioxide molecule, (g) a mite (a very small arthropod that can only be seen when magnified), and (h) the egg cell in an egg from a chicken.

5. Draw a diagram of a cell and label as many parts as you can.

The previous questions assess Objectives 1 through 3. To assess understanding of Objective 4 (Identify the main roles of the cytoskeleton), you will need to ask another question that could be "open book." For example:

6. Open your textbook to page 181 and answer the following question: Write a paragraph of 50 to 100 words on the *nature* and *functions* of the cytoskeleton. Be sure to address both the nature (characteristics or structure) of the cytoskeleton and at least three key functions.

To address Objective 5 (Compare and contrast cell functions with functions of whole, multicellular organisms), you will need to add another question such as the following: (Note: This could also be an "open book" test item.)

7. List five life functions such as responding to stimuli, movement, using food, growth, reproduction, and excretion that are carried on by all living things and show how these occur in a multicellular organism such as a dog or a tree, in single-cell organism such as an amoeba, and in a cell that is part of a multicellular organism. The following chart may be helpful in organizing your information. In the first row of the table, write the name of the organisms you choose in the blanks in columns 2 and 3. Add the life functions you select in column 1. Then complete the chart.

Life Function	Multicellular organism (_____)	Single-cell organism (_____)	A cell that is part of a multi-cellular organism
Responding to stimuli			
Movement			

Another effective assessment item is suggested in the *Biology* textbook on page 181, question 4. It asks, "How is a cell like a factory?" You might also wish to ask students to consider in what ways the factory metaphor is a sound one for thinking about a cell and where it fails to be effective.

Assessment of Objective 6 (Describe key elements of the long history of development of contemporary concepts of cell structure and function and link them to technological developments in microscopy) may vary depending on how you develop the historical background. However, one possibility is to ask a question such as the following:

Describe how our understanding of cells has depended on technological developments related to microscopy. Compare and contrast understandings of cells that emerged with simple microscopes such as those used by Hooke and van Leeuwenhook in the seventeenth century, with compound microscopes in the nineteenth century, and with electron microscopes in the twentieth century. How did other technologies, such as staining and tools for preparation of thin sections, also add to the advancement of our knowledge of cells?

Reflection & Discussion Questions

1. Are there other items you would recommend for the summative assessment?

2. What about using a lab-based item, such as the "Quick Lab" on page 180 of the *Biology* textbook, as part of your summative assessment?

Formative Assessment Ideas and approaches for formative assessment will be presented along with the learning activities in the following section of the plan.

Reflection & Discussion Questions

Return to Figure 9.2 and rate the development on assessment according to the plan outlined in Chapter 9. Rate each item as S, P, or N, based on your interpretation of the adequacy of the development up to this point. It is obvious that VII.D will receive a rating of N.

Categories III Through V: Learning Activities

1. The preassessment items contain useful starting points for this lesson sequence. I suggest that you employ one or more of these, as they can be useful engaging activities and also will provide you with important information about your students' ideas and reasoning about cells. Also, you will need to engage students in this work by helping them realize the central place of cells in the functioning of all organisms, including themselves. Helping students realize that individual cells in organisms need to carry out most of the basic life functions that whole organisms must also carry out can be one step in building understanding about the unity of life that can add to engagement. Activities 2 and 3 below also will be useful in facilitating engagement.

2. Earlier in the textbook, in Section 7-1, page 168, it was suggested that students be given the opportunity to look at a variety of cells through a microscope. It is recommended that they examine slides of plant leaves and stems, nerve cells, bacteria, and paramecia. I would add slides such as epithelial cells from inside students' cheeks, tissue from between layers of onions, and prepared slides of muscle cells. In these students will see some of the larger structural parts of cells, including cell walls and membranes, and nuclei, and cytoplasm, but they will miss most of the smaller organelles because they will not be able to discern them with their light microscopes. However, this activity is useful to give students a sense of what cells actually look like to a scientist who is studying them with mid-levels of magnification provided by light microscopes.

3. On page 175, the Teacher Guide portion includes an activity called "Build Science Skills." This activity provides students with another opportunity to gain experiences with observing slides of plant and animal cells and creating meaning from the visual information contained therein. It is important to give students such opportunities.

4. At an appropriate point in this introductory sequence, you could ask students to reflect on what they already know about cells and what else they would like to know. A ground rule in this activity is that students cannot answer "nothing." Giving students an opportunity to reflect on what they know and what else would be important to know allows students to develop some sense of control over their learning. This can add to engagement and is a valuable formative assessment task.

What should you do if the results of this task are disappointing? For example, what would the appropriate next steps be if students show little or no interest in learning about cells? One possibility is to have students read and discuss the following note from Dr. Miller, one of the authors of the *Biology* textbook, about his personal history with cells (Figure 11.2). His enthusiasm for biology was partly a result of his teacher's enthusiasm. Obviously there is a lesson here for all teachers!

What if students' desires for new knowledge are "thin" and seem low level to you? This suggests "where your students are" at this time. You can take their limited concerns and interests seriously and also nurture them. For example, you can respond by saying, "This is an interesting idea. Let's think about how we can make this fit into our high school biology class." Then ask the class, "How might a biologist think about this point?" By asking questions like these, you give credibility to students' ideas and also help to enrich them.

5. You may wish to have students recall Activity 2 in this section and also show some electron photomicrographs and have them describe what can be seen in these pictures that can't be seen with ordinary, light microscopes. At this point, you can introduce the term *organelles* and use the examples that are familiar to the students such as the nucleus and chloroplasts. Comparison of Figure 7-6 on *Biology* textbook page 175 (an illustrator's representation of the structure of a cell) with observations made through their microscopes and with electron microscope images would be an important next step. This will provide a basis for guiding students through the remaining pages of Section 7-2, in which the structure and function of different organelles is described and sometimes pictured. In addition, the students will need

FIGURE 11.2

Unit **3**

Dear Colleague,

I can still remember the first time I looked through a microscope and saw a living cell. It was in Mr. Zong's ninth-grade biology class in my hometown in New Jersey. After carefully instructing us in the proper use of the microscope, our teacher placed a drop of water on every student's slide and told us to have a look.

I couldn't believe my eyes. Glistening creatures swam across the field of view. They twisted and turned, I thought, almost as if they were alive. I think I said that out loud, because I can remember Mr. Zong's deep, gentle laugh and a pat on my shoulder. "They *are* alive, Kenny! They're alive just like you and me."

Mr. Zong was famous among my classmates at Rahway High for his devotion to the "practicum" style of exam. Every other Friday, we walked into the classroom to be confronted by 30 "stations," one at the desk of every student. Each station had a specimen—a leaf, a butterfly, a seed, or a drop of water under a microscope. Taped to each desk was a question about that specimen.

We had 90 seconds to look at the specimen, read the question, and write down an answer. Then, we each moved on to the next station. No timeouts, no chances to go back. Forty-five minutes went by like a flash.

At first, I feared these semiweekly exams. After a while, however, I grew to love the challenge. In a way, I suppose, we sensed the passion in our teacher's insistence that the mysterious world of nature held stories— great stories. We students, he thought, could be expected to read, to learn, and then to tell those stories from the material of life itself.

As fall turned toward winter, I remember my parents' surprise when I told them what I hoped to find under our Christmas tree that year— a microscope.

Only a few weeks later, I had transformed a tiny corner of the room I shared with my brother into a miniature laboratory. A tiny desk lamp glowed day and night, providing energy for nearly a dozen test-tube colonies of *Euglena.* At the end of the year, those cells would become a science project, the very first research I would ever do on my own.

I won second place that year in our school's science fair for my study of light's effect on the growth of *Euglena.* Although I have long since misplaced the ribbon my project was given, I hope I never lose the greater gift that came from a year of study in Paul Zong's classroom—a sense of amazement that returns every time I sit down at a microscope in my laboratory.

I hope that you and your students will find some of that amazement written into the pages of this unit. As a cell biologist, I especially hope to give students an appreciation of the roles that cells play in every aspect of life. In these four chapters, we have done our best to explain how cells live and grow, how they transform energy, and how they pass information along from one generation to the next.

I have been lucky enough to make biology my career, using the electron microscope as my primary research tool. Not all of your students can expect to do this, of course. But we can hope that with your guidance, each and every one of them will experience the same thrill I did when they focus their microscopes on living cells for the very first time.

Sincerely,

Ken Miller

166   *Unit 3*   *Unit 3*   **167**

Note: Please note that the actual text pages are full color.

Source: From *Prentice Hall Biology* by Kenneth R. Miller and Joseph Levine © 2004 by Pearson Education, Inc., publishing as Pearson Prentice Hall. Used by permission.

guidance in using analogies that are presented in the textbook.

You may be asking why should high school students be spending time working with electron photomicrographs? The purpose is twofold. First, students need to base their concepts about cell structure and organelles on actual experiences instead of textbook diagrams like Figure 7-6. Although students may not be able to engage in firsthand inquiry that relates to the actual development of science concepts about cell organelles, examining some of the experiential data that scientists were confronted with when electron microscopes became part of their set of tools will help them to see how these concepts about the cell came to be. Second, using photomicrographs will help students grasp the connection between technology and ideas. For example, van Leeuwenhoek was able to see very limited structure of cells with his simple microscope. Compound light microscopes allowed greater opportunities to see cell structure. Electron microscopes added substantially to scientists' knowledge of cells. This progression can help students see how science and new research technologies progress hand in hand.

As stated earlier, finding good electron microscope photos of cell organelles will require some searching. Web sites do not seem to offer many good examples of something as mundane as cell organelles. It may be valuable for you to send your students on a search for good photomicrographs of cells to add to your efforts on this dimension. The following site, identified earlier, is useful even though it has only one photo:

http://ghs.gresham.k12.or.us/science/ps/sci/soph/ cells/anat/cellquiz.htm

Another good source is the following:

h t t p : / / w w w . u n i - m a i n z . d e / F B / M e d i z i n / Anatomie/workshop/EM/EMAtlas.html

The language is a mixture of English and German, and photos are labeled in German.

Students also will need to gain some indirect experiences with the various organelles found in cells. This could be through reading or investigating various organelles on the Web or from other resources, as suggested in Activities 8 and 9 on the following pages, or from illustrated lectures that you present. Or you could present a short, illustrated "lecture of the day" on each of the organelles that you choose to include. This responsibility could be given to small groups of students. Consider how you will provide students with a base of experience about the structure of cells and the functions of a selected set of organelles that comprise them. Also, you need to consider how this part of the lesson sequence can stimulate students' intellectual engagement in learning about cells and about scientific inquiry.

Whatever vehicle you use to provide students with the needed base of experience about cell organelles and structure, you also will need to provide time and opportunities for them to process the new information, to make sense of it, and to make connections with what they already know. A small-group discussion, combined with writing, may be appropriate here. For example, you could ask students to write a brief summary about how the organelles that have been introduced work together to help cells stay alive. You also might ask how the structure of organelles enables them to do "their job." Once you give students this task, you can observe, question, and guide students toward valid actions.

One part of the cell structure that needs special attention is the cytoskeleton (see *Biology* textbook page 181). Understanding the nature of the cytoskeleton is an essential part of understanding cells. Therefore, as you and your students work through the structure and function of the various organelles, you also should give some attention to the overall structure of cells, including the cytoskeleton.

6. When students complete this extended task and produce a written product, you may want to collect their reports, read them, and then use them further as the basis for small-group or whole-class discussion about any difficulties you noted in them. Retyping a few responses that fall short of the desired understandings or that represent misconceptions, and then presenting them anonymously for clarification, correction, or elaboration either by groups or by the whole class, can be a very productive learning activity for all.

Reflection & Discussion Questions

1. What options did you consider for providing your students with a base of experience about the structure of cells and the functions of a selected set of organelles that comprise them? What approach did you find most appropriate for you and your students? Why did you select this approach above the others on your list?

2. What tasks did you include for helping students process and form understanding from the experience-building activities?

Note: These are examples of decisions you need to make as you plan lesson sequences for your students.

7. A useful activity is suggested in the upper right hand corner of page 175, asking for students to make predictions about the kinds of organelles (or structures) cells would need to carry out essential life functions. This would be a good group activity that might last for ten minutes or more, depending on the engagement of students in it, followed by a whole-class discussion. It also would be a useful vehicle for embedded assessment as you watch and listen to students at work in their small groups, and as you listen to and record students' comments and questions in the whole-class discussion.

Thinking about how cells get food, water, and oxygen and eliminate wastes would be a good starting point. Then you could have students consider how cells transform food into products that the cell needs for growth and how cells "burn" (transform) the food to obtain energy. That is, *how do materials cycle through cells and how does energy flow through them?* You can build on earlier work on the chemistry of life (Unit 1) in which students learned that food consists of complex molecules with high-energy bonds and that living organisms transform into simple molecules with low-energy bonds. This releases energy for organism functions. Living organisms also transform complex molecules into other complex molecules that enable replacement of cells and growth. Maintaining form and shape, movement, and reproduction are also topics that could be part of this discussion. (Caution: This activity could take on a life of its own to the point that students could become lost in its details, while forgetting its purpose as a lead-in to the study of parts of a cell. Therefore, after students have spent some time on this activity, you will need to refocus their thinking into looking at cell organelles and how scientists have discovered their functions.)

8. Use of analogies is included on page 181 of the *Biology* textbook in the upper right hand corner under the heading "Cytoskeleton." The framing of a house and the cytoskeleton are compared and contrasted. This could be a useful group discussion activity that could also provide a vehicle for writing about this analogy and its strengths and limitations (Treagust and Harrison, 1994).

9. An interesting mystery story can be developed from the science of cells, as advances in microscopy over the past century have uncovered new organelles and fueled inquiry about their functions. Although you may not be able to engage class members in all segments of this developmental history, you may want to select a few as examples of how science advances in response to new technologies and new scientific perspectives. One possibility is to use the examples in the Teachers'

Guide section at the bottom of pages 176 and 177, about two of the research studies that led to an understanding of how the nucleus controls the cell. These are interesting examples of how scientists have uncovered new understanding through research. They are also useful in helping students learn how science functions.

An embedded assessment question that could follow a short lecture or discussion of these two research vignettes would ask students to state the hypothesis that these scientists set out to test with this investigation. Then you could also ask how the data supported (or failed to support) the hypothesis. A question like this serves the dual purpose of teaching and assessing. Also it shows examples of actual inquiries that scientists have conducted to advance the understanding of cells.

10. Another approach, which could be used in addition to the previous one, would be to assign an organelle to each of several small groups of students as a short-term project, with each group to produce some information on one or two research studies that were important in determining the function of that organelle. This could result in a poster that had the following components:

   a. A title like the following: "Research That Led To an Understanding of the Function of _____" where the blank space includes the name of a specific organelle.

   b. A description of the discovery of that organelle, including the date of discovery, how it was discovered, and the names of the scientists responsible for discovering and naming it.

   c. The names of the scientists and the dates of their work to determine the organelle's function.

   d. The hypothesis that they tested.

   e. The key experiments or investigations conducted by these scientists.

   f. A summary of their findings including relevant data collected.

   g. The meaning that was given to their data including how the data supported their hypothesis.

Students should make presentations about their studies of the research on organelles to the whole class and, if possible, to other groups such as parents or other community members. Presentations to the whole class could be assessed by other students, as well as by you, using a rubric with a four-point scale, such as the following:

Criteria Rating	1	2	3	4
Was the presentation engaging?				
Did the presenters demonstrate the accuracy of their information by showing their sources?				
Was the information presented so I could understand it?				
Did the presentation generate questions about the organelle and its relation to other parts of the cell?				
Do I have a better understanding of the organelle as a result of this presentation?				
Do I have a better understanding of how scientists work as a result of this presentation?				
Total Points /24				

NOTE: A discussion of the rating form should occur before students begin their preparation of presentations, as they begin to give them, and again after two or three presentations have been completed to be sure students are using the rubric to advantage.

As students work on preparation of their reports and present them, you will have many opportunities to engage in formative assessment. To make the most of these opportunities, you will need a short list of questions that can elicit information about students' ideas and reasoning about their work. Be sure to include questions about (1) the structure and function of their organelle, (2) how structure and function are connected, (3) the organelle's relationship to the functioning of the cell, (4) how scientists learned all of this, and (5) what this work by scientists conveys about the nature of science and inquiry.

11. Creating a large model of a cell with its organelles and the cell built to scale is suggested in the "Quick Lab" on page 180 of the *Biology* textbook. This could be a useful motivating activity for students that could be suggested early in the lesson sequence and tied to Activity 7, with students learning about both the history of the discovery of cell organelles and their function. Also, as suggested earlier, it could provide information for summative assessment.

12. Early in this chapter, during the analysis of objectives, the following statement from *Benchmarks for Science Literacy* was included:

Within every cell are specialized parts for the transport of materials, energy transfer, protein building, waste disposal, information feedback, and even movement. (Project 2061, 1993, p. 113)

This statement suggests a valuable organizing framework for students and for your lesson sequence. I recommend that you help your students create a table similar the following to help students see the role of the different organelles in cells. The table could be as detailed and elaborated as you think is appropriate for your students. However, it does provide a visual organizer to focus students on the key functions of cells and their organelles. Coupling this with a model (Activity 11) or a diagram or photomicrographs of cells will help students gain a visual image that can aid understanding and organizing information. The framework gives added meaning and purpose to what can be perceived as a long list of organelles.

Organelle	Transport Materials	Energy Transfer	Protein Building	Waste Disposal	Information Feedback	Movement
Cell membrane	x					
Nucleus					x	
Mitochondria			x			

As part of your planning process, you now must formulate a sequence of activities that is developmentally sound for your students. You also will need to integrate your formative assessment activities into your plan, as suggested in several places, along with your ideas about how to respond to students who are having difficulties understanding the subject matter. In your planning, you will need to think about each of the elements contained in the modified Project 2061 Categories and Criteria, as well as how to engage students and help them maintain enthusiasm for learning about this topic.

As you plan this lesson sequence, you should return occasionally to Figure 9.2 and check out the criteria associated with Categories III, IV, and V to be sure that you are developing a lesson sequence that has the potential for engaging students, developing a sound information base about cells, developing understanding of that information, and learning how to apply this knowledge to subsequent learning and applications outside of school.

Reflection & Discussion Questions

1. Are you becoming more confident about your capability to plan lesson sequences that foster understanding?

2. In what ways are the tools for planning, such as teaching models and the modified Categories and Criteria, of value to you in addressing the complex task of planning lesson sequences?

3. What new visions, approaches, and skills have you attained through this process?

4. What additional techniques and skills do you feel you need? How can you attain these?

Reflection & Discussion Questions

Return to Figure 9.2 and rate the development of learning activities according to the plan outlined in Chapter 9. Rate each item as S, P, or N, based on your interpretation of the adequacy of the development up to this point.

Journal Questions

In your journal, reflect on how the process of planning this lesson sequence has *deepened your understanding* and *strengthened your skills* related to:

1. The subject matter concepts that are incorporated in the textbook chapter.

2. Inquiry and the process of science.
3. The nature of science including the historical development of scientific concepts as well as the connections that exist between concepts and processes.
4. Applications of science to your students' experiential world.
5. Students' ideas, reasoning, and conceptual difficulties including potential misconceptions.
6. Instructional models and approaches to teaching.
7. The complexity of the planning process.

Chapter 12

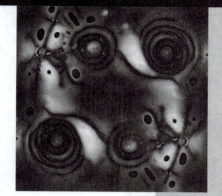

Planning a High School Lesson Sequence on Stoichiometry

Stoichiometry is a challenging topic for many beginning chemistry students, because they have difficulty in understanding the combination of chemical principles and logical reasoning behind it. Instead, students often try to learn how to solve mathematical problems by learning some procedures, without understanding the underlying principles of chemistry. Helping students to understand these principles requires integration of several ideas that have been developed over several weeks of an introductory chemistry course. Moreover, the reasoning involved is unfamiliar to many students. Like the topic itself, this chapter is challenging and dense. Therefore, you should give it time and careful thought.

Description of *Prentice Hall Chemistry*

Prentice Hall Chemistry (Wilbraham et al., 2005) has many resources built into it that provide support to teachers in their work with students. This book begins with a lengthy Teachers' Guide, which lays out one-page briefs on many helpful topics related to teaching chemistry that includes topics such as inquiry, reading, mathematics, and problem solving in the science classroom. Other relevant topics presented deal with *National Science Education Standards*, assessment, technology, and differentiated instruction to help teachers address the individual needs of students. The introductory Teachers' Guide concludes with support materials, including a planning guide, materials lists, and instructions on how to set up a small-scale chemistry laboratory that can enhance safety and reduce both costs and potential for environmental pollution.

In its design, the *Chemistry* textbook, like many others, draws on the knowledge and experience of the high school and university chemistry teachers who comprise the author team. Moreover, the teacher supports that are embedded within the pages of the chapter on stoichiometry also are invaluable.

Also, note that the placement of this chapter on stoichiometry is near the middle of the book, which implies that much prior knowledge of chemistry is needed in order to comprehend this topic. By the time that students reach Chapter 12 on stoichiometry, they have experienced considerable work related to chemical reactions and the theoretical background of chemistry. The two previous chapters deal with percentage composition of chemical

FIGURE 12.1 ■ Selected Pages from *Prentice Hall Chemistry*

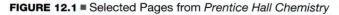

CHAPTER **12** Stoichiometry Planning Guide		Use these planning tools Lesson Plan Book Teacher Express

SECTION OBJECTIVES	STANDARDS NATIONAL STATE		ACTIVITIES and LABS
12.1 The Arithmetic of Equations, pp. 353–358 1 block or 2 periods **12.1.1 Explain** how balanced equations apply to both chemistry and everyday life. **12.1.2 Interpret** balanced chemical equations in terms of moles, representative particles, mass, and gas volume at STP. **12.1.3 Identify** the quantities that are always conserved in chemical reactions.	A-2, B-3		**SE** Inquiry Activity: How Many Can You Make?, p. 352 **L2** **TE** Teacher Demo: Interpreting a Chemical Equation, p. 357 **L2** **LM** Lab 19: Quantitative Analysis **L2** **LP** Lab Practical 12-1: Stoichiometry in a Reaction **L2**
12.2 Chemical Calculations, pp. 359–367 1 block or 2 periods **12.2.1 Construct** mole ratios from balanced chemical equations and **apply** these ratios in stoichiometric calculations. **12.2.2 Calculate** stoichiometric quantities from balanced chemical equations using units of moles, mass, representative particles, and volumes of gases at STP.	A-2, B-3		**SE** Small-Scale Lab: Analysis of Baking Soda, p. 367 **L2** **TE** Teacher Demo: Interpreting a Chemical Equation, p. 361 **L2** **TE** Class Activity: Stoichiometric Flash Cards, p. 365 **L2** **LM** Lab 19: Quantitative Analysis **L2** **SSLM** Lab 18: Weight Titrations: Measuring Molar Concentrations **L2** **SSLM** Lab 19: Mass Titrations: Measuring Molar Concentrations **L2** **PLM** Analysis of Baking Soda **L2** **LP** Lab Practical 12-2: Limiting Reagent **L2**
12.3 Limiting Reagent and Percent Yield, pp. 368–377 1 block or 2 periods **12.3.1 Identify** and use the limiting reagent in a reaction to calculate the maximum amount of product(s) produced and the amount of excess reagent that remains unreacted. **12.3.2 Calculate** theoretical yield, actual yield, or percent yield given appropriate information.	A-2, B-3		**SE** Quick Lab: Limiting Reagents, p. 372 **L2** **TE** Teacher Demo: Limiting Factor, p. 369 **L2** **TE** Class Activity: Actual Yield and Heat, p. 373 **L2** **LM** Lab 20: Balanced Chemical Equations **L2**

352A   Chapter 12

Note: Please note that the actual text pages are full color.
Source: From *Prentice Hall Chemistry* by Anthony C. Wilbrahm, Dennis D. Staley, Michael S. Matta, and Edward L. Waterman © 2005, 2002, 2000, 1997 by Pearson Education, Inc., publishing as Pearson Prentice Hall. Used by permission.

FIGURE 12.1 (Contd.)

Ability Levels	Components
L1 For students who need additional help	**SE** Student Edition **LM** Laboratory Manual **GCP** Graphing Calculator **T** Transparencies
L2 For all students	**TE** Teacher's Edition **SSLM** Small-Scale Chemistry Problems **CA** Chem Alive and Chemistry
L3 For students who need to be challenged	**GRSW** Guided Reading and Lab Manual **TTT** Test-Taking Tips with Field Trips DVD
	Study Workbook **LP** Laboratory Practicals Transparencies, **iT** Interactive Textbook with
	CTR Core Teaching Resources **PLM** Probeware Lab Manual Grades 9–12 Science ChemASAP
	SSG Spanish Study Guide **VCL** Virtual Chemistry Labs **STP** Standardized Test **GO** Go Online Internet
	CTB Computer Test Bank Preparation Workbook Resources

RESOURCES PRINT and TECHNOLOGY	PROBLEMS and ASSESSMENT
GRSW Chapter 12, Section 1 **L1**	**CP** 12.1, Interpreting a Balanced Chemical Equation
T T122–T125 **L2**	**SP** 12.1, Using a Balanced Equation as a Recipe
GO Chapter 12, Section 1 **L2**	**SE** Section 12.1 Assessment, p. 358
	iT Section 12.1
GRSW Chapter 12, Section 2 **L1**	**SP** 12.2, Calculating Moles of a Product
T T126–T132 **L2**	**SP** 12.3, Calculating the Mass of a Product
	SP 12.4, Calculating Moles of a Product
	SP 12.5, Volume-Volume Stoichiometric Calculations
	SP 12.6, Finding the Volume of a Gas Needed for a Reaction
	SE Section 12.2 Assessment, p. 366
	iT Section 12.2
GRSW Chapter 12, Section 12.3 **L1**	**SP** 12.7, Determining the Limiting Reagent in a Reaction
T T133–T138 **L2**	**SP** 12.8, Using a Limiting Reagent to Find the Quantity of a Product
GO Chapter 12, Section 3 **L2**	**SP** 12.9, Calculating the Theoretical Yield of a Reaction
	SP 12.10, Calculating the Percent Yield of a Reaction
	SE Section 12.3 Assessment, p. 375
	iT Section 12.3

Go Online

Go Online SCLINKS
Web Code: cdn-1121
Web Code: cdn-1123

MATERIALS List

Quantities for each group

STUDENT EDITION

Inquiry Activity, p. 352
20 metal paper clips (symbol M), 20 identically colored vinyl-coated paper clips (symbol C), plastic sandwich bag

Small-Scale Lab, p. 367
Baking soda, 3 plastic cups, soda straw, balance, pipets of HCl, NaOH, and thymol blue, PH sensor (optional)

Quick Lab, p. 372
Graduated cylinder, balance, 3 250-mL Erlenmeyer flasks, 3 rubber balloons, 4.2 g magnesium ribbon, 300 mL $1.0M$ hydrochloric acid

TEACHER'S EDITION

Teacher Demo, p. 357
2.5–3.5-cm strip of magnesium, 50 mL $1M$ HCl(aq) in a 100-mL beaker baking soda

Teacher Demo, p. 361
Prior to the demonstration prepare $0.1M$ solutions of potassium iodide and lead(II) nitrate. Measure 50.0 mL of $Pb(NO_3)_2$ and 150 mL of KI into separate 250-mL beakers. 250-mL beaker

Class Activity, p. 365
8 index cards, 1 colored index card or colored cardboard cut to size, paper punch, 2 brass paper fasteners

Teacher Demo, p. 369
15 plastic bottles, 30 plastic caps to fit the bottles, and 6 containers to hold 5 caps each

Class Activity, p. 373
3 styrofoam cups, a thermometer, 100 mL of $1.0M$ HCl, and approximately 200 mL of $1.0M$ NaOH

Chapter Assessment

CHAPTER ASSESSMENT
SE Chapter Assessment, pp. 379–382
CTB Chapter 12

iT Chapter 12

STANDARDIZED TEST PREP
SE Chapter 12, p. 383
STP Topic 3

iT Interactive Textbook with Assessment at PHSchool.com

Stoichiometry **352B**

Note: Please note that the actual text pages are full color.

FIGURE 12.1 (*Contd.*)

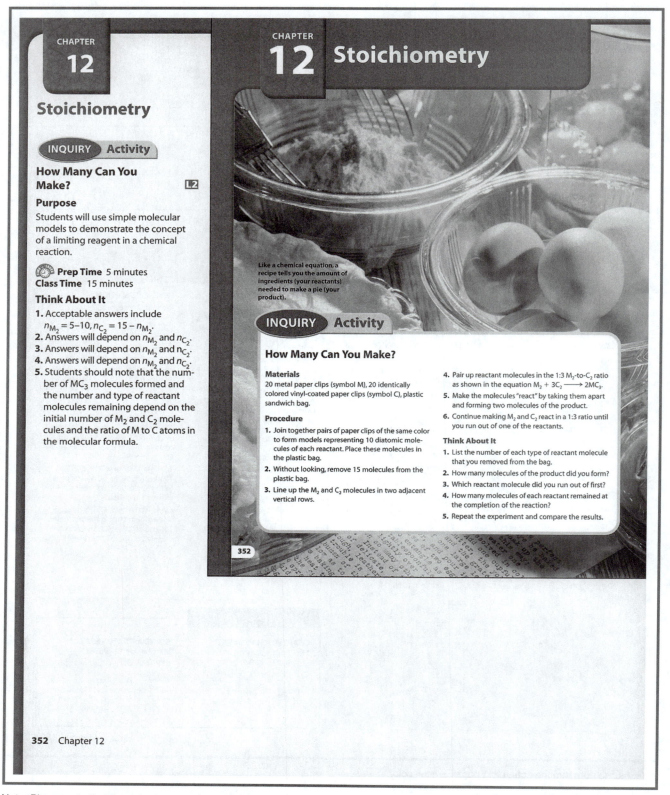

CHAPTER
12

Stoichiometry

INQUIRY Activity

How Many Can You Make? L2

Purpose
Students will use simple molecular models to demonstrate the concept of a limiting reagent in a chemical reaction.

Prep Time 5 minutes
Class Time 15 minutes

Think About It
1. Acceptable answers include $n_{M_2} = 5–10$, $n_{C_2} = 15 – n_{M_2}$.
2. Answers will depend on n_{M_2} and n_{C_2}.
3. Answers will depend on n_{M_2} and n_{C_2}.
4. Answers will depend on n_{M_2} and n_{C_2}.
5. Students should note that the number of MC_3 molecules formed and the number and type of reactant molecules remaining depend on the initial number of M_2 and C_2 molecules and the ratio of M to C atoms in the molecular formula.

CHAPTER
12 Stoichiometry

Like a chemical equation, a recipe tells you the amount of ingredients (your reactants) needed to make a pie (your product).

INQUIRY Activity

How Many Can You Make?

Materials
20 metal paper clips (symbol M), 20 identically colored vinyl-coated paper clips (symbol C), plastic sandwich bag.

Procedure
1. Join together pairs of paper clips of the same color to form models representing 10 diatomic molecules of each reactant. Place these molecules in the plastic bag.
2. Without looking, remove 15 molecules from the plastic bag.
3. Line up the M_2 and C_2 molecules in two adjacent vertical rows.
4. Pair up reactant molecules in the 1:3 M_2-to-C_2 ratio as shown in the equation $M_2 + 3C_2 \longrightarrow 2MC_3$.
5. Make the molecules "react" by taking them apart and forming two molecules of the product.
6. Continue making M_2 and C_2 react in a 1:3 ratio until you run out of one of the reactants.

Think About It
1. List the number of each type of reactant molecule that you removed from the bag.
2. How many molecules of the product did you form?
3. Which reactant molecule did you run out of first?
4. How many molecules of each reactant remained at the completion of the reaction?
5. Repeat the experiment and compare the results.

352

Note: Please note that the actual text pages are full color.

FIGURE 12.1 (*Contd.*)

12.1 The Arithmetic of Equations

12.1

Connecting to Your World   Silk is one of the most beautiful and luxurious of all fabrics. It is spun from the cocoons of silkworms. Silk manufacturers know from experience that to produce enough silk to make just one elegant Japanese kimono they will need over 3000 cocoons. In a similar fashion, chemists need to know how much reactant is needed to make a certain amount of product. The answer lies in chemical equations. From a balanced chemical equation, you can determine the quantities of reactants and products in a reaction.

> In the student version of the text, a picture of geisha in a kimono appears here.

Using Everyday Equations

When you bake cookies, you probably use a recipe. A cookie recipe tells you the precise amounts of ingredients to mix to make a certain number of cookies, as shown in Figure 12.1. If you need a larger number of cookies than the recipe provides, you can double or triple the amounts of ingredients. **A balanced chemical equation provides the same kind of quantitative information that a recipe does.** In a cookie recipe, you can think of the ingredients as the reactants, and the cookies as the products.

Here is another example. Imagine you are in charge of manufacturing for the Tiny Tyke Tricycle Company. The business plan for Tiny Tyke requires the production of 640 custom-made tricycles each week. One of your responsibilities is to be sure that there are enough parts available at the start of each workweek to make these tricycles. How can you determine the number of parts you need per week?

> In the student version of the text, a picture of a recipe card and ingredients for oatmeal cookies appears here.

Guide for Reading

Key Concepts

- How is a balanced equation like a recipe?
- How do chemists use balanced chemical equations?
- In terms of what quantities can you interpret a balanced chemical equation?
- What quantities are conserved in every chemical reaction?

Vocabulary

stoichiometry

Reading Strategy

Using Prior Knowledge Before you read, jot down three things you know about balanced chemical equations. When you have read the section, explain how what you already knew helped you learn something new.

Figure 12.1 A cookie recipe tells you the number of cookies that you can expect to make from the listed amounts of ingredients. **Using Models** *How can you express a cookie recipe as a balanced equation?*

Section 12.1 The Arithmetic of Equations   **353**

12.1

1 FOCUS

Objectives

12.1.1 Explain how balanced equations apply to both chemistry and everyday situations.

12.1.2 Interpret balanced chemical equations in terms of moles, representative particles, mass, and gas volume at STP.

12.1.3 Identify the quantities that are always conserved in chemical reactions.

Guide for Reading

Build Vocabulary   L2

Paraphrase Introduce the term stoichiometry in your own words. Stress that stoichiometry allows students to calculate the amounts of chemical substances involved in chemical reactions using information obtained from balanced chemical equations.

Reading Strategy   L2

Relate Text and Visuals Have students construct tables similar to Figure 12.3 to interpret balanced chemical equations for stoichiometric problems. Students need to use only those levels of interpretation—particles, molecules, moles, mass, or gas volumes—appropriate to the problem.

2 INSTRUCT

Connecting to Your World

Have students study the photograph and read the text that opens the section. Ask, **How many cocoons would be required to produce enough silk for two Japanese kimonos?** *(twice as many, or 6000 cocoons)* **How did you calculate the number of cocoons?** *(by multiplying the number needed for one kimono by two)*

> **Answers to...**
>
> **Figure 12.1** Acceptable answers will list ingredients as reactants and cookies as the product.

Stoichiometry   **353**

Section Resources

Print

- **Guided Reading and Study Workbook,** Section 12.1
- **Core Teaching Resources,** Section 12.1 Review
- **Transparencies,** T122–T125
- **Laboratory Manual,** Lab 19

Technology

- **Interactive Textbook with ChemASAP,** Problem Solving 12.1, 12.4, Assessment 12.1
- **Go Online,** Section 12.1

Note: Please note that the actual text pages are full color.

FIGURE 12.1 (*Contd.*)

Section 12.1 (continued)

Using Everyday Equations
Discuss L2

Write this statement on the board:"A frame, a seat, wheels, a handlebar, and pedals are needed to assemble a complete tricycle." Have students look at the visual representation of how a tricycle is assembled and ask, **Does this statement correctly describe the process?** *(no)* **What is the correct statement?** *(A frame, a seat, three wheels, a handlebar, and two pedals are needed to assemble a complete tricycle.)*

Using Balanced Chemical Equations
Discuss L2

Remind students that during a chemical reaction, atoms are rearranged into new combinations and groupings. It is somewhat similar to changing silk cocoons into a kimono. Just as a chemical reaction has reactants and products, the cocoon is the reactant and the kimono is the product. Much like having the proper supply of silk cocoons, chemists must have an adequate supply of reactants for a chemical reaction.

Word *Origins* L2

The term *spectrometry* means "the study of light or spectrum."

To simplify this discussion, assume that the major components of the tricycle are the frame (F), the seat (S), the wheels (W), the handlebars (H), and the pedals (P), in other words, your reactants. The figure below illustrates how an equation can represent the manufacturing of a single tricycle.

$$F + S + 3W + H + 2P \longrightarrow FSW_3HP_2$$

The finished tricycle, your product, has a "formula" of FSW_3HP_2. The balanced equation for making a single tricycle is

$$F + S + 3W + H + 2P \longrightarrow FSW_3HP_2$$

This balanced equation is a "recipe" to make a single tricycle: Making a tricycle requires assembling one frame, one seat, three wheels, one handlebar, and two pedals. Now look at Sample Problem 12.1. It shows you how to use the balanced equation to calculate the number of parts needed to manufacture a given number of tricycles.

Using Balanced Chemical Equations

Nearly everything you use is manufactured from chemicals—soaps, shampoos and conditioners, CDs, cosmetics, medicines, and clothes. In manufacturing such items, the cost of making them cannot be greater than the price they are sold at. Otherwise, the manufacturer will not make a profit. Therefore, the chemical processes used in manufacturing must be carried out economically. This is where balanced equations help.

A balanced chemical equation tells you what amounts of reactants to mix and what amounts of product to expect. ⬡ **Chemists use balanced chemical equations as a basis to calculate how much reactant is needed or product is formed in a reaction.** When you know the quantity of one substance in a reaction, you can calculate the quantity of any other substance consumed or created in the reaction. Quantity usually means the amount of a substance expressed in grams or moles. However, quantity could just as well be in liters, tons, or molecules.

The calculation of quantities in chemical reactions is a subject of chemistry called **stoichiometry.** Calculations using balanced equations are called stoichiometric calculations. For chemists, stoichiometry is a form of bookkeeping. For example, accountants can track income, expenditures, and profits for a small business by tallying each in dollars and cents. Chemists can track reactants and products in a reaction by stoichiometry. It allows chemists to tally the amounts of reactants and products using ratios of moles or representative particles.

✔**Checkpoint** *How is stoichiometry similar to bookkeeping?*

Word *Origins*

Stoichiometry comes from the combination of the Greek words *stoikheioin*, meaning "element," and *metron*, meaning "to measure." Stoichiometry is the calculation of amounts of substances involved in chemical reactions. **What do think the term *spectrometry* means?**

Note: Please note that the actual text pages are full color.

FIGURE 12.1 (Contd.)

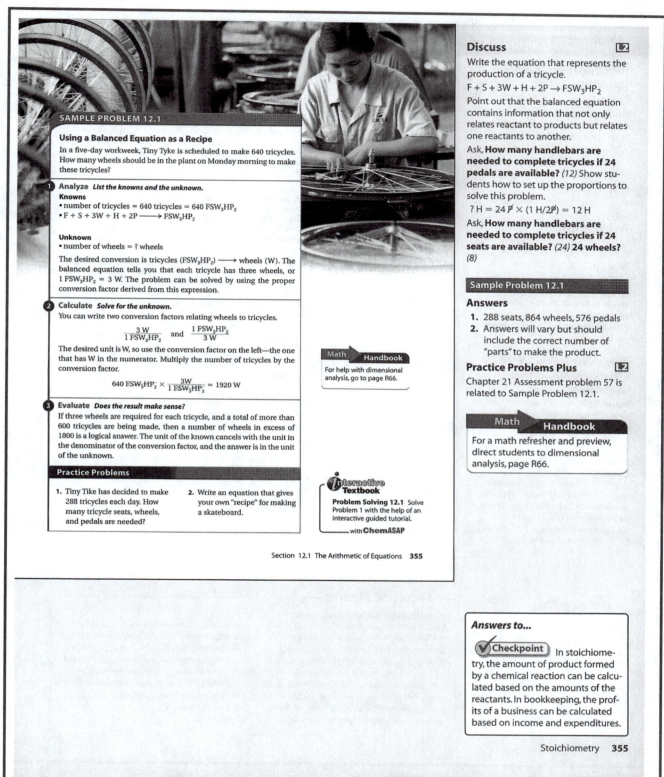

SAMPLE PROBLEM 12.1

Using a Balanced Equation as a Recipe

In a five-day workweek, Tiny Tyke is scheduled to make 640 tricycles. How many wheels should be in the plant on Monday morning to make these tricycles?

① Analyze *List the knowns and the unknown.*

Knowns
• number of tricycles = 640 tricycles = 640 FSW_3HP_2
• F + S + 3W + H + 2P ⟶ FSW_3HP_2

Unknown
• number of wheels = ? wheels

The desired conversion is tricycles (FSW_3HP_2) ⟶ wheels (W). The balanced equation tells you that each tricycle has three wheels, or 1 FSW_3HP_2 = 3 W. The problem can be solved by using the proper conversion factor derived from this expression.

② Calculate *Solve for the unknown.*

You can write two conversion factors relating wheels to tricycles.

$$\frac{3\,W}{1\,FSW_3HP_2} \quad \text{and} \quad \frac{1\,FSW_3HP_2}{3\,W}$$

The desired unit is W, so use the conversion factor on the left—the one that has W in the numerator. Multiply the number of tricycles by the conversion factor.

$$640\;FSW_3HP_2 \times \frac{3\,W}{1\,FSW_3HP_2} = 1920\;W$$

③ Evaluate *Does the result make sense?*

If three wheels are required for each tricycle, and a total of more than 600 tricycles are being made, then a number of wheels in excess of 1800 is a logical answer. The unit of the known cancels with the unit in the denominator of the conversion factor, and the answer is in the unit of the unknown.

Practice Problems

1. Tiny Tike has decided to make 288 tricycles each day. How many tricycle seats, wheels, and pedals are needed?

2. Write an equation that gives your own "recipe" for making a skateboard.

Math ▶ Handbook

For help with dimensional analysis, go to page R66.

ⓘnteractive Textbook

Problem Solving 12.1 Solve Problem 1 with the help of an interactive guided tutorial.

— with **ChemASAP**

Section 12.1 The Arithmetic of Equations **355**

Discuss 🔲2

Write the equation that represents the production of a tricycle.

F + S + 3W + H + 2P → FSW_3HP_2

Point out that the balanced equation contains information that not only relates reactant to products but relates one reactants to another.

Ask, **How many handlebars are needed to complete tricycles if 24 pedals are available?** *(12)* Show students how to set up the proportions to solve this problem.

? H = 24 P × (1 H/2P) = 12 H

Ask, **How many handlebars are needed to complete tricycles if 24 seats are available?** *(24)* **24 wheels?** *(8)*

Sample Problem 12.1

Answers

1. 288 seats, 864 wheels, 576 pedals
2. Answers will vary but should include the correct number of "parts" to make the product.

Practice Problems Plus 🔲2

Chapter 21 Assessment problem 57 is related to Sample Problem 12.1.

Math ▶ Handbook

For a math refresher and preview, direct students to dimensional analysis, page R66.

Answers to...

✔**Checkpoint** In stoichiometry, the amount of product formed by a chemical reaction can be calculated based on the amounts of the reactants. In bookkeeping, the profits of a business can be calculated based on income and expenditures.

Stoichiometry **355**

Note: Please note that the actual text pages are full color.

FIGURE 12.1 (Contd.)

Interpreting Chemical Equations

Discuss L2

Review balancing chemical reactions by writing several unbalanced equations on the board. For example:

$CuO(s) + NH_3(aq) \rightarrow$
$$Cu(s) + H_2O(l) + N_2(g)$$

$NH_3(g) + O_2(g) \rightarrow NO(g) + H_2O(g)$

$KClO_3(s) \rightarrow KCl(s) + O_2(g).$

Have students balance the equations as shown.

$3CuO(s) + 2NH_3(aq) \rightarrow$
$$3Cu(s) + 3H_2O(l) + N_2(g)$$

$4NH_3(g) + 5O_2(g) \rightarrow 4NO(g) + 6H_2O(g)$

$2KClO_3(s) \rightarrow 2KCl(s) + 3O_2(g)$

Ask, **Why is it not correct to balance an equation by changing the subscripts in one or more of the formulas?** *(Changing the subscripts in a formula changes the chemical identity of the substance.)*

Mass Conservation in Chemical Reactions

Use Visuals L1

Figure 12.3 Remind students that the term STP represents "standard temperature and pressure." Ask, **What are the values of STP?** *(0°C and 101.3 kPa)* **Why is the volume of a gas usually measured at STP?** *(The volume of a gas is usually measured at STP because its volume varies with temperature and pressure.)* **What is the molar volume of any gas at STP?** *(22.4 L/mol)* **How many particles does it contain?** *(22.4 L of any ideal gas at STP contains 6.02×10^{23} particles of that gas.)*

Figure 12.2 Gardeners use ammonium salts as fertilizer. The nitrogen in these salts is essential to plant growth.

Interpreting Chemical Equations

In gardens such as the one shown in Figure 12.2, fertilizers are often used to improve the growth of flowers. As you may recall from Chapter 10, ammonia is widely used as a fertilizer. Ammonia is produced industrially by the reaction of nitrogen with hydrogen.

$$N_2(g) + 3H_2(g) \longrightarrow 2NH_3(g)$$

The balanced chemical equation tells you the relative amounts of reactants and product in the reaction. However, your interpretation of the equation depends on how you quantify the reactants and products. ○→ A **balanced chemical equation can be interpreted in terms of different quantities, including numbers of atoms, molecules, or moles; mass; and volume.** As you study stoichiometry, you will learn how to read a chemical equation in terms of any of these quantities.

Number of Atoms At the atomic level, a balanced equation indicates that the number and type of each atom that makes up each reactant also makes up each product. Thus, both the number and types of atoms are not changed in a reaction. In the synthesis of ammonia, the reactants are composed of two atoms of nitrogen and six atoms of hydrogen. These eight atoms are recombined in the product.

Number of Molecules The balanced equation indicates that one molecule of nitrogen reacts with three molecules of hydrogen. Nitrogen and hydrogen will always react to form ammonia in a 1:3:2 ratio of molecules. If you could make 10 molecules of nitrogen react with 30 molecules of hydrogen, you would expect to get 20 molecules of ammonia. Of course, it is not practical to count such small numbers of molecules and allow them to react. You could, however, take Avogadro's number of nitrogen molecules and make them react with three times Avogadro's number of hydrogen molecules. This would be the same 1:3 ratio of molecules of reactants. The reaction would form two times Avogadro's number of ammonia molecules.

Moles A balanced chemical equation also tells you the number of moles of reactants and products. The coefficients of a balanced chemical equation indicate the relative numbers of moles of reactants and products in a chemical reaction. This is the most important information that a balanced chemical equation provides. Using this information, you can calculate the amounts of reactants and products. In the synthesis of ammonia, one mole of nitrogen molecules reacts with three moles of hydrogen molecules to form two moles of ammonia molecules. As you can see from this reaction, the total number of moles of reactants does not equal the total number of moles of product.

✓ Checkpoint *What do the coefficients of a balanced chemical equation indicate?*

--- **Facts and Figures** ---

Ammonia in the Nitrogen Cycle

Earth's atmosphere contains 0.01 parts per million of ammonia, and small amounts of ammonia occur in volcanic gases. Most ammonia cycles through the living world without returning to the atmosphere. Ammonia plays a role in several stages of the nitrogen cycle. Nitrogen-fixing bacteria form nodules, or swellings, on the roots of plants in the legume family, such as beans and clover plants. These bacteria change atmospheric nitrogen into ammonia molecules or ammonium ions. Other bacteria break down the nitrogenous material in dead plants and animals into ammonia molecules. Certain soil bacteria oxidize these molecules into nitrate ions, the form readily absorbed by plant roots. When a plant dies, this cycle begins again.

Note: Please note that the actual text pages are full color.

FIGURE 12.1 (*Contd.*)

Mass A balanced chemical equation obeys the law of conservation of mass. This law states that mass can be neither created nor destroyed in an ordinary chemical or physical process. As you recall, the number and type of atoms does not change in a chemical reaction. Therefore, the total mass of the atoms in the reaction does not change. Using the mole relationship, you can relate mass to the number of atoms in the chemical equation. The mass of 1 mol of N_2 (28.0 g) plus the mass of 3 mol of H_2 (6.0 g) equals the mass of 2 mol of NH_3 (34 g). Although the number of moles of reactants does not equal the number of moles of product, the total number of grams of reactants does equal the total number of grams of product.

Volume If you assume standard temperature and pressure, the equation also tells you about the volumes of gases. Recall that 1 mol of any gas at STP occupies a volume of 22.4 L. The equation indicates that 22.4 L of N_2 reacts with 67.2 L (3×22.4 L) of H_2. This reaction forms 44.8 L (2×22.4 L) of NH_3.

Mass Conservation in Chemical Reactions

Figure 12.3 summarizes the information derived from the balanced chemical equation for the formation of ammonia. As you can see, the mass of the reactants equals the mass of the products. In addition, the number of atoms of each type in the reactants equals the number atoms of each type in the product. ⟐ **Mass and atoms are conserved in every chemical reaction.** However, molecules, formula units, moles, and volumes are not necessarily conserved—although they may be. Consider, for example, the formation of hydrogen iodide,

$$H_2(g) + I_2(g) \longrightarrow 2HI(g)$$

In this reaction, molecules, moles, and volume are all conserved. But in the majority of chemical reactions, they are not.

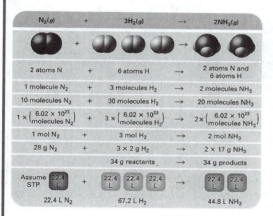

Figure 12.3 The balanced chemical equation for the formation of ammonia can be interpreted in several ways. **Predicting** *How many molecules of NH_3 could be made from 5 molecules of N_2 and 15 molecules of H_2?*

Section 12.1 The Arithmetic of Equations   **357**

For: Links on Conservation of Mass
Visit: www.SciLinks.org
Web Code: cdn-1121

Download a worksheet on **Conservation of Mass** for students to complete and find additional support for NSTA SciLinks.

TEACHER **Demo**

Interpreting a Chemical Equation

Purpose Students interpret a balanced equation of the reaction of magnesium and hydrochloric acid.

Materials 2.5–3.5-cm strip of magnesium, 50 mL 1*M* HCl(*aq*) in a 100-mL beaker, baking soda

Safety Wear safety glasses and an apron. Neutralize remaining HCl(*aq*) with baking soda before flushing down the drain.

Procedure Identify the two reactants as magnesium and hydrochloric acid. Have students observe the reaction as you carefully add the magnesium strip to the acid. Ask students to write a balanced chemical equation for the reaction of magnesium and hydrochloric acid. [*Mg(s) + 2HCl(aq) → MgCl$_2$(aq) + H$_2$(g)*] Have students interpret the equation in terms of particles, moles, and molar masses.

Expected Outcome Students should express the balanced equation at the particle level as one atom of magnesium reacts with two molecules of hydrogen chloride to produce one formula unit of magnesium chloride and one molecule of hydrogen gas. Similarly, one mole of magnesium reacts with two moles of hydrogen chloride to produce one mole of magnesium chloride and one mole of hydrogen gas. Finally, 24.31 g Mg + 72.92 g HCl produces 95.21 g MgCl$_2$ + 2.02 g H$_2$.

Answers to...
Figure 12.3 10 molecules NH_3

✓**Checkpoint** the relative numbers of representative particles, the relative numbers of moles, and, for gases, the relative volumes

Stoichiometry   **357**

Differentiated Instruction

Less Proficient Readers   **L1**
Have students construct a table like the one shown in Figure 12.3 for the reaction of hydrogen gas with oxygen gas to form water. Students should begin by writing the balanced equation. Encourage students to draw pictures as shown in Figure 12.3 to represent reactants and products. Have students use the completed table to answer questions such as, "How many moles of water are produced by reacting 4 moles of hydrogen gas with excess oxygen?" Other reactions for students to analyze:
$CO(g) + 2H_2(g) \rightarrow CH_3OH(l)$
$CH_4(g) + 2O_2(g) \rightarrow CO_2(g) + 2H_2O(g)$

Note: Please note that the actual text pages are full color.

FIGURE 12.1 (Contd.)

Section 12.1 (continued)

CONCEPTUAL PROBLEM 12.1

Answers

3. 2 molecules H_2 + 1 molecule $O_2 \rightarrow$
$\qquad$ 2 molecules H_2O
2 mol H_2 + 1 mol $O_2 \rightarrow$ 2 mol H_2O
44.8 L H_2 + 22.4 L $O_2 \rightarrow$ 44.8 L H_2O

4. 2 mol C_2H_2 + 5 mol $O_2 \rightarrow$
$\qquad$ 4 mol CO_2 + 2 mol H_2O
44.8 L C_2H_2 + 112 L $O_2 \rightarrow$
$\qquad$ 89.6 L CO_2 + 44.8 L H_2O
212 g reactants $\rightarrow$ 212 g products

Practice Problems Plus [L2]

Balance the following equation:
$C_5H_{12}(g) + O_2(g) \rightarrow CO_2(g) + H_2O(g)$

Interpret the balanced equation in terms of relative number of moles, volumes of gas at STP, and masses of reactants and products. [1 mol $C_5H_{12}(g)$ + 8 mol $O_2(g) \rightarrow$ 5 mol $CO_2(g)$ + 6 mol $H_2O(g)$; 22.4 L $C_5H_{12}(g)$ + 179 L $O_2(g) \rightarrow$ 112 L $CO_2(g)$ + 134 L $H_2O(g)$; 328 g reactants $\rightarrow$ 328 g products]

③ ASSESS

Evaluate Understanding [L2]

Have pairs of students write a balanced chemical equation for a simple reaction. Have pairs exchange equations and write quantitative relationships between reactants and products in terms of mass, moles, particles, and, where appropriate, volumes.

Reteach [L1]

Remind students that the coefficients in a balanced chemical equation state the relationships among substances involved in the reaction.

Writing ▶ Activity

Moles of reactants and products are conserved for some reactions, but this is generally not the case.

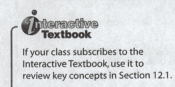 **Interactive Textbook**

If your class subscribes to the Interactive Textbook, use it to review key concepts in Section 12.1.

——with **ChemASAP**

CONCEPTUAL PROBLEM 12.1

Interpreting a Balanced Chemical Equation

Hydrogen sulfide, which smells like rotten eggs, is found in volcanic gases. The balanced equation for the burning of hydrogen sulfide is:

$$2H_2S(g) + 3O_2(g) \longrightarrow 2SO_2(g) + 2H_2O(g)$$

Interpret this equation in terms of
a. numbers of representative particles and moles.
b. masses of reactants and products.

> In the student version of the text, a picture of volcanic gases appears here.

① Analyze *Identify the relevant concepts.*
a. The coefficients in the balanced equation give the relative number of molecules or moles of reactants and products.
b. A balanced chemical equation obeys the law of conservation of mass.

② Solve *Apply concepts to this situation.*
a. 2 molecules H_2S + 3 molecules $O_2 \longrightarrow$
$\qquad$ 2 molecules SO_2 + 2 molecules H_2O
2 mol H_2S + 3 mol $O_2 \longrightarrow$
$\qquad$ 2 mol SO_2 + 2 mol H_2O

b. Multiply the number of moles of each reactant and product by its molar mass:
2 mol H_2S + 3 mol $O_2 \longrightarrow$ 2 mol SO_2 + 2 mol H_2O.

$$\left(2 \text{ mol} \times 34.1\tfrac{g}{mol}\right) + \left(3 \text{ mol} \times 32.0\tfrac{g}{mol}\right) \longrightarrow$$
$$\left(2 \text{ mol} \times 64.1\tfrac{g}{mol}\right) + \left(2 \text{ mol} \times 18.0\tfrac{g}{mol}\right)$$

68.2 g H_2S + 96.0 g $O_2 \longrightarrow$ 128.2 g SO_2 + 36.0 g H_2O
164.2 g = 164.2 g

Practice Problems

3. Interpret the equation for the formation of water from its elements in terms of numbers of molecules and moles, and volumes of gases at STP.

$$2H_2(g) + O_2(g) \longrightarrow 2H_2O(g)$$

4. Balance the following equation.

$$C_2H_2(g) + O_2(g) \longrightarrow CO_2(g) + H_2O(g)$$

Interpret the balanced equation in terms of relative numbers of moles, volumes of gas at STP, and masses of reactants and products.

Interactive Textbook

Problem-Solving 12.4 Solve Problem 4 with the help of an interactive guided tutorial.
——with **ChemASAP**

12.1 Section Assessment

5. ⏺ **Key Concept** How is a balanced equation similar to a recipe?
6. ⏺ **Key Concept** How do chemists use balanced equations?
7. ⏺ **Key Concept** Chemical reactions can be described in terms of what quantities?
8. ⏺ **Key Concept** What quantities are always conserved in chemical reactions?
9. Interpret the given equation in terms of relative numbers of representative particles, numbers of moles, and masses of reactants and products.

$$2K(s) + 2H_2O(l) \longrightarrow 2KOH(aq) + H_2(g)$$

10. Balance this equation: $C_2H_5OH(l) + O_2(g) \longrightarrow CO_2(g) + H_2O(g)$. Show that the balanced equation obeys the law of conservation of mass.

Writing Activity

Explanatory Paragraph Explain this statement: "Mass and atoms are conserved in every chemical reaction, but moles are not necessarily conserved."

Interactive Textbook

Assessment 12.1 Test yourself on the concepts in Section 12.1.
——with **ChemASAP**

Section 12.1 Assessment

5. Both a balanced equation and a recipe give quantitative information about the starting and end materials.
6. as a basis to calculate how much reactant is needed or product is formed in a reaction
7. numbers of atoms, molecules, or moles; mass; and volumes
8. mass and atoms

9. 2 atoms K + 2 molecules $H_2O \rightarrow$
$\qquad$ 2 formula units KOH + 1 molecule H_2
2 mol K + 2 mol $H_2O \rightarrow$
$\qquad$ 2 mol KOH + 1 mol H_2
78.2 g K + 36.0 g $H_2O \rightarrow$
$\qquad$ 112.2 g KOH + 2.0 g H_2
10. C_2H_5OH + 3$O_2 \rightarrow$ 2CO_2 + 3H_2O
46.0 g C_2H_5OH + 96.0 g $O_2 \rightarrow$
$\qquad$ 88.0 g CO_2 + 54.0 g H_2O
142.0 g reactants $\rightarrow$ 142.0 g products

Note: Please note that the actual text pages are full color.

FIGURE 12.1 (*Contd.*)

12.2 Chemical Calculations

Connecting to Your World   Air bags inflate almost instantaneously upon a car's impact. The effectiveness of air bags is based on the rapid conversion of a small mass of sodium azide into a large volume of

In the student version of the text, a picture of a crash test dummy being cushioned by an inflated airbag appears here.

gas. The gas fills an air bag, preventing the driver from hitting the steering wheel or dashboard. The entire reaction occurs in less than a second. In this section you will learn how to use a balanced chemical equation to calculate the amount of product formed in a chemical reaction.

Writing and Using Mole Ratios

As you just learned, a balanced chemical equation provides a great deal of quantitative information. It relates particles (atoms, molecules, formula units), moles of substances, and masses. A balanced chemical equation also is essential for all calculations involving amounts of reactants and products. For example, suppose you know the number of moles of one substance. The balanced chemical equation allows you to determine the number of moles of all other substances in the reaction.

Look again at the balanced equation for the production of ammonia from nitrogen and hydrogen:

$$N_2(g) + 3H_2(g) \longrightarrow 2NH_3(g)$$

The most important interpretation of this equation is that 1 mol of nitrogen reacts with 3 mol of hydrogen to form 2 mol of ammonia. Based on this interpretation, you can write ratios that relate moles of reactants to moles of product. A **mole ratio** is a conversion factor derived from the coefficients of a balanced chemical equation interpreted in terms of moles. ⊂⊃ In chemical calculations, mole ratios are used to convert between moles of reactant and moles of product, between moles of reactants, or between moles of products. Three mole ratios derived from the balanced equation above are:

$$\frac{1 \text{ mol } N_2}{3 \text{ mol } H_2} \qquad \frac{2 \text{ mol } NH_3}{1 \text{ mol } N_2} \qquad \frac{3 \text{ mol } H_2}{2 \text{ mol } NH_3}$$

Mole-Mole Calculations   In the mole ratio below, W is the unknown quantity. The values of a and b are the coefficients from the balanced equation. Thus a general solution for a mole-mole problem, such as Sample Problem 12.2, is given by

$$x \text{ mol } G \times \frac{b \text{ mol } W}{a \text{ mol } G} = \frac{xb}{a} \text{ mol } W$$

Given   Mole ratio   Calculated

Guide for Reading

⊂⊃ **Key Concepts**
- How are mole ratios used in chemical calculations?
- What is the general procedure for solving a stoichiometric problem?

Vocabulary
mole ratio

Reading Strategy
Relating Text and Visuals As you read, look closely at Figure 12.9. Explain how this illustration helps you understand the relationship between known and unknown quantities in a stoichiometric problem.

Figure 12.4 Manufacturing plants produce ammonia by combining nitrogen with hydrogen. Ammonia is used in cleaning products, fertilizers, and in the manufacture of other chemicals.

In the student version of the text, a picture of chemical tanks appears here.

1 FOCUS

Objectives

12.2.1 Construct mole ratios from balanced chemical equations and **apply** these ratios in stoichiometric calculations.

12.2.2 Calculate stoichiometric quantities from balanced chemical equations using units of moles, mass, representative particles, and volumes of gases at STP.

Guide for Reading

Build Vocabulary   L2

Paraphrase Have students work with a partner to define the term *mole ratio* in their own words. They may do so by reading this section and by using what they already learned about balanced chemical equations. Have student pairs read their definitions to the class.

Reading Strategy   L2

Identify Main Ideas/Details As you read the material under the heading *Mass-Mass Calculations*, identify and list the main ideas presented by the text.

2 INSTRUCT

Connecting to Your World

Have students study the photograph and read the text that opens the section. Write the equation for the decomposition of sodium azide with heat as one of the products $2NaN_3(s) \rightarrow 2Na(s) + 3N_2(g) + \text{heat}$. Ask, **How can stoichiometry be used to calculate the volume of a gas produced in this reaction?** *(The number of moles (and volume) of nitrogen gas formed by this reaction depends on the number of moles of sodium azide that decompose.)*

Section Resources

Print
- **Guided Reading and Study Workbook,** Section 12.2
- **Core Teaching Resources,** Section 12.2 Review
- **Transparencies,** T126–T132
- **Laboratory Manual,** Lab 19

- **Small-Scale Chemistry Laboratory Manual,** Labs 18, 19
- **Probeware Laboratory Manual,** Section 12.2

Technology
- **Interactive Textbook with ChemASAP,** Simulation 13, Problem-Solving 12.12, 12.13, 12.15, 12.19, Assessment 12.2

Note: Please note that the actual text pages are full color.

FIGURE 12.1 (Contd.)

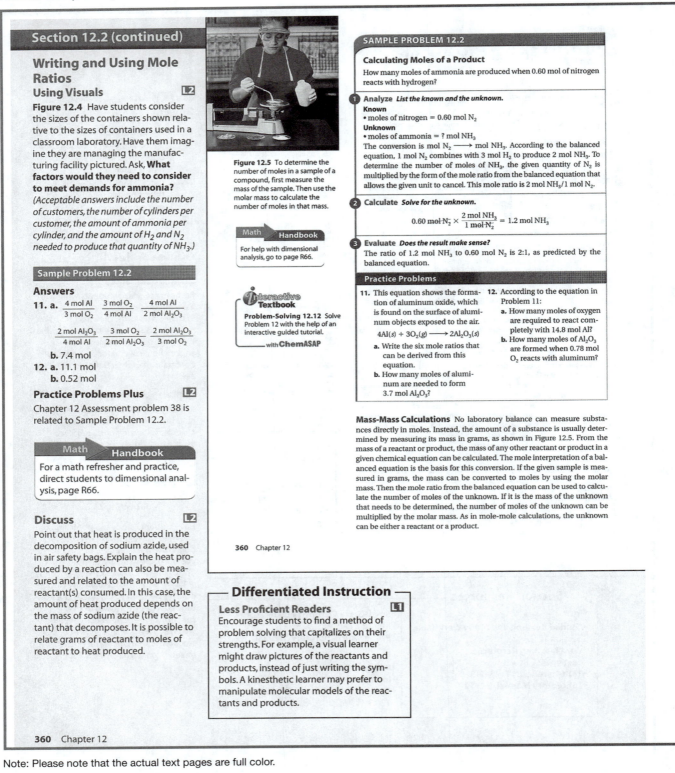

Section 12.2 (continued)

Writing and Using Mole Ratios
Using Visuals   L2

Figure 12.4 Have students consider the sizes of the containers shown relative to the sizes of containers used in a classroom laboratory. Have them imagine they are managing the manufacturing facility pictured. Ask, **What factors would they need to consider to meet demands for ammonia?** *(Acceptable answers include the number of customers, the number of cylinders per customer, the amount of ammonia per cylinder, and the amount of H_2 and N_2 needed to produce that quantity of NH_3.)*

Sample Problem 12.2

Answers

11. a. $\dfrac{4 \text{ mol Al}}{3 \text{ mol O}_2}$ $\dfrac{3 \text{ mol O}_2}{4 \text{ mol Al}}$ $\dfrac{4 \text{ mol Al}}{2 \text{ mol Al}_2\text{O}_3}$

      $\dfrac{2 \text{ mol Al}_2\text{O}_3}{4 \text{ mol Al}}$ $\dfrac{3 \text{ mol O}_2}{2 \text{ mol Al}_2\text{O}_3}$ $\dfrac{2 \text{ mol Al}_2\text{O}_3}{3 \text{ mol O}_2}$

     b. 7.4 mol
12. a. 11.1 mol
     b. 0.52 mol

Practice Problems Plus   L2

Chapter 12 Assessment problem 38 is related to Sample Problem 12.2.

> **Math**   **Handbook**
>
> For a math refresher and practice, direct students to dimensional analysis, page R66.

Discuss   L2

Point out that heat is produced in the decomposition of sodium azide, used in air safety bags. Explain the heat produced by a reaction can also be measured and related to the amount of reactant(s) consumed. In this case, the amount of heat produced depends on the mass of sodium azide (the reactant) that decomposes. It is possible to relate grams of reactant to moles of reactant to heat produced.

Figure 12.5 To determine the number of moles in a sample of a compound, first measure the mass of the sample. Then use the molar mass to calculate the number of moles in that mass.

> **Math**   **Handbook**
>
> For help with dimensional analysis, go to page R66.

interactive
Textbook

Problem-Solving 12.12 Solve Problem 12 with the help of an interactive guided tutorial.

— with **ChemASAP**

SAMPLE PROBLEM 12.2

Calculating Moles of a Product

How many moles of ammonia are produced when 0.60 mol of nitrogen reacts with hydrogen?

1 **Analyze** *List the known and the unknown.*

Known
• moles of nitrogen = 0.60 mol N_2

Unknown
• moles of ammonia = ? mol NH_3

The conversion is mol $N_2 \longrightarrow$ mol NH_3. According to the balanced equation, 1 mol N_2 combines with 3 mol H_2 to produce 2 mol NH_3. To determine the number of moles of NH_3, the given quantity of N_2 is multiplied by the form of the mole ratio from the balanced equation that allows the given unit to cancel. This mole ratio is 2 mol NH_3/1 mol N_2.

2 **Calculate** *Solve for the unknown.*

$$0.60 \text{ mol } N_2 \times \frac{2 \text{ mol } NH_3}{1 \text{ mol } N_2} = 1.2 \text{ mol } NH_3$$

3 **Evaluate** *Does the result make sense?*

The ratio of 1.2 mol NH_3 to 0.60 mol N_2 is 2:1, as predicted by the balanced equation.

Practice Problems

11. This equation shows the formation of aluminum oxide, which is found on the surface of aluminum objects exposed to the air.

$$4\text{Al}(s) + 3\text{O}_2(g) \longrightarrow 2\text{Al}_2\text{O}_3(s)$$

   a. Write the six mole ratios that can be derived from this equation.
   b. How many moles of aluminum are needed to form 3.7 mol Al_2O_3?

12. According to the equation in Problem 11:
   a. How many moles of oxygen are required to react completely with 14.8 mol Al?
   b. How many moles of Al_2O_3 are formed when 0.78 mol O_2 reacts with aluminum?

Mass-Mass Calculations No laboratory balance can measure substances directly in moles. Instead, the amount of a substance is usually determined by measuring its mass in grams, as shown in Figure 12.5. From the mass of a reactant or product, the mass of any other reactant or product in a given chemical equation can be calculated. The mole interpretation of a balanced equation is the basis for this conversion. If the given sample is measured in grams, the mass can be converted to moles by using the molar mass. Then the mole ratio from the balanced equation can be used to calculate the number of moles of the unknown. If it is the mass of the unknown that needs to be determined, the number of moles of the unknown can be multiplied by the molar mass. As in mole-mole calculations, the unknown can be either a reactant or a product.

360 Chapter 12

Differentiated Instruction

Less Proficient Readers   L1

Encourage students to find a method of problem solving that capitalizes on their strengths. For example, a visual learner might draw pictures of the reactants and products, instead of just writing the symbols. A kinesthetic learner may prefer to manipulate molecular models of the reactants and products.

Note: Please note that the actual text pages are full color.

FIGURE 12.1 (*Contd.*)

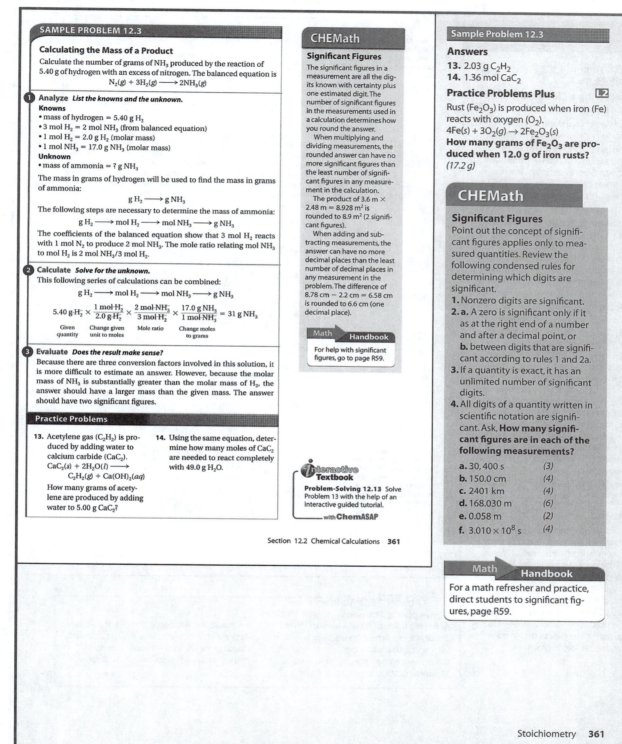

Calculating the Mass of a Product

Calculate the number of grams of NH_3 produced by the reaction of 5.40 g of hydrogen with an excess of nitrogen. The balanced equation is

$$N_2(g) + 3H_2(g) \longrightarrow 2NH_3(g)$$

1 **Analyze** *List the knowns and the unknown.*

Knowns
- mass of hydrogen = 5.40 g H_2
- 3 mol H_2 = 2 mol NH_3 (from balanced equation)
- 1 mol H_2 = 2.0 g H_2 (molar mass)
- 1 mol NH_3 = 17.0 g NH_3 (molar mass)

Unknown
- mass of ammonia = ? g NH_3

The mass in grams of hydrogen will be used to find the mass in grams of ammonia:

$$g\ H_2 \longrightarrow g\ NH_3$$

The following steps are necessary to determine the mass of ammonia:

$$g\ H_2 \longrightarrow mol\ H_2 \longrightarrow mol\ NH_3 \longrightarrow g\ NH_3$$

The coefficients of the balanced equation show that 3 mol H_2 reacts with 1 mol N_2 to produce 2 mol NH_3. The mole ratio relating mol NH_3 to mol H_2 is 2 mol NH_3/3 mol H_2.

2 **Calculate** *Solve for the unknown.*

This following series of calculations can be combined:

$$g\ H_2 \longrightarrow mol\ H_2 \longrightarrow mol\ NH_3 \longrightarrow g\ NH_3$$

$$5.40\ \text{g } H_2 \times \frac{1\ \text{mol } H_2}{2.0\ \text{g } H_2} \times \frac{2\ \text{mol } NH_3}{3\ \text{mol } H_2} \times \frac{17.0\ \text{g } NH_3}{1\ \text{mol } NH_3} = 31\ \text{g } NH_3$$

Given quantity | Change given unit to moles | Mole ratio | Change moles to grams

3 **Evaluate** *Does the result make sense?*

Because there are three conversion factors involved in this solution, it is more difficult to estimate an answer. However, because the molar mass of NH_3 is substantially greater than the molar mass of H_2, the answer should have a larger mass than the given mass. The answer should have two significant figures.

Practice Problems

13. Acetylene gas (C_2H_2) is produced by adding water to calcium carbide (CaC_2).
$$CaC_2(s) + 2H_2O(l) \longrightarrow$$
$$C_2H_2(g) + Ca(OH)_2(aq)$$
How many grams of acetylene are produced by adding water to 5.00 g CaC_2?

14. Using the same equation, determine how many moles of CaC_2 are needed to react completely with 49.0 g H_2O.

CHEMath

Significant Figures

The significant figures in a measurement are all the digits known with certainty plus one estimated digit. The number of significant figures in the measurements used in a calculation determines how you round the answer.

When multiplying and dividing measurements, the rounded answer can have no more significant figures than the least number of significant figures in any measurement in the calculation.

The product of 3.6 m × 2.48 m = 8.928 m² is rounded to 8.9 m² (2 significant figures).

When adding and subtracting measurements, the answer can have no more decimal places than the least number of decimal places in any measurement in the problem. The difference of 8.78 cm − 2.2 cm = 6.58 cm is rounded to 6.6 cm (one decimal place).

Math ▶ Handbook

For help with significant figures, go to page R59.

ínteractive Textbook

Problem-Solving 12.13 Solve Problem 13 with the help of an interactive guided tutorial.

— with **ChemASAP**

Section 12.2 Chemical Calculations   **361**

Answers
13. 2.03 g C_2H_2
14. 1.36 mol CaC_2

Practice Problems Plus   **L2**

Rust (Fe_2O_3) is produced when iron (Fe) reacts with oxygen (O_2).
$$4Fe(s) + 3O_2(g) \rightarrow 2Fe_2O_3(s)$$
How many grams of Fe_2O_3 are produced when 12.0 g of iron rusts?
(17.2 g)

CHEMath

Significant Figures
Point out the concept of significant figures applies only to measured quantities. Review the following condensed rules for determining which digits are significant.
1. Nonzero digits are significant.
2. **a.** A zero is significant only if it as at the right end of a number and after a decimal point, or
   b. between digits that are significant according to rules 1 and 2a.
3. If a quantity is exact, it has an unlimited number of significant digits.
4. All digits of a quantity written in scientific notation are significant. Ask, **How many significant figures are in each of the following measurements?**

a. 30,400 s   *(3)*
b. 150.0 cm   *(4)*
c. 2401 km   *(4)*
d. 168.030 m   *(6)*
e. 0.058 m   *(2)*
f. 3.010×10^8 s   *(4)*

Math ▶ Handbook
For a math refresher and practice, direct students to significant figures, page R59.

Stoichiometry   **361**

Note: Please note that the actual text pages are full color.

FIGURE 12.1 (*Contd.*)

Section 12.2 (continued)

TEACHER   Demo

Interpreting a Chemical Equation   **L2**

Purpose Students interpret a balanced equation in terms of moles and mass.

Materials Prior to the demonstration prepare 0.1*M* solutions of potassium iodide and lead(II) nitrate. Measure 50.0 mL of $Pb(NO_3)_2$ and 150 mL of KI into separate 250-mL beakers.

Safety Wear safety glasses and apron.

Procedure Tell students that you are going to mix 0.005 moles of lead(II) nitrate with excess potassium iodide. Have student observe as you combine both solutions in the 250-mL beaker. Have students write a balanced chemical equation for the observed reaction.

$[2KI(aq) + Pb(NO_3)_2(aq) \rightarrow$
$\qquad\qquad 2KNO_3(aq) + PbI_2(s)]$

Have students predict the number of moles of product produced. *(0.005 moles PbI$_2$ assuming the reaction was complete)* Note that, in an actual reaction, the amounts of reactants often are not present in the mole ratios predicted by the coefficients in a balanced equation. Explain the importance of the mole ratios in an equation for calculating relative quantities. Ask, **What is the mass of lead(II) nitrate reacted and the mass of lead(II) iodide produced?** *(1.66 g Pb(NO$_3$)$_2$ and 2.30 g PbI$_2$)*

Expected Outcome A bright yellow precipitate will form.

Discuss   **L2**

Students sometimes try to do mass-mass conversions by incorrectly using the mole ratio as a mass ratio. (That is, they use grams instead of moles as the units in the mole ratio, and then skip the mass-mole conversion step.) Stress that because the number of grams in one mole of a substance varies with its molar mass, a mass-mole conversion is a necessary intermediate step in mass-mass stoichiometric problems.

Figure 12.6 In this Hubble Space Telescope image, clouds of condensed ammonia are visible covering the surface of Saturn.

In the student version of the text, a picture of Saturn appears here.

If the law of conservation of mass is true, how is it possible to make 31 g NH_3 from only 5.40 g H_2? Looking back at the equation for the reaction, you will see that hydrogen is not the only reactant. Another reactant, nitrogen, is also involved. If you were to calculate the number of grams of nitrogen needed to produce 31 g NH_3 and then compare the total masses of reactants and products, you would have an answer to this question. Go ahead and try it!

Mass-mass problems are solved in basically the same way as mole-mole problems. Figure 12.7 reviews the steps for the mass-mass conversion of any given mass (*G*) and any wanted mass (*W*).

Steps in Solving a Mass-Mass Problem

1. Change the mass of *G* to moles of *G* (mass *G* $\longrightarrow$ mol *G*) by using the molar mass of *G*.

$$\text{mass } G \times \frac{1 \text{ mol } G}{\text{molar mass } G} = \text{mol } G$$

2. Change the moles of *G* to moles of *W* (mol *G* $\longrightarrow$ mol *W*) by using the mole ratio from the balanced equation.

$$\text{mol } G \times \frac{b \text{ mol } W}{a \text{ mol } G} = \text{mol } W$$

3. Change the moles of *W* to grams of *W* (mol *W* $\longrightarrow$ mass *W*) by using the molar mass of *W*.

$$\text{mol } W \times \frac{\text{molar mass } W}{1 \text{ mol } W} = \text{mass } W$$

Figure 12.7 also shows the steps for doing mole-mass and mass-mole stoichiometric calculations. For a mole-mass problem, the first conversion (from mass to moles) is skipped. For a mass-mole problem, the last conversion (from moles to mass) is skipped. You can use parts of the three-step process shown in Figure 12.7 as they are appropriate to the problem you are solving.

Figure 12.7 This general solution diagram indicates the steps necessary to solve a mass-mass stoichiometry problem: convert mass to moles, use the mole ratio, and then convert moles to mass. **Inferring** *Is the given always a reactant?*

$$\boxed{aG \longrightarrow bW}$$
(given quantity)   (wanted quantity)

$$\boxed{\text{mass of } G} \times \boxed{\frac{1 \text{ mol } G}{\text{mass } G}} \rightarrow \boxed{\text{mol } G} \times \boxed{\frac{b \text{ mol } W}{a \text{ mol } G}} \rightarrow \boxed{\text{mol } W} \times \boxed{\frac{\text{mass } W}{1 \text{ mol } W}} \rightarrow \boxed{\text{mass of } W}$$

Mass-mole conversion   Mole ratio from balanced equation   Mole-mass conversion

---

Facts and Figures

Atmospheric Ammonia

Ammonia is found in trace amounts in the atmospheres of three Jovian planets—Jupiter, Saturn, and Uranus. In Jupiter's atmosphere, the clouds of ammonia consist of frozen ammonia droplets changing to liquid ammonia droplets nearer the planet's surface. Because of colder temperatures, the ammonia clouds in the atmosphere of Saturn and Uranus consist of frozen ammonia droplets.

Note: Please note that the actual text pages are full color.

FIGURE 12.1 (*Contd.*)

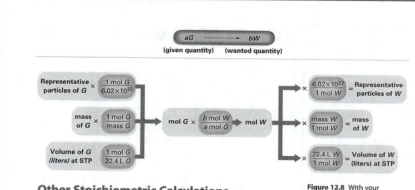

Other Stoichiometric Calculations

As you already know, you can obtain mole ratios from a balanced chemical equation. From the mole ratios, you can calculate any measurement unit that is related to the mole. The given quantity can be expressed in numbers of representative particles, units of mass, or volumes of gases at STP. The problems can include mass-volume, particle-mass and volume-volume calculations. For example, you can use stoichiometry to relate volumes of reactants and products in the reaction shown in Figure 12.8. ⟳ **In a typical stoichiometric problem, the given quantity is first converted to moles. Then the mole ratio from the balanced equation is used to calculate the number of moles of the wanted substance. Finally, the moles are converted to any other unit of measurement related to the unit mole, as the problem requires.**

Thus far, you have learned how to use the relationship between moles and mass (1 mol = molar mass) in solving mass-mass, mass-mole, and mole-mass stoichiometric problems. The mole-mass relationship gives you two conversion factors.

$$\frac{1 \text{ mol}}{\text{molar mass}} \quad \text{and} \quad \frac{\text{molar mass}}{1 \text{ mol}}$$

Recall from Chapter 10 that the mole can be related to other quantities as well. For example, 1 mol = 6.02×10^{23} representative particles, and 1 mol of a gas = 22.4 L at STP. These two relationships provide four more conversion factors that you can use in stoichiometric calculations.

$$\frac{1 \text{ mol}}{6.02 \times 10^{23} \text{ particles}} \quad \text{and} \quad \frac{6.02 \times 10^{23} \text{ particles}}{1 \text{ mol}}$$

$$\frac{1 \text{ mol}}{22.4 \text{ L}} \quad \text{and} \quad \frac{22.4 \text{ L}}{1 \text{ mol}}$$

Figure 12.8 summarizes the steps for a typical stoichiometric problem. Notice that the units of the given quantity will not necessarily be the same as the units of the wanted quantity. For example, given the mass of *G*, you might be asked to calculate the volume of *W* at STP.

✓ **Checkpoint**   *What conversion factors can you write based on the mole-mass and mole-volume relationships?*

Figure 12.8 With your knowledge of conversion factors and this problem-solving approach, you can solve a variety of stoichiometric problems.
Identifying *What conversion factor is used to convert moles to representative particles?*

ⓘ **Interactive Textbook**

Simulation 13 Strengthen your analytical skills by solving stoichiometric problems.
with **ChemASAP**

Section 12.2 Chemical Calculations   **363**

Discuss   L2

Initiate a discussion with students by asking whether the law of conservation of mass is always true. If not, ask them to give an example. (Nuclear reactions are the only cases where this law does not hold true.) Ask, **Why isn't there a "law of conservation of moles"?** (*In reactions involving rearrangements of atoms, reactants can combine or decompose to produce fewer or greater numbers of moles of product. Although the total mass of reactants and products is constant, the number of moles of particles can increase or decrease depending on the final grouping of atoms.*) **Give an example of a reaction in which the number of moles of products is greater than the number of moles of reactants.**
$[2H_2O(l) \rightarrow 2H_2(g) + O_2(g)]$
Give an example of a reaction in which the number of moles of products is less than the number of moles of reactants.
$[2Mg(s) + O_2(g) \rightarrow 2MgO(s)]$

Other Stoichiometric Calculations
Discuss   L2

On the board, write equations for reactions in which the reactants are both gases or are a gas and a solid. Ask students how the reactants and products in each reaction would most likely be measured. Have students relate these measurements to the concept of a mole.

Answers to...

Figure 12.7 No; the given could be a product.

Figure 12.8 6.02×10^{23} representative particles/1 mol

✓ **Checkpoint**

$\dfrac{1 \text{ mol}}{\text{molar mass}}$	$\dfrac{\text{molar mass}}{1 \text{ mol}}$
$\dfrac{22.4 \text{ L}}{1 \text{ mol}}$	$\dfrac{1 \text{ mol}}{22.4 \text{ L}}$

Stoichiometry   **363**

FIGURE 12.1 (*Contd.*)

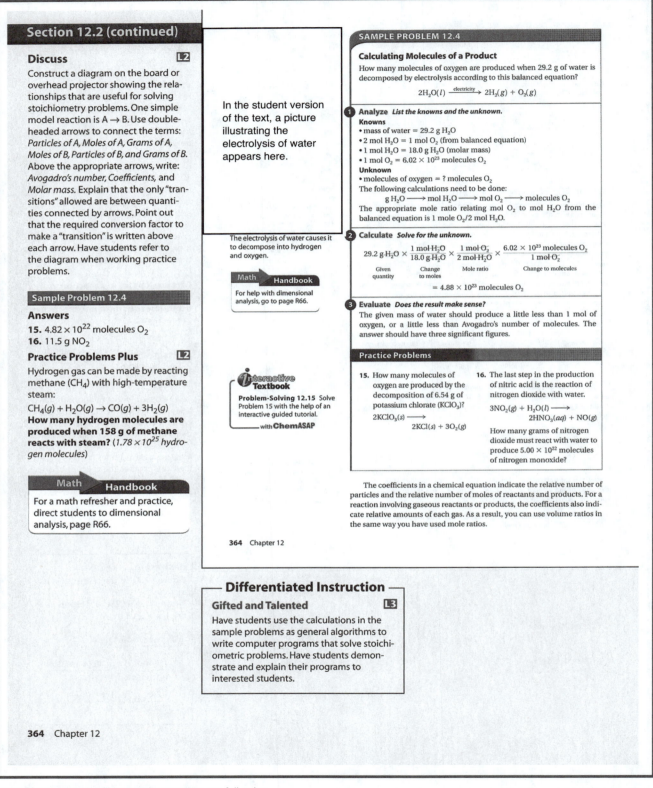

Section 12.2 (continued)

Discuss · L2

Construct a diagram on the board or overhead projector showing the relationships that are useful for solving stoichiometry problems. One simple model reaction is A → B. Use double-headed arrows to connect the terms: *Particles of A, Moles of A, Grams of A, Moles of B, Particles of B,* and *Grams of B.* Above the appropriate arrows, write: *Avogadro's number, Coefficients,* and *Molar mass.* Explain that the only "transitions" allowed are between quantities connected by arrows. Point out that the required conversion factor to make a "transition" is written above each arrow. Have students refer to the diagram when working practice problems.

Sample Problem 12.4

Answers
15. 4.82×10^{22} molecules O_2
16. 11.5 g NO_2

Practice Problems Plus · L2

Hydrogen gas can be made by reacting methane (CH_4) with high-temperature steam:

$CH_4(g) + H_2O(g) \rightarrow CO(g) + 3H_2(g)$

How many hydrogen molecules are produced when 158 g of methane reacts with steam? (*1.78×10^{25} hydrogen molecules*)

— Math ► Handbook —
For a math refresher and practice, direct students to dimensional analysis, page R66.

In the student version of the text, a picture illustrating the electrolysis of water appears here.

The electrolysis of water causes it to decompose into hydrogen and oxygen.

Math ► Handbook
For help with dimensional analysis, go to page R66.

interactive **Textbook**
Problem-Solving 12.15 Solve Problem 15 with the help of an interactive guided tutorial.
— with **ChemASAP**

SAMPLE PROBLEM 12.4

Calculating Molecules of a Product
How many molecules of oxygen are produced when 29.2 g of water is decomposed by electrolysis according to this balanced equation?

$$2H_2O(l) \xrightarrow{\text{electricity}} 2H_2(g) + O_2(g)$$

1 Analyze *List the knowns and the unknown.*

Knowns
• mass of water = 29.2 g H_2O
• 2 mol H_2O = 1 mol O_2 (from balanced equation)
• 1 mol H_2O = 18.0 g H_2O (molar mass)
• 1 mol O_2 = 6.02×10^{23} molecules O_2

Unknown
• molecules of oxygen = ? molecules O_2

The following calculations need to be done:

g $H_2O \longrightarrow$ mol $H_2O \longrightarrow$ mol $O_2 \longrightarrow$ molecules O_2

The appropriate mole ratio relating mol O_2 to mol H_2O from the balanced equation is 1 mole O_2/2 mol H_2O.

2 Calculate *Solve for the unknown.*

$$29.2 \text{ g } H_2O \times \frac{1 \text{ mol } H_2O}{18.0 \text{ g } H_2O} \times \frac{1 \text{ mol } O_2}{2 \text{ mol } H_2O} \times \frac{6.02 \times 10^{23} \text{ molecules } O_2}{1 \text{ mol } O_2}$$

| Given quantity | Change to moles | Mole ratio | Change to molecules |

$$= 4.88 \times 10^{23} \text{ molecules } O_2$$

3 Evaluate *Does the result make sense?*
The given mass of water should produce a little less than 1 mol of oxygen, or a little less than Avogadro's number of molecules. The answer should have three significant figures.

Practice Problems

15. How many molecules of oxygen are produced by the decomposition of 6.54 g of potassium chlorate ($KClO_3$)?

$2KClO_3(s) \longrightarrow$
$\qquad 2KCl(s) + 3O_2(g)$

16. The last step in the production of nitric acid is the reaction of nitrogen dioxide with water.

$3NO_2(g) + H_2O(l) \longrightarrow$
$\qquad 2HNO_3(aq) + NO(g)$

How many grams of nitrogen dioxide must react with water to produce 5.00×10^{22} molecules of nitrogen monoxide?

The coefficients in a chemical equation indicate the relative number of particles and the relative number of moles of reactants and products. For a reaction involving gaseous reactants or products, the coefficients also indicate relative amounts of each gas. As a result, you can use volume ratios in the same way you have used mole ratios.

⸻ Differentiated Instruction ⸻

Gifted and Talented · L3

Have students use the calculations in the sample problems as general algorithms to write computer programs that solve stoichiometric problems. Have students demonstrate and explain their programs to interested students.

Note: Please note that the actual text pages are full color.

FIGURE 12.1 (*Contd.*)

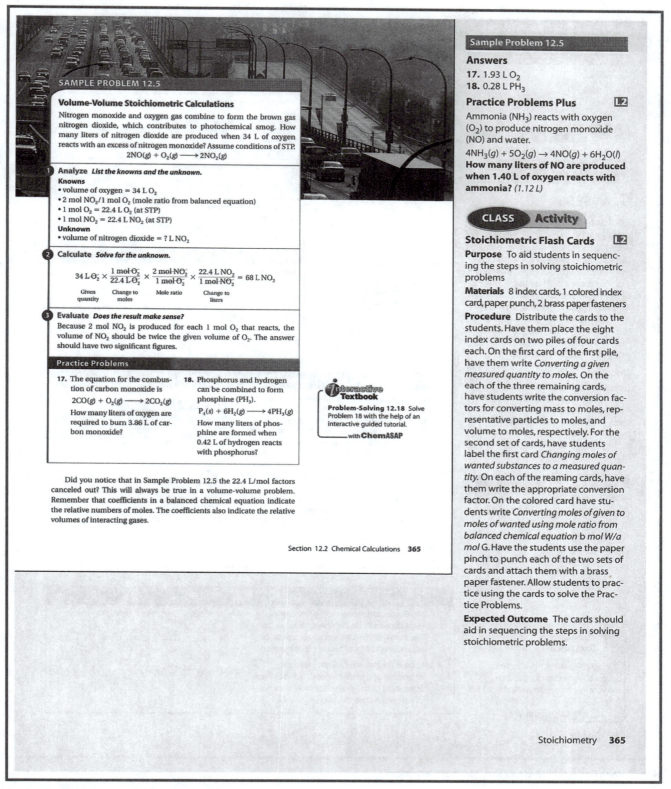

SAMPLE PROBLEM 12.5

Volume-Volume Stoichiometric Calculations

Nitrogen monoxide and oxygen gas combine to form the brown gas nitrogen dioxide, which contributes to photochemical smog. How many liters of nitrogen dioxide are produced when 34 L of oxygen reacts with an excess of nitrogen monoxide? Assume conditions of STP.

$$2NO(g) + O_2(g) \longrightarrow 2NO_2(g)$$

1 **Analyze** *List the knowns and the unknown.*

Knowns
- volume of oxygen = 34 L O_2
- 2 mol NO_2/1 mol O_2 (mole ratio from balanced equation)
- 1 mol O_2 = 22.4 L O_2 (at STP)
- 1 mol NO_2 = 22.4 L NO_2 (at STP)

Unknown
- volume of nitrogen dioxide = ? L NO_2

2 **Calculate** *Solve for the unknown.*

$$34\ \text{L}\ O_2 \times \frac{1\ \text{mol}\ O_2}{22.4\ \text{L}\ O_2} \times \frac{2\ \text{mol}\ NO_2}{1\ \text{mol}\ O_2} \times \frac{22.4\ \text{L}\ NO_2}{1\ \text{mol}\ NO_2} = 68\ \text{L}\ NO_2$$

Given quantity   Change to moles   Mole ratio   Change to liters

3 **Evaluate** *Does the result make sense?*

Because 2 mol NO_2 is produced for each 1 mol O_2 that reacts, the volume of NO_2 should be twice the given volume of O_2. The answer should have two significant figures.

Practice Problems

17. The equation for the combustion of carbon monoxide is

$$2CO(g) + O_2(g) \longrightarrow 2CO_2(g)$$

How many liters of oxygen are required to burn 3.86 L of carbon monoxide?

18. Phosphorus and hydrogen can be combined to form phosphine (PH_3).

$$P_4(s) + 6H_2(g) \longrightarrow 4PH_3(g)$$

How many liters of phosphine are formed when 0.42 L of hydrogen reacts with phosphorus?

Interactive Textbook

Problem-Solving 12.18 Solve Problem 18 with the help of an interactive guided tutorial.
—— with **ChemASAP**

Did you notice that in Sample Problem 12.5 the 22.4 L/mol factors canceled out? This will always be true in a volume-volume problem. Remember that coefficients in a balanced chemical equation indicate the relative numbers of moles. The coefficients also indicate the relative volumes of interacting gases.

Section 12.2 Chemical Calculations   **365**

Answers
17. 1.93 L O_2
18. 0.28 L PH_3

Practice Problems Plus   L2

Ammonia (NH_3) reacts with oxygen (O_2) to produce nitrogen monoxide (NO) and water.

$$4NH_3(g) + 5O_2(g) \rightarrow 4NO(g) + 6H_2O(l)$$

How many liters of NO are produced when 1.40 L of oxygen reacts with ammonia? *(1.12 L)*

CLASS **Activity**

Stoichiometric Flash Cards   L2

Purpose To aid students in sequencing the steps in solving stoichiometric problems

Materials 8 index cards, 1 colored index card, paper punch, 2 brass paper fasteners

Procedure Distribute the cards to the students. Have them place the eight index cards on two piles of four cards each. On the first card of the first pile, have them write *Converting a given measured quantity to moles*. On the each of the three remaining cards, have students write the conversion factors for converting mass to moles, representative particles to moles, and volume to moles, respectively. For the second set of cards, have students label the first card *Changing moles of wanted substances to a measured quantity*. On each of the reaming cards, have them write the appropriate conversion factor. On the colored card have students write *Converting moles of given to moles of wanted using mole ratio from balanced chemical equation b mol W/a mol G*. Have the students use the paper pinch to punch each of the two sets of cards and attach them with a brass paper fastener. Allow students to practice using the cards to solve the Practice Problems.

Expected Outcome The cards should aid in sequencing the steps in solving stoichiometric problems.

Stoichiometry   **365**

Note: Please note that the actual text pages are full color.

FIGURE 12.1 (*Contd.*)

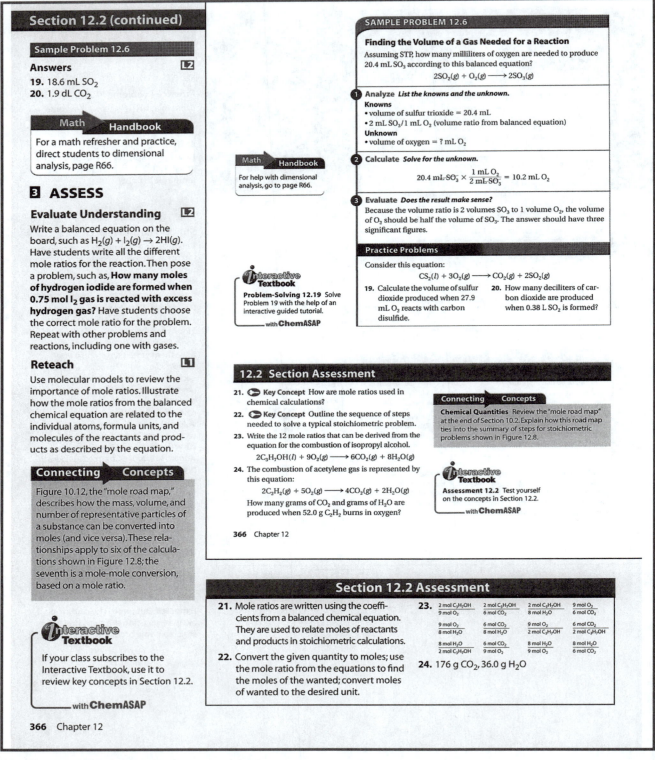

Section 12.2 (continued)

Sample Problem 12.6

Answers [L2]

19. 18.6 mL SO_2
20. 1.9 dL CO_2

> **Math ▶ Handbook**
> For a math refresher and practice, direct students to dimensional analysis, page R66.

❸ ASSESS

Evaluate Understanding [L2]

Write a balanced equation on the board, such as $H_2(g) + I_2(g) \rightarrow 2HI(g)$. Have students write all the different mole ratios for the reaction. Then pose a problem, such as, **How many moles of hydrogen iodide are formed when 0.75 mol I_2 gas is reacted with excess hydrogen gas?** Have students choose the correct mole ratio for the problem. Repeat with other problems and reactions, including one with gases.

Reteach [L1]

Use molecular models to review the importance of mole ratios. Illustrate how the mole ratios from the balanced chemical equation are related to the individual atoms, formula units, and molecules of the reactants and products as described by the equation.

> **Connecting ▶ Concepts**
> Figure 10.12, the "mole road map," describes how the mass, volume, and number of representative particles of a substance can be converted into moles (and vice versa). These relationships apply to six of the calculations shown in Figure 12.8; the seventh is a mole-mole conversion, based on a mole ratio.

> **Interactive Textbook**
> If your class subscribes to the Interactive Textbook, use it to review key concepts in Section 12.2.
> —with **ChemASAP**

SAMPLE PROBLEM 12.6

Finding the Volume of a Gas Needed for a Reaction

Assuming STP, how many milliliters of oxygen are needed to produce 20.4 mL SO_3 according to this balanced equation?

$$2SO_2(g) + O_2(g) \longrightarrow 2SO_3(g)$$

❶ Analyze *List the knowns and the unknown.*

Knowns
• volume of sulfur trioxide = 20.4 mL
• 2 mL SO_3/1 mL O_2 (volume ratio from balanced equation)

Unknown
• volume of oxygen = ? mL O_2

❷ Calculate *Solve for the unknown.*

$$20.4 \text{ mL } SO_3 \times \frac{1 \text{ mL } O_2}{2 \text{ mL } SO_3} = 10.2 \text{ mL } O_2$$

❸ Evaluate *Does the result make sense?*

Because the volume ratio is 2 volumes SO_3 to 1 volume O_2, the volume of O_2 should be half the volume of SO_3. The answer should have three significant figures.

> **Math ▶ Handbook**
> For help with dimensional analysis, go to page R66.

> **Interactive Textbook**
> **Problem-Solving 12.19** Solve Problem 19 with the help of an interactive guided tutorial.
> —with **ChemASAP**

Practice Problems

Consider this equation:

$$CS_2(l) + 3O_2(g) \longrightarrow CO_2(g) + 2SO_2(g)$$

19. Calculate the volume of sulfur dioxide produced when 27.9 mL O_2 reacts with carbon disulfide.

20. How many deciliters of carbon dioxide are produced when 0.38 L SO_2 is formed?

12.2 Section Assessment

21. ◖▶ **Key Concept** How are mole ratios used in chemical calculations?

22. ◖▶ **Key Concept** Outline the sequence of steps needed to solve a typical stoichiometric problem.

23. Write the 12 mole ratios that can be derived from the equation for the combustion of isopropyl alcohol.

$$2C_3H_7OH(l) + 9O_2(g) \longrightarrow 6CO_2(g) + 8H_2O(g)$$

24. The combustion of acetylene gas is represented by this equation:

$$2C_2H_2(g) + 5O_2(g) \longrightarrow 4CO_2(g) + 2H_2O(g)$$

How many grams of CO_2 and grams of H_2O are produced when 52.0 g C_2H_2 burns in oxygen?

> **Connecting Concepts**
> **Chemical Quantities** Review the "mole road map" at the end of Section 10.2. Explain how this road map ties into the summary of steps for stoichiometric problems shown in Figure 12.8.

> **Interactive Textbook**
> **Assessment 12.2** Test yourself on the concepts in Section 12.2.
> —with **ChemASAP**

Section 12.2 Assessment

21. Mole ratios are written using the coefficients from a balanced chemical equation. They are used to relate moles of reactants and products in stoichiometric calculations.

22. Convert the given quantity to moles; use the mole ratio from the equations to find the moles of the wanted; convert moles of wanted to the desired unit.

23.

$\frac{2 \text{ mol } C_3H_7OH}{9 \text{ mol } O_2}$	$\frac{2 \text{ mol } C_3H_7OH}{6 \text{ mol } CO_2}$	$\frac{2 \text{ mol } C_3H_7OH}{8 \text{ mol } H_2O}$	$\frac{9 \text{ mol } O_2}{6 \text{ mol } CO_2}$
$\frac{9 \text{ mol } O_2}{8 \text{ mol } H_2O}$	$\frac{6 \text{ mol } CO_2}{8 \text{ mol } H_2O}$	$\frac{9 \text{ mol } O_2}{2 \text{ mol } C_3H_7OH}$	$\frac{6 \text{ mol } CO_2}{2 \text{ mol } C_2H_7OH}$
$\frac{8 \text{ mol } H_2O}{2 \text{ mol } C_3H_7OH}$	$\frac{6 \text{ mol } CO_2}{9 \text{ mol } O_2}$	$\frac{8 \text{ mol } H_2O}{9 \text{ mol } O_2}$	$\frac{8 \text{ mol } H_2O}{6 \text{ mol } CO_2}$

24. 176 g CO_2, 36.0 g H_2O

Note: Please note that the actual text pages are full color.

FIGURE 12.1 (*Contd.*)

Small-Scale LAB

Analysis of Baking Soda

Purpose
To determine the mass of sodium hydrogen carbonate in a sample of baking soda using stoichiometry.

Materials
- baking soda
- 3 plastic cups
- soda straw
- balance
- pipets of HCl, NaOH, and thymol blue
- pH sensor (optional)

Procedure

Probeware version available in the Probeware Lab Manual.

A. Measure the mass of a clean, dry plastic cup.
B. Using the straw as a scoop, fill one end with baking soda to a depth of about 1 cm. Add the sample to the cup and measure its mass again.
C. Place two HCl pipets that are about 3/4 full into a clean cup and measure the mass of the system.
D. Transfer the contents of both HCl pipets to the cup containing baking soda. Swirl until the fizzing stops. Wait 5–10 minutes to be sure the reaction is complete. Measure the mass of the two empty HCl pipets in their cup again.
E. Add 5 drops of thymol blue to the plastic cup.
F. Place two full NaOH pipets in a clean cup and measure the mass of the system.
G. Add NaOH slowly to the baking soda/HCl mixture until the pink color just disappears. Measure the mass of the NaOH pipets in their cup again.

Analyze
Using your experimental data, record the answers to the following questions below your data table.

1. Write a balanced equation for the reaction between baking soda (NaHCO₃) and HCl.
2. Calculate the mass in grams of the baking soda.

(Step B − Step A)

3. Calculate the total mmol of 1*M* HCl.
Note: Every gram of HCl contains 1 mmol.

(Step C − Step D) × 1.00 mmol/g

4. Calculate the total mmol of 0.5*M* NaOH.
Note: Every gram of NaOH contains 0.5 mmol.

(Step F − Step G) × 0.500 mmol/g

5. Calculate the mmol of HCl that reacted with the baking soda. *Note:* The NaOH measures the amount of HCl that did not react.

(Step 3 − Step 4)

6. Calculate the mass of the baking soda from the reaction data.

(0.084 g/mmol × Step 5)

7. Calculate the percent error of the experiment.

$$\frac{(\text{Step 2} - \text{Step 6})}{\text{Step 2}} \times 100\%$$

You're the Chemist
The following small-scale activities allow you to develop your own procedures and analyze the results.

1. **Analyze It!** For each calculation you did, substitute each quantity (number and unit) into the equation and cancel the units to explain why each step gives the quantity desired.

2. **Design It!** Baking powder consists of a mixture of baking soda, sodium hydrogen carbonate, and a solid acid, usually calcium dihydrogen phosphate (Ca(H₂PO₄)₂). Design and carry out an experiment to determine the percentage of baking soda in baking powder.

Small-Scale Lab **367**

Small-Scale LAB

Analysis of Baking Soda   L2

Objective
Students calculate the mass of NaHCO₃ in a sample using stoichiometry.

⏱ **Prep Time** 1 hour
Materials Baking soda; plastic cups; soda straws; mass balances; pipets of HCl, NaOH, and thymol blue; pH sensor (optional)

Advance Prep

Solution	Preparation
0.5*M* NaOH	20.0 g in 1.0 L
1.0*M* HCl	82 mL of 12*M* in 1.0 L **Caution** *Always add acid to water carefully and slowly.*
0.04% TB	100 mg in 21.5 mL of 01*M* NaOH; dilute to 250 mL

Class Time 30 minutes
Safety Have students wear safety glasses and follow the standard safety procedures.

Teaching Tips
- Stress that the procedure measures the amount of excess HCl that is not reacted with the baking soda (Step 4). Because this excess HCl reacts with the NaOH in a 1:1 mole ratio, the moles of NaOH equal the moles of HCl in excess. Subtracting the excess moles of HCl from the total moles used in the experiment (Step 5) yields the moles reacted with the baking soda, which is 100% NaHCO₃.
- If the mixture does not turn red when thymol blue is added, the student should find the mass of a third pipet and add just enough HCl to turn the mixture cherry red. Then the student should find the mass of the half-empty pipet so the mass of HCl added can be calculated and added to the total mass used.

Expected Outcome
Sample data: Step A. 2.83 g, B. 3.28 g, C. 10.70 g, D. 4.29 g, F. 10.53 g, G. 8.78 g

---

Analyze

1. HCl + NaHCO₃(s) → CO₂(g) + H₂O + NaCl
2. 3.28 g – 2.83 g = 0.45 g
3. (10.70 – 4.29)g × 1.00 mmol/g = 6.41 mmol
4. (10.53 – 8.78)g × 0.500 mmol/g = 0.875 mmol (0.875 mmol HCl unreacted)
5. 6.41 mmol total – 0.875 mmol unreacted = 5.53 mmol (5.53 mmol NaHCO₃)
6. (0.0840 g/mmol) × 5.53 mmol = 0.46 g
7. (0.46 – 0.45) g/0.45g × 100% = 2% error (assuming baking soda is one hundred percent sodium hydrogen carbonate)

You're the Chemist

1. See Steps 2–7.
2. Repeat Steps A–G and 1–7 using baking powder instead of baking soda. The percent error is the percent of baking soda in baking powder, assuming no other errors.

For Enrichment   L3

Ask students to predict how much baking soda and 1*M* HCl are needed to produce enough CO₂ to fill a 1-L plastic bag. Have them write a procedure and then carry out the experiment.

Stoichiometry **367**

Note: Please note that the actual text pages are full color.

compounds and chemical reactions. This knowledge forms the basis for learning about stoichiometry.

Reflection & Discussion Questions

1. As you review this material from the text, what ideas come to mind about how to use it as a resource to guide students in developing an understanding of stoichiometry?

2. What objectives and purposes come to mind?

3. What ideas and reasoning do you feel that students will bring to their study of this lesson sequence?

4. What resources does the material provide that will help you teach, and your students learn, this content and reasoning process?

Planning the Lesson Sequence

In this chapter, we will apply planning tools that have been developed in previous chapters. We will use the modified Project 2061 Criteria, which are summarized in Figure 9.2, and we will draw on the learning model first presented in Figure 6.2, which is a blend of the 5E model, conceptual change, and the apprenticeship model. We also will examine and employ the learning model that is part of the text itself.

Categories I and VII: Goals, Purposes, and Learning Environment

As in Chapters 10 and 11, we will begin the planning process with Categories I and VII from Project 2061 by considering the learning goals, purposes of the lesson sequence, and the classroom environment.

The goals of the first two sections on stoichiometry (Sections 12.1 and 12.2) are stated on page 352A as follows.

12.1 The Arithmetic of Equations, pp. 352–358

　12.1.1 Explain how balanced equations apply to both chemistry and everyday life.

　12.1.2 Interpret balanced equations in terms of moles, representative particles, mass, and gas volume at STP.

　12.1.3 Identify the quantities that are always conserved in chemical reactions.

12.2. Chemical Calculations, pp. 359–367

　12.2.1 Construct mole ratios from balanced chemical equations and apply these ratios in stoichiometric calculations.

12.2.2 Calculate stoichiometric quantities from balanced chemical equations using units of moles, mass, representative quantities, and volumes of gases at STP. (Wilbraham et al.,2005, p. 352A)

This chapter builds on earlier work in balancing chemical equations and takes it to a new level of both conceptual and quantitative understanding. These objectives are very specific and highly descriptive of what is expected of students, and they are at a level of specificity that is not found in *National Science Education Standards* or Project 2061 *Benchmarks*, where goals are much more general. Also these objectives are quite demanding and present substantial challenges to students and their teacher. These objectives are a central part of understanding chemistry, and they allow students to comprehend and predict the outcomes of chemical reactions, including how much of a product can result from a reaction between specified amounts of reactants. Further, it also is interesting to note how the authors have connected stoichiometry to daily life through comparison to recipes for cooking and assembly of tricycles.

In establishing a sense of purpose for the lesson sequence, the approaches in the *Chemistry* textbook are helpful, but a more general sense of purpose lies in how stoichiometry helps to deepen students' understanding of chemistry. It can help to establish and expand the sense of wonder and awe that chemistry can hold for students if the technical details are put in a proper perspective. Therefore, the sense of purpose of this lesson sequence on stoichiometry can focus on increasing understanding of the predictability of the reactions between substances that are represented in balanced chemical equations. It provides an opportunity to connect theory with practical experience.

The objectives presented on page 352A of the textbook form a sound basis for the lesson sequence if you augment them with the ideas in the previous paragraph. Therefore, the recommended objectives for this lesson sequence will include both the technical objectives and applications included in the textbook and the affective objectives described above.

After studying this chapter on stoichiometry, students should be able to

1. Explain how balanced equations apply to both chemistry and everyday life.
2. Understand and interpret balanced equations in terms of moles, representative particles, mass, and gas volume at STP.
3. Describe and identify the quantities that are always conserved in chemical reactions.
4. Construct mole ratios from balanced chemical equations and apply these ratios in stoichiometric calculations.

5. Calculate stoichiometric quantities from balanced chemical equations using units of moles, mass, representative quantities, and volumes of gases at STP.
6. Describe their appreciation of the way in which stoichiometry enables prediction of the amount of product that results from chemical reactions when the amounts of reactants are known.
7. Conversely, describe their appreciation of the predictability of the amount of reactants needed to produce a specified amount of product.
8. Show satisfaction with their new capability to determine these quantities from examining chemical equations.

Reflection & Discussion Questions

Are there other goals or purposes that you would like to include in this lesson sequence? One possibility is to include some work on the history of the development of chemistry, showing how chemists in the nineteenth century developed these ideas, which would enhance students' understanding of the nature of science.

The classroom environment for this lesson sequence may be different from some others because this content requires integration of several ideas that are still relatively new to students. Lots of support will be needed to help students who have difficulty with this level of integration of ideas and with using mathematical reasoning. Careful reasoning will need to be nurtured. You also need to decide on how much lab work you will employ, and when you will let students struggle and when you will intervene to help them. Most important, you will need to think about the kinds of questions you should ask at particular points in the lesson that will help students in reasoning through the processes that underlie this lesson sequence.

This lesson sequence also needs a driving question that stimulates interest in the topic. Figure 12.3 on textbook page 357 provides a basis for this question. This figure shows the amount of NH_3 produced when specific amounts of N_2 and H_2 are combined chemically. The reactants and product are expressed in terms of atoms, molecules, moles, masses, and volumes. The fact that it is possible to determine so many levels of specificity shows the power of the stoichiometric approach. Therefore, the driving question could be as follows:

How much will be produced when known amounts of reactants are combined?

A conversation about textbook Figure 12.3 could be a good starting point about this lesson sequence. Placing this figure on a large poster paper or section of the chalkboard for frequent reference could be both engaging and supportive of students as they develop understanding of stoichiometry.

Reflection & Discussion Questions

Return to Figure 9.2 and rate the development on objectives and purposes according to the plan outlined in Chapter 9. Rate each item as S, P, or N, based on your interpretation of the adequacy of the development up to this point. Be reflective in assigning your ratings. It may be useful to have a group or whole-class discussion based on this task.

Be sure to note which items from Figure 9.2 will receive more attention later in your planning for this topic.

Categories II and VI: Students' Ideas and Assessment

Moving on to students' ideas and assessment (Categories II and VI in Figure 9.2) as part of the planning process, attention needs to be given to prerequisite knowledge and skills (Criterion II.A). Students need to be skilled in writing and balancing chemical equations, in calculating molecular weights of substances from formulas, and in identifying how balanced chemical equations represent the number of moles of each substance in the equation. Students also need to be clear in the connection between a weight of a mole of a gaseous substance, its 22.4 liter volume at STP, and the number of particles in a mole (6.023×10^{23}). Reinforcing these connections and reviewing the prerequisite knowledge is important. You may want to create a bulletin board display or other display of these essentials that you can refer to as you teach and use this topic. Visuals like these and textbook Figure 12.3 are useful supports for students as they try to keep track of the multiple elements underlying stoichiometry.

Students have few misconceptions related to stoichiometry because it is not a topic about which they have given much thought prior to the experiences they will have in this lesson sequence. This may be one of the places where students have a reasonably "blank slate" on which you and they can build new ideas. However, the task you and they face here is one of integrating several prior elements of chemistry into a complex quantitative, conceptual understanding that is not easy to grasp.

Your next task is to think about preassessments, embedded or formative assessments, and summative assessments for this lesson sequence. Preassessments should include those items mentioned earlier regarding balancing equations, calculating molecular weights, and knowledge of the connection between moles of a gaseous substance and its volume at STP. Therefore, your pretest should include questions like the following:

1. Write and balance the chemical equation for the decomposition of water into its elements.
2. How many moles of each substance are represented by the equation?
3. How many liters of each substance at STP are represented by this equation?
4. What is the molecular weight of each substance in this reaction?
5. Write and balance the chemical equation for the reaction between sulphuric acid and sodium hydroxide.
6. Answer questions 2 and 4 for this reaction.
7. Why is it not relevant to answer question 3 for this reaction?

Each of these questions also can be useful as formative assessment questions to embed into this lesson sequence. More will be said about formative assessment as we work through the learning activities for students.

Two sound summative assessments are built into the *Chemistry* textbook on pages 366 and 367. The Section 12.2 Assessment is a paper-and-pencil test, and the Small-Scale Lab—Analysis of Baking Soda—could be a lab-based assessment that also requires a more advanced level of activity and more time. The section assessment questions are numbered 21 through 24. I recommend that you require an additional task on question 24, such as the following: "In a couple of sentences, describe how you arrived at your answers for question 24." To round out the summative assessment, you could select additional items from the Section 12.1 Assessment questions 5 through 10 on page 358. If you have used these questions as part of your lesson, then you can modify them as shown in the example below for question 10:

Balance the equation $H_3PO_4 + Ca(OH)_2 \rightarrow Ca_3(PO_4)_2 + H_2O$ and show how the balanced equation follows the law of conservation of mass.

Reflection & Discussion Questions

1. What are the benefits and losses if you were to use the questions on page 358 of the textbook as part of your formative assessment and then repeat them in the summative assessment?
2. How could you ensure that this repetition was not diminishing students' understanding of the topic?

As occurred in Chapter 10, a time plan for activities needs to be finalized. I anticipate that this lesson

sequence may require about a week to aid students in developing the needed level of understanding to be successful with it. However, it will need recurring activities throughout the remainder of the course so that the learning is reinforced and sustained.

Reflection & Discussion Questions

Return to Figure 9.2 and rate the development on students' ideas and reasoning and assessment that you have prepared, according to the plan outlined in Chapter 9. Rate each item as S, P, or N, based on your interpretation of the adequacy of the consideration of students' ideas and reasoning in the section above. Are there ideas that need further development? If so, what are they?

Categories III through V: Learning Activities

Four "engagement" activities have been included in the *Chemistry* textbook on pages 352 through 354 to connect students with the idea of stoichiometry. These begin on page 352 with a hands-on activity that provides a quantitative simulation chemical reaction. This is followed on pages 353 through 355 by two activities about recipes that could be used as points of discussion to an activity that involves manufacture of tricycles. These represent examples of stoichiometry that lie outside of chemistry. On page 354, the authors introduce chemical stoichiometry with definitions, followed by an example based on the manufacture of tricycles.

One possible plan would be to assign pages 352 through 357 as reading for high-level students followed by discussion of these six activities in class. The discussion should focus on engaging students with the idea of stoichiometric calculations through the combination of nonchemical and chemical contexts that are presented on textbook pages 352 through 355. The remainder of the lesson would focus on the last two pages of the reading. These pages deal with important foundational ideas about stoichiometry, which are summarized in the graphic (Figure 12.3) on page 357. As mentioned in the previous section of this chapter, textbook Figure 12.3 could be an excellent vehicle for engaging students in the study of stoichiometry, for generating the driving question for this lesson sequence, and for visually supporting students' developing understanding of the topic. The context used is the synthesis of ammonia from nitrogen and hydrogen. Understanding the meaning contained in this graphic is an essential step in understanding and becoming skilled in using balanced chemical equations in stoichiometric calculations. An important feature of this figure is its potential for helping students visualize the integrated nature of the various levels of meaning underlying this topic.

A potential homework problem is suggested at the bottom of textbook page 357 under the heading "Differentiated Instruction." However, this task would be excellent practice for all students because it would help students to integrate essential ideas about stoichiometry as represented in the graphic.

If your class lacks the motivation or skills to gain knowledge from reading, then textbook pages 352 through 357 could form the basis of a set of guided activities, where students carry out the hands-on activity on page 352 and use it as a basis for engaging with stoichiometry. You may choose to discuss the recipe and tricycle assembly metaphors on textbook pages 353 and 354, but leave out the calculations in Sample Problem 12.1 on page 355 as it may cause more confusion than benefit. Instead you could move directly from the section on Using Balanced Chemical Equations on page 354 to the example of stoichiometry with ammonia synthesis on pages 356 and 357. Recommended homework or supervised classroom activity would be the same as above.

![icon] ***Reflection & Discussion Questions***

As you proceed through this introductory lesson, what formative assessments will you incorporate? Reflect on this before continuing reading.

For the inquiry activity on textbook page 352, the questions listed under "Think About It" will be useful formative evaluation items. Also you should observe students at work to see that they are doing the activity correctly and getting the meaning from it. Asking students to explain to you what they are trying to show with this paper clip activity will help them from merely perfunctory actions.

Further formative assessments could include asking students to describe how recipes and balanced equations are similar and how they are different. You also should ask students about how balanced equations show *each* of the following:

Numbers of atoms and molecules

Numbers of moles

Masses of substances

Volumes of substances

For students to be facile with stoichiometry, they will need to be very clear on these points! They also need to be clear that the first two in the list above are a matter of counting or reading from a balanced equation, whereas the last two will require calculation based on the equation. Figure 12.3 in the *Chemistry* textbook (p. 357) can also serve as both discussion point and the basis of formative assessment questions.

The previous activities would constitute initial work on stoichiometry requiring one or two days follow.

With these foundational understandings in place, students are now ready to engage in learning about how to carry out stoichiometric calculations. This begins on textbook page 358. I suggest that you make this section the basis of a teacher-centered introduction in which you guide students through the application of what they have learned in the initial activities about the information contained in balanced chemical equations. This would involve about ten minutes of teacher-centered activity followed by about fifteen minutes of small-group work on the two practice problems (3 and 4) provided, where you observe and provide students with needed guidance. In terms of the apprenticeship model, you will model, or demonstrate, then coach and fade as students try the questions in small groups.

While the students are working, and you are observing, you can ask questions such as the following:

- How many moles of each substance are represented in the equation?
- How many grams of each substance would that be? Tell me how you would calculate this quantity.
- How many moles of each of the substances are represented in the equation for the combustion of acetylene? How would you calculate the volume at STP of each of the reactants and products?
- Why must you balance the equation before you can answer the previous question and begin to do your calculations?

Questions like these may also be a desirable part of a discussion to follow the group work for about ten minutes. This would allow students to reflect on and verbalize their understandings and misunderstandings that may be emerging as they get more deeply involved in this work. It will be an important part of formative assessment.

![icon] ***Reflection & Discussion Questions***

1. How have the preceding paragraphs helped you understand how assessment is embedded into instruction?

2. Do you agree that most learning activities are also assessment activities and most assessment activities are also learning activities?

You should conclude this discussion with an agreed-upon procedure for approaching stoichiometric problems. The steps should include

1. Write and balance the equation for the reaction.
2. Determine the number of moles of each substance from the prefixes.
3. Determine the molecular weight of each substance in the reaction.
4. Determine the mass of each substance in the reaction as the arithmetic product obtained by multiplying the molecular weight and the number of moles shown in the equation.

I also recommend that you give students an additional problem to be completed individually in the form of a quiz that you correct and return to them the next day. That problem could be as follows:

> Write and balance the equation for the reaction of zinc and hydrochloric acid and identify the moles of each substance that are represented in the equation. Then calculate the mass of each substance if 130 grams of zinc are used up in the reaction. Also calculate how many liters of hydrogen at STP are produced. (Note: A simpler problem can be produced if you specified 65 grams of zinc, which is about 1 mole.)

You can evaluate this quiz using the following criteria:

- Can the student write and balance the equation?
- Does the student use the prefixes for each substance to represent the number of moles?
- Does the student recognize that mass and atoms are conserved in the equation and in the reaction that it represents?
- Can the student calculate the molecular weight of each substance?
- Does the student recognize that 130 grams of zinc is approximately 2 moles?
- Does the student show that 2 moles of zinc will require 4 moles of HCl and produce 2 moles of $ZnCl_2$ and 2 moles of H_2?
- Does the student calculate the masses of each reactant and product correctly based on the balanced equation?
- Does the student calculate the volume of H_2 correctly as 44.8 liters?

You should correct these quizzes and return them for discussion at the beginning of the next class. This will provide you and your students with information that can be used to guide next steps.

If students did well on the quiz, then you can proceed with further work on chemical calculation in Section 12.2 with confidence. If not, then you should go over the questions and the criteria that are listed above. As a further step to assist students, you could give a similar problem for a small-group activity and have the more facile students assist those who are having difficulties. Your supervision of this group task will be important. Careful monitoring of students' ideas and reasoning, diagnosis of individuals' difficulties, coupled with thoughtful and patient support of students as they work through examples will yield the intended results. For some students, you will need to build their confidence, as these students may suffer more from lack of self-confidence in doing quantitative work than in lack of ability. Often, students have difficulty putting the pieces of this puzzle together in a coherent way. Reference to *Chemistry* textbook Figure 12.3 can help students grasp relevant connections that lead to understanding.

Section 12.2 Chemical Calculations. This section of the textbook begins with an interesting application of chemistry in automobile safety. There is a connection to the work on chemical calculations since sodium azide (NaN_3) converts to a gas (N_2) to inflate air bags. The amount of gas produced from this reaction must be controlled to ensure that air bags inflate properly. Some of your students may wish to explore this reaction and the technology behind it. It could be an interesting problem of both chemistry and engineering.

The objectives of this section, shown on textbook page 359, are a continuation of the objectives in Section 12.1—to construct and apply mole ratios in making chemical calculations and calculate stoichiometric quantities from balanced equations.

The first topic in Section 12.2 deals with writing and using mole ratios. This is both straightforward and important. However, the algebraic modeling used in the textbook for mole-mole calculations, such as that found at the bottom of textbook page 359, can be confusing to students. The Sample Problem 12.2 on textbook page 360 makes this much clearer. However, you will need to guide students in reading this part of the text so that the calculations on textbook page 359 become helpful instead of an impediment.

You will need to "walk students through" this section and the next one on mass-mass calculations near the bottom of textbook page 360. Again the Sample Problem 12.3 supplements and clarifies the written paragraph that precedes it. Textbook page 362 provides an elaboration on mass-mass calculations, and students will need your help in understanding it as the symbolism in the graphics (Figure 12.7) and the message in the written text on page 362 can be difficult to some students.

I recommend that you spend ten to fifteen minutes in whole-class lecture-discussion of these pages and then give students some practice problems to work on in small groups. The difference here is that the quantities are not molar quantities as in Section 12.1. Here the quantities are fractions of moles or odd amounts greater than one mole. In guiding students to do calculations on practice problems, you may want to refer to the procedures used in Section 12.1 to make sure students maintain their understanding of the chemistry that underlies the calculations and avoid "getting lost in the math."

Keeping the "logic" of stoichiometry straight is important if students are to understand chemical calculations. Students need to remember that all calculations begin with writing and balancing a chemical equation. A balanced equation gives students the number of moles of each substance represented by the equation. They now also know or can calculate the molecular weights of all substances. Knowing these facts that are represented by the equation, and knowing the quantity of the material given in the problem, they then can use ratios and proportions to calculate the specific mass required. The procedures shown on textbook page 362, and on later pages in this section of the textbook, assume that students know and apply these facts. Unfortunately, students don't always hold on to these foundations, and when they don't, they run into difficulties. This is why it is important to give students sufficient practice in applying all of the steps, including writing and balancing chemical equations and then reasoning about what that equation can tell them about each calculation problem that is presented. To be successful with this work, students need to understand the underlying theory *and* apply it systematically. Having students "talk through" problems can be of great help in developing necessary understanding and skill.

The remaining pages in Section 12.2 (textbook pages 363 through 367) deal with other calculations, including calculation of the number of molecules produced from a given mass of a reactant and volumetric calculations. Again, the logic of all of these calculations has been developed in Section 12.1 and is represented in the graphic in Figure 12.3 on page 357. As you work through pages 363 through 367 with your students, you should refer to this graphic as it is a powerful representation of the concepts underlying stoichiometry.

As previously, I recommend that you work through the material on textbook pages 363 through 367 with your students in a series of short whole-class lecture-discussions and then assign similar practice problems in calculating masses, volumes, and numbers of molecules

as small-group tasks. This reapplies the apprenticeship model of learning: modeling, coaching, and fading. As students work through problems in small groups, be sure to use continuous assessment, observing them and asking questions on key points, including both the logic employed and their algebraic strategies. These tasks should be followed by whole-class discussion about difficulties encountered and strategies to overcome them. Individual tasks should also be provided so that students develop confidence in their ability to read, organize, and solve different types of calculations. Group work can be beneficial in learning strategies and talking through tasks. However, students need to develop the independence and confidence that comes from individual work. Therefore, a combination of whole-class teacher-led activities, small-group work, and individual work is useful in becoming fluent in stoichiometric calculations.

Reflection & Discussion Questions

Return to Figure 9.2 and rate the development of learning activities according to the plan outlined in Chapter 9. Rate each item as S, P, or N, based on your interpretation of the adequacy of the development up to this point. Which criteria need to receive more attention?

Journal Questions

In your journal, reflect on how the process of planning this lesson sequence has *deepened your understanding* and *strengthened your skills* related to:

1. The subject matter concepts that are incorporated in the textbook chapter.
2. Inquiry and the process of science.
3. The nature of science including the historical development of scientific concepts as well as the connections that exist between concepts and processes.
4. Applications of science to your students' experiential world.
5. Students' ideas, reasoning, and conceptual difficulties including potential misconceptions.
6. Instructional models and approaches to teaching.
7. The complexity of the planning process.

Chapter 13

Planning a High School Lesson Sequence on Refraction

Physics has a reputation for being a difficult subject. Teaching physics for understanding holds special fascination to me for two reasons: its reputation as a difficult subject and the fact that early in my career I taught high school physics along with other secondary sciences. It was both exciting and challenging to work with students who came to my classes with some trepidation and to help them develop confidence and understanding of this subject. The challenge of high school physics is similar to the challenge we have already discussed in Chapter 12 that relates to high school chemistry. In both subjects students must add a dimension to their science work that does not appear as starkly in earlier courses as it does in these two. Expanding slightly on what the *National Science Education Standards* says in the chapter on Content Standards about developing understanding, I offer the following:

> High-school students develop the ability to relate the macroscopic properties of substances that they study in grades K-8 to the microscopic structure of substances. This development in understanding requires students to move among three domains of thought—the macroscopic world of observable phenomena, the [abstract and often] microscopic world of [energy, electromagnetic waves], molecules, atoms, and subatomic particles, and the symbolic and mathematical world of chemical formulas, equations, and symbols. (National Academy of Sciences, 1996, p.177) [author's additions]

It is this integration of ideas and experiences with mathematics that often presents a deep challenge to students. However, when approached as a new, exciting way of thinking about the world around us, it becomes more intriguing. That added motivation and intrigue makes it more exciting and worthy of the added effort.

1. How does the point of view expressed in the opening paragraphs of this chapter relate to your experiences?

2. Are you able to help students find the excitement and awe among the observations, abstractions, and the symbolic/mathematical character of science?

3. How does this relate to the idea of developing connections among observations and experiences, patterns, and explanations?

Description of *Conceptual Physics*

In this chapter, I will use a section on refraction from Paul Hewitt's book *Conceptual Physics* (2002) as the basis for a lesson plan. Paul Hewitt has devoted his professional life to making physics more understandable and appealing to students. He has developed resources for teaching physics for conceptual understanding at both the college and high school levels. His approach differs from the mathematical approaches more common in high school and college physics. As the title of his book implies, he takes a conceptual approach that is closely aligned with the approach described in *Science for All Americans*, which was described in the previous chapter on cells. "*Conceptual Physics* features the concepts-before-computation approach pioneered by Paul Hewitt" (Hewitt, 2002, p. T3) that involves three phases:

1. Exploration to ignite students' interest with meaningful examples and activities,

2. Conceptual development to expand understanding with engaging narrative, visuals, and a wide range of conceptual development questions and exercises, and

3. Application to reinforce key concepts with problem solving, critical thinking and the immediacy of laboratory work. (Hewitt, 2002, p. T3)

The selected pages from *Conceptual Physics* are presented below. I urge you to read them carefully as they present an exciting story about refraction of waves in general and refraction of sound and light. Strong connections are made to practical applications of the concepts that pertain to refraction. You also will see that this is not a stand-alone book, but it needs the supplemental materials that accompany it in the program that Hewitt and the publisher have created. Three additional resources may be used as part of the planning process to foster understanding of refraction—the *Laboratory Manual, Conceptual Development Practice*

Book, and *Next-Time Questions*—all of which are part of this program.

1. As you read this section from *Conceptual Physics*, what were your reactions? Did you find his approach engaging and motivating?

2. What perceptions did you have about how students would react to this text?

3. What strengths and shortcomings did you find in the approach?

4. What ideas do you have for the lesson sequence on refraction?

Planning the Lesson Sequence

In this chapter, I will continue to apply the integrated model of teaching introduced in Chapter 5. Further, as in previous chapters, we will use the modified Project 2061 Categories and Criteria developed in Chapters 8 and 9 to guide our planning process. Therefore, we will begin with Categories I and VII as usual. Also, as in the previous chapter, I will leave some of the decision making about the details of your instructional plan for this topic to you and your colleagues, with whom you may be working to improve your teaching. This is consistent with the apprenticeship model, where we now are in a "fading" stage, turning more of the responsibility over to you as an advanced learner. However, this reinforces the need for you to have spent time on Chapters 10 through 12 even though these may not coincide with your subject matter background or the subjects you intend to, or currently, teach.

Categories I and VII: Goals, Purposes, and Learning Environment

In spite of its importance as part of high school physics and its multiple applications in real life, refraction is not included in *Benchmarks for Science Literacy*. The entry that most closely pertains to refraction in *National Science Education Standards* is found in Content Standard B under Interactions of Matter and Energy, and even that is a "stretch." The statement is as follows:

> Waves, including sound and seismic waves, waves on water, and light waves, have energy and can transfer energy when they interact with matter. (National Academy of Sciences, 1996, p.180)

Additional statements of objectives about the specifics of refraction are not easy to find on Web sites or in other resources. More specific standards on refraction are quite limited, but teaching resources

Selected Pages from *Conceptual Physics*

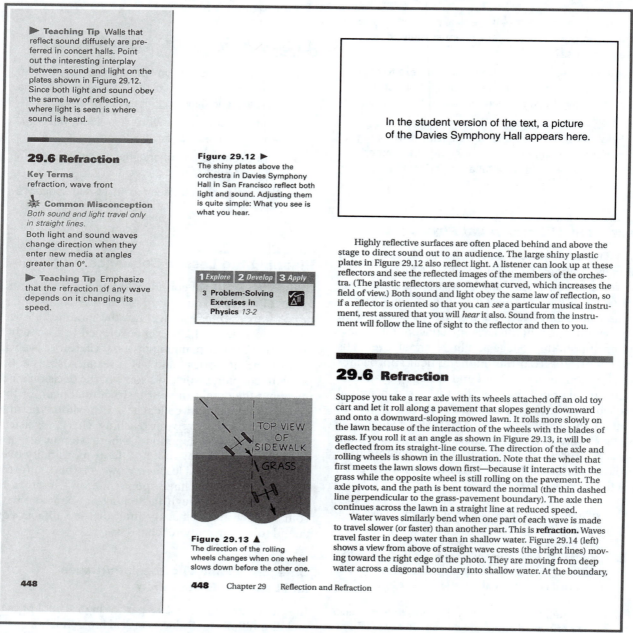

▶ **Teaching Tip** Walls that reflect sound diffusely are preferred in concert halls. Point out the interesting interplay between sound and light on the plates shown in Figure 29.12. Since both light and sound obey the same law of reflection, where light is seen is where sound is heard.

29.6 Refraction

Key Terms
refraction, wave front

✳ **Common Misconception**
Both sound and light travel only in straight lines.
Both light and sound waves change direction when they enter new media at angles greater than 0°.

▶ **Teaching Tip** Emphasize that the refraction of any wave depends on it changing its speed.

In the student version of the text, a picture of the Davies Symphony Hall appears here.

Figure 29.12 ▶
The shiny plates above the orchestra in Davies Symphony Hall in San Francisco reflect both light and sound. Adjusting them is quite simple: What you see is what you hear.

1 *Explore*	2 *Develop*	3 *Apply*

3 Problem-Solving Exercises in Physics *13-2*

Highly reflective surfaces are often placed behind and above the stage to direct sound out to an audience. The large shiny plastic plates in Figure 29.12 also reflect light. A listener can look up at these reflectors and see the reflected images of the members of the orchestra. (The plastic reflectors are somewhat curved, which increases the field of view.) Both sound and light obey the same law of reflection, so if a reflector is oriented so that you can *see* a particular musical instrument, rest assured that you will *hear* it also. Sound from the instrument will follow the line of sight to the reflector and then to you.

29.6 Refraction

Suppose you take a rear axle with its wheels attached off an old toy cart and let it roll along a pavement that slopes gently downward and onto a downward-sloping mowed lawn. It rolls more slowly on the lawn because of the interaction of the wheels with the blades of grass. If you roll it at an angle as shown in Figure 29.13, it will be deflected from its straight-line course. The direction of the axle and rolling wheels is shown in the illustration. Note that the wheel that first meets the lawn slows down first—because it interacts with the grass while the opposite wheel is still rolling on the pavement. The axle pivots, and the path is bent toward the normal (the thin dashed line perpendicular to the grass-pavement boundary). The axle then continues across the lawn in a straight line at reduced speed.

Water waves similarly bend when one part of each wave is made to travel slower (or faster) than another part. This is **refraction.** Waves travel faster in deep water than in shallow water. Figure 29.14 (left) shows a view from above of straight wave crests (the bright lines) moving toward the right edge of the photo. They are moving from deep water across a diagonal boundary into shallow water. At the boundary,

Figure 29.13 ▲
The direction of the rolling wheels changes when one wheel slows down before the other one.

Note: Please note that the actual text pages are full color.
Source: From *Conceptual Physics* by Paul G. Hewitt © 2002 by Pearson Education, Inc., publishing as Pearson Prentice Hall. Used by permission.

(Contd.)

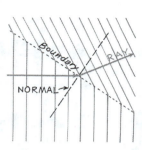

In the student version of the text, a picture of the refraction of a water wave appears here.

Figure 29.14 ▲
(Left) Photograph of the refraction of a water wave at a boundary where the wave speed changes because the water depth changes. (Right) Diagram of wave fronts and a sample ray. The ray is perpendicular to the wave front it intersects.

the wave speed and direction of travel are abruptly altered. Since the wave moves more slowly in shallow water, the crests are closer together. If you look carefully, you'll see some reflection from the boundary.

In drawing a diagram of a wave, as in Figure 29.14 (right), it is convenient to draw lines that represent the positions of different crests. Such lines are called **wave fronts.*** At each point along a wave front, the wave is moving perpendicular to the wave front. The direction of motion of the wave can thus be represented by rays that are perpendicular to the wave fronts. The ray in Figure 29.14 (right) shows how the water wave changes direction after it crosses the boundary between deep and shallow water. Sometimes we analyze waves in terms of wave fronts, and at other times in terms of rays. Both are useful models for understanding wave behavior.

29.7 Refraction of Sound

Sound waves are refracted when parts of a wave front travel at different speeds. This happens in uneven winds or when sound is traveling through air of uneven temperature. On a warm day, for example, the air near the ground may be appreciably warmer than the air above. Since sound travels faster in warmer air, the speed of sound near the ground is increased. The refraction is not abrupt but gradual (Figure 29.15). Sound waves therefore tend to bend away from warm ground, making it appear that the sound does not carry well.

---

* Wave fronts can also represent the positions of different troughs—or any continuous portions of the wave that are all vibrating the same way at the same time.

449

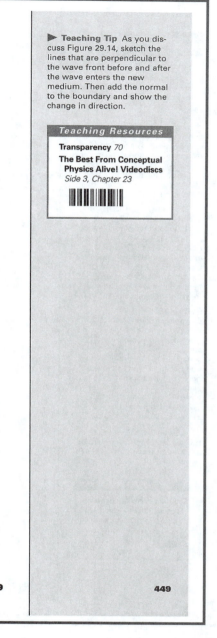

▶ **Teaching Tip** As you discuss Figure 29.14, sketch the lines that are perpendicular to the wave front before and after the wave enters the new medium. Then add the normal to the boundary and show the change in direction.

Teaching Resources

Transparency *70*
The Best From Conceptual Physics Alive! Videodiscs
Side 3, Chapter 23

449

Note: Please note that the actual text pages are full color.

(Contd.)

29.7 Refraction of Sound

▶ **Teaching Tip** Note the sound of a bugle being refracted both upward and downward in Figure 29.15. In the figure the reason for refraction is the change in speed through different air densities. Different wind speeds can also cause sound refraction. The upper illustration could represent faster ground winds, and the lower illustration faster upper winds. Listing all variables helps.

▶ **Teaching Tip** Discuss the useful application of sound refraction in medicine, ultrasound imaging, and how it can replace the use of X-rays in examining internal organs. This technique is useful in examining unborn children in pregnant women and is relatively free of dangerous side effects.

▶ **Teaching Tip** Another example of sound refraction which makes detecting submarines with sonar very difficult. Thermal gradients in the ocean and the resulting refractions of sonar waves leaves gaps or "blind spots" in the water, which are used to advantage by submarines. Otherwise, submarines would easily be detected by sonar.

✐ **Check Question** What is the key factor for refraction (of any kind of wave)? *(A change in wave speed)*

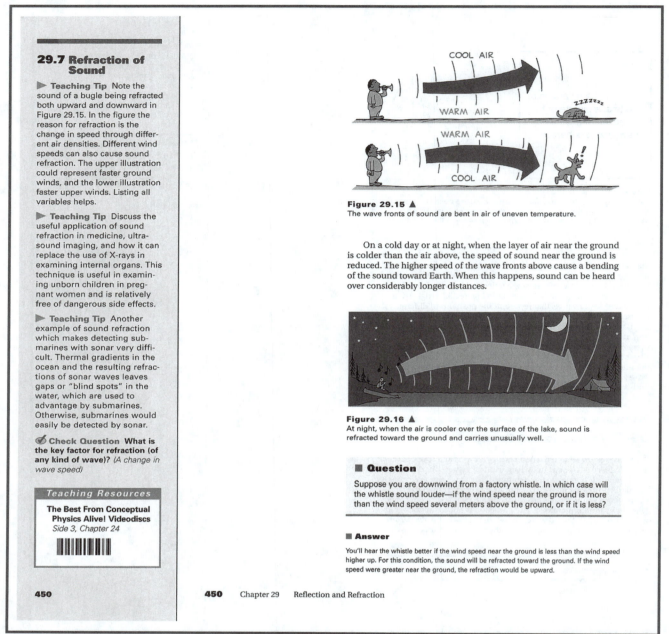

Figure 29.15 ▲
The wave fronts of sound are bent in air of uneven temperature.

On a cold day or at night, when the layer of air near the ground is colder than the air above, the speed of sound near the ground is reduced. The higher speed of the wave fronts above cause a bending of the sound toward Earth. When this happens, sound can be heard over considerably longer distances.

Figure 29.16 ▲
At night, when the air is cooler over the surface of the lake, sound is refracted toward the ground and carries unusually well.

■ **Question**

Suppose you are downwind from a factory whistle. In which case will the whistle sound louder—if the wind speed near the ground is more than the wind speed several meters above the ground, or if it is less?

■ **Answer**

You'll hear the whistle better if the wind speed near the ground is less than the wind speed higher up. For this condition, the sound will be refracted toward the ground. If the wind speed were greater near the ground, the refraction would be upward.

Note: Please note that the actual text pages are full color.

(Contd.)

29.8 Refraction of Light

A pond or swimming pool both appear shallower than they actually are. A pencil in a glass of water appears bent, the air above a hot stove seems to shimmer, and stars twinkle. These effects are caused by changes in the speed of light as it passes from one medium to another, or through varying temperatures and densities of the same medium—which changes the directions of light rays. In short, these effects are due to the refraction of light.*

Figure 29.17 shows rays and wave fronts of light refracted as they pass from air into water. (The wave fronts would be curved if the source of light were close, just as the wave fronts of water waves near a stone thrown into the water are curved. If we assume that the source of light is the sun, then it is so far away that the wave fronts are practically straight lines.) Note that the left portions of the wave fronts are the first to slow down when they enter the water (or right portion if you look along the direction of travel). The refracted ray of light, which is at right angles to the refracted wave fronts, is closer to the normal than is the incident ray.

Compare the refraction in this case to the bending of the axle's path in Figure 29.13. When light rays enter a medium in which their speed decreases, as when passing from air into water, the rays bend toward the normal. But when light rays enter a medium in which their speed increases, as when passing from water into air, the rays bend away from the normal.

Figure 29.18 shows a laser beam entering a container of water at the left and exiting at the right. The path would be the same if the light entered from the right and exited at the left. The light paths are reversible for both reflection and refraction. If you can see somebody by way of a reflective or refractive device, such as a mirror or a prism, then that person can see you (or your eyes) by looking through the device also.

---

*   The ratio *n* of the speed of light in a vacuum to the speed in a given material is called the *index of refraction* of that material.

$$\text{index of refraction } n = \frac{\text{speed of light in vacuum}}{\text{speed of light in material}}$$

The quantitative law of refraction, called *Snell's law*, was first worked out in 1621 by Willebrod Snell, a Dutch astronomer and mathematician. According to Snell's law,

$$n \sin \theta = n' \sin \theta'$$

where *n* and *n'* are the indices of refraction of the media on either side of the boundary, and θ and θ' are the respective angles of incidence and refraction. If three of these values are known, the fourth can be calculated from this relationship.

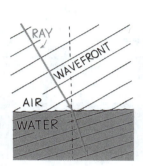

1 *Explore*	2 *Develop*	3 *Apply*

2 Concept-Development Practice Book *29-3, 29-4*

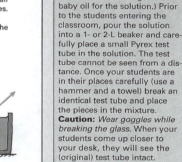

Figure 29.17 ▲
As a light wave passes from air into water, its speed decreases. Note that the refracted ray is closer to the normal than is the incident ray.

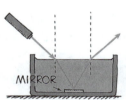

Figure 29.18 ▲
The laser beam bends toward the normal when it enters the water, and away from the normal when it leaves.

451

29.8 Refraction of Light

▶ **Teaching Tip** Refer back to Figure 27.7 on page 410. Stress that different frequencies of light travel at different speeds in a transparent material—red slowest, and blue and violet fastest.

DEMONSTRATION

Prepare a mixture of 590 ml carbon tetrachloride and 410 ml benzene (approximately 10 : 7 by volume), **Caution:** *Both carbon tetrachloride and benzene are hazardous. Prepare the mixture in a well-ventilated space and cover the container until just before use.* The mixture has almost the same index of refraction as Pyrex. (*Note:* If you wish, you can substitute one of several brands of vegetable or baby oil for the solution.) Prior to the students entering the classroom, pour the solution into a 1- or 2-L beaker and carefully place a small Pyrex test tube in the solution. The test tube cannot be seen from a distance. Once your students are in their places carefully (use a hammer and a towel) break an identical test tube and place the pieces in the mixture. **Caution:** *Wear goggles while breaking the glass.* When your students come up closer to your desk, they will see the (original) test tube intact.

▶ **Teaching Tip** Students might be interested to see how light behaves in mirrors that are silvered on the back: Light first refracts as it enters the glass and then reflects off the back surface. As it leaves the glass, it refracts again.

451

Note: Please note that the actual text pages are full color.

(Contd.)

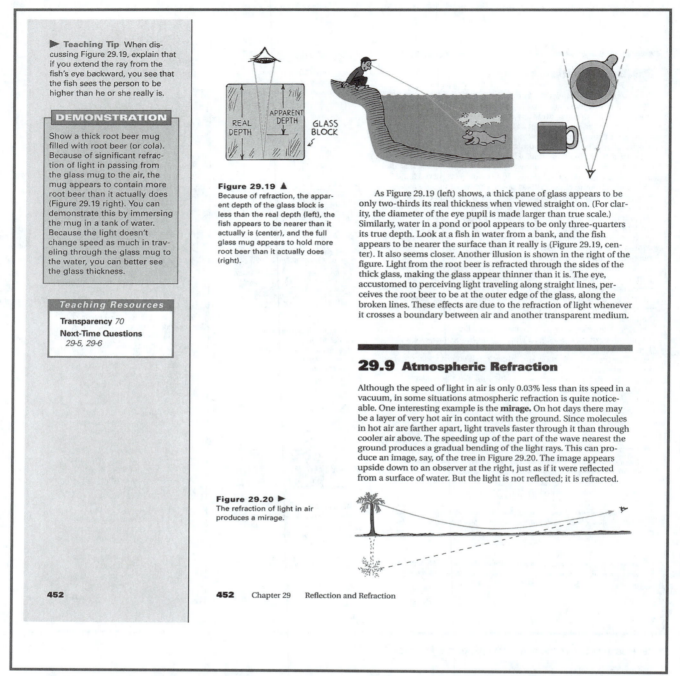

Figure 29.19 ▲
Because of refraction, the apparent depth of the glass block is less than the real depth (left), the fish appears to be nearer than it actually is (center), and the full glass mug appears to hold more root beer than it actually does (right).

As Figure 29.19 (left) shows, a thick pane of glass appears to be only two-thirds its real thickness when viewed straight on. (For clarity, the diameter of the eye pupil is made larger than true scale.) Similarly, water in a pond or pool appears to be only three-quarters its true depth. Look at a fish in water from a bank, and the fish appears to be nearer the surface than it really is (Figure 29.19, center). It also seems closer. Another illusion is shown in the right of the figure. Light from the root beer is refracted through the sides of the thick glass, making the glass appear thinner than it is. The eye, accustomed to perceiving light traveling along straight lines, perceives the root beer to be at the outer edge of the glass, along the broken lines. These effects are due to the refraction of light whenever it crosses a boundary between air and another transparent medium.

29.9 Atmospheric Refraction

Although the speed of light in air is only 0.03% less than its speed in a vacuum, in some situations atmospheric refraction is quite noticeable. One interesting example is the **mirage.** On hot days there may be a layer of very hot air in contact with the ground. Since molecules in hot air are farther apart, light travels faster through it than through cooler air above. The speeding up of the part of the wave nearest the ground produces a gradual bending of the light rays. This can produce an image, say, of the tree in Figure 29.20. The image appears upside down to an observer at the right, just as if it were reflected from a surface of water. But the light is not reflected; it is refracted.

Figure 29.20 ▶
The refraction of light in air produces a mirage.

Note: Please note that the actual text pages are full color.

(Contd.)

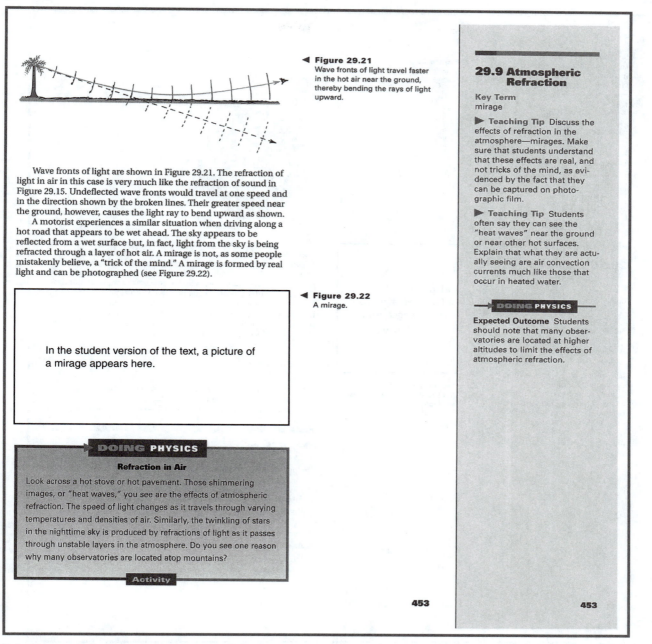

◀ **Figure 29.21**
Wave fronts of light travel faster in the hot air near the ground, thereby bending the rays of light upward.

Wave fronts of light are shown in Figure 29.21. The refraction of light in air in this case is very much like the refraction of sound in Figure 29.15. Undeflected wave fronts would travel at one speed and in the direction shown by the broken lines. Their greater speed near the ground, however, causes the light ray to bend upward as shown.

A motorist experiences a similar situation when driving along a hot road that appears to be wet ahead. The sky appears to be reflected from a wet surface but, in fact, light from the sky is being refracted through a layer of hot air. A mirage is not, as some people mistakenly believe, a "trick of the mind." A mirage is formed by real light and can be photographed (see Figure 29.22).

◀ **Figure 29.22**
A mirage.

In the student version of the text, a picture of a mirage appears here.

DOING PHYSICS

Refraction in Air

Look across a hot stove or hot pavement. Those shimmering images, or "heat waves," you see are the effects of atmospheric refraction. The speed of light changes as it travels through varying temperatures and densities of air. Similarly, the twinkling of stars in the nighttime sky is produced by refractions of light as it passes through unstable layers in the atmosphere. Do you see one reason why many observatories are located atop mountains?

Activity

29.9 Atmospheric Refraction

Key Term
mirage

▶ **Teaching Tip** Discuss the effects of refraction in the atmosphere—mirages. Make sure that students understand that these effects are real, and not tricks of the mind, as evidenced by the fact that they can be captured on photographic film.

▶ **Teaching Tip** Students often say they can see the "heat waves" near the ground or near other hot surfaces. Explain that what they are actually seeing are air convection currents much like those that occur in heated water.

DOING PHYSICS

Expected Outcome Students should note that many observatories are located at higher altitudes to limit the effects of atmospheric refraction.

453

453

Note: Please note that the actual text pages are full color.

(Contd.)

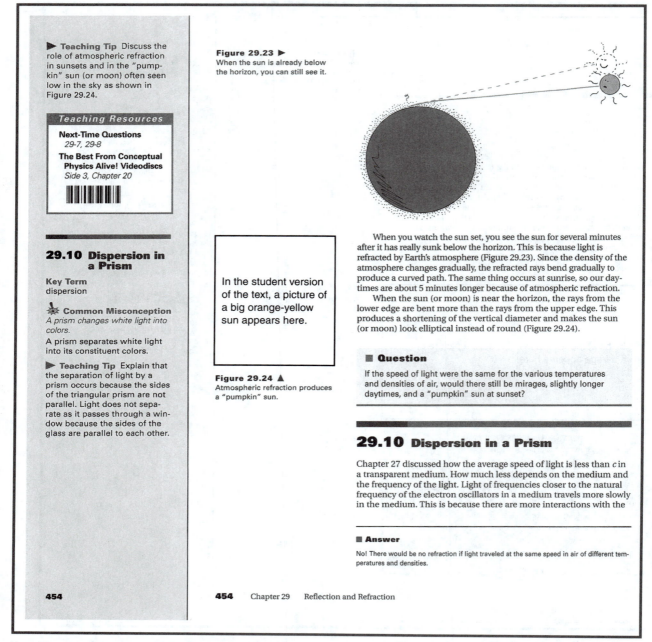

▶ **Teaching Tip** Discuss the role of atmospheric refraction in sunsets and in the "pumpkin" sun (or moon) often seen low in the sky as shown in Figure 29.24.

Teaching Resources

Next-Time Questions
29-7, 29-8

The Best From Conceptual Physics Alive! Videodiscs
Side 3, Chapter 20

29.10 Dispersion in a Prism

Key Term
dispersion

※ **Common Misconception**
A prism changes white light into colors.

A prism separates white light into its constituent colors.

▶ **Teaching Tip** Explain that the separation of light by a prism occurs because the sides of the triangular prism are not parallel. Light does not separate as it passes through a window because the sides of the glass are parallel to each other.

Figure 29.23 ▶
When the sun is already below the horizon, you can still see it.

In the student version of the text, a picture of a big orange-yellow sun appears here.

Figure 29.24 ▲
Atmospheric refraction produces a "pumpkin" sun.

When you watch the sun set, you see the sun for several minutes after it has really sunk below the horizon. This is because light is refracted by Earth's atmosphere (Figure 29.23). Since the density of the atmosphere changes gradually, the refracted rays bend gradually to produce a curved path. The same thing occurs at sunrise, so our daytimes are about 5 minutes longer because of atmospheric refraction.

When the sun (or moon) is near the horizon, the rays from the lower edge are bent more than the rays from the upper edge. This produces a shortening of the vertical diameter and makes the sun (or moon) look elliptical instead of round (Figure 29.24).

■ **Question**

If the speed of light were the same for the various temperatures and densities of air, would there still be mirages, slightly longer daytimes, and a "pumpkin" sun at sunset?

29.10 Dispersion in a Prism

Chapter 27 discussed how the average speed of light is less than *c* in a transparent medium. How much less depends on the medium and the frequency of the light. Light of frequencies closer to the natural frequency of the electron oscillators in a medium travels more slowly in the medium. This is because there are more interactions with the

■ **Answer**

No! There would be no refraction if light traveled at the same speed in air of different temperatures and densities.

Note: Please note that the actual text pages are full color.

(Contd.)

medium in the process of absorption and reemission. Since the natural or resonant frequency of most transparent materials is in the ultraviolet part of the spectrum, visible light of higher frequencies travels more slowly than light of lower frequencies. Violet light travels about 1% slower in ordinary glass than red light. The colors between red and violet travel at their own intermediate speeds.

Since different frequencies of light travel at different speeds in transparent materials, they will refract differently and bend at different angles. When light is bent twice at nonparallel boundaries, as in a prism, the separation of the different colors of light is quite apparent. This separation of light into colors arranged according to their frequency is called **dispersion** (Figure 29.25). Dispersion is what enabled Isaac Newton to produce a spectrum.

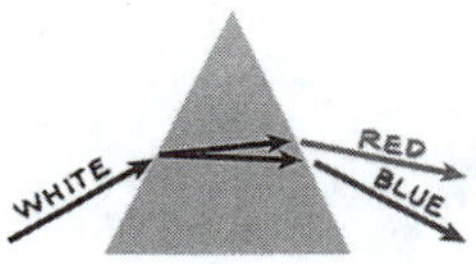

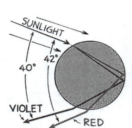

Figure 29.25 ▲
Dispersion through a prism.

29.11 The Rainbow

A spectacular illustration of dispersion is the rainbow. The conditions for seeing a rainbow are that the sun be shining in one part of the sky and that water droplets in a cloud or in falling rain be in the opposite part of the sky. When you turn your back to the sun, you see the spectrum of colors in a bow. Seen high enough from an airplane, the bow forms a complete circle. All rainbows would be completely round if the ground were not in the way.

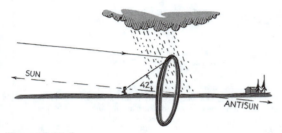

Figure 29.26 ▲
The rainbow is seen in a part of the sky opposite the sun and is centered on the imaginary line extending from the sun to the observer.

To understand how light is dispersed by raindrops, consider an individual spherical raindrop, as shown in Figure 29.27. Follow the ray of sunlight as it enters the drop near its top surface. Some of the light here is reflected (not shown), and the rest is refracted into the water. At this first refraction, the light is dispersed into its spectral colors. Violet is bent the most and red the least.

Figure 29.27 ▲
Dispersion of sunlight by a single drop, which produces a rainbow. Light is concentrated at the angles shown.

455

29.11 The Rainbow

▶ **Teaching Tip** Point out that there are not distinct bands of color in the rainbow, but rather the colors merge from one hue to another. We separate the rainbow into the colors we have learned to identify.

▶ **Teaching Tip** Figure 29.26 shows a single arc. If the raindrop region is thicker, more arcs will form and the rainbow will be brighter. Students can think of the arcs as concentric rings around a cone with an apex at the viewer's eye.

▶ **Teaching Tip** State that all rainbows are complete circles, but the ground gets in the way so only half of the circle is seen.

I have seen complete circles of both primary and secondary bows from a helicopter over Kauai. Spectacular!
PAUL

▶ **Teaching Tip** Explain that rainbows cannot be seen when the sun is more than 42° above the horizon because the bow is below the horizon where no water drops are to be seen. Hence rainbows are normally seen early and late in the day. We don't see rainbows in midday in summer in most parts of the world (except from an airplane, where they are seen as full circles).

▶ **Teaching Tip** Point out a significant, yet commonly unnoticed, feature about the rainbow—the disk segment bounded by the bow is appreciably brighter than the rest of the sky. The rainbow is similar to the chromatic aberration around a bright spot of projected white light.

455

Note: Please note that the actual text pages are full color.

216   Chapter 13

(Contd.)

▶ **Teaching Tip** The different sizes of raindrops affect the proportions of color seen in a rainbow. Drops between 0.5 and 1 mm in diameter create the most brilliant colors. Drops of 1–2 mm in diameter show very bright violet and blue with scarcely any green. Larger drops produce poor rainbows because they depart from a truly spherical shape due to flattening caused by air pressure and the oscillations they undergo. In drops smaller than 0.5 mm, red is weak. In the 0.02–0.3 mm range, red is not seen. At 0.08 to 0.10 mm, the bow is pale with only violet vivid. Smaller drops produce weak bows with a distinct white stripe. And as a sheet of Polaroid or a pair of Polaroid sunglasses will show, rainbows are polarized.

The rays reach the opposite part of the drop to be partly refracted out into the air (not shown) and partly reflected back into the water. Part of the rays that arrive at the lower surface of the drop are refracted into the air. This second refraction is similar to that of a prism, where refraction at the second surface increases the dispersion already produced at the first surface. This twice-refracted, once-reflected light is concentrated in a narrow range of angles.

Each drop disperses a full spectrum of colors. An observer, however, is in a position to see only a single color from any one drop (see Figure 29.28). If violet light from a single drop enters your eye, red light from the same drop falls below your eye. To see red light you have to look at a drop higher in the sky. You'll see the color red when the angle between a beam of sunlight and the dispersed light is 42°. The color violet is seen when the angle between the sunbeam and dispersed light is 40°.

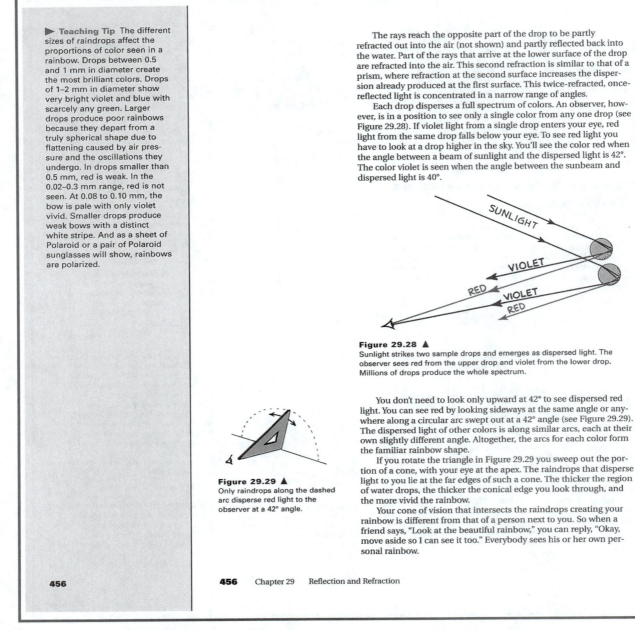

Figure 29.28 ▲
Sunlight strikes two sample drops and emerges as dispersed light. The observer sees red from the upper drop and violet from the lower drop. Millions of drops produce the whole spectrum.

Figure 29.29 ▲
Only raindrops along the dashed arc disperse red light to the observer at a 42° angle.

You don't need to look only upward at 42° to see dispersed red light. You can see red by looking sideways at the same angle or anywhere along a circular arc swept out at a 42° angle (see Figure 29.29). The dispersed light of other colors is along similar arcs, each at their own slightly different angle. Altogether, the arcs for each color form the familiar rainbow shape.

If you rotate the triangle in Figure 29.29 you sweep out the portion of a cone, with your eye at the apex. The raindrops that disperse light to you lie at the far edges of such a cone. The thicker the region of water drops, the thicker the conical edge you look through, and the more vivid the rainbow.

Your cone of vision that intersects the raindrops creating your rainbow is different from that of a person next to you. So when a friend says, "Look at the beautiful rainbow," you can reply, "Okay, move aside so I can see it too." Everybody sees his or her own personal rainbow.

456

456   Chapter 29   Reflection and Refraction

Note: Please note that the actual text pages are full color.

(Contd.)

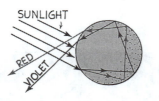

SUNLIGHT

RED

VIOLET

◀ **Figure 29.30**
Double reflection in a drop produces a secondary bow.

So when you move, your rainbow moves with you. This means
you can never approach the side of a rainbow, or see it end-on as in
the exaggerated view of Figure 29.26. You *can't* get to its end. Hence
the expression "looking for the pot of gold at the end of the rainbow"
means pursuing something you can never reach.

Often a larger, secondary bow with colors reversed can be seen arch-
ing at a greater angle around the primary bow. The secondary bow is
formed by similar circumstances and is a result of double reflection
within the raindrops (Figure 29.30). Because some light is refracted out
the back during the extra reflection, the secondary bow is much dimmer.

■ **Question**

If light traveled at the same speed in raindrops as it does in air,
would we still have rainbows?

29.12 Total Internal Reflection

When you're in a physics mood and you're going to take a bath, fill
the tub extra deep and bring a waterproof flashlight into the tub with
you. Turn the bathroom light off. Shine the submerged light straight
up and then slowly tip it and note how the intensity of the emerging
beam diminishes and how more light is reflected from the water surface to the bottom of the tub.

At a certain angle, called the **critical angle**, you'll notice that the
beam no longer emerges into the air above the surface. The intensity
of the emerging beam reduces to zero where it tends to graze the
surface. When the flashlight is tipped beyond the critical angle (48°
from the normal in water), you'll notice that the beam cannot enter
the air; it is only reflected. The beam is experiencing **total internal
reflection.** The only light emerging from the water surface is that
which is diffusely reflected from the bottom of the bathtub.

■ **Answer**

No. If there is no change in speed, there is no refraction. If there is no refraction, there is
no dispersion of light and hence, no rainbow!

457

457

Note: Please note that the actual text pages are full color.

(Contd.)

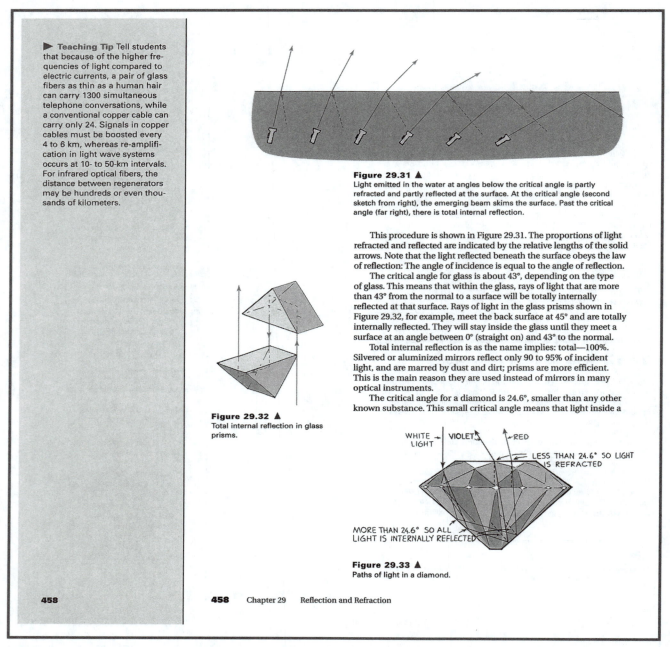

▶ **Teaching Tip** Tell students that because of the higher frequencies of light compared to electric currents, a pair of glass fibers as thin as a human hair can carry 1300 simultaneous telephone conversations, while a conventional copper cable can carry only 24. Signals in copper cables must be boosted every 4 to 6 km, whereas re-amplification in light wave systems occurs at 10- to 50-km intervals. For infrared optical fibers, the distance between regenerators may be hundreds or even thousands of kilometers.

Figure 29.31 ▲
Light emitted in the water at angles below the critical angle is partly refracted and partly reflected at the surface. At the critical angle (second sketch from right), the emerging beam skims the surface. Past the critical angle (far right), there is total internal reflection.

This procedure is shown in Figure 29.31. The proportions of light refracted and reflected are indicated by the relative lengths of the solid arrows. Note that the light reflected beneath the surface obeys the law of reflection: The angle of incidence is equal to the angle of reflection.

The critical angle for glass is about 43°, depending on the type of glass. This means that within the glass, rays of light that are more than 43° from the normal to a surface will be totally internally reflected at that surface. Rays of light in the glass prisms shown in Figure 29.32, for example, meet the back surface at 45° and are totally internally reflected. They will stay inside the glass until they meet a surface at an angle between 0° (straight on) and 43° to the normal.

Total internal reflection is as the name implies: total—100%. Silvered or aluminized mirrors reflect only 90 to 95% of incident light, and are marred by dust and dirt; prisms are more efficient. This is the main reason they are used instead of mirrors in many optical instruments.

The critical angle for a diamond is 24.6°, smaller than any other known substance. This small critical angle means that light inside a

Figure 29.32 ▲
Total internal reflection in glass prisms.

WHITE LIGHT   VIOLET   RED
LESS THAN 24.6° SO LIGHT IS REFRACTED

MORE THAN 24.6° SO ALL LIGHT IS INTERNALLY REFLECTED

Figure 29.33 ▲
Paths of light in a diamond.

Note: Please note that the actual text pages are full color.

(Contd.)

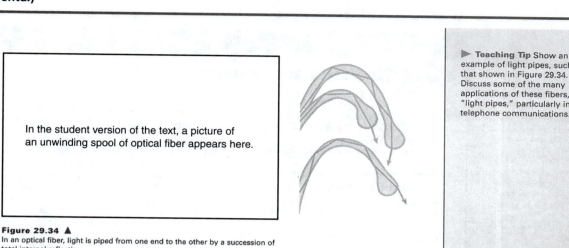

In the student version of the text, a picture of an unwinding spool of optical fiber appears here.

Figure 29.34 ▲
In an optical fiber, light is piped from one end to the other by a succession of total internal reflections.

diamond is more likely to be totally internally reflected than to escape. All light rays more than 24.6° from the normal to a surface in a diamond stay inside by total internal reflection. When a diamond is cut as a gemstone, light that enters at one facet is usually totally internally reflected several times, without any loss in intensity, before exiting from another facet in another direction. That's why you see unexpected flashes from a diamond. A small critical angle, plus the pronounced refraction because of the unusually low speed of light in diamond, produces wide dispersion and a wide array of colors. The colors seen in a diamond are quite brilliant.

Total internal reflection underlies the usefulness of **optical fibers,** sometimes called *light pipes.* As the name implies, these transparent fibers pipe light from one place to another. They do this by a series of total internal reflections, much like the ricocheting of a ball bearing inside a steel pipe. Optical fibers are useful for getting light to inaccessible places. Mechanics and machinists use them to look at the interiors of engines, and physicians use them to look inside a patient's body. Light shines down some of the fibers to illuminate the scene and is reflected back along others.

Optical fibers are important in communications. In many cities, thin glass fibers have replaced thick, bulky, and expensive copper cables to carry thousands of simultaneous telephone messages between major switching centers. Undersea copper cables are also being replaced by optical fibers. More information can be carried in the high frequencies of visible light than in the lower frequencies of electric current. Optical fibers are more and more replacing electric circuits and microwave links in communications technology.

Teaching Tip Show an example of light pipes, such as that shown in Figure 29.34. Discuss some of the many applications of these fibers, or "light pipes," particularly in telephone communications.

1 *Explore* **2** *Develop* **3** *Apply*

3 Problem-Solving Exercises in Physics *13-3*

459

459

Note: Please note that the actual text pages are full color.

(Contd.)

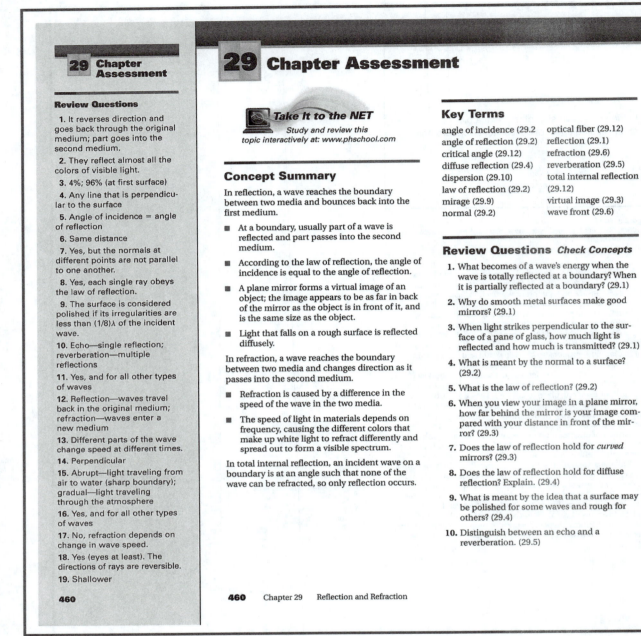

29 Chapter Assessment

Review Questions

1. It reverses direction and goes back through the original medium; part goes into the second medium.

2. They reflect almost all the colors of visible light.

3. 4%; 96% (at first surface)

4. Any line that is perpendicular to the surface

5. Angle of incidence = angle of reflection

6. Same distance

7. Yes, but the normals at different points are not parallel to one another.

8. Yes, each single ray obeys the law of reflection.

9. The surface is considered polished if its irregularities are less than $(1/8)\lambda$ of the incident wave.

10. Echo—single reflection; reverberation—multiple reflections

11. Yes, and for all other types of waves

12. Reflection—waves travel back in the original medium; refraction—waves enter a new medium

13. Different parts of the wave change speed at different times.

14. Perpendicular

15. Abrupt—light traveling from air to water (sharp boundary); gradual—light traveling through the atmosphere

16. Yes, and for all other types of waves

17. No, refraction depends on change in wave speed.

18. Yes (eyes at least). The directions of rays are reversible.

19. Shallower

460

Take It to the NET

Study and review this topic interactively at: www.phschool.com

Concept Summary

In reflection, a wave reaches the boundary between two media and bounces back into the first medium.

■ At a boundary, usually part of a wave is reflected and part passes into the second medium.

■ According to the law of reflection, the angle of incidence is equal to the angle of reflection.

■ A plane mirror forms a virtual image of an object; the image appears to be as far in back of the mirror as the object is in front of it, and is the same size as the object.

■ Light that falls on a rough surface is reflected diffusely.

In refraction, a wave reaches the boundary between two media and changes direction as it passes into the second medium.

■ Refraction is caused by a difference in the speed of the wave in the two media.

■ The speed of light in materials depends on frequency, causing the different colors that make up white light to refract differently and spread out to form a visible spectrum.

In total internal reflection, an incident wave on a boundary is at an angle such that none of the wave can be refracted, so only reflection occurs.

Key Terms

angle of incidence (29.2)	optical fiber (29.12)
angle of reflection (29.2)	reflection (29.1)
critical angle (29.12)	refraction (29.6)
diffuse reflection (29.4)	reverberation (29.5)
dispersion (29.10)	total internal reflection
law of reflection (29.2)	(29.12)
mirage (29.9)	virtual image (29.3)
normal (29.2)	wave front (29.6)

Review Questions *Check Concepts*

1. What becomes of a wave's energy when the wave is totally reflected at a boundary? When it is partially reflected at a boundary? (29.1)

2. Why do smooth metal surfaces make good mirrors? (29.1)

3. When light strikes perpendicular to the surface of a pane of glass, how much light is reflected and how much is transmitted? (29.1)

4. What is meant by the normal to a surface? (29.2)

5. What is the law of reflection? (29.2)

6. When you view your image in a plane mirror, how far behind the mirror is your image compared with your distance in front of the mirror? (29.3)

7. Does the law of reflection hold for *curved* mirrors? (29.3)

8. Does the law of reflection hold for diffuse reflection? Explain. (29.4)

9. What is meant by the idea that a surface may be polished for some waves and rough for others? (29.4)

10. Distinguish between an echo and a reverberation. (29.5)

Note: Please note that the actual text pages are full color.

(Contd.)

11. Does the law of reflection hold for both sound waves and light waves? (29.5)

12. Distinguish between reflection and refraction. (29.1, 29.6)

13. When a wave crosses a surface at an angle from one medium into another, why does it "pivot" as it moves across the boundary into the new medium? (29.6)

14. What is the orientation of a ray in relation to the wave front of a wave? (29.6)

15. Give an example where refraction is abrupt, and another where refraction is gradual. (29.6–29.7)

16. Does refraction occur for both sound waves and light waves? (29.7–29.8)

17. If light had the same speed in air and in water, would light be refracted in passing from air into water? (29.8)

18. If you can see the face of a friend who is underwater, can she also see you? (29.8)

19. Does refraction tend to make objects submerged in water seem shallower or deeper than they really are? (29.8)

20. Is a mirage a result of refraction or reflection? Explain. (29.9)

21. Is daytime a bit longer or a bit shorter because of atmospheric refraction? (29.9)

22. As light passes through glass or water, do the high or low frequencies of light interact more in the process of absorption and reemission, and therefore lag behind? (29.10)

23. Why does blue light refract at greater angles than red light in transparent materials? (29.10)

24. What conditions are necessary for viewing a rainbow in the sky? (29.11)

25. How is a raindrop similar to a prism? (29.11)

26. What is the *critical angle* in terms of refraction and total internal reflection? (29.12)

27. Why are optical fibers often called *light pipes*? (29.12)

Think and Explain *Think Critically*

28. Suppose that a mirror and three lettered cards are set up as in the figure. If a person's eye is at point P, which of the lettered cards will be seen reflected in the mirror? Explain.

29. Why is the lettering on the front of some vehicles "backward," as seen here?

30. Trucks often have signs on their backs that say, "If you can't see my mirrors, I can't see you." Explain the physics here.

31. Contrast the types of reflection from a rough road and from the smooth surface of a wet road to explain why it is difficult for a motorist to see the roadway ahead when driving on a rainy night.

32. Cameras with automatic focus bounce a sonar (sound) beam from the object being photographed, and compute distance from the time interval between sending and receiving the signal. Why will these cameras not focus properly for photographs of mirror images?

33. Why is an echo weaker than the original sound?

34. Does the reflection of a scene in calm water look exactly the same as the scene itself only upside down? (*Hint*: Place a mirror on the floor between you and a table. Do you see the top of the table in the reflected image?)

461

20. Refraction. It only apears to be a reflection.

21. Longer

22. High frequencies

23. Blue interacts more and slows more than red.

24. The observer must be between a low sun and the water drops.

25. Both refract and disperse light.

26. The angle at which light doesn't refract, but reflects

27. They literally pipe light along the fiber.

Think and Explain

28. By the law of reflection, only light from card B reaches his or her eyes.

29. It will be seen in proper form in the rearview mirrors of cars in front.

30. Light that takes a path from one point to another will take the same path when it goes in the reverse direction.

31. A dry road causes diffuse reflection of headlight beams and only a small part of the reflected light returns to the driver's eyes. A wet road acts more like a plane mirror, so most of the light is reflected ahead (causing glare for oncoming motorists!).

32. Sound is bounced from the mirror surface rather than from the image, so sonar cameras will not ordinarily focus properly for a mirror image.

33. Sound, like any wave, spreads as it travels and is diluted with distance.

34. No, the reflected view of an object is seen from a lower angle, as from a point as far below the reflecting surface as the viewer is above it. The geometrical difference is most noticeable when closer objects and their reflections are viewed.

461

Note: Please note that the actual text pages are full color.

(Contd.)

Think and Explain *(cont.)*

35. Below. The fish appears to be closer to the surface than it really is, because of the refraction of light that leaves the fish and travels to your eye in the air above the water; No, laser light will travel back along the same path as the light from the fish, so you would have to aim directly at the fish's image.

36. Yes. Your head is directly between the sun and the center of the bow.

37. Both show illusions, but the encased bottle shows a truer view (refraction at curved bottle shrinks cola a bit). More refraction occurs for the bottle in air, which shows much more cola than exists.

Think and Solve

38. About 92% because each boundary reflects 4% (96% gets through the first boundary, and 96% of 96%, or 92.2%, gets through the second boundary.)

39. Relative to each other, you and your image approach at 2 m/s.

40. A one-way trip takes 0.5 s so $d = vt = (340 \text{ m/s})(0.5 \text{ s}) = 170 \text{ m}$

41. A one-way signal takes 3 s, so $d = vt = (1530 \text{ m/s})(3 \text{ s}) = 4590 \text{ m}$

Activities

42. Half your height

43. No difference

44. Its high index of refraction

Teaching Resources

TestWorks™ CD-ROM
Chapter 29

---

35. If you were spearing a fish with a spear, would you aim above, below, or directly at the observed fish to make a direct hit? Would your answer be the same if you used laser light to "spear" the fish? Defend your answer.

36. A rainbow viewed from an airplane may form a complete circle. Will the shadow of the airplane appear at the center of the circle? Explain with the help of Figure 29.26.

37. The photo below shows two identical cola bottles, each with the *same* amount of cola. The right bottle is in air, and the left bottle is encased in solid plastic that has nearly the same "index of refraction" as glass (the speed of light in the plastic and in glass are nearly the same). Which bottle shows an illusion of the amount of cola? How does the other bottle give a truer view of its contents?

Think and Solve
Develop Problem-Solving Skills

38. When light strikes glass perpendicularly, about 4% is reflected at each boundary. How much light is transmitted through a pane of window glass?

39. Suppose you walk toward a mirror at 1 m/s. How fast do you and your image approach each other? (The answer is *not* 1 m/s.)

---

40. A bat flying in a cave emits a sound and receives its echo in one second. How far away is the cave wall?

41. An oceanic depth-sounding vessel surveys the ocean bottom with ultrasonic waves that travel 1530 m/s in sea water. Find the depth of the water if the time delay of the echo to the ocean floor and back is 6 s.

Activities *Performance Assessment*

42. Stand in front of a mirror and put two pieces of tape on the glass: one piece where you see the top of your head, and the other where you see the bottom of your feet. Compare the distance between the pieces of tape with your height. If a full-length mirror is not handy, use a smaller mirror and find the minimum length of mirror to see your face. Mark where you see the top of your head and the bottom of your chin. Then compare the distance between the marks with the length of your face. What must be the minimum length of a plane mirror in order for you to see a full view of yourself?

43. What effect does your distance from the mirror have on the answer to Activity 42? (*Hint:* Move closer and farther from your initial position. Be sure the top of your head lines up with the top piece of tape. At greater distances, is your image smaller than, larger than, or the same size as the space between the pieces of tape?) Surprised?

44. If available, look at a diamond or similar transparent gemstone under bright light. Turn the stone and note the flashes of color that refract, reflect, and refract toward you. When the flash encounters only one eye instead of two, your brain registers it differently than for both eyes. The one-eyed flash is a sparkle! What causes the brilliant sparkle of a diamond?

More Problem-Solving Practice
Appendix F

Note: Please note that the actual text pages are full color.

about refraction are abundant and from these it is possible to infer objectives and purposes. One useful site is *http://www.physicsclassroom.com/Class/refrn/refrntoc.html*

This Web site presents six component topics related to refraction of light as follows:

1. Refraction at a Boundary
2. The Mathematics of Refraction
3. Total Internal Reflection
4. Interesting Refraction Phenomena
5. Image Formation by Lenses
6. The Eye

Examination of these materials suggests that the objectives coincide with those of *Conceptual Physics*.

Given the importance of refraction in understanding so many familiar phenomena, I feel that studying refraction is an important part of physics, deserving a place in a high school physics course. It certainly has an important place in most physics textbooks, including Dr. Hewitt's. Chapter 29, Reflection and Refraction, contains twelve sections, seven of which relate to refraction. He lists the following objectives on refraction, with the first two being quite general followed by others that are more specific:

- Describe what happens to light when it strikes different materials.
- Explain the change in direction in a wave when it crosses the boundary between media.
- Describe the effects of refraction of sound waves.
- Describe the effects of refraction of light.
- Explain how mirages are formed.
- Explain how a prism separates white light into colors.
- Describe how a rainbow is formed.
- Describe total internal reflection, its effects, and its applications.

Other applications of refraction to vision, lenses, and optical instruments such as microscopes and telescopes could also be part of this unit, but they are not addressed in Hewitt's book.

For the objectives for this lesson sequence, I recommend the following:

On completion of this lesson sequence, students should be able to

1. Describe what happens to light when it strikes different materials.

2. Explain the change in direction in a wave when it crosses the boundary between media and describe factors affecting the amount of change.
3. Describe the effects of refraction of sound waves and light that are a familiar part of people's experiences.
4. Use the concepts of refraction and total internal reflection to explain common phenomena, including mirages, rainbows, and the effects of lenses and prisms on light.

In planning your lesson sequence on refraction, these objectives give you considerable latitude in choosing examples and experiences. However, they do focus your attention on development of basic understandings and their applications.

The purpose of this lesson sequence is to help students understand the general nature of refraction as a scientific phenomenon, which will explain several observable phenomena involving both light and sound. You could also generalize the experience to show that other wave-based entities including x-rays, microwaves, and water waves also are subject to the laws of refraction.

Reflection & Discussion Questions

1. What objectives will you choose for your lesson sequence on refraction? Objectives 1 and 2 address observations and theory, whereas Objectives 3 and 4 concern applications.

2. What might cause you to change the emphasis proposed here?

3. Do these objectives provide you with sufficient guidance or do you feel that they leave you with too much latitude or uncertainly? Explain your reasoning behind your responses to these questions.

4. In what ways does the statement of purpose clarify or complicate the issue?

The classroom environment supported by Hewitt in *Conceptual Physics* includes three levels of student involvement—exploration, concept development, and application. The textbook and its ancillary materials support this instructional model. Therefore, as you plan your lesson sequence, you should draw on these resources to create the learning environment that will be engaging and helpful to your students.

The Hewitt textbook has little emphasis on the history of development of ideas about refraction. *Optics*, by Isaac Newton, is a delightful report on his experiments and observations relating to light, with considerable emphasis on refraction. It is an excellent resource for you and your students on important history that is relevant to this topic. In addition, it shows Newton as a superb experimental scientist, when so often we only are presented with his theoretical contributions.

Reflection & Discussion Questions

As you will see in the remaining pages of this chapter, I am supporting a classroom environment that provides many opportunities for students to experience new ideas about familiar phenomena and then to have time to process these ideas through discussion, writing, and organizing thoughts for presentation. This takes you back to an early model of learning with understanding developed in Chapter 3 (Figure 3.1) that entailed three components: (1) building a base of information, (2) developing understanding of the information through sense making and connecting it with other experiences and ideas, and (3) applying the new understanding. What kind of classroom environment will you establish for this lesson sequence? How will it differ from the normal classroom environment you strive for?

Reflection & Discussion Questions

Return to Figure 9.2 and review how you have completed the first phase of planning for this lesson sequence on refraction. Do the objectives, purposes, and environment for this lesson sequence correspond favorably to the Categories and Criteria defined in the first part of that figure?

Categories II and VI: Students' Ideas and Assessment

There does not appear to be extensive research about high school students' ideas about refraction. Hewitt lists only one misconception in the teacher materials on page 448. The work by Driver and colleagues (1994) on secondary science has only one report on refraction—a study by Shapiro that deals with why a pencil in a glass of water appears broken. Respondents gave varied responses, including "the water makes the light rays bend," "the shape of the beaker makes it look broken," or "a combination of the water and the shape of the beaker make it look bigger" (Driver et al., 1994, p. 131)

However, experience shows that many students believe the bending of light in lenses prisms occurs *inside* of the object, such as a prism, instead of at the *boundaries* where light moves from one medium to another. Students apparently perceive that some materials, like glass, have the power to bend light. Therefore, the idea that refraction results as light goes from a medium of one optical density to a medium of a different optical density has not entered into their thinking about refraction. In addition, the "bending" that is perceived often is thought of as curving, like bending a

metal rod, instead of angular. Diagrams of mirages, which involve refraction of sound or light in air, where refraction results in curved "rays" due to the changing optical density of air with differing temperature or air pressure, contribute to the formation and persistence of this misconception.

Some instructional materials may contribute to this misunderstanding that refraction occurs inside of lenses or other transparent objects instead of at the boundary. This is described in a Web site that shows a diagram similar to Figure 13.1, where light rays bend within the lens instead of at the boundaries as shown in Figure 13.2.

This Web site states that

> Many introductory physics books show lens ray diagrams in which the light rays mysteriously change direction along the midplane of the lens. In reality the change in direction always occurs at the lens **surfaces**, where there's a discontinuity in the index of refraction.
>
> This example is from a text often used in introductory college physics courses. . . . We don't identify the title, author, or publisher, to protect the guilty. (*http://www. lhup.edu/~dsimanek/scenario/miscon.htm*)

Another pitfall for students is understanding the *normal*, which is a line perpendicular to a surface. In the case of curved surfaces, which are so common in studying phenomena related to light, the normal is perpendicular to the tangent to the surface at any point.

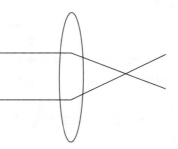

FIGURE 13.1 ■ An Erroneous Ray Diagram. Light rays bend at the boundaries of the lens, not in the middle.

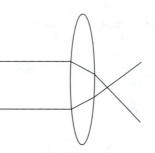

FIGURE 13.2 ■ A More Accurate Ray Diagram. Light rays bend at the surface of the lens.

Perhaps the most difficult idea for students to maintain a hold on is that anything we see is the result of light coming to our eyes from the object we are seeing. Too often students slip back to a childish idea that we see objects because something goes from our eyes to the object. With such phrases as "Look at. . . " and "Cast your eyes on. . . ," our everyday language reinforces these concepts, as do cartoons that children watch in which seeing an opponent (like Roadrunner and Wile E. Coyote) is represented by a dotted line that goes from the eye of the observer to the observed. You will need to keep this in mind as you work with students on several activities and assessments. Also, you may want to spend time discussing and drawing diagrams that help students get a clearer idea about this misconception and help you understand a major source of students' difficulties. This will be especially important when you deal with Activities 4 through 6 in my list that follows in the section on Categories III, IV, and V.

Reflection & Discussion Questions

From your experience, can you add to this list of misconceptions about students' ideas and reasoning? As you work with your students, be sure to note any additional misconceptions or alternative reasoning patterns that impede students' understanding of this topic, as well as how you dealt with it. Also, consider how you will record these for future use, so that the next time you teach refraction that information is available to you.

Preassessment. Students should be given several tasks that engage them in thinking about the interaction of light with various materials. The benefit you and your students will gain from this preassessment lies in the "spin" you put on it. The tasks should be presented as interesting ones to explore and not as a "test" that will merely expose their ignorance or result in low grades. (Note: Several of the following items were inspired by diagrams and questions in the selected pages of the *Conceptual Physics* textbook that are presented in the early part of this chapter. Page 461 was especially useful.)

1. Describe at least three things that can happen to light as it strikes objects that are made of different kinds of materials, including materials that are transparent, translucent, and opaque. Use diagrams to aid your descriptions.

2. Observe and describe the pathways of light through thick blocks of transparent glass and plastic objects of different shapes (prisms, lenses, blocks) using light boxes that emit parallel beams

of light. Provide as thorough an explanation as possible of why light follows these pathways.

3. Draw the pathway of the beams of light through the rectangular block of glass and the lens represented by the diagram below. (Note: The straight lines to the left of each object represent impinging light rays.)

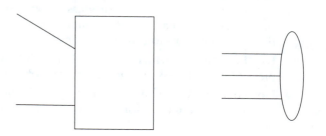

4. What is the difference between reflection and refraction?

5. Can both sound and light be refracted? How sure are you of your answer? (1—Just a guess, 2—Quite sure, 3—Very sure)

6. What else can be refracted? Name several "refractables." How sure are you of your answer? (1—Just a guess, 2—Quite sure, 3—Very sure)

7. What are the characteristics of "refractables"?

Reflection & Discussion Questions

I thought you might want a hint here! Since light and sound are both wave-based forms of energy, it appears that other "refractables" would include any of the components of the electromagnetic spectrum and any other waves such as water waves. What is your judgment on this? How would you answer the questions above? At the appropriate time, this could serve as the basis for an interesting class discussion.

8. How does a prism disperse white light into its colors?

9. Why does a diamond ring sparkle more than one made of glass?

10. How can fiber optic cables carry so much more information than copper wires? Give at least two reasons.

Summative Assessment. As you plan your summative assessment, keep the objectives in mind and prepare items that assess each of them. As before, *Conceptual Physics* textbook pages 460 through 462 can be an excellent source of material for the summative assessment. (Note: I have organized assessment items with each of the objectives below, and I have indicated page numbers for you to examine as sources of some items below.)

1. Describe what happens to light when it strikes different materials.

   ■ Describe as many different real events that you can think of that can occur when a beam of light hits a piece of clear plastic or glass. How does the angle at which the light beam hits affect this? Use diagrams to clarify your answer.

   ■ Do the same for when a beam of light hits a piece of frosted glass or other translucent object.

   ■ Do the same for when a beam of light hits an opaque object, such as a piece of paper or a person.

2. Explain the change in direction in a wave when it crosses the boundary between media and describe factors affecting the amount of change.

   ■ Use a combination of a diagram and narrative writing to explain why a wave changes direction, or "pivots," when it crosses the boundary from one medium to another. (Item 13, page 461)

   ■ Use a combination of a diagram and narrative writing to show the difference in orientation of a ray (or beam) of light and its wave front. (Item 14, page 461)

   ■ Use diagrams to show how a beam of light is affected by a convex lens, an equilateral prism, and a rectangular block of glass. Make your diagrams large to show the change of direction of the beam of light at the relevant points. Be sure to include the normal at the relevant points. Represent the beam of light as a solid line and the normal as a dashed line. Include a narrative description and labels to clarify the meaning of the diagram.

3. Describe the effects of refraction of sound waves and light that are a familiar part of people's experiences.

   ■ Explain why sound travels better on clear nights than at other times.

   ■ Examine the photograph of a mirage (Figure 29.22) and explain how mirages occur. Use diagrams to show how light travels from the car (as represented in the photo) to your eye to produce the mirage.

   ■ Air also refracts both light and sound. Diagrams in your textbook pages show that refraction in air results in a curve in the propagation of the light and sound waves, but in glass, water, and other materials the diagrams all show light traveling in straight lines except at the boundaries between the media. How can you explain the difference between these two different types of drawings about the effects of air and other materials on refraction? (Said another way, why do light rays and sounds curve in air and not in other media?)

4. Use the concepts of refraction and total internal reflection to explain common phenomena, including mirages, rainbows, and the effects of lenses and prisms on light.

   ■ Blue light refracts at greater angles than red light when it strikes a prism. Show a diagram of white light entering a prism and then being dispersed.

   ■ How many different colors result when white light passes through a prism and produces a spectrum? (a) 7, (b) more than 100, (c) more than 1,000, (d) more than a 10,000. Explain your reasoning.

   ■ Use diagrams and written narrative to explain how a rainbow forms.

   ■ What conditions are necessary for viewing a rainbow? (Item 24, p. 461)

   ■ We all learned that light travels in straight lines. Explain how light moves through fiber optic cables that are not straight. Also explain why fiber optic cables can carry more messages than copper or other metal wires.

   ■ Explain why diamonds are cut as they are. How does this enhance the brilliance and sparkle of a diamond? What characteristics of a diamond make it such a good choice for sparkling jewelry?

Reflection & Discussion Questions

1. Are there other items you would like to add to this summative assessment?

2. Would you make this into a test to be given on a particular day or would you intersperse these activities during the lesson sequence? What are the advantages of these two approaches?

3. Why is retaining a summative test at the end of instruction on a topic or unit of value from an educational standpoint?

Embedded assessment will be incorporated into the activities that follow.

Reflection & Discussion Questions

Return to Figure 9.2 and review how you have completed the second phase of planning for this lesson sequence on refraction. Does the attention given to students' ideas and reasoning, and to assessment, for this lesson sequence correspond suitably to the Categories and Criteria defined in the second part of that figure?

Categories III through V: Learning Activities

I suggest modifying the sequence of presentation in the Conceptual Physics textbook as follows: Sections 29.6, 29.8, 29.9, 29.7, 29.10, 29.11, 29.12. This sequence seems more logical to me. Beginning the study of refraction in the simpler instances where light passes from one medium to another making an abrupt change should provide students with experiences that will lead to a fundamental understanding of the phenomenon. Once that level of understanding is accomplished, a foundational understanding is available to take on the more complex instances of refraction of light in air that enables an understanding of mirages and the effect of the atmosphere on light that enters it. This can then be followed by the refraction of sound in the atmosphere, which is even more experientially remote. Finally, you can deal with prisms, dispersion of white light into its colors, rainbows, and total internal reflection. This sequence brings together a good balance among experience, patterns, and theory as you help students develop understanding of refraction.

Throughout the activities that follow, you will need to do some guiding and explaining, but be sure that the students have plenty of opportunity to engage in actual experience with phenomena, interpretation of textbook narrative, construction of diagrams, explaining ideas and diagrams to you and their peers, and writing explanations. Be sure that learning is active! You will need to hold back in giving answers. Instead you should ask questions that prompt students to generate their own answers and express reasons why they answered as they did. Students should not only be active learners, but also be encouraged to become more self-critical and self-evaluative about their ideas and explanations.

You are trying to engage people in analytical thought like that of scientists. To accomplish this, you also are trying to bring the potential of this textbook to life as you plan ways to use it effectively as an important resource for learning. You need to vary your approaches during lessons so that they don't seem "plodding" and dull. A mixture of demonstrations, discussions, listening to and discussing students' ideas, and carefully planned writing assignments can help to make the work enjoyable and meaningful.

Reflection & Discussion Questions

1. Many people tend to think of textbooks as boring. As you read the pages from Hewitt's *Conceptual Physics*, what different ideas emerged about the potential of textbooks? Did you find it intriguing?

2. How can you "enliven" textbooks and make your instruction engaging as you incorporate this textbook and others into it?

3. How can you use textbooks as effective tools in instruction?

4. How can you include other resources to further enrich your teaching and students' learning?

To help you create your sequence of activities for this lesson sequence, I offer the following ideas as a set of possible starting points.

1. Begin with an engaging, exploratory activity such as the one described in Preassessment Activity 2. An activity like this one will have a positive effect on students' engagement with refraction as it enables immediate visualization of the phenomenon. Ask questions to guide observations and interpretations, such as "Where do the light rays bend?" "In what directions do they bend?" "Do they bend more or less if you change the angle at which the light hits the surface?"

2. At some point early in the lesson sequence, take a few minutes to do or discuss Preassessment Activity 1 to clarify that the three major interactions of light with objects are that light can be reflected, refracted, or absorbed. Moreover, most commonly, light is reflected in a diffuse manner instead of directly from a mirror.

Reflection & Discussion Questions

1. What do you think about using these two activities for a combination of preassessment and engagement activities? Also, how could you use them as formative assessment activities?

2. What response should you make when students' answers to questions you asked while students were exploring in Activity 1 showed that students' interpretations were incorrect?

3. Figures 29.13 and 29.14 could be the basis of some explanation by you or they could be the basis of a small-group task where students "unpack" the meaning contained in these diagrams and the accompanying text. The goal of this activity is to help students formulate a *model for refraction* that has light bending toward the normal at the entry boundary of a more optically dense medium and bending away from the normal as it leaves a more dense medium and enters a less optically dense one. What questions will you ask to ensure that students are getting the appropriate meaning as they analyze the text and diagrams? How will you help them comprehend this model? Are students integrating the two sources of information? Are your students interpreting that light changes speed as it refracts?

In this activity and many others that follow, students are not only learning physics but also learning how to draw meaning from experience and text. How will you support both kinds of learning?

4. You should then skip to Section 29.8 and use the narrative and the two figures on textbook page 451 (Figures 29.17 and 29.18) as the basis for the next activity. It could involve a short lecture-demonstration using a laser beam or any other columnar beam of light passed through glass or water with a bit of cornstarch added so that the path of the light is visible. (One clarification needed with Figure 29.17 is the connection between the motion of a wave front and the change in direction of the beam of light that is shown there. This diagram could be confusing if you don't help students see the meaning implied by both lines. Also, as mentioned in the section on misconceptions, students have difficulty with the concept of the "normal" probably because it is an abstract idea. Therefore, you should give that appropriate attention.)

(Note: If you use a laser for this demonstration, safe use of lasers should be incorporated into the lesson.)

5. If you choose to incorporate the quantitative side of this work with Snell's law, you will need to plan and carry out a presentation and appropriate activities that will help students understand it. Be sure to give students some experience with the phenomenon so that they can see patterns in the data, and then create the mathematical argument based on this set of experiences and patterns. (Don't just "pull this out of the air!") A demonstration or a short lab showing how different liquids affect the path of a laser beam can be effective here. However, the changes are small and you will need an accurate way to measure the differences, such as noting the position of the refracted beam on a millimeter ruler at the bottom of the container in which different liquids are placed. You also need to exert caution if students handle the lasers. Also, the *Handbook of Chemistry and Physics* or other resources, including many physics textbooks, will carry tables of Index of Refraction of several materials. You may wish to have this reference available for students if you elect to go this route. As you do this activity, you will need to be sure that students are making the connection between the phenomenon and the mathematical representations of it. To understand Snell's law ($n \sin \theta = n' \sin \theta'$), students must have a connection with the observations. Empirically, you know the index of refraction for air. You also can measure the two angles θ and θ';

therefore, you can calculate the fourth element in this equation—the index of refraction of water or any other transparent substance. Then you can use the first equation shown to determine the speed of light in these materials.

Questions for students would be essential to guide them through this logical reasoning, as it is not immediately obvious from reading the small section at the bottom of textbook page 451. You might begin by asking what students know about the elements included in this section—the speed of light in vacuum, in other materials, and the angles of incidence and refraction. Which are facts that have been determined by others? Which are facts that can be determined empirically? How do we use what we know or what we can measure to determine what we don't know?

6. Figure 29.19 on textbook page 452 is a treasure for helping students understand refraction of light in water and glass as well as everyday experiences that relate to it. However, students will need help in interpreting ray diagrams. Several activities can be developed around this figure and the narrative that accompanies it. Some examples follow:

a. Discuss each diagram to help students understand its meaning, especially how the observation and its cause are represented in the diagram. For example, in the left hand diagram, why does the observer perceive that the glass block is thinner than it is? How do the lines representing light rays help people understand why people's perception is affected?

b. Have students explain why the fish in the center diagram looks higher in the water than it really is. Also have them discuss how a person in the diagram trying to spear fish would need to aim a spear in order to connect with the fish. This may require that the students create a ray diagram that shows the path of light from the fish to the person's eyes. Be sure students include the normal at the appropriate place in the diagram. Also, be sure they grasp why we only draw one ray instead of several, when light from the fish is being reflected in many different directions.

As students draw these diagrams, observe their work carefully to ensure that they are using ray diagrams in ways that help them apply the principles learned in Activities 3 and 4 to understand the ideas underlying these activities. Frame questions about movement of light in and out of water. Also, be sure that students grasp the idea that light rays coming to the eye determine what is perceived. Therefore, seeing the fish in the center diagram in Figure 29.19 results from light coming from the fish to the observer. Too often students "slip away" from this fundamental idea and relapse to more childish ideas!

c. Another challenge is to show a ray diagram that would indicate where the person would be seen by the fish. Use the same detail as in Item b. As part of this activity, you may include a discussion of how refraction affects the ability of people to sneak up on unsuspecting fish to spear them from shore.

d. The right hand diagram in Figure 29.19 provides another challenge for which students need to draw ray diagrams from the mug to the observer's eye. To do so will require a substantial enlargement so that the path of the rays from the contents of the glass can be represented as they enter and leave the glass and then travel to the observer.

e. The diagram on textbook page 462 that is part of Item 37 is another variation on this idea. You could have students spend some time discussing this question partly in small groups, then coming together for a whole-class summary and discussion of the last two questions that are part of this activity.

In all of these activities you will need to be observant about students' diagrams and mindful that they may be slipping into a childlike perception of how we see what we see. Be sure to note how students draw, describe, and explain why objects appear different than they really are when refraction of light occurs. When you see that students are having difficulties, a first clue you should look for would be finding out how students are drawing and describing the movement of light. Are they showing that it goes from the object to the observer's eye?

Reflection & Discussion Questions

1. In the previous list, I recommend that you have a mixture of whole-class, small-group, and individual activities. What are the advantages of each of these in helping students learn with understanding?

2. How does each enhance motivation and engagement?

3. Why is it important to use a combination of these organizational structures?

7. Next you can address Sections 29.9 and 29.7 dealing with atmospheric refraction of both light and sound. Mirages are a fascinating topic that is not limited only to visions that people have crossing

deserts. We can often see mirages on our streets and highways. We also hear the effects of refraction of sound when we hear a train or other sounds in the distance on a cold night. In the activities that follow, you and your students will unpack ideas about atmospheric refraction.

a. Use Figure 29.22 to initiate discussion of mirages. Have students describe their observations of this phenomenon. (Note: You may want to introduce this figure early in the lesson sequence as an engaging activity and allow students to see if they can observe it themselves. The teaching of this phenomenon would be more meaningful and interesting if students had experienced it firsthand, instead of only through a picture in a book. Having students recall or look for mirages adds to vicarious experiences with photos. Then follow up with a discussion of Figures 29.20 and 29.21.

Again it will be essential to explore how students are representing and interpreting the direction of movement of light and how an observer sees.

b. Arctic mirages are also an interesting phenomenon from a historical perspective. When weather conditions in the North Atlantic were just right, it is thought that early Norse adventurers could see distant islands, beyond the horizon, which gave them courage to seek them out. Over time, it enabled them to reach North America long before Columbus. Arctic mirage is explained similarly to others. Air close to the surface is warmed, in this case by water, causing the upward bending of light rays to produce the mirage.

c. Figures 29.3 and 29.4 are further examples of atmospheric refraction of light that can serve as the basis for additional small-group discussion and deepening of understanding through added application of the ideas to sunsets and other observations about variations in the duration of twilight at different latitudes and times of year.

d. Some discussion of the question in the middle of textbook page 454 can be beneficial here. However, this discussion should entail more than a yes or no answer. Students must be able to back up their choice with scientific reasons.

e. This would be an appropriate time to return to Section 29.7 on refraction of sound, using Figures 29.15 and 29.16. Again this is an opportunity for you to make a short presentation and then have students engage in group work to develop sound explanations of the meaning of the diagrams, to determine their application in daily life, and to answer the question at the bottom of page textbook 450.

Reflection & Discussion Questions

1. Let's think more about formative assessment. What will you look for and listen for as your students engage in these activities that will provide you with feedback on students' progress?

2. How will you "make sense" of what you see and hear about students' ideas and reasoning?

3. What actions will you take when you find that some students are holding onto or forming inappropriate ideas and reasoning patterns?

To answer the questions above, you need to look and listen for students' ideas and reasoning about the tasks they are engaged in. How are they applying the principles of refraction that underlie the phenomena they are addressing in these tasks? Do they show understanding of the model of refraction developed in Activity 3 that has light bending toward the normal as it enters a more dense medium and away from the normal as it goes from more dense to less dense media? Are they also able to apply this model to the phenomena that are part of the tasks? In answer to the last question in this box, you can help students use the model of refraction as part of their explanation if they are not doing so consistently. It also could help students if you were to discuss some of the difficulties that you see your students having as a whole class. This often works best if the particular students who are having the difficulties remain anonymous. You can introduce difficulty by saying:

> I saw a few students were finding it difficult to apply the rule that light bends toward the normal when entering a more dense medium and away from the normal when leaving it. Let's discuss why this is an important rule in thinking about the refraction of light in two instances— first, when the medium is like a block of glass or plastic that has a uniform optical density, and second, when the medium is like air and has a variable optical density depending on its temperature.

A discussion about this can be helpful to all students including those who have not experienced the difficulty as it helps all students reinforce the need to use the model.

8. As you begin Section 29.10, Dispersion in a Prism, students should have some experience with prism, as well as a demonstration by you that shows the beauty of dispersion of light into the visible spectrum. Also, in planning activities, be sure to give students opportunities to process the information included in the textbook on pages 454 and 455 and

in Figure 29.25 as well as any presentation and demonstrations you give. Such processing can most effectively be carried out with small-group work and writing, and whole-class discussion of questions students have about what they are experiencing.

Reflection & Discussion Questions

1. What is your objective for this activity?

2. Are your students able to draw the path of light through a prism using a rule such as "when light slows down, it bends toward the normal, and when it speeds up, it bends away from the normal"?

3. Do they know that higher frequency light is affected more than lower frequency light on both entering and leaving a medium like glass? How does this latter concept enable understanding of dispersion?

4. Do your students understand the concepts of refraction and dispersion sufficiently to be able to apply them to rainbows? If not, what actions can you take to help them?

9. Rainbows are such attractive phenomena but understanding them is not easy. The diagrams in some textbooks can be confusing to many people. The teaching tips on textbook pages 455 through 457 and Figures 29.26 through 29.30 are quite helpful as the presentation is both detailed and clear. I encourage you to use this as a group activity, plus homework, to have students try to develop a succinct explanation using one hundred words or less of how rainbows form. Each group could prepare overhead transparencies with their explanation and diagrams for presentation. Then each group could be critiqued by class members. A rubric could be assembled to guide students' critique that includes criteria dealing with accuracy, clarity, and engagement of audience.

Subsequent questions for discussion groups could involve such phenomena as double rainbows, circular rainbows, and halos around the moon and sun. The connection of halos to weather prediction lore can also be included, since ice crystals in cirrus clouds are both the cause of halos and indicators of an approaching warm front, which usually is accompanied by precipitation.

An engaging homework activity would be to have students use a garden hose and spray nozzle to create rainbows. To do so, they would need to create a list of requirements for rainbows and for viewing them. The experience would be a memorable and excellent synthesis of their study of this topic.

Reflection & Discussion Questions

Why is this better as a homework activity than as an outdoor classroom activity?

10. Total internal reflection is another attractive phenomenon because of its connections with diamonds and fiber optics. Although the latter has little to do with refraction, the former combines both concepts of refraction and reflection. Here are some ideas about how to approach this topic.

    a. Figure 29.31 can be presented as part of a demonstration if you seal a flashlight or a laser pen in a plastic bag and use chalk dust in the air to make the emerging beam visible. This can be an engaging initial activity for this topic. It is a good lead-in to the textbook narrative on pages 457 through 459.

    b. Figure 29.32 and the two paragraphs adjacent to it can be a useful base for a small-group activity that would allow students to process and apply information from the previous activity and the related text. It also is a valuable embedded assessment, as you will be able to monitor students' grasp of the topic as they work in groups to answer questions such as "How are prisms used to make binoculars more compact?" and "Why are only right angle prisms typically used in compact, high-quality binoculars?" (Note: You may need to remind students that angles of reflection and refraction are always measured from the normal, not from the surface.)

    c. Diamonds and other jewels have a natural fascination for many people. A diamond ring under a strong light can be quite engaging when accompanied by a discussion of Figure 29.33 and the related text paragraph. Questions such as "Why do diamonds sparkle so brightly?" and "Why are they cut as they are?" provide motivating material for discussing, processing, and writing about new ideas and experience by students.

    d. It may also be desirable to view other kinds of jewels such as topaz, which comes in many colors and is a commonly used semiprecious stone. You could have students find out its critical angle, and compare the structure of cut topaz with cut diamonds. Making sense of similarities and differences between jewelry made of the two materials would involve some thoughtful reasoning and discussion. A question about the design for cutting semiprecious stones would also be an interesting activity. A question to prompt this discussion might be, "Given the difference in critical angles of diamond and topaz, how would you design the cuts on a topaz to maximize its sparkle?"

    e. Fiber optics is also included in this section on total internal reflection. Because of their very small diameter, light waves stay inside of optical fibers, which act like "light pipes" because of the large angle of incidence and angle of reflection between the light rays and the normal to the inner surface of the fiber. These angles are always greater than the critical angle for the material of which the fibers are made.

        The teaching tips on textbook pages 458 and 459 provide you with useful ideas, diagrams, and narrative. The latter deals with underlying scientific principles, and the former addresses an important application.

        Decorative fiber optic lamps are now available at a very modest cost (only a few dollars), and these make a "good attention getter" and useful source of firsthand experience for students as they approach this topic. It would be helpful if each student could observe a fiber optic lamp close-up for a few minutes to see that nearly all of the light that enters the fibers stays within them, and emerges from the other end. They also should recognize that some light is lost through the sides of the fiber optic tubes and consider the observational evidence that supports this interpretation.

        A possible learning task would be to have small groups of students design experiments to show the ratio of input to output of a fiber optic lamp. Another possible task is to consider empirical ways of finding out how much light is emitted through the walls of the fibers and to see how it compares with the difference between light input and output.

        Finally, the teaching tip on textbook page 458 provides you with the basis for an analysis of application of fiber optics in communication. Using the information presented, you could ask students to consider the advantages of fiber optic cables over copper or aluminum cables in communication technology. You could also have students identify questions that are not answerable about the comparison between glass and metal cables. Some possible questions could be: "How is fiber transmission able to carry so many messages compared to wire?" "How do the cost of installation and maintenance of the two compare?" "Must fiber optic cables be installed underground to protect them from movements and possible breakage from wind?" Your students can generate similar questions and others.

FIGURE 13.3 ■ Scheduling Activities.

Day	Activity	Time	Purpose
	Pretest Activity 1	15	Obtain data on students' entry-level knowledge of the topic
1	2	20	Address Objective 1
	3	30	Start initial work on Objective 2
2	4	20	Continue work on Objective 2 to help students build a model of how light bends during refraction
	3 and 4	30	Enable students to make sense of the new model and learn how to use it
3	5	50	Discuss Snell's law (Note: You may choose to eliminate this activity if it does not match your goals.)
4	6	50	Start initial activities to address Objectives 3 and 4
5	Discussion/ assessment	25	Allow students to process information from Activity 6 and obtain feedback on students' grasp of these applications
	7	35	Give presentation on atmospheric refraction and mirages, allow time for students to process this information and you to do formative assessments during group work or class discussion
6	8 and 9	50	Use refraction rules to understand prisms and rainbows; include formative assessment to monitor students' progress toward understanding
7	10	50	Use refraction rules to understand total internal reflection, why diamonds sparkle, and fiber optics
8	Response to questions	30	Respond to students' questions and review how the model of refraction is useful in understanding many different phenomena; consolidate understanding of Objectives 3 and 4
9	Summative Test	30	Administer summative test. Facilitate posttest discussion of the test

Reflection & Discussion Questions

Return to Figure 9.2 and review how you have completed the third phase of planning for this lesson sequence on refraction. Does the attention to engaging students, to developing their understanding of the science content and reasoning, and to formative assessment for this lesson sequence correspond suitably to the Categories and Criteria in Figure 9.2?

Sequencing Activities

Figure 13.3 shows one possible scenario of how this lesson sequence would be enacted. You should feel free to create your own scenario.

Reflection & Discussion Questions

What sequence of activities and plan for enactment of this lesson sequence would you create if you were to teach it?

Journal Questions

In your journal, reflect on how the process of planning this lesson sequence has *deepened your understanding* and *strengthened your skills* related to:

1. The subject matter concepts that are in incorporated in the textbook chapter.
2. Inquiry and the process of science.
3. The nature of science including the historical development of scientific concepts as well as the connections that exits between concepts and processes.
4. Applications of science to your students' experiential world.
5. Students' ideas, reasoning and conceptual difficulties including potential misconceptions.
6. Instructional models and approaches to teaching.
7. The complexity of the planning process.

Chapter **14**

Planning a Middle School Lesson Sequence on Weather

Weather is an important topic in middle school science programs. Understanding weather requires application of ideas from physical sciences to the earth sciences. Also, a study of weather provides many opportunities for inclusion of inquiry, and it is an excellent vehicle for application of fundamental science concepts in real-world contexts.

This chapter will consider planning a lesson sequence that deals with a small, but essential component of understanding weather—water in the atmosphere, with special emphasis on understanding evaporation and condensation. It will focus on part of a unit from the FOSS Middle School Science Program, which contains nine topical units for grades 5 though 8—three life science, four physical science, and two earth science. Each unit might occupy as much as half a school year if students were to develop a sound understanding of the content and inquiry processes that are part of each one. Therefore, the potential exists for choice of topics in building a middle school program.

Description of *Weather and Water*

The unit, titled *Weather and Water*, which authors of the program prepared for students in grades 6 or 7, "emphasizes the use of knowledge and evidence to construct explanations for the movement and change in air and water that result in weather on Earth" (Full Option Science System [FOSS], 2005, p. 2). The authors also state that the program is based on *National Science Education Standards*, including standards relating to science as inquiry, along with science and technology, physical science, and earth science content knowledge (FOSS, 2005, p. 2).

The *Weather and Water* unit contains nine component topics labeled "Investigations" as follows:

1. What Is Weather?
2. Where's the Air?
3. Seasons and Sun
4. Heat Transfer
5. Convection
6. Water in the Air
7. The Water Planet
8. Air Pressure and Wind
9. Weather and Climate

The topic chosen for this chapter is from Investigation 6, Water in the Air. Investigation 6 is comprised of five parts as follows:

Part 1 Is Water Really There?—helps students understand that water vapor is present in the air

Part 2 Evaporation and Humidity—helps students understand how water gets in the air and how relative humidity is measured

Part 3 Condensation and Dew Point—extends the ideas about humidity to explore the temperature at which water vapor in the air condenses into liquid form

Part 4 Clouds and Precipitation—explores how temperature of air can be modified by changes in pressure and how clouds form when rising air cools to the dew point

Part 5 Weather Balloons—uses a multimedia presentation about weather balloons to help students clarify ideas about cloud formation and humidity by interpreting temperature data at increasing elevations, from four different cities

Specifically, this chapter will focus on development of a lesson sequence that demonstrates the presence of water in the air, leading to a more detailed study of evaporation and condensation. The remainder of Investigation 6 includes clouds, precipitation, and weather balloons, which are not part of my chapter due to limitations of space. This chapter of *Teaching Science for Understanding* will focus on Parts 1 and 2 of Investigation 6.

Selected pages from the unit have been reproduced here for your convenience. These include materials from the Teacher Guide and the students' Lab Notebook. The sections chosen do not contain materials from *Weather and Water Resources*, a book of readings for students, nor do they employ material from the accompanying compact disk that is also included with the program as these two resources did not contain material related to these two parts of Investigation 6.

Selected Pages from *Weather and Water*

These pages should be studied carefully to determine the intended objectives, instructional content, inquiry process, and suggested instructional strategies that can serve as the basis for planning an instructional sequence on water in the atmosphere. Teacher Guide pages 1, 2, and 177 provide an overview and connections to *National Science Education Standards* to enable you to see where evaporation and condensation fit into the big picture of this unit and Investigation 6. Pages 182 through 184 contain a part of the Scientific and Historical Background for Investigation 6 that is provided in the Teacher Guide. Pages 190 through 199, 336, 337, 455, and 465 contain detailed material from the Teacher Guide. The remaining pages (1, 31, and 33) are from the Lab Notebook that is used in data recording and in interpretation. These are the key resources provided by the program authors that serve as the basis for planning the sequence of lessons on evaporation and condensation.

One important feature of this program is that it is different from any of the textbook-based programs that served as the basis for Chapters 10 through 13. It has far less reading material for students than those textbooks. Moreover, the teacher material is much more detailed and elaborated. This makes the planning activity and classroom enactment quite different from the previous four chapters.

Reflection & Discussion Questions

1. How does each section of the materials from FOSS help you as a teacher?

2. What can you learn from Teacher Guide pages 182 through 184? For example, what important understandings does the section titled "Humidity and Vapor Pressure" add or review for you? What about other sections?

3. What teaching resources did you find to be most promising?

Note: I have provided you with a very small portion of the FOSS *Weather and Water* material. Some important resources have been omitted such as the compact disk that accompanies the program, and you have only seen a very limited segment of the program. Therefore, you should not make judgments about the program based on the limited information contained in this book.

Selected Pages from *Weather and Water*

FULL OPTION SCIENCE SYSTEM—Middle School

FOSS

OVERVIEW
WEATHER AND WATER COURSE

WELCOME TO FOSS WEATHER AND WATER

The **FOSS Weather and Water Course** focuses on Earth's atmosphere, weather, and water. As part of their study, students delve into topics that may seem unrelated to weather, including a good dose of physics and a bit of chemistry. These scientific disciplines support many areas in the earth sciences. A good understanding of meteorology as an earth science isn't complete without an introduction to concepts that cross into the realm of physics and chemistry.

Understanding weather is more than reading a thermometer and recording air-pressure measurements. Students need to grapple with ideas about atoms and molecules, changes of state, and heat transfer before they can launch into the bigger ideas involving air masses and fronts, convection cells and winds, and the development of severe weather.

Earth's atmosphere is composed of a variety of gases, with nitrogen and oxygen the most abundant. But Earth wouldn't be the same if it weren't for one keystone gas, water vapor. When you look at the percentages, water vapor is a relatively minor and variable component of the atmosphere. But without water vapor and its liquid and solid forms, both on the surface and in the atmosphere, there would be no weather. There would be neither clouds nor precipitation. If precipitation didn't occur, we wouldn't have runoff to create the streams and rivers that erode mountains, deposit deltas, and replenish lakes and oceans. An atmosphere without water vapor would be an alien and hostile place. The importance of water on Earth is a major element of this course.

(Contd.)

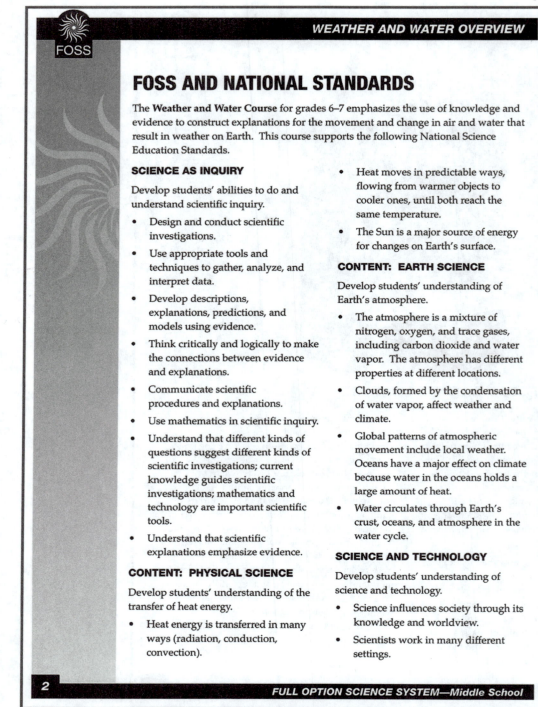

FOSS AND NATIONAL STANDARDS

The **Weather and Water Course** for grades 6–7 emphasizes the use of knowledge and evidence to construct explanations for the movement and change in air and water that result in weather on Earth. This course supports the following National Science Education Standards.

SCIENCE AS INQUIRY

Develop students' abilities to do and understand scientific inquiry.

- Design and conduct scientific investigations.
- Use appropriate tools and techniques to gather, analyze, and interpret data.
- Develop descriptions, explanations, predictions, and models using evidence.
- Think critically and logically to make the connections between evidence and explanations.
- Communicate scientific procedures and explanations.
- Use mathematics in scientific inquiry.
- Understand that different kinds of questions suggest different kinds of scientific investigations; current knowledge guides scientific investigations; mathematics and technology are important scientific tools.
- Understand that scientific explanations emphasize evidence.

CONTENT: PHYSICAL SCIENCE

Develop students' understanding of the transfer of heat energy.

- Heat energy is transferred in many ways (radiation, conduction, convection).

- Heat moves in predictable ways, flowing from warmer objects to cooler ones, until both reach the same temperature.
- The Sun is a major source of energy for changes on Earth's surface.

CONTENT: EARTH SCIENCE

Develop students' understanding of Earth's atmosphere.

- The atmosphere is a mixture of nitrogen, oxygen, and trace gases, including carbon dioxide and water vapor. The atmosphere has different properties at different locations.
- Clouds, formed by the condensation of water vapor, affect weather and climate.
- Global patterns of atmospheric movement include local weather. Oceans have a major effect on climate because water in the oceans holds a large amount of heat.
- Water circulates through Earth's crust, oceans, and atmosphere in the water cycle.

SCIENCE AND TECHNOLOGY

Develop students' understanding of science and technology.

- Science influences society through its knowledge and worldview.
- Scientists work in many different settings.

2

Note: Please note that the actual text pages are full color.

(Contd.)

FOSS WEATHER AND WATER COURSE

INVESTIGATION 6:
WATER IN THE AIR

GOAL

In *Water in the Air* students investigate humidity—the water vapor in the air—to understand some of the variables that influence its transition from liquid to gas and from gas to liquid.

OBJECTIVES

SCIENCE CONTENT

- Water changes from liquid to gas (vapor) by evaporation.
- Water changes from gas to liquid by condensation.
- Relative humidity is the percentage of water vapor in air compared to the amount of water vapor needed to saturate that air at a specific temperature.
- Dew point is the temperature at which air is saturated with water vapor.

CONDUCTING INVESTIGATIONS

- Use ice water to cool air to produce condensation.
- Measure changes in temperature due to evaporation.
- Observe changes in temperature due to pressure change.
- Determine dew point by cooling water in a container until condensation occurs on the container.
- Use pressure to produce a cloud in a bottle.

BUILDING EXPLANATIONS

- Explain how dew and clouds form when humid air cools to its dew point and condenses.
- Predict cloud formation by analyzing radiosonde sounding data.

FULL OPTION SCIENCE SYSTEM **177**

(Contd.)

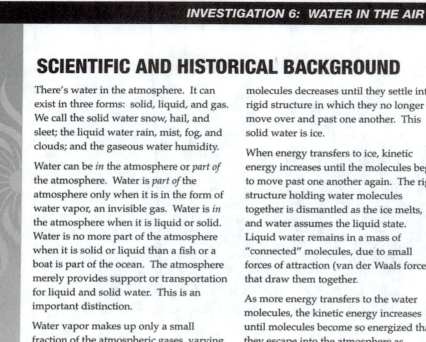

SCIENTIFIC AND HISTORICAL BACKGROUND

There's water in the atmosphere. It can exist in three forms: solid, liquid, and gas. We call the solid water snow, hail, and sleet; the liquid water rain, mist, fog, and clouds; and the gaseous water humidity.

Water can be *in* the atmosphere or *part of* the atmosphere. Water is *part of* the atmosphere only when it is in the form of water vapor, an invisible gas. Water is *in* the atmosphere when it is liquid or solid. Water is no more part of the atmosphere when it is solid or liquid than a fish or a boat is part of the ocean. The atmosphere merely provides support or transportation for liquid and solid water. This is an important distinction.

Water vapor makes up only a small fraction of the atmospheric gases, varying from practically none at all to 4% by volume. Water-vapor content is higher at the tropics and decreases toward the poles. Although water vapor is only a few percent of Earth's total atmosphere, the amount of water that those few percent represent is awesome. Water vapor moving in Earth's atmosphere is the principal mechanism for resupplying water around the globe. The atmospheric redistribution of water is a key element in the water cycle.

THE CHANGING STATES OF WATER

Water is the only substance on Earth that exists in substantial quantities in all three fundamental states: solid, liquid, and gas. Heat is the primary variable that determines what state water will assume at any moment. When heat transfers from liquid water, kinetic activity of water

molecules decreases until they settle into a rigid structure in which they no longer move over and past one another. This solid water is ice.

When energy transfers to ice, kinetic energy increases until the molecules begin to move past one another again. The rigid structure holding water molecules together is dismantled as the ice melts, and water assumes the liquid state. Liquid water remains in a mass of "connected" molecules, due to small forces of attraction (van der Waals forces) that draw them together.

As more energy transfers to the water molecules, the kinetic energy increases until molecules become so energized that they escape into the atmosphere as individual molecules, unfettered by forces of attraction between one another. Invisible water vapor, a gas, becomes part of the atmosphere and, as such, subject to the pressures, energy transfers, and movements that determine the behavior of the atmosphere, and thus the weather.

A CLOSE LOOK AT EVAPORATION

Evaporation is the process by which liquid water becomes water vapor. One way to produce water vapor is to put a pot of water on the range, crank up the heat, and bring it to a boil. After a spell the water will all evaporate. When liquid water reaches 100°C, it doesn't get any hotter; it evaporates, becoming a gas, water vapor.

That's only one instance of evaporation, however. Clothes hanging on the line, puddles on the sidewalk, dishes parked in the drainer, and golden retrievers all dry

Note: Please note that the actual text pages are full color.

(Contd.)

WEATHER AND WATER COURSE

without being heated to 100°C (212°F). What happens in these cases?

Close analysis of the physical interactions reveals that, during virtually all evaporation, some water molecules are leaving the liquid state and going into the gas state, and others are going from the gas state into the liquid state. Which way a molecule goes depends on its energy when it reaches the interface between the mass of liquid water and the atmosphere. Every mass of water has molecules with low energy states and others with high energy states. The same is true of water-vapor molecules in the atmosphere. Water molecules are always going both ways.

The thing that determines if and at what rate evaporation will proceed is the *net* movement of molecules between liquid and gas. If more molecules are going into the gas phase, evaporation will occur. If more molecules are going into the liquid phase, condensation will occur. The greater the transfer of energy into the liquid, the greater the rate of evaporation.

Evaporation will continue until equilibrium is obtained, that is, until the number of water molecules escaping into the atmosphere is exactly equal to the number of water molecules returning to the liquid. The physical phenomenon is called **vapor pressure.** Every gas pushes with a pressure that depends on its concentration and a number of other variables. We won't go into detail in this course, but the next level of understanding of gas/liquid interactions requires knowledge of vapor pressures.

HUMIDITY AND WATER VAPOR

As the amount (concentration) of water vapor in a volume (of air) increases, its vapor pressure increases. Eventually the vapor pressure of water vapor will be great enough to, in effect, push water molecules back into the water as fast as new molecules are being pushed into the air. This is the **equilibrium vapor pressure.**

When the equilibrium vapor pressure is reached, the concentration of water vapor in the air cannot increase any more. This condition is popularly called **saturation.** It is often described as the point at which the air can hold no more water vapor, even though it has nothing to do with air's ability to "hold" water. Even so, it is a convenient and more intuitive model for middle school students to get their arms around. So, in this course, we will compromise scientific accuracy in order to start students along a difficult conceptual path.

Equilibrium vapor pressure changes with temperature; the warmer the air, the more water it can hold. To take this a step further, it would appear that, the warmer the air, the more water vapor it will take to saturate the air. This is true. Cold, arctic air saturates with only a trace of water vapor, but warm, tropical air soaks up a lot of water vapor before it is saturated.

Water vapor in the air is **humidity.** It can be described in different ways, including absolute humidity and relative humidity. **Absolute humidity** is simply the mass of water vapor present in a volume of air,

Note: Please note that the actual text pages are full color.

(Contd.)

usually a cubic meter. That seems straightforward enough, but there is a problem with the idea of absolute humidity. A cubic meter of air containing 5 g of water has an absolute humidity of 5 g/m^3. If that cubic meter of air is compressed to half its volume, that same 5 g of water is in half a cubic meter of air, so the air's absolute humidity is now twice what it was before, or 10 g/m^3. This changeable nature of absolute humidity makes it a difficult measurement for monitoring moisture in air masses.

Most often meteorologists describe the moisture in the air in terms of relative humidity. **Relative humidity** is the amount of water vapor in the air compared to the amount of vapor needed to saturate the air at its current temperature. Relative humidity describes how close to saturation the air is.

Because it takes more water vapor to saturate warm air, relative humidity changes with the temperature. Consider 1 kg of air containing 5 g of water vapor. If the air sample cools to 5°C, the sample will be saturated (see the table). When a sample of air is holding as much water vapor as it can (is saturated), the relative humidity is 100%.

If we heat the sample to 25°C, however, the air can hold more water vapor. The sample is no longer saturated, so the

Water/air saturation points	
Air temp. (°C)	Grams of water per kilogram of air (g/kg)
−40	0.1
−30	0.3
−20	0.8
−10	2.0
0	3.5
5	5.0
10	7.0
15	10.0
20	14.0
25	20.0
30	26.5
35	35.0
40	47.0

relative humidity is less than 100%. The table shows that the saturation point for air at 25°C is 20 g/kg. The 5 g of water vapor now represents only 25% of that needed to saturate 1 kg of air. Air that has 5 g/kg has a relative humidity of 25% when heated to 25°C. At what temperature would our sample have a relative humidity of 50%? According to the table the temperature would be 15°C.

CONDENSATION

As discussed earlier, water molecules are continuously transitioning between liquid and gas phases. At equilibrium the numbers going in each direction are equal. When there is a net flow from one phase to the other, either evaporation or condensation occurs. Generally, when energy transfers into the system, the phase shifts toward gas; transfer of energy out of the system produces condensation.

Condensation is the change from gas to liquid. Net condensation occurs when relative humidity reaches 100%. Actually, condensation starts to accumulate when the relative humidity *exceeds* 100% by a little bit, because 100% relative humidity is still an equilibrium condition. Condensation happens on surfaces. The surface can be large, like the surface of a cold soda can or a bathroom mirror, or small, like a piece of dust or a molecule of salt.

Note: Please note that the actual text pages are full color.

(Contd.)

MATERIALS FOR PART 1
IS WATER REALLY THERE?

FOR EACH GROUP

2	Plastic cups, large, 500-ml
4	*Weather and Water Lab Notebooks*
•	*Class Weather Chart*, page 1

FOR THE CLASS

1	Set of weather tools
•	Thermometers
•	Syringes
•	Graduated cylinders
•	Containers, such as pie plates, cups, and bottles (optional) *
•	Food coloring
•	Water *
•	Pitchers or other water containers *
•	Ice *
•	Zip bags
•	Plastic wrap (optional) *
1	Overhead projector *
1	Transparency of *Class Weather Chart for Period_____* (from Investigation 1)

FOR ASSESSMENT

•	*Assessment Chart for Investigations 5 and 6*
*	Supplied by the teacher

190

Note: Please note that the actual text pages are full color.

(Contd.)

GETTING READY FOR PART 1

1. BEGIN SECOND ROUND OF WEATHER OBSERVATIONS

Have students begin collecting another 8–10 days of weather observations, using the weather tools in the kit. Add the observations to the class weather chart used in Investigation 1. Enter the data on the multimedia spreadsheet if possible. Students will analyze these data later.

2. CONSIDER HUMIDITY

Find out what your local dew point is before beginning this investigation. You can find dew points by checking your favorite weather website.

If the dew point is 5°C (41°F) or higher, students should be able to condense water vapor on a cold surface. If the dew point is below 5°C, as it can be in the Southwest, producing condensation will be difficult.

3. PROMOTE INQUIRY

Most students have had personal experience with evaporation and condensation—wet objects dry by themselves and dew forms on cold drinks, for instance. Where does the water go and where does it come from? Give students time to engage these questions and be prepared to accommodate as many of their plans for acquiring evidence as you can. This may mean waiting a day for students to bring in materials from home for their investigations.

4. PLAN FOR ICE

This part requires plenty of ice. Make sure you have an adequate supply ready for all your classes.

5. THINK ABOUT ADDITIONAL MATERIALS

Depending on their investigation plans, students may want to use zip bags or plastic wrap. You can use the zip bags in the kit, but these are not consumable and should be dried out and returned to the kit. Plastic wrap is optional. You could either supply it or have students bring it in.

6. CONSIDER FOOD COLORING

Students will probably figure out a way to include food coloring in their investigations. You should be in charge of the food coloring.

7. PLAN ASSESSMENT: TEACHER OBSERVATION

In Step 8, when students make their presentations to the class, score them on three aspects of inquiry: planning and conducting the investigation, constructing a reasonable explanation, and communicating their ideas.

Note: Please note that the actual text pages are full color.

(Contd.)

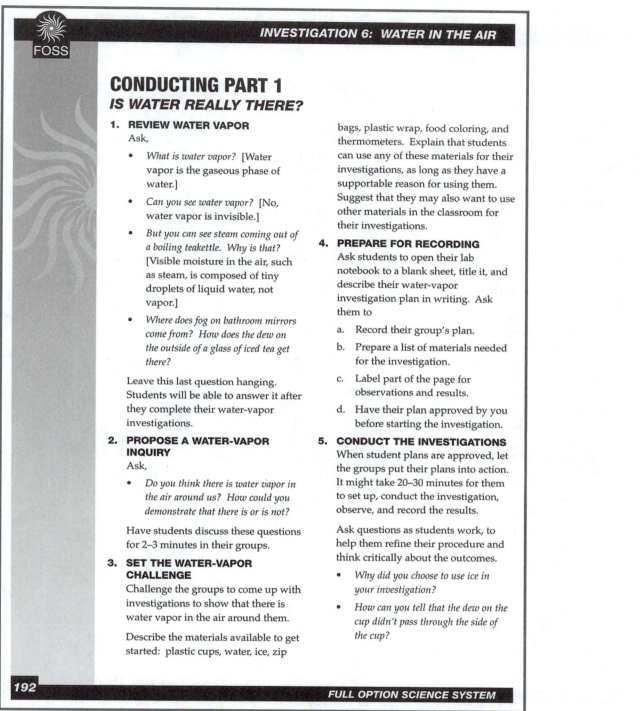

CONDUCTING PART 1
IS WATER REALLY THERE?

1. **REVIEW WATER VAPOR**
   Ask,

   - *What is water vapor?* [Water vapor is the gaseous phase of water.]

   - *Can you see water vapor?* [No, water vapor is invisible.]

   - *But you can see steam coming out of a boiling teakettle. Why is that?* [Visible moisture in the air, such as steam, is composed of tiny droplets of liquid water, not vapor.]

   - *Where does fog on bathroom mirrors come from? How does the dew on the outside of a glass of iced tea get there?*

   Leave this last question hanging. Students will be able to answer it after they complete their water-vapor investigations.

2. **PROPOSE A WATER-VAPOR INQUIRY**
   Ask,

   - *Do you think there is water vapor in the air around us? How could you demonstrate that there is or is not?*

   Have students discuss these questions for 2–3 minutes in their groups.

3. **SET THE WATER-VAPOR CHALLENGE**
   Challenge the groups to come up with investigations to show that there is water vapor in the air around them.

   Describe the materials available to get started: plastic cups, water, ice, zip bags, plastic wrap, food coloring, and thermometers. Explain that students can use any of these materials for their investigations, as long as they have a supportable reason for using them. Suggest that they may also want to use other materials in the classroom for their investigations.

4. **PREPARE FOR RECORDING**
   Ask students to open their lab notebook to a blank sheet, title it, and describe their water-vapor investigation plan in writing. Ask them to

   a. Record their group's plan.

   b. Prepare a list of materials needed for the investigation.

   c. Label part of the page for observations and results.

   d. Have their plan approved by you before starting the investigation.

5. **CONDUCT THE INVESTIGATIONS**
   When student plans are approved, let the groups put their plans into action. It might take 20–30 minutes for them to set up, conduct the investigation, observe, and record the results.

   Ask questions as students work, to help them refine their procedure and think critically about the outcomes.

   - *Why did you choose to use ice in your investigation?*

   - *How can you tell that the dew on the cup didn't pass through the side of the cup?*

Note: Please note that the actual text pages are full color.

(Contd.)

- *What causes dew to form only on cups of ice water?*

- *Could you get dew to form on a cup of room-temperature water?*

- *Sometimes fog forms on your glasses or on a bathroom mirror. How is that related to your investigation?*

6. **CLEAN UP AND SUMMARIZE**
    Once students finish, have them clean up their materials and return them to the materials station.

    Give them 5 minutes to discuss, organize, and record their conclusions.

7. **ORGANIZE RESULTS FOR CLASS PRESENTATION**
    Tell students that each group will present its results to the rest of the class. Their presentations should include a

    a. Statement of the challenge.

    b. Description of what they did.

    c. Statement of their conclusions and the evidence supporting those conclusions.

8. **MAKE THE PRESENTATIONS**
    Have each group make a short presentation. Allow time for student questions and critique. Ask questions to enrich the presentations.

    - *Why did you set up your investigation in this particular way?*

    - *How did you determine that the water didn't soak through the cup or container?*

    - *Why did you place the cup with water in the zip bag?*

    - *What evidence do you have that the water on the side of the cup came from the air?*

9. **ASSESS PROGRESS: TEACHER OBSERVATION**
    As students make their presentations, score them on how well they planned and conducted their investigations, whether they constructed reasonable explanations, and how well they communicated their ideas. Make note of any elements of inquiry where the class performance needs improvement or where they performed particularly well.

10. **DEFINE "CONDENSATION"**
    Tell students,

    Water can exist in three phases or states: solid ice, liquid water, and gaseous vapor. When water changes from gas to liquid, it is called **condensation.** *Water vapor condenses to form liquid water. The dew on cups of ice water is water that condensed from gas to liquid.*

11. **POLL THE CLASS**
    Take a poll of the class to find out whether the students think that, as a whole, their investigations demonstrated that water vapor exists in the air. Ask them to recall any other examples of condensation that they may have seen—situations in which water vapor condensed into liquid water.

Note: Please note that the actual text pages are full color.

(Contd.)

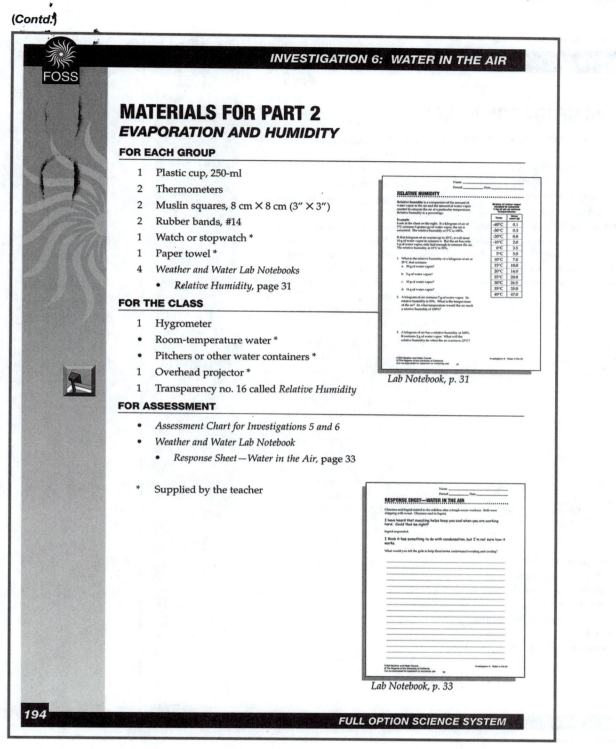

MATERIALS FOR PART 2
EVAPORATION AND HUMIDITY

FOR EACH GROUP

- 1   Plastic cup, 250-ml
- 2   Thermometers
- 2   Muslin squares, 8 cm × 8 cm (3" × 3")
- 2   Rubber bands, #14
- 1   Watch or stopwatch *
- 1   Paper towel *
- 4   *Weather and Water Lab Notebooks*
  - •   *Relative Humidity*, page 31

FOR THE CLASS

- 1   Hygrometer
- •   Room-temperature water *
- •   Pitchers or other water containers *
- 1   Overhead projector *
- 1   Transparency no. 16 called *Relative Humidity*

FOR ASSESSMENT

- •   *Assessment Chart for Investigations 5 and 6*
- •   *Weather and Water Lab Notebook*
  - •   *Response Sheet—Water in the Air*, page 33

*   Supplied by the teacher

Lab Notebook, p. 31

Lab Notebook, p. 33

194

Note: Please note that the actual text pages are full color.

(Contd.)

GETTING READY FOR PART 2

1. **PLAN FOR ROOM-TEMPERATURE WATER**
   Put aside a couple of liters of tap water to reach room temperature before beginning this part.

2. **CUT MUSLIN**
   Muslin is supplied in 16-cm squares in the kit. Use scissors or a paper cutter to cut the squares into four 8 cm × 8 cm pieces. Cut enough for each pair of students to have a small square.

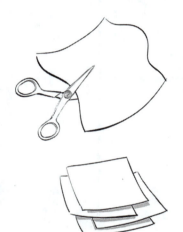

3. **CONSIDER HUMIDITY**
   In Step 7, students use a wet-bulb thermometer to measure the decrease in temperature that occurs when they wave the thermometer. The decrease will be greater on days when the relative humidity is low (60% or less).

Use the hygrometer in the kit to estimate relative humidity in your room. Try to do this part when the relative humidity is below 80%.

4. **PLAN ASSESSMENT: RESPONSE SHEET**
   Students complete a response sheet in Step 13. Read through students' responses and make notes about common understandings of the relationship between temperature and evaporation and condensation. Use this information to guide your teaching in Part 3.

   If the class as a whole does not provide good answers to the response sheet, hold a self-assessment session. Provide samples at various levels of accuracy and completeness and ask students to evaluate them. Return the response sheets to students. Ask them to score their own and revise or add information as necessary. This is also a good way to convey to students your expectations for the science writing they should be producing. See the scoring guide in the Assessment chapter.

Note: Please note that the actual text pages are full color.

(Contd.)

CONDUCTING PART 2
EVAPORATION AND HUMIDITY

1. REVIEW PART 1

Ask one or two students to recount the activities they conducted in Part 1 and to review the evidence that water vapor is indeed in the air. They should cite the condensation observed on different surfaces.

2. PONDER EVAPORATION

Ask,

- *We have pretty good evidence that there is water vapor in the air. How does water vapor get into the air?*

Many students will be familiar with evaporation from earlier experiences. They may suggest that water evaporates from oceans, lakes, and pavement and that it goes into the air.

Have them write this definition in their notebooks.

Evaporation is the process by which liquid water becomes a gas called water vapor.

3. DISCUSS THE EFFECT OF WIND

Have the GETTERs get a cup of water for their group. Ask students to dampen a small area on the back of both hands, then gently blow on the wet spot on their left hand to simulate wind.

Ask,

- *What effect does wind have on the wet spot?* [The water dries up faster; the area on the left hand is cooler than the right hand.]

- *Where did the water go that was on your hands?* [It evaporated and went into the surrounding air.]

- *Why did the wet spot feel cold?* [It takes heat to turn liquid water into water vapor. Heat transfers from your hand to the water by conduction. The reduced heat on your hand sends a "cold" signal to your brain.]

4. INTRODUCE MEASURING TEMPERATURE CHANGE

Tell students that you have some materials that they can use to find out more about temperature change during evaporation.

Show them the thermometers, muslin, rubber bands, and cups of water. Ask,

- *How could you use these materials to measure temperature change during evaporation?*

Have students discuss this question in their groups and come up with ways they might accomplish this task. Encourage them to consider conditions they need to control, for example, dry thermometer versus wet thermometer. Have them write their ideas in their lab notebooks. After 5 minutes, have groups share their ideas.

5. DESIGN THE INVESTIGATION

Use a variation of the ideas from Step 4, or modify students' ideas to come to the following procedure:

a. Each group gets two thermometers, two pieces of muslin, two rubber bands, a paper towel, and a cup of water.

Note: Please note that the actual text pages are full color.

(Contd.)

FOSS

b. Record the starting temperature of the thermometers.

c. Wrap a piece of muslin around the bulb end of both thermometers. Secure the muslin with rubber bands.

d. Dip the muslin end of *one* thermometer into water. It shouldn't be dripping wet, so blot excess water from the fabric.

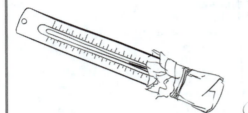

Students often propose blowing on the damp muslin. Suggest that they can accomplish the same effect by waving the fabric end of the thermometers back and forth rapidly in the air. They don't need to wave the thermometers with sweeping motions, just 10–15 cm (4–6″) back and forth in the air. They should rest their elbows on the table and flick their wrists back and forth.

Demonstrate how to do this with a simple wrist action.

NOTE for Step 7

You may want to help students design a chart for recording temperature data before they begin waving the thermometers.

6. SET UP THERMOMETERS
Have GETTERs get two thermometers, two pieces of muslin, two rubber bands, a paper towel, and one cup half-filled with water for their group. Remind them to record the starting temperature before attaching the muslin.

7. WAVE THERMOMETERS
When each team has dampened the fabric on one of its thermometers, time 1 minute. Ask students to read the temperatures on the thermometers. Ask,

- *How can you increase the amount of evaporation from the fabric?*

Let the waving begin. Students should take turns doing the waving, 20–30 seconds at a time. They should read the temperature on both thermometers between turns.

After about 5 minutes, ask the groups to record final temperature readings.

8. REPORT THE RESULTS
Have students calculate the difference between the starting and ending temperatures for each thermometer. Students should find that the temperature decreased for the wet-bulb thermometer. Call on each group to report its temperature changes.

Note: Please note that the actual text pages are full color.

(Contd.)

INVESTIGATION 6: WATER IN THE AIR

9. DISCUSS THE RESULTS

Ask,

- *What happened to the water on the fabric when you waved the thermometer around in the air?* [It evaporated.]

- *What caused the temperature to go down?*

Have students discuss this question in their groups for a minute. If students struggle for an answer, tell them,

Water can change from liquid to vapor only when energy is available. Evaporation requires energy. Energy in the form of heat in the environment is usually the source of energy to make evaporation happen.

Continue the analysis of results.

- *What is required for evaporation to happen?* [Heat energy has to transfer to the water.]

- *Where did the heat come from?* [From the surrounding environment, including the water in the cloth, the cloth, the thermometer, and the air.]

- *When you take heat energy away from an object, does the object get warmer or cooler?* [Cooler.]

- *What object or objects got cooler, when the water evaporated from the cloth?* [The cloth, the water in the cloth, the thermometer, the air.]

- *Where did the heat energy go?* [Water molecules in the liquid water absorbed the heat energy. The extra energy caused the molecules to speed up and evaporate.]

10. INTRODUCE "HUMIDITY"

Ask,

- *When water evaporates from a surface, like the piece of cloth or the ocean, what happens to the amount of water vapor in the air?* [It increases.]

Refer to the definitions on transparency no. 16, *Relative Humidity*, as you tell students,

*Water vapor in the air is called **humidity**. When there is a lot of water vapor in the air, the air is **humid**. Humid air usually makes you feel sticky.*

The amount of water vapor in the air changes as the temperature changes. The warmer the temperature, the more water vapor the air can hold. As air gets colder, it holds less water vapor.

*When air contains as much water vapor as it can, it is **saturated**. It takes a lot of water vapor to saturate warm air, but only a little bit of water vapor to saturate cold air.*

*Meteorologists often describe the amount of water vapor in the air in terms of **relative humidity**. Relative humidity is measured in percentages. Relative humidity compares the amount of water vapor in the air to the amount of water vapor needed to saturate the volume of air.*

You might hear that the humidity today is 50%. That means that the air contains 50% of the amount of water vapor needed to saturate the air at today's temperature. For example, 1 kg of air at 25℃ can hold 20 g of water vapor. If it's holding 10 g of water vapor, the relative humidity is 50%.

198

FULL OPTION SCIENCE SYSTEM

Note: Please note that the actual text pages are full color.

250 Chapter 14

(Contd.)

WEATHER AND WATER COURSE

BREAKPOINT

11. INTRODUCE STUDENT SHEET

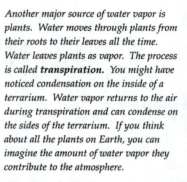

Ask students to open their lab notebooks to page 31, *Relative Humidity.* Use the transparency called *Relative Humidity,* as you introduce the sheet. Work through the example together. Give students 10–15 minutes to work on the three problems. See the answer sheet in the Teacher Answer Masters.

Discuss students' answers. They may need a little assistance with the percentage calculations and some guidance with the logic imbedded in the questions.

12. SUMMARIZE WATER VAPOR IN THE AIR

Tell students,

Water vapor is part of air. Water vapor gets into the air several different ways. As we found out, liquid water can evaporate when it absorbs energy. Energy transferred to water, either by radiation or conduction, can increase the kinetic energy enough to change liquid water into gas.

Sometimes the humidity can reach 100%. That means that the air contains as much water vapor as possible at that time.

- *When temperature increases and the amount of water vapor stays the same, the relative humidity decreases.*

- *When temperature stays the same but the amount of water vapor increases, relative humidity increases.*

Another major source of water vapor is plants. Water moves through plants from their roots to their leaves all the time. Water leaves plants as vapor. The process is called **transpiration.** *You might have noticed condensation on the inside of a terrarium. Water vapor returns to the air during transpiration and can condense on the sides of the terrarium. If you think about all the plants on Earth, you can imagine the amount of water vapor they contribute to the atmosphere.*

All terrestrial animals exhale water vapor when they breathe. The amount of water that enters the atmosphere as a result of respiration is significant as well. Also, fires, internal combustion engines, and volcanic eruptions add water vapor to the atmosphere.

13. ASSESS PROGRESS: RESPONSE SHEET

Have students open their lab notebooks to page 33, *Response Sheet— Water in the Air.* Ask them to respond individually to the statements on the sheet. Collect the lab notebooks when students are through.

WATER IN THE AIR
199

Note: Please note that the actual text pages are full color.

(*Contd.*)

RELATIVE HUMIDITY

Humidity is the amount of water vapor in the air.

Saturate means to fill up completely.

Relative humidity gives a measure of water vapor in the air compared to how much water vapor is needed to saturate the volume of air. Relative humidity is measured as a percentage.

Example

Suppose 1 kg of air at 25°C can hold 20 g of water vapor. If it is holding only 10 g of water vapor, it is holding half as much as it can. The relative humidity is 50%.

$$10 \text{ g} / 20 \text{ g} = 0.5 \qquad 100 \times 0.5 = 50\%$$

- When temperature increases and the amount of water vapor stays the same, the relative humidity decreases.

- When temperature stays the same but water vapor increases, relative humidity increases.

- Warm air can hold more water vapor than cooler air.

- Air under low pressure holds more water vapor than air under higher pressure.

336

(Contd.)

HUMIDITY CALCULATOR

Dry-bulb temp. (°C)	Relative humidity (%) Difference between wet- and dry-bulb temperature (°C)																			
	1°	2°	3°	4°	5°	6°	7°	8°	9°	10°	11°	12°	13°	14°	15°	16°	17°	18°	19°	20°
−10	67	35																		
−9	69	39	9																	
−8	71	43	15																	
−7	73	48	20																	
−6	74	49	25																	
−5	76	52	29	7																
−4	77	55	33	12																
−3	78	57	37	17																
−2	79	60	40	22																
−1	81	62	43	26	8															
0	81	64	46	29	13															
1	83	66	49	33	17															
2	84	68	52	37	22	7														
3	84	70	55	40	26	12														
4	85	71	57	43	29	16														
5	86	72	58	45	33	20	7													
6	86	73	60	48	35	24	11													
7	87	74	62	50	38	26	15													
8	87	75	63	51	40	29	19	8												
9	88	76	64	53	42	32	22	12												
10	88	77	66	55	44	34	24	15	6											
11	89	78	67	56	46	36	27	18	9											
12	89	78	68	58	48	39	29	21	12											
13	89	79	69	59	50	41	32	23	15	7										
14	90	79	70	60	51	42	34	26	18	10										
15	90	80	71	61	53	44	36	27	20	13	6									
16	90	81	71	63	54	46	38	30	23	15	8									
17	90	81	72	64	55	47	40	32	25	18	11									
18	91	82	73	65	57	49	41	34	27	20	14	7								
19	91	82	74	65	58	50	43	36	29	22	16	10								
20	91	83	74	66	59	51	44	37	31	24	18	12	6							
21	91	83	75	67	60	53	46	39	32	26	20	14	9							
22	92	83	76	68	61	54	47	40	34	28	22	17	11	6						
23	92	84	76	69	62	55	48	42	36	30	24	19	13	8						
24	92	84	77	69	62	56	49	43	37	31	26	20	15	10	5					
25	92	84	77	70	63	57	50	44	39	33	28	22	17	12	8					
26	92	85	78	71	64	58	51	45	40	34	29	24	19	14	10	5				
27	92	85	78	71	65	58	52	47	41	36	31	26	21	16	12	7				
28	93	85	78	72	65	59	53	48	42	37	32	27	22	18	13	9	5			
29	93	86	79	72	66	60	54	49	43	38	33	28	24	19	15	11	7			
30	93	86	79	73	67	61	55	50	44	39	35	30	25	21	17	13	9	5		
31	93	86	80	73	67	61	56	51	45	40	36	31	27	22	18	14	11	7		
32	93	86	80	74	68	62	57	51	46	41	37	32	28	24	20	16	12	9	5	
33	93	87	80	74	68	63	57	52	47	42	38	33	29	25	21	17	14	10	7	
34	93	87	81	75	69	63	58	53	48	43	39	35	30	28	23	19	15	12	8	5
35	93	87	81	75	69	64	59	54	49	44	40	36	32	28	24	20	17	13	10	7

(Contd.)

ASSESSMENT CHART FOR INVESTIGATIONS 5 AND 6

5—CONVECTION
6—WATER IN THE AIR

STUDENT NAME	5.1 Density Calculating (RS)	5.2 Layering Hot and Cold (SS)	5.3 Convection Chamber (SS)	5.3 Written Communication (TO)	Mid-summative Exam 5	6.1 Plan and Conduct (TO)	6.1 Construct Explanation (TO)	6.1 Communication (TO)	6.2 Evaporation and Cooling (RS)	6.3 Dew-Point Questions (SS)	6.4 Temp and Pressure (TO)	6.5 Self-Assess (OW)	Mid-summative Exam 6	informal notes
1.														
2.														
3.														
4.														
5.														
6.														
7.														
8.														
9.														
10.														
11.														
12.														
13.														
14.														
15.														
16.														
17.														
18.														
19.														
20.														
21.														
22.														
23.														
24.														
25.														
26.														
27.														
28.														
29.														
30.														
31.														
32.														

Assessment Charts
No. 3—Assessment Sheet

(Contd.)

MID-SUMMATIVE EXAM 6 ···

1. Martha's mom hung the sheets out to dry instead of putting them in the dryer. The process in which the sheets get dry is called_____.

2. Samantha was thirsty and poured some lemonade over ice. A few minutes later she noticed the outside of the glass was wet.

   This is an example of_____.

3. Cindy said the news reported yesterday that the relative humidity was 55. She thought it should have been reported as 55_____ (add the unit of measure), to show that relative humidity is a comparison between _____ and _____ .

4. When temperature increases and the amount of water vapor in the air stays the same, what happens to the relative humidity?

   _____

5. One day the dew point was reported as 20°C, and on another day it was reported as 15°C. Why isn't the dew point always the same?

   _____

   _____

   _____

6. Draw a diagram and write a short paragraph to explain how clouds form. (Use the back of this sheet or another piece of paper if you need to.)

465

(Contd.)

CLASS WEATHER CHART

Name _____

Period _____ Date _____

Date/time	Temp. (°C)	Air pressure (mb)	Relative humidity	Wind speed	Wind direction	Visibility	Other observations

Date/time	Temp. (°C)	Air pressure (mb)	Relative humidity	Wind speed	Wind direction	Visibility	Other observations

FOSS Weather and Water Course
© The Regents of the University of California
Can be duplicated for classroom or workshop use.   1

Investigation 1: What Is Weather?
Student Sheet

Source: Pages 1, 31, 33, from FOSS® (Full Option Science System®) *Weather and Water* Lab Notebook.
© The Regents of the University of California and published by Delta Education. Used with permission.

(Contd.)

Name _____

Period _____ Date _____

RELATIVE HUMIDITY ·

Relative humidity is a comparison of the amount of water vapor in the air and the amount of water vapor needed to saturate the air at a particular temperature. Relative humidity is a percentage.

Example
Look at the chart on the right. If a kilogram of air at 5°C contains 5 grams (g) of water vapor, the air is saturated. The relative humidity at 5°C is 100%.

If that kilogram of air warms up to 15°C, it will need 10 g of water vapor to saturate it. But the air has only 5 g of water vapor, only half enough to saturate the air. The relative humidity at 15°C is 50%.

Grams of water vapor needed to saturate 1 kg of air at various temperatures

Temp.	Water vapor (g)
–40°C	0.1
–30°C	0.3
–20°C	0.8
–10°C	2.0
0°C	3.5
5°C	5.0
10°C	7.0
15°C	10.0
20°C	14.0
25°C	20.0
30°C	26.5
35°C	35.0
40°C	47.0

1. What is the relative humidity of a kilogram of air at 25°C that contains
   a. 20 g of water vapor?

   b. 5 g of water vapor?

   c. 10 g of water vapor?

   d. 16 g of water vapor?

2. A kilogram of air contains 7 g of water vapor. Its relative humidity is 50%. What is the temperature of the air? At what temperature would the air reach a relative humidity of 100%?

3. A kilogram of air has a relative humidity of 100%. It contains 2 g of water vapor. What will the relative humidity be when the air warms to 25°C?

(Contd.)

Name _____

Period _____   Date _____

RESPONSE SHEET—WATER IN THE AIR
· ·

Christine and Ingrid trotted to the sideline after a tough soccer workout. Both were dripping with sweat. Christine said to Ingrid,

I have heard that sweating helps keep you cool when you are working hard. Could that be right?

Ingrid responded,

I think it has something to do with condensation, but I'm not sure how it works.

What would you tell the girls to help them better understand sweating and cooling?

_____

_____

_____

_____

_____

_____

_____

_____

_____

_____

_____

_____

_____

_____

_____

_____

_____

_____

_____

Planning the Lesson Sequence: Purposes, Objectives, and Learning Environment

Project 2061 and *National Science Education Standards* include several points related to weather, in general, and evaporation and condensation, in particular. Some of these are incorporated in the selections below, including both background commentary and goals for elementary, middle, and high school to show the progression of learning that is anticipated for these topics. For example, evaporation and condensation can be understood at one level as disappearance and reappearance of water, whereas understanding that involves conservation of matter based on a molecular view of matter, and the structure of molecules, represent higher levels. Applying these latter constructs to the water cycle brings about an even higher level of understanding.

Benchmarks for Science Literacy

SELECTED CONNECTIONS TO WEATHER

Evaporation and condensation will mean nothing different from disappearance and appearance, perhaps for several years, until students begin to understand that the evaporated water is still present in the form of invisibly small molecules. (*Benchmarks*, Grades 3–5)

- **When liquid water disappears, it turns into a gas (vapor) in the air and can reappear as a liquid when cooled, or as a solid if cooled below the freezing point of water. Clouds and fog are made of tiny droplets of water. (*Benchmarks*, Grades 3–5)**

Water offers another important set of experiences for students at this level. Students can conduct investigations that go beyond the observations made in the earlier grades to learn the connection between liquid and solid forms, but recognizing that water can also be a gas, while much more difficult, is still probably accessible. Perhaps the main thrust there is to try to figure out where water in an open container goes. This is neither self-evident nor easy to detect. But the water cycle is of such profound importance to life on earth that students should certainly have experiences that will in time contribute to their understanding of evaporation, condensation, and the conservation of matter. (*Benchmarks*, Grades 6–8)

- **The cycling of water in and out of the atmosphere plays an important role in determining climatic patterns. Water evaporates from the surface of the earth, rises and cools, condenses into rain or snow, and falls again to the surface. The water falling on land collects in rivers and lakes, soil, and porous layers of rock, and much of it flows back into the ocean. (*Benchmarks*, Grades 6–8)**

National Science Education Standards

SELECTED CONNECTIONS TO WEATHER

As students mature, the concept of evaporation can be reasonably well understood as the conservation of matter combined with a primitive idea of particles and the idea that air is real. Condensation is less well understood and requires extensive observation and instruction to complete an understanding of the water cycle. (NSES, Physical Science, Grades 5–8)

OBJECTS IN THE SKY

- The sun provides the light and heat necessary to maintain the temperature of the earth. (NSES, Content Standards—Earth and Space Science, grades K–3)
- Water, which covers the majority of the earth's surface, circulates through the crust, oceans, and atmosphere in what is known as the "water cycle." Water evaporates from the earth's surface, rises and cools as it moves to higher elevations, condenses as rain or snow, and falls to the surface where it collects in lakes, oceans, soil, and in rocks underground. (NSES, Content Standards—Earth and Space Science, Grades 5–8)

WATER IS A SOLVENT

- As it passes through the water cycle it dissolves minerals and gases and carries them to the oceans.
- The atmosphere is a mixture of nitrogen, oxygen, and trace gases that include water vapor. The atmosphere has different properties at different elevations.
- Clouds, formed by the condensation of water vapor, affect weather and climate. Global patterns of atmospheric movement influence local weather. (NSES, Content Standards—Earth and Space Science, Grades 5–8)
- Materials can exist in different states—solid, liquid, and gas. Some common materials, such as water, can be changed from one state to another by heating or cooling. (NSES, Physical Science, Grades 5–8).
- Solids, liquids, and gases differ in the distances and angles between molecules or atoms and therefore the energy that binds them together. In solids the structure is nearly rigid; in liquids molecules or atoms move around each other but do not move apart; and in gases molecules or atoms move almost independently of each other. (NSES Physical Sciences, Grades 9–12)

As you can see from Teacher Guide page 177, the goal and objectives for a substantial part of Investigation 6 deal with investigating and understanding factors that influence humidity in the atmosphere. This understanding is grounded in an understanding of evaporation and condensation. Therefore, the purpose of this lesson sequence is to assist middle school students in coming to realize that water vapor is in the air and that under particular circumstances more water can be added to it, or removed from it, through processes of evaporation and condensation.

Three ideas that underlie Parts 1 and 2 of Investigation 6 are

1. that water vapor is present in the air,

2. what happens to water when it evaporates and condenses, and

3. what factors influence the amount of water in the air.

These concepts lie at the heart of understanding many weather-related phenomena, and as you will see as we address students' ideas in the next section of planning, they are problematic for many middle school students, and even for some high school students and adults. These facts about students' entry-level understanding lead to formulation of the following objectives, based on the resources from *Weather and Water*, ideas from the reform documents including National Science Education Standards and Project 2061 resources, and our understanding of the background and needs of middle school students. Therefore, I suggest the following objectives for this lesson sequence:

On completion of this lesson sequence, students should be able to

1. Describe evaporation and condensation as changes of state of water from liquid to a gas (water vapor) and from a gas to a liquid that add water to, and remove water from, air.

2. Investigate evaporation and condensation of water and accompanying changes in temperature, and draw meaning from these investigations.

3. Explain that evaporation requires the addition of heat energy to water, which cools the surroundings, and that condensation requires the removal of heat energy from water vapor, which usually warms the surroundings.

4. Define relative humidity as the percentage of water vapor that is in air at any particular temperature compared to the amount needed to saturate air at that temperature.

5. Describe and conduct an investigation to determine relative humidity as a component of weather observations.

Further elaborating the purpose of this lesson sequence, you may wish to provide a more practical emphasis such as the following: The purpose is to understand that water vapor is present in the air in varying amounts at different times and locations, depending on temperature of the air and the availability of water. Also the amount of water vapor usually is related to where the air has been recently. That is, water that has passed over cold or dry areas contains less water vapor than air that has passed over warm, moist land or bodies of water.

The learning environment fostered in Investigation 6 is one in which students explore their own ideas to generate a question for inquiry, plan and carry out the investigation, organize and make sense of the information from the investigation, and then use the new ideas for the next round of exploring ideas. Parts 1 and 2 are components of an inquiry-centered program that aims to advance students' understanding and application of science content. The teacher's role is central in guiding students as they explore their own ideas and raise meaningful new questions that lead to productive investigations. The teacher also has a central role in guiding interpretation of the data from inquiry and in supporting new understanding that is based on the interaction of students' developing ideas and their inquiry-based experiences. Therefore, the teacher must be careful to assist students when needed, but not give so much assistance that students become overly dependent on him/her. Guiding students toward scientifically valid conclusions and meanings, while requiring that students develop their own critical-thinking skills, requires the teacher to be a thoughtful and patient listener. It also requires that the teacher have a firm understanding of the instructional goals and content.

Reflection & Discussion Questions

1. Think about how the learning environment described in the previous paragraph relates to the objectives and the design of the textbook pages. In what ways are these three compatible?

2. How will students acquire the information and form the concepts that they need to understand and apply the science content about evaporation, condensation, and humidity?

3. What responsibilities are placed on students and teachers by this design?

4. How will you engage students in a way that causes them to accept these responsibilities?

5. How is this dependent on the learning environment that you and your students create?

As you think about this lesson sequence, recall the initial planning model introduced in Chapter 3. You should remember that it emphasized three aspects set in the context of continuous assessment. The three aspects of this model were (1) building a base of information about the topic at hand through varied means, including reading, listening, and investigating; (2) developing understanding of the ideas contained in the information base; and then (3) learning how to use this newly constructed knowledge to further expand and demonstrate understanding. Of course, engagement of students in all of these processes is essential. You may wish to combine teaching and learning models, adding the 5E model, conceptual change, or the apprenticeship model to the initial planning model. Regardless of how you approach the teaching-learning model, you also need to consider how you will answer the questions for reflection and discussion that precede this paragraph.

Planning the Lesson Sequence: Students' Ideas and Assessment

Students' Ideas

Middle school students may come to science classes with varied views about evaporation, condensation, and humidity. Teachers must understand students' ideas and reasoning because of their importance in planning, teaching, and assessing students' entry-level knowledge and their progress toward the learning objectives for this lesson sequence. Even more important, discerning students' ideas about these phenomena should be part of the planning and assessment related to these topics.

Evaporation holds some mystery for younger children, but by middle school age, students have some sense that matter is conserved during evaporation. That is, most comprehend that disappearance of water, as it evaporates, does not mean that the water no longer exists. However, one day, in a serious conversation with a teacher from an upper elementary school, it became evident that she was confusing evaporation of liquids with a figure of speech in which "evaporate" means to disappear—as in "I laid down my pencil and it must have *evaporated* since I can no longer find it." Therefore, even though most middle school students apply a form of the principle of conservation of matter, in which they believe that the disappearing liquid must have gone somewhere (Driver et al., 1994, p. 81), it may be beneficial to be alert that some students may have not formed this view. Careful listening to students' conversations, or use of thoughtful questions can be a source of information about this.

Even though middle school students have some concept of conservation of matter, it may not be generalized. For example, Driver and colleagues (1994) also report a study of Israeli students by Stavy in which she demonstrated evaporation of acetone in a sealed tube. Only 5 percent of nine-year-olds demonstrated conservation of weight, but this increased to 80 percent of fourteen-year-olds. Their reason related to their belief that gaseous substances weighed less than their liquid counterpart. Thus for students in grades 6 and 7, it is reasonable to infer that perhaps half or more of the students may not hold the same views as you regarding conservation of matter in every example of evaporation.

Students' ideas about condensation are even more complex. The common observation that water drops form on a cold container brings out many alternative viewpoints about where the water droplets came from, such as

- the coldness turns to water,
- the cold comes through the container and turns to water,
- liquid inside the container seeps through the container and collects on the outside, and
- coldness caused hydrogen and oxygen in the air to form water.

Only a small percentage of ten- to twelve-year-olds said that the water from the air condensed on the sides of the cold container. With students ages twelve to seventeen, the percentages increased from 10 to 55 percent. Other studies show that students of middle and high school age have poorly organized views about condensation and the structure of matter that conform very little to accepted scientific views (Driver et al., 1994). This shows that middle school students need considerable help in understanding condensation and evaporation in a scientifically sound manner.

These findings place great importance on pre-assessment and formative assessment as part of your instructional plan.

Reflection & Discussion Questions

1. Why is understanding conservation of matter an important part of understanding evaporation and condensation?

2. Why is it important to understand the particulate view of matter in order to understand these two phenomena?

3. How do these constructs (conservation and particle nature of matter) lie at the heart of understanding evaporation and condensation, in particular,

and other weather phenomena such as humidity, the water cycle, cloud formation, and precipitation, in general?

Preassessment

Preassessment for this lesson sequence is important because it can serve to engage students in the topics and give you needed information about students' entry-level knowledge, beliefs, and attitudes about condensation, evaporation, and humidity. You could set up some tasks for students to consider and write about individually as a form of pretest. Some items for this pretest are listed below including some that have been adapted from pages 191 through 199 of the Teacher Guide.

1. Over several days, the water level in an aquarium becomes lower. The aquarium contains fish and plants, but has no cover.

   (a) Describe what happened to the water.

   (b) Where has the water gone?

2. (a) What is water vapor?

   (b) What is humidity?

   (c) What is meant by the term relative humidity?

3. When you remove a can of soft drink from the refrigerator and set it on the counter for few minutes, drops of liquid can often be seen on the outside. Where did these drops come from and how did the drops get there?

4. When a can of soft drink that has not been in the refrigerator is placed on the same counter as the cold can of soft drink, drops of liquid do not form on the outside of the can. Tell why the cold can has drops of water on it and the other can does not.

5. This question asks for your self-assessment of your understanding of the ideas in questions 1 through 4. Choose the response (a, b, c, or d) that best describes your background knowledge for each of the questions above (1a, 1b, 2a, 2b, 2c, 3, and 4). The choices are:

   (a) I feel that I understand this idea very well.

   (b) I have heard of this idea, and partly understand it.

   (c) I have heard of this idea, but don't understand it at all.

   (d) I have not heard of this idea.

   Place the letter (a, b, c, or d) that corresponds to your sense of how much you know about the answer to questions 1 through 4 in the spaces provided below for each question.

   1. a. _____

       b. _____

   2. a. _____

       b. _____

       c. _____

   3. _____

   4. _____

Reflection & Discussion Questions

1. Describe your reaction to question 5.

2. What can question 5 show you about students' ideas and reasoning?

3. Would question 5 be more reliable if students had some experience or practice with making such judgments under your guidance? Give your reasons for your answer.

Summative Assessment

Examine the "Mid-Summative Exam" on page 465 from the Teacher Guide. Questions 1 through 4 are relevant to this lesson plan. A draft of some additional questions for the summative assessment follows:

1. Almost anything you remove from the refrigerator will show some evidence of condensation of moisture on the outside if left in air that is warmer than the refrigerator. Tell what it is composed of, where the moisture came from, and how it accumulated on the object.

2. Describe what happens to water on your body when you leave a swimming pool. In your description, be sure to also tell why you frequently feel cold after leaving the pool, even though the air is warm.

3. A kilogram of air at room temperature can hold about 16 grams of water. If the relative humidity of the air is 75 percent, how much water is in a kilogram of air? Show how you calculated the answer.

4. When measuring the relative humidity of air, a student obtained the following readings:

Wet bulb thermometer	22° C
Dry bulb thermometer	17° C

   Use your Humidity Calculator chart to determine the relative humidity.

5. How would you convince a grade 5 student, who has not studied about evaporation and condensation, that there is water in the air? Describe some demonstrations that would show that there is water in the air, and also tell how you would make a convincing argument that the air around us contains water.

6. (Bonus Question) If evaporation is a cooling process, why should you also believe that condensation is a warming process?

Reflection & Discussion Questions

If you wish to add questions to this formative assessment, feel free to do so. As part of your consideration about adding other questions, check to see that all of the objectives for Parts 1 and 2 have been addressed by this draft of the summative assessment. Be sure to add questions for objectives that have not been adequately addressed.

Planning the Lesson Sequence: Activities that Promote Learning with Understanding

Examine the materials provided in the pages of the Teacher Guide to gather ideas for learning activities. Think about the model of teaching and learning that is implied in Part 1 of the Teacher Guide and the model you want to use for this planning activity. How will you engage your students? How will you help them build the knowledge base that is essential for understanding the concepts that are incorporated in the objectives? How will you nurture the understanding and applications that are included in the objectives? How will you monitor the progress students are making toward the objectives? How do the activities and materials in the Teacher Guide support you and the students in teaching and learning the content and inquiry processes that comprise this lesson sequence?

Pages 190 and 194 of the Teacher Guide provide a list of materials that are needed for the activities suggested in the succeeding pages. Most of these materials would be available to teachers who have access to the equipment kits that accompany the program. The exceptions are asterisked. Pages 191 and 195 give users of the program instructions about how to prepare the needed equipment and materials for teaching the two parts from Investigation 6 that have been selected for this chapter. Pages 192 and 193 and pages 195 through 199 of the Teacher Guide provide suggestions about how to approach the teaching and learning activities for these two parts.

Before you go further in your preparation, look back at the beginning of this chapter and see the list of topics that students have studied in Investigations 1 through 5. As you can see, these have focused mainly on heating and cooling of the atmosphere and making some basic weather observations. Previous topics will influence students' background knowledge.

Recommended Step 1 on page 191 of the Teacher Guide calls for return to regular weather observations. It is implied that relative humidity will be added to the list with students collecting that data at some time during the enactment of Part 2 of Investigation 6. Also, the local temperature and humidity will have a considerable effect on how you approach these two parts of Investigation 6. For good condensation results, you need high humidity, but for good evaporation results, lower humidity is better. Where you live in the country and the time of year you choose to do this lesson in your class will influence how well the students will be able to experience the phenomena. It may take some creativity on your part to "pull it off" effectively. For example, on some winter days in cold climates, indoor air is so dry that condensation is not easily demonstrated. This also can occur in very dry climates such as in the southwestern desert. However, you can create a small humid environment in a covered aquarium with an inch of water in the bottom. In such an environment, a refrigerated can of soft drink can be placed on a small stand that keeps it above the level of the water to show how drops of liquid will form on the cold can. Similarly, potential difficulties that exist in your local environment often can be circumvented by planning or discussion with colleagues.

Page 192 of the Teacher Guide provides a strategy for addressing the objectives that relate to answering the question of Part 1—Is water really there? Activity 1 on page 192 can be made more engaging if some actual examples of the phenomena are available to the students. A flask of water boiling on the demonstration desk, clear plastic glasses filled with some ice and water located where the students can observe them close up to see condensation, and a closed aquarium with water that is condensed on the lid all make good focal points for engaging observations and discussion. You can begin by having students in small groups make careful observations of these three examples and describe their observations within groups. Follow this with groups reporting to the whole class, so that all observations are represented by verbal description. Ask if there are similarities among the three examples to cause students to think about observing connections and patterns.

Then you can return to a small-group setting and have students work on questions such as the following that are designed to direct their attention to water vapor in the air:

Note what is happening to the boiling water in the flask. A cloud of water droplets can be seen above the flask. Where did that cloud come from? What is the cloud composed of? What happens to the cloud? Does it remain about the same or does it increase in size? Why doesn't it fill the room, making it foggy?

As students are discussing these questions, you have an excellent opportunity to listen and observe as a way of assessing students' preconceptions about water in the air and evaporation. Another opportunity for preassessment can occur when groups report their conclusions after a few minutes of discussion. A third opportunity for preassessment lies in the use of the pretest described in the previous section of this chapter. The advantage of the written preassessment is that you will have information from individual students, whereas the other approaches give you a blend of ideas from group members, which are more difficult to interpret. However, if you ask questions to clarify ideas from individual students, you can gain useful information.

Another round of questions about the ice water in the clear plastic glasses can also foster engagement. Tasks such as "Describe your observations about the glass of water and ice" and "Where did the drops of liquid on the outside of the plastic come from?" also present opportunities for formative assessment.

After discussion of these responses, you can then begin with the questions in Activity 1 on page 192 of the Teacher Guide to complete the engagement activity. This discussion can lead to Activity 2 on page 192—students planning an investigation that will demonstrate the presence of water vapor in the air. You may modify it slightly, however, to use the information already gained from the engagement activities. That could be prompted by asking, "How can you provide convincing evidence to show the presence of water vapor in the air?" This prompt could be used as a basis for short, small-group discussions, followed by reporting to the whole class with you tabulating the ideas on the board. Some discussion of these ideas would be valuable to highlight different kinds of evidence that students suggest. Students could rank different suggestions as high, medium, or low, regarding how convincing each might be. As part of the ranking, students should also give their rationale for their choices. Such an approach not only provides students with an important learning activity that connects to the lesson content about water in the air and to inquiry, but also provides valuable formative assessment data on students' ideas and reasoning.

Reflection & Discussion Questions

1. How does the discussion, ranking, and presentation of rationales for choices help students learn about the lesson content?

2. How does it help them learn about inquiry?

3. What information does it give you about students' developing understanding of the topic and inquiry?

4. Why is this detailed preparation important for the investigation outlined in Activities 3, 4, and 5 on page 192 of the Teacher Guide?

With this background, you now are ready for students to choose one or more approaches to collecting convincing evidence about the presence of water vapor in the air. Students should have a clear picture of what they are trying to support with evidence from the investigation. Therefore, the plan set out in Activities 3, 4, and 5 provide a way of proceeding to the next level—gathering evidence to support their idea about water vapor in the air. The questions at the end of Activity 5 (Teacher Guide pages 192 and 193) provide you with important tools for probing students' thinking as you observe the work of small groups carrying out their investigations. Asking questions such as these, at the same time you supervise students closely during group investigations, is an important strategy for sound classroom management and for helping students keep the science concepts and investigation techniques in mind. Without this kind of monitoring and interaction, activities like this frequently fail to achieve their potential.

Activities 6, 7, and 8 on Teacher Guide page 193 describe a plan for the next activity, which involves making sense of the data collected. Students are advised to reflect on their data from the investigation, to organize it for a report, and to make a presentation. Adding the first question in Activity 8 (*Why did you set up your investigation in this particular way?*) may be a good addition to the directions given in Activity 7 to make it a standard part of the report. This would prompt students to think about this question as they prepare for their presentation, instead of it coming during the report. A more thoughtful answer may result.

The connections between items b and c in Activity 7 are keys to meaningful outcomes from Part 1 in Investigation 6 about Water in the Air. Also the second and fourth questions in Activity 8 are key questions that students must answer. The purposes of this set of activities in Part 1 of Investigation 6 are to (1) engage students in thinking deeply about a question, (2) identify an investigation to provide some data (evidence) to answer the question, (3) make sense of the data, and (4) draw a conclusion based on the data. The four questions provide a way for students to meet these purposes through careful reflection on their work as they prepare to present it to their classmates. These actions, along with observing and reflecting on the results of others, provide a powerful way for students to confront the commonplace naïve conceptions about water in the air. Understanding that air contains water vapor is an essential prerequisite to understanding important ideas that relate to weather, including condensation, evaporation, precipitation, and the water cycle.

Although these questions are important to ask during the oral presentations, I also recommend that they become a writing task for students a day or two later in the sequence. The results of this writing task will be an important source of information for you about how each student has grasped the idea about water vapor in the air. Here is a possible prompt for this writing task, which could be given at the beginning of a class a few days after you conclude Part 1 (Writing Task 1):

> At home on a warm summer day, I took a jar of pickles out of my refrigerator. A few minutes later, I noticed that the outside of the jar was covered with small drops of a clear liquid that looked and tasted like water. Where did this liquid come from? How did it get there? How could I know that the liquid did not come from inside the jar?

Reflection & Discussion Questions

1. Why must students address these commonplace naïve conceptions about water vapor in the air as part of a study of weather?

2. Why is so much time and energy given to this concern?

3. How does this sequence of activities in Part 1 help students come to a new understanding about water vapor in the air and about science?

Activity 9 reiterates the importance of collecting information about students' performance and then keeping the information available to guide further work. This reiterates the formative assessment cycle that was introduced in Chapter 7. Activity 10 formalizes the ideas from Part 1 of Investigation 6. Use of the term *condensation* to describe the observations, giving meaning to that term in its connection both to change of state and to observations that exemplify it, are part of sound instructional practice. A visual that summarizes this could be a helpful tool for students if it were to have a prominent place in the classroom and enlarged as new ideas were introduced, as in Part 2 of Investigation 6. An example follows:

Term	Meaning	Relevant Observations
States of matter	Water and other substances can exist in three states	Liquid water, solid water (ice), and gaseous water (water vapor)
Condensation	Change from a gas to a liquid	Water droplets form on cold glass that is exposed to warmer air. Water droplets form on a mirror in a bathroom when a person is showering.
Evaporation		
Humidity		

The closing activity in Part 1, the Poll of the Class, would be a useful review and another tool for assessing

students' understanding about water vapor in the air and condensation. In addition, the writing prompt given previously about removing the pickle jar from the refrigerator on a warm summer day provides another, potentially better assessment.

Reflection & Discussion Questions

In what ways were the set of activities for Part 1 consistent with the criteria for planning from Chapter 9, including engaging students with phenomena, developing and using scientific ideas, and promoting student thinking about experiences and ideas?

Part 2 of Investigation 6 begins on Teacher Guide page 194 with a listing of the materials needed. Page 195 provides some important preparatory steps. Steps 1 and 3 are quite simple, but very important for the success of the laboratory-type activities in this section. You should consider why they are so important.

Step 4 gives a recommendation about formative assessment and possible modifications to Part 3 if students are not grasping the connections among temperature, evaporation, and condensation.

Thirteen activities for Part 2 are found on pages 196 through 199. Activities 1, 2, and 3 provide a segue into Part 2 and some direct experiences on which to build conceptual understanding of humidity, evaporation, and its cooling effect.

Reflection & Discussion Questions

1. Why was it important to set aside a few liters of water to come to room temperature as advised on page 195, Step 1?

2. What steps does the Teacher Guide recommend for engaging students in Part 2? How could you make this even more engaging?

3. When would you introduce the definition of evaporation?

4. Activity 3 presents a conceptual conflict for many students—evaporation is a cooling process, but evaporation requires heat. It is logically explained at the end of Activity 3, page 196, but how can you help students deal with potential confusion on this point?

Activity 3 is a simple, but powerful experience that packs a lot of meaning! It is important to help students give it the time and thought that it needs. The logic of the development on page 196 is useful and can be helpful to you and the students. Before going on to Activity 4, I recommend that you employ small-group discussion, followed by whole-class discussion and possibly a writing task that deals with the three questions that are bulleted in Activity 3. Careful thought is needed on all of them to connect experience and ideas. However, the third question, "Why did the wet spot feel cold?," lies at the heart of understanding evaporation, temperature, and energy flow. Helping students make significant meaning out of the explanation that follows the question is important. I recommend not only that you spend time at this point helping students grasp the meaning, but also that you return to this idea a few times during the remainder of the unit. It is an example that serves as the basis for an important understanding that has many applications both to weather and to the physiology of plants and animals.

A writing task based on Activity 3 could be conducted as a "quick write" at the beginning of the following class. A possible prompt follows (Writing Task 2):

> When you are physically active during exercise or hard physical work, your body temperature increases and you perspire. Describe how perspiration cools your body.

Activity 4 is an engagement activity that begins the exploration of measuring relative humidity. It has three parts. First, you work with the students to establish the problem for the investigation. Second, students work in small groups for a few minutes to think collectively about how to carry out an investigation to address the problem. Third, you guide the students in sharing the results of their small-group discussion.

Activities 5, 6, and 7 contain descriptions of how to proceed with the investigation. Read these carefully. The transition from Activity 4 to Activity 5 will need some added attention before proceeding to be sure that students are clear about the purpose, the actions that are needed, and the reasons for doing them. After students are clear about what they are trying to accomplish with this series of activities, and the reasons underlying each action, you should attend to the note in the upper right hand corner of page 197 about designing a chart for recording data. The significant data include the temperatures shown by the two thermometers (wet and dry) and the difference between them after a few minutes of waving them through the air. Other data are not essential to the outcome.[1]

Activities 8 and 9 are designed to help students bring added meaning to the results of the investigation. Groups should record their data on a class chart so that the results of the work of all groups can be analyzed and interpreted. After examining the data, the ques-

tions in Activity 9 form the basis for a productive whole-class discussion. Understanding why the "wet" bulb showed a lower temperature involves understanding the flow of energy as evaporation occurs. This is essential to understanding how the results can be used as a measure of relative humidity, which comes in Activities 10, 11, and 12. Therefore, it is important that students create personal meaning from the discussion of the questions in Activity 9.

I strongly recommend that this activity be given the time it deserves and that it is followed by a writing activity. One prompt for writing that could be helpful at this point is (Writing Task 3):

> Explain why the temperature of the "wet" bulb is lower than the temperature of the "dry" bulb. Be sure to describe how energy flowed as the water evaporated from the moist cloth. Also tell why the temperature of the "dry" thermometer did not change as it was waved in the air.

This writing could serve as a small-group activity for about fifteen minutes on one day and as an individual writing task at a later time. Another strategy would be to have it as an individual writing task for about ten minutes and then turn it into a group writing task where students in the group review and improve the individual writing.

Reflection & Discussion Questions

1. Why is a writing task so important at this juncture in the lesson sequence?

2. What understandings need to be integrated to understand relative humidity?

3. How does this writing task reinforce these ideas and their integration?

4. What would be an alternative writing task at this point?

In Activity 10, the concepts of *humidity, relative humidity*, and *saturation* are introduced formally. I recommend that the information contained in Activity 10 be presented to students in written form because of its importance and the number of ideas. A handout with the information for students will be a helpful resource. Reading the information can be helpful to some students, but it also will need to be supplemented by explanation by the teacher, especially for the last two paragraphs from Activity 10. (Note: You could make one handout that presents the information in Activities 10 and 12. The information for Activity 12 will need to be held for use when that activity is enacted.)

Before concluding Activity 10, I suggest that you guide students through determining relative humidity using the data from Activity 9. The Humidity Calculator on Teacher Guide page 337 will be essential for this.

---

[1] You may want to show that the temperatures of the water and the room are the same at the outset of the investigation. This is an observation that may differ from students' belief, as students generally perceive that the water at room temperature feels colder than the air. [This is definitely an excursion from the main idea that you may wish to consider.]

If the dry bulb thermometer reading was 20°C and the wet bulb thermometer reading was 15°C, use the chart to look up the intersection of 20 and 5 (the difference between the two readings) and you find that the relative humidity was 59 percent. You may also wish to create some additional examples for students to practice as follows:

Dry Bulb °C	Wet Bulb °C	Difference °C	Relative Humidity %
20	10		
25	10		
20	7		
22	21		

Activity 11 builds on and applies this new information. Transparencies 16 and 17 (pages 336 and 337) and page 31 from the student book comprise resources for this activity. Activity 11 also further clarifies the meaning of the term *relative humidity* by helping students understand how much water vapor is needed to saturate the air at various temperatures. This is shown in the table on page 31 of the student book. The directions on page 31 and in the Teacher Guide page 199 are clear. However, students may need some guidance in transforming the words and actions in this activity into understanding.

Reflection & Discussion Questions

1. How do Activities 9, 10, and 11 complement each other? How can you help students make this set of connections?

2. What tasks would you give the students to facilitate this?

3. How would you nurture their integration of these ideas?

4. How would you assess their progress toward understanding?

Activity 12 provides students with information about how water vapor gets into the atmosphere. Up to now, the emphasis has been on change of state from liquid water to water vapor through the process of evaporation. Activity 12 reviews that important idea and adds two others: (1) transpiration from plants, which helps them move minerals from their roots to leaves and also helps to control the temperature of plants as evaporation requires heat energy, and (2) the exhaling of water by animals as a product of their burning food to release energy for their body functions. Given the numbers of plants and animals, these two processes account for a large amount of water vapor. This activity deserves a serious discussion to help students give it

the meaning it deserves. Questions like the following can be helpful to students in creating understanding of these ideas:

1. What effects does transpiration have on the temperature of the leaves of plants and on the air around them? Explain why this is the case.

2. Would you expect that the air inside a dairy barn with a large number of cows would have a lower or a higher humidity than the air outside? Tell why you think this.

3. Why does the air in schoolrooms tend to be so dry in the winter months? Why do many homes use humidifiers in the winter months? How would you predict that the relative humidity in a schoolroom might change during the first hour of class each day? Explain why you made that prediction.

Activity 13 is an application activity about the cooling effect of perspiration. This is an idea that requires some thought for most people as they associate sweating with being hot, instead of its cooling effect.

Reflection & Discussion Questions

1. How can this lesson sequence be improved?

2. What would you add to it to make it more effective?

Note: These are two questions you should ask each time you plan a lesson sequence!

Sequencing Activities

What follows (Figure 14.1) is one possible scenario of how this lesson sequence would be enacted. You should feel free to create your own scenario.

FIGURE 14.1 ■ Scheduling Activities

Day	Activities
1	Begin Part 1, Activity 1—Engagement of Students
2–3	Activities 2–7—Investigation
4	Activities 8–11
5	Writing Task 1. Begin Part 2, Activities 1–3
6–7	Writing Task 2, Activities 4–8
8	Activity 9, Writing Task 3—Individually followed by group analysis of group members' writing
9	Activities 10–11
10	Activities 12 and 13
11	Summative Test

Journal Questions

In your journal reflect on how the process of planning this lesson sequence has *deepened your understanding* and *strengthened your skills* related to:

1. The subject matter concepts that are incorporated in the textbook chapter.
2. Inquiry and the process of science.
3. The nature of science including the historical development of scientific concepts as well as the connections that exist between concepts and processes.
4. Applications of science to your students' experiential world.
5. Students' ideas, reasoning, and conceptual difficulties including potential misconceptions.
6. Instructional models and approaches to teaching.
7. The complexity of the planning process.

Chapter 15

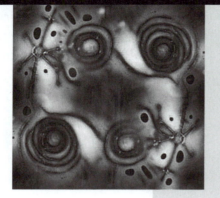

Continuing Your Professional Development

Congratulations on progressing to this point with this book. I hope that your efforts have provided you with an exciting professional challenge. Moreover, I hope that you see the work that was prompted by this book was an important step in your long-range professional development and that you are serious about continuing to move along this pathway with additional activities in the weeks, months, and years ahead.

Obviously, it is easy to say that you will continue to work on improving your teaching and your students' learning, but it also is easy to fall back into familiar, old patterns of behavior. Without the continual reminders of assignments, group members, and a group leader for your professional development activities, daily pressures tend to overwhelm the good intentions that you may now have to apply what you have learned to your daily work. You already may be thinking about the "loose ends" that have been left in other parts of your life while you were engaging in this professional development experience. To avoid this tendency you need a plan for continuing this work on your own or with one or two colleagues.

The Importance of Teamwork

A small-team effort is very useful. In my own experience as a secondary school science teacher, I had the privilege of working with one or two colleagues who taught with me in adjacent rooms. Although the "cast of characters in my life drama as a secondary science teacher" changed over the years, all of them were extremely helpful in stimulating my professional growth. In my first two years at a small rural school, Eric, Maggie, and

Janet, who taught science, mathematics, and English, provided me with so much guidance about how to deal with the cultural milieu, the curriculum, and helping students' learn. In a new position over the next six years, John, Paul, and Art were my loyal science teaching companions with whom I planned work, organized lessons, and discussed difficulties in engaging and nurturing our students in grades 7 through 12. Subsequently, both Paul Joslin and I entered doctoral programs to enable us to work as teacher educators in universities. Paul's career continued at Drake University and mine at Stanford, Governors State, and Michigan State Universities.

During much of my time as a secondary school teacher, I also was an active member of a multicounty organization in western New York State called the Central Schools Science Teachers Association, a group of about thirty teachers who met monthly at different schools to discuss assessment and science laboratory activities. The organization allowed us to share ideas about how to improve our teaching and students' achievement. We shared concerns and experiences. We even wrote a piece of legislation, which was passed and made into law by the New York State legislature. But the most important contributions of these sessions resulted from a continuing forum among a dedicated group of professionals about specific issues in teaching and learning science. I benefited greatly from the collective expertise of the group members.

In my many years as a university faculty member, the professional associations with colleagues and students at Michigan State University and other venues were essential elements of my continued growth and development. Among the most significant of these are the long-term interactions I have had with middle school science teachers in Toledo, Ohio, and Lansing, Michigan, which lasted for twelve years in two parallel projects. Both of these had a powerful impact on my thinking and understanding about teaching and learning. In turn, they also had a powerful impact on teachers in these two cities, because they fostered extended interaction about teaching and learning.

These examples of small-team efforts with close colleagues are included here because they demonstrate the importance of a team approach that provides personal motivation and shared professional expertise for continuing professional growth. One of the "lessons" we learned was that many of the problems we were encountering as teachers could be resolved. The collective groups, both on the small scale within a school building or department and in the multischool setting, enabled us to take actions that improved our work and our professional outlook. On the other hand, we had colleagues who were not willing to engage with us, and instead of taking positive action on their problems they tended to blame others—students, parents, administrators, and the school board—and continued to suffer in their inaction.

From these experiences, I learned that teachers can choose to take action to resolve the difficulties that they face in their work, or they can be victims of the circumstances in which they work and live. Being a victim is neither productive nor enjoyable. It leads to frustration and unhappiness. Therefore, the proactive approach appears to me to be the only viable choice.

Reflection & Discussion Questions

1. What examples can you give of teachers collaborating for professional growth? What were the salient factors that made these successful?

2. Were there also factors that inhibited them from being as successful as they might have been? What were these?

3. How can you deal with colleagues who are not willing to engage in improvement and choose to blame others for difficulties we encounter as teachers?

One of the places where I have seen teachers fall into the "victim trap" relates to school-based professional development. Many school districts set aside a few days each year for professional development activities. Often, these involve a speaker or other large-group activity that carries little meaning for the audience. Although the speaker or activity may have something important to offer, the teachers often have not been prepared to be active learners. As a result, they often take a passive, and sometimes resistant, stance toward the professional development day. On the other hand, approaching the activity with a more positive attitude of "what can I learn from this" could make a difference. An even greater difference could arise from taking an active stance with the district in planning the nature and organization of these professional development days. As teachers, we need to take charge of all aspects of our professional development, including our personal, daily reflection on our own teaching, the professional organizations we join and become active in, the journals and books we read, and how we interact in with our peers and administrators.

Reflection & Discussion Questions

1. In what ways have you taken charge of your professional development?

2. Does reflection on your own work and your students' achievement hold a place in your daily routine?

3. Is interaction with peers and administrators about teaching and learning an important part of your activity?

4. Are professional organizations and reading professional literature part of your routine?

Initiating Work with Colleagues

I often hear from new teachers and energetic experienced ones that their colleagues are "set in their ways" and unwilling to try new approaches. Moreover energetic teachers feel that some of their peers belittle their efforts to improve. As a result, they feel both frustrated and isolated, which can have the effect of diminishing the intensity of their efforts.

One solution is to engage one or two of your colleagues in working with you on teaching science for understanding. But the question is, "How can you begin to work with your peers?" On this I have three levels of advice:

1. Begin by asking your colleagues for guidance or help with a particular difficulty you are facing in your teaching. Be quite specific. For example, you could begin a conversation about a difficulty that you encountered in teaching a particular lesson about change of state, for example. As the conversation progresses you could ask, "How do you help students understand that when evaporation occurs, matter is not lost? Some of my students use the term *evaporate* in the commonplace sense that it disappears—it is gone!"

    Asking for advice is a form of compliment, which can be irresistible to even the most hardened colleague. Once you have engaged colleagues in thinking about the problem you can carefully shift the conversation to related issues that are at a higher level, such as "How can you tell if the students really understand evaporation, and are not just repeating phrases that they have read or heard?" or "How do you get students to approach lab work more holistically, or in a more engaged manner instead of just following steps in a 'cookbook' approach?"

2. As you work with colleagues on this first level, you probably find differences in the engagement that such conversations engender. Some colleagues will give only superficial responses, but others will engage in ways that seem more interested and be more reflective. The latter group of colleagues probably offer more promise for longer-term work, and it only takes one or two peers to provide you with an effective group for continuing your professional development. The next step is to continue to talk on a regular basis, at lunch, during planning periods, or before or after school. The essential element is that you take some time to do this, and that the conversations stick to issues related to teaching,

learning, assessment, and curriculum. Moreover, be specific so that conversations are productive in resolving particular difficulties that you are encountering with students' developing understanding of the content of science. Having an agenda is essential.

On the other hand, don't be too single-minded. It is important to recognize that you need to keep the attention on understanding and assessing students' learning, and that the topic of lessons will change frequently as you progress through each week and month. Therefore, you and your colleagues will have an unending array of new instructional topics to deal with, and each presents new challenges in clarifying appropriate objectives, identifying misconceptions that students bring with them or develop from your teaching, and structuring engaging, meaningful, high-quality activities and assessments. Such an approach to teaching and learning can be energizing for you and for your colleagues, as new horizons are continually encountered.

Work on this level can continue for a long time, as new challenges will arise that will engage you and your co-workers for months and years. You will continue to learn and grow professionally from interacting about teaching and learning with one or more co-workers. Also, your circle of colleagues may grow as you talk about the work you are doing at lunchtime or other occasions.

An additional consideration: Just as you should keep a journal about your interactions with students in your classes, and reflections about this work, you also should keep a journal on your interactions with peers and their impact on your teaching. It should include the questions you ask of your colleagues, their responses, and how these influenced your teaching. This information can be important for your reflection about how to engage your colleagues in discourse about teaching and learning science for understanding, and the ways you are capitalizing on interactions with them. It may be that their direct input on your teaching is not great, but the thought you put into interactions with them results in deeper insights about what you are intending to teach and how to teach and assess it.

Your journal should contain a report of interactions and your reflections about them that you write at least once each week. I recommend a daily journal, so that you don't forget important events and interactions. It also should contain information on ideas you tried in your classes as well as questions that you used to generate interactions with peers. You can keep your journal on your laptop or it can be handwritten in a notebook. The important matter is to keep a cumulative record of your interactions and how they have affected your thinking and teaching.

Reflection & Discussion Questions

1. How can you engender the kind of environment implied in levels 1 and 2 in your school or department?

2. How can you engage one or two of your colleagues to talk about, and think with you about, teaching and learning science for understanding?

3. How long do you think you would need to spend at the first level before you can engage with one or two colleagues at level 2? Will it be weeks or months?

4. If your peers are unresponsive or negative about such interactions, how will you avoid becoming discouraged and isolated or simply giving up on them?

5. How could the journal recommended in the previous paragraph be of help to you?

3. Success at the second level leads directly into the third—planning action research. However, this may not be an immediate outcome. On the other hand, it can add a deeper focus to your work. In addition, it provides a vehicle for you to share your work with others both within and beyond your school.

What is action research? Much has been written about action research during the last quarter century (Mills, 2000; Hubbard and Power, 1999). In a nutshell, action research is an important tool that teachers can use to continue their professional growth by studying their own teaching and students' learning in a systematic way. Action research, like most scientific research, is question-driven and involves thoughtful planning about how to collect and interpret data to answer the question.

Questions for action research can be either of a scientific nature, to gain new knowledge about teaching and learning, or more like those used by engineers, to improve effectiveness and efficiency of teaching practice and student learning. Scientific questions can address students' thinking and how it changes as a result of specific learning activities and contexts. Engineering questions can address how to design lessons that increase the number of students who attain a desired level of performance or decrease the time needed to attain a particular objective.

To carry out an action research project, you first must think about the research question that will guide it. Choosing the appropriate question often is a long process as we often ask questions that are difficult to answer systematically. Therefore, questions often undergo revision and narrowing to make them manageable. Broad questions that deal with motivating students are quite common as beginning points when teachers think about action research, and these must be narrowed to questions that deal with engaging students with specific instructional topics or activities. On the other hand, these narrower questions can be reset in a broader context as you generalize from specific investigations to a larger set of concerns.

As you work to frame the question for an action research project, you also need to think about the methods you will use to carry out the research. Often this takes on the character of a set of lesson plans with activities that form a "treatment" and assessments that form the "criterion measure" for your research. And as you formulate each of these components, you will find that the process is iterative with the question, treatment, and criterion measure each being modified as you work through the process.

To conclude this brief discussion of action research, I offer the following recommendations that are aimed at guiding your work in this promising area:

- *Don't be overly ambitious with your first action research project.* Identify a question about students' learning on a topic you teach that you can answer in a project of short duration with a clear criterion measure. For example, a biology teacher teaching a lesson sequence on cells could explore the ideas that students hold at the beginning and at the end of the lesson sequence about the levels of organization and sizes of molecules, macromolecules such as proteins, cell organelles, and whole cells. This could test the effectiveness of the lessons in helping students with an important biological understanding. The criterion measure could be a question such as the following:

   List the following items in order of increasing size: a cell, an oxygen molecule, a carbon dioxide molecule, a protein molecule, a glucose molecule, a cell nucleus, a mitochondrion. Then write a few sentences to explain why you placed these items in the order you did, including any uncertainties you had in doing so.

   This criterion measure can be administered at the beginning and the end of the lesson sequence. It also could be administered a third time, a few weeks after the end of the unit to test for retention.

Analysis of the pretest data would be useful in helping you determine where students need help in their understanding of levels of organization. Analysis of posttest and delayed posttest results will give you useful information on the effects and effectiveness of your instruction. It would also help you in thinking about any difficulties that students have in constructing scientifically sound reasoning about levels of organization in biology. Although this is just one objective of a biology course, it is an important one, and similar themes for research can be found in every science subject and instructional unit.

- *Work with a colleague who can offer constructive criticism.* As you plan this action research project, talk with a colleague about it and have him/her review your plans and the criterion measures you will use. Wording and the approach to presenting pretests and posttests to students can have a big impact on how seriously students engage in them, which will affect the results of your study. Discuss these matters with your colleague so that you make the process engaging and nonthreatening to your students. Also discuss the lessons you plan on this topic that will be part of your instructional approach, to ensure that it will have a positive effect beyond simply memorizing an ordered list. Early in the study, you also should discuss pretest results with your colleague, so that you can benefit from "another set of eyes" on your initial data and its relationship to your plans.

  Your rapport with your students also is an important factor. Letting your students know that you are working to improve your teaching and their learning can have a big impact on your work.

- *Find out what others have done on this topic.* You probably are not the first person to think about your research question. Therefore, a search for prior work on the topic using libraries, *http://scholar.google. com*, and other Web-based sources can lead you to valuable information about prior research on the topic.

- *Set time limits for planning, preparing, and conducting the research, and for analyzing data and writing a report.* Given the demanding schedules that teachers live with daily,

you will need to be efficient in preparing for, doing, and following up on your action research project. Also, since the pretest data should have an important influence on your teaching plans, timely analysis of these data and reviewing them with your colleague will be essential.

Most important, you should write a report of your findings and interpretations of them. This can be done in stages, beginning with writing up your plans for the study, which will help you in reviewing the study design and criterion measures with your colleague. Writing the plans will help you think about details you might miss if you only planned in your mind. Further, you can write a report of the pretest data as soon as that is available. You can also report the posttest data as soon as they are collected. Last, you can write about your interpretations and conclusions from the study.

One of the biggest difficulties facing anyone who does research is *not writing* component reports at each stage in the work. Then the task of writing becomes monumental. Alternatively, writing at each stage makes the task manageable, and you are able to use the results of your writing to guide you at the next step. Each step may only entail a few pages, which is an easy writing task, especially since the work is fresh in your mind. Conversely, by delaying writing, the task multiplies in extent and becomes more remote due to time and intervening elements in your life. Too often the result is that the written report is not completed. Thus the study fails to achieve its potential value.

- *Present the results of your research to your peers.* This would include your colleagues at school at a faculty meeting and at a meeting of a professional organization such as your state science teachers association or a regional or national meeting. For some situations, a poster describing the study, your findings, and your interpretations will be adequate. For most situations, an oral presentation augmented by PowerPoint slides or hard-copy handouts will be required. Typically, presentations at professional meetings are limited in duration to ten or fifteen minutes. Therefore, concise presentation of highlights is essential.

  Presentation at meetings of professional organizations has multiple benefits.

First, you will receive feedback on your own research that will help you refine your work. Second, you will learn about research and development activities that will keep you up to date with new ideas and products. Third, you will find "kindred souls" who are interested in improving teaching and learning. With electronic communication, you can broaden your professional contacts and associations on a continuing basis as a result of meeting colleagues from other locations. Fourth, you will be energized by the opportunity to talk about your work and other developments with a broader spectrum of colleagues.

Reflection & Discussion Questions

1. Is action research for you? It may seem daunting, but it is a valuable tool for continuing professional growth. Several of our beginning teachers developed action research projects based in their work, and they have made presentations at Michigan Science Teachers Association annual meetings. This put them on a sound professional pathway with many long-term benefits.

2. What actions will you take in the next few weeks and months to proceed along this pathway?

Impediments to Teaching and Learning Science for Understanding

Awareness of the factors that impede teaching science for understanding can be of help as you work to improve your teaching and your students' learning. Tobin, Rennie, and Fraser (1990) prepared a report on this topic that outlines several key factors that make it difficult for teachers to teach for understanding. In the introduction to this monograph, they state that

> Despite bold rhetoric in school brochures and textbook forwards, science programs typically are not inquiry oriented, do not have laboratory emphasis and do not excite the majority of students. Students learn from textbooks and lectures and the curriculum is focused by tests which emphasize rote learning of facts and procedures. (Tobin, Rennie, and Fraser, 1990, p. 1)

Further, these authors state that the cognitive demand of many classroom and homework activities is at a low level, involving search of textbooks to answer end-of-chapter questions and write brief summaries of complex information. Much of this work involves little more than transcription of information from the source to their notes, worksheets, or homework. They add,

> There is little evidence that the majority of science teachers are concerned with the extent to which students understand what they are to learn or with implementing the curriculum to emphasize student understanding or science. Rather, findings of research suggest that most teachers feel constrained to prepare students for tests and examinations and to cover science content from textbooks. This practice deprives many students of opportunities to learn with understanding. (Tobin, Rennie, and Fraser, 1990, p. 1)

This is a strong indictment of both teachers and the system in which they work. Although they qualify this statement subsequently, it does highlight major impediments to learning and teaching science for understanding. Teachers need to change their approach to teaching, which is what the previous chapters have been about. In addition, teachers, parents, students, and school administrators need to think differently about what teaching should involve. For more than a quarter century, since the publication of *A Nation at Risk*, we have been aware that old models of teaching are inadequate. But many teachers—and most parents, school administrators, and political leaders—have not taken the messages of that report seriously. National, state, and local district policies have wavered on this point. School administrators have placed more emphasis on memorization of facts as a way of improving students' scores on external examinations, and they have not fostered emphasis on longer-term goals that are in the national interest of producing a new generation of school graduates that can meet the challenges of the twenty-first century. There is more concern about immediate test results than on students' long-range needs to understand and be able to use science.

Teachers have been given mixed signals about how they should approach the curriculum and assessments. These "old-school messages," which include much of their experience as learners in universities, their interactions with colleagues, and directives from school leaders, reinforce emphasis on content coverage, memorization, and test scores over understanding. These messages also reinforce conformity over critical thinking. The reform messages about understanding and application of science knowledge as preparation for participation in the twenty-first century are overshadowed as teachers are called to work on the immediate, short-term goal to improve scores on tests that have little to do with long-range societal and personal needs.

Reflection & Discussion Questions

Serendipitously, during the week that I was drafting this chapter, one of my students wrote the following comment about an essay prepared by a group of her peers in my class: "Your conclusion really says it all: teachers need to revolutionize the way they teach. I think the profession has been a one-way street for too long, where the teacher delivers knowledge and the students 'receive' it. What happens to knowledge inside a child's mind is often a mystery. . . . I often wonder to myself how kids devise the understandings or misunderstandings they demonstrate" (Thompson, 2005). How does this statement capture the essence of the foregoing section of this chapter? How would you state your reactions to this section to your colleagues?

How Exemplary Teachers Overcome Impediments

Not all teachers have acquiesced to the demands of the "old school" or its recent rejuvenation in national, state, and local policies. A strong core of concerned teachers recognizes the longer-term needs of students to understand science. They also are clear that their students will score well on external examinations *precisely because they understand and can apply their science knowledge.* A group of these teachers were studied by Fraser and Tobin (1990). They worked with educational leaders to identify a group of science and mathematics teachers that were deemed to be exemplary. Their research then involved comparative study of twenty-two exemplary teachers and a parallel sample of nonexemplary teachers. Classrooms of teachers from both groups were observed over several days to learn about their practices and the learning environment in their classrooms. Classroom environment questionnaires were also used to obtain a quantified picture of life in these classrooms from the students who resided in them daily (Tobin and Fraser, 1987).

As a result of this study, Fraser and Tobin made the following assertions:

1. *Exemplary teachers used management strategies that facilitated sustained student engagement.* Studies showed substantial differences in management styles of exemplary teachers when compared with others in the study. "The exemplary teachers had well ordered classes with a relaxed atmosphere characterized by pleasant interactions with students and subtle use of humor" (Fraser and Tobin, 1990, p. 5), which allowed exemplary teachers to concentrate on teaching and learning rather than on keeping control of student behavior. Although the interactive styles of exemplary teachers varied, it appeared that they were able to establish a productive working relationship with students that less able teachers could not form.

Based on my experiences in observing a wide range of teachers over long durations, I strongly believe that much of the difference in teachers' success or frustration with management results from actions taken by teachers in the first month of

each school year or semester. In that period, new relationships are created among students and between the students and the teacher. These relationships must be guided toward formation of a productive learning environment, where serious, yet enjoyable, work patterns are developed, distractions are kept to a minimum, and appropriate behaviors are subtly rewarded. This is a tall order! However, the consequences make it important to give considerable attention to the establishment of a productive work environment during the first month of school and to its maintenance throughout the year.

Reflection & Discussion Questions

1. How do/will you treat the first month of your work with students?

2. How do/will you use that time to nurture an engaging learning environment where students and you can work cooperatively on learning with understanding?

3. Do you feel that this needs greater attention?

4. Also how do/will you work through the remainder of the year or semester to maintain that high-quality learning environment?

2. *Exemplary teachers used strategies designed to increase student understanding of science.* Among the essential strategies identified in this comparative study of exemplary teachers and those who were not considered as such, a focus on making abstract science concepts more meaningful through concrete examples was high on the list. "However, the key to teaching with understanding was the verbal interaction which enabled teachers to monitor student understanding of science and mathematics concepts. Exemplary teachers were effective in a range of verbal strategies which included asking questions to stimulate thinking, probing student responses for clarification and elaboration, and providing . . . students with additional information" (Fraser and Tobin, 1990, p. 6).

Reflection & Discussion Questions

What strategies are part of your work with students to ensure development of understanding? After working through the preceding chapters of this book, you probably have a list longer than that reported above by Fraser and Tobin. Now would be a good time to make a list of the essential strategies that you use in teaching for understanding. The modified list of Categories and Criteria in Chapters 8 can serve as a framework for thinking about these strategies from clarifying goals and objectives to identifying students' ideas and reasoning.

In using the Categories and Criteria, you will make visible the planning and thought that lies behind classroom performance, as well as the techniques and approaches that are part of classroom work with students. As you prepare this list, share it with others. The discussion that results should be of value!

3. *Exemplary teachers used strategies that encouraged students to participate in learning activities.* An important difference between the classrooms of the two groups of teachers in this study was how exemplary teachers made the classroom a supportive environment for students to express ideas and raise questions about the subject matter. Exemplary teachers "appeared to be able to maintain focus on meaningful learning and make it safe, in an emotional sense, for students to engage in whole-class, small-group, and individualized activities. For example, one exemplary teacher always treated students and their contributions with the utmost respect and endeavored to work from a given answer to the understanding he wanted a student to have" (Fraser and Tobin, 1990, p. 6). Exemplary teachers avoided embarrassing students if they erred, and when a student was unable to answer a question, they tended to persist by rephrasing it or asked supplementary questions until the student could contribute. In addition they showed interest in students' ideas by engaging them with probing questions to help them clarify their ideas. Therefore, formative assessment was an integral part of the exemplary teachers' classrooms.

4. *Throughout all of this, respect for each student's ideas was paramount to maintain a supportive atmosphere.*

Reflection & Discussion Questions

1. In what ways do/will you make your classroom a place that encourages and supports students to be active learners?

2. How do/will you make it "safe" for students to be open about their ideas and reasoning, without fear of, embarrassment in, exposing their thoughts and learning difficulties?

5. *Exemplary teachers maintained favorable classroom learning environments as perceived by their students.* This aspect of the comparative study was assessed by having students complete a Classroom Environment Scale (Tobin and Fraser, 1987; Tobin, Treagust, and Fraser, 1988), which appraised stu-

dents' perceptions of six dimensions of classroom environments (Involvement, Affiliation, Teacher Support, Task Orientation, Order and Organization, and Rule Clarity). The results from students in exemplary teachers' classrooms were more positive than those in other classes on all six scales with the greatest differences in Involvement, Teacher Support, and Order and Organization. That is, students in these classes, compared with students in nonexemplary teachers' classes, felt much more involved in learning, perceived greater support from their teacher, and saw the classroom as more organized and psychologically secure. Further, these ratings also included scales on the "desired" and the "actual" classroom environments. Students in exemplary teachers' classrooms scored these two dimensions with little difference, indicating satisfaction with the learning environment in their classrooms. On the other hand, students in the comparison group showed greater differences between the actual and desired environments, which suggest less satisfaction with the learning environment.

Reflection & Discussion Questions

1. The connection between greater student involvement, more teacher support, and more organized classrooms as central elements of effective teaching and increased learning emerges in this study. It also appears that many problems that teachers face in their interactions with students are diminished when students are more satisfied with the classroom environment. Are these connections evident to you?

2. What can you do to enhance these dimensions in your classroom?

6. *Teachers' beliefs about teaching, learning, students, and science itself had a major impact on their enactment of the curriculum and their interactions with students.* I will address these four elements in reverse order. Exemplary teachers tend to hold the view that science is more than just a body of facts to be mastered. They appear to see science as multidimensional, in line with the content standards of *National Science Education Standards.* They also view science as comprehensible and connected with the real world of students. As a result, exemplary teachers work to make science comprehensible and connected.

Exemplary teachers also view their students in a positive light, while recognizing that they have limited experience and need support in learning. They rarely focus on the negative characteristics of students. Teachers' expectations of the students are high, and they endeavor to engage all of their students in learning.

Learning is viewed as a continuous enterprise, and exemplary teachers recognize that there are many levels of understanding. They grasp the meaning of Wiggins and McTighe's facets of understanding (described in Chapters 2), in an operational sense, even though they may not articulate them spontaneously.

Exemplary teachers also recognize that they can make a difference in students' lives by providing an organized, psychologically safe learning environment, by providing meaningful learning experiences and scaffolding their learning in a variety of ways, by continually assessing students and providing supportive feedback to them, and by listening to their ideas and reasoning, and responding to them in ways that are supportive.

Reflection & Discussion Questions

1. How do your beliefs about teaching, learning, students, and science coincide with those of exemplary teachers?

2. Are you as positive and confident, yet realistic, as they are?

3. How can you develop and maintain the beliefs and attitudes that contribute to exemplary teaching and effective learning for all students?

7. *Knowledge limitations of teachers increased focus on memorization of facts and decreased emphasis on teaching for understanding.* Observations of teachers teaching within and outside of their field of expertise showed substantial differences in the approaches used. For example, it was found that teachers with a biology major teaching both biology and chemistry, taught very differently in the two courses. In chemistry class, teaching was "from the book" and lacked the richness and support of understanding that occurred in biology class. The same features were noted among general science teachers who taught topics closely related to their field of expertise with much more emphasis on understanding than in topics where their knowledge of the subject was more limited. An important difference for teachers teaching in and out of their field relates to the connections—grasping relationships among ideas. When teaching topics that are not part teachers' subject matter strength, connections and relationships often are not clearly developed in lessons, frequently resulting in both teachers and the students missing the essential understandings of the lesson or topic. Therefore, teacher knowledge of the subject matter taught was found to be an essential element in teaching for understanding. However, as we all know, it is not the only ingredient needed as witnessed from some college courses where a particular professor had a high level of knowledge of subject matter, yet was ineffective as a teacher.

Reflection & Discussion Questions

1. Teachers often are required to teach topics or subjects for which they are not fully qualified. If you are faced with this situation, what can you do to minimize the negative effects of your limited knowledge of the content?

2. How can you do more than simply keep a few pages ahead of the students?

3. How will careful planning of lesson clusters and units of instruction help you in this circumstance?

Becoming a Leader in Your Field

As you work with your colleagues to continue your professional growth, you will advance toward a position of leadership as a science teacher. You may not have a title to go along with this position, but your efforts will not go unnoticed. You will be able to help yourself and your colleagues improve as teachers. The students in the school will learn more science and enjoy the process more. By participating in professional associations, you will continue to learn from others outside your school. By reading professional journals and participating in workshops and related programs, you will continue on a pathway toward excellence in your profession. The lessons from studies of excellence also provide you with new tools to aid your development as an expert teacher.

Your continuing professional growth will be enhanced if you set goals for your own interactions with your students and with your colleagues. Instead of "just letting it happen," be proactive about your professional growth. Make a plan and seek out opportunities to learn more about this exciting field. Set goals for each week or month. Goals should be consistent with the natural flow of the school year. The first month provides opportunities to work in establishing an effective learning environment with each of your classes. Learning about how to work effectively with the students in each class at the different times of day that you meet them can be an important initial goal. In addition, learning the skills about how to sustain the learning community that you establish early in the year also is an important, persistent goal. Subsequent goals can be more focused on specific elements of content learning and on varied teaching approaches. Action research plans can be an important element in this work.

As you continue on your professional journey toward becoming an exemplary science teacher, keep in mind that it is an exciting, life-long venture. There always are new skills and techniques to be refined. There is new subject matter to be understood more richly and deeply. There are new students, with different backgrounds and resources, to engage, and new colleagues to interact with. The excitement, opportunities, challenges, and rewards are endless if you seek them.

Journal Questions

Add to your journal by revisiting the following questions that will help you monitor your progress as you make a paradigm shift in your teaching and your understanding of your students' learning for understanding and application in science.

1. What were the purposes or objectives of this chapter?
2. What were the key ideas presented in this chapter? (Note: These two could be combined as a two-column table to show the parallel between the purposes of each chapter and the big ideas presented.)

3. What important additions have you made to your vision of teaching science for understanding and application by studying this chapter and discussing with others? This should be an ongoing narrative that highlights development of your personal paradigm for teaching and learning science.
4. I also recommend that you create a concept map that portrays your understanding about teaching and learning science for understanding and application and add new concepts and connections as you study each chapter of this book. This concept map can provide a visual representation of your developing new vision or paradigm of science teaching and learning that you developed in the previous item.
5. What new skills and techniques do you find you need to develop in order to enact your vision of science teaching? What progress are you making in developing those skills and techniques?
6. Finally, what concerns do you have about being able to implement your new vision, your new paradigm of science teaching with your students, in your classroom, laboratory, and fieldwork? How will you respond to these concerns?

References

Chapter 1

Bracey, G. (2003). April Foolishness: The 20th Anniversary of *A Nation at Risk*. *Phi Delta Kappan* 84(8): 616–621.

Bransford, J., A. Brown, and R. Cocking. (2000). *How People Learn: Brain, Mind, Experience, and School*. Washington, DC: National Academies Press.

Forgione, P. D. Jr. (1998). *Achievement in the United States: Progress Since* A Nation At Risk? Washington, DC: National Center for Education Statistics.

Gallagher, J. (2000). Teaching for Understanding and Application of Science Knowledge. *School Science and Mathematics* 100(6): 310–318.

Mintzes, J., J Wandersee, and J. Novak. (1997). *Teaching Science for Understanding: A Human Constructivist View*. San Diego: Academic Press.

Morris, W. (1980). *The American Heritage Dictionary of the English Language*. Boston: Houghton Mifflin.

National Association of State Telecommunications Directors. (1998). Finding and Keeping Skilled IT Personnel: The Problem Is Real, States Fight Back. *NAST Backgrounder* 2(4): 1–7.

National Commission on Excellence in Education. (1983). *A Nation at Risk: The Imperative for Educational Reform*. Washington, DC: U.S. Department of Education.

National Research Council. (1996). *National Science Education Standards*. Washington, DC: National Academies Press.

Project 2061. (1993). *Benchmarks for Science Literacy*. New York: Oxford University Press.

Project 2061. (2001). *Atlas of Science Literacy*. Washington, DC: National Science Teachers Association.

Roth, K. J., S. L. Druker, H. Garnier, M. Lemmens, C. Chen, T. Kawanaka, Y. Okamoto, D. Rasmussen, S. Trubacova, D. Warvi, P. Gonzales, J. Stigler and R. Gallimore. (in press). *Teaching Science in Five Countries: Results from the TIMSS 1999 Video Study*. Washington, DC: U.S. Department of Education, National Center for Education Statistics, NCES 2005-020.

Rothkopf, E. (1970). The Concept of Mathemagenic Activities. *Review of Educational Research* 40(3): 325–336.

Rutherford, J., and A. Ahlgren. (1989). *Science for All Americans*. New York: Oxford University Press.

Shulman, L. S. (1986). Those Who Understand: Knowledge Growth in Teaching. *Educational Researcher* 15(2): 4–14.

Washington Post. (2004). December 7, 2004.

Wiggins, G. and J. McTighe. (1998). *Understanding by Design*. Alexandria, VA: Association for Supervision and Curriculum Development.

William, D. and P. Black. (1996). Meanings and Consequences: A basis for distinguishing the formative and summative functions of assessment. *British Educational Research Journal*, 22(5): 537–548.

William, D., C. Lee, C. Harrison, P. Black. (2004). Teachers developing assessment for learning: impact on student achievement. *Assessment in Education: Principles, Policy & Practive*, Volume 11, Number 1. London: Routledge.

Wiske, M. (1998). *Teaching for Understanding: Linking Practice with Research*. San Francisco: Jossey-Bass.

Yang, J. R. (October 2003). Personal communication.

Chapter 2

Anderson, C. W. (2003). Teaching science for motivation and understanding. Unpublished manuscript, East Lansing, MI: Michigan State University.

Tobin, K. (1993). *The Practice of Constructivism in Science Education*. Kenneth Tobin (Ed.). Hinsdale, NJ: Erlbaum.

White, R., and R. Gunstone. (1992). *Probing Understanding*. London: Falmer.

Wiggins, G., and J. McTighe. (1998). *Understanding by Design*. Alexandria, VA: Association for Supervision and Curriculum Development.

Wiske, M. (1998). *Teaching for Understanding: Linking Research with Practice*. San Francisco: Jossey-Bass.

Chapter 3

Appleton, K. J. (1997). *Teaching Science: Exploring the Issues*. Rockhampton, Qld.: Central Queensland University Press.

Bransford, J., A. Brown, and R. Cocking. (2000). *How People Learn: Brain, Mind, Experience, and School*. Washington, DC: National Academies Press.

Freyberg, P., and R. Osborne. (1985). *Learning in Science: The Implications of Children's Science*. Aukland: Heineman.

Brooks, J., and M. Brooks. (2001). *In Search of Understanding the Case for Constructivist Classrooms*. Upper Saddle River, NJ: Merrill/Prentice Hall.

Lave, J., and E. Wenger. (1991). *Situated Learning: Legitimate Peripheral Participation*. New York: Cambridge University Press.

National Research Council. (1996). *National Science Education Standards*. Washington, DC: National Academies Press.

Resnick, L. B. (1983). Mathematics and Science Learning: A New Conception. *Science* 220(4596): 477–478.

Ross, F., E. Enger, R. Otto, and R. Kormelink. (1996). *Diversity of Life*. Dubuque, IA: Wm. C. Brown.

Tobin, K. (1990). Social Constructivist Perspectives on the Reform of Science Education. *Australian Science Teachers Journal* 36(4): 29–35.

Von Glasersfeld, E. (1989). Cognition, Construction of Knowledge, and Teaching. *Synthese* 80(1): 121–140.

White, R., and R. Gunstone. (1992). *Probing Understanding*. London: Falmer.

Wiggins, G., and J. McTighe. (1998). *Understanding by Design*. Alexandria, VA: Association for Supervision and Curriculum Development.

Wiske, M. (1998). *Teaching for Understanding: Linking Research with Practice*. San Francisco: Jossey-Bass.

Yager, R. E. (1991). The Constructivist Learning Model. *The Science Teacher* 58, 52–57.

Chapter 4

Anderson, C. W. (2003). Teaching Science for Motivation and Understanding. Unpublished manuscript, East Lansing, MI: Michigan State University.

Anderson, C. W., and E. L. Smith. (1986). Children's Conceptions of Light and Color: Understanding the Role of Unseen Rays (Research Series No. 166). East Lansing, MI: Michigan State University, Institute for Research on Teaching.

Anderson, C. W., A. Sharma, J. Lockhart, A. Carolan, F. Moore, T. Parshall, and J. Gallagher. (2004). Environmental Literacy Blueprint Draft. Unpublished paper, Michigan State University.

Atkin, M., and R. Karplus. (1962). Discovery or Invention? *The Science Teacher* 29: 45–61.

Bransford, J., A. Brown, and R. Cocking. (2000). *How People Learn: Brain, Mind, Experience, and School*. Washington, DC: National Academies Press.

Bybee, R. W. (1997). *Achieving Scientific Literacy*. Portsmouth, NH: Heinemann.

Cajas, M. F. (1998). *Teaching Science for Understanding and Applications: The Role of Technology*. Unpublished doctoral dissertation, Michigan State University.

Collins, A., J. S. Brown, and S. E. Newman. (1989). Cognitive Apprenticeship: Teaching the Craft of Reading, Writing, and Mathematics. In L. B. Resnick (Ed.), *Knowing, Learning, and Instruction: Essays in Honor of Robert Glaser*. Hillsdale, NJ: Lawrence Erlbaum Associates, pp. 453–494.

Donovan, S., J. Brandsford, and J. W. Pellegrino. (1999). *How People Learn: Bridging Research and Practice*. Washington DC: National Academies Press.

Driver, R., E. Guesne, and A. Tiberghien. (1985). *Children's Ideas in Science*. Philadelphia: Open University Press.

Driver, R., A. Squires, P. Rushworth, and V. Wood-Robinson. (1994). *Making Sense of Secondary Science: Research into Children's Ideas*. London: Routledge.

Eisenkraft, A. (2003). Expanding the 5E Model. *The Science Teacher* 70(6): 56–59.

National Research Council. (2000). *Inquiry and the National Science Education Standards: A Guide for Teaching and Learning*. Washington, DC: Author.

Osborne, R., and P. Freyberg. (1985). *Learning in Science: The Implications of Children's Science*. Aukland: Heineman.

Piaget, J. (1950). *The Psychology of Intelligence*. (M. Piercy and D. Berlyne, Trans.). London: Routledge & Kegan Paul.

Strike, K., and G. Posner. (1992). A Revisionist Theory of Conceptual Change. In R. Duschl and R. Hamilton (Eds.), *Philosophy of Science, Cognitive Psychology, and Educational Theory and Practice*. Albany: State University of New York Press, pp. 147–176.

Strike, K., and G. Posner. (1982). Conceptual Change and Science Teaching. *European Journal of Science Education* 4(3):231–240.

Weiss, I. (1979). *Report of the 1977 National Survey of Science, Mathematics, and Social Studies Education*. Research Triangle Park, NC: Center for Educational Research and Evaluation.

Chapter 5

Anderson, C. W. (1999). Inscriptions and Science Learning. *Journal of Research in Science Teaching* 36: 973–974.

Baumeister, M. (1992). *Think-Pair-Share: The Effects on Oral Language, Reading Comprehension, and Attitudes*. Unpublished doctoral dissertation. University of Maryland.

Cohen, E. G. (1994). *Designing Groupwork: Strategies for the Heterogeneous Classroom*. New York: Teachers College Press.

Gabelnick, F., J. MacGregor, R. S. Matthews, and B. L. Smith. (Eds.). (1990). *Learning Communities: Creating Connections Among Students, Faculty, and Disciplines*. New Directions for Teaching and Learning, no. 41. San Francisco: Jossey-Bass.

Gallagher, J. J. (2000). Teaching for Understanding and Application of Science Knowledge. *School Science and Mathematics* 100: 310–318.

Gonzales-Lantz, D. (1998). Personal communication.

Hand, B., C. W. Wallace, and E. Yang. (2004). Using a Science Writing Heuristic to Enhance Learning Outcomes from Laboratory Activities in Seventh-Grade Science: Quantitative and Qualitative Aspects. *International Journal of Science Education* 26: 131–149.

Heath, S. B. (1983). *Ways with Words: Language, Life and Work in Communities and Classrooms*. Cambridge: Cambridge University Press.

Hogan, K., and M. Maglienti. (2001). Comparing the Epistemological Underpinnings of Students' and Scientists' Reasoning about Conclusions. *Journal of Research in Science Teaching*, 38(6): 663–687.

Keys, C., B. Hand, V. Prain, and S. Collins. (1999). Using the Science Writing Heuristic as a Tool for Learning from a Laboratory Investigations in Secondary Science. *Journal of Research in Science Teaching* 36(10): 1065–1084.

Koslowski, B. (1996). *Theory and Evidence: The Development of Scientific Reasoning*. Cambridge, MA: MIT Press.

Kuhn, D. (1991). *The Skills of Argument*. Cambridge: Cambridge University Press.

Lazarowitcz, R. (1994). Learning Science in a Cooperative Setting: Academic Achievement and Affective Outcomes. *Journal of Research in Science Teaching* 31: 1121–1131.

Lonning, R. A. (1993). Effect of Cooperative Learning Strategies on Student Verbal Interactions and Achievement during Conceptual Change Instruction in 10th Grade General Science. *Journal of Research in Science Teaching* 30: 1087–1101.

McManus, S. M., and M. Gettinger. (1996). Teacher and Student Evaluations of Collaborative Learning and Observed Interactive Behaviors. *Journal of Educational Research* 90: 13–22.

Mitchell, S., R. Reilly, and G. Bramwell. (2004). Friendship and Choosing Group Mates: Preferences for Teacher-Selected vs. Student-Selected Grouping in High School Science Classes. *Journal of Instructional Psychology* 31 (1): 20–32.

National Research Council. (1996). *National Science Education Standards*. Washington: National Academy Press.

Osborne, J.F., S. Erduran, and S. Simon. (2004) Enhancing the Quality of Argument in School Science. *Journal of Research in Science Teaching* 41(10): 994–1020.

Ochsner, R., and J. Fowler. (2004). Playing Devil's Advocate: Evaluating the Literature of the WAC/WID Movement. *Review of Educational Research* 74: 117–140.

Rivard, L. P., and S. B. Straw. (2000). The Effect of Talk and Writing on Learning Science: An Exploratory Study. *Science Education* 84: 566–593.

Roth, K. J. (1997). Food for Plants. Unpublished document. East Lansing MI: Michigan State University

Rowell, P. M. (1997). Learning in School Science: The Promises and Practices of Writing. *Studies in Science Education* 30: 19–56.

Shapiro, N. S. and J. H. Levine. (1999). *Creating Learning Communities*. San Francisco: Jossey-Bass.

Sharan, Y., and S. Sharan. (1992). *Expanding Cooperative Learning through Group Investigation*. New York: Teacher's College Press.

Stoddart, T., A. Pinal, M. Latzke, and D. Canaday. (2002). Integrating Inquiry Science and Language Development for English Language Learners. *Journal of Research in Science Teaching* 39: 665–687.

Treagust, D. F., R. Jacobowitz, J. J. Gallagher, and J. Parker. (2001). Using Assessment as a Guide in Teaching for Understanding: A Case Study of a Middle School Science Class Learning about Sound. *Science Education* 85: 137–157.

Wiggins, G., and J. McTighe. (1999). *Understanding by Design*. Alexandria, VA: Association for Supervision and Curriculum Development.

Webb, N., and A. S. Palincsar. (Eds.). (1996). *Group Processes in the Classroom*. New York: Prentice Hall.

Chapter 6

A Plant Exploration Unit: How Plants Really Get their Food Available http://ed-web3.educ.msu.edu/rothk/

National Research Council. (1996). *National Science Education Standards*. Washington: National Academies Press.

Project 2061. (1993). *Benchmarks for Science Literacy*. New York: Oxford University Press.

Chapter 7

Ames, C., and J. Archer. (1998). Achievement Goals in the Classroom: Students' Learning Strategies and Motivation Processes. *J. Education Psychology*. 80(3): 250–257.

Brophy, J. and T. Good (1986). Teacher Behavior and Student Achievement. In M. C. Whitrock (E.), *Handbook of Research on Teaching* (Third Edition). Chicago: Rand McNally.

Bybee, R. (1997). *Achieving Science Literacy: From Purposes to Practices*. Portsmouth, NH: Heinemann.

Driver, R., E. Guense, A. Tiberghien. (1985). *Children's Ideas in Science*. Philadelphia: Open University Press.

Driver, Rosalind, A. Squires, P. Rushworth, and V. Wood-Robinson (1994). *Making Sense of Secondary Science: Research into Children's Ideas*. London: Routledge.

Duggan-Haas, D. (2000). *Scientists Are from Mars, Educators Are from Venus: Relationships in the Ecosystem of Science Teacher Preparation*. Unpublished doctoral dissertation, Michigan State University.

Floden, R., and J. Gallagher. (1994). Blueprint for Teacher Education. In Project 2061. *Blueprint for Reform: Science, Mathematics and Technology Education*. New York: Oxford University Press.

Gallagher, J. J. (2000a). Teaching for understanding and application of science knowledge. *School Science and Mathematics* 100: 310–318.

Gallagher, J. (2000b). Unpublished study of the impact of professional development on student achievement. Michigan State University.

Gallagher, J., and J. Parker. (1996a). *Structure of Matter*. East Lansing, MI: Michigan State University.

Gallagher, J., and J. Parker. (1996b). *Improving Teaching & Learning Using Assessment in Middle School Science: A Resource for Teachers and Those Who Teach Them*. East Lansing, MI: Michigan State University.

Gallagher, J., and S. Wilcox. (1995). Report to National Science Foundation, Project Number MDR9252881. Michigan State University.

Jeranyama, L. (2001). Reshaping Teacher Thinking, Planning, and Practice Using Embedded Assessment: Case Studies of Three Middle School Science Teachers. Unpublished Doctoral Dissertation. Michigan State University.

Keys, C. (1999). Revitalizing instruction in scientific genres: Connecting knowledge production with writing to learn in science. *Sci Ed* 83: 115–130

Magnusson, S. J., M. Templin, and R. Boyle. (1997). Dynamic Science Assessment: A New Approach for Investigating Conceptual Change. *Journal of the Learning Sciences* 6(1): 91–142.

National Research Council. (1996). *National Science Education Standards*. Washington, DC: National Academies Press.

Project 2061. (1993). *Benchmarks for Science Literacy*. New York: Oxford University Press.

Salish I Research Project. (1997). *Secondary Science and Mathematics Teacher Preparation Programs: Influences on New Teachers and Their Students*. Iowa City: University of Iowa.

Schmidt. W., C. McKnight, L. Cogan, P. Jakwerth, and R. Houang.(1999). *Facing the Consequences: Using TIMSS for a Closer Look at U.S. Mathematics and Science Education*. New York: Springer.

Tyson, H. (1994). *Who Will Teach the Children: Progress & Resistance in Teacher Education*. San Francisco: Jossey-Bass.

Wiggins, G., and J. McTighe. (1998). *Understanding by Design*. Alexandria, VA: Association for Supervision and Curriculum Development.

William, D., and P. Black. (1996). Meanings and Consequences: A Basis for Distinguishing the Formative and Summative Functions of Assessment. *British Educational Research Journal* 22(5): 537–548.

William, D., C. Lee, C. Harrison, and P. Black. (2004). Teachers Developing Assessment for Learning: Impact on Student Achievement. *Assessment in Education: Principles, Policy & Practice* 11(1): 49–65.

Wiske, M. (1998). *Teaching for Understanding: Linking Practice with Research*. San Francisco: Jossey-Bass.

Chapter 8

Driver, R., E. Guesne, and A. Tiberghien. (1985). *Children's Ideas in Science*. Philadelphia: Open University Press.

Driver R., A. Squires, P. Rushworth, and V. Wood-Robinson. (1994). *Making Sense of Secondary Science: Research into Children's Ideas*. London: Routledge.

Gunckel, K. (2003). The Nature of Science in Curriculum Materials and Possible Implications for Achieving Scientific Literacy. Unpublished paper, Michigan State University.

National Research Council. (1996). *National Science Education Standards*. Washington, DC: National Academies Press.

Project 2061. (2000). *Mathematics and Science Instructional Categories and Criteria*. Available http://www.project2061.org/tools/textbook/mgsci/crit-used.htm

Chapter 9

Ausubel, D. P. (2000). *The Acquisition and Retention of Knowledge: A Cognitive View*. Kluwer.

Blumenfeld, P., E. Soloway, J. Marx, J. Krajcik, M. Guzdial, and A. Palincsar. (1991). Motivating Project-Based Learning: Sustaining the Doing, Supporting the Learning. *Educational Psychologist* 26: 369–398.

Boulanger, F. D. (1981). Instruction and Science Learning: A Quantitative Synthesis. *Journal of Research in Science Teaching* 18: 311–327.

Kesidou, S., and J. Roseman. (2002). How Well Do Middle School Science Programs Measure Up? Findings from Project 2061's Curriculum Review. *Journal of Research in Science Teaching* 39(6): 522–539.

Malone, T. W., and M. R. Lepper. (1987). Making Learning Fun: A Taxonomy of Intrinsic Motivations for Learning. In R. Snow and M. Farr (Eds.), *Aptitude, Learning, and Instruction: Cognitive and Affective Process Analyses*, Vol. 3. Hillsdale, NJ: Lawrence Erlbaum, pp. 223–253.

Project 2061. (1993). *Benchmarks for Science Literacy*. New York: Oxford University Press.

Project 2061. (2000). *Mathematics and Science Instructional Categories and Criteria*. Available: http://www.project2061.org/tools/textbook/mgsci/crit-used.htm

Tasker, R., and P. Freyberg. (1985). Facing the Mismatches in the Classroom. In R. Osborne, and P. Freyberg (Eds.), *Learning in Science: The Implications of Children's Science*. Auckland: Heinemann, pp. 66–80.

Wiggins, G., and J. McTighe. (1998). *Understanding by Design*. Alexandria, VA: Association for Supervision and Curriculum Development.

Wise, K. C., and J. R. Okey. (1983). A Meta-analysis of the Effects of Various Science Teaching Strategies on Achievement. *Journal of Research in Science Teaching* 20: 419–435.

Chapter 10

Driver, R., A. Squires, P. Rushworth, and V. Wood-Robinson. (1994). *Making Sense of Secondary School Science: Research into Children's Ideas*. London: Routledge.

Project 2061. (1993). *Benchmarks for Science Litreracy*. New York: Oxford University Press.

Prentice Hall Science Explorer Focus on Physical Science, California Version, Teacher's Edition. (2001). Upper Saddle River, NJ: Prentice Hall.

Project 2061. (2001). *Mathematics and Science Instructional Categories and Criteria*. Available: http://www.project2061.org/tools/textbook/mgsci/crit-used.htm

Chapter 11

Driver, R., A. Squires, P. Rushworth, V. Wood-Robinson. (1994). *Making Sense of Secondary Science: Research into Children's Ideas*. London: Routledge.

Miller, K., and J. Levine. (2004). *Biology*. Upper Saddle River, NJ: Pearson Prentice Hall.

Project 2061. (1993). *Benchmarks for Science Literacy*. New York: Oxford University Press.

Project 2061. (2001). *Atlas of Science Literacy*. Washington, DC: National Science Teachers Association.

Rutherford, J., and A. Ahlgren. (1989). *Science for All Americans*. New York: Oxford University Press.

Treagust, D., and A. Harrison. (1994). Analogies: Avoid Misconceptions with This Systematic Approach. *The Science Teacher* (April): 41–43.

Wiggins, G. and J. McTighe. (1998). *Understanding by Design*. Alexandria, VA: Association for Supervision and Curriculum Development.

Chapter 12

Wilbraham, A., D. Staley, M. Matta, and E. Waterman. (2005). *Chemistry*. Needham, MA: Pearson Prentice Hall.

Chapter 13

Driver, R., A. Squires, P. Rushworth, and V. Wood-Robinson. (1994). *Making Sense of Secondary Science: Research into Children's Ideas*. London: Routledge.

Hewitt, P. (2002). *Conceptual Physics: The High School Program*. Upper Saddle River, NJ: Prentice Hall.

National Academy of Sciences. (1996). *National Science Education Standards*. Washington, DC: National Academies Press.

Newton, I. (1730). *Optics: A Treatise of the Reflections, Refractions, Reflections and Colours of Light*, 4th ed. London.

Chapter 14

Driver, R., A. Squires, P. Rushworth, V. Wood-Robinson. (1994). *Making Sense of Secondary Science: Research into Children's Ideas*. London: Routledge.

Full Option Science System. (2005). *Weather and Water*. Nashua, NH: Dell.

National Research Council. (1996). *National Science Education Standards*. Washington, DC: National Academies Press.

Project 2061. (1993). *Benchmarks for Science Literacy*. New York: Oxford University Press.

Chapter 15

Fraser, B., and K. Tobin. (1990). *Environments for Learning Science and Mathematics: Key Centre Monograph Number 1*. Perth: Curtin University, Key Centre for School Science and Mathematics.

Hubbard, R., and B. Power. (1999). *Living the Questions: A Guide for the Teacher Researcher*. York, ME: Stenhouse.

Mills, G. (2000). *Action Research: A Guide for the Teacher Researcher*. Columbus, OH: Merrill.

Thompson, J. (2005). Response to class members. Personal communication regarding TE 861A Teaching Science for Understanding, Feb. 15, 2005.

Tobin, K., and B. Fraser. (1987). *Exemplary Practice in Science and Mathematics Education*. Perth: Curtin University of Technology.

Tobin, K., L. Rennie, and B. Fraser. (1990). *Barriers to Learning Science with Understanding: Key Centre Monograph Number 1*. Perth: Curtin University, Key Centre for School Science and Mathematics.

Tobin, K., D. Treagust, and B. Fraser. (1988). An Investigation of Exemplary Biology Teaching. *American Biology Teacher* 50(3): 142–147.

Name Index

Subject Index